On the Rez

Also by Ian Frazier

Coyote v. Acme (1996)

Family (1994)

Great Plains (1989)

Nobody Better, Better Than Nobody (1987)

Dating Your Mom (1986)

On the Rez

. . .

Ian Frazier

Farrar ▪ Straus ▪ Giroux / New York

Farrar, Straus and Giroux
19 Union Square West, New York 10003

Copyright © 2000 by Ian Frazier
Distributed in Canada by Douglas & MacIntyre Ltd.
Printed in the United States of America
Designed by Jonathan D. Lippincott
First edition, 2000
Second printing, 2000

Library of Congress Cataloging-in-Publication Data
Frazier, Ian.
On the rez / Ian Frazier. — 1st ed.
p. cm.
ISBN 0-374-22638-5 (alk. paper)
1. Oglala Indians.   2. Pine Ridge Indian Reservation (S.D.)
3. War Lance, Le.   4. Indians of North America—Great Plains.
5. Big Crow, SuAnne.
I. Title.
E99.03F73   2000
978.3′66—dc21   99-28353

Parts of this book first appeared in *The Atlantic Monthly*.

For Cora and Thomas

Contents

On the Rez

This book is about Indians, particularly the Oglala Sioux who live on the Pine Ridge Reservation in southwestern South Dakota, in the plains and badlands in the middle of the United States. People want to know what a book is about right up front, I have found. They feel this way even if the book does not yet exist, if it is only planned. When I describe the subject to non-Indians, they often reply that it sounds bleak. "Bleak" is the word attached in many people's minds to the idea of certain Indian reservations, of which the Oglala's reservation is perhaps the best example. Oddly, it is a word I have never heard used by Indians themselves. Many thousands of people—not just Americans, but German and French and English people, and more—visit the reservations every year, and the prevailing opinion among the Indians is not that they come for the bleakness. The Indians understand that the vistors are there out of curiosity and out of an admiration which sometimes even reaches such a point that the visitors wish they could be Indians, too. I am a middle-aged non-Indian who wears his hair in a thinning ponytail copied originally from the traditional-style long hair of the leaders of the American Indian Movement of the 1970s, because I thought it looked cool. When I'm driving across a field near the town of Oglala on the Pine Ridge Reservation and I see my friend Floyd John walking across it the other way, I stop, and he comes over to the car and leans in the window and smiles a big-tooth grin and says, "How ya' doin', wannabe?"

I kind of resent the term "wannabe"—what's wrong with wanting to be something, anyway?—but in my case there's some truth to it. I don't want to participate in traditional Indian religious ceremonies, dance in a sun dance or pray in a sweat lodge or go on a vision quest with the help of a medicine man. The power of these ceremonies has an appeal, but I'm content with what little religion I already have. I think Indians dress better than anyone, but I don't want to imitate more than a detail or two; I prefer my clothes humdrum and inconspicuous, and a cowboy hat just doesn't work for me. I don't want to collect Indian art, though pots and beadwork and blankets made by Indians remain the most beautiful art objects in the American West, in my opinion. I don't want to be adopted into a tribe, be wrapped in a star quilt and given a new name, honor though that would be. I don't want to stand in the dimness under the shelter at the powwow grounds in the group around the circle of men beating the drums and singing ancient songs and lose myself in that moment when all the breaths and all the heartbeats become one. What I want is just as "Indian," just as traditional, but harder to pin down.

In 1608, the newly arrived Englishmen at Jamestown colony in Virginia proposed to give the most powerful Indian in the vicinity, Chief Powhatan, a crown. Their idea was to coronate him a sub-emperor of Indians, and vassal to the English King. Powhatan found the offer insulting. "I also am a King," he said, "and this is my land." Joseph Brant, a Mohawk of the Iroquois Confederacy between eastern New York and the Great Lakes, was received as a celebrity when he went to England with a delegation from his tribe in 1785. Taken to St. James's Palace for a royal audience, he refused to kneel and kiss the hand of George III; he told the King that he would, however, gladly kiss the hand of the Queen. Almost a century later, the U.S. government gave Red Cloud, victorious war leader of the Oglala, the fanciest reception it knew how, with a dinner party at the White House featuring lighted chandeliers and wine and a dessert of strawberries and ice cream. The next day Red Cloud parleyed with the government officials just as he was accustomed to on the prairie—sitting on the floor. To a member of a Senate select committee who had delivered a tirade against Sitting Bull, the Hunkpapa

Sioux leader carelessly replied, "I have grown to be a very independent man, and consider myself a very great man."

That self-possessed sense of freedom is closer to what I want; I want to be an uncaught Indian like them.

Another remark which non-Indians often make on the subject of Indians is "Why can't they get with the program?" Anyone who talks about Indians in public will be asked that question, or variations on it; over and over: Why don't Indians forget all this tribal nonsense and become ordinary Americans like the rest of us? Why do they insist on living in the past? Why don't they accept the fact that we won and they lost? Why won't they stop, finally, being Indians and join the modern world? I have a variety of answers handy. Sometimes I say that in former days "the program" called for the eradication of Indian languages, and children in Indian boarding schools were beaten for speaking them and forced to speak English, so they would fit in; time passed, cultural fashions changed, and Hollywood made a feature film about Indians in which for the sake of authenticity the Sioux characters spoke Sioux (with English subtitles), and the movie became a hit, and lots of people decided they wanted to learn Sioux, and those who still knew the language, those who had somehow managed to avoid "the program" in the first place, were suddenly the ones in demand. Now, I think it's better not to answer the question but to ask a question in return: What program, exactly, do you have in mind?

We live in a craven time. I am not the first to point out that capitalism, having defeated Communism, now seems to be about to do the same to democracy. The market is doing splendidly, yet we are not, somehow. Americans today no longer work mostly in manufacturing or agriculture but in the newly risen service economy. That means that most of us make our living by being nice. And if we can't be nice, we'd better at least be neutral. In the service economy, anyone who sat where he pleased in the presence of power or who expatiated on his own greatness would soon be out the door. "Who does he think he is?" is how the dismissal is usually framed. The dream of many of us is that someday we might miraculously have enough money that we could quit being nice, and everybody would then have to be nice to us, and niceness would surround us like a warm dome. Certain speeches we would love to make accompany this dream, glorious, blistering tellings-off of those to whom we usually hold our tongue. The eleven people who actually have enough money to do that are icons to us. What we read in newsprint and see on television always reminds us how great they are, and we can't disagree. Unlike the rest of us, they can deliver those speeches with no fear. The freedom that inhered in Powhatan, that Red Cloud carried with him from the plains to Washington as easily as air—freedom to be and to say, whenever, regardless of disapproval—has become a luxury most of us can't afford.

From a historical perspective, this looks a lot like where America came in. When Columbus landed, there were about eleven people in Europe who could do whatever they felt like doing. Part of the exhilaration of the age was the rumored freedom explorers like Columbus found. Suddenly imagination was given a whole continent full of people who had never heard of Charlemagne, or Pope Leo X, or quitrents, or the laws of entail, and who were doing fine. Amerigo Vespucci, the explorer whose name and the continent's would be the same, brought back news that in this land "every one is his own master." If this land new to Europeans was the setting, the lives of these untrammeled people suggested the plot: we could drop anchor in the bay, paddle up the river, wade up the creek, meet a band of Indians, and with them disappear forever into the country's deepest green. No tyranny could hold us; if Indians could live as they liked, so could we.

The popular refrain about Indians nowadays is that they and their culture were cruelly destroyed. It's a breast-beatingly comfortable idea, from the destroyers' point of view. In the nineteenth century, with white people firmly established on the continent, common wisdom had it that the Indian must eventually die out. That meant die, literally, and give way in a Darwinian sense to the superiority of the Anglo-Saxon. "Adieu, red brother! You are going to join the Mastodon and the Scthysaurus," wrote humorist Bill Nye in 1891, shortly after the massacre at Wounded Knee. In the twentieth century, stories of the Indians' destruction, set mostly in the past tense, made a follow-up to this comfortable idea. From one century to the next, the destruction of the Indians was such a common theme that if they did not die out in fact, by the sound of it they might as well have. But beyond the sphere of

rhetoric, the Indians as a people did not die out, awful though the suffering was. Killing people is one thing, killing them off is another. The
Sand Creek Massacre, one of the bloodiest episodes on the Western
frontier and a permanent scar on the history of the state of Colorado,
killed at least two hundred, mostly women and children, of Chief Black
Kettle's band of Southern Cheyenne in 1864. Today there are more
than four thousand descendants of Sand Creek Massacre survivors; they
hope for restitution and a reservation of their own. New England's Pe-
quots, a tribe "extinct as the ancient Medes," according to Herman
Melville, rebounded from a recent time when just two members were
still living on the reservation and now run a gambling casino which
takes in x billion dollars a year. The Mohicans, of whom we were supposed to have seen the last in the 1750s, recently prevented Wal-Mart
from building a multiacre discount store on land they consider sacred in
upstate New York. In 1900, there were fewer than a quarter of a million
Indians in the United States. Today there are two million or more. The
population of those claiming Indian descent on the census forms has
been growing four times as fast as the population as a whole, making
Native Americans the fastest-growing ethnic group in the country.

Like many comfortable stories, the story of the Indians' destruction
hides other stories that are less so. For starters, it leaves out that the destruction was and is actually worse than can be easily described. A well-
informed person probably knows of the bigger and more famous
massacres, but big and small massacres took place in many states over
the years. Killing Indians was once the official policy of the state of California, which spent a million dollars reimbursing Indian-hunters for
the ammunition they used. Helen Hunt Jackson's history of Indian-
white relations, *A Century of Dishonor*, published in 1881, recounted
episodes of killing and mistreatment which have long faded into the
past. Its modern reader can weep at descriptions of massacres he has
never heard of—does anyone besides those who live in the town of
Gnadenhutten, Ohio, know of the slaughter in 1780 of the peaceful Indians at the Moravian mission there? Jackson's book could be revised
and reissued today, with another hundred years added to the title. After
the frontier gunfire died down, violence and untimely death found
other means. The Indian was supposed to be heading off to join his ancestors in the Happy Hunting Ground, and the path he might take to

get there (alcoholism? pneumonia? car wreck? the flu epidemic of 1918?) apparently did not need to be too closely explained. The violence continued, and continues today. Among the Navajo, the largest tribe in the United States, car accidents are the leading cause of death. Especially in Western towns that border big reservations, stabbings and fights and car wrecks are a depressingly regular part of life.

Also, the destruction story gives the flattering and wrong impression that European culture showed up in the Americas and simply mowed down whatever was in its way. In fact, the European arrivals were often hungry and stunned in their new settlements, and what they did to Indian culture was more than matched for years by what encounters with Indians did to theirs. Via the settlers, Indian crops previously unknown outside the Americas crossed the Atlantic and changed Europe. Indian farmers were the first to domesticate corn, peanuts, tomatoes, pumpkins, and many kinds of beans. Russia and Ireland grew no potatoes before travelers found the plant in Indian gardens in South America; throughout Europe, the introduction of the potato caused a rise in the standard of living and a population boom. Before Indians, no one in the world had ever smoked tobacco. No one in the Bible (or in any other pre-Columbian text, for that matter) ever has a cigarette, dips snuff, or smokes a pipe. The novelty of breathing in tobacco smoke or chewing the dried leaves caught on so fast in Europe that early colonists made fortunes growing tobacco; it was America's first cash crop. That the United States should now be so determined to stamp out all smoking seems historically revisionist and strange.

Surrounded as we are today by pavement, we assume that Indians have had to adapt to us. But for a long time much of the adapting went the other way. In the land of the free, Indians were the original "free"; early America was European culture reset in an Indian frame. Europeans who survived here became a mixture of identities in which the Indian part was what made them American and different than they had been before. Influence is harder to document than corn and beans, but as real. We know that Iroquois Indians attended meetings of the colonists in the years before the American Revolution and advised them to unite in a scheme for self-government based on the confederacy that ruled the six Iroquois nations; and that Benjamin Franklin said, at a gathering of delegates from the colonies in Albany in 1754, "It would be a strange thing if six nations of ignorant savages should be capable of forming a scheme for such a union and be able to execute it in such a manner as that it has subsisted for ages and appears indissoluble, and yet that a like union should be impracticable for ten or a dozen English colonies." His use of the term "ignorant savages" is thought to have been ironical; he admired the Iroquois plan, and it formed one of the models for the U.S. Constitution. We know, too, that Thomas Jefferson thought that American government should follow what he imagined to be the Indian way. He wrote: ". . . were it made a question, whether no law, as among the savage Americans, or too much law, as among the civilized Europeans, submits man to the greatest evil, one who has seen both conditions of existence would pronounce it to be the last . . . It will be said, that great societies cannot exist without government. The savages, therefore, break them into small ones."

Indian people today sometimes talk about the need to guard their culture carefully, so that it won't be stolen from them. But what is best (and worst) about any culture can be as contagious as a cold germ; the least contact passes it on. In colonial times, Indians were known for their disregard of titles and for a deep egalitarianism that made them not necessarily defer even to the leading men of their tribes. The route this trait took as it passed from Indian to white was invisible. Probably, contagion occurred during official gatherings, as when an exalted person arrived at a frontier place from the governor's palace or across the sea. The Indians spoke to the exalted person directly, equals addressing an equal, with no bowing or scraping or bending of the knee. Then, when their white neighbors got up to speak, perhaps ordinary self-consciousness made it hard to act any differently—to do the full routine of obeisance customary back in England—with the Indians looking on. Or maybe it was even simpler, a demonstration of the principle that informal behavior tends to drive out formal, given time. However the transfer happened, in a few generations it was complete; the American character had become thoroughly Indian in its outspokenness and all-around skepticism on the subject of who was and was not great.

We often hear that Indians traditionally believed in the Great Circle of Being, the connectedness of all creation, and the sacredness of every blade of grass. That the example of individual freedom among the Indians of the Americas inspired writers from Thomas More to Locke to

Shakespeare to Voltaire is seldom mentioned these days. (None of those writers, for their part, seem to have heard of the Great Circle of Being.) The Indians' love of independence and freedom has dwindled in description in recent years to the lone adjective "proud." Any time the Apache, for example, or the Comanche, or a noted Indian leader is described, that adjective is likely to be someplace close by. We are told that the Comanche or the Apache were or are "a proud people," and we get used to hearing it, and we forget what it means: centuries of resistance to authority, intractibility and independent-mindedness have won them only that brief epithet. The excitement of new discoveries in the Americas fired all sorts of fantasies about Indians in the minds of Europeans, and Indians remain the objects of fantasy today. The current fantasy might be summed up: American Indians were a proud people who believed in the Great Circle of Being and were cruelly destroyed.

I don't doubt that Indians in general saw all parts of creation as holy; references to such beliefs come up often in translated and transcribed speeches of Indians from years ago. At a treaty council between General Oliver O. Howard and the Nez Perce in 1877, Howard got tired of what he called "the oft-repeated dreamer nonsense" of the Indians, and told them, "Twenty times over I hear that the earth is your mother, and about the chieftainship of the earth. I want to hear it no more." What strikes me as fishy is that white people, having had no apparent interest in the Great Circle of Being for centuries, should find it so compelling now. I think its appeal has partly to do with its vague and unthreatening environmentalism, the genial Earth Day sort that leaves larger problems aside. Beyond that, I think the idea of connectedness is its key selling point. It reminds me of an advertisement for a telephone company, the one that used to say, "We're all connected." That statement could be further from the truth, but not much; no matter how many wires we thread into our homes, no matter the increasing complexity of the machines we hook them to, we are getting more disconnected all the time. People with money and without, people of different races and sexual identities, people in tinier and tinier areas of specialization, people in various categories off in gated communities by themselves—we are divided and a scattered every which way. Whiskey-trading forts on the Western frontier had special entrance enclosures where goods could be exchanged under guard, with escape doors at the other end for the traders in case negotiations got out of hand. That's essentially the connectedness the modern "we're-all-connected" world provides.

The Indian inclination toward personal freedom, no matter the consequences, made for endless division and redivision among tribes. Social problems often were solved geographically: you and I don't get along, so you stay here and my family and friends and I will move over there. Also, of course, splitting up into smaller groups was an efficient way to use the wild resources of the land. To give an accurate picture of any tribe, you need not just an identifying name or two but plenty of subcategories as well. For example, the Sioux, a populous and powerful tribe west of the Great Lakes when white men arrived, got that name apparently from a French corruption of the word *nadowesioux,* which was said to mean "little snakes" in the language of their enemies the Chippewa. Among themselves, the Sioux used (and use) the name Lakota, or variations of it, to indicate the tribe as a whole. Lakota means "allies." Setting aside the Assiniboine Sioux, a more northerly tribe, the Sioux in the United States were of three kinds: the Eastern, or Santee Sioux, who lived near the Mississippi in and around what is now Minnesota; the Yankton Sioux, a central branch, who lived between them and the Missouri; and the Western, or Teton Sioux, who lived farther to the west, on the Great Plains. The Santee were divided into a number of tribes, including the Sisseton, the Wahpekute, and the Mdewakanton. The Yankton had two subgroups—the Yankton and the Yanktonai. The Teton Sioux were of seven tribes, also called the seven council fires. They were the Sicangu, the Minnecojou, the Oohenumpa, the Itazipcho, the Sihasapa, the Hunkpapa, and the Oglala. Each name has a Lakota meaning whose origin is more or less obscure. One translation of Oglala is "dust scatterers." It may have come from a time when members of that tribe tried unsuccessfully to farm in the unwatered soil of the plains. After the Western Sioux got horses, they thrived as buffalo hunters on the plains. The Oglala tribe grew in numbers, and spread out and divided into bands. Important moments in Oglala history involved a conflict between a band of Oglala called the Bad Faces and a band called the Cut Off People. There were other bands of Oglala as well.

Historians have said that this kind of social division was a reason for the Indians' defeat. Inability to unite in common interest ruined the conspiracy of Pontiac, and the alliance Tecumseh tried to create among tribes resisting white encroachment in 1811. Indians lost battles because they couldn't keep together and attack all at the same time, like the white soldiers. Indian leaders often worried more about enemies within the tribe than about threats from outside, and survived wars with the whites only to die at the hands of Indian rivals. Certainly, pursuit of individual freedom among Indians has had a dreadful downside in quarreling and jealousy. Some Indians say that jealousy is a bigger problem for their people than alcohol. On Indian reservations nationwide, it is hard to find one that has no ongoing intratribal dispute.

Any smugness at the thought of this urge to division in Indian society ignores how powerful it has been in the United States at large. From a certain perspective, the history of the United States has been the history of schism. Whether we would be one nation or many has perplexed us from the start. The Civil War seemed to decide the question in favor of unity. Many Northerners who cared nothing for the fate of enslaved blacks had been persuaded to fight to preserve the union; "Union!" was the wartime rallying cry that echoed in the names of national companies like the Western Union Telegraph Company and the Union Pacific Railroad that prospered after the war. As a plot device, union proved ideal. It gave the American story a clarity of outcome and a vista of happily-ever-after. Out of many, so we were told, we had become one.

Disunion, on the other hand, is complicated and ambiguous and inconclusive, and more difficult to describe. In our history whose winner is union, disunion is the bad guy, the loser. Its story is less often told. But it holds there, right below the surface of American history, threatening to turn the story of our union into countless numbers of stories too complicated to follow or tell. We know, for example, that the United States has been a Protestant-majority nation since it began. That fact seems simple, white-bread, monochrome. But the origin of Protestantism was protest and argument. Especially in the early nineteenth century the Protestants in America argued and disagreed and divided into factions so prolifically as to make the Indian tribes seem unanimous by comparison. A glance into the can of worms that is the Baptist sects, the Hard-Shell and Foot-Washing and Six Principle and Free

Will and Primitive and so on, or at the multiplicity of Presbyterian sects strewn across the range of opinion on the doctrine of predestination, suggests why there is not yet any comprehensive and coherent account of the Protestant Churches of America. Like Indian tribes, Protestant Churches split up into smaller groups, solved disputes geographically, and took advantage of the immensity and variety of the land. America was resettled by Protestant division, as it had been settled by Indian division before. Confidently *unum,* we looked down on the Indian *pluribus*; but we have always been at least as *pluribus* as they.

So, to the question "Why can't Indians get with the program?" one might reply that we have already gotten with theirs. Immigrants did not simply reproduce in America the life they had left behind overseas. They adapted instead to the culture they found here, a native culture that was immeasurably old and that still survives today. The latest version of American history tends to describe the meeting of white and Indian in terms of despoilment, with the Indian getting the worst of it, as indeed occurred. But such accounts can't do justice to the thrilling spark of freedom in the encounter—the freedom the Indians had, the freedom that white people found. As surely as Indians gave the world corn and tobacco and potatoes, they gave it a revolutionary new idea of what a human being could be. Thanks to Indians, we learned we didn't have to kneel to George III. In the droning sameness of history, this was front-page, glorious news: we could walk the earth the equal of anyone we met, no princeling's inferior, unobliged to kiss anyone's hand in subjugation or to have anyone kiss ours. As with other inventions, this one succeeded because it met people who were ready for it, and Enlightenment-era Europeans in particular were. Generations of thought about the right relationship of people to God and to each other had already moved Europeans away from the oppressions of feudalism; but the example of freedom and equality among Indians provided a resounding real-life confirmation of theory. The pursuit of freedom drove the social revolutions that occupied much of the world over the last two centuries, and reform in the name of equality produced great improvements and disasters.

Now, in America, we have gotten used to freedom. We heard about it in school, we know we have it, theoretically; and so what? With regard to its original thrill, we are like frequent fliers grown so used to the routine of modern air travel that we've lost the heart-lifting joy people felt at the sight of Wilbur Wright flying past the New York skyline and circling the Statue of Liberty in his homemade biplane back in 1909. But like the principles of flight, the idea of freedom still survives. It is what makes people all over the world still want to come to America, and still have hopes for what America can be and do. It is part of the allure in American advertising, and in American popular music, and in the images we export of gangsters and bikers and heavily armed lone-wolf fighters of evil. Freedom illuminates the cheapest made-in-Taiwan feathers in the toy-store Indian costume and provides the theme of every Western movie, in which the irresponsible and too-free freedom of wild Indians and outlaws yields inevitably to the more responsible, less-free freedom which we townsfolk understand.

And now we look out upon the traffic jam and wonder, "Is this the land of the free?" We turn on the television along with the rest of America every evening and wonder whether this is the equality the Founders had in mind. Yes, we do kiss a hand now and then, the boss's or the loan officer's or the preferred customer's—it's just part of life, no big deal—and we take a certain pleasure in having our own hand kissed as well. (Though our kissing metaphor, like the rest of our culture, has moved a bit lower down.) The day after tomorrow the earth will be so crowded you won't be able to turn around without stepping on someone's toes, and what will be the purpose of freedom then? In our spare moments we worry about what the world's coming to, and our worry breeds proposals: one expert reveals that the solution is all in education, in improving the public schools and in hiring more teachers to reduce the number of students per classroom. Another says the solution requires the perfection of the electric car. Others talk of changing the policies of the Federal Reserve Bank, of campaign-finance reform, of making new laws or getting rid of laws we already have. Not long ago I read in the newspaper about new kinds of bioengineered trees that will produce nearly thirty times the annual growth of ordinary trees, thereby supposedly saving the rain forests and providing us with lumber and protecting the ozone until kingdom come.

But even if we somehow do all the experts say we should, and even if the solutions work better than we could expect, will we be free? Will the question even be mentioned at all? Will anything remain of that urge to freedom that drove people across oceans and continents, and caused them to struggle and die, and inspired them to speechify in such high-flown terms? In our smaller public school classes, at the wheels of our electric cars, in control of our bank policies and our politicians' campaign spending, listening to the rustling of our frantically photosynthesizing trees, what kind of people will we be? Will we be a free people, will that idea have meaning anymore?

When I go to Indian reservations in the West, and especially to the Pine Ridge Reservation, I sometimes feel unsure where to put my foot when I open the car door. The very ground is different from where I usually stand. There are fewer curbs, fewer sidewalks, and almost no street signs, mailboxes, or leashed dogs. The earth here is just the earth, unadorned, and the places people walk are made not by machinery but by feet. Those smooth acres of asphalt marked with lines to tell you where to park and drive which cover so much of America are harder to find on the reservations. If the Iroquois hadn't resisted the French in the 1600s, the Northeast would be speaking French today; if the Comanche hadn't opposed the Spanish, the American Southwest would now be Mexico. The Oglala Sioux reservation, actively or otherwise, continues to resist the modern American paving machine. Walking on Pine Ridge, I feel as if I am in actual America, the original version that was here before and will still be here after we're gone. There are windblown figures crossing the road in the distance who might be drunk, and a scattering of window-glass fragments in the weeds that might be from a car accident, and a baby naked except for a disposable diaper playing in a bare-dirt yard, and an acrid smell of burning trash—all the elements that usually evoke the description "bleak." But there is greatness here, too, and an ancient glory endures in the dust and the weeds. The way I look at it, this is the American bedrock upon which the society outside its borders is only a later addition. It's the surviving piece of country where "the program" has not yet completely taken hold.

Of course I want to be like Indians. I've looked up to them all my life. When I was a young man my number-one hero was the Oglala leader Crazy Horse. I read every source I could find about him, went to many places of importance in his life, and studied his history as an example of what a person should be. I discovered many others who felt as strongly about Crazy Horse as I did. Crazy Horse was born about 1840 into the Bad Faces band of Oglala at Bear Butte, near where Sturgis, South Dakota, is today. He grew up in the neighborhood of Fort Laramie on the prairie in what is now southeastern Wyoming, made his reputation as a young man in battles with the Crow and other tribes, and won his greatest fame for his part in Indian victories over the Army, most notably the killing of General Custer and others of his command at the battle of the Little Bighorn. The following spring Crazy Horse agreed to stop fighting and come in to the Red Cloud Agency—the early version of the Pine Ridge Reservation, located then in western Nebraska. The Army put him under arrest and killed him, under confused and shameful circumstances, that fall. A large plaque erected in 1964 on the reservation just off Highway 18 by the turnoff to the village of Wounded Knee recounts his biography in some detail. As a rule, historical markers on the reservation get hit pretty hard by vandalism. Almost any unattended point of interest, it seems, will attract a scrawl of spray paint or a hurled Budweiser bottle sooner or later. But I have never seen a speck of graffiti or a sliver of glass on the marker commemorating Crazy Horse. Evidently, even the most hell-bent drunks leave it alone. When its lettering begins to age, someone carefully paints it in again.

I wrote a lot about Crazy Horse in a book I published in 1989, and I continued to refer to his example when wondering how I should act in certain situations. I had decided that Crazy Horse's one mistake was in coming into the agency, where his halfhearted efforts at accommodation led only to intrigue, jealousy, and death. When faced with a possibly compromising decision, I would ask myself, "Is this 'coming into the agency'?" Having lunch with certain people in the magazine business or applying for an arts grant was 'coming into the agency,' I believed. My wife and I bought a cooperative apartment in Brooklyn, and it had a shabby kitchen, and my wife decided to remodel it. She went to a remodeling firm, then sat down with me to go over the estimates. I asked myself, "Would Crazy Horse have spent this much to remodel a kitchen?"

Crazy Horse's recent popularity dates from the years of the Vietnam War, when a lot of people began to see the sense in his resistance to the

U.S. government. The political activists who made up the American Indian Movement loved Crazy Horse. AIM leaders often repeated the few quotations attributed to him—"One does not sell the earth on which the people walk"; "Today is a good day to die!"—and took inspiration from his warlike determination to be himself no matter what. Watching AIM leaders on the news in those days, I sometimes found them scary, with their improvised protest demonstrations and violent talk. But I admired them, too. Most of them were of the same age as the older guys I had looked up to in school. AIM guys—and AIM was very much a "guy" organization—usually came from city-Indian backgrounds and dressed in an eclectic combination of street tough and Indian traditional that no one had seen before. To a press conference, an AIM leader might wear a beaded black leather vest, black chinos, and black boots, with his hair in waist-length braids wrapped in strips of red felt and otter fur. Violence and dissension and FBI informers did in AIM eventually, and its members ended up scattered, more than a few in jail. But AIM changed the way people regarded Indians in this country, and the way Indians regarded themselves; in an assimilationist America, they showed that a powerful Indian identity remained. A while ago I was reminded of my admiration for Clyde Bellecourt, a Chippewa from Minnesota and one of the founders of AIM. Back in 1973, as a result of a long-standing dispute between AIM factions, an AIM member named Carter Camp shot Clyde Bellecourt in the stomach on the Rosebud Reservation in South Dakota. Clyde Bellecourt survived the shooting and refused to press charges, and Carter Camp went free. What reminded me was a recent item in an Indian newspaper saying that Clyde Bellecourt's daughter Mary, a tenth-grader, was about to receive a high award in her Girl Scout troop. To have survived a shooting *and* to have a daughter who wins a high award in Girl Scouts—how much cooler can a middle-aged father be?

I'd like to be a hero myself, especially for dramatic, action-hero exploits of some kind. Riding the subway from Brooklyn to Manhattan, I used to daydream of rescuing a helpless person from armed muggers, of knocking guns to the subway floor and subduing criminals and turning them over nonchalantly to the Transit Police. Other fantasies, even more far-fetched and Walter Mittyish than that, sometimes ran through my mind; a few scenarios I now know so well I have them nearly memorized and could direct the film versions to the smallest detail. In reality, I've never performed any heroic feat, and I'm glad that no mugging has ever taken place in front of me to reveal what I would actually do. On a subway train I often rode, but at a time when I was not there, someone once set off a firebomb in a car filled with rush-hour passengers. The bomb burned forty-seven people, some of them critically. A passenger who survived the blast ran back into the burning car to rescue a number of injured people who were still on fire. In news stories that followed, when reporters asked the rescuer about his deed he always said, "I'm no hero." This, I have found, is a constant in modern-day news stories in which heroic acts are involved. You will meet the disclaimer by the third paragraph, almost without fail. Regardless of the courageous, dangerous, lifesaving thing the person has done, he or she always insists, "I'm no hero."

Most everybody wants to be rich, millions want to be famous, but no one today wants to be mistaken for a hero. This recent change in our psychology is baffling to me. It is also profoundly un-Indian. Indians who were heroes generally came out and said so. For many tribes, life revolved around heroism. Young men dreamed of setting off from camp alone and on foot, and of returning days or weeks later on a fine mount with eight other ponies captured from the Snakes; the old women would cry their praises, the drummers would compose songs in their honor, the chiefs would hold feasts and giveaways, and the young women would look at them over the tops of their shawls. For many Indians, autobiography was just a series of brave exploits strung together over years. Naturally, Indian culture produced heroes of all sizes in plentiful supply. Bil Gilbert, biographer of Tecumseh, says that the Indians of North America resembled the ancient Greeks in their ability to produce heroes, and that both societies considered heroism more important than wealth or power. In American history, the names of Sequoyah and Osceola and Black Hawk and Roman Nose and Chief Joseph and Looking Glass and Satank and Quanah Parker and Cochise and Geronimo ring like names of heroes out of Homer.

The Western Sioux, who never numbered more than seventy thousand souls in all, have given America and the rest of the world heroes in quantity far out of proportion to the size of the tribe. Sitting Bull, the Hunkpapa warrior and medicine man, became one of the most famous

Americans of all time. Spotted Tail, of the Sicangu or Brule Sioux, was perhaps the greatest Indian diplomat and negotiator. Other Sioux, like Rain in the Face and Gall and Pawnee Killer, were known mainly for deeds in battle. Among the Oglala, the number of heroes is unusually high. Besides Crazy Horse, the Oglala included Red Cloud, who spoke to power in Washington and New York as no Indian had done before. Oglala chiefs like Little Wound and Red Dog and American Horse and He Dog and Young Man Afraid of His Horses attained eminence within the tribe and beyond. One of the greatest Oglala heroes was a holy man, Nicholas Black Elk, who held on to his people's ancient religion during a time when it was actively suppressed. Toward the end of his life he conveyed some of the holy teachings in print, most notably in the book *Black Elk Speaks*, written with the help of Nebraska poet John G. Neihardt. *Black Elk Speaks*, published in 1932, became a classic of religious literature, familiar to readers around the world.

A surprising amount of Oglala culture is the same today as it was in pre-reservation times. The Oglala still produce heroes, despite the fact that the wider market for them seems to have waned. If you want to see a lot of combat veterans in one place, go to a Veterans' Powwow in Pine Ridge village on an August afternoon. There's probably more foreign shrapnel walking around the small towns of the reservation than there is in similar towns anywhere in America; some Oglala families can give you a genealogy of warriors that begins at Operation Desert Storm and continues back to the Little Bighorn and before. The Oglala have always honored warriors, and they honor children as well. The Lakota word for child, *wakanyeja*, translates literally as "the child is also holy." An Oglala hero of recent history was a girl athlete who died just before she turned eighteen. She starred for the Lady Thorpes, the girls' basketball team at Pine Ridge High School, from 1987 through 1991. I have only heard about her and read local news stories about her, but words fail me when I try to say how much I admire her. Her name was SuAnne Big Crow.

CHAPTER

2

So Le War Lance and I became friends. I mentioned him in a book, the same one in which I wrote about Crazy Horse, and in the same chapter; I said that I had noticed an Indian waiting to cross the street in front of my apartment in New York City, that I had asked on impulse if he was Sioux, and that he had replied, "I'm an Oglala Sioux Indian from Oglala, South Dakota." I described a conversation Le War Lance and I had on the subject of Crazy Horse and how he had told me, "Crazy Horse was my gran'father!" Le War Lance liked what I wrote about him; he said that I told the truth. I included a photograph of him in the book, and for a while he was carrying a paperback copy around in his back pocket so he could show the photo to people from time to time. He said he even used it for a picture ID once or twice. I kept running into him in various parts of the city: by the statue of Garibaldi in Washington Square Park at two in the morning as I was returning from some party, or on a park bench in Columbus Circle in the middle of the afternoon. He wrote down his phone number for me and added mine to the long list of phone numbers he keeps in his head. He called me often, and he still does. I've known Le War Lance now for going on twenty years. All my other friends I met in school, at work, or through connections from work. Le War Lance is the only friend I have who I met originally on the street.

Le's appearance has varied over those years. He is about six feet tall, and he has a broad face rather like the actor Jack Palance's. Le's eyes can be merry and flat as a smile button, or deep and glittering with malice or slyness or something he knows and I never will. He is fifty-seven years old. I have seen his hair, which is black streaked with gray, when it was over two feet long and held with beaded ponytail holders a foot or so apart, and I have seen it much shorter, after he had shaved his head in mourning for a friend who had died. He has big hands which can grip a basketball as easily as I can hold a softball, and long arms. He is almost never able to find shirts or coats with long-enough sleeves. I've seen him in fancy tooled cowboy boots, in oversize Italian loafers with metal buckles, and in running shoes; in many different cowboy hats, in an orange-and-white knit ski cap bearing the name of an insurance company, and in snowmobiler caps with fur earflaps. I've seen him fat and thin. For a while he was about 260 pounds, a pro-football heft. Then he became slim and rangy-looking. He told me he was losing weight because he had cancer. I asked what kind of cancer he had and he replied, "Generic." He told me he would be dead in six weeks, and even gave the date on which he would die, which he said had been revealed to him in a dream. That was about eight years ago. He has gained back a lot of the weight since then.

Le and I have fallings-out from time to time. He often is not a very nice guy. If he has done only a few of the things he says he has done, it's amazing he isn't in jail. (Evidently he did go to prison for car theft and writing bad checks back in the early sixties.) When he's drinking, which is frequently, he tells me all kinds of stories. I don't completely disbelieve any of them. For years I thought his story about jumping off the Space Needle in Seattle attached by just a Band-Aid to the end of a bungee cord in a promotional stunt for the Johnson & Johnson company might have a grain of truth to it somewhere. When I reminded him of it recently, he laughed and said if he had told me that he was just having fun with me. Other stories that are only slightly less wild have turned out to be true.

He calls me every few weeks, it seems, to ask for money. It's good that he does, I suppose, to keep me from getting sentimental when I think of him. Even now I can feel my words want to pull him in a wrong direction, toward a portrait that is rose-tinted and larger than life, while he is pulling the other way, toward reality. Sometimes when he calls, his voice is small and clear, like neat printed handwriting; other times, depending on his mood and how much he's had to drink, his voice is sprawling and enlarged, like a tall cursive signature with flourishes on the tail letters and ink blots and splatters alongside. I have wired him money many times, for more purposes than I can remember—to help a friend who was stranded at a Micmac Indian reserve in Canada, to resole a pair of boots, to fix a heater, to buy any number of car parts and tanks of gas, to provide a wreath on a coffin, to provide a suit of clothes for a relative who had just died, to buy a used mobile home, to buy steamer trunks to hold the presents at a giveaway ceremony, to pay a DWI fine. After a while the wire-transfer company sent me a good-customer card that lets me take a dollar or so off the service charge. I get a satisfaction from these transactions which would be complicated to explain. Of course, I also often get annoyed. Once when I said I had no money to send, Le became angry and told me he would not be seeing me again, that he expected soon to die. Then he told me to "suck on a banana and make it real," and hung up. I didn't hear from him for a year or more after that, and I began to worry that maybe he actually had died. At Christmas I sent a card to his girlfriend's address and inquired about him. Four or five days after I mailed the card, I found a message on my answering machine: Le's voice, the extra-large version, in a rising volume: "Hey—Little Brother—I hear you forgot my NAME!" I played it over several times. I was delighted to hear from him again.

One Sunday morning I was lying in my bed in lower Manhattan when I got a call from Le. He said he had been partying the night before with Jimmy Page of Led Zeppelin and had just gotten home. He planned to take a nap, he said, and after that he wanted me to come by his apartment for a visit. Then he told me he was going to buy an Appaloosa mare and asked if I would like to have one of her colts. He said he would raise the colts on land he owned on the reservation. He said he planned to go back to the reservation that spring and trap an eagle there. He said he trapped eagles by going up on a butte and burying himself in the earth and covering his face with sagebrush and holding a live rabbit on the sagebrush. When the eagle came down for the rabbit, he said, he grabbed the eagle by the leg. The last one he had caught, he said, beat its wings so hard it pulled him out of the earth. I said that I would not want to try that, that I would be afraid the eagle would peck my eye out. Le said, "Nothing eats me."

I told him I would be there about one o'clock. Le was living in Washington Heights at the time. The A train, which stopped below my apartment, took me right there. Washington Heights is at the far northern end of Manhattan, where the island is so rocky it's almost mountainous. I rode an elevator many stories from the subway up through the rock, walked around some hilly streets, and finally found his building, Cabrini Terrace, on 191 Street. A Hasidic man all in black with side curls pointed it out to me. I climbed the stairs to Apartment 5K and knocked on the door. Le opened it, shirtless, barefoot, in brown pegged pants rolled up at the cuffs and curled under at the waistline, where his stomach overhung. He had his hair piled high on his head and held with elastic bands so that it fanned out above in sort of a delta shape; it looked like a nineteenth-century hairstyle of a Plains Indian in a portrait by Catlin or Bodmer. The room was full of the smell of stew cooking. Light came from a lamp or two and from the blue glow of a large TV against one wall. There was no daylight; all the windows were covered completely with aluminum foil. Le saw me notice the foil. "My girlfriend's paranoid. She just discovered she was an orphan," he explained.

Le was drinking a sixteen-ounce can of Budweiser beer. He asked me to sit, and he offered me one. As I got accustomed to the light, I saw sixteen-ounce Budweiser cans everywhere—not scattered around carelessly, but set upright neatly among the furniture, on the end table, in the shelves of the bookcase, under the television, in the corners; it was like a brain-teaser drawing: "How many beer cans can you find in this picture?" He introduced me to his cat, Hey Baby, and to Coyote, his dog. Coyote was small and waggy and blind in one eye. A painting of an eagle with wings spread covered an entire wall. It was done in sketchy strokes of brown on the wall itself, and one of the legs in particular was so detailed and eagle-like, with careful feathering and sickle-shaped claws, that I thought it possible he had gotten as close to a real eagle leg as he said he had. In the middle of the eagle he had pasted a poster advertising the Longest Walk, a demonstration organized by the American

Indian Movement in 1978 to protest anti-tribal legislation then before Congress. Le said he had participated in the walk, which began in California and ended in Washington, D.C., and that he had worn out four pairs of boots, three pairs of tennis shoes, and two pairs of other shoes along the way. He said concrete just eats shoes up. Then he told me to look at the ceiling; a sketch of a buffalo head done in carpenter's pencil, full face, stared down. He walked to different parts of the room and pointed up. "Here is his horns . . . here is his eyes . . . here is his nose . . . here is his beard." The ceiling was white; this was a sacred white buffalo, he said.

He said, "I want to tell you my movie," and for the next forty minutes or so, he did, almost frame by frame. He said that Howard Hughes's lawyer either had given him money to make it or was about to give him money to make it. The plot involved a woman who wakes up in the morning ("The sun comes up and kisses the sky and paints Mother Earth in all the colors of the day . . ."), rummages in a cupboard, makes herself some tea, drinks it, and drives into town. She goes into a café and sits down. Everybody knows her. She's a model. She's beautiful. She looks out the window of the café and sees an Indian painting a picture. She gets up and goes out and looks at it. It's a picture of an old Indian. Suddenly she's reminded of a time when she was at the café and the café was robbed and the robbers took her away in an airplane and the airplane crashed and she was the only one who survived and she slid down the wing with a broken leg, broken ribs, two broken arms, and a concussion. When she came to, she saw this old Indian—the same one as in the picture—on an Appaloosa horse looking down at her. (Here Le did an imitation of a man sitting on horseback with the reins in two hands resting one atop the other on the saddlehorn.) The Indian took her and made a sweat bath for her and took off all her clothes except her slip and put red-hot rocks in the sweat lodge, and the woman picked up one of them, and suddenly she was sitting outside the lodge in the middle of nowhere. Then she put the rock down and she was back in the sweat lodge. Then she picked up some sage and suddenly she's in her own garden smelling a flower. She put it down and she's back in the sweat lodge again. The old Indian cured her and took her back to the highway, where somebody could pick her up, and as she's about to get in the car she turns around and he has disappeared. But nobody can explain the buffalo-hide splints on her arms and legs. She remembers all this, and she asks the Indian painting the picture who the man in it is, and the Indian says, "That was my grandfather." So she goes in and finishes eating and comes out and gets in her car, and in her rearview mirror as she drives away you see the old Indian sitting on his horse looking after her.

Le put on a shirt and pulled on some boots, and we went out for more beer. He had a cheerful word for the doorman in the lobby, a woman watching two children on the sidewalk out front, and the man behind the deli counter. He took two six-packs of sixteen-ounce Budweisers from the cooler; I paid. As we came back down his hall, he pointed to the door next to his and said, "The lady who lives there is a Holocaust survivor." Angling for approval, I said that he was kind of a holocaust survivor, too. He said, "You got that right, bro."

The stew was ready. Le called it soup and a Lakota word I didn't catch. He took me into the kitchen and showed it to me, ladling through it with a big spoon. Its main ingredients were pieces of cow stomach and intestines and Indian corn. The long boiling had caused the individual kernels to expand to the size of pieces of popcorn. I had only seen this kind of corn on colorful dried corncobs in autumn displays on suburban front doors; I had never realized it was a food. Le filled a big bowl for me, and I cleared away some magazines and Budweiser cans on a small table and set it down. The soup was good, hot and strong-tasting; but when I looked close up at the intricacies of a piece of stomach wall, for a second I blanched. After that I ate without looking, keeping my eyes instead on the television, which had never been off since I arrived. Le looked at the television, too. After a moment he said, "I've seen this movie before. It's called *Body Heat*—it's a pretty raunchy movie. That woman is Kathleen Turner."

"No, it isn't," I said. "I've seen this movie, too. That's an actress named Kim Zimmer. I know, because she's married to a guy who used to live across the street from me in Ohio. She plays Reva Lewis in the soap opera *Guiding Light*."

Le leaned forward to the screen and examined it. Then he turned back to me. "You're right," he said. "That *is* Kim Zimmer."

We each had another bowl of soup, and more cold Budweiser to go with it. Then we sat back, content. "I see you like the soup," Le said, using the Lakota word for it. I agreed it was very good. Again shirtless, Le began to point out his scars to me and tell the stories he said were behind them. On one arm and shoulder he said he had 250 scars the size of a matchhead, from flesh offerings he had made at sun dances. On the other shoulder, a more visible pale zipper of a scar he identified as the result of a rotator cuff operation. He had been a minor league pitcher, he said, and once pitched against fastballer Nolan Ryan. After his arm blew up he couldn't pitch again, despite the operation, and had to switch to his left arm when he went back to riding bulls in the rodeo. He held on with his left hand and used his injured right arm for balance when he rode. He was once fourth in the world championship rodeo in bull riding, he said.

He told me that he had worked sorting potatoes and sewing potato bags shut in a field near Hemingford, Nebraska, for three dollars an hour; that he had worked as a gandy dancer fixing the Northern Pacific tracks from Gillette, Wyoming, clear across the state for twelve hundred dollars a week; that he had once helped a shady guy on the reservation rustle cattle for a flat fee of two hundred dollars and no questions asked. He said he had played professional basketball for the Denver Truckers in the Amateur Athletic Union, had driven stunt cars in the movies, and had driven an Oppenheimer Lotus racing car in a race in Antwerp, Belgium, at a clocked speed at 190.280 miles per hour. He said he was a good friend of Scottish racer Jim Clark, and had given up racing for good after Clark died in a crash at Indianapolis. He described, by my count, seven or eight guys he had killed—all in self-defense. The telephone rang. He picked it up, said "Yo!" into the receiver, and slammed it down. He said it was his girlfriend checking in from Montclair, New Jersey, where she was taking care of her mother. How that squared with her being an orphan puzzled me, but I did not ask.

Occasionally he sang Lakota songs. His voice went from deep and throaty to wavery and high in a song whose words he translated as "Young Lakota man, come into the center of the circle, so the young women can see your pheasant dance!" Another song he said was an old one that had been sung first by Red Cloud. Its words went:

You ask me to be a Lakota,
And that is the hardest thing in the world to be.
I am a Lakota,
So I suffer for my people.

Sometimes he idly leaned forward and turned the TV channels, never finding anything that held his attention for long. Suddenly the Winter Olympics was on, and he stopped talking. The announcer said the next event would be the Women's Figure Skating. Le said, "I have to see this. I want Katarina Witt to win. She'll be skating the compulsory figures. I told everybody, 'If Katarina Witt finishes any higher than fifth in the compulsories, she's got the whole thing sewed up.' "

"Why is that?" I asked.

"Because she *hates* the compulsories—it's her worst event. All she has to do is place fourth or higher." He sat with his elbows on his knees and watched, his piled-up hair silhouetted against the screen.

For a while I was seeing Le every few weeks. When he happened to be downtown he stopped by my apartment, and on weekend afternoons I sometimes made the trip up to Washington Heights. Most visits were like my first one: we sat around and drank beer and talked and watched TV. Though I didn't meet Le's girlfriend, I met a number of his Lakota friends and relatives who were staying in his apartment. There was a skinny guy with glasses named Will, who Le introduced as his brother; they looked so unlike that I asked Will if he really was Le's brother, and Will said, "Well, that's what he introduces me as." Another guy, Thomas Yellow Hair, I recognized right away. He was the marcher featured prominently in the Last Walk photograph in the poster hanging on Le's wall. A guy in a Western shirt and blue jeans who was so thin his beaded belt seemed to go around him twice Le also introduced as his brother. In this case, he really was a brother—Floyd John, born five years and five days after Le. Floyd John said little the first time I saw him. Le told me that Floyd John was a veteran who had served two tours in Vietnam, and that after he had signed up for the second tour, their uncle had given him his own name, Loves War. To make conversation, I asked Floyd John which branch of the service he had been in. Floyd

John said, "Army." He said nothing else to me the rest of the afternoon.

I usually showed up with beer. Once I brought a six-pack of a beer called Moosehead, which I happened to have in my refrigerator because a guest had left it. It was not a brand I would have bought myself. When I pulled it out of the shopping bag, the shouts of derision from Le and Floyd John (who had begun talking to me by then) were something to hear. I might as well have pulled an actual moosehead out of the sack. How could I have been so peculiar as to bring this extremely non-Budweiser, off-brand beer? Le and Floyd John never got over it. They still remind me of that Moosehead incident to this day. If this were 150 years ago and I were an eccentric white traveler passing through the Oglala camps, I have no doubt what my Indian name would be.

With other people around, Le did not tell yarns the way he did the first time I visited. Mostly we all sat in Le's living room and watched television. Le's TV got the cable channels, and one of them showed old Western movies. Generally Le and the others preferred Westerns to anything else that was on. I did, too. My TV didn't get cable, and the other channels in New York didn't seem to care about Westerns at all. When I first moved to the city I had complained about this, and pointlessly told people that the only movie I ever could find on television in New York was *Daddy Long Legs,* starring Fred Astaire. Most of my favorite movies are Westerns. That sound of Indians screaming and yipping and firing guns as they circle the wagon train was the basic TV background noise of my childhood.

Perhaps it should have occurred to me that those TV and movie war cries were made by actual people with names. It didn't, though, until I watched Westerns in Le's living room. Often an Indian would cross the screen to tomahawk a soldier or catch a bullet and fall, and (depending on the movie) Le or Floyd John would say, "That's Burgess Red Cloud."

"No," the other would reply, "that's what's-his-name, Kills Enemy. Lived over there with Mildred? Was it Bob? Bob Kills Enemy?"

"No, not Bob."

"Burgess Red Cloud was the guy in the buffalo-horn hat in *How the West Was Won.*"

"No, man—Burgess wasn't in that movie."

"That guy—*there*—that's Marvin Thin Elk."

"Yeah, that's Marvin."

"That's Vince LaDuke. He played the Indian guy on *Bonanza*."

"That guy that just got shot off the roof—I forget his name—wasn't he the guy the Mennonites gave a trailer house to over by Manderson? Died of alcoholism?"

"I don't know. Now that guy right there, that's Matthew Two Bulls as a younger man. You can't hardly recognize him. He's the greatest Lakota drummer and singer of all time. Of course, they had to get Victor Mature to play Crazy Horse."

"Victor Mature as Crazy Horse! It's insane!"

One time a face appeared and Le said, "There's Lot Cheyenne! Hang on, Lot!" and both he and Floyd John began to laugh. Le said to me, "Lot Cheyenne lives near where we used to over by Oglala on the reservation, and he told us about this movie or maybe it was another one—anyway, him and these other Indians was supposed to attack a wagon train, and they all had it in their contracts that they was gonna get twenty-five dollars a day, and if any of them fell off his horse he'd get a bonus of fifty dollars. So Lot and them went riding and hollering up to the wagon train, and a cowboy sticks his head out and fires one shot with a pistol, and immediately all thirty Indians go sprawling off their horses onto the ground!"

A footnote:

Thousands of Indians have been in movies. They appeared in some of the first movie footage ever made; starting in 1894, Thomas Edison filmed documentary scenes of Indian life and Indian performers in Buffalo Bill Cody's Wild West Show. The first American hit movie was a ten-minute-long Western called *The Great Train Robbery*, made in 1903. It had no Indians, but many films that imitated it did, as the Western became the basic American movie genre. As in the Wild West Shows, some movie directors preferred to use "real" Indians. By that they generally meant Plains Indians like Sioux or Cheyenne. Around 1910, a moviemaker named Thomas Ince brought a group of Sioux to his studio near Los Angeles and set them up in a village there so as to have a ready supply. To the many categories of Sioux, a new one was added: the Inceville Sioux, as these movie-actor Indians were sometimes called.

Buffalo Bill Cody had his own moviemaking company, and in 1913 he went to the Pine Ridge Reservation and places nearby to film a movie about the Plains Indian wars of forty years before. The federal bureaucracy that ran the reservations let over a thousand Sioux be in the movie. Some were old men who had fought in the actual battles portrayed. Short Bull, one of two Indians listed by name in the credits, was the same man who had been among the leaders of the Ghost Dance on the reservation back in 1890 and 1891. After Wounded Knee, and after the Army had suppressed the dance and imprisoned him and others, he had gone on to become a performer for Buffalo Bill.

Westerns tended to use actors who didn't look even remotely Indian in Indian roles, but Indian actors like William Eagleshirt and Chief Thundercloud and Chief Big Tree and Lois Red Elk and Jay Silverheels played those parts, too. Generally their names were pretty far down in the credits, their characters called simply "Indian" or "Indian Brave." John Ford, perhaps the greatest director of Westerns, often used the dramatic landscape of Arizona's Monument Valley for the setting of his films. Monument Valley is on the Navajo Reservation, and the Indian actors in John Ford Westerns are usually Navajo. In one movie they play Comanche, in another Arapahoe, in another Cheyenne; whenever background dialogue was required, they spoke Navajo regardless. If you look closely at the Navajo in a John Ford Western—for example, when they are Apache waiting along a ridgetop for the approach of the unsuspecting cavalry in *Fort Apache*—sometimes they seem to be trying hard not to smile.

The real boom in Westerns came in the 1950s and early 1960s, when scores of Western TV shows filled the air. Many Indians had bit parts then; it's not uncommon to find that a Sioux of sixty-five or older has appeared briefly in a TV show or film. By the 1970s, eighty-one movies had been made about the Sioux alone. (Only the Apache, with 104, had more.) About that time the Western briefly died. It soon revived, and casting directors again returned to the reservations. As happened with Short Bull, Indians who had formerly scared white people seemed to have a theatrical advantage; AIM leaders Russell Means and Dennis Banks and John Trudell have all appeared in movie roles.

Despite the participation of Indians in American moviemaking from its very beginnings, Hollywood has never given them much credit or praise. Of the many Indians who have appeared in movies, only three have been nominated for Academy Awards: Dan George, for Best Supporting Actor in the movie *Little Big Man*; Graham Greene, for Best Supporting Actor in *Dances with Wolves*; and Buffy Sainte-Marie, for writing the theme song "Up Where We Belong" for *An Officer and a Gentleman*. The only Indian ever to win an Academy Award is Buffy Sainte-Marie.

After a few months, my visits to Le's apartment came to an end. One day I got a call from him saying that he and his girlfriend had moved to near the town of Monsey, in upstate New York. He and I made many arrangements to meet when he said he was coming to town, but usually he didn't show up. Once he called and said he would be at a performance of the American Indian Dance Theater on West Nineteenth Street, and I went and waited outside, on the off chance. He and his girlfriend were among the first through the door when the show was over. Le was wearing a red turtleneck pullover, a fringed leather jacket, a straw cowboy hat, baggy stonewashed jeans, and snakeskin cowboy boots. He introduced me to his girlfriend, Noelle, a short, dark-haired woman with glasses and slightly out-of-sync eyes. She had on a sweater that buttoned and a white blouse with a gold print. The three of us went to a restaurant by the theater. Le and I had Budweisers and mozzarella sticks, and Noelle had coffee. They said they had just been out to the Pine Ridge Reservation to attend the August powwow and an honoring ceremony for Le's ninety-year-old father, Asa, known as Ace. Noelle said the reservation was like a black hole to her, with all that drinking and driving around on bumpy dirt roads, and that she had been glad to leave. She said they had gotten lost in the middle of the night on a dirt road somewhere in the badlands, and Le was passed out in the back seat, and she turned to ask him where they were; he woke up, looked around, said, "The New Jersey Turnpike," and went back to sleep. Le told me that they had gone to Wounded Knee and had taken some photographs of the mass gravesite, but the film had come back blank. He said that always happens when you photograph there.

Another time, Le and a half-Sioux, half-Micmac friend of his named Sequoyah and a woman friend of Sequoyah's and the woman's eleven-year-old son stopped by my apartment one evening when I was away at an art opening. My wife and I had moved to Brooklyn by then, and our daughter was three years old. My wife was sick with the flu and didn't answer the buzzer, but Le persisted, showing our upstairs neighbor the picture of him in my book and telling the neighbor that he was dying. The neighbor held the front door for them, and Le and his friends slept for a while on the floor in the basement of our building, then came up and knocked at our door. They sat around the apartment for several hours, smoking and talking with my wife and playing with my daughter. Later, when I asked her what she thought of Le, she said he had a "rough, gruff voice," but she liked him.

Le and Sequoyah rang the buzzer again a few nights later, and I went down and met them in the vestibule. My wife was still sick, so I didn't ask them in. Instead, we sat in Sequoyah's car, Le and I in the front seat, Sequoyah in the back, all of us about waist-deep in a rubble of Budweiser cans. We watched the passersby on Tenth Street through windows streaked with dried beer foam as Le told about the spiritual advantages of eating dog. He said that a faithful, fat puppy was best for eating, and that if you ever got lost wandering in the spirit world, the dog's faithfulness would recall you to yourself. Le got out of the car for a moment just as a neighbor of mine passed by walking his dog. Le said to him, conversationally, "I don't eat those. I just eat little puppies." The neighbor hurried away up the sidewalk. Sequoyah and I got out, too, and Le opened the trunk. He said he had a present for me and pulled out a Western-style saddle and laid it in the street next to the car. Its stirrups stretched almost from one side of Tenth Street to the other. He said it was mine. I said I had no horse. He tried to persuade me to take it, then reluctantly put it back in the trunk, meanwhile asking me for $500. I said I didn't have $500 either, at the moment. Le said I would get it tomorrow, that he would call me in the morning and I would give it to him.

Then for a long while I didn't see him, only heard from him by phone. Misfortune became the theme of his calls. He had been in a car wreck on the New York Thruway. A car in which he was riding had skidded and crashed into a culvert, and a screw jack under the front seat had come loose and cracked his kneecap, and his face hit the metal dashboard three times, and he had to go to a special Indian hospital in

Omaha for plastic surgery. A house he and Noelle had bought turned out to be on land which had not belonged to the seller, and the owner of the land was trying to evict them. He had pleaded guilty to a drunk-driving charge due to the incompetence of his lawyer and had been sentenced to a year in state prison as a repeat offender. A highway patrolman had come to his house with drawn gun and had taken him away. A judge had released him. He needed money for a new lawyer. His attempts to avoid prison had failed, and he had been given a date to begin to serve his sentence. He told me he would rather be dead than go to prison again.

One afternoon he called me from the Port Authority Bus Terminal in Manhattan. I remembered that this was the day he was supposed to go to prison. I went downstairs and got on the subway and met him by the Greyhound ticket counter. He looked tired and hungover, but otherwise better than I expected; I would not have noticed the scars on his face from his car accident if he hadn't pointed them out. He said he was going back to South Dakota. I said becoming a fugitive was a bad idea. We argued about this for a while. Finally he agreed to go back upstate and report to jail. I bought him an Adirondack Trailways bus ticket using my credit card, so the ticket could not be refunded. Then we went to a nearby cash machine and I took out fifty dollars and gave it to him. He was wearing a gray felt cowboy hat with a tall, uncreased crown and an eagle feather hanging from the back on a buckskin thong. He took off the hat and untied the eagle feather and handed it to me. He said it was a present for my son, then only a month or two old. We shook hands, and I wished him luck. He said as soon as he had gotten himself some Chinese food he would catch the next bus home. On the subway back to Brooklyn, three people asked me about the eagle feather. A black man in an Indian-style choker necklace made of pipe beads asked if I would be interested in selling it. I smiled and said no.

Le did not take the next bus home, or the bus after that. Noelle and I exchanged several anxious phone calls. About a week later, he called from a truck stop just east of Rapid City, South Dakota. He said he needed money for carfare; he was going back to the reservation.

CHAPTER 3

A while later, my family and I moved to Montana. It was either there or Russia. I had finished writing a long book, I became restless, I wanted a change. I went to Moscow to check it out and stayed in the apartment of a friend of mine's mother who was visiting the United States. I got my daughter enrolled in the first grade at the American School on Leninsky Prospect without too much difficulty (although the high tuition I would have to pay surprised me). Finding an apartment proved more of a challenge. I asked around among friends of friends, but no one knew of anything in the size and price range I wanted. I went to Moscow University and copied some telephone numbers from apartment ads on a bulletin board there. When I called the numbers, however, the people who answered all spoke Russian. Even flipping quickly through my Russian-English dictionary I could not keep up. After I came back to Brooklyn, my wife and I talked it over and decided, with some relief, on Missoula, Montana, instead. Having already moved to Montana once before when restlessness overcame me, I felt a bit self-conscious about doing it again. A friend in Montana told me that it was nothing to worry about; he had moved to Missoula seven times already, he said.

We put our apartment on the market, we attended farewell parties, we packed up our stuff. One hot morning in August a moving van came, and five black moving men working hard emptied the apartment in a few hours, never commenting to us on the dozens of cardboard boxes labeled TOYS and the scores of heavy cardboard boxes labeled BOOKS. We took a final look around the apartment and locked the door for the last time. We had lived there for six and a half years. We stopped at the dry cleaners on the corner and picked up my poplin suit, drove up to my sister's husband's parents' place in Connecticut, stayed there with my sister's family for a day or two, and set out across the country in our rented car.

The moving company had told us that the van might take as long as seventeen days to get to Missoula, so we didn't hurry. We visited my brother in Cleveland and ancestral graves in Norwalk, Ohio. My daughter saw her first rainbow in Nappanee, Indiana. My wife took pictures of Amish laundry hanging on clotheslines because she liked how all the garments were black and the same. Rows of corn wound around hills in Iowa like threads on a screw; woodlots sat on the prairie horizon suspended on a shimmering, like hovercraft. In Nebraska, while I was driving and perversely defending a recent magazine column by George Will that said the late Jerry Garcia of the Grateful Dead was responsible for America's drug problem, a column I didn't even agree with, I was stopped by a highway patrolman barely out of puberty and given a ninety-dollar ticket for speeding. When I got back in the car, humbled, the children looked at me with fearful eyes. My wife, who had been angrily arguing the anti–George Will position, could not stop laughing. She couldn't have been happier if ninety dollars had just flown in the window, instead of out the other way.

We passed through western South Dakota not far from the Pine Ridge Reservation; I wanted to go there and visit Le, but we didn't, choosing by majority vote to go to a reptile garden instead. I sulked about that as we drove through the Black Hills. When we called in the evening to check with the moving company, they said there had been a change of schedule and the van would be in Missoula in two days. We hurried across Montana to beat them there. Our friends Bryan and Dee, who had found us a house to rent near theirs in town, met us when we arrived. Bryan had given the wooden frame of the swing in the back yard of our house a new coat of paint, bright blue. We slept on the floor that night, and the next morning the van arrived. Three moving men from Seattle carried our stuff in, making derisive note of all the boxes of toys and books. "Books and toys, toys and books," they kept saying. The van driver told me that the movers in New York who had loaded our stuff into the van had all been crackheads, and I told him that they definitely weren't crackheads and that he wasn't from New York and that he had no idea what he was talking about. After that he was disagreeably polite.

When the van had left and we had unpacked the essentials, I went around town looking at cars with FOR SALE signs in people's yards. I found a 1988 Chevy Blazer in good condition—owned by an optometrist—and I bought it. A few days later, I drove back 780 miles to Oglala, South Dakota, to visit Le.

I was on the road by 6:45 in the morning. Mist rose from the Clark Fork River and hung up in the bushes beside it like packing material; a man stood on the front of a log loader and wiped the mist off the windshield with full gestures of his arm. I took Interstate 90 almost all the way—up the Clark Fork valley to Butte, over the Continental Divide, over more ranges of mountains, then along the valley of the Yellowstone River to Billings. Beyond Billings the road headed south into Wyoming, past the site of the battle of the Little Bighorn, then across the creased and empty near-desert in the northeastern part of that state. At first I had the visor down against the sunrise. Five hundred miles later, the sun was way behind me, bouncing off my rearview mirror and tinting the buttes and strips of plowed ground a red like the red that runs along the gutter by a brownstone being sandblasted in Brooklyn.

Full dark had fallen by the time I reached Rapid City. I followed South Dakota Highway 79 heading through town and then south, toward Le's house on the reservation about eighty miles away. Just beyond the city's last lights, an Indian hitchhiker appeared suddenly on the roadside. The wind had come up, and his long hair flew in the headlights. I didn't stop. The sameness of the interstate seemed far behind me now. On the dark, narrow two-lane, the occasional cars coming the other way seemed to blast by at highest speed. In this part of the country, Indians have an average life expectancy about eleven years shorter than that of Americans as a whole. As I approached the reservation, I imagined I could feel the life expectancy drop, as palpable as a sudden drop in temperature. Just before the little town of Hermosa, South Dakota, my headlights picked out a group of the white reflecting-metal highway markers which South Dakota puts up at places where fatal car accidents have occurred. I counted eight markers—eight souls—set in a row that ascended from the ditch by the road and up the grassy incline beside it.

Over the next four years, I traveled back and forth to the reservation many times. Usually I went via the interstate and Highway 79, and I noted those markers whenever I passed. If I had the radio on, I turned it off, and I said a prayer. I wondered about the markers, so I called the South Dakota Department of Transportation, and a man in the accident records division found the accident report and sent it to me. The crash had happened at eight minutes after nine o'clock on the evening of Friday, June 27, 1986. A northbound car went out of control and collided with a southbound car, and both cars caught fire. Seven members of a Sioux family originally from the Rosebud Reservation died in the southbound car. Three of them were children under seven years old. The family's name was Dismounts Thrice. The northbound driver, who had a bottle of whiskey of a brand the highway patrol did not specify with only an inch left in it in his car, and whose blood alcohol content was three times the legal limit, also died. The Indian driver had no alcohol in his blood. The drunk driver was not an Indian. He worked for the Better Business Bureau.

I searched out local newspaper stories about the crash and read about the heat of its flames, the immense rising pillar of dark-black smoke, and the thunderstorm that poured down not long afterward. I pursued even further, found the apartments where the people in the southbound car had lived in the mostly Indian housing developments north of Rapid City and the convenience store where they had bought their last tank of gas. I went to the small Western city where the drunk driver had grown up and saw the ample brick house he had grown up in, his picture in his high school yearbook, the apartment where his parents lived. After a couple of years, it occurred to me that maybe by now God had granted some peace to the people who had died in the crash and to those who loved them, and that I should, too.

The first time I saw the markers, I decided I did not want to drive anymore. I had gone 720 miles since morning. I pulled over in Hermosa and parked in a shadowed place behind a gas station–convenience store–casino–restaurant. I picked a spot by the aluminum-can recycling Dumpster where I hoped my car wouldn't be too conspicuous, folded down the back seat, unrolled my sleeping bag, and went to sleep. At an unknown hour of the night, I came half awake in a flood of light from a brilliant source at my back window. In my sleep I thought I was dreaming of that floodlit moment in the movies when the alien spaceship descends. The light seemed to be coming from a giant vehicle parked behind me. I got up on one elbow. Someone rapped on the driver's-side window with something metal—a flashlight—and asked me to roll the window down. The flashlight was in the hand of a short, blond, crewcut man in a blue denim coat and jeans with a big pistol in a black holster on his hip. He asked for my driver's license and I groggily fumbled it to him. He beamed the light on it, asking me quick questions all the while. Finally, looking at his denim outfit, I said, "Who are *you*?" He said, with a drawling flourish, "I'm the local law." Then he disappeared, the mothership ascended, and I went back to sleep.

At dawn, I took a back road from Hermosa to the reservation. There was no one else about. I had the radio tuned to KILI, the Pine Ridge radio station, which broadcasts from the reservation near the village of Porcupine. It was playing Lakota singing and drumming. Under an overcast sky, the prairie looked drained of color. Here and there I saw burned patches, the black extending in tongues where the wind had pushed it. In the middle of one burned patch was a car seat, also burned. A wheel rim with shreds of tire still on it hung from a fencepost. Two rows of tires lay flat on the roof of a turquoise-colored trailer, anchoring the roof against the wind. I followed the road into a wide valley, crossed a bridge over the Cheyenne River, and was on the reservation.

How many boundaries this reservation has had over the years! About a century and a half ago, the lands set aside for the Sioux by treaty stretched from the Powder River to the west, to the Heart River in the north, to the Missouri River in the east, to the North Platte River in the south—an immense expanse in the middle of the continent, covering parts of the present states of Montana, Wyoming, North Dakota, South Dakota, and Nebraska. Since then, Sioux lands have shrunk and shrunk again, leaving behind vestigial boundaries like a drying sea. In 1868, after the Sioux had won the Powder River war, a new treaty actually increased their lands somewhat, giving them hunting rights as far north as the Yellowstone River and as far west as the Bighorn Mountains. A provision of that treaty, which the Indians may have overlooked, however, required them to make their permanent homes only in a smaller part of their lands, in what was called the Great Sioux Reservation, most of which lay within the half of present South Dakota west of the Missouri River. After the Indian victory over Custer and the Seventh Cavalry at the Little Bighorn, a punitive spirit in the United States led to the so-called sell-or-starve agreement of 1876: the Sioux got a token land exchange for much of their original territory, and the Great Sioux Reservation was relieved of its westernmost part, which included the gold-rich Black Hills. If the Sioux refused to sign, the government commissioners told them, the food-ration payments which had begun with earlier treaties would be cut off. Even with this threat, the commissioners could not collect the signatures of three-fourths of the adult males of the tribe as required by law. Congress went ahead and ratified the agreement anyway the following year.

In 1889, the federal government unilaterally broke up what remained of the Great Sioux Reservation, and gave nine million acres of it to the new states of North Dakota and South Dakota. Again, the Sioux had no say. The Sioux tribes ended up with six reservations within the former Great Sioux Reservation's boundaries. The Oglala got a piece of land in southwestern South Dakota about ninety miles long and fifty-five miles wide at its widest point. Its southern boundary was the Nebraska state line. On paper, the Oglala reservation included almost three million acres; another act of Congress, however, had the long-term effect of removing much of that from Indian hands. The Dawes Act of 1887, called the Allotment Act, intended to make Indians full citizens through ownership of land. Tribal holdings were allotted to individual tribal members in parcels of 160 acres per head of household. Lands left over, called "surplus lands," were open for settlement by non-Indians. The people who wrote the act considered themselves friends of the Indian, and they put in various clauses and safeguards to see that Indians kept the land they received. In fact, the Dawes Act proved an efficient means for the further drastic reduction of Indian lands. Individual ownership of land, that notion imported from Europe, generally did not make much sense to Indians. White ranchers and farmers and speculators found taking land from Indians one at a time to be simpler and more legal than previous methods of taking it from the tribe as a whole.

By 1934, when another act of Congress ended the allotment program, Indian lands had decreased from 138 million acres to 47 million acres nationwide. On the Oglala reservation, about a million acres passed from Indian ownership. Perhaps believing the nineteenth-century dictum that the Indian must soon disappear, the authors of allotment did not provide for the possibility the Indian populations would expand. Indians often were not fond of making wills, and many died intestate, with many heirs, leaving allotted lands to be divided into equal shares. Over generations, this occurred again and again. Today, on Pine Ridge and other reservations, some Indians own parcels of original allotments which are measured not in acres but in square yards, feet, and inches.

Past the village of Red Shirt inside the border of the reservation, the road entered a piece of grassy tableland which descends steeply at its edges into badlands. Locals call this the Red Shirt Table Road. At certain places beside the road, the badlands are like an erosion carnival opening at your feet. Travelers on the Red Shirt Table Road, frustrated by its lack of public restrooms, sometimes pull over, step out, stroll a short distance away from the car, and accidentally plunge into the chasms below. Some of the pillars of rock still have a flat piece of prairie on top the size of a living-room rug, from which the eroded rock face complicatedly declines hundreds of feet to the canyon floor. Some of the monoliths are jagged on top, like newspaper torn against the grain. Others are rounded and smooth, and shiny as old pants. In places the ranks recede, one eroded gray-and-pink wall of rock behind the other, all the way to the horizon. The Red Shirt Table Road is the worst paved road I have ever driven. Even here on the flat, the badlands seem to want to make their point. Sinks afflict the road's asphalt, creating places where you drive down in and then up the other side. Plates of roadway lurch upward toward you, bumper-high. Potholes slurp and open wide. Not every road on Pine Ridge or in its vicinity is as bad as this, but anyone who visits the reservation more than twice learns that Pine Ridge is a difficult place to get to. No major thoroughfare or rail line runs to it, or even very close by. This may seem at first to be a coincidence of geography or bad planning. In fact, it is deliberate. To oversimplify only a little, it is the result of the bad conscience of General William Tecumseh Sherman.

The Oglala Sioux, pre-reservation, lived mostly west of here, in present Wyoming west and south of the Black Hills. If their nation had had a capital, it would have been there on the prairies in the valley of the North Platte River, perhaps near the fur-trading post at Fort Laramie. The Oglala liked to trade at the fort, then move into the Powder River country to the north, for the good buffalo hunting and the convenient raiding distance from the Crow. The Oregon Trail ran along the North Platte Valley, and the Oglala found the wagon trains interesting. After they had chased the Army out of Wyoming's Powder River country in 1868, they could not understand why General Sherman and the other treaty commissioners kept insisting that they move well away from the Platte, preferably to the northeast and out of Wyoming Territory entirely. Which is to say, they did not understand about the railroad. In 1868 the Union Pacific Railroad was building the first transcontinental line on a route that ran through southern Wyoming. The government had issued the railroad millions of dollars in bonds and needed to get the line completed fast. Nobody in the government or in the employ of the railroad wanted the warlike Oglala anywhere near the railroad line.

General Sherman, who led the government negotiators, no doubt had a more personal vision of what the Oglala might do to it; he had himself torn railroad lines to shreds all over the South during the Civil War just a few years earlier. He knew how easy it was to wreck a railroad, and maybe even how much fun it was. Still fighting the previous war, as generals do, Sherman thought first of securing the railroad. He and many others wanted to move the Oglala all the way back east to the shores of the Missouri River; steamboat contracts to supply them there had already been let. The struggle went on for ten years, Red Cloud and the Oglala pulling to stay in the West, the government pushing them east. This corner of South Dakota somewhere between each's desire became the final compromise. Red Cloud accepted it, but didn't like it. Sherman and the railroad builders were satisfied; no one was ever going to try to lay railroad tracks through those badlands anyway.

Within fifteen miles or so, the Red Shirt Table Road left the bumpiness of the tableland and became a good gravel surface running straight through an expanse of little bare-top clay hills like gray haystacks, then through rolling prairie with low buttes to the east and west. The road turned to asphalt again, this section smooth and newly paved. Up ahead a magpie flapped black and white across it like a checkered flag. Occasional dirt driveways to either side dwindled to house trailers, each one solitary in the distance, blue wood smoke rising from the stovepipes. Next to almost every lonesome trailer, you could see the silhouette of a basketball backboard and pole. James Naismith, who in 1891 invented the game of basketball, never made any money from it; but, he wrote, "I am sure that no man can derive more pleasure from money or power than I do from seeing a pair of basketball goals in some out of the way place." I crossed the bridge over the White River and soon saw a water tower on the horizon. When I came up to it, I could read the word LONEMAN in black letters on its silver side. It's in the little community of Loneman, uphill from a housing development and the Loneman Elementary School. Past Loneman I continued to the junction of Highway 18, turned left, and drove on a mile or so to the village of Oglala. A woman sorting mail in the gray cement post office told me how to find the house of a woman named Sarah Brave, who told me through her closed screen door how to find Le.

His house stood by a bend in the road with no other houses around, singular as a letter in an alphabet book. It was a standard government-built house of the kind often seen on military bases or Indian reservations. It was one-story, with faded brown siding and a yard run mostly to weeds. Six or eight cars and a pickup truck, in various stages of dilapidation, made a loose semicircle around one corner. I pulled into the rutted mud driveway, opened the door, and stepped out onto a flattened Budweiser can. Le was standing in the yard. We had not seen each other in a year and a half, since that time at the Port Authority Bus Terminal. He greeted me without surprise. We hugged each other and shook hands, and Le felt the pulse in my wrist with his thumb. He said, "*Hoka hey*, Little Brother. I am honored to be in your presence." His breath was Budweiser and a chemical I couldn't place. He was wearing cowboy boots, faded pegged blue jeans, a red cowboy shirt with buttons of blue imitation mother-of-pearl, and a neck brace in a color sometimes called "flesh" extending from his collarbone up to his ears. On the front of the neck brace, just above the collarbone, large raised letters said FRONT. He had his hair in the piled-high style I'd seen before. Combined with the brace, it gave him the look of a starched-collar lady from out of the past.

"I was in a car wreck three weeks ago," he explained. "Me and this guy named Archambault that I went to Indian boarding school with was drinking in White Clay, Nebraska, and in the afternoon we started hitchhiking back to Pine Ridge. We got picked up by Joe Red Star and Mark Goings, and me and Archambault got in the back seat, and I hadn't hardly got in when them guys floored it and we was flyin' up Highway 407, and then suddenly we was off the road on the right and I looked up and saw the light pole comin' at us. I was yellin', 'Hey, hey, hey!' and we took out the light pole and rolled four times. I went flyin' over the front seat and hit the windshield with the back of my head and shoulders, and I had the top of the car pressed right against my face. Man, there was a whole lot of moanin' and groanin' in that car. It took the emergency medical technician guys three and a half hours to cut us out. We backed up traffic on 407 for miles. It was *hot* in that car, too. I could hear people sayin', 'Why can't they get 'em *out*?' Finally they had the top cut off and one of the EMT guys took hold of my head to see if my neck was broken and I let out a bloodcurdling scream. They put a big plastic thing under my head and put me on a slab of wood and then onto a gurney and took me to Rapid City Regional Hospital. I was in surgery for about four hours. They fixed the broken vertebrae in my neck—I think they used some bone taken from my hip. Everybody came to the hospital to visit. Elliott Gould called to tell me to get better, and his daughter Molly called, too. David Carradine called, and Robert Altman, the movie director. My sister Norma sat by my bedside and prayed for me for eight straight hours. I was out of the hospital in a week. The other guys didn't have nothin' serious—broken ankle, broken nose, bruises and scrapes. Last week I ran into Archambault, and he said, 'If we'd known those guys was so drunk, we'd've waited for the next car.' "

Le invited me in, and we climbed the single cinder block he used for a doorstep. His door latch was a green-and-white plastic fish stringer, which he tied to a nail inside. He asked if I'd had breakfast and offered me a beer. I replied that I had quit drinking. He said, "That reminds me—I've got to take my pills again." He produced half a dozen pill bottles of various sizes and shook pills from them into his palm. Hospitably, he first offered a large orange capsule to me: "Want one?" I declined, with thanks. Then he washed them all down with a few swigs of beer. He sat on a stove log and I on the only chair. The amount of stuff in his house overthrew my attempt to take it in. There was a non-working clock on the wall, and a brown hole near it where the oven pipe used to be, and a cast-iron woodstove, and a plastic milk crate full of silver tinsel Christmas wreaths, and a yellow hard hat, and a photograph of a statuesque Indian woman in a T-shirt smiling and holding a .357 Magnum revolver ("That's my nephew's wife, Deborah. She's a rowdy from the Fort Apache Reservation"), and a rolled-up section of snow fence, and a poster from the movie *Incident at Oglala,* and a copy of the collected short stories of Ernest Hemingway, and several sports trophies, and the paperwork from Le's recent hospital bills. A door just behind me opened into a room filled several feet deep with suitcases, plastic picnic coolers, backpacks, baby carriers, trunks, and heavyweight canvas tote bags. I remembered when Le had just moved from New York City up to Monsey, and I had commiserated with him, saying how hard it was to move. He had replied, "It's not hard for me. I'm nomadic."

I asked if this stuff was his. He said, "Most of it belongs to my sister Florence. She lived here for a while with her kids and grandkids, until the tribe gave her a new house in a development in Oglala on the other side of Highway 18. Before that, my dad lived here. It was his house originally, and they all moved in here with him. He needed a house close to the highway like this because he had cancer and had to get back and forth over to the clinic for treatment. He lost a quarter of his stomach and one and a half of his lungs, and he still was smokin' three packs a day. He didn't care what brand—any tobacco he could get, as long as he could blow smoke. The tribe or the BIA or someone moved this house here from the Army munitions depot over in Igloo, South Dakota. I think that at one time it might have been near to some nuclear weapons. A while ago they tested it and it was really radioactive. It still will get a Geiger counter going pretty good. It had a fire in '83, and when they fixed it up afterward they didn't put in no insulation, so when the temperature drops it can get pretty chilly in here. When winter comes I'll just get me a fat woman and let her sleep on the windy side."

Back in the yard, he led me on a brief tour of the accumulated cars. All of them, according to him, were much closer to being drivable than they appeared. He kept saying, "Oh, it'll run. Put a new battery and a windshield and a new set of tires and some gas in it, and it'll run." Then he said, "Let's go—I'll take you to see my mom and dad." We got in my car. He did not put on his seat belt, but I insisted that he put on his seat belt. We headed north, on the road I had driven from Red Shirt Table. I asked him if anyone on the reservation called him Le. I knew his birth name was Leonard Thomas Walks Out; Sarah Brave had referred to him as Leonard. "There's people here who call me Le or Laid-Back, but most call me Leonard," he said. "Or Lenny. And there's still a few real old-timers who remember when I was the baby of my family, before Floyd John was born. One old lady, Leonora Fast Horse, saw me at the post office the other day and said, 'Look! It's Baby Leo!' I mean, here I'm goin' on fifty five years old!"

After about three miles Le directed me onto a grassy track leading off to the right. In the high weeds next to it were pieces of a broken guitar. The track led onto a low rise with a barbed-wire fence around a small plot of gravestones and crosses; set back from and above the road, it would be hard to spot if you didn't know it was there. Le braced his chest against the gatepost, reached around it with both arms, and pulled hard to free the gate end from the taut loop of barbed wire that latched it; then he dragged the gate open and laid it on the ground (not bad, I thought, for a person with a broken neck). I took off my baseball cap and walked quietly as we entered the cemetery grounds. The more Le talked, the quieter I became. On this little patch of earth, a vastness of suffering and disaster had converged. Among the murders, suicides, and car accidents the headstones could not describe, these three seemed central to Le's life:

Albert C. Walks Out; Feb. 23, 1933–Aug. 3, 1957. "This was my brother," Le said. "Albert was nine years older than me. He joined the Army during the Korean War. He had only an eighth-grade education, but he became a war hero and got a battlefield commission as a sergeant first class when he was only twenty years old. He was a really tough guy, and a lot of people around here were jealous of him. When he was home on leave, he stopped to help some guys whose car had a flat tire on the county road eight miles east of Oelrichs, South Dakota, and they beat him to death with a tire iron. I was fifteen years old at the time. The guys who killed him were Jonas and Franklin Belt and Charles Blind Man. They were drunk when they did it. They all went to prison, and they're all dead now. I believe one or two of them are buried in this cemetery, too."

Elizebith Walks Out; May 22, 1906–April 7, 1958. "This is my mom. She was born on the Cheyenne River Reservation, by Eagle Butte. We still have inheritance land over there. She and my dad got married in 1926, and they had eleven children. I'm the eighth. Her maiden name was Blacksmith, and I've got a lot of Blacksmith relatives around here and on Cheyenne River. Her grandfather Moses Blacksmith was a Canadian Frenchman with a light-colored, curly hairdo like George Washington's. Her dad had a ranch with racehorses and pigs and chickens and ducks on the Moreau River near Thunder Butte. But then her mom died and her dad moved over here and married Edna Loafer and became a member of the Oglala Tribe. After they moved here was when my mom met Asa Walks Out, my dad. She got killed in an accident on Highway 87 between Rushville and White Clay, Nebraska. She had gone over there shopping with Amos Red Paint and they ran out of gas and they were pushing the car by the side of the road when a bootlegger from White Clay with no headlights ran into them from behind. She got both her legs cut off and died seven days later. My dad lived to be ninety-one. He died just last summer. We buried him on top of her, but we don't have a marker for him yet."

Elda Asa Walks Out; March 7, 1935–Feb. 14, 1959. "My mom died eight months after Albert, and Elda—we called him Eldee—died ten months after my mom. Eldee was just out of the Army and he could kick anyone's ass. He didn't even care if he got his own ass kicked once in a while. He'd get back in the car with his nose all bloodied and say, 'Well, at least I got the anger out of me!' He was running my dad's spread near here, and me and him had gone up to Rapid to buy sixteen hundred pounds of cattle feed, and we were coming back in the pickup drinking whiskey and beer, and he started telling me that he'd made a terrible mistake. He said he had married too young and in a Catholic ceremony and now he couldn't get out of it, and he was in love with a fifteen-year-old girl. So we got back to his place and I was outside unloading the truck when one of his kids come running out of the house saying, 'Mommy and Daddy is fightin'.' So I picked the kid up and comforted him and went inside and asked what they were fightin' about, and Eldee said, 'We're not fightin', we're just talkin'.' Then he takes me out in the yard and says, 'She won't give me a divorce. I'm goin'.' I said, 'Where to? I'll go with you.' He says, 'Where I'm goin' you can't follow. Take care of my kids.' He gets a rifle out of the truck and I think, Whoa, I better get the kids back in the house. I go in and right away I hear BLAM—he shoots himself right in the head. I run out and he's flat on his back and blood is gushing from his forehead eighteen inches in the air. I ran to a white rancher's house and said, 'Call the fuckin' ambulance! My brother has shot himself in the head!' By the time I got back, there was blood all over the place but nobody there.

"After that I went crazy for a while, writing bad checks. I got caught, went to prison, got out, stole a government truck, ended up back in prison again. When Eldee shot himself I was sixteen years old."

As we walked back to my car, Le stopped by an unmarked grave near the middle of the cemetery. He said, "This is my grandfather James Walks Out. He was born in 1861, and he lived to be an old man. When I was a little boy, I lived with him for a few years. He raised me, more than my mom and dad. One of his Lakota names was Woz'aglai, which means Gatherer of the Spirits. He was a famous medicine man. He was really good at helping people to find stuff they had lost. He had special ceremonies for that; white people and Indians used to come to him from all around. He was a boy at Fort Robinson when Crazy Horse was killed, and he helped smuggle Crazy Horse's bones from a grave there. Him and a few other young guys took the bones at night to near Chadron Creek and met up with Crazy Horse's parents, and the parents carried them from there. Woz'aglai was one of the few people who knew where Crazy Horse was buried. Once my oldest brother, Hermus, asked him where that was. Hermus said he would go and dig the bones up and sell them and make a lot of money. Woz'aglai refused to tell, and after that he never talked about where Crazy Horse was buried anymore."

Le closed the cemetery gate, again pulling on it hard, and he latched it with the loop of wire. Then we drove back the way we had come. As we approached his house, Le said, "Floyd John ought to be awake by now. Let's go eat up his food." We drove on, and he directed me to turn onto a puddled road just past the Loneman School. The ruts were deep and the car jounced, and Le's neck caused him to wince with each jounce. The going got muddier and muddier. I stopped and shifted into four-wheel drive. The ruts then split up into an every-man-for-himself profusion across a mudflat, and I must have guessed wrong, because soon I was roaring across it at maximum rpms slewing back and forth, going nearly sideways sometimes, and hurling up flying mud around me like a magnetic field. Floyd John heard us coming—anyone would have—and he was standing outside his green tar-paper shack as we squished to a stop in his yard. The car had mud on the hood and the windshield and the side windows. I turned off the steaming engine. Floyd John walked to the car, looked me over, and asked, "Well, bro, are you likin' the rez as much as you liked New York?"

"Tell me, Floyd John—when are they going to finish building the subway out to your house?"

"Any day, any day. The bull snakes and the king snakes are workin' on it right now."

CHAPTER

4

Floyd John had put on some weight since I'd last seen him, and now he walked with a limp and used a cane. He began to tell me how he had been working on a modular home over at the air base by Rapid City and a wall had fallen on him and crushed his hip. Then he described which new benefits this entitled him to. The paperwork of it, between agencies of the state and the federal government and the tribe, was so complicated that I couldn't have kept up if he'd explained it to me five times. Le asked him if he had any red beans with hot sauce we could eat, and Floyd John said he had no food in the house. He wasn't due to pick up his commodities for a couple of days. He said that his girlfriend, Wanda Kindle, who worked for the tribal police, was due to get paid that afternoon. He climbed with difficulty into the back seat, and we roared and crawfished our way back to the paved road.

First we stopped at the Oglala post office so Le and Floyd John could check their mail. The postmaster usually has all the mail sorted and in the boxes by 10:30, a time known thereabouts as "mail": "I'll see you tomorrow morning after mail." Not many on the reservation get their mail brought to where they live; most people have to go in and pick it up, either from a post office box or by asking at the window for general delivery. In the later years of Red Cloud's life, his two-mile trip to the post office and back was the big event of his day. At 10:45 that morning, the rutted lot by the Oglala post office was full of idling cars, some of them making plenty of noise and smoke. Le and Floyd John got out and exchanged a few words with the woman in the station wagon next to us. Then they went into the building and came out again in a second, disappointed and blue. "Nothing," Le said. "A lot of days there's nothing. I usually check it anyway. You never know. A few weeks ago I got a letter from the Attorney General of New York saying that he wasn't gonna come after me and make me go to jail as long as I never set foot in New York State again. It was a pretty friendly letter, all in all."

Like many of the other cars, we then pulled out of the post office lot and headed for the village of Pine Ridge fifteen miles away. Pine Ridge is the largest town on the reservation. The center of tribal government is there, and the reservation headquarters of the U.S. Bureau of Indian Affairs, and the Indian Health Services hospital. Many days on the reservation include a trip to Pine Ridge. The road from Oglala follows the valley of White Clay Creek much of the way. For some distance the creek bottom and a reservoir are on one side, then the creek crosses to the other. To the north and south are uplands leading to low, chalk-colored buttes that rise from the prairie like molars from a gumline. Groups of the yellow pines that give Pine Ridge its name fit themselves into the upland creases and folds. On unsettled days, cumulus clouds pile up for miles above. We passed a tipi made of white canvas, a tipi made of weathered white plyboard, a Quonset hut, a Seventh-Day Adventist church. Trailer homes and one-story houses appeared here and there, mostly set far apart. Wherever their driveways met the road, deltas of muddy tire tracks spread across the pavement. Le made me retell for Floyd John the story about the policeman in Hermosa who had awakened me the night before. They said the cop was famous for giving a hard time to Indians on their way through town. He and Floyd John kept repeating, *"I'm the local law!"* and laughing.

A rise brought us in view of the Pine Ridge water towers—most towns on the reservation have a water tower fixing them in place, but Pine Ridge has four—and the rise after that showed a slow line of cars below us moving to the only traffic light on the reservation, at the intersection of Highways 18 and 407, in downtown Pine Ridge. The intersection has had a traffic light for only five years or so. Before, it was a four-way stop. People on the reservation called it "the four-way," and many still call it that today. The four-way is the main crossroads of the Oglala nation. On one corner is a wooden bench whose back is a square concrete planter containing weeds and a small pine tree. A large concrete pot full of earth nearby perhaps was once intended to grow flowers. People sit on the bench and cross their legs and talk for hours, just as old men used to do years ago, long before the bench and the flowerpot, telling about the time Queen Victoria kissed them when they were young children in England with Buffalo Bill. "Bullshit Corner" is this corner's unofficial name. On another corner is the Pine Ridge post office, which shares a large brick building with an auditorium called Billy Mills Hall, where most of the important indoor community gatherings are. On another corner is a two-story brick building containing tribal offices and the offices of the Oglala Department of Public Safety—the tribal police. Floyd John got out and went to look for Wanda there. On another corner is a convenience store–gas station which then was called Big Bat's Conoco and now is called Big Bat's Texaco. Le and I parked and went in.

In Pine Ridge, Big Bat's is the place you go. If you're just passing through or visiting, you go to Big Bat's because it's one of the few places on the reservation that look like what you're used to in paved America. Big Bat's has a big, highway-visible, red-and-white sign, and rows of pumps dispensing gasoline and diesel fuel, and full-color cardboard advertisements affixed to the top of the pumps, and country music playing from speakers in the canopies above; inside, it has the usual brightly lit shelves of products whose empty packages will end up on the floor of your car, and freezers and beverage coolers set into the wall, and a deli counter highlighted in blue neon and staffed by aproned young people who use disposable clear plastic gloves to put cold cuts on your six-inch or twelve-inch submarine sandwich, and video games, and TV monitors just below ceiling level showing CNN or country-music videos, and plastic tables and window booths where you can sit and eat or just sit, and a row of pay telephones. If you live on the reservation, if you're not just passing through, you go to Big Bat's because that's where everybody goes.

The original Big Bat was Baptiste "Bat" Pourier, a trader who married into the Sioux and who often served as an interpreter between them and government officials in the second half of the nineteenth century; he was called Big to distinguish him from another interpreter, Baptiste "Little Bat" Garnier. Big Bat's name comes up often in chronicles of the Plains Indian wars. The present Big Bat, also a Pourier, is the original Bat's four-greats grandson. He is a well-built man in his forties with a close-cropped head, a round, boyish face, and dark eyes that register minute changes in the progress of his enterprise. Often, they gleam with triumph; Big Bat's is always busy. No other small-town place I know of has such a plentiful and varied clientele. There are Indians, of course, of all blood degrees, full-blood as well as almost blond. Employees of the tribe and of the BIA and tribal politicos come in for breakfast and for coffee afterward, prolonging conversations that are elliptical and hard to eavesdrop on. Drunks who have been up all night nurse cups of coffee they have bought with change and use the john. There are truck drivers running overweight and avoiding the weigh stations on the main roads, Oglala teenagers in groups of four or five wearing the colors of Denver street gangs, Methodist ministers on their way to local volunteer jobs, college professors leading tours of historical sites, TV crews shooting documentary footage, Mormon missionary ladies in polyester raincoats and with scarves tied around their heads. In the summer, tourists multiply—mid-Americans wearing clothes so casual they might as well be pajamas and toting large video cameras, and fiftyish English couples having one of those bitter, silent arguments travelers have, and long-haired New Age people smelling of patchouli oil, and Australian guys with leather Aussie hats and lissome girlfriends, and college kids from Massachusetts singing in a fake-corny way songs they just heard on the radio in their van, and black families in bright sportswear, and strangely dressed people speaking Hungarian, and ashblond German women backpackers in their early twenties effortlessly deflecting the attentions of various guys trying to talk to them, and Japanese people by the occasional busload, and once in a while a celebrity with an entourage. Observers who noted about a hundred years ago the disappearance of the American frontier have turned out to be wrong; America will always have its frontier places, and they will always look like Big Bat's.

Le and I each got twelve-inch club combo sandwiches with everything, including jalapeños, and medium sodas. Total cost: $10.62. The sandwiches lasted all day, because half was enough to fill us up, and we saved the rest for later. We sat at a table and ate, and Floyd John and Wanda joined us. Wanda was a short, unsmiling woman with long hair parted in the middle. She wore a heavy shirt unbuttoned like a jacket over a dark pullover and blue jeans. Her wary eyes took me in at a glance when Floyd John introduced us. He said she was the only person on the reservation who knew how to run the computer system for the police department. Wanda accepted this without comment; as we talked, she mostly listened, adding only a remark or two in a small, clear voice quieter than a whisper. Le made me tell for the third time the story about the cop in Hermosa, and when I finished Wanda just nodded, as if she'd heard it before.

Le turned to three guys seated at a table next to ours and began talking to them in Sioux. He stopped for a moment to introduce me to one of them, who he said was his cousin, but I didn't catch the name. Floyd John joined the discussion, which went back and forth and seemed to be verging on an argument. After the three guys had left, I asked Le what it had been about. "White guys dancing," he said. "My cousin was saying that there was too many white guys dancing at the sun dances on the reservation last summer. Him and his friends think letting white guys or any non-Indians in ruins the ceremonies. They don't think outsiders should be allowed even as helpers or water carriers. They say that you let white guys buy the food and the firewood, the way some sun dances do, and then you've gotta let 'em dance, and then pretty soon people who don't know anything are running the whole ceremony. And he's right that there was *hundreds* of white guys goin' to the sun dances last summer. But I say, If a person's heart is good, let him participate in a respectful way. There's non-Indian people that love the sun dance and are really sincere. You just have to be sure that you have elders and medicine men who run the ceremony as it's supposed to be."

Over the next summers, the question of white guys dancing would become one of the most controversial on the reservation. Some traditionalists wanted the tribal council to pass a law banning all non-Indians from sun dances held on Pine Ridge. People who favored open sun dances answered that they would use guns to defend their right to practice their religion with whomever they chose. At least one respected leader kept his sun dance strictly closed. Some dances were open, others were semi-open but had entrances with many checkpoints at which undesirables could be turned away, others were small and secret and held in remote places where passersby and tourists would never see. A hundred years ago Oglala who continued to practice their traditional ceremonies despite the government's ban did so in secret, for fear of white people finding out and shutting them down; today the fear is of white people finding out and wanting to join.

The first afternoon I spent on the reservation can stand for many: we went to Big Bat's, then gassed up, got supplies, and drove around. That day, Le and Floyd John wanted to show me around the reservation, which meant a lot of driving, but being on the reservation almost always does. Two 32-mile round trips between Oglala and Pine Ridge in a day were not uncommon. Then there were the longer drives up to Rapid City to see doctors or relatives, trips to Chadron, Nebraska, to take a television to a repair shop, trips to Hot Springs, South Dakota, to drop Floyd John off at the Veterans' Hospital, trips to see a medicine man who lives miles off the paved road. It seemed as if every time I looked at the gas gauge it was falling back to empty, and every time I checked the odometer I had added another 300 miles. The Oglala may have lost the prairie vastnesses they used to hunt, but they are still obliged to roam. The supplies we picked up beforehand were usually beer. Afternoons almost always began with a trip to the town of White Clay, Nebraska, a mile and three-quarters from the town of Pine Ridge and just across the Nebraska line. Selling alcohol is illegal on the reservation, but legal in Nebraska. I will say more about White Clay later. I dreaded going there.

The reservation landscape is dense with stories. As we drove around, Le told me some of them, and Floyd John occasionally joined in. In the valley of the White River northwest of Oglala, on paved roads and gravel roads near where they grew up, Le said:

"I was riding over this bridge one night with the He Crow boys when we saw a ghost. We heard the hoofs of a horse climbing out of the creek bottom, and then the sound came onto the road right in front of us, and there wasn't nothin' there. Then just for a second we saw the face and body of this Indian rider. The ghost said, 'Hey'—and man, did we go gallopin' hell for leather out of there! We didn't stop till we reached the ridgetop. I never laughed so hard.

"That flat ground above the creek over there is where Francis Slow Bear died. He was playin' cards one night at his brother's cabin back in the hills, and he decided to walk home, and everybody told him to stay till morning, but he went anyway. It was late November, and a blizzard hit. A cowboy found him the next morning froze to death just above his cabin. He had got lost in the blizzard, probably snow-blind. His tracks showed he had walked in circles before he died.

"All back there along the river is Earl Charging Thunder's land. Earl had a string of good buckin' horses he used to hire out to rodeos, and sometimes he let the kids around here practice on 'em. I learned to ride broncs at Earl's.

"Everybody around here used to have horses. Us kids used to ride up on those ridgetops and spread out along 'em just at dark, and then one of us would hold up a lighted kitchen match, and then pretty soon all of us would be holdin' up matches, and you could see the little lights in a line strung out for miles.

"One time me and some guys was huntin' along here, and Timothy Bear Nose said, 'I'm gonna shoot me a mule deer, and if I can't find a deer I'm gonna shoot me a cow.' So here we saw a deer grazin' about a hundred yards away. We roll down the window and Timothy Bear Nose sticks his rifle out and sights it and pulls the trigger and the gun goes off really loud, and there's a puff of dust in front of the deer and the deer trots away. And immediately a cow about three hundred yards on up the hill falls flat on its side! It was a freak shot—he'd been aimin' at the deer, but the bullet ricocheted and hit the cow. Of course, there was nothin' we could do but drive over there and butcher it out.

"I used to walk along here with a buddy of mine when I was about fifteen sniffin' that white-gas gasoline. We'd keep it in a gallon bleach bottle and sniff it out of a rubber tube. It will really get you high. We huffed regular gas sometimes, too. That was back before unleaded gas, though, and the lead was bad for you. There was some guys around here almost died of lead poisoning from it. I only did it for about three months.

"Our family's cabin was over there. It was a pretty good-sized log house, actually. That's where Eldee shot himself. The cabin was torn down a long time ago.

"That bare patch of ground where you can still see foundations is where our community center used to be. It was a long log house with big barrel stoves at each end, and when there was dances we'd bring in a lot of firewood and get those stoves so hot they glowed bright red. Everybody around here used to come to the dances in their horse-and-buggies or spring wagons. Back then, not many had cars. The main families were the Makes Shines, the Blue Horses, the No Waters—they were related to the No Water who shot Crazy Horse in the face after Crazy Horse stole No Water's wife—the Dreaming Bears, the Bear Noses, the Bores a Holes, the Helpers, the Porcupines, the Little Soldiers. A lot of the families still live around here."

Le's stories with horses in them tended to be happier than his stories involving cars; as he talked, and as the miles passed in the vicinity of Oglala and Pine Ridge, remembered car wrecks strewed the roadside. I gripped the steering wheel tightly with both hands. Le offered me a beer, and I told him again that I had quit drinking. I was nervous even breathing the fumes as he and Floyd John went through one after the next and crumpled the cans on the floor underfoot. It was broad daylight, the weather was clear, and I drove expecting at any second the cymbals-crash of the collision that would end our lives. Le pointed out the place where a man had backed up over the man's sister and killed her when they stopped at the White River to get water, and where the ambulance driver fell asleep and went off the road and her passenger hit the dashboard and died, and where the Porcupine boys crashed, and where a nephew hit a bridge abutment and the steering wheel crushed his chest and killed him, and where a car Floyd John was riding in with six other kids spun out at an S-curve at a hundred-plus miles an hour and rolled over many times and the engine block just kept going and ended up fifty yards farther down the road (nobody killed), and where a drunk driver on his way back from White Clay hit two pedestrians and sheared off parts of their arms and legs. Generally his stories did not coincide with the fatality markers which the state has put along the roads. Those markers were for crashes he didn't know about, that happened when he was living away from the reservation, Le said. Occasionally we passed a fatality marker that had been damaged in a subsequent crash.

In the past, the Pine Ridge Reservation has gone through periods of small-scale war. A recent bloody time was in the mid-1970s, when supporters of the American Indian Movement and supporters of the tribal government under tribal chairman Dick Wilson battled each other with gang-style violence that ranged from beatings to firebombings to murder. In a two-year span, 1973–75, there were dozens of unexplained deaths on the reservation. Many AIM supporters lived in the village of Oglala, and a lot of the violence took place around there. Three miles east of Oglala, Le and Floyd John told me to turn off into a pasture pocked with prairie-dog holes. This was the site of the best-known single incident of the 1970s war, the killing of FBI agents Jack Coler and Ronald Williams when they came to question some AIM people staying at the Jumping Bull residence on June 26, 1975. Of the suspects in the killings, only Leonard Peltier was eventually convicted, and he is now serving consecutive life sentences in federal prison. The agents were hit by rifle fire they didn't expect soon after they turned onto the property, and they died from bullets fired at close range as they lay wounded by their cars. Le and Floyd John showed where AIM member Joe Stuntz was killed in the shoot-out with police that followed. They pointed with pride to the gullies and ravines through which everybody else on the Jumping Bull place made their escape through the police cordon. Le and Floyd John laughed at how stupid the police were, but I could see nothing here but murder and sorrow. This nondescript piece of ground—the grass growing in bunches, the gray dirt, the black crickets crawling—seemed unequal to the violence it had borne. We stood there for a while without conversation, then got back in the car.

Driving again, still in the vicinity of Oglala and Pine Ridge, Le providing the commentary: "The people who lived in that house raised a deer. It grew up big and used to run with their dogs and chase cars. One day it heard the call of the wild and disappeared . . . My aunt Rose White Magpie lives back there. There's a black pickup truck in her yard that was in the movie *Thunderheart* . . . Just the other side of the hill is where somebody shot down the FBI helicopter that was lookin' for fugitives after the FBI guys was killed . . . The guy in that house sent

away to the *National Enquirer* for a white woman, and he got one, too."
(Floyd John: "He didn't *send away.* He just mentioned in a story they
did about Pine Ridge that he was lookin' for one, and a woman over in
Europe somewhere read it and came here and met him and married
him.") "That's where Uncle John Bank lived. He always drank Four
Roses whiskey . . . That was Spencer Crow's place. Spencer was our fat
guy. Every town on the rez has its fat guy, and he was Oglala's. He
weighed 470 pounds. He was *strong.* I seen Spencer once pick up a car
engine and bring it to his middle and bump it into the back of a pickup
with his belly. When he died, they needed fourteen pallbearers to carry
his casket, and as they were lowering it with ropes into the grave it almost pulled them in . . . The woman who runs that church is named Sister Kate. She's a nun. She's Wanda's sister . . . That little red house is
where a Frenchman named Daniel lived. He came through the rez on a
vacation years ago and he liked it so much that he stayed. One time him
and me was sittin' around drinking red wine and eatin' kidneys and he
told me that he was an expert at *sabata,* what they call French kick-
boxing. He said he could kick my ass with it. So I said, 'Let's get it on,'
and we went out in the yard and he kicked at me and I hit him on the
side of the head and he fell flat. Then we went back in and started
drinkin' again . . . Down that road is where Alex Scabby Face used to
live . . . That's where the great Lakota singer Matthew Two Bulls lives
. . . In one of them junk cars lives a guy who I ran into years ago in the
Dawes County Jail in Chadron, Nebraska. I was in for something or
other and all these Indian guys in there was moanin' about how the
judge had give 'em thirty days or ninety days, and that guy comes strut-
tin' in so happy—I forget what his crime was—but he was overjoyed,
doin' the quail dance, gettin' down real low and singin' Indian, and he
shouts out, 'Boys, I got two years!' . . . That's where Lyman Red Cloud
lives, old Chief Red Cloud's great-grandson . . . That's where the Young
Man Afraid of His Horses family lives . . . Edison Red Nest lived there
. . . Marvin Dreaming Bear's place . . . Vera Fast Horse's . . . My sister
Aurelia's . . . The sun-dance grounds . . . That's where we used to gather
sweet grass, at a wet place up the creekbed, but the tribe put some new
houses back there and the sewage runoff killed it off . . . Somebody
dumped three 55-gallon barrels of toxic waste in that schoolyard a few
weeks ago . . . That's Tobacco Road, where the Tobaccos lived . . ."

After a stretch of silence, Le added, "But August 1977 was the really sad time on the reservation. They ran out of black crepe in all the stores around here, and all the women on the reservation were cryin'."

"What happened in August 1977?" I asked.

"What *happened*? Elvis died!"

Like many visitors to the reservation, I wanted to see that most famous of Indian places, Wounded Knee. It's about fifteen miles from Pine Ridge. I knew that there isn't much there. The general store that once stood by the Y where two roads meet in the valley of Wounded Knee Creek is gone, as is the Catholic church with the tall bell tower that used to be on a hill above. What remains of the village has moved a half mile up the road, where the tribe has put in a small development of one-family houses. At the Wounded Knee junction, about the only reference points the eye can find are the silhouettes of cemetery gates and stone monuments on the hilltop, the roof of a small church beyond the cemetery, and a couple of pole structures holding pine boughs to shade people selling dream catchers and beadwork at a graveled pullout next to the road. The museum which once adjoined the store was ransacked by rioters in 1972, and its contents dispersed and lost. Students of Lakota history say that among the artifacts were the only known copies of two ancient tanned hides that held the Lakotas' accumulated knowledge of the stars. Now only the museum's stone chimney still stands.

Wounded Knee, the event, has two dates: 1890 and 1973. The history of the Lakota over the last 150 years hangs on those dates like wire on telephone poles. As markers, the years are so prominent that they have become important in the larger history of America as well. The first was the year of the massacre. On December 29, 1890, shots broke out as a cavalry regiment was attempting to disarm Chief Big Foot's band of Minnecojou Indians camped on Wounded Knee Creek, and once the soldiers started shooting they didn't stop until well after all the Indians had fallen or run away. At least 146 Indians died, including 44 women and 18 children. Perhaps 30 soldiers also died. Many of Big Foot's band had participated in the Ghost Dance on the Standing Rock Reservation, and had fled there for Pine Ridge after official attempts to suppress the dance led to the killing of Sitting Bull. The soldiers at

Wounded Knee were also on Pine Ridge because of the Ghost Dance; they had been dispatched to watch and intimidate Ghost Dancing Indians there.

Probably no dance in history ever scared people more than the Ghost Dance scared white people back in 1890. Essentially, the Ghost Dance was an Indian version of the religious revivals so popular on the frontier; but in this case, the Promised Land it evoked would be here on earth, with all the Indians who had ever lived restored to life, and the buffalo herds as well. In this paradise the earth itself would be renewed and would cover all white people and their works to a depth five times the height of a man. What believers must do to hurry the arrival of paradise was dance, leaders of the Ghost Dance said. As the Indians did—as they danced for days, fell in exhaustion, went into trances, awoke, told of the ancestors they had visited on the Morning Star, showed pieces of the Morning Star they had brought back as proof— and as the dance spread quickly on the hungry reservations of the West in 1890, people living near the reservations inclined to panic. The government called out the troops by the thousands. Some of them (the Seventh Cavalry, for example, General Custer's old regiment, ordered to Wounded Knee) were ready to kill, and horror came to pass. The photograph of the frozen body of Chief Big Foot with its fingers contorted and its legs twisted as if trying to get purchase to rise became America's most famous image of homegrown massacre. Killings associated with the Ghost Dance did not stop at Wounded Knee, and two hundred or more died in white–Indian and Indian–Indian violence on the Pine Ridge Reservation in the months that followed.

Wounded Knee's other prominent date, 1973, was the year in which the American Indian Movement occupied the village as a protest demonstration. The occupation, sometimes called Wounded Knee II, lasted for seventy-one days between February and May. AIM members holding the village made demands for political changes and negotiated with the government while various federal agencies, the tribal police, and local volunteer opponents of AIM surrounded them in a porous state of siege. Wounded Knee II was the last in a series of major occupations staged nationwide by Indian protest groups beginning in 1969, when West Coast activists seized the abandoned federal prison on Alcatraz Island in San Francisco Bay. The Alcatraz occupation didn't accomplish much of substance, but it got a lot of press over the eighteen months it lasted, and other occupations followed. Protesters took over an abandoned Coast Guard station in Milwaukee, a Lutheran Church conference in South Dakota, a museum in Los Angeles, the top of Mount Rushmore, the replica ship *Mayflower II* in Massachusetts on Thanksgiving Day, and the headquarters of the Bureau of Indian Affairs in Washington, D.C. The American Indian Movement, founded in Minneapolis in 1968, led most of the big takeovers and emerged as the important voice of Indian miltancy. AIM leaders often talked about Indian self-determination and tribal sovereignty, ideas that had been overlooked in the recent past, when government policy had emphasized moving Indians from reservations into the American mainstream and terminating the official status of many tribes. AIM's real flair was for the defiant gesture in the face of authority. That, combined with its strong sense of Indian history, made it conservative and radical at the same time.

The bloody history of the place was why AIM chose Wounded Knee. The occupiers often said that they were prepared to die there, and that they expected to be wiped out as Big Foot's band had been. Setting aside the occupiers' demands for Senate investigations of all Indian treaties and of the Bureau of Indian Affairs and of all Sioux reservations in South Dakota, the main issue at Wounded Knee II came down to a conflict between progressives and traditionalists on the Pine Ridge Reservation. Loosely subsumed in that were other reservation conflicts—mixed-bloods versus full-bloods, the village of Pine Ridge versus outlying areas, pro–Vietnam War versus anti–, and local politicians versus activists of no fixed abode. Tribal chairman Dick Wilson spoke for the progressives. He wore his hair in a bristly crew cut and called AIM members and their supporters lawbreakers, unpatriotic scum, and Communist agitators. AIM leaders called Wilson a dictator, a thug, and a puppet of the BIA. Traditionalists on the reservation generally sided with AIM. Repeated regularly among the occupiers' demands was Wilson's immediate removal as tribal chairman. AIM said that many Wilson supporters were goons who intimidated people with violence. The Wilson men accepted the name with pride, saying that it was an acronym for Guardians of the Oglala Nation and that they had thought it up themselves. Groups of goons maintained their own roadblocks on the roads leading into Wounded Knee, and in their eagerness for a fight with AIM sometimes drew guns on federal marshals who were trying to restrain them and ended up in jail.

The federal government, for its part, had a legal responsibility to protect life and property on the reservation. Any desire the government might have had to attack the occupiers with full force was balanced by the Nixon administration's fear of another Wounded Knee massacre; the Watergate hearings had just begun, and the administration needed no more bad press. Yet there wasn't much the feds could do about the occupiers' demands, because the crucial one, getting rid of Dick Wilson, could not be granted without involving the government illegally in the sovereign government of the tribe. Whatever the accusations against him, Wilson had been duly elected; the feds feared that if a tribal government could be overthrown by force, the whole structure of government on the reservations would fall apart. Hence, the seventy-one-day standoff, punctuated with many long-range firefights. Bullets probably from the besiegers' rifles killed two occupiers, one of them a man whose grandmother had survived the first Wounded Knee, and a bullet from the occupiers' compound hit a federal marshal and paralyzed him from the waist down.

A fact of Indian political life is its tendency to descend into mind-numbing complications and small print. A good example of this would be the catalogue of proposals, counterproposals, negotiations broken down, negotiations resumed, new negotiating teams, near-settlements, AIM leaders' appearances before Congress, and eventual surrender terms that marked the long occupation. AIM succeeded in the realm of theatrics; its images of long-haired Indians painted for war and carrying high-powered rifles appeared regularly on the TV news, and made a larger point about Indian militancy. But when the occupiers left Wounded Knee not long after the second death there, none of their main demands had been met, and the government's promises led only to a few meetings with low-level officials which most people considered a joke. As at the first Wounded Knee, the events at the second proved to be part of a longer struggle. For years afterward the reservation remained violently divided between AIM and goon. Houses caught fire in the night, shots came through car windows, people usually uncomfortable with guns felt they had to carry them, and the jumpy paranoia that seemed to be everywhere in America in those days reached a high pitch on the reservation. Trying to solve crimes in the midst of this undeclared civil war, the FBI sent its agents. After two of them died at Oglala in June 1975, and FBI men were suddenly all over the place in search of the killers, some residents wondered why the recent deaths of Indians by the dozens hadn't produced a similar response.

Le and Floyd John and I were approaching Wounded Knee from the south. Le said, "During the occupation there were goons right at this junction, the Wounded Knee turnoff. This was where the first roadblock was. From here on you could get shot at, all the way to Wounded Knee. And we're still seven miles away."

Floyd John: "Them goons'd sit around in their trucks drinkin' coffee, drinkin' whiskey. Any civilians that tried to get through, they'd put a gun in their face and turn 'em around."

Le: "At the start, people came from all over to show solidarity with AIM. But if the goons saw a car they didn't recognize—it's easy to tell a rez car—they'd run 'em off the road, terrorize 'em, stay on 'em till they left the rez."

Floyd John: "Wilson made a law that nobody but tribal members could be on the rez if they didn't have official business here. He wouldn't even let that Frank guy that got shot at the occupation be buried here."

Le: "Up ahead is where the pigs had one of their main bunkers—"

(Me: "The pigs?")

Le: "The marshals, the FBI—the *pigs,* man. At the top of that rise was where their lines began. From here their perimeter ran all the way around the Knee, fourteen miles."

Floyd John: "Every so often they put another bunker like the one was here—on high ground so they could shoot down into the village and at the AIM bunkers by the church."

Le: "Them marshals was really gung-ho. You'd see 'em sometimes when they was off duty, down in Gordon or Rushville or up in Rapid. A lot of 'em dressed kind of mod—big wide belts and pants with big stripes on 'em and little caps. They thought they were some cool dudes."

Floyd John: "Sometimes guys'd oink at 'em on the street, but that was about all. Everybody knew when the pigs was off duty they wasn't supposed to mix it up with nobody."

Le: "The marshals and FBI was just the tip of the iceberg. All kinds of military was here—advisers, like in 'Nam. The 82nd Airborne from Ellsworth Air Force Base was ready to take the whole place out in a minute, if they'd got the call."

Floyd John: "There was armored personnel carriers, choppers, reconnaissance planes. After the occupation was over they burned down the church, so nobody could tell from all the holes in it that the pigs'd been usin' 50-caliber machine guns."

Le: "Charley Red Cloud said the only branch of the service that wasn't here was the Navy, and they would've been, too, if the rez had had any water."

Floyd John: "From all the bunkers they was shootin' up flares, every night. One flare after another—and when the flares came down on places where there wasn't no snow, they set the grass afire. The ground was black everywhere."

Le: "They had the guns and they loved to shoot 'em. The pigs must've fired ten million rounds. After they finally left, there was metal cartridge cases layin' all over the place. Some kids went around collectin' 'em, and guys that do traditional crafts made 'em into breastplates and chokers, like they used to in the old days with pipe beads. I heard they sold those cartridge breastplates for a lot of money."

We coasted down the hill to the Wounded Knee junction. Just ahead of us was a Volkswagen bus with oval license plates. It hesitantly turned left, then inched onto the drive that led up to the massacre monument and the site of the Catholic church. The driveway to the monument at America's most famous massacre site is a deeply rutted single-lane dirt track so unpromising as to give any car owner pause. History here has had little time to reflect; it seems to be waiting for further developments, perhaps Wounded Knee III or IV. I parked next to the VW and we got out. Le and Floyd John showed me the long, shallow depression of the mass grave from the first Wounded Knee and the large marker of gray granite with the name of Lawrence "Buddy" Lamont, the Wounded Knee survivor's grandson killed at the second Wounded Knee. They said he was an easygoing guy, a former tribal employee, who was shot in the head by an FBI sniper one morning while on his way to the sweat lodge. His monument had an engraving of an Indian waving as he leaves camp, and a long inscription in Sioux. I picked up the visitors' sign-in list on a clipboard that was chained to a folding chair. Many of the visitors gave European addresses in elegant and unfamiliar handwriting styles.

We looked at the foundations of the church and rectory, and at the places where the bunkers used to be. Vietnam vets among the protesters had deployed and built them, Le said. They were made double-walled, several feet thick, of plywood frames filled with dirt. Now the hill felt as exposed as a countertop; I could not imagine spending seventy-one days surrounded there, bunkers or no. Along the base of the hill runs the narrow valley of Wounded Knee Creek, a winding line of brush, where so many Indians died trying to get away from the soldiers in 1890. Le pointed to a draw a mile or more away to the north. "When I was sneakin' into the Knee at night, I came through that gully," he said. "I snuck in here past the feds eighteen times, carryin' seventy-five- to ninety-pound packs of food, medicine, ammunition, tobacco. I got rides to a drop-off point four or five miles past that butte and walked in through that gully the rest of the way."

(Me:) "Why couldn't the feds just seal the place off?"

Floyd John: "At night they was afraid to get out of their APCs, man. They could see with their nightscopes, but they was afraid to do anything."

Le: "The spirits of the dead at Wounded Knee were up and walking around. Sometimes the feds could see them in the moonlight, hear horses whinnying and babies cryin'. But they'd shoot and it would be just a ghost."

Floyd John: "The marshals set up trip wires and stuff, but that didn't stop nothin'."

Le: "One night I was comin' through the gully with a white guy and a Mexican guy, all of us carryin' packs, and somebody tripped a wire and a flare went off and we hit the ground and crawled on our bellies for a hundred yards faster than you could run. We was laughin' so hard—the flare was bright as daylight, but nobody came after us or shot at us. Some nights I'd get here, drop off the pack, and turn around and sneak back out before morning. Other nights I'd stay—just grab a sleeping bag and crash anywhere. Lots of times there was gunfire. Gunfire at night is like when you bring a new baby home and it cries in the night—you don't have much choice but to get up and pay attention to it. But after a while you get used to it, and you pay attention to it without really waking up."

Le then began to tell a long story about the Indian protest movement and his part in it, by way of explaining how he had come to Wounded Knee. He said that he got out of prison in 1968 and went to San Francisco and participated in the occupation of Alcatraz, where he slept in a room in the guards' quarters from November 1969 until June 1971. After Alcatraz, he joined a number of other protests in the Far West—at Pit River Reservation in Northern California, where there was a dispute over fishing rights, and at a store run by the Puyallup tribe in Washington State, fighting for their right to sell cigarettes without collecting state sales tax. He said that in 1972 he went to a convention of Indian traditionalists and protesters and their supporters north of San Francisco and became disillusioned and depressed. Everybody was talking about traditional Indian spirituality and getting it all mixed up with mystical beliefs that had nothing to do with it. ("They were talking about stuff like kundalini sweat lodges. *There are no kundalini sweat lodges!*") He said that after the conference he gave up on the protest movement and the whole bunch of them. He wanted to be by himself for a while, and he knew some people in Los Angeles. So, he said, he decided to walk from San Francisco to Los Angeles along the beach.

He said he set out in February 1972 with a backpack, a sleeping bag, four hundred dollars, and 4,600 hits of mescaline. Sometimes he couldn't walk on the beach, because there were only cliffs, and sometimes he had to walk around large beachfront installations like Fort Ord, ninety miles south of San Francisco. Along the way he met migrant workers, fishermen who shared their fish with him, avocado ranchers, farmers growing roses by the hundreds of acres for use on floats in the Rose Bowl Parade, mission Indians, golf course employees. People usually recognized him for an American Indian—he always wore two eagle feathers in his hair. He said that on the beach near Carmel he met the movie actress Kim Novak painting a watercolor. She was with her Great Dane, and she brought him back to her house and showed him her other animals, including a pygmy goat, llamas, cows, horses, a cockatoo, and little birds in cages. He said that before he left, she gave him an autographed photo.

He said that from Oxnard south to L.A., the beach is all privately owned and closed. He had worn out his shoes by that point and was walking barefoot. It was now July, he had been walking for five months. A man and his daughter gave him a ride all the way to Santa Monica, and when he got there he went under the pier and soaked his feet in the ocean for a long time. Then he walked into a shoe store and told the salesperson his story, and she let him have the most expensive pair of running shoes in the place for five dollars. From Santa Monica he went to his friends' place in Laurel Canyon for a while. Then he hitchhiked to Boulder, Colorado, where he stayed with friends for several months. Then he got a ride to the Rosebud Reservation and stayed at Crow Dog's Paradise, home of the Lakota spiritual leader Leonard Crow Dog. He was living at his aunt's place in Oglala in February 1973 when the occupation began at Wounded Knee.

His mention of the actress Kim Novak made me curious. I wrote her a letter asking if she remembered Le, and sent it to her in Carmel. It came back stamped REFUSED. A friend in New York found me the phone number of Kim Novak's manager, and I called her. The manager said that Kim Novak does not accept mail, but if I were to fax my letter to her (the manager), she would read my fax to Kim Novak. I did, and the manager soon called me back. She said Kim Novak had a vague memory of the incident Le described, but she couldn't be sure, it was so long ago. She said that Kim Novak said that all the details he mentioned—the painting, the house, the animals—were right.

This partial success encouraged me to get in touch with other celebrities Le has mentioned. Apparently he lived in Los Angeles during much of the 1970s after Wounded Knee, and in his stories of that time he sometimes mentions the actor Elliott Gould. A friend of a friend gave me Elliott Gould's phone number, and I left a message on his answering machine. Elliott Gould called me back from New Orleans, where he was touring in a production of *Deathtrap*. He said he certainly did remember Le. He had met him, as I had, on the street. He said that he picked him up hitchhiking in Malibu Canyon and later invited him to his house. He remembered Le afterward coming to his house late one night so high on drugs and alcohol that his body was giving off a ripple effect. He said that he also remembered watching a football game on TV with him, and that Le might have done a curing ceremony for his daughter, Molly, when she had open-heart surgery. He said that the actor David Carradine knew Le much better than he did, and that Le even appears in Carradine's autobiography, *Endless Highway.*

In fact, Carradine devotes an entire chapter of *Endless Highway* to Le. The chapter title is "Lee Warlance"; Carradine explains that he always called him Lee to discourage him from getting too conceited about his Oglala heritage. (Le pronounces his name more like "Leh" or "Lay," in the Lakota style.) Carradine describes Le as an "extremely beautiful man" who came by his house one day and introduced himself because people had told him that he and Carradine looked alike. They got to know each other; "I trusted him. I trusted his instincts and his mystic concepts," Carradine says. According to Carradine, Le said that he was a Vietnam veteran who had a bullet lodged in his head which hospitals were afraid to touch, but which he suddenly felt in his mouth and spit out in the middle of a sweat lodge curing ceremony. (Despite what Le might have said, he is not a Vietnam veteran.) Le apparently also told Carradine stories about Wounded Knee unlike any that he told me; for example, that he helped some reporters and women to escape from the occupation, and that when pursuers shot at them his dog confronted the pursuers and was killed, saving their lives. Of these and other stories, Carradine says, "I was more a listener than an investigator." Carradine also says that through Le he met a number of Indian militants "considerably wilder" than Le. He does not mention that one evening Le brought some of these people and their friends to Carradine's house, that they found no one home, that they hung around for a while, that three of them left in a taxicab, that Le stayed behind, and that the taxicab driver later turned up dead, stabbed many times and stuffed into a drainpipe. Police questioned Carradine about the murder, and Le says that he (Le) was held on suspicion of it for over a month. Le adds that neither he nor Carradine had anything to do with the murder of the taxi driver.

Dennis Banks, with Russell Means the best-known of the leaders of

AIM and a main spokesman for the occupiers at Wounded Knee, more recently headed an American Indian program in Newport, Kentucky. I wanted to ask him questions on several subjects, so I telephoned him there. In the course of our conversation I asked him if he knew Le. He said that he did, and that Le had indeed been at the occupation of Wounded Knee.

CHAPTER

5

Indians are embedded deeply in America. You find them every-where—in remote places where almost no one else could live, in small towns, and in the biggest cities. 30.9 percent of Indians have incomes below the national poverty line, more than any other race or ethnic group, so the neighborhoods where they live tend to be run-down. But Indian tribes also own high-priced real estate in Las Vegas, Nevada, and Palm Springs, California; five tribes operate gambling casinos that gross $100 million or more a year. The federal government has granted offi-cial tribal status to 570 tribes. Over 150 others remain unrecognized but continue to exist all the same. From time to time you read of an-other officially overlooked tribe turning up in a makeshift community under a highway bridge or in the desert between two Western cities. Of the almost two million people who identify themselves as American In-dians on the U.S. census form, about half are enrolled members of a federally recognized tribe.

Most Indians live west of the Mississippi River. More than half the Indians in the United States live within a 300-mile radius of Albu-querque, New Mexico; Los Angeles has the largest concentration of off-reservation Indians in the country. Every Western state has at least one Indian reservation, with the exception of Missouri, Arkansas, and Hawaii. (Of course, native peoples live in those states as well.) Fewer of the Eastern states have reservations. In the nineteenth century, most Eastern states favored removal of all Indian tribes to points west far from their boundaries, they didn't care where. But some Indians refused to go and continued inhabiting unwanted lands where their neighbors often assumed they had died out. Scattered reservations of various sizes, from a quarter-acre on up, remain in many parts of the East.

You could fix a map of the lower forty-eight states to a wall with pins stuck in reservations at each of the four corners. In the Northeast, the Maliseet Reservation is at the very end of Interstate Highway 95, on the border between Maine and Canada. Many of the Maliseet live on the Canadian side. During the hostage crisis in Iran, the chairman of the Maliseet tribe's land-claims committee sent a letter to the Islamic government of Iran asking for financial aid, citing the indifference of the United States to the tribe's complaints. Congress eventually gave the Maliseet a $900,000 claims settlement, which they used for buying riverfront land. Near the other end of I-95, at the tip of Florida in the southeastern United States, the Miccosukee Indians live on a reservation which includes thousands of acres of Everglades swamp. The Florida Miccosukee are descendants of Indians the government couldn't catch and move to Oklahoma after the expensive and bloody Seminole War of the 1830s and '40s. Some Miccosukee villages can be reached only by pirogue or airboat. In the far northwest of the forty-eight states, on the end of the Olympic Peninsula in Washington, is the Makah Reservation. The Makah are seagoing Indians who still build and race large cedar war canoes. Their language is unlike that of any other tribe, but only a few native Makah speakers remain. Recently the International Whaling Commission granted the Makah's request to be allowed to harpoon whales, as the tribe had done in the past for as long as it can remember; in May of '99 the tribe killed its first whale since the 1920s. In the southwest corner of the map, you could put dozens of pins in the many small reservations the United States made of the old Indian missions of the Spanish in Southern California. Some of those reservations are just a ten-mile hike from the Mexican border. Their landscape is mostly hilly desert scribbled with low, spiky greenery. On the horizon stretches the carbon-streaked sky of San Diego and the approaching blue curve of the Pacific Ocean.

Even in the middle of the country, Indians somehow manage to live on the edges. Wherever you are traveling, if your eye pauses on some distant and inhospitable-looking spot, chances are an Indian has already been there, or lives there now. Indians live on islands in the Great Lakes, and at the tip of Louisiana near where the Mississippi empties into the Gulf, and on the Rio Grande border with Mexico. Our wheeled and plumbed and wired society prefers landscapes of a temperate and level kind, but Indian occupation predates the requirements of technology. The Havasupai tribe lives thousands of feet down in a canyon in Arizona that connects to the Grand Canyon. Many of the 650 tribal members still speak Havasupai. The Havasupai's main industry is a tourism business that brings tens of thousands of hikers to the canyon bottom every year. The Timbisha Shoshone have no official reservation, but continue to live in the desert in southeastern California, where summer temperatures reach 134°. In arid parts of Arizona and New Mexico, Hopi and other Indians live in pueblos that are the oldest continually inhabited sites in North America. The Acoma Pueblo, on a butte in west-central New Mexico, is at least a thousand years old, and at the San Juan Pueblo, some of the dwellings have been lived in for seven hundred years. The Hopi Pueblo of Old Oraibi, in Arizona, is even older. Parts of Old Oraibi were built in about A.D. 500. The Spanish explorer Francisco Vásquez de Coronado went there in his search for cities of gold in 1540; the pueblo has had electricity since 1963.

And if the distant place your eye pauses upon happens to be man-made—the top of the Golden Gate Bridge in San Francisco, say, or New York's Empire State Building—Indians have been there, too. For many years, Mohawk Indian high-steel construction crews worked on bridges and skyscrapers from one end of the country to the other. They liked the difficulty and danger of the job, as well as the travel. Sometimes the Mohawks would get bored working on a skyscraper in Manhattan and all pile into their cars and take off for a new job they heard about, three thousand miles away.

Indians are twice as likely as non-Indians to live in a mobile home. The reason for this has partly to do with laws against repossession of tribal land: banks will loan money on reservations only for property which, in the event of default, can be towed away. Ninety thousand or more Indian families are homeless, living on the street or sharing housing with relatives. Forty percent of Indian households are over-crowded or have inadequate dwellings, compared to about 6 percent for the population at large. Indians are about twice as likely as non-Indians to be murdered. Their death rate from alcoholism is four times the national average, and the rate of fetal alcohol syndrome among their children is thirty-three times higher than for whites. Indian babies are three times as likely as white babies to die of sudden infant death syndrome (SIDS). Indians smoke more than non-Indians, and smoking is their leading cause of cancer death. They commit suicide at rates that in certain circumstances approach the epidemic. The American Medical Association says that one in five Indian girls and one in eight boys attempts suicide by the end of high school. In an Indian town in northern Canada, an Indian teenager dead of alcohol poisoning was found to have a blood alcohol content higher than any ever recorded in North America. On and on, the saddening statistics multiply. Any modern study of Indians lists them, unavoidably. They tend to overwhelm the few positive numbers one can point to—the increase in Indian life expectancy over the last twenty years, or the growth in the numbers of Indian college graduates, or the success of the many new tribal colleges, or the large decline in the percentage of Indians living in poverty over the last ten years.

A good example of what Indians have done to survive since white people came is the much-traveled Kickapoo tribe, who to most people are no more than a colorful name. The first reports of the Kickapoo were from French frontiersmen who found them in present Wisconsin in the early 1700s. In the 1760s the Kickapoo moved south to present Illinois and Indiana, home of their relatives the Fox and the Sauk. The Kickapoo fought for the British in the Revolutionary War and in the War of 1812, and with the Fox and Sauk continued fighting the United States in Black Hawk's War. A treaty signed as part of the removal of Indians in the 1830s to lands west of the Mississippi known as Indian Territory—the present states of Kansas, Nebraska, and Oklahoma—gave the Kickapoo land in northeastern Kansas, along with other Eastern tribes. When the United States was deciding what to do about the extension of slavery into the Kansas and Nebraska Territories, no one on either side of the question gave a serious thought to the fate of the Indians recently relocated there. In a unanimity of racism similar to that which would help reknit the country after the Civil War, pro-slavery and anti-slavery politicians agreed on their right to do as they pleased with the Indians of Kansas and Nebraska. The creation of the Kansas Territory greatly reduced the Kickapoo's lands. A large band of Kickapoo who didn't like the outcome simply left their Kansas reservation and relocated a thousand or more miles away, across the border into Mexico.

In 1862, the Kickapoo still in Kansas lost most of their remaining lands in a treaty whose result was the transfer of those lands to the Atchison and Pikes Peak Railroad Company. About a hundred Kickapoo who liked this even less than the high-handedness of ten years before decided to join their relatives in Mexico. There the Kickapoo refugees lived on their own for many years, occasionally raiding across the border. In the 1870s some of the Kickapoo in Mexico were induced to come back to Kansas, to the reduced reservation which remained. The Mexican government eventually gave the Mexican Kickapoo some land, but during a drought in the 1940s a band of them moved north again, to the Texas side of the Rio Grande. In 1981 there were 620 of these Mexican Kickapoo living in reed huts beneath the International Bridge on the U.S. border by Eagle Pass, Texas. An American charitable organization bought them 125 acres along the Rio Grande in Texas in the same year, and in 1983 the U.S. government granted them official tribal status as the Kickapoo Traditional Tribe of Texas. Books about Indians which I read as a child usually divided tribes into geographic categories, such as Woodland Indians, Indians of the Prairies, or Indians of the Southwest; such books never mentioned that a harried tribe might end up falling into two categories, or three.

The most famous removal of Indians, of course, was the removal of the Cherokee from Georgia westward to Indian Territory in 1838 and 1839. There are many accounts of the forced march that came to be known as the Trail of Tears—of the Cherokee's previous peaceableness and prosperity on their lands in Georgia; of the Georgia settlers' hatred of Indians and desire for those lands; of the mercilessness of President Andrew Jackson; of Supreme Court Justice John Marshall's ruling that the removal was illegal; of Jackson's response: "He has made his law. Now let him enforce it"; of the opposition of people as diverse as Ralph Waldo Emerson and Davy Crockett to the removal; of the U.S. soldiers' roundup of the Georgia Cherokee; of the Cherokee's suffering in the stockades and along the trail; of the death of more than four thousand Cherokee, about a third of the population of the tribe, before the removal was through. The Cherokee had their own written language, with an alphabet devised by the Cherokee leader Sequoyah during the 1820s. But their success at following the ways of the whites proved no defense. As would happen again elsewhere, building houses and farms only gave the Indians more to lose when government policy changed.

Some Cherokee escaped the soldiers and stayed in the mountains of their original territory, surviving on little more than bark and grass. Eventually they moved down into North Carolina. Today they have a reservation there and are known as the Eastern Cherokee. The Cherokee who were forced west in the 1830s have no reservation but live spread out through a fourteen-county area in eastern Oklahoma. Their tribal capital is in the Oklahoma town of Tahlequah. Both the Eastern Cherokee and the Cherokee of Oklahoma commemorate the Trail of Tears march with a large outdoor pageant every year. Also, Indians and other people on spiritual quests sometimes walk the historic route of the trail. A Cherokee woman recently walked it from Rattlesnake Springs, Tennessee, all the way to Tahlequah, a distance of 1,100 miles. In 1996, a Pomo Indian minister of an interdenominational church spent four months walking the route carrying a seventy-pound wooden cross.

The Cherokee are among the three or four best-known American Indian tribes. "Cherokee" is especially popular as a brand name, appearing on products from cars and airplanes to hospital scrubs and soda pop. If a person claims to have a little Indian blood, chances are the tribe mentioned will be the Cherokee; Bill Clinton says he is one-eighth Cherokee. In both Oklahoma and North Carolina, the Cherokee are involved in many business ventures, including gambling, tourism, manufacturing, and ranching. In Oklahoma the tribe issues its own VISA card. The Cherokee are sometimes called the largest American tribe. Of those who identify themselves as American Indian on the census form, more say they are Cherokee than say they belong to any other tribe.

The Cherokee are an Iroquoian tribe. That means that their language resembles others—including Tuscarora, Huron, and Erie—which ethnologists have grouped into the Iroquoian language family.

Other Native American language families are the Algonquian, the Muscogean, the Siouan, the Uto-Aztecan, and the Athapascan, each of whose speakers occupied a more or less distinct part of the continent. Of the Iroquoian tribes, only the Cherokee and a few others were not part of the Iroquois Confederacy, perhaps the most powerful Indian force in America at the time white men arrived. The Iroquois Confederacy consisted of five tribes: the Cayuga, Oneida, Mohawk, Seneca, and Onondaga. (A sixth tribe, the Tuscarora, joined later.) The Iroquois lived in present New York State and ruled themselves by a set of laws orally passed down in a tradition of ceremonial recitation which the Mohawk tribe continues today. In domestic matters, government was left to the individual tribe. But in larger questions of war or of relations with other governments or tribes, leaders from each tribe in the confederacy met in council at a longhouse among the Onondaga. These leaders, or sachems, reached decisions through formal debate, and although they had no power of enforcement, their authority compelled obedience. The Iroquois Confederacy could operate effectively on a larger scale than other tribes, and helped the Iroquois to overpower the mostly Algonquian-speaking tribes around them. If Europeans had never come to this continent, perhaps eventually a lot of it would have become an Iroquois dominion, in the way that the Mediterranean and parts of Europe were Romanized in classical times.

As fighters, the Iroquois were fierce. Their large and far-ranging war parties reduced to misery Indian nations as distant as the Illinois on the shores of the Mississippi, the Huron north of Lake Superior, and the Erie south of the lake that has their name. The Iroquois enjoyed torturing captives. Returning from their conquests, they usually made an event of it, with the women and children joining in. To incapacitate enemy warriors immediately after capture, the Iroquois would break the captives' fingers with their teeth. Many accounts of Iroquois torture have come down through records of the early colonial period, especially among the Canadian French. When the torture phase was done, the Iroquois often adopted the survivors. An elaborate system of adoption, with captives parceled out to tribes according to their losses, helped the confederacy to grow.

White people in colonial times and after seem to have feared and admired the Iroquois more than any other tribe. The Iroquois were said to be the bravest, the smartest, the noblest, and the best-looking of all Indians. The American portrait and history painter Benjamin West, upon first seeing the statue of the Apollo Belvedere in the Vatican, cried, "By God, a Mohawk!" I have mentioned above that the example of the Iroquois Confederacy influenced the Founding Fathers of the United States; it also influenced the founders of Communism, Friedrich Engels and Karl Marx. They read about the Iroquois in an 1877 book called *Ancient Society*, by the American anthropologist Lewis Henry Morgan, and made special note of the symmetry between the democracy of Iroquois society and its communal ownership of property. To Marx and Engels, the Iroquois were Communists in a natural state.

With the help of the Iroquois Confederacy, the English had driven the French colonial empire from Canada and the Northeast by 1763. The victory turned out to be bad news for the tribe, however. Once the English no longer had the French to fear, they neglected their Iroquois allies and gave them fewer weapons and presents. Most of the Iroquois remained on the side of the English in the American Revolution, and when the Americans won, Iroquois power dwindled still further. Much of the tribe went to Canada, where its descendants now live on the Six Nations Reserve in Ontario. Other Iroquois stayed; the Cayuga today share a reservation with Seneca in Oklahoma, but the other five tribes of the confederacy still have reservations in upstate New York. When the United States gave all Indians within its borders citizenship in 1924, the Iroquois refused it. They said they were citizens of their own nation and didn't need to belong to another. The tradition of tribal sovereignty, built over centuries, is still strong among the tribes of the Iroquois. They are quick to defend their tribal status, and other Indians look to them for leadership. A few years ago, when the governor of New York State tried to collect sales tax on gasoline and cigarettes sold in Iroquois convenience stores, the tribe stood on their centuries-old treaty rights exempting them from state taxes on reservation lands. The state persisted; the Iroquois protested and set fires along the highways and blocked traffic and threatened to charge tolls on highways crossing their lands. Finally the state of New York backed down.

Two tribes of the Iroquois Confederacy, the Tuscarora and the Oneida, broke with the English during the Revolution. Most Tuscarora and Oneida warriors either remained neutral or fought on the side of the Americans. The English told the tribes that for this disloyalty their lands would be forfeit; after the war, the U.S. Congress rewarded them by letting them stay where they wanted to be. The Tuscarora ended up with a reservation about ten miles square along the Niagara River, in the vicinity of the Falls. In 1790, George Washington told the Tuscarora and the other Iroquois tribes that their lands were theirs to sell or not, as they chose. Federal land-allotment policy after 1887 put much of the land into individual ownership, as happened on reservations nationwide, but for years the boundaries of the Tuscarora Reservation remained the same as they had been in 1784.

Then, in 1959, Robert Moses, head of the New York State Power Authority, decided he needed a big piece of the Tuscarora Reservation for a power station reservoir. He duly had the land condemned, and construction began. The Tuscarora organized protest rallies, blocked the bulldozers, and filed suit to stop him. The suit went all the way to the Supreme Court, which ruled for Moses. The Court's majority held that since much of the reservation land was privately owned, it could be condemned for public use like other private land. Justice Hugo Black, for the minority, said that this was ridiculous, that everyone knew the land was part of an Indian reservation and that "great nations, like great men, should keep their word." Soon afterward Robert Moses printed at Power Authority expense a pamphlet he wrote defending his action. He referred to the Tuscarora with irony as "the noble red men," said they hadn't been doing anything with the land anyway, and advised them to "join the United States."

Other tribes of the East: the Pamunkey and Mattapony, descendants of the Powhatan Confederacy, relatives of Pocahontas, whose state reservations in eastern Virginia are 340 years old and who renew their treaty with gifts of turkey, fish, and deer brought to the governor of Virginia every fall; the Passamaquoddy of Maine, who won $40 million in a land claims settlement with the United States in 1980, and increased it to $100 million by good investments, and bought a cement company and sold it a few years later for a profit of $60 million, and became a parable of smart business dealings in a course taught at Harvard Business

School; the Independent Traditional Seminole Nation of Florida, a tribe without a reservation or federal recognition, which recently won a lawsuit against the county where they live when its inspectors tried to force them to bring their cypress-thatched chickees into compliance with local housing codes; the Shinnecock of Long Island, whose name is also that of an exclusive golf course; the Schaghticoke and the Golden Hill Paugusset and the Paucatuck Pequot and the super-wealthy Mashantucket Pequot of Connecticut; the Ramapough tribe of Mahwah, New Jersey, recently denied federal recognition on the grounds that they were not Indians but descendants of African and Dutch settlers who moved to New Jersey from Manhattan Island in the late 1600s; and the Lumbee of North Carolina, a tribe which has lived for a hundred years in the mountains around Lumberton unrecognized by anyone but themselves; and the Catawba tribe of South Carolina, whose language became extinct in 1996 with the death of its last speaker, a seventy-six-year-old man named Red Thunder Cloud.

A myth about America which we learn early is the story of the first Thanksgiving, when Indians and Pilgrims met to celebrate the harvest in Plymouth Colony in Massachusetts in 1621. The Indians in the story were of the Wampanoag tribe, led by Chief Massasoit, a friend to the whites. He and ninety other Wampanoag attended the Thanksgiving feast and contributed five deer. Squanto, the English-speaking Indian said to have taught the Pilgrims to bury a fish in each hill of corn, was a Wampanoag. About fifty years after the first Thanksgiving, the Wampanoag and other New England tribes rose against the whites in a widespread series of battles called King Philip's War, which killed perhaps a thousand settlers and nearly wiped out many tribes. After that, the Wampanoag seemed to disappear from history for several centuries. In the 1800s, they were among the tribes said to have become extinct. However, they continued to live in the vicinity where the Pilgrims found them in eastern Massachusetts. The Mashpee-Wampanoag have a reservation near Mashpee on Cape Cod, and the Wampanoag tribe of Gay Head has one on the island of Martha's Vineyard. In the late 1970s the Mashpee-Wampanoag filed suit against the town of Mashpee to reclaim land they said was theirs, but a federal jury in Boston decided that the tribe had stopped being a tribe at several key points in their history and so ruled against them. In 1989 a group of Wampanoag on Martha's

Vineyard petitioned Jacqueline Kennedy Onassis for control of an acre
and a half of beachfront which she said she needed to keep celebrity
seekers at a distance from her property and which the Wampanoag said
was the burial site of an ancestor and thus sacred land. (Lawyers for
Mrs. Onassis settled the dispute with a land exchange.) Chappaquid-
dick is the name of a tribe of the Wampanoag.

The tribe with the most enrolled members and the most land is the
Navajo. The Navajo Reservation covers 17.5 million acres in Arizona,
New Mexico, and Utah, an expanse bigger than New England. It is divided into Western, Central, and Eastern regions, and includes desert,
canyonlands, mountains, and badlands. The eroded red-rock spires that
have become a visual shorthand for the American West in movies and
advertisements are one of its features. Some of the best-preserved pre-
Columbian ruins on the continent are in Navajo country, as is the
Canyon de Chelly National Monument, with its cliff dwellings dating to
A.D. 348 and its ancient cliff-face handprints and pictographs. In 1880,
there were about 9,000 Navajo; about 200,000 live on the reservation
today, and another 60,000 live elsewhere. Of all North American Indian
languages, Navajo has by far the most speakers. Many Navajo children
speak it; at a time when tribes are trying to keep their languages alive,
Navajo children sometimes must be taught English before they can enter school. In parts of the reservation there are Navajo who speak no
English. KTNN, the tribal radio station, broadcasts part of the time in
Navajo, and does live coverage in Navajo of Phoenix Suns pro basketball games.

At least 20,000 Navajo on the reservation are homeless. Some
Navajo spend their time drinking in "border towns"—places like Gallup, New Mexico, or Winslow, Arizona—just across the reservation's
border. The border towns make much of their income selling liquor to
the Navajo; travelers who stop in peaceful-looking Gallup on the night
of a big rodeo may be surprised at how wild a night in Gallup can be.
The big tank, the cell in the Gallup jail where drunks are thrown, holds
five hundred. It is said to be the largest jail cell in the country. Navajo
by the score have been killed walking back to the reservation along the
"hell highway"—a seven-and-a-half-mile stretch of U.S. 666 north of

Gallup. After years of trying, Nancy Bill, an official at the Indian Health Services in the tribal capital of Window Rock, got streetlights installed along that stretch, and the fatality rate went way down. Some Navajo live in hogans, traditional round dwellings of rock, timber, and adobe, and continue to worship the hundred or so deities who help in different aspects of Navajo life. Not long ago a family in a remote part of the reservation said they received a visit from two of these deities, who warned them that the Navajo were risking great danger by giving up their traditions. When the news of the visit got out, thousands of Navajo made pilgrimages to the family's hogan to pray and scatter sacred corn pollen.

People may assume that gambling casinos are now the only business enterprise on the reservations. The Navajo tribe has twice held referendum votes on whether to allow casinos on the reservation, and twice Navajo voters have rejected the idea. Unemployment among the Navajo is around 30 percent. Still, thousands of Navajo work in the coal and uranium mines on the reservation, or in harvesting the reservation's timber, or raising sheep, or in the Navajo's large tourist industry. The Navajo are especially known for their turquoise jewelry and their silversmithing, and are the only tribe in the Southwest who still weave rugs. The tribe encourages its young people to go to college. Dr. Fred Begay, the only American Indian physicist I know of, is a Navajo. He works at the National Laboratory at Los Alamos, New Mexico, not far from the reservation. Dr. Lori Arviso Alvord is the only Navajo woman ever to become a surgeon. Her practice on the reservation emphasizes *mizhoni*, which means walking in beauty, a measuredness and harmony among all things. She was head resident in surgery at Stanford Medical School in 1990–91, and now is a dean at Dartmouth Medical School.

It's remarkable that the Navajo don't want casinos; hundreds of other tribes do. Since the boom in Indian casinos began about ten years ago, 184 tribes have built casinos, a few tribes have made billions of dollars, and lots of tribes are trying to open casinos of their own. Nowadays, in many people's minds casinos and Indians are one and the same. No other story about Indians in recent decades has received anywhere near as much attention as the casino story, and the image of the casino-rich

Indian has become the latest in a long series of too-simple images pasted over the reality of Indian life. But like most such images, this one is not completely wrong. No tribal enterprise in history has succeeded even remotely as well as tribal casinos. Some tribes with imagination and persistence and reservations convenient to large population centers have become vastly rich with casino dollars, and the rise of tribal gambling has given some tribes economic power greater than Indians have known since the years when they had the continent to themselves.

The success of Indian casinos has largely to do with tribal sovereignty. Basically, a reservation is like a state; federal laws apply to it, but it makes its own local laws, among which are laws regulating gambling. In the 1980s, perhaps revived by the new awareness of tribal sovereignty that was part of the Indian protest movement of the decade before, some tribes realized that they could offer gambling opportunities (larger jackpots, for example) in their little bingo parlors, which the states surrounding them did not allow. The speed with which the new Indian gambling enterprises grew and prospered alarmed the states, mainly because tribal gambling can't be taxed—any more than a state can tax another state's lottery winnings, or the federal government can tax a state's. Frightened at the idea of tribes amassing untaxable gambling riches and building gambling empires within their borders, the states pressed Congress to pass a law regulating Indian gambling. This law, the Indian Gambling Regulatory Act of 1988 (IGRA), gave the states some control over Indian gambling. The IGRA said that a federally recognized tribe could offer gambling on its reservation only after entering into a compact agreement with the state in which its reservation lies. The practical result of this was usually some kind of compromise between the tribe and the state involving a sharing of casino revenues in lieu of tax. After the IGRA passed, the structure it provided helped the Indian gambling boom to take off.

Unlike, say, Christianity or individual ownership of land, gambling was actually part of Native American tradition. Before European contact many tribes played games of chance, often with dice-like stones and marked bones. White travelers who met Indians far from the settlements wrote of their passion for gambling, and recounted with disapproval how some Indians spent long winter nights in riotous gambling, how they sometimes kept playing until they had lost horses, lodges, wives, and everything down to their breechclouts. In the nineteenth century, gambling joined the list of supposed vices which the civilizers of the Indian wanted to eradicate. When Geronimo, the famed war chief of the Chiricahua Apache, lived on a reservation in Oklahoma, he was kicked out of the Dutch Reformed Church for gambling.

The idea to build Indian casinos turned out to be lucky itself. At about the time that the IGRA passed, and in the years since, Americans went gambling crazy. I don't know why. Maybe the reason has to do with the aging of much of the population, and the fact that retirees have more money than younger people, and more free time; certainly, on any given day, people with white hair make up a good segment of the players at most casinos' slot machines. Maybe the reason involves the heralded global victory of capitalism, and the vaulting rise of financial markets using money to make more money without clear connection to anything real. Maybe gambling is just our era's acceptable form of group hysteria. Whatever the cause, the gambling phenomenon is on the order of a continental drift. In the 1990s Americans began to spend more money on gambling than on all other forms of entertainment combined. Gambling meccas like Atlantic City and Las Vegas greatly expanded their hotels and casinos, referred to what they offered as "gaming" to remove any gangsterish tinge, and retooled to accommodate middle-class families. In 1988, the year of the IGRA, Indian casinos took in about $121 million. By 1994, they were making about $4.5 billion. In 1997, Americans bet $638.6 billion—*billion*—on the various forms of legal gambling, and lost about $51 billion of it. The total revenue for Indian casinos in that year was about $7 billion.

Casino money has completely changed the lives of some tribes. Exhibit A is always the Mashantucket Pequot, that small tribe of multimillionaires in Ledyard, Connecticut, just off Interstate 95. Their Foxwoods Casino is sometimes described as the largest casino in the Western Hemisphere, sometimes as the largest in the world. The tribe has become one of the leading employers in the state; it builds museums, funds ballets, builds its own high-speed ferryboats to haul customers from along the seaboard. Recently, the 25 percent of its slot-machine take, which it pays by compact agreement to the state of Connecticut, came to over $14 million in a single month. In other urbanized parts of the country tribal casinos bring in tens or hundreds of millions of dollars every year. Gambling revenues have enabled some tribes to reduce or eliminate unemployment, pay for schooling, hire tribal historians, build clinics and roads and houses, get tribal members off welfare, and in some cases give members per capita payments ranging from thousands to hundreds of thousands of dollars a year.

The fact remains, however, that most Indian reservations are not good sites for gambling casinos. Reservations tend to be far from anywhere, on less-traveled roads, and difficult to promote to gamblers, who, if they travel, usually go to Vegas. Just a few of the tribal casinos—under a dozen—take in half of the gambling dollars. Along with the Pequot, the biggest moneymakers are the Mdewakanton Sioux near Minneapolis, the Oneida of Wisconsin, the Fort McDowell Reservation near Phoenix, and the Sandia Pueblo between Albuquerque and Santa Fe. Hundreds of other Indian tribes don't have casinos, and of those who do, most are making modest profits or just breaking even. A majority of Indians still live close to or below the poverty line. In short, profits from the gambling boom have had little effect on most Indians' lives.

I have been to big-money tribal casinos on both coasts and in Minnesota, and they tend to run together in the mind. They are of a sameness—the vast parking lots, the low, mall-like, usually windowless buildings, the arbitrary Indianish decor, the gleeful older gamblers rattling troves of quarters in their bulging pants pockets, the unromantic expressions in the employees' eyes. Also, going to a major Indian casino is so much like going to a non-Indian one, in Atlantic City or someplace, that you may have to remind yourself exactly why Indian casinos enjoy tax advantages non-Indian casinos don't. The idea of Indian tribal sovereignty, a bit elusive to begin with, can fade out entirely behind the deluge of generic gambling dollars. In the last few years, some state and federal legislators have begun to view tribal casinos in just this skeptical way. Their renewed attacks on tribal sovereignty usually include a lot of rhetoric about the supposed great gambling wealth of Indian tribes nowadays. Regrettably, the resentment against Indian casinos, whose largest benefits go to only a few tribes, may end up threatening the sovereignty of all tribes. Many Indians have worried more about loss of sovereignty since the casino boom began. Some say that entering into compacts with the states is itself a wrong idea, because it accepts state jurisdiction where none existed before. Concern for sovereignty has been a main reason why the Navajo have rejected casino gambling. A Navajo leader said that tribes who accept outside oversight of their gambling operations have allowed a violation of tribal sovereignty; he added, "The sovereignty of the Navajo Nation and the Navajo people is not and should never be for sale."

Tribes do make money at other kinds of enterprises. The Santa Ana tribe, about a hundred households on a small reservation north of Albuquerque, has been able to remain an agricultural tribe by growing many tons of blue corn every year to sell to The Body Shop, a British-based cosmetics company, which makes a blue-tinted natural face cleanser from it. (More recently, the tribe has built a casino, and used its profits to build a multimillion-dollar resort.) The Choctaw tribe of Mississippi, formerly sharecroppers and paupers, have become one of the largest employers in the state; Choctaw factories make circuit boards, wiring-harnesses for automobile dashboards, automotive speakers, and hand-finished greeting cards for the American Greeting Card Company. Almost all Mississippi Choctaws still speak Choctaw. The Bois Forte (Nett Lake) Chippewa Reservation in northern Minnesota grows world-famous wild rice, which the tribe harvests by traditional methods in early fall. Harvesters make their way among the rice stalks in canoes and beat the kernels into the boats with sticks, a method which fills the harvesters' faces with chaff. Waterfowl love the rice, and the Bois Forte Reservation has fine duck hunting.

Wisconsin's Menominee tribe, which has been where it is for five thousand years, occupies a reservation of 235,000 acres in the east-central part of the state. Most Menominee land is managed forest; the tribe had 1.2 billion standing board feet of timber in 1850, has harvested 2 billion board feet since then, and still maintains a healthy forest of 1.5 billion board feet. A tribal corporation limits the annual timber cut and plants replacement trees. The Lac du Flambeau Chippewa, also of Wisconsin, operate Ojibwe Brand Pizza, a chain in seven states; the Eastern Cherokee own the largest mirror company in the United States; the Ak-Chin Community in Maricopa, Arizona, grow top-quality pima cotton; and the Skull Valley Band of Goshute Indians own a rocket-motor test site on tribal land in northwestern Utah. Recently the Goshute have come up with a plan to provide temporary storage on the reservation for spent nuclear fuel.

Many tribes get revenue from energy leases. Although Indian reservations contain just 4 percent of the nation's land, they hold 16 percent of its coal reserves and 4 percent of its petroleum and natural gas. On some reservations, oil has been the major source of non-government income. The Fort Peck Assiniboine Reservation in Montana used to hold a powwow every August to celebrate the discovery of oil there in 1952. On the Wind River Reservation in Wyoming, the Shoshone and Arapahoe tribes made money during the high oil prices of the 1970s; after the prices dropped in the 1980s, the reservation suffered a corresponding rise in suicides.

People who took land from Indians in the nineteenth century thought in terms of farms, railroad rights-of-way, and mines. If they had thought in terms of energy and of what energy resources might be worth someday, Indians might have been left with no land at all. The value of a piece of land, like character, can take time to be revealed. Uranium, for example, turned out to be plentiful in landscapes which no nineteenth-century farmer would have looked at twice—in just the sorts of places where America pushed Indians. Half the nation's uranium reserves now lie under Indian lands. Many of these reserves are in a large mineral belt west of Albuquerque; the reservation of the Laguna Pueblo, near the middle of the deposit, has the largest uranium strip mine in the world. During the Cold War, Navajo miners helped dig the uranium used to make nuclear weapons. When some of them developed lung cancer and sued the government for not warning them of the danger, the government cited the arms race and the need for national security. Tribal revenues from uranium mining, like the uranium business nationwide, have been in decline ever since the near-disaster at the nuclear power plant at Three Mile Island.

One place where you find a lot of Indians is in the Army. Indians have always made good soldiers and have gotten along better in all branches of the service than they often did elsewhere in the non-Indian world. Indians fought in every American war from the Revolution on. Iroquois and other Eastern tribes served in the Continental Army; a while ago the Daughters of the American Revolution gave membership to a full-blooded Indian woman named Neana Neptune Lent, descendant of a Penobscot Indian in that war. Winnebago and Iroquois fought for the North in the Civil War, while Cherokee and Choctaw fought for the South. Stand Watie, a Cherokee politician and soldier, who led a regiment of Cherokee cavalry, was the last Southern general to surrender.

Though most Indians were not U.S. citizens at the time of the First World War, they volunteered at a rate greater than that of any other group. Afterward, partly out of gratitude, Congress passed the law extending citizenship to all Indians. In the Second World War, they again volunteered by the thousands—a thousand from the Oglala alone—and bought lots of war bonds with their scarce dollars and put tribal funds at the disposal of the government. Indians in the service tended to acquire the nickname "Chief," and to win more decorations than their comrades. Notable among Indian heroes of that war was the Pima Ira Hayes, a Marine pfc and winner of two Bronze Stars for gallantry. After a *Life* magazine photographer took the famous picture of Hayes and other Marines hoisting the flag on Iwo Jima, higher-ups brought Hayes back to the United States to make appearances at patriotic rallies and fund-raising events. Hayes quickly tired of the attention and received permission to return to the war.

Biographies of Indian men in their seventies and older almost always include a reference to the Second World War: "He survived the sinking of the U.S.S. *Waters* off Okinawa, one of only thirty-eight found alive from a crew of five hundred"; "He was captured with others of the 36th Texas Division in the South of France, then freed by the 3rd Division, and afterwards wounded by machine gun fire. He had four bullets and one kidney removed, and still has one bullet in his body"; "He served as a fireman and gunner aboard the U.S.S. *Benham* in the years 1944 through 1946 and was awarded five battle stars"; "When a Japanese suicide plane flew into the ship, he was in the water for 52 hours before being rescued." Recently the Ranger Hall of Fame at Fort Benning, Georgia, inducted a Ranger veteran named Norman Janis. Mr. Janis, an Oglala Sioux and a descendant of Red Cloud, was cited for his service with a special unit called Merrill's Marauders in the North Burma campaign. The citation said that once, when his platoon was surrounded, Pfc Janis used his sharpshooting abilities to kill eight Japanese soldiers with eight bullets, all to the head.

In Vietnam, Indian soldiers were more likely to see combat than those of other groups. Many Indians were killed or wounded there; of those missing in action, scientists at first had trouble identifying the remains, because of the similarity of Indian skulls to the skulls of Asian people like the Vietnamese. Indian veterans angry about the war made a large percentage of the membership of AIM and contributed to its militancy. The tradition of Indians in the armed services did not end with that war, however. One of the first U.S. soldiers to die in Operation Desert Storm was a member of the San Carlos Apache tribe named Michael Noline; among the Navy technicians firing Tomahawk missiles at Saddam Hussein was a Crow Indian, Fire Controlman Third Class Wesley Old Coyote. In recent years, many Indian women have joined the military as well.

The military often builds its bases in the neighborhood of Indian reservations. The same remoteness, emptiness, and general unfarmability that resulted in the reservations being where they are proved ideal for the training purposes of the Army and Air Force. Military aircraft on training exercises fly over reservation land all the time. If you drive on Western reservations, sooner or later a B-52 bomber will roar over the roof of your car so close you could almost throw a rock at it, or a Phantom 115 jet fighter will pop out like a genie from around a butte and flit by in spooky silence a second ahead of the sky-filling thunder of its engine. Military overflight has become such a reservation commonplace that some tribes have considered the possibility of restricting their air space. And naturally, every so often a plane flying over an Indian reservation will crash.

On the night of May 10, 1995, an F-117-A Nighthawk Stealth fighter on a training mission crashed into Pia Mesa on the Zuñi Indian Reservation in western New Mexico. Zuñi who saw the plane coming down thought it was a falling star. The plane made a thirty-foot crater and burned, and Zuñi search-and-rescue teams and police and firefighters were the first to reach the crash. Afterward, the Air Force gave all the Zuñi who had been there a detailed health questionnaire. The burning materials in the plane included beryllium, carbon graphite, depleted uranium, radar-absorbent materials, and thermoplastic; Air Force scientists wanted to know what the effects of exposure to such smoke and fumes might be. "I guess they want to know if we are going to mutate into something," Zuñi responder Clay Dillingham said.

The name of this plane, the Nighthawk Stealth fighter, is misleading. It is not a supersonic dogfighting airplane like the Phantom. In fact, its top speed is about that of a commercial jet, well in the subsonic range. The Stealth is designed to fly slowly, undetected by radar, and to drop one or two bombs. It is about the size of a fighter plane and looks like a cross between a boomerang and a grand piano. Its delta-wing shape, futuristic though it may be, suggests to the observer uninformed about aeronautics that the plane might not fly very well. In this case, aeronautics notwithstanding, the doubt would seem to be well founded; of the fifty-nine Stealth built so far, six have crashed, and another caught fire and burned on landing. There has also been a question about the ability of the plane's radar-absorbing skin to resist certain kinds of weather, particularly rain.

As part of most Indian treaties, the United States promised to educate Indian children. Because of this, the Bureau of Indian Affairs is responsible for the public schools on Indian reservations. Recently the BIA has announced that a large number of its reservation school buildings are falling apart. Some buildings are in such bad shape that students have been injured in them, and some have been shut down and replaced with temporary structures until repairs can be made. In 1995 the BIA estimated that the 187 schools it runs nationwide needed between $650 million and $800 million for repairs. The Stealth that crashed on the Zuñi reservation cost $45 million. The fifty-nine Stealths built so far have cost about $2.7 billion. BIA funding in general has been cut in recent years. Its funds for all school repairs and improvements nationwide in 1998 were $32 million, about enough to buy two-thirds of a Nighthawk Stealth airplane.

One of the pleasures of reading about Indians is in the names. In American history, you come across Indians with names like Arm Blown Off (who carried a message between Red Cloud and the soldiers in 1877), or Civility (a Conestoga Indian in Pennsylvania who made a speech to Thomas Penn), or William Shake Spear (an Arapahoe interpreter at the

St. Stephen's Mission in Wyoming in the 1890s) or Spy (a Sioux scout for the Army), or Buttock On Both Ends (a warrior in the Custer battle). In an Army census of about fifteen hundred Indians at the Red Cloud Agency in 1876 and 1877, about seventy Indians gave names which were, by our standards, remarkably obscene. The previous generation or two of pop culture left the impression that most Indians had names like Running Bear or Little White Dove or Running Water. In fact, Indians had and have names of almost every kind, from simple and de-ethnicized to complicated and traditional. Reading about Indians in recent years turns up names like Goofy Killsnight, Toby Shot to Pieces, Rufus White Woman, Gerben D. Earth, Montgomery Ward Two Belly, Heather Whiteman Runs Him, and Whisper Black Elk. Some names are complete sentences, like Randy Falls Down or Michael Stops or Frank Fools Crow or Peter Catches or Bobby Talks Different. An Oglala tribal member sometimes mentioned in news stories about the Pine Ridge Reservation is a woman named Carla Respects Nothing. Then there's Pius Moss, Smile White Sheep, Exactly Sonny Betsuie, Louis Pretty Hip, Melanie Shoot Dog, Octa Keen, Charley Zoo, the brothers Roy and O'Ray Dog, and Frizzell Frizzell, the nation's only American Indian golf course superintendent.

Many Indian last names recall the colonial powers in North America. A few Indians have Dutch last names, more have names that are Spanish, English, or French. In the far Pacific Northwest, where the Russians once built trading posts, some Aleut and Inuit Native Americans still belong to the Russian Orthodox Church and have Russian last names. Bill Prokopiof is the name of an Aleut artist from the Pribilof Islands four hundred miles off the coast of Alaska in the Bering Sea. As the original people on the continent, Indians absorbed groups who came later, and they continue to absorb them. Ethnologists predict that in the next century the number of pure-blood Indians will dwindle to almost none, a prospect which disturbs the many tribes who require that their members be of a certain percentage of tribal blood—usually a quarter or an eighth.

Very likely, future membership in an Indian tribe will depend as much on family tradition and personal affinity as on blood degree, further complicating the already fraught problem of Indian identity. Also, due to the widespread practice of putting Indian babies up for adoption by non-Indian families back in the assimilationist 1950s and 1960s, many adoptees now in search of their parentage are finding that they are Indian. There is even an organization, the Lost Bird Society, to help people find their Indian roots; the tribal enrollment office of the Gila River Pima-Maricopa tribe in Arizona said not long ago that it was getting an average of three requests a day from adoptees in search of their birth parents. A few years past a woman named Yvette Silverman Melanson who had grown up Jewish in New York discovered that she had been born a Navajo. "I thought [Indians] were extinct, like the dinosaur," she told a newspaper.

The idea of belonging to a tribe not by blood but by affinity is less vague than it sounds. Some Indians preferred (and prefer) to live with bands or tribes other than the ones they were born into. An Oglala of the Cut Off band might move in with his mother's relatives among the Bad Faces, a Santee Sioux might journey west from Minnesota and join the Oglala, a Sioux might be adopted into the Cheyenne or a Cheyenne into the Arapahoe. Today there are Oglala descended from Minnecojou Sioux who stayed on Pine Ridge after the massacre at Wounded Knee, or from Cheyenne who came to the reservation and stayed partly due to the friendship of Red Cloud. The power of affinity applies to non-Indians as well. Some people with no Hopi or Zuñi blood at all love the Pueblo Indian culture, and study it and buy its artifacts, and talk about the Pueblo tribes as if no other existed. Germans who like Indians often seem to choose the Sioux or the Apache, while the French favor more northerly tribes like the Blackfeet and Cree. Among Western history buffs it is possible to get into long arguments about which is the coolest tribe, with strong opinions on a number of sides. Every buckskinner—buckskinners are historical re-enacters who dress in buckskin and shoot black powder rifles, for a hobby—has a favorite tribe, and usually a favorite band within that tribe.

Indeed, the Indians of America are so varied that I think you could find an appropriate tribe for almost anyone. The tribes' historical variety is like that of America today, but in seed-crystal form. As we get older, we learn our affinities—for certain foods or kinds of music or seats in an airplane or professions or physical types among the sex we happen to be attracted to. Just through an affinity for a particular part of the country, a person narrows down the number of tribes that would be right for him or her. In the same way that I have gotten used to my liking for hot sauce and my aversion to crowds, I accept that my affections veer toward the Oglala Sioux. Many names of Indian tribes, translated from the original, have a self-praising meaning like "the True People" or "the Human Beings," and Indians will sometimes tell you privately that their tribe is the best of all. Much as I like Indians in general, when it comes to the Oglala, my inclination is to agree. By blood and circumstances, I can never be an Oglala; but by long-standing affinity, the Oglala are my tribe.

CHAPTER

6

I spent the night in a motel in Chadron, Nebraska—the Pine Ridge Reservation has no motels—and in the morning drove the thirty-some miles back to Le's. His door was tied shut with the fish stringer, and on the door was a note addressed to me: "Went to Floyd John's across the river. See U. —Le." I wasn't sure what that meant, so I drove over to Pine Ridge, went to Big Bat's, and had a sandwich. I walked around Pine Ridge for a while, then went to Le's again. This time his door was open and he was sitting unsteadily on several piled-up sofa cushions and looking out through the screen. In his hand was a 24-ounce can of Olde English Malt Liquor. He told me to come in, and then he said, "Listen—I want to tell you something—you know I'm a dog soldier, right? You know what that means? It means I fight for my people, that I'm a warrior. You understand? I'm a dog soldier, today is a good day to die! It's a good day to change the world! I'm standing on my own two feet on the bosom of our mother earth. I go where I want, I do what I want. I take no orders from anybody. The *spirits* tell me what to do. I'm just a man . . ." He began to cry.

He took some dried sage tied in a narrow bundle with red thread, lit it with a paper match, and began to swish its smoke around the room. He was singing Lakota, but so quietly that only occasionally did audible phrases emerge. He said, "I talk to you because you—" He stopped.

"Because I'm your friend," I finished for him.

"I talk to you because you have a curious mind and an innocent heart. And you're not my friend. You're my brother." He set the smoldering sage in an empty can that had once held commodity pears. He sang some more, then took me by both arms and prayed for me, asking that I see with clear eyes that do not judge. He shook hands with me complicatedly, feeling the pulses in my wrists with his thumbs.

We got in my car and drove a few miles north on the highway, then turned off into a pasture. He said that he wanted to collect some more sage and that he knew a good place for it by the sun-dance grounds. We went through several fenced fields, Le getting out to open the gates. Then we came down a small embankment and into an open flat surrounded by cottonwood trees. In the center of it stood a sun-dance arbor—a shelter in the shape of an O, tree-limb posts supporting crossbeams laid over with a roof of bushy pine boughs—and in the center of the O stood the sun-dance pole. From the pole's top fluttered strips of cloth in the four sacred colors, which are red, black, yellow, and white. A sun dance had taken place there a week or so before, and the grasses were still trampled down, and the dusty ground exhaled a good fragrance I couldn't identify. There was not a scrap of litter anywhere. Near the sun-dance arbor remained the willow frame of a sweat lodge, a delicate sketch of a dome just big enough to sit under. By the lodge frame I saw a few remaining pieces of split cottonwood of a deep yellow, a heap of stones, and a sort of whisk made of long-needle pine boughs tied with baling twine. Aside from the twine, the fastenings of blue nylon cord on the sweat-lodge frame, and the cloth at the top of the sun-dance pole, everything in this ceremonial place was made from natural materials found close at hand. Most religious structures look as if they had descended upon the landscape from above; these looked as if they had risen on their own out of the ground.

Le cut sprigs from sage bushes growing at the clearing's edge, singing again in Lakota and telling me Lakota words I should know. The Wild West smell of the sage mingled with the liquidity of the words: *oskí-ski*, which means badlands, and *ih'é-swu-la*, the little stones found sometimes on anthills, and *péji wacaṅga*, sweet grass, and *mitakuye oyasin*, the phrase you say when the heat becomes too intense inside the sweat lodge and you want to get out. It means "all my relatives." Le took a generic-brand cigarette from a pack in his shirt pocket and scattered the tobacco from it to the four directions and said a prayer before we left.

From there we went to Floyd John's. The road to his place had dried to deep ruts, and I walked each tire through them slowly, so as not to jounce Le's neck. Floyd John was on the ground by the propane tank outside his cabin, lying on his back propped up on both elbows. His hair was every which way and his eyes were remote and intent at the same time. He gestured for me to sit on the ground beside him and I did. Then he turned to me and said, "What is love? Love is a piece of shit." He began to talk about love, about the woman and the man, and how one does this and the other does that, and how all of it is shit; meanwhile, he held my right hand in his, emphasizing his points with various shakes and squeezes. I felt something sticky, and when I finally retrieved my hand, I found the palm blotched with drying blood. He and Wanda had had a fight, he explained, and he had broken a glass and cut his hand. Wanda came around the corner of the cabin, gave us an unencouraging look, and went back inside.

The day before, I had loaned Floyd John $20.85 to buy a new regulator for a car he was trying to get running, and he wanted to pay me back. He went in the cabin and came out with an Army fatigue shirt in a jungle camouflage pattern that he had worn in Vietnam. I didn't want to accept it, but I did, thanking him a lot. Then he went in again and this time came out with a belt buckle of embossed and painted leather he had made himself. In the middle of the buckle was the head of a bald eagle in profile superimposed on a black spade, with the word NAM above and the years " '66 '68" below. The edge of the buckle was black leather hand stitching, and stamped on the back was Floyd John's name. I really did not want to take this, and I protested as much as I could, saying that I could never wear it, that I hadn't been in Vietnam. He kept saying he had made it in the V.A. hospital and he wanted me to have it because I was his bro. Finally I took it.

In Pine Ridge I had seen a sign advertising a rodeo west of town that evening, and I wanted to go to it. I had already asked Le if he wanted to go. Now he persuaded Wanda and Floyd John to come along, too. I wasn't crazy about this development, because it looked to me as if the fight they'd been having was far from done. But we all four then piled into my car and drove to Pine Ridge, Wanda and Floyd John continuing to exchange words in the back seat, though I could hear only Floyd John's. In Pine Ridge he told me to pull over at the four-way so we could get out and look at his name on the Vietnam Veterans' Memorial beside the road. Then, by a three-to-one majority, we elected to go to White Clay to buy a case of beer.

We pulled up by the door of the Arrowhead Inn—I am still not ready to describe the town of White Clay—and I gave Le seventeen dollars. He went in and bought a case of Budweiser and three 24-ounce cans of Olde English Malt Liquor. He and Floyd John said they would tell me how to get to the rodeo grounds. On the way there, Floyd John began to tell me about a poem he had written at Khe Sanh, and to lean in my ear and say loud remarks that were hard to respond to. I was in my extra-careful driving mode. Le and Wanda told him to shut up. We missed the turnoff for the rodeo grounds, stopped, and went back. The turnoff was unmarked except by the tracks of many tires, and it led quite a ways off the paved road, over one swell in the prairie and then another, and finally to a gate at a four-strand wire fence where some women were taking admission. It cost us four dollars apiece to get in; again I paid. We drove on to the arena, a corral with nine banks of lights on high poles around it and stock chutes at the far end. There were no grandstands, so we did the same as everyone else and pulled up to the corral fence to watch from our car. Some people had spread blankets on their car hoods to lie on.

There were the usual rodeo preliminaries—the riders guiding carefully-stepping horses among the cars, the bellows from the roping stock, the country music from the scratchy loudspeakers, the small parade featuring the American flag and the flag of the Oglala tribe. The arena lights seemed to get brighter as the sun went down. The first event, the folksy rodeo announcer said, would be Mutton Bustin', a bucking-sheep-riding contest for kids. At an end of the arena the small contestants assembled in a line, many in hats so big and pants so pegged they looked like tacks. One at a time they climbed into the bucking chutes, got aboard, and came out on sheep who flung themselves around more vigorously than I would have believed sheep could move. Some of the kids were quite little and got bucked off quickly. A few began to cry and ran for their dads to the accompaniment of the announcer's uncomforting folksy commentary. Other kids hung on like burrs until the sheep quit bucking, and a swell of applause and honking car horns rose from the spectators. One successful ride prompted the announcer to say that the Oglala ought to consider raising sheep for a living. Perched on my car hood, Floyd John yelled back, "*Sheep?* We ain't no goddamn Navajos!" This got a big laugh, and he yelled it several times more.

I told Le I was going to take a walk and look around. I circled the arena, then headed off across the prairie, stopped on the crest of a rise, and sat down. From here the arena was just a cloud of bright dust rising into the lights, in a vague encirclement of vehicles. The prairie silence stretched on every side to the darkening horizon, and the announcer's voice and the sound of the car horns were faint and faraway. After a while I got up and walked back slowly. Nearer the arena, I noticed that someone seemed to be sitting in the driver's seat of my car. I hurried over to see who it was; I didn't want anyone sitting there. The person turned out to be a cowboy named Jimmy Yellow Boy, an acquaintance of Le's and Floyd John's. He was drinking Budweiser and bully-ragging with them, while Floyd John made threats about kicking his ass. I could not tell for sure how serious he was.

I introduced myself to Jimmy Yellow Boy in a way which I hoped said, "Get out of my car." Jimmy Yellow Boy took no notice, talking instead about the bad bull he had drawn to ride and about bad bulls he had ridden in the past. He said he had been hurt by a bull named Peggy Sue—"I'm all broken up, man. You don't mess with those bulls"—and he showed me his hands. Their multiple breaks and rehealings had given them an odd look, as if they had been drawn by one of those plentiful artists who can't draw hands. Le finally told him to get the hell out so I could sit down, and Jimmy Yellow Boy did, cheerfully telling us to honk our horn for him when he rode.

Each event seemed to take longer than the one before it to get under way. Often a roping steer or a bull would wedge himself crosswise in the chute and bellow and kick and send people leaping back. Many of the hazers and stock handlers had cans of beer in Styrofoam can caddies at convenient spots on the ground along the corral fence and occasionally stepped away from their tasks for long sips, which worked to their disadvantage in dealing with the angry, lively, and sober bucking stock. The announcer called Jimmy Yellow Boy's name, and suddenly we saw the wide blue-and-white stripes of his shirt bouncing from the chute on top of a dark, grunting blur. He had slid to the ground before I remembered to honk the horn. Le and Floyd John were now arguing on a repetitive theme, so I left again and stood behind the bucking chutes. A tall bull rider grinned broadly at a pregnant girl in light-blue cutoffs and asked, "If I ride him, will you name your baby after me?" Then he climbed into the chute, got settled, gave a nod, and went flying off at the second or third buck.

When the rodeo was winding down, Le wanted me to drive around among the parked cars looking for a friend of his, but I ignored him and joined the traffic honking and jockeying at the fence gate in the headlight beams full of exhaust smoke and dust. Le and Floyd John had begun to argue about the Vietnam War, Le calling Floyd John a chump for going and Floyd John calling him worse for not going, keeping up a running argument with Wanda all the while. As we approached Pine Ridge, we came over a rise and saw the lights of the village spread out across the dark prairie. I remarked that they looked like the lights of Los Angeles seen from Mulholland Drive, and said how pretty it was. Wanda said, more clearly than I ever heard her say anything, "It looks pretty, but it's just a slum."

As we drove on toward Oglala, the three-way argument escalated to threats about who would do what to whom. My driving terror reached its peak. In every set of oncoming headlights—or single headlight, or car with no headlights at all—I imagined I was seeing the final frame before the film goes blank. I wondered how I would control the car if the argument suddenly came to blows. Old-time plainsmen used to say you haven't seen a fight until you've seen Sioux fighting Sioux. Then we were bouncing along the drive to Floyd John and Wanda's dark cabin. Because of his bad leg and uncertain balance, Floyd John had a hard time getting out of the back seat, but he finally made it, with a few parting shots at Le and a last complicated handshake for me, along with a promise to introduce me to a rancher named Warren who had known his dad. Le discovered that Floyd John had forgotten his cane in the back seat, and he got out to give it to him. "You're still my bro, Bro," Le said to Floyd John.

Then I drove Le to his house while he told me about two guys he had killed with his bare hands when he was in prison. I backed my car around in his drive to light with my headlights his way into the electricity-less house. He turned at the door and waved and disappeared behind it, like an actor behind a lit curtain. Then I beat it back to Chadron and the motel.

Le had been up for a long time when I got to his house the next day about noon. He had gone to the post office, stacked some firewood, put on a clean shirt, and read some of Stephen Oates's biography of Abraham Lincoln. I noticed it lying on his bed and commented on it. He said he hated Lincoln for hanging thirty-eight Sioux in Mankato, Minnesota, after the Santee Sioux Uprising in that state in 1862. I said that the Minnesotans had wanted to hang three hundred or more, that Lincoln had wanted to pardon most of them, and that thirty-eight was the compromise they made. Le said all the same it was the largest mass execution in U.S. history, and he would always hate Lincoln for it. He said George Washington was another Indian-killer and he hated him, too. I tried to put in a few good words for Lincoln, but failed to dent his opinion.

Florence Cross Dog, Le's older sister, had told Le that she wanted to meet me, so we went to her house at the end of a gravel street of new one-story single-family homes. But Florence had gone to the clinic in Porcupine for her regular kidney dialysis treatment. Le considered for a while and then said, "Well then, let's go see Uncle Edgar." Edgar High White Man, Le's uncle in only the honorific and affectionate sense, lived in a house at the junction of the highway and a gravel road a few miles west of Oglala. Le told me that Edgar High White Man's mother had survived the massacre at Wounded Knee. We pulled into his driveway and got out, and Le called through the back door screen, and Edgar High White Man came out and talked with us as he leaned with one foot propped on the running board of his new red pickup truck. He was short, deeply wrinkled, eighty-six years old, with bowlegs like parentheses. He wore a straw cowboy hat with red, yellow, and black feathers in the hatband; a blue-and-white-checked shirt; blue jeans; blue suspenders; and the gold watch he received on his retirement after thirty years driving the Loneman school bus.

In 1976 Edgar High White Man had testified before Congress as part of the Sioux's attempt to get reparations from the government for Wounded Knee. His mother, Dora, was nine years old at the time of the massacre. She was with her grandmother there, and after her grandmother got shot, Dora ran away over a ridge. A wagon picked her up and carried her to Oglala, where she afterward remained. Edgar High White Man went inside and brought out the transcripts of the hearings, in a thick paperbound volume swollen a bit with water damage that happened when someone he had loaned it to didn't take proper care. He said he testified to the senators about his mother's sufferings for a long time. He and the other descendants of Wounded Knee survivors had hoped the government would agree to reparation payments similar to those given to Japanese interned during the Second World War; but one of the South Dakota senators was working on the Sioux's behalf while the other was working just as hard against them, he said, and nothing came of the hearings in the end.

I asked him if he knew where the name High White Man came from. He said, "Well, that's quite a story. My great-granpa was a respected man and sometimes he would get into a group of younger men talking about expeditions they would like to go on. They'd plan where they wanted to go and they always wanted an older, well-experienced man like him to lead. One older man would lead and another would bring up the tail part, with the younger fellows in between, everybody walking single file just close enough so they could hear each other's steps. Well, on this one expedition they were down south of where Scottsbluff, Nebraska, is now. They never went on the flat like this ground around here, where an enemy could see them. They followed the higher ground just below the ridgeline, and every so often the leader would go up on the ridge and use a bush for cover and look all around. Then he'd go to the next hill and do the same thing.

"Well, my great-granpa was on a hill looking around and he sighted this wagon train coming. So he said to the others, 'This is a tight place. I'll go on ahead and meet the wagon train, and if anything happens to me you can get them when they come through here.' So he went to the wagon train a long way around so they wouldn't know where he had come from, and the fellows that were watching saw the whole wagon train stop. Then they saw the wagon master come over to my great-granpa, and they saw the wagon master shake his hand. The wagon master was a very tall guy with red hair. Well, they saw that, and they decided they had another name for my great-granpa. They said, 'We'll call him Washicun Wankatuya, High-up White Man.' The wagon master gave my great-granpa molasses and bread, and all the others came to the wagon train and got molasses and bread, too, so they didn't have to attack 'em. Our family has had that name ever since.

"It's funny you should ask me that question," Edgar High White Man said. "Just a few weeks ago an auto-glass repairman in Nebraska asked me the same thing."

(I am glad I got a chance to meet Edgar High White Man. He died January 18, 1996.)

On another afternoon, we found Florence Cross Dog at home. Her car was in her driveway, so we pulled in behind it and walked around to the back door, past a black pickup truck with a dead porcupine on the hood. Le said that one of Florence's sons was using the quills for decorative quillwork on a rattle he was making. Le rapped on the screen and someone called to him from inside and we went in. There were a lot of people in the house, and that first time I didn't get them all straight. Several little kids—Florence's grandchildren—came up to us and stared at me and smiled at Le, and held up their puckered lips so he could bend down and be kissed. A girl named Tabitha showed him her new mood ring, and a baby named RaeDawn, wearing only a disposable diaper, yelled something up at us I couldn't understand and then yelled it again and laughed. RaeDawn's mother, Florence's daughter Flora, known as Tweet, was sitting in the living room watching TV. Florence's son John lay asleep on a couch. Le said John was a medicine man and had to stay up all night.

Florence came out from her bedroom, where she had been sewing. She is a big-boned woman with short dark hair, high eyebrows, and eyes that take quick measure of what they see. She had on a loose-fitting short-sleeved dress and bandages in the crooks of both arms, from the dialysis. She said that she'd heard so much about me from Le. I said she sure had cute grandkids, pointing down at RaeDawn. Florence said, "That one was born the same day I had my kidney removed, and the papers got the two things confused and wrote that I was in the hospital and had this baby. And I'm five years older than Leonard! I'm sixty years old!"

Immediately she asked me if I would like to buy a star quilt. This is a traditional Sioux style of quilt which has a star at the center with usually eight points radiating to the edges on a plain background, usually white. The star part of the quilt is made of diamond-shaped pieces of cloth all the same size fitted together and sewn on the off side. The pieces can be of all kinds of fabrics and colors, as in any quilt, and their combination and arrangement is a difficult art. I like star quilts, so I told Florence I'd be happy to see hers. She brought out a queen-sized quilt with a star of lavender, light pink, and light blue floral print on a white background. It was not finished yet, and still had blue marks on it from the quilting chalk. She said she wanted $200 for it and needed the money right away. I didn't have $200, but I said I liked the quilt, and I gave her a deposit of $50. I asked her how she had learned to quilt. She led me into her bedroom and showed me her sewing machine.

"It came to me one night in a dream," Florence said. "I never learned quilting from anybody—I just dreamed how to do it. I've been making star quilts for thirty-five years. And I've used this same Singer sewing machine the entire time. You can see how the wood here that the cloth goes over has all the finish worn off, and a layer or two of the plyboard, too. I've made hundreds of plain star patterns, and stars with pictures in the middle—buffalos and eagles and porcupines, and that picture called *The End of the Trail*. The Red Cloud Museum by Pine Ridge only pays $100 a quilt, and the Prairie Edge store up in Rapid only pays $200, and sometimes they turn around and sell them for a lot more, so I don't sell to them no more. Most of my customers are just people who've heard about me, people from all over."

From a bureau drawer she took out a stack of Polaroid photos of star quilts she had made. Reduced to this size, the stars in the middle of each quilt seemed to pulse. Some stars blended colors of the wildest gaudiness into a whole so simple that the eye had to go back over, color by color, to see how the effect had been achieved; others used pastel shades varying in subtle sequence from the center of the star to the tip of the points. Then she showed me a calendar with star quilt photos from the Rosebud Reservation, to compare. On those quilts the colors looked more random, bright but competing with each other in the eye. "Those Rosebudders are good sewers," Florence said, "but they don't understand about the colors, how to put 'em together."

Tabitha and her older sister, Amanda, seeing I was interested in such things, got out their jingle dresses to show me. Le's sister Norma, their great-aunt, had made them. The jingle dress is a ceremonial Sioux garment that goes back at least to the fur trade days. It can be of soft buckskin or cloth, and its main feature is the many little tin cones that hang from it from yoke to hem and that jingle together when the wearer moves. The dress is worn in a traditional women's dance called the jingle dance; Tabitha held her dress to her and did some jingle-dance steps so I could hear how it sounded. Jingle dresses sometimes have 365 cones on them, each representing a prayer for a different day of the year. A woman moving in a jingle dress is a multiplicity of small and soft sounds, like a treeful of dried seedpods rustling in the wind or a river with lots of shards of ice. Under certain circumstances, the effect on the ear can be as beguiling as perfume is on the nose. In former times, the cones were made of tin cut from containers of snuff bought at the trader's. I looked more closely at Amanda's and Tabitha's dresses and saw that on one, every cone was of tin cut from the top of a Redwood chewing tobacco can, and on the other, every cone was from a Copenhagen chewing tobacco can.

Flora took the baby RaeDawn and gave her a bath, and RaeDawn then ran around wrapped in a towel, showing off. John woke up, and he and his brother Rex and Le sat on the couch and began to watch a sit-com called *Major Dad*. Le had seen this episode already and he explained the plot to them. A grandchild of Florence's named E.J. asked if it was okay if he and another little boy went across the street to play on a backhoe at the construction site there. Florence let them. RaeDawn pulled a cushion from an armchair onto the floor and began to do som-

ersaults on it. Le and Rex began to talk about a car, a Volare, that someone was trying to fix up. It had carburetor problems. Florence joined
the conversation, and it briefly switched to Lakota, mixed with occasional English words like "air-filter cover." Through the front window I
could see E.J. and the other little boy climbing all over the backhoe in a
haze of dust blowing down the street.

Another afternoon, Le and I visited his sister Aurelia Two Crow. She is
eight years older than Florence, and shorter and more spry. After her
husband died a few years ago, she moved back to Oglala. She has
medium-length, mostly gray hair and she wears glasses with big round
frames that give her an owlish expression. Her manner is querulous and
lyrical, and her sentences sometimes trail off in a gentle "Uh-huh . . . oh
yes . . ." Her house is far from the road in a grove of tall cottonwood
trees. Her car, an older-vintage Chrysler, was parked among them. We
found her just beginning to wash it. "I was in Rapid, and I wanted to
wash my car it was so dirty," she said. "But they wanted two dollars and
fifty cents for a car wash up there, and I decided I'd rather have a fish
sandwich than a clean car, so I waited to wash it till I got home."

Aurelia's conversation, spoken as much to the car and herself as to
us, proceeded in phases between filling a heavy black plastic bucket at
the pump, soaping the car from roof to fenders, rinsing with splashes of
clean water, and polishing it dry with a rag.

"I went up there to visit at the hospital," she said, soaping, "and I
wanted to stay longer, but a storm came up, and I told Floyd John I was
worried about getting back, so we left. The wind started to blow and
tumbleweeds was running back and forth across the road and the sky
got so dark we had the headlights on. Floyd John drove fast on the
wrong side of the road most of the way. He said we was the only people
crazy enough to be out there anyway in that weather, so it didn't matter.
Yes, mm-hmm . . .

"I got Wisconsin license plates on this 'cause I been living over there
with my daughter. I should be in a nursing home, I'm so old. But instead I'm living in this old place now. I came back here last December
for the holidays and I been here ever since. My kids are all gone, New
Mexico and Wisconsin, and I'm out here by myself. Florence said I

ought to get out and do something, that I'm just vegetating. I said, 'If you think I'm vegetating, I'll run a race against you.' I can still get around good. Oh yesss . . .

"I'm feeling good now that I'm back home out of that damp Wisconsin climate. And I feel a *lot* better now that I don't drink so much anymore. Florence said she quit drinkin' and lost all her friends. Well, I didn't go that far—I have a few beers, but I don't drink so much wine and whiskey like I used to. And I don't try to drink with these guys [gesturing to Le]. I was drinkin' all the time a few years ago and some people told me I was drinkin' too much, that it was terrible. I said, 'Well, all right, Mr. Know-It-All. I worked for fifteen years as a cook at the senior center, makin' Indian food, fresh bread and biscuits and fry bread every day, not boughten bread and crackers like they serve now. And I had my kids and I raised 'em up right, and now they're off and gone, and I don't have no responsibilities no more. So why can't I do what I feel like and drink sometimes if I want to?' Yes, that's so . . ."

She finished polishing the chrome and threw the rags into the empty bucket. Then she stood back and admired her work. "This is a pretty good old car, mm-hmmm . . . Some mornings when it's real cold it don't like to start. But I just take a steel baking sheet from the kitchen and put hot cinders from the stove on it, and then I slide that baking sheet on the ground right under the engine block, and in a half hour or so it starts up just fine. Mm-hmmm . . ."

Aurelia invited us in and gave us mugs of hot tea with honey. She stirred something in a pot on the stove, and Le told me to come look, that she was cooking bull snake. I peered into the pot and saw slices of canned luncheon meat. I said it was a convenient sort of snake, to slice up so nice that way. Aurelia moved boxes of cloth scraps from the couch so we could sit. Late-season flies were buzzing at the windowpanes like wind-up toys running down, and Aurelia swatted vexedly at them with her hand. Then she went and got an aerosol can of hair spray, shook it, and sprayed it at the flies. They dropped in a heap on the sill. She said, "Not a lot of people know that hair spray kills insects almost as good as insect spray—mmm-hmm, it's so."

On the reservation, I noticed that people often told me tips like that. The tips, usually quite specific and informed by experience, reminded me of the woodcraft we were taught sometimes in the Cub Scouts or the Boy Scouts under the heading Indian Lore. That sort of woodcraft seemed to apply to situations that seldom came up—walking backwards in one's own footprints to confuse pursuers, for example, or rubbing two sticks together to make a fire when there were no matches around. But after years of talking to Indians and reading about them, I have found that they do indeed know a lot of more practical precepts that could be described as Lore, such as:

The smoke from anemone flowers burned on hot coals can cure headaches.

When you see cranes flying north, you know the really cold weather is over and spring is on the way. Other birds can tell you the same thing, but cranes are the most reliable.

You find fish in a river wherever there is a whirlpool.

Rainbow-hued sun dogs—bright spots on either side of the sun—mean an enemy is approaching.

If you hear a loud knock on your door and you open it and no one is there, it means that somebody you love has died.

An owl crossing your path can foreshadow tragedy.

After a powwow, there's almost always a party, usually in a motel room or a field. The party is called a forty-nine.

It is impossible to get bloodstains out of wallpaper.

The only way to kill a turtle so its heart stops beating is to boil the turtle for fifteen minutes.

If you kill a rattlesnake to eat, cut off the top six inches of the snake along with the head, because when the snake's muscles contract in death, the poison sometimes works back into the meat.

You cannot claim money that is wired to you by Western Union unless you show a picture ID.

Mussed or frayed eagle feathers may be restored by being dipped in a weak solution of shampoo in water and then hung up to dry.

A good way to break off a cast is by rubbing it on a curbstone.

If you find a dead person in your yard, you must call a sun dancer to come and purify your house.

Ashes will absorb wet blood from a wood floor.

Red willow bark to smoke in a sacred pipe must be gathered in the winter, after the first frost of fall and before the first thunders of the spring.

Deer meat that hasn't been hung up to cure will give you the runs.

If you're out drinking and you get rolled, watch your mailbox, because sometimes your wallet will come back in the mail.

A good fishing line may be made of the white hairs of a horse's tail, braided together.

Warming the hide of a drumhead with a blow dryer before you play it makes the drum sound better.

Hall's Mentholyptus lozenges make singers' voices sound sweeter.

In the old days, big storms always arrived at the death of the moon, but now even the moon lies.

If you're trying to move a house and you can't get it to skid onto the blocks, lubricate the way with liquid dishwashing soap.

Copperhead snakes smell like cucumbers.

A bluish-gray weed called lightning weed, if tied to your golf cart, will keep you from getting hit by lightning on the golf course.

Snakes always come out when it's windy and warm.

That fall a hard winter was on the way. It gave a preview of itself early, as such winters often do. One day we were driving on the reservation in hot sunshine with our sleeves rolled up and the windows down, road dust caking in our sweat. The next morning as I drove to Le's I came over a rise and saw a long, quite low cloud extending before me like the bill of a giant cap. In another minute I was in a white-out blizzard. The snow clouds must have been thin, because the sun lit the whirling whiteness all around until it was almost too bright to look at. I turned the radio off and drove at a slow speed. Soon I had emerged into shafts of sunshine coming down like stilts from among high, fast-moving clouds. To the west I could see more clouds lined up in ranks all the way to the Black Hills.

Le had to go to Rapid City to get a note from his doctor verifying his disability from the car accident, so that he could apply for free firewood and other emergency assistance from the tribe. I went by his house and then we drove to Rapid City and back, almost 160 miles round trip, me watching the weather all the way. The errand took about five hours. Then Le wanted to get his propane fuel tank refilled; besides using the fuel to cook with, he said, he could leave the oven burning and its door open for extra heat on cold days. A friend had disconnected the tank from the inlet out back for him. The tank was the height of a man and a foot or more across, and with his injuries Le couldn't move it by himself. Together we rolled it on its base and wrestled it crosswise into the back of my Blazer.

We drove to PTI Propane, south of Pine Ridge almost to the town of White Clay. PTI Propane is an acre or so of fenced ground with white storage tanks, a trailer house for an office, and a loading dock and scales. I backed up to the loading dock while Le went into the office and paid. Then two women, Patty and Faith, came out with him to fill the tank. We roll-walked the tank to the filler hose, and Patty began to try to open the tank's valve. As she did she told us she was Patty Pourier, wife of Big Bat. He is part-owner of PTI. We talked about him and about his famous ancestor as we each took a turn at trying to get the valve open. Patty is short, apple-cheeked, pretty, and strong. After giving the valve a final hard try, she said it must be rusted shut. She said she could get it fixed for us, but not right away. Le said that he knew where he could find another tank in the meantime and that we'd return soon.

We drove back toward Oglala. Le said he had a tank that someone had stolen from him in a field nearby. He directed me to turn off onto a dirt road which the morning's blizzard had turned to muck. At a place where the road led up a steep embankment, I got out to reconnoiter. Not only was the road muddy and slick and furrowed with small gullies, but its grade slanted toward the downhill side. I walked to the top and concluded my car couldn't make it. As I turned to go back, several dogs at a house beside the hill saw me and set out for me at a run, barking and growling with their teeth bared. I walked quickly but did not run, fearing to enrage them further. I calculated that our paths would converge just about at the car. I was a few feet from it and they were a few yards from me when Le heard the racket, stuck his head from the car door, and growled a word at them in Sioux. His growl was throaty and loud, like that of a dog much bigger than they. The dogs stopped so fast they left skid marks in the mud, and then ran yelping back home. The word Le had said to them sounded familiar. I asked him what it was. He said, "I said to them, '*Wahampi!*' It means soup." (And then I remembered—it was the word he had used for the soup we ate in his apartment in New York.) "Dogs on the reservation know the word *wahampi* because they know they might end up in some soup themselves. Eat a dog once in a while, it teaches the other dogs a healthy respect."

After further complications, and with the help of Floyd John, who we met along the road, we found a propane tank we could borrow. Then we drove back to the propane place. Patty was alone there—it was late in the day by then and Faith had gone home—and she came out to the loading dock when she saw us pull in. We rolled the propane tank up to the filler hose, and she opened the valve and attached the hose. Two guys in a pickup truck had pulled in right after us, and the driver asked if I would mind moving my car away from the dock so he could back his truck up to it. I got in my car and was about to turn the ignition when I heard a pop and a cry and then a loud hissing noise. In the rearview mirror, I saw white fumes billowing. I turned the ignition and pulled the car a few feet ahead. Patty came running at me and yelling, "Turn off your car! Turn off your car!"

I got out and looked back. The filler hose had ruptured at the point where the rubber met the nozzle, and propane gas was spewing out all over. The smell of propane filled the air as the white cloud of gas rose waist-deep around the loading dock and spread slowly across the compound. Le and Floyd John were holding the hissing hose while Patty ran around turning valves, to no effect. Then she told them to let go the hose and get away, and she sprinted for the trailer. Le and Floyd John came over to me, and Le said, "Let's get out of here—the whole place is gonna blow." I remembered when the propane distribution place blew up on the Santee Reservation in Nebraska some years ago. My main thought was that I hated to lose my car. Like an idiot, I went to it and started it again. Patty burst from the trailer waving both arms over her head and screaming at me not to start my car, was I crazy? I turned it off and left it regretfully. Then Le and Floyd John and I jog-walked away down the drive.

A white propane truck came speeding to the bottom of the drive and stopped. The driver jumped from the cab and ran up to the loading dock, leaped onto it, and disappeared behind the tanks. In another second the hissing stopped; he had found the cutoff valve. We waited a while longer, until the gas cloud had dispersed, and then we walked back up the drive. I got in my car while Le and Floyd John went up on the loading dock. In the rearview mirror I watched them talking with Patty. Then I thought I saw them laugh. I looked again; yes, they were laughing, while Patty shook her head and looked at the ground. Then she looked up and began to laugh, too.

When they got in the car I asked them what they had been laughing about. "Oh, we just made some joke about us almost getting blown up," Le said. "Patty told us that wasn't nothin' to laugh about. But then she kind of saw the humor in it, too."

"I don't think it's very funny," I said.

"Well, that's the Indian way," Le said. "We'd rather laugh about still being alive than moan about how we almost died."

Le and Floyd John speculated as we drove off about how big the explosion would have been if the place had blown, and what size crater it would have left. A hundred yards across? Two hundred yards? We got beer in White Clay and then headed back to Oglala. Le and Floyd John were laughing about where we would all be now if my car had happened to backfire when I started it just after the hose ruptured. I had never seen either of them in a better mood. Floyd John's driveway had returned to its liquid state, and we four-wheeled up it and got out and stood by his cabin deciding what to do. The wind had begun to blow hard. Dark-blue, silvery clouds bore down from the northwest, and prefatory snowflakes whirled. Florence's daughter had asked Le to bring me to her house for dinner, but I was all in. My nerves were twanging. I took another look at the clouds and decided to head for home.

I asked Le and Floyd John to make my apologies to Florence's daughter, and said to tell her that I'd come another time, that I'd be back soon. Le imparted some final dog-soldier precepts to me, and asked for forty dollars to get his reading glasses fixed. I gave him two twenties, and a twenty to Floyd John. After last farewells, I four-wheeled out to the highway. I took deep breaths as the mud clonked around in the wheel wells, and as the tires ran smoothly again on the pavement after the mud was gone.

CHAPTER

7

I came back in November. By then several snowstorms had been and gone, and the grasses lay flat on the prairie waiting for the next. A friend had brought the refilled propane tank to Le's house and hooked it up. Now Le could cook on his stove and use it for heat. He had acquired a too-small green overcoat and an orange-and-white ski cap with the words STATE FARM INSURANCE knit into the design in big letters. His neck brace would come off in a couple more weeks, he said. Floyd John and Wanda were now living in a trailer house across from the Oglala post office. Le said Floyd John had bought it with a VA loan. We drove over there and found Floyd John inside on a couch watching Court TV. He and Le began talking about a car a cousin of theirs had left in the town of Oelrichs, twenty-six miles away, which the cousin had said Floyd John could have if he could get it running before the car crusher came for it tomorrow. The three of us spent the morning and early afternoon in a meandering storyline involving this car.

A mile or two west of Pine Ridge we passed a bearded man in a black cassock and a gray beret who was picking up trash along the highway. Le said he was probably one of the Jesuit fathers from the Red Cloud Indian School nearby. After the car project petered out, I dropped Le and Floyd John off in Oglala and went back to the school to talk to him. The Red Cloud School is a group of brick buildings, some over a hundred years old, south of the highway about three miles from Pine Ridge. The school is down in an expanse of ground between low ridges which give the campus and its drive lined with cottonwoods a sheltered feel. I went into a likely-looking building and found the office of Eva Bordeaux, the school's publicity director. The original Bordeaux in these parts was James Bordeaux, a trader who came to the Plains in the 1830s and married into the Oglala. He remained alive and in business for forty more years, a real achievement back then. At Fort Laramie in 1854 he had the good sense not to accompany the headstrong Lieutenant Grattan when Grattan went to a Sioux camp to arrest those responsible for the theft of a cow from a Mormon immigrant train, and thus avoided the Grattan massacre, which the historians point to as the beginning of the wars between the Sioux and the Army. A marker near the site of Bordeaux's trading post east of Chadron, Nebraska, says that Bordeaux may have sold the Sioux weapons used against Custer's men at the battle of the Little Bighorn.

Eva Bordeaux, a stocky young woman with glasses and a PR director's forthcoming style, said that she was a six-greats granddaughter of James Bordeaux. There are lots of Bordeaux around, she said. I described the man I had seen picking up along the highway and she said that must have been Brother Simon. She led me back through hallways to an office cluttered with papers and livened with hanging plants and goldfish in tanks. There, brother C. M. Simon, S.J., a small man with a spade-shaped gray beard and a long tobacco-stained mustache, greeted me as cheerily as if I had an appointment and was right on time. Eva Bordeaux left us to talk. Brother Simon said he had nothing better to do at the moment; he runs the school's museum of Indian arts and crafts and had to be in his office while an auditor from a firm reviewing the school's books went over his inventory. The auditor, a tall, transparent man, asked occasional questions about one item or another, and Brother Simon answered him in between talking to me. Brother Simon speaks with a stutter which, years ago, kept him out of the Army. Once I caught on to it, I found it more pleasant to listen to than ordinary speech. (I'll omit it here.)

"Yes, I do pick up the trash in the ditches along the road every week or so, just in the vicinity of the school," he said. "One must participate in the community, you know, and occasionally I find some little keepsake, and of course I can recycle the aluminum cans. I am not a teacher at the school. I've been here for thirty-five years, but I've taught nothing, except by my bad example. I've worked in the treasurer's office, and when we had a herd of prize Charolais cattle I handled the paperwork for that, doing yearling weights and genealogies and so on, and for eighteen years I've run the museum and the exhibition of Indian art we have at the school every year. Now, I'm sure in what you'll write you'll say that I'm a monk. Writers always refer to me as a monk when they do stories about me—they get things so balled up. Jesuits are not monks. Jesuits are brothers or priests. I'm a Jesuit brother, which means that I have no sacramental powers. The responsibility of the brothers is to do the labor of the mission. Priests perform the sacraments and teach—although they'll be happy to tell you that when it comes to labor, teaching teenagers all day is mighty hard work.

"The painted buffalo skull? That's on consignment. It's listed under 'Items on Hock.'

"I was trained in Florissant, Missouri, and came here from a seminary in Mound, Minnesota. My assignment here just happened by circumstance, or maybe because no other house wanted me. Whatever the reason, I came and I stayed. I love the country and I love the people. We have had many fine graduates over the years—Dave Archambault, the former president of Standing Rock College; Shirley Plume, the first woman agent for the BIA; Chuck Trimble, an official in the Nixon administration; Tim Giago, founder and editor of the newspaper *Indian Country Today*; Phyllis DeCory, coordinator of Indian Education for the diocese; Birgil Kills Straight, past president of Oglala Lakota College; so many more. I knew people on both sides of the conflict during and after Wounded Knee. Everybody knows everybody around here, but you have to be neutral. Religion and politics don't mix. Even now, I'd rather not say anything about the Wounded Knee years. It's all still too awful fresh.

"No, no, no—heavens, no. That's not two dozen quillwork armbands, it's only two. See, it's listed here . . .

"There are five brothers and nine priests at the mission, and we cover the entire reservation—eighteen parishes. I believe our church has the most members of any on the reservation. (It depends on who's doing the counting.) The Sioux have traditionally been a Catholic tribe, going back to Father De Smet and the other Jesuit missionaries of the nineteenth century. Of course, there are other churches here as well— Episcopalians, Presbyterians, Seventh-day Adventists, three different Body of Christ fundamentalists, Latter-Day Saints. Then there's the Native American Church, and the traditional Lakota religious cere- monies like the sun dance. Many of our parishioners attend sun dances, too. We don't consider any of the faiths to be competition, and we're glad they're all here.

"The black van door with the windmill painted on it? I don't know what it goes for—I'll have to check.

"It's remarkable, really, when you think about it, how much of their tribal culture the Sioux have retained. Certainly they've retained a lot more than the rest of us. Take me, for example. Two of my grandpar- ents came to Minnesota from Alsace-Lorraine. But would you by any stretch of the imagination consider me an Alsatian? The family has lost its memory of ever coming from there. The old language is lost, the dress is lost, the dance is lost. The Oglala still dance as their ancestors did centuries ago. Can you still do the dances your forefathers did long ago back in Scotland or wherever? For most of us, the only thing we've got left of our Old World ethnic culture is the food. Often in a family a traditional dish or two will survive, but that's about it. I thought it was funny a while ago when Newt Gingrich was trying to get a bill through Congress which would make English the official language of the U.S.A. If we did that, we'd have to hire English teachers from England, be- cause what we speak here isn't English at all, it's American. And, as in any culture that's alive, the American language is changing all the time."

Brother Simon hooked his hands into the cincture of his cassock and leaned back in his chair. The transparent man conferred with him about a clock in the shape of a horse, then faded into columns of numbers again. "I travel sometimes because of the work I do," Brother Simon said. "I go to exhibits of Native American art in cities like Washington and Detroit, but the truth is that I always feel safer here. I think the reservation cops, in general, do a great job. Imagine how hard it is to be a policeman in a place where everyone is a relative—how hard to arrest a cousin or a brother. I do make it a policy never to go out after dark, however. I'm afraid I might run into something on the highway. There are the drunks, of course, especially after the checks come at the first of the month. And perhaps you've noticed that most of the cows around here are black. They don't show up very well at night, even in the headlights. What could be harder to see at night than a black cow?"

When I came out from talking to Brother Simon, the temperature seemed to have dropped about twenty degrees. Full dark had fallen, and wind blew through the tops of the cottonwood trees. I began to see what Brother Simon meant about the dark; on Pine Ridge, dark is darker, somehow. I drove back toward Chadron on the road that led through White Clay. That town was busy. Crowds stood silhouetted in the lighted doors of the package stores, and waiting cars just off the road here and there idled loudly, their brake lights beaming red.

I was going about fifty miles an hour south of White Clay when something hit my car. The impact was so sudden and so loud that I thought at first I must have been shot and could not believe my car was continuing to drive. I thought to pull over, but the road was narrow and cars were speeding by. Neither the car nor I seemed to show any ill effects. I looked all over inside for any evidence of damage I could find, by the dashboard's lonesome greenish light. When I reached the intersection of Highway 20, I pulled over and got out. All along the car, on the driver's side, was a windblown spatter of frozen suds. I took some between my thumb and forefinger and smelled: beer. Scattered among the suds were fragments of brown glass so tiny they had almost returned to sand and a few little pieces of foil label colored red, white, and blue.

Back at the motel, I examined the car again. The bottle, probably thrown from an oncoming car, had hit at the lower driver's-side corner of the windshield frame by the strut that holds the rearview mirror. At that height, if the bottle had hit anywhere but those few square inches, it would have shattered the windshield or the windows on that side. When I went to Le's house the next morning, I pointed out the dent the bottle had made. "Oh, that happens all the time," Le said. "Why do you think there are so many cars on the rez with broken windshields or with left-side headlights gone? You should've chased down the guys that threw it. That's what I'd've done. The last time that happened to a car I was in, we hung a U-turn and chased down the guys that done it and ran 'em off the road. We showed 'em the headlight they'd broke, and they said they was sorry, they hadn't even known the bottle hit us. Then they gave us five bucks to buy ourselves some wine."

A person on the reservation who I especially wanted to meet is Charlotte Black Elk. She is in her early forties, and is the great-granddaughter of the holy man Nicholas Black Elk. Her grandfather, Ben Black Elk, often posed for tourists at Mt. Rushmore in traditional garb and was said to be the most photographed Indian in the world. I had seen Charlotte Black Elk in a documentary on public television talking about the history of the Sioux and about their desire for the return of the Black Hills. I admired her persistent manner, her abrasiveness, and her long dark hair. Because I appeared briefly in that documentary myself, I thought she might remember my name. I called her on the telephone, and although she didn't seem to, she said I could come by and talk to her. The only problem was that she had a bad case of the flu. She told me to call again in a couple of days. "By then I'll be either better or dead," she said.

When I called again she was better, and she told me how to get to her house. She lives on a road that branches from the road between Manderson and Wounded Knee, in the hollow of a creek called Pepper Creek. She said her house looks like a structure built on top of a mine shaft, and it sort of does. It is a gray, two-story house with small four-sided towers and wings and additions that seem to have been built as the need arose. I parked in the narrow drive and knocked on the door. A teenage girl let me in without comment and went back to watching TV; at the time, Charlotte was raising nine children, only one of them her own. I found her in the kitchen kneading apricot-sunflower bread dough on a red-tile countertop under racks of hanging pots and pans. She is a slim, fine-boned woman, and the hand she offered, after rinsing it of flour, was delicate and thin. The part in her long, straight hair is directly in line with the bridge of the round-lens glasses she wears, and she has a smile I didn't remember from TV.

She and her (then) husband, Gerald Clifford, an engineer and accountant who has held many positions with the tribe, are among the leaders in the movement to get Congress to return the Black Hills to the Sioux. Gerald Clifford worked for years as coordinator of the legislative effort of the Black Hills Steering Committee. Charlotte supports the Sioux's claim with a theory based on astronomy and ancient Sioux tradition. Her theory, which she presented during congressional hearings on the Black Hills question, involves the astronomical dating of certain star groups of importance to the yearly rituals of the tribe. Like the Greeks and others, she says, the Sioux had star groups which they named and gave mythic significance to. And like the constellations of the zodiac, certain Sioux constellations were associated with certain times of year. The "Dried Willow" group of stars, for example, once coincided with the sun at the spring equinox. According to tradition, when the path of the sun passed through the "Dried Willow" group, the time had come to break winter camps, begin a series of ceremonies, and follow the buffalo herds.

Due to a fact of the heavens known as precession of the equinoxes, the sun no longer passes through the constellations of the zodiac the same way it did two thousand years ago, when those constellations were named. A slight wobble in the earth's rotation, caused mostly by the gravitational pull of the earth and the moon, causes the path of the sun to cross the plane of the earth's orbit slightly farther to the west all the time, which results in a westerly rotation of the equinoxes totaling a full degree every seventy-two years (and a full 360 degrees every 26,000 years). Precession slowly changes the position of the sun in relation to other bodies in the sky. Today the sun is no longer "in" any of the zodiac constellations at the times of year associated with those signs; its path has moved about thirty degrees westward over the past two thousand years. Similarly, Charlotte argues, precession can be used to date the cultural age of the ceremonial constellations of the Sioux. At the spring equinox, the path of the sun is now thirty to fifty degrees to the west of the "Dried Willow" group of stars. Multiplying those numbers by seventy-two years for each degree of precession, she concludes that the "Dried Willow" star group, as a Sioux cultural artifact, must be between 2,160 and 3,600 years old.

Further, she says, tradition and certain ancient star maps drawn on tanned hide link Sioux constellations to places on the earth, specifically to places in and around the Black Hills. "Seven Little Girls," a constellation identical to the Pleiades, is linked through story to Harney Peak, the "Bear's Lodge" constellation to Devils Tower, the "Race Track" to the red clay valley encircling the Hills, and so on. Using the same calculations of precession as she did for the "Dried Willow" group, she dates the tribe's occupation of the Black Hills between two thousand and three thousand years old. Indeed, it may well be even older, she believes. She scorns ethnologists who, using linguistic similarities between the Sioux language and the languages of Eastern tribes, place the Sioux's more distant origins in the Carolinas. She believes that years immeasurable have made the Sioux and the Black Hills as one. She often refers to the Black Hills as "the heart of our home, and the home of our heart."

When I pulled up a stool and sat at her kitchen counter, she explained her theory to me almost before we talked about anything else. She knows more astronomy and math than I do, and at first I did not follow all of what she said. Later, I found a book with a basic description of the theory, written by her. When I had a better idea of it, I found it less persuasive than she does; historical evidence of the Sioux's migrations over the last 250 years just seems more believable to me. As for the tribe's claim to the Black Hills, the case in their favor is so strong, based simply on facts of history over the last century and a half on which both sides agree, that adding a theory open to debate seems poor strategy. While Charlotte talked, however, I got a sense of what it might be like to live in a place where one believed one's ancestors had lived from the remote obscurities of time. It made me feel like a transient, and a descendant of transients, by comparison.

I asked Charlotte about her great-grandfather, and about his book, *Black Elk Speaks.* "To tell you the truth, I've never had the inclination to sit down and read it," she said. "Being related to someone like Black Elk brings a sense of responsibility that's not very gratifying sometimes, especially when you're a kid. I guess I never really felt I had to read it. As my Granpa Ben told me, 'The book is about this much [thumb and forefinger an inch apart] and you already know this much [arms wide apart].' You probably remember that Black Elk traveled all over Europe with Buffalo Bill's Wild West Show. Well, he spent quite a while in Paris, and when he was there he lived with a Frenchwoman named Charlotte, and that's who I'm named after. I'm named after my great-granpa's chick. Another of my great-grandfathers was Little Big Man.

People think of him as the friend of Crazy Horse who was with him when Crazy Horse was stabbed. But not many people know that Little Big Man wasn't Oglala or Minnecojou—he was a Santee Sioux who fled Minnesota after the Sioux War of 1862 and met up with the Oglala at Rawhide Buttes, near Bear Butte. Little Big Man's brother was one of the Santee captured and hanged after the war. The brother's name was Man Who Stands upon the Earth. I named my son after him. My son is nine now. Usually we don't call him by the whole name. Usually we call him Maka, which means Earth.

"A lot of the Crazy Horse people who stayed on Pine Ridge came to this part of it, in and around Manderson. The Good Thunders, Little Wolfs, He Dogs, Willow Shields, Chips, Little Bulls, Black Tail Deers, Kills Braves, Plenty Wolfs, Protectors—those were the major families. And since a lot of them were ghost dancers in 1889 and '90—Kicking Bear, the ghost-dance leader, settled in Manderson, too—and since the ghost dancers were sentenced to a choice between prison or joining the Wild West Show, there were a lot of Wild West Show veterans around here. The town of Manderson has always been a totally different creature from the town of Pine Ridge. People in Pine Ridge are descended from "friendlies" and treaty-signers who acculturated to white ways back in the 1850s. Some of them were mixed-bloods, who served as interpreters—the Lakota word for mixed-blood, *ieska,* even means interpreter. But a lot of the families around here, around Manderson, became reservation people only very late. Some didn't come in until the 1890s, and some have relatives who never came in, who stayed in Canada. There's a real division between us and the Pine Ridge people to this day. A while ago, when Gerald and I and some others from Manderson walked into a meeting in Pine Ridge, Oliver Red Cloud said, 'Here come the hostiles.' I'm proud of being a hostile.

"When I was younger I used to travel around quite a bit. In general, though, now I stay home. This valley is very quiet. When the snow falls here, it falls straight down, while out on the prairie it's a gale. We've got turkeys and deer around the house, and feral dogs. Actually, I think they're wolf-dog hybrids. They don't bark, and once they kill something, they don't stop eating until they've eaten it all. They ate one of our horses a while ago. With nine kids in the house, I've got enough to keep me occupied here. I don't have all the skills the elders used to have—I

Pine Ridge landscape

Amos Bad Heart Bull drawing of the Manypenny Commission council of 1876
(*courtesy of the University of Nebraska Press*)

Red Cloud about 1872
*(courtesy of the National
Anthropological Archive,
Smithsonian Institution)*

Red Cloud
(courtesy of the Nebraska State Historical Society)

Red Dog
(courtesy of the Nebraska State Historical Society)

American Horse
(Richard Throssel, 1907. Courtesy of the William Hammond Mathers Museum, Indiana University)

Short Bull and Joseph Horn Cloud
(courtesy of the Nebraska State Historical Society)

Little Wound
(courtesy of the James R. Walker Collection, Colorado Historical Society [negative number F-26, 996])

Reverend Eugene Buechel, S.J.,
c. 1938
(William J. Moore, S.J. Courtesy of Marquette University)

Custer's Last Fight—Anheuser-Busch used this painting
by Otto Becker in its advertisements for years
(*courtesy of the Anheuser-Busch Archives*)

Bill's Bar (now The Stockman) in Buffalo Gap, South Dakota

Tribal president Dick Wilson at Wounded Knee
(*courtesy of Corbis*)

AIM leader Dennis Banks
(*AP Wide World Photos.*
Courtesy of The Chicago Tribune)

AIM leader Russell Means
(*Con Marshall*)

Le War Lance (*above*);

Aurelia Two Crow (*right*)

Florence Cross Dog (*above*)

Le's niece Flora (*right*)

SuAnne Big Crow in third grade

Clockwise from center: her mother, Leatrice "Chick" Big Crow; her sisters, Frances (Pigeon) and Cee Cee; and her niece, Jamie Lea

In the uniform of the National Indian Team

SuAnne in cheerleader uniform

SuAnne in a 1989 playoff game

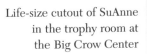

Life-size cutout of SuAnne
in the trophy room at
the Big Crow Center

remember watching my grandmother cut a piece of buffalo meat for drying. She'd go to work on it with her knife, a cigarette hanging out of the corner of her mouth, and when she was done that sucker would be a single piece of meat almost as big as this table, thin as tin foil and not a hole in it. I don't know if I could do that. But then I do stuff they never did. When I finish this apricot-sunflower bread I'm going to make cinnamon rolls, and last week we got some piñon nuts and I made piñon–black olive bread, and it was gone in about a second. Going to New York or wherever is interesting once in a while, but basically I try to leave here as seldom as I can. This is where I want to be. My days of being ready to bum at the drop of a hat are long gone."

Le had told me that a medicine man should bless the eagle feather he had given me for my son in the Port Authority Bus Terminal, and that I should bring it with me. I did, and it was hanging by its buckskin thong from a garment hook in my car. One morning I went by Le's house, and then we picked up Floyd John and set out in search of a medicine man named Zachary Bear Shield. Le said that you always must bring a present for the medicine man, so we stopped first at Yellow Bird's store in Pine Ridge and got four packs of king-size generic cigarettes in a brown paper sack. Zachary Bear Shield lived a long way off the pavement in the Wounded Knee district. The dirt drive to his place led over hills and around hollows. At the dicier spots, I first got out and scouted ahead on foot, then proceeded in four-wheel drive. Finally we stopped by two trim house trailers in a pine glen. No cars were parked nearby, the blinds were down. A sleeping dog roused itself and looked at us and yawned; Zachary Bear Shield must get a lot of visitors. Le knocked on the door anyway. No answer. After a few minutes he said, "Well, let's see if we can find Earlie Janis.

"Earlie Janis is a pipe carrier," he continued, getting into the car. "That means he is allowed to hold the sacred pipe at the sun dances and perform other ceremonies. It's not the same as being a medicine man, but almost. Earlie's been around a long time. He's a funny guy. Back in the sixties, when the BIA had this big push to get Indians off the reservations and relocate them in the cities, they came out here to make an instructional film to show to Indians all over the country and they asked

Earlie to be in it. He was supposed to play a young Indian guy headin'
off down the highway with his suitcase in his hand hitchhiking to Rapid
City or somewhere. So he's walking along with his suitcase, and the film
crew is in a car filming him right behind, and this carload of guys he
knows pulls up and tells him to hop in. Earlie says he can't, he's being in
a movie. The guys're all drunk, and they say, 'A movie? Bull*shit*, Earlie!'
and they haul him and his empty suitcase into the car and take off down
the road, with the film crew chasing along behind."

Earlie Janis proved not to be at the end of several long driveways we
tried. Sometimes Le got out and asked directions of people we passed
along the way. One set of directions led to a slab of concrete with wires
and pipes sticking from it, but no walls or roof or other sign of a house
at all. Le said the house had probably just been moved. As we bounced
back toward pavement, I was contemplating a drive to Pine Ridge and a
sandwich at Big Bat's. Then Le said, "Let's go borrow that gun."

He directed me to the town of Porcupine, and to a small blue house
in a row of similar houses with a red school bus parked out front. We
pulled up by the school bus and a skinny white woman in a gray sweat
suit and unlaced fleece-lined boots came out of the house and gave Le
a hug. Le introduced her as Raven. She invited us in. Drying laundry
was hanging everywhere, and there wasn't much of anyplace to sit, so
we stood and conversed around the clothes. We met Raven's nine-year-
old son, Cameron, and her husband, Adam, a quiet, curly-headed blond
man in a blue T-shirt and a blue-and-white-print head rag. We had evidently interrupted Raven in the middle of a speech about what she
would do to her landlady if her landlady did such-and-such to her, and
she picked up again where she had left off. On the floor by my feet was
a copy of *Archaeology* magazine with a cover story on birth control
methods of early man. After the landlady had been taken care of, Raven
started in on the tribal policeman who had come to the house investigating an untrue complaint about Cameron. Le and Floyd John and I
stood nodding politely.

During a pause, Le said that the three of us were going hunting and
wanted to borrow Adam's gun. This was the first I had heard of any
hunting. Adam seemed surprised at the request, but he agreed. From a
back room he brought the gun, a semiautomatic .22 rifle, wrapped in a
crocheted shawl. Then he rummaged around in a gym bag full of or-

ange pill bottles and found the gun clip and a black cloth pouch full of hollow-point bullets, magnum size. He gave the gun to Le, and Le immediately gave it to me, I don't know why. I was uncomfortable standing there in the laundry with it, so I went out to my car and opened the back and laid the gun inside. Then I took the paper bag of cigarettes we had intended for Zachary Bear Shield and gave them to Raven, who was walking Le and Floyd John back to the car. She looked in the bag and then said, "Sir, I thank you," inclining her head and giving me her thin hand. Le told her that we planned to go hunting Sunday morning and would have the gun back to them sometime next week.

Then we drove to Pine Ridge, and to White Clay for the customary purchase. A guy who had promised to cut firewood for Le needed 50-weight motor oil for the chainsaw, so we bought some at the Pine Ridge supermarket, Sioux Nation. Then we headed back to Oglala. I asked Le what the story was with this hunting expedition. He said, "There's lots of mule deer in the hills behind Aunt Rose White Magpie's house. She says she sees them every day. You and me and Floyd John will drive as far back in there as we can get an hour before sunup on Sunday morning and stake out a canyon when they're comin' down to drink, and we'll get us a deer." I dropped him and Floyd John off at Floyd John's trailer and gave them the rifle, happy to have it out of my car. I said I would pick them up about 5:30 Sunday morning, gave Le five dollars he asked for, and left.

On my way I stopped off at Florence's to see if my star quilt was ready yet. I had never been to her house by myself. One of her grandsons saw me through the storm door and called to her, "There's a white guy here!" She came to the door with her face set hard enough to scare away whoever it might be. Then she recognized me and smiled. The transformation from fierce to friendly was so sudden it dazzled me. She said my quilt wasn't done yet, that she'd sent it to the lady who does her batting for her. It should be ready by tomorrow, she said. I paid the balance I owed her and said I'd pick the quilt up on Sunday.

This time I went back to Chadron via a reservation road that's mostly gravel. The sun had gone down, and the sky at the horizon was multicolored, shining pink on the bottoms of dark clouds above. Viewed from high ground, the brightness in the west made the landscape to the horizon a deep silhouette-black, with occasional pieces of silver sky reflected in little stock ponds. But when the road led down into a hollow and out of the glare, then the details—the junipers, the ravines, the fence poles, the grasses—emerged in the twilight. I passed almost no houses, just occasional road signs riddled to steel mesh with bullet holes. I went by what appeared to be a thick paperback lying open in the middle of the road, and I stopped and went back to see. It was a collection of plays by Jean-Paul Sartre, including *The Flies, Dirty Hands*, and *The Respectful Prostitute*. It was in pretty good shape. I brought it with me. Ahead, on a small bluff by the side of the road, I saw two boys standing on a ridge, one in a dark hooded jacket. As a car passed coming the other way, one of the boys suddenly and expertly threw something at it, bending at the waist with a quick sidearm motion.

I will now describe the town of White Clay, Nebraska. One morning when I had nothing else planned I walked around the town. White Clay, White Clay! Site of so many fistfights, and of shootings and beatings and stabbings! Next-to-last stop of so many cars whose final stop was a crash! Junkyard, dusty setting for sprawled bodies, vortex consuming the Oglala Sioux! Sad name to be coupled with the pretty name of Nebraska! White Clay, White Clay!

A man who worked for years as a bartender at the Jumping Eagle Bar in White Clay once spread his ten fingers before me and showed me the many scars on his hands from fistfights he'd been in there. He said he often broke up fights with a pump handle, and kept a loaded shotgun hanging behind the bar. So many mournful Oglala stories have White Clay at their end. When I was a kid I liked movies about Wild West towns, those saloon-filled places where a cowboy riding in on Main Street always heard raucous laughter, and a gunshot or two, and glass breaking, and the tinkling of a barroom piano. White Clay is a Wild West town survived into the present that shows how uncongenial such a place would really be. In White Clay, decades of barroom violence have smashed all the saloon windows and mirrors and broken all the stools over people's heads, and now no bars remain. Elsewhere, Indian bars bolt stools and other furniture immovably to the floor and serve drinks only in flimsy plastic cups that can't be used as weapons.

White Clay has gone even further—there are abandoned houses and grain silos where you can drink protected somewhat from the weather, but the town's liquor sales are now all carry-out. Today no commercial establishment in White Clay allows its customers to drink indoors.

White Clay is two rows of stores and houses that line its main street, Nebraska Highway 87, for about a block and a half. Some of the buildings are of wood, with porch roofs extending over the dirt sidewalk and high false fronts like town buildings in Western movies. Others are made of cinder blocks, with thick windows of opaque glass bricks or small, slitlike window openings with bars and steel mesh imprisoning red neon Budweiser signs. About two dozen people live in White Clay. The town has four stores that sell alcoholic beverages—beer and malt liquor only. It also has a Napa auto-parts store (now closed), a Big A auto-parts store (also closed), a car-repair shop that sells auto parts, and a convenience store that sells some auto parts. There's a post office, a secondhand store, two grocery stores, and a pawnshop. Some of the buildings on the main street are boarded shut. The side streets are all unpaved. A wreckage of beer cans and bottles, with other miscellany—a broken shopping cart, a baby's shoe—accumulates in drifts here and there.

Even at 9:30 in the morning, White Clay effervesces and bubbles as if acid were eating it away. On this particular Saturday, there were loud cars cruising slowly, laughter, shouts. A group of tall men drinking 24-ounce beers stood by the side door of the Jumping Eagle Inn, a package store which is not an inn. Two gray-faced women in heavy plaid flannel shirts conferred by the side of the road, then smiled together and set out at a walk. Because White Clay is within walking distance of the reservation, the town usually has a lot of pedestrians. When the crowds get too big or unruly, the Nebraska highway patrol comes and makes everybody who's on foot walk back across the Pine Ridge border. Groups of evictees stagger along the highway out of town; when they see the Nebraska patrolman leave, they come back. Nebraska police made fifty-six alcohol-related arrests in White Clay in 1997. White Clay businesses paid almost $88,000 in Nebraska state liquor taxes in 1997, and another $152,000 in state sales tax, and more than 90 percent of their customers came from the reservation. But Pine Ridge residents jailed in Nebraska can't really get treatment at state-subsidized alcohol treatment centers in Nebraska. Those facilities are intended only for state residents.

Seen from the air, White Clay would look like a small appendage to a multiacre expanse of junk cars. The junkyard, on the prairie behind the Arrowhead Inn, is enclosed by a rambling fence made of corrugated iron alternating with chain-link mesh. The fence is permeable, and the cars provide some of the customers of the Arrowhead Inn with a place to sit as they drink. Women too preoccupied with drinking to be called prostitutes accompany men into the junkyard in exchange for a car radio or a bottle of wine. Large auto junkyards like this one are a common feature of Western towns that sell alcohol on the borders of Indian reservations.

I had brought Le to the Arrowhead Inn a number of times, but had never gone inside it myself. I expected it to be a dive, dark and dank and bestrewn. I was surprised at the near-clinical orderliness I met when I pulled open the heavy steel door. There was an expanse of bare floor ending at a waist-high counter that ran clear across the room, and behind the counter glass-front coolers full of beer in bottles and cans. A man in the back room heard me enter and he came quickly to the counter, ready for business this Saturday morning. Improvising, I asked for a 24-ounce can of Olde English Malt Liquor. He got me one from the cooler and charged me a dollar. He was short, round-cheeked, round-nosed, and bespectacled—like a small Santa Claus, but unsmiling and with security cameras for eyes. He wore jeans, a plaid shirt, suspenders, and a billed wool cap with a ball tassel on top. As I paid, I asked him where all the junk cars out back came from.

"Off the rez, mostly," he said.

"People bring 'em to trade?"

"They bring 'em to sell, trade. Yeah."

"Does the junkyard belong to you?"

"I'm the owner."

"Of this store and the junkyard both?"

"Uh-huh."

I said, "Thanks a lot," and picked up the beer and turned to go. In almost any store in the rural West, the person behind the counter will say, "So long" or "Have a good day," when you leave. But the owner of the Arrowhead Inn and adjoining junkyard said nothing, just watched me as I went out the door.

In the past, I had always thought of the devil as a wild, out-of-control figure—as a half-mad guy lit dramatically from below by leaping flames as his maniacal laughter echoed, a being of chaos caught up in the chaos he spawned. When I came out of the Arrowhead Inn, I had a new thought: If the devil exists, he's probably sober.

On Sunday morning I got up in my motel room at 4:30 and drove to Le's to go hunting. I took the back road from Chadron and saw one other car in thirty-eight miles. I was aware of the dusty smell of the car heater, the staticky uselessness of the radio, and the veering of the headlights back and forth across the darkness as the car swerved through the windings of the road. When I pulled into Le's driveway, I turned off the engine and the lights and stood for a while in the darkness beside the car and looked at the stars. One problem the Pine Ridge Reservation does not have is light pollution. The stars were like bullet holes, the galaxies like patterns of birdshot. I climbed the cinder block by Le's door and knocked. He got up immediately and came out of his dark house, and we went to Floyd John's.

Oglala was dead quiet. Le pounded on the door of Floyd John and Wanda's trailer, the sound distinct and singular in the stillness. A dog began to bark. It took a lot of pounding before a light came on inside, and a while longer before they opened the door. A single pale streak had appeared above the bluffs to the east. I thought we were just there to pick up Floyd John and go, but Le took off his coat and sat down on the couch and began to read a copy of *Reader's Digest*. I had brought some packaged doughnuts and a quart of orange juice, and I set them both on the kitchen counter. Nobody seemed much interested, but Wanda took a doughnut. She wasn't looking at any of us. I did not know her well enough to judge, but I got a feeling she was angry we were there. Le began reading out loud an article about a girl trapped under a derailed train in New Zealand. An infomercial was playing on the TV—about how troubled marriages could be saved through certain unspecified lovemaking techniques which the spokeswoman said were described in more detail on a video you could order by phone.

Outside, the sky was getting lighter. I couldn't understand the delay, but accepted this as the Indian way. Wanda and Floyd John were talking desultorily about a standoff between tribal factions at the Ojibwa

Reservation at Keweenaw Bay, Michigan. They said Oglala policemen might be called in to assist, because of the Oglala's familiarity with such problems. Floyd John began to clean up some messes the cat had made on the lineoleum, and a strong disinfectant smell filled the room. He said something to Le in Lakota, and they went into the hall and talked in Lakota there. After a few minutes Le came back and said that we couldn't go hunting because they didn't have the gun anymore. I asked where the gun was. Le said that it was in Oelrichs, that Floyd John had hocked it with a guy there. They said maybe we could get it back, so we drove the twenty-six miles to Oelrichs and Le and Floyd John knocked on the door of a house behind a gas station at 7:15 in the morning. But they returned empty-handed, and we drove back to Oglala.

And that was it for the hunting expedition. What exactly happened with the gun, and whether Adam and Raven ever saw it again, I never found out for sure. Oddly, I had sort of been looking forward to going hunting. Le had said that if we got a deer we would divide it up and give parts to different relatives. But after that morning we didn't mention hunting again. Back at the trailer, we stood around outside for a while. I had planned to begin the drive home today, so I figured I might as well get going. I said goodbye to Le and Floyd John. I remember seeing Wanda at the door of the trailer, but I don't remember whether I said goodbye to her or not.

Given how the morning had gone so far, I thought there wasn't much point in stopping by Florence's to pick up my star quilt. But I did anyway, and when I knocked at this early hour she answered right away and handed a large black plastic leaf bag with the quilt in it through the door. I put the quilt in the back without looking at it and drove home stopping only for gas—about eight hundred miles in about fourteen hours. My wife was still awake when I arrived. We sat for a while in the living room, and then I remembered the quilt and brought it in from the car. I took it from the plastic bag and unfolded it and laid it on the living-room floor. It was a bit larger than queen size. I could not stop looking at it—at the intricacy of the stitching, at the modulations in the colors, at the parts close up and the whole from farther away. I lay down on it, got up, looked some more. The quilt was like a map of the reservation, with the gravel roads and dirt lanes and one-water-tower towns and little houses in the middle of nowhere stitched together and made shiningly whole. I wished I had a gallery to hang it in.

Bad things seemed to happen on Pine Ridge on holidays in those years. On a Christmas morning, a man named Beto James Rodriguez shot three men with a rifle outside his house in the Eastridge housing in Pine Ridge village. Two were seriously wounded and the other died. They had apparently come to Rodriguez's house at 5:00 a.m., and a fistfight started. Rodriguez later pleaded guilty to manslaughter and got six and two-thirds years in prison. On a Good Friday, the Holy Rosary Church at the Red Cloud School burned down. For unknown reasons a fire started early in the morning in the small chapel on one side of the church and quickly spread through the building. When firemen came they could do little but watch it burn, and the church was a total loss.

I got home from the reservation a few days before Thanksgiving. The day after Thanksgiving, Le called. He said that early Thanksgiving morning Wanda Kindle had been run over and killed by a car. She had driven to Chadron apparently to do the laundry and was returning by herself to Oglala on the reservation road when her car quit on her. It was about two in the morning. Very likely, no other cars came along. She began to walk. She made it to Highway 18, and as she was walking east toward Oglala, at the junction of the road to Loneman, she got hit by a pickup truck. The truck left the scene, and her body was not discovered until several hours after the accident. The driver, a woman, had been arrested on charges including leaving the scene of an accident and DWI.

I wired some money for her funeral expenses. I had talked to her just five days before. I thought of her leaving the car on that back road from Chadron and walking along in the night. I remembered her eyes that I never saw lit by joy, and the quiet, almost uninflected way she talked, and her dark silence as she moved about her kitchen making coffee on the morning we didn't go hunting. Mostly I remembered the complete conviction, free from any trace of hope, with which she said, "It looks pretty, but it's just a slum," as the lights of Pine Ridge village spread before us on the night when we were returning from the rodeo.

A week or two after her funeral, the newspaper *Indian Country To-day* ran an obituary:

> OGLALA—Wanda V. Kindle, 45, died Nov. 23, 1995, in Oglala, due to injuries received in an apparent hit-and-run accident.
>
> Survivors include three sons, Shane Herrod and Shaun Herrod, both of Oglala, and Sheldon Herrod, Lawrence, Kan.; one daughter, Sonya Herrod, Ada, Okla.; three brothers, Fred Kindle, Ben Kindle and Ceferino Kindle, all of Oglala; four sisters, Kate Kindle and Catherine Starr, both of Oglala, Minnie Kindle, Columbus, Ohio, and Audrey Wallace, Dallas, Texas; and one grandchild.
>
> Services were at Brother Rene Hall with the Rev. Asa Wilson and the Rev. Simon Looking Elk officiating . . .

Recently, I visited her grave. It's in a corner of Makasan Presbyterian Cemetery, behind the Presbyterian church west of Oglala. Her gravestone is of dark-pink granite carved with two blooming roses above her name. She must have liked roses; a wreath on a marker at the site of the accident always has an arrangement of artificial roses, and someone changes them from time to time. White quartzite stones decorate her grave plot, along with artificial flowers and a pinwheel of bright plastic. Tulips grow by the headstone. Like all the headstones in the cemetery, it faces east, where the view is of a plowed field and the Loneman water tower. To the north is more plowed ground and prairie rolling to distant pink-and-gray buttes wrinkled like old skin. To the west, the horizon is a wavering line. From the south comes the sound of cars on the highway where she died.

CHAPTER

8

Time was, a person could hitch a ride from the reservation up to Rapid
City and drink in bars like Fitzgerald's, the Rainbow Ballroom, and the
Coney Island Bar. They were "real humdingers," according to old men
who remember them, with fights and prostitutes and wild goings-on.
The Coney Island and the others are no more; many of the old bars
along Main Street washed away in the big flood of 1972. From Rapid
City a person could hop a freight and wake up the next day in Billings,
Montana. As the train moved slowly, clanging through the center of
town, a person could roll off onto the gravel right-of-way and take his
pick among dozens of bars lining the tracks for blocks on both sides. A
person might begin drinking in Billings one morning in midwinter and
still be drinking there in spring. Old-timers remember Billings as a
friendly place to drink, well supplied with ranchers who drank themselves and were usually ready to buy.

Streets in Billings are so wide they seem to bend slightly with the
curvature of the earth. On the streets along the train tracks were bars
called the Buffalo Bar, the Mexican Star, the Yukon, the Oasis, the
Wheeler, the Mint, the Western. Of those, only the Western remains;
recently, a patron at the Western looked up and down the long bar,
whose lines seemed to converge at a vanishing point in the far distance,
and asked the only other patron, "Is it always this quiet in here?" The

bartender, overhearing, apologized, "Yes, looks like it's going to be pretty quiet tonight." On the adjoining blocks, the other bars are gone. At the Oasis Bar, the neon sign remains, pieces of broken neon tubing hanging down. The sign depicts a camel and a saguaro cactus, an unlikely but thirst-provoking combination. On the building's fake log front, Toni Whitewolf, or someone thinking of her, has penciled her name. At the Mint Bar on April 6, 1947, a ranch hand named John H. Emery was heard to say to a truckdriver named Clyde Kipp, his wife's ex-husband, "You think I'm kidding." Then he pulled a .38 pistol and shot Clyde Kipp dead. Emery was sentenced to life in prison. 2619 Montana Avenue, where the Mint Bar used to stand, is now a lot for guest and employee parking at the Sheraton Billings Hotel.

Why do neon signs look more beautiful in arid places? Take the signs of Los Angeles or Las Vegas, for example—maybe it has to do with the clarity of light in dry desert air. The neon signs of the bars by the railroad tracks in Billings used to be something to see, especially on a summer evening when the sunset was fading in the west and the wind brought the smell of dust and cattle and diesel exhaust. Prominent among these signs was one for a bar called Casey's Golden Pheasant. On top, the sign had a long-tailed bird outlined in neon of yellow-gold, and below that the name of the bar in red and blue. At the bottom of the sign was the word FIREWATER, not in neon but painted, in letters slanted to the right with multicolor flames coming off them. The word suggested that Indians drank in this bar, which was true. A veteran Indian drinker of the 1950s and '60s called Casey's Golden Pheasant "the preeminent Indian bar in this country."

Indians from many tribes drank at Casey's. Its owner, Casey Collett, encouraged them to come; advertising firewater in his sign might have meant that he considered them good for business, too. The reservation of the Crow tribe is closest to Billings, and there were often Crow Indians in the bar. Sioux and Cheyenne drinkers sometimes harassed the Crow for their history of service as scouts for the U.S. Army in the last century, and particularly for guiding Generals Crook and Custer in the Little Bighorn campaign of 1876. The anti-Crow drinkers had a song that ended *"You helped Custer! Yaaaaaaaa!"*—after which the barroom melee usually began. Casey handed out business cards for his bar bearing the motto "All Kinds of Drinks," but the Indian drinkers in Casey's often preferred gallon jugs of wine. Patrons at the bar sometimes chipped in for a gallon of Virginia Dare red to send to the Indians in the back room. That room was called the Snakepit, and according to reputation, awful things went on in there.

2622 Minnesota Avenue, where Casey's Golden Pheasant used to be, is now a vacant lot. It's as you might expect—low heap of concrete rubble, dead pigeon, ground-hugging weeds, water-stained paperback copy of *Fade the Heat*, by Jay Brandon. You can see the shadow outline of the building on the wall of the boarded-up building still standing alongside. I paced off twenty steps from the sidewalk as a guess of where the back room called the Snakepit might have been. If the brawls and gang rapes said to have occurred there left any ghostly traces, they were undetectable by me. It's just a vacant lot like any other. In Billings, an establishment called Casey's Golden Pheasant remains. It's now a restaurant and bar, under different ownership—Casey Collett died years ago—on North Broadway, a few blocks away. It still has Casey's original neon sign. It specializes in Cajun dishes like gumbo and blackened halibut, and has signed photos of celebrities like Lou Gossett Jr., and Tommy Smothers hanging on the walls. I have never seen Indians in there, but then I have been there only a few times. I don't think it is any longer the preeminent Indian bar.

I knew that the old bars in White Clay, Nebraska—Kelley's Cove and Toad's Tavern and the Jumping Eagle, and others—had all closed down. But as I traveled the country and asked sometimes about Indian bars, I found that they seemed to be disappearing elsewhere, too. In Brooklyn, New York, in the neighborhood where the Mohawk high-steel men once lived, the famous Indian bar used to be the Nevins Bar & Grill, at other times called the Wigwam. Joseph Mitchell wrote about it in his great magazine piece "The Mohawks in High Steel." The bar he described was crowded with Indians, and it stocked one Montreal ale and two Montreal beers, for its Mohawk customers from Canada and vicinity. When it was the Wigwam, it had a sign over the door that said, THE GREATEST IRON WORKERS IN THE WORLD PASS THROUGH THESE DOORS. Today there is a take-out pizza place where the Nevins Bar & Grill used to be. It receives money and dispenses pizzas through a security barricade of steel gratings and thick glass or plastic. I hollered through a metal slit to a man back there, and he said that he was the owner and that the Indians now drink at the Doray Tavern, at the corner of Third and Atlantic nearby.

In the Doray Tavern, I found one Indian, a stocky man named Ronnie Tarbell, on a stool at the bar. He wore metal-rim glasses, a blue work shirt, and his thinning brown hair combed straight back. With a Brooklyn accent, he said that he had worked for thirty years as a high-steel foreman and was now retired. Mohawk Indians used to rule this neighborhood, but not anymore, he said. They used to be able to beat up everybody, even the Italians; but where there used to be three hundred Mohawk families on these blocks, now there was maybe one. Bars with mostly Indian customers like the Spar and the Wigwam, he said, were now long gone. Though he spoke of local Mohawks mainly in the past tense, several times he remarked of guys walking by, "He's married to an Indian." The current state of affairs seemed to dishearten him not at all. "I'm not an American and I'm not a Canadian," he said. "I'm a North American from the Kahnawake Reserve, which is older than the U.S. and older than New York State and older than Canada. My people are the natural people, the people of the earth. We've always been here and we'll always be here. After the white man has destroyed everything, and even after the buildings we built for him have fallen down and disappeared, we'll still be here."

Los Angeles, the city with more American Indians than any other, used to have lots of Indian bars. The Columbine, the Ritz, the Shrimp Boat, and the Irish Pub are among the names that people recall. A while ago when I was in L.A. I went looking for those bars without success. I did, however, find the L.A. landmark called Indian Alley. The name appears on no map or street sign, but Indians everywhere know it, and many thousands have been to it. It's one of the most famous unofficial public spaces in the country—a narrow alley in the skid row district of downtown L.A., in the middle of the block bounded by Main Street, Los Angeles Street, Winston Street, and Fifth. The alley also continues partway down the block between Fifth and Sixth. Back walls of commercial buildings enclose it on both sides, and it has the usual skid-row litter of flattened cardboard packing crates, squashed fruit, Styrofoam take-out containers and broken glass. But the tribal names spray-painted on the bricks, the AIM slogans, the sketches of eagle feathers and war ponies, and the scrawled names and hometowns of Indians from reservations all over the country give it an aura of unceded territory, of native ground.

There's an Indian Health Service crisis intervention center at the corner of the alley and Winston Street. Near it I found a tall, copper-red man with pockmarked skin and long gray hair standing with a smaller man in a Hawaiian shirt and black jeans. I asked them if they knew where I could find the Irish Pub—I had read it was in that neighborhood. They said they both had heard of it, but that it closed down long ago. The names of other bars I mentioned rang no bells. A middle-aged woman in a T-shirt that said HOPI came out of the crisis center and joined the discussion, as did two other guys walking by. "There's no bars around here where Indians can drink anymore," the pockmarked man said. "They kick you right out on the street." They all agreed that in L.A. there are no more Indian bars.

Same thing in Minneapolis–St. Paul, in Phoenix, and in Butte, Montana—the bars mentioned in Indian stories from the not-distant past seem mostly to have vanished without a trace. Perhaps new ones have replaced them that I haven't heard of yet. But the Red Front, the Harbor Bar, the Silver King, the Trade Winds, the Busy Bee are forgotten and gone; or perhaps the former bar has been subsumed into a nineties-era hangout for college students, its name changed to Grandma's Saloon & Deli and with a volleyball court added alongside. Bars have an odd relationship to history. Generally they spring up in a moment, provide a setting for all that transpires when people drink, close down without warning, and become a copy shop or similar place containing no clue of what used to be there. Rarely, a momentous event will single out a bar for longer-lasting fame: for example, the No. 10 Saloon in Deadwood, South Dakota, where Jack McCall shot and killed the gambler and gunfighter James "Wild Bill" Hickok as he sat playing poker and holding a pair of aces and a pair of eights, the hand now known as the Dead Man's Hand. Hickok's shooting, in August 1876, was so storied that the bars succeeding the No. 10 on the site have never forgotten it, and posted homemade signs about it that survive in the current occupant to this day. Usually, though, people don't go to bars to remember, and after a particular bar is gone no one much wants to remember it. Not long ago I was walking down the Main Street in Miles City, Montana, where many old Western bars still survive. On the front of the Montana Bar I saw a metal plaque that said this bar, in existence since 1902, had been entered in the National Register of Historic Places. That brought me up short; I had never seen a historic marker on a bar before.

Once in a while I came across a bar I'd heard of that seemed pretty much unchanged. On Highway 39 in southeastern Montana just before the Northern Cheyenne Reservation I stopped at the Jimtown Bar, a drinking hangout of the Northern Cheyenne. It achieved minor fame when it appeared in the 1989 movie *Powwow Highway*. Its door is of splintered plywood painted red and its door handle is a piece of twine, and inside it's your basic Western roadhouse—video poker games, neon beer signs, Beach Boys music on the jukebox. One unusual feature is the bar stools of thick pine log cross-sections bolted to the floor. Outside on a weekend morning eight Indians sat against the wall in the sunshine, waiting for opening time. On the bar's sign on the roof is a large silhouette of that too-common image in Indian country, *The End of the Trail*—the Indian warrior slumped forward on his pony, after the famous sculpture. George Custer passed by the site of the Jimtown Bar in June 1876 as he led the Seventh Cavalry up the Rosebud River valley on the way to the battle of the Little Bighorn. Just across the Rosebud valley and within sight of the Jimtown Bar are the Deer Medicine Rocks, tall sandstone outcroppings carved with Indian pictographs. The pictographs are of buffalo, sheep, the sun, horses, and a convincingly rendered grizzly bear. One of the rocks is marked with a long gray-blue line where lightning struck it. At the base of the lightning mark, and pointing to it with what appears to be a feathered lance, is a carving of a figure in a headdress said to be a medicine man.

The most authentic Western bar I found is the Longhorn Saloon, in Scenic, South Dakota, a little town in badland country about seven miles north of the Pine Ridge Reservation line. The Longhorn used to have a prominent sign in Lakota on its front telling Indians to go away, but changed that policy long ago. It is perhaps best described as a cowboy *and* Indian bar. Its history is long; I know of one murder that has taken place in the Longhorn, though what other acts of violence there may have been I did not ask. The name Scenic is a laconic understatement to describe the landscape that surrounds the town. The immense horizontals stretch all across and around, the long, low buttes and pastel badlands varying endlessly under open sky. The entry to the Longhorn Saloon is beneath a porch roof propped up by unfinished posts and topped with coils of barbed wire. All along the roof and the building's false front are dozens of cow skulls, affixed in decorative profusion. Once you're inside, the skulls make more sense. The saloon's ceiling is low, no more than eight feet high, and the floor is ankle-deep in fresh wood shavings: in the vastness of this near-desert, the saloon suggests the cozy burrow of a predator, complete with an accumulation of bones just outside.

Cattle brands decorate the ceiling. On the walls are pairs of long-horn cattle horns, chaps, spurs, and cartoons of ranching mishaps signed by a cowboy artist named Gumbo Pete. I played the video gambling games and quickly lost fifteen dollars while listening to a weathered blond barmaid tell a story: "He was *old* and he was *bald* and he had *no teeth*, and she was pretty and about twenty-two, so in love with him she sat right here at the end of the bar while he was talking and just *stared!*" The wind-scoured South Dakota sky over the badlands was a bright blue that afternoon, but in the Longhorn Saloon cigarette smoke hung thick. A column of sunlight slanting through it from a window made a luminous gray shaft above an unoccupied table piled with perhaps three dozen empty Budweiser cans.

On the reservation and elsewhere in Indian country you get used to seeing images of the Budweiser brand. If you notice a speck on the roadside up ahead and guess that it is an empty Budweiser case, very often you will be right. Often a trash barrel full to the top will turn out to contain mostly Budweiser cans. The ground at popular outdoor drinking spots—by the cement picnic tables near the powwow grounds, or at a parking area beside a swimming hole on the White River—will often be a mosaic of pieces of broken brown-glass Budweiser bottles, some of the pieces still held together by the paper labels. Bottles thrown at bridge supports and other targets are often Budweiser bottles. The sweetish smell of Budweiser hangs around the places where the bottles are smashed, and in seat covers where Budweiser is spilled, and on people's clothes, and probably sometimes on DWI victims in the morgue. It's a smell you encounter often on the reservation. The distributor of Anheuser-Busch products for northwestern Nebraska sells more Budweiser in White Clay, Nebraska, than in any other town in his territory; package stores in White Clay account for about a third of his total Budweiser sales.

People sometimes say they'd like to buy a whole beer truck full of Budweiser and drink it dry. On the Standing Rock Sioux Reservation in northern South Dakota, a man from the town of Bullhead did. Some years ago the man received an oil settlement of $30,000 and spent $25,000 of it on a Budweiser delivery truck stocked with three hundred cases of beer. He parked the truck beside his house, which it was longer than, and had a nonstop party until all three hundred cases were gone.

Once, as Le and I were driving somewhere, we passed an unusual abundance of Budweiser cases along the road. I asked Le why there were so many of them. Misunderstanding me, he replied, "Used to be you never saw empty beer cases, because everyone on the rez had woodstoves, and they saved the cases and tore 'em up to start their fires. Now, though, people mostly have gas heat. So they just throw the cases away."

"No, I mean why are they all *Budweiser* cases?"

"Well, Budweiser is the biggest maker of beer in the world, so it figures Indians would drink a lot of it. And then Budweiser has all that advertising. Indians buy because of advertising, same as anyone else."

Indeed, Budweiser beer and Sioux Indians have been linked in the company's advertising for more than a hundred years. The brand was created by Anheuser-Busch Breweries in St. Louis in the late 1800s and became the first nationally distributed beer. Adolphus Busch, president of Anheuser-Busch, believed that advertising was vital to selling a beer nationwide. Part of his promotional plans involved "point-of-sale" items—plaster wall mountings, scenes of the Budweiser brewery painted on glass, jackknives bearing Busch's picture, and so on— distributed to bars. In 1888 Busch bought a St. Louis saloon which displayed a large diorama painting of Custer's Last Stand. He hired an artist named Otto Becker to paint a smaller version of the battle scene and make a lithograph of it. Becker produced a 24 by 40–inch painting showing Custer with his sword raised at the center of a maelstrom of Indians and cavalrymen, with Indians on horseback riding from the rear to finish him off and a dust-obscured prairie landscape beyond. (Some of the fallen figures in the painting's foreground Becker took from Gustave Doré's illustration for Dante's *Inferno*, as a scholar recently pointed out.)

Becker finished the painting and had it lithographed in 1896, and the company printed 15,000 copies of the picture bearing the title *Custer's Last Fight*, along with the company's name. Since 1896 Anheuser-Busch has reprinted the picture many times, in over a million copies, and it has hung behind countless bars. Many hours of barroom contemplation have been spent staring at this scene of the final moments of Custer, a circumstance that might have amused him, considering that after an embarrassing episode at the age of twenty-one he never had another drink in his life. In 1939 Otto Becker sold the original of the painting to Anheuser-Busch, and it hangs today in the company's corporate headquarters, where people probably don't think much about the fate of the actual Sioux Indians who drink their beer.

Many fortunes have been made selling alcohol to Indians. John Jacob Astor, America's richest man in the early nineteenth century, amassed his original wealth in the furs-for-whiskey trade as owner of the American Fur Company of New York City. Among the many Indians on the losing end of the trade were the Oglala Sioux, who suffered from the competition between Astor's company and others as traders used free whiskey to lure customers away. Fights brought on by whiskey in the Oglala camps caused deaths and the separation of bands, leaving enmity between them that lasted into reservation times. Throughout the 1800s Congress passed law after law prohibiting the sale of "ardent spirits" in Indian country, to little effect. A man who sold whiskey to Indians on the northern Plains after the Civil War called the laws against the trade "practically a dead letter," in a book he wrote about his career. "I make no excuse for the whiskey trade," he wrote. "It was wrong, all wrong, and none realized it better than we when we were dispensing the stuff."

In the early reservation years, old-timers recalled, alcohol use actually went down. On the Oglala reservation, laws against being caught drinking were enforced with high fines and sentences of a year and a day in tribal jail. But the same act that did away with allotment of tribal lands—the Indian Reorganization Act of 1934, which also provided for tribal constitutions and representative government—allowed for more leniency in anti-drinking laws. By 1940, the alcohol problem on Pine Ridge had become severe. A House Resolution in Congress in 1953 finally removed the old federal laws prohibiting Indians from buying guns, liquor, and ammunition. Control of alcohol on the reservations has since been left up to individual tribes, and today only 91 of America's 293 reservations allow liquor sales. On Pine Ridge, although the suffering from alcohol is ancient, help for it remains hard to find. As far as I know, no one who made money from selling alcohol to Indians has ever contributed anything toward repair of the damage alcohol has done. And although statistics say the alcoholism rate among adults on Pine Ridge is above 65 percent, there is as yet no alcohol treatment center on the reservation.

The late Frank Fools Crow, an Oglala traditionalist, medicine man, and supporter of AIM, still affectionately referred to by some as "Granpa Frank," said in a biography of him published in 1979, "Alcohol is the bitterest curse we have, and it has done more to weaken and destroy us than anything else. We had no strong drink, no such thing as whiskey, before the white men came to our country. We didn't need it then and we don't need or want it now."

About fifteen miles west of the reservation line, by its northwest corner, is the little town of Buffalo Gap, South Dakota. The town is named for a prominent geographic feature about a mile away—a gap in the Black Hills made by the valley of a creek which once provided the buffalo herds with an easy way in and out of the Hills. Charlotte Black Elk says that Sioux cosmology assigned a particular star to Pte Tali Yapa, the Sioux name for Buffalo Gap. She says that in former times, when the star we call Mirfak in the constellation Perseus began to approach the sun, it signaled the beginning of the buffalo's spring migrations through the gap. Wesley Whiteman, a Cheyenne holy man, said that the sun dance sacred to many Plains tribes originated at Buffalo Gap, where the buffalo themselves first performed it and later taught it to the Indians. Two low hills rise on either side of the entrance to the gap; they are hard to miss from Highway 79 as you cross Beaver Creek just east of the Hills. If you turn off onto the gravel road leading up the gap, you proceed along the creek and follow a little north-south sidle around some bluffs. In the next moment you have gone from rolling prairie to mountain canyon as easily as switching geographic channels. In another moment, mountain landscape has enclosed you on all sides. The gap is one of the magical places of the West.

Indians used the gap to enter or leave the Black Hills, and fur trappers and other early white travelers followed them. After the discovery of gold on French Creek in the Black Hills in 1874, thousands of miners and fortune seekers came into the Hills, many of them from the east by way of the gap. A merchant heading for the Hills in 1876 described for a Wisconsin newspaper how his party shot and wounded an Indian who he said sneaked up on their camp in the night; in the morning they found a lariat and some blood nearby, and the place where a pony had been staked, and more blood, about a quarter mile away. The merchant wrote that this happened "at Buffalo Gap where half a dozen battles have already been fought."

In 1885 the Fremont, Elkhorn & Missouri River Railroad built an extension north from Chadron, Nebraska, along the eastern edge of the Hills. The tracks stopped on the prairie near the gap, and there the town of Buffalo Gap was founded. During its time as the railroad terminus and a departure point for the gold mines in the Hills, Buffalo Gap became one of the wildest Western towns ever. It soon had a population of 3,000, many buildings made of green lumber, and hundreds of dwellings of tent canvas. A local history says that it also had "four blacksmith shops, 23 saloons, 17 hotels and eating places, two sporting houses and a whole row of small ones, four general stores, two drug stores, four Chinese laundries . . ." George Boland, the town's first postmaster, responded with irritation to a U.S. postal inspector concerned about Boland's handling of the mail, which he had sorted into the different pigeonholes of a wooden beer-bottle crate. "There's your god damned Post Office, Mr. Inspector," Boland said, throwing the beer crate out the back door of his saloon. "Now you git."

A Frenchman named Galiot François Edmond, Baron de Mandat-Grancey, visited the young town of Buffalo Gap while traveling the West in 1887. He was wry about the real-estate frenzy that had possessed the inhabitants: "The experts predict that Third Avenue is going to become the meeting place of the elite, the fashionable resort—but they ask themselves if Pine Street will be able to contain all the banks which will accumulate there." One night during the baron's stay, some cowboys from a local ranch rode through town and shot out windows in the middle of the night, and when the citizens returned fire, two of the cowboys were killed. The next day the cowboys came back and threatened to burn Buffalo Gap to the ground. The baron noted that what seemed to worry the citizens most about the incident was what it would do to the value of the town's lots.

Like the dreams of many Great Plains towns, Buffalo Gap's did not materialize. The completion of the railroad to Rapid City in 1896 ended the town's importance as a terminus and caused a decline. A big fire one winter destroyed much of the town. The residents built an imposing three-story schoolhouse of red sandstone on a hill, but people continued to move away. By 1910, the population of Buffalo Gap had fallen to 280. The town's reputation for nightlife and "rather wide open dances" (as a county history puts it) endured its change of fortunes, and rowdy evenings still occurred. A shooting just outside the community auditorium in the late 1950s, one longtime resident recalled, "slowed the dances for a while." The last passenger train stopped in Buffalo Gap in 1954; the last high school class graduated in 1963. The Southern Hills Bank, founded in Buffalo Gap in 1910, survived the Depression, only to close in 1994. The schoolhouse continued to hold classes for the elementary grades, but in 1997 it also closed, and the children now go to school in Hot Springs, about twelve miles away. Fewer than two hundred people live in Buffalo Gap today.

I walked around Buffalo Gap's red dirt and gravel streets one summer afternoon a while ago. Though the town has shrunk, the streets remain as optimistically wide as they were in 1895. A Methodist church, gleaming white and with a sign saying EVERYONE WELCOME, anchored one street, tall rows of silver maples held down others. There were some neat one-story houses, a few houses falling down, and a house under construction, evidently abandoned, also falling down. Some of the storefronts had elaborate pressed-tin fronts, boarded-shut doors, and blank display windows. The grain elevators by the railroad tracks were still active, with sparrows eating spills of grain on the ground nearby. Against the side of a building behind the elevator an assortment of galvanized-metal stock tanks of various sizes leaned on their sides, the ten-foot ones inside the twenty-foot ones inside the thirty-footers, like a set of nesting cups.

On a corner stood Buffalo Gap's neat frame post office, a definite improvement on a beer-bottle crate. Across the street was a bar called the Stockman. The doors to the bar, front and side, were locked, and no cars were parked nearby. I walked around the building and looked at it from roof to ground. Its siding was of overlapping fiberboard painted a barn red now so faded you could see in places that it used to be a light bluish-green, with rows of inch-wide unfinished lath running vertically every foot or so for decoration or to help hold the siding on. A rickety false front made the building's single story look taller from that angle, but from the side you could see the roof, half of it wood-shingled and the other half covered with tar paper. Rising from the tar paper was a chimney of cinder blocks extended with a piece of corrugated-iron pipe. If it weren't for the big air-conditioning unit bulging from a window, and the air-conditioner filters lying below it in the heap of silver-maple leaves, the building would have looked just like the ad hoc frontier structures in photos of Buffalo Gap from its boom times over a hundred years ago. People in town believe this building may even be that old.

Twenty-seven years ago this bar was owned by a man named Bill Zuber. Back then it was called Bill's Bar. Zuber bought it from a man named Degnan and remodeled it to make it more homey. He put in a fireplace, enlarged the dance floor, and hired bands on the weekends. Lots of young people came. On Saturday, January 20, 1973, a thirty-year-old man named Darld Schmitz who worked in a gas station in the Black Hills town of Custer drove to Bill's Bar with a friend, Harold Wheeler, and two women they had picked up earlier in the evening in a bar in Hot Springs. Schmitz was an Air Force veteran and father of three. His wife had had their third child in Rapid City just the day before, and Schmitz had visited her there before going drinking with Wheeler. Schmitz and the others had four or five drinks apiece at Bill's Bar and stayed until closing time.

While they were there, a twenty-two-year-old Oglala man named Wesley Bad Heart Bull arrived with some friends. Just outside the bar an argument began, and the bouncer didn't let Bad Heart Bull in. He remained in the street out front rattling an eighteen-inch log chain he carried with him and threatening departing customers. Bad Heart Bull was from Hot Springs and had a record of nineteen arrests for assault and public intoxication. The Bad Heart Bulls were of the same Oglala band as Red Cloud, the *Ite Sica* (Bad Faces), and Wesley's relative Amos Bad Heart Bull was a well-known artist whose ledger book drawings from the late 1800s and early 1900s are an important source for the pre-reservation history of the tribe. Wesley was still standing outside under the single streetlight at 2:00 a.m., when the bar closed and the patrons began to leave.

A man named James Geary, nicknamed "Mad Dog," had words with Bad Heart Bull when he came out. Trina Bad Heart Bull, Wesley's younger sister, later said that Geary picked the fight, jumping from his car and shouting that he could "lick an Indian." All witnesses including Geary agreed that he and Bad Heart Bull began to fight, and most said that Bad Heart Bull then knocked Geary unconscious with the log chain. Darld Schmitz and his companions had left the bar just before the fight started. Schmitz said that they got in their car and saw the fight in the street, and that he and Wheeler and Jane LaChelt, one of the women with them, got out. Mrs. LaChelt ran over to try to get Bad Heart Bull to stop. She said Bad Heart Bull was continuing to beat Geary on the ground, but other witnesses said he had stopped. She knew Bad Heart Bull and was distantly related to him. She said she tried to grab him, but someone pulled her away.

Schmitz said he took out his pocketknife and told Bad Heart Bull to drop the chain. He and other witnesses said that Bad Heart Bull came at him and swung the chain at him. Schmitz said he ducked, tried to push Bad Heart Bull back with his left hand, and stabbed him with the knife in his right hand. Several witnesses said that at about this time they heard gunshots, a coincidence that was never explained. A friend of Bad Heart Bull's tried to hit Schmitz over the head with a bottle, but some people stopped him. Bad Heart Bull fell to the ground, got up, and said, "I've been stabbed." Schmitz said he saw blood on his knife and left immediately.

Bad Heart Bull collapsed again, and friends helped him to a car and drove off toward Hot Springs to take him to the hospital. On the way the car ran out of oil and burned out its engine. The car taking Geary to the hospital passed the stalled car along the road, came back, and loaded Bad Heart Bull in with his victim. The delay occupied some time. Schmitz's knife had just penetrated Bad Heart Bull's aorta, and he bled to death before he reached the hospital.

Bad Heart Bull was stabbed on the morning of January 21. Police arrested Darld Schmitz in Custer the same day. He admitted the stabbing and gave police the knife he had used. After questioning he was released on a $5,000 bond and ordered to appear before the county court in Custer on January 22. Hobart Gates, the Custer County district attorney, did not think he could get a jury to convict Schmitz of any crime more serious than second-degree manslaughter, so he charged him with that. A judge set a date for a preliminary hearing about a month away and released Schmitz on continuation of bond.

At the time of the Bad Heart Bull stabbing, the American Indian Movement had just finished a busy year. In February 1972 it had led a successful protest over the beating and death of an Indian named Raymond Yellow Thunder in Gordon, Nebraska, south of the reservation. AIM had brought hundreds of people from Pine Ridge to Gordon for a rally which shook up the town, got the authorities to make a number of concessions, and won the admiration of a lot of people on the reservation. The big flood in Rapid City in June killed 238 people, nearly half of them American Indian, and AIM helped provide food and housing for the survivors. In October AIM organized the Trail of Broken Treaties, a car caravan that crossed the country from Seattle and San Francisco to Washington, D.C., to remind America of the many treaties made with Indian nations that remained unfulfilled. That protest led in early November to the takeover and occupation of the Bureau of Indian Affairs headquarters in Washington, a much-reported event that lasted seven days.

When AIM learned of the Bad Heart Bull killing, it demanded that the charge against Schmitz be changed to first-degree murder. AIM leaders claimed that witnesses had heard Schmitz say he was "going to kill him an Indian" earlier on the night of the twentieth, that Bad Heart Bull was set upon by white youths who goaded him to fight, and that he was stabbed many times. AIM leader Russell Means called for a conference on the Bad Heart Bull case with county officials to take place in Custer on the morning of February 6, and AIM told its supporters that there would be a mass rally at the courthouse on that day. Custer County had never had a riot before, but people there had seen enough of AIM in the newspapers and on TV to fear one. The county assembled highway patrolmen, federal officers, and FBI agents to keep order, a force of perhaps seventy in all. The governor put the South Dakota National Guard on alert.

An AIM caravan of cars with two hundred people arrived in front of the courthouse early in the afternoon of the sixth. The courthouse was a Victorian-era brick building with high windows and wide front steps leading to wooden doors. The county sheriff met the protesters at the top of the steps and said that only four AIM people would be allowed inside at a time, so AIM leaders Dennis Banks and Russell Means and two others went in. Means, an Oglala on his father's side who had grown up mostly in California, was known for his oratory and his dark, photogenic good looks. He had organized an Indian center in Cleveland, Ohio, and had gained national notice for a protest he led against Chief Wahoo, the caricature-Indian mascot of the Cleveland Indians baseball team. Dennis Banks, a Chippewa from the Leech Lake Reservation in Minnesota, was more a politician and less an actor than Means. He had founded AIM with two other Minnesota Indians, and said that the decision to work for Indian justice had come to him while he was serving time in prison. Craggy-faced as the Indian profile of popular imagination, he sometimes smiled an easygoing smile like a person just having a good time.

When Hobart Gates began to explain to the AIM delegation the reasons for the manslaughter charge, Dennis Banks replied with a long speech about the continuing injustices Indians suffered, pointing out that if the killer had been an Indian and the victim white the charge would certainly have been more severe. Gates tried to answer, but the AIM people kept talking on top of his words. The conference became mostly angry speeches from the AIM side. Russell Means later wrote that the riot started when police on the front steps beat Sarah Bad Heart Bull, Wesley's mother. Other sources say it started when the protesters outside threw rocks through the courthouse windows and broke down the front doors.

Police and protesters began to fight inside and outside the building. The highway patrolmen had recently been issued new riot sticks, but had not been trained in their use, and Indians took the sticks from some of them and clubbed them. The police had helmets, and more Indians than police ended up with head injuries. Outside, two police cars were vandalized and burned. Means says that inside he and his brothers and a Choctaw with a black belt in karate were mowing the policemen down, and that at one point he scratched D.A. Hobart Gates across the face with his long fingernails. AIM supporters did some damage to the gas station where Darld Schmitz worked, and took gasoline to set the courthouse on fire. (Means says the fire was caused by tear-gas canisters police shot in through the window.) A nearby log-cabin building that housed the Chamber of Commerce burned to the ground (also the result of tear gas, says Means), but firemen stopped the courthouse blaze. Amazingly, no one was killed. A former Custer County district attorney who has watched a video of the riot says that for a few frames you can see the finger of a highway patrolman reach for the trigger of his gun, but he has gloves on—snow had begun to fall—and he can't get his finger through the trigger guard.

Police arrested thirty-six Indians, including Dennis Banks and Russell Means. Banks was charged with burglary, arson, rioting while armed with a dangerous weapon, and assault without intent to kill. Means was charged with two counts of arson and one count of rioting. Both were released on bond. On February 9, riots occurred in Rapid City, with damage to several bars and more arrests. A big AIM rally in Sturgis, South Dakota, met a larger force of police and deputized volunteers, and ended peacefully. After the Custer riot, county authorities got reinforcements from the Custer County Civil Defense, the Forest Service, and the Volunteer Fire Department, and no further violence happened there.

Events went rolling on. Darld Schmitz's trial was moved from Custer to Rapid City, but by the time it began, AIM's attention had gone elsewhere: the occupation was in progress at Wounded Knee. AIM's charges against Darld Schmitz did not prove out in court. Schmitz's defense attorney, in his summation, said that Wesley Bad Heart Bull had taken up the sword and had perished by the sword. The jury agreed and acquitted Schmitz. Although the national news had given much play to the Custer riot, Schmitz's acquittal received almost no mention. Wounded Knee had claimed the front pages; no other story on the subject of Indians would get such notice nationwide until a few tribes began to make millions of dollars from casino gambling in the early 1990s. In the midst of the occupation, the actor Marlon Brando, an AIM sympathizer, won an Academy Award for his portrayal of Don Corleone in the movie *The Godfather.* During the televised awards ceremony he sent an Apache actress named Sacheen Little-feather to refuse the award as a protest against the movie industry's treatment of Indians. Among most people who were following the news back then, this is the moment of Native American protest that today remains clearest in their minds.

The Wounded Knee occupation ended in May, and the government arrested over a hundred people in connection with it. Federal prosecutors put some on trial and sent some to jail. Dennis Banks and Russell Means, as leaders, were tried together on charges including grand larceny and conspiracy. A team of lawyers led by William Kunstler and Mark Lane defended them. After a trial of ten months in federal court in St. Paul, Minnesota, the judge dismissed all charges and said he was ashamed of how the government had handled the case. Nine months later, in June 1975, Dennis Banks finally stood trial for the charges resulting from the Custer courthouse riot. As that trial was going on, the two FBI agents were murdered in Oglala. A jury found Banks guilty on the counts of rioting while armed with a dangerous weapon and assault without intent to kill, but acquitted him on the arson and burglary charges. In August he failed to appear for his sentencing hearing and fugitive warrants were issued for him.

After further adventures which the FBI said included aiding the escape of fellow fugitive Leonard Peltier, Dennis Banks eventually turned up in California. Police arrested him in a suburb of San Francisco in January 1976 for the flight charge and the charges from the Custer riot. Banks fought extradition to South Dakota, with California's then governor, Jerry Brown, on his side. In 1978 Brown announced that he would not extradite Banks, and Banks remained in California working at an alternative university he helped found near Davis. When Brown left the governorship in '82 to run for the Senate and law-and-order Republican George Deukmejian succeeded him, Banks fled to the Onondaga Iroquois Reservation in New York State and asked New York governor Mario Cuomo to grant him sanctuary. Cuomo temporized, but the

Onondaga gave Banks permanent sanctuary and said they would protect him. A year later Banks complained that having to stay on the
reservation all the time to avoid arrest was like being in prison. In 1984,
more than eleven years after the Custer courthouse riot, Banks surrendered to police in Rapid City, South Dakota, to face the flight charges
and the sentencing for his riot convictions. His lawyer, William Kunstler, provided the judge with testimonies to Banks's good character
from Jesse Jackson, Harry Belafonte, and César Chávez. The judge sentenced Banks to three years in prison for the riot. Banks served a little
over a year in the South Dakota Penitentiary. After his release, in November 1984, he lived in Rapid City and started his own limousine
service; later he began to work for the cause of Indian sobriety by pro-
moting alcohol-free powwows.

Russell Means stood trial on the Custer courthouse riot charges in
Sioux Falls, South Dakota, in April 1974. His federal trial on the
Wounded Knee charges was then still going on, but the judge allowed
him time off to go to Sioux Falls. At the Sioux Falls trial, another riot
occurred. Means and his co-defendants and their supporters refused to
stand when the judge entered the room, the judge ordered police to
clear the court, and the police and the defendants began to fight.
Means ended up with a number of new felony charges as a result. The
federal judge dismissed all the charges from Wounded Knee in September 1974. Some months later, Means went with a group of friends
to the Longhorn Saloon in Scenic, South Dakota. In the saloon's men's
room, he and an AIM member named Richard Marshall had an encounter with a Lakota from Pine Ridge named Martin Montileaux, and
left Montileaux lying on the floor with a .22 caliber bullet in his head.
Means and companions fled the saloon and drove toward Rapid City at
high speeds with police in pursuit until they were caught on the city's
outskirts. When Montileaux died of his wound, Means and Marshall
were charged with murder. Marlon Brando paid Means's bail.

A few months after that, a BIA policeman on the Standing Rock
Reservation shot Means in the back with a .357 pistol during a traffic
stop. The bullet hit no vital organs and Means was soon out of the hospital. The next month, on the Rosebud Reservation, someone shot at
him from a passing car. The bullet grazed his head but did no serious
harm. In December 1975 a jury found him guilty of rioting to obstruct

justice in the Sioux Falls courtroom brawl. The judge sentenced him to four years in prison but allowed him to remain free on bond. At a party some months later on the Yankton Sioux Reservation, Means and his bodyguard got into an argument with two younger AIM members, who pulled guns and shot them. Means was hit with a .222 rifle bullet in the chest, again not suffering much damage. The bodyguard, shot in the head, also survived.

Means went on trial for the Montileaux murder in July 1976. The other defendant, Richard Marshall, had already been convicted and given a life sentence. Andy Warhol had asked several times that Means come to New York so that Warhol could do his portrait, and Means figured that since he might be in jail for the rest of his life if convicted, he should go to New York now. He flew to New York the weekend before the final arguments in the murder trial. Warhol took many Polaroids of him and entertained him with a night on the town. They and some friends went to dance clubs where Means, a former dance teacher, had a wonderful time. He later called Warhol "a great host." Returning to Rapid City, Means decided that if he was found guilty he would kill the prosecutors and the judge. He and two confederates smuggled pistols into the courtroom in their boots before the verdict was read. Luckily, he was found not guilty. Soon after, he plea-bargained the Custer riot charges to a single misdemeanor and got thirty days in jail and a $100 fine.

In the late 1970s, Means participated in more protest demonstrations and served over a year in prison on the Sioux Falls riot charges. In prison someone stabbed him in the chest with a prison-made knife, but the blade deflected on a rib, and after some stitches he was fine. When he got out he began to work for the return of federal lands in the Black Hills to the Sioux and occupied some Forest Service land there with a settlement he called the Yellow Thunder Camp, named after the man killed in Gordon, Nebraska, in '72. The settlement finally dispersed in the early 1980s after someone was murdered there. In 1983 Means briefly joined the campaign of pornographer Larry Flynt for the Republican presidential nomination, running as Flynt's vice president. In '84 Means traveled to Libya, and in '85 and '86 he went to Nicaragua. His reports of the Sandinistas' brutal treatment of Nicaraguan Indians, and his description of a bombing raid conducted by Sandinista planes on a peaceful Miskito Indian village which he said he saw, lost him support among leftists. The Reverend Sun Myung Moon's Unification Church paid for him to go around the country speaking on the abuses of the Sandinistas. In 1987 Means campaigned in forty-six states for the presidential nomination of the Libertarian Party, but lost a close vote at the party's national convention in San Francisco.

A casting director from Hollywood called him in 1991 and asked if he would try out for the part of Chingachgook in an upcoming movie of *The Last of the Mohicans*. Means went to California and New York to read for the part, scoffing at the script and saying that wasn't how Indians talked. His improvised dialogue impressed the director, who cast him. While filming the movie Means fell in love with acting and decided to make a career of it. In 1995 he did the voice of Chief Powhatan for the Disney animated feature *Pocahontas*. When the movie came out he gave interviews to promote it, calling Disney "revolutionary" for their portrayal of Indians, and adding, "Anybody that nitpicks this movie has buried their childhood, they've buried the child within them."

During the years after Wounded Knee, Means married for the third time, got divorced, then married for the fourth time. He had many children in his four marriages. His oldest son, Hank, went to the South Dakota State Penitentiary in 1982 for his part in a robbery during which one of the victims—a Jesuit priest—died. In 1996, Means's sixteen-year-old daughter Tatewin, his only child by his third wife Peggy Phelps Means, was chosen Miss Teen South Dakota and represented her state in the Miss Teen U.S.A. Pageant.

I thought about this long skein of consequences as I stood in the gravel street where Wesley Bad Heart Bull fell in front of the former Bill's Bar. Then I went into the post office, the one public place in Buffalo Gap that seemed to be open on that afternoon. The only person in the post office was the postmaster, Loretta Schroth, a blond, blue-eyed, frank-faced woman of indeterminate middle age and friendly disposition—another evident improvement over the Buffalo Gap of 1885. We got to talking, and I asked her if she was living here at the time Wesley Bad Heart Bull was killed. "Yes, I was," she said. "Well, not *here*—my husband and I run a ranch just outside of town. When that killing happened my husband was fire chief of Buffalo Gap and he helped organize the men into neighborhood patrols. AIM was having that uprising over in Custer, and we didn't want any uprising here. That bar was a lively place when Bill Zuber had it. The killing didn't hurt business at all—helped it, maybe. Bill's was still a pretty lively place afterward. There's been a lot more that happened there—a car ran into the front of it, there were fights, the law had to be called. Bill Zuber's dead now. He sold the bar some years ago to Jim and Jo Hayes, who came up from Colorado. They had it for a while and then sold to Georgia Loberg, who was an immaculate type of person and a wonderful cook, and she put in a café and did real well with that. Then she sold it to Sid Hussey, who sold it to Bill Hartshorn. Bill's not really a bar person—he'd be the first to tell you that himself. His wife's part-Indian and her relatives had a band and people weren't too crazy about all the activity that was bringing in. He tried to keep it open just in the afternoons, but he just wasn't getting the business, so he closed down. I believe he's been trying to sell it.

"What hurt these little bars more than anything else is these new laws that say you lose your license if you drink and drive. We're down to one bar in Buffalo Gap now. People go to Jeannie's—it's a big brown wood building, one block down and take a left. The fellow who runs it, he's not a very sociable-type man, and he's got a gun and Mace and so forth, and the Indians mostly don't go there. Mostly they go to Hot Springs or Oelrichs. Hard to believe that once there were fifty or more bars in this town. Well, there's always been a bar in Buffalo Gap, and I guess there always will be."

CHAPTER

9

The winter after Wanda Kindle died, it snowed and snowed. I stayed at home waiting for a break in the weather and read a book I had bought on a side trip to the Rosebud Reservation—the *Lakota-English Dictionary*, compiled by Rev. Eugene Buechel, S.J. Father Buechel began his work among the Sioux in 1902 and continued it until his death, at the age of eighty, in 1954. He began collecting Lakota words and definitions in 1910, spoke the language fluently himself, and spent much of his free time discussing its intricacies with elders on the Rosebud Reservation. His book of Lakota grammar came out in 1939, but he didn't finish the dictionary in his lifetime. Jesuit colleagues went through his 30,000 note cards and edited them, and the Red Cloud Indian School published the dictionary in 1970. In a picture on page iii, Father Buechel appears as a sagacious-looking man with a high, wrinkled forehead, spectacles, and a well-trimmed gray beard. People on Pine Ridge have told me that the dictionary is overly Christian in tone, and that Father Buechel's informants left out the racy side of the language, an important part of Lakota, because they felt self-conscious talking to a priest.

But Mary Brave Bird, in her book (with Richard Erdoes) *Ohitika Woman*, says that Father Buechel traveled all over the reservation by horse and buggy to say Mass in such remote hamlets as Upper Cut Meat and He Dog, and that the Sioux people liked him for his knowledge of their language, his willingness to eat any food he was served, and the little gifts he brought in his pockets for the children. Mary Brave Bird says that her mother said that she not only learned English from Father Buechel's books but learned her own language better as well.

The dictionary has 853 pages, and I read them all. Father Buechel notes with care a word's shades of meaning, its different uses, and how it changes with prefix and suffix and in idiom. His explanations are always specific, often accompanied with examples. Sioux has lots of words that mean "to bite"; a horse bites with one word, but a mosquito with another. Many Sioux words convey a basic meaning of "to hit or strike," but vary according to the circumstances in which the hitting is done. There are slightly different two-syllable words that mean to make pigs cry by striking, to make dogs cry by striking, and to make boys tough by striking. The act of shooting has a whole palette of words to itself. The word for shooting with an arrow is different from that with a gun, to shoot and miss is a different word from to shoot and hit, to shoot to many pieces is different from to shoot in two.

Sometimes when I travel in the West—on the Great Plains, especially—I find myself in a place too unimportant for people to pay it much attention nowadays; and yet it's a real place, unlike any other and specific to itself, and it always makes me wonder what the lost Indian name for it was. Father Buechel's dictionary contains many words for which the object or action or condition described will probably never come up in ordinary conversation again—that is, the word remains, but what it describes has now been forgotten or lost. Will the Sioux ever again have much use for the word *tacaka*, which means the roof of a buffalo's mouth? Many of the Lakota words in the dictionary are ones I wish we had equivalents of in English. As I read the dictionary, I kept a list of those words and others. Father Buechel devised a complicated orthography for conveying Lakota sounds that don't exist in English; the dictionary's introduction suggests a simpler version of it that uses symbols available on a typewriter. Among my favorite words were:

aca´hsu, v. To form ice on something in little drops, as on trees, grass, etc.

anpta´niya, n. Breath of day, the very first glimmerings of morn, vapors raised by the sun.

cui´yohe, n. Moccasins made of old hides that have served as tents.

glinun´wan, v. To arrive at home swimming.

hepi´ya, n. The side or flank of a hill.

hia´kigle, v. To set the teeth firmly, as a dying person does.

heku´, n. The foot of a hill back from a river.

hena´gi, n. The shadow of a hill.

ica´konta, v. To cut a groove in, as one branch resting on another will do when swayed by the wind.

iwa´glamna, n. An extra or fresh horse.

iyu´s´o, v. When a man rides through water and gets wet in spite of lifting his legs.

jiji´lowan, v. To sing in a low, whispering, drawling manner.

kable´blesic´iya, v. refl. To rest one's mind by walking around after hard work.

mniagla´pepeya, v. To make a flat stone skip on the water.

nakpi´, v. To crack with the foot, as boys do with the eyes of butchered cattle.

opa´skan, v. To melt by lying on.

opu´hli, v. To stuff anything into, as an old coat into a broken window.

pa´blaska, n. The broad bill of a duck.

Ptegle´ska canli´, n. Bull Durham tobacco.

tiyo´heyunka, n. Frost settling on the inside wall of houses or tents.

tacan´hahaka wapa´ha, n. A headdress made from the upper end of the buffalo's spinal column.

waya´gla, v. To draw out or uncoil, as a dog does when eating the fat from entrails.

wica´natasloka, n. A dry human skull.

wo´econla, v. To consider something hard work but it is not.

yugwa´, v. To soften by hand.

yuhmin͟´ yan, adv. Off sideways, crookedly, as a ball might go; sliced, as in golf.

yupo´ ta, v. To tear to pieces, as does an eagle a rabbit with the bill and not by scratching.

Just after New Year's, Le called from Oglala and said he was going to Los Angeles soon. He said he needed a full-body CAT scan to qualify him for certain disability payments, and that a friend in Los Angeles had told him she would pay for the test if he had it done there. He was going by car with friends, taking a northern route through Seattle, and said that on their way they would stop and visit me. I had my doubts, as usual. When weeks went by and he didn't arrive, I decided that the trip must have fallen through. Then one Saturday afternoon in late January I got a call from a woman who said that her name was Wendy Cody and that she was with Leonard Walks Out at the corner of Orange Street and Broadway in Missoula. This news startled and worried me. I said my wife was out and I was taking care of the kids, and asked if I could call her back. Wendy said no, she was at a pay phone. I asked her to hold on, and I put the phone down and went into another room and paced around.

I am sorry to say that being generous and hospitable to my friend was not the first thing on my mind. Mainly I was afraid that Le and his friends would come over to my house drunk, and then never leave. But Wendy sounded pretty normal. I picked up the phone again and said they could come by for just a little bit. She said that she'd been driving all night and needed to stop. I gave her directions to my house.

I put on a pot of coffee and did a quick cleaning up of the downstairs. When I looked out the front window, an orange station wagon was pulling into the drive. Le got out of the front seat and stood in the snowy yard with his arms spread wide. I had forgotten what long arms he has. He said, "Give me a hug. I've been lonely out on the highway." His hair was down in his eyes and he no longer wore a neck brace. He was medium drunk—I had seen him drunker. He introduced me to Wendy, the driver, a red-haired white woman in her thirties with blue eyes, one of them bloodshot. Then Le said, "That's Mike Shot in the back seat." Mike did not seem to want to get out and had to be coaxed.

Wendy talked to him for a minute or two, he got out, and we all went inside.

Mike Shot was wearing high laced combat-style boots, a black leather jacket, and big amber-tinted dark glasses. He was in his mid-twenties, and his straight dark-brown hair hung to the middle of his back. He seemed to be about as drunk as Le. Both he and Le had on a lot of cologne. My kids, then four years old and almost eight, came to the front hall to say hello—to stare, really—and Le and Mike hugged them the way sailors who had just survived a shipwreck might hug the beach. The embrace went on and on; Le and Mike didn't say anything, and the kids stood there and let themselves be hugged. Then we sat in the living room, and Le held my daughter, Cora, on his lap on the couch and told her that he was her Indian. I nervously went to the kitchen and brought out cups of coffee. Cora, a talkative child, told Le that she was in first grade and that boys on the playground at school tried to beat her up sometimes. Le said, "You tell them that you have a friend who's an Oglala dog soldier, and that he'll destroy them if they do anything to you!" While he was holding her he spilled hot coffee on her leg, but I had told her to be nice, so she didn't say anything about it until later.

My son, Thomas, wanted to fight with Mike, and stood beside his chair hitting at his knees. Mike parried the attack with one hand. He told me that he had recently gotten out of the Marine Corps. He took off his sunglasses, and I recognized him—I had met him on the reservation the summer before, when I passed him picking chokecherries by the side of the road. He had two big black plastic bags of chokecherries with him then, and he had mentioned the Marine Corps. He had told me that he was about burned out on chokecherries. As I described this incident and what he had said, he slowly remembered it, and smiled a shy, brilliant smile.

Wendy asked me if I wanted to buy a dream catcher Mike had made. A dream catcher is a hoop whose center is strung with a sort of cat's-cradle web of thread or fine string; hung beside a bed, the dream catcher is supposed to intercept bad dreams. I said I'd like to look at it, and Wendy brought it in from the car. Mike had made the hoop part of the catcher from deer antlers bolted together, with the antler points on the outside and a net of tightly strung deer sinew in the center. He had painted the antlers with red and white streaks of lightning and blue deer tracks. I asked Wendy how much they wanted for it and she said $150. I said I didn't have that much money with me, but I could pick it up at a cash machine before they left.

I was acting very flustered and dropped-in-upon, constantly hopping up and fussing with the coffee and so on. I said I didn't know what I could give them for lunch—would peanut butter and jelly be okay? Wendy asked if we had any tuna fish, and I said that was a good idea and went to the kitchen and made a bunch of tuna-fish sandwiches, managing distractedly to use about twenty different utensils in the process. Mike told Wendy to help me, and as she did, she told me that she lived on the reservation and worked with senior citizens, and that she was going to Seattle and L.A. to try to raise money to buy a vehicle to ferry Oglala elders without means to get around. When the sandwiches were done I called Mike and Le, and they sat down at the dining-room table. Le lifted the top piece of bread from his sandwich, stared awhile at the tuna fish, and asked if I had any hot sauce. "Hot sauce? On a tuna-fish sandwich?" I asked.

"Do I look like a white boy to you?" he growled. I brought him a bottle of Louisiana Red and he poured it all over the tuna and began to eat. I gave the kids sandwiches, too, and Mike reached over to Thomas in his high chair and tousled his hair and said to me, "You got beautiful children." That reminded me of the eagle feather Le had given me for Thomas, so I jumped up from the table and went down to my office in the basement and got it. I showed it to everybody and passed it around, and then absentmindedly set it on the table among the lunch fixings. Mike winced slightly and picked the feather up with the tips of his fingers and handed it back to me: I recalled that an eagle feather isn't something you leave lying around next to the mayonnaise. I took the feather and went downstairs again and put it away.

Le sat close by Cora at the table, sketching a picture of her on some paper she brought him and telling her again that he was her Indian and that he was a dog soldier. He asked her if she remembered when she was a little girl and he came to our apartment in Brooklyn and they played on the floor. She said she did. I was eyeing the weather from the dining-room window; the snow had started to fall pretty hard. Suddenly

Mike stood up and said, "It's time to go." Silently grateful, I appeared with everybody's hats and coats. Le took his scarf and wrapped it around Cora's head as a present for her. Just at this point my wife got home, which prolonged the leave-taking. Le hugged me and said a lot more stuff to me, but I disengaged myself and practically pushed him into the car. Mike and Wendy said goodbye and got in, too. Then Wendy hopped out again. She had forgotten her gloves, and she ran back into the house to get them. Such a display of presence of mind gave me confidence in her ability to lead this journey. I had her follow me in their car to the Bi-Lo Supermarket, where I ran in and got $150 from the cash machine for the dream catcher. As I gave the money to Wendy through her window, she asked if I thought that Lolo Pass on Highway 12 would be open in this weather. I said, "Probably," and wished them luck. Then I got back in my car and left them in the supermarket parking lot.

I was not too happy about how I had behaved. Here Le had shown me around the reservation, introduced me to his friends and family, and I could hardly find it in myself to invite him in for a sandwich. I hesitate even to mention this incident, for fear of offending readers who expect likability in the people they read about. But there it is—I was kind of a jerk to Le and his friends when they came to visit me. The memory of my unkindness stayed with me, and had a part in events that came later.

During a clear, cold spell soon after, I went back to the reservation. Around Oglala the wind had blown the prairie free of snow in most places, except for little drifts on the lee side of bushes and tufts of grass. Next to snow fences and in road cuts, big and frozen snowdrifts overlapped on each other, blue as shaving gel in their creases. The badlands looked even more wrinkled on their rock faces than usual, the snow in their eroded fissures bringing the texture into plain relief. The late-February wind just would not quit. Sometimes I couldn't get the car door open against it, other times if I opened it a crack it yanked the door open all the way. Wind sent empty plastic soda bottles skittering across the parking lot at Big Bat's and scattered children as they got off the school buses in the afternoon. Metal clips on the pulley rope kept banging against the flagpole in front of BIA headquarters. Beside the highway tribal policemen sat in their idling cars drinking coffee and chewing sunflower seeds.

On this trip I talked to almost no one. Mainly I read local histories about Pine Ridge in libraries in Custer and Rapid City, and newspaper stories on microfilm at the library at Chadron State College in Chadron, Nebraska, and back issues of the *Sheridan County Star* at the paper's offices in Rushville, Nebraska. One afternoon I went to Oglala and stopped in at Florence's house. She had gone to her dialysis treatment and no one was home but her son, Rex. He told me that Le had gotten back from California a week or so ago and that Florence had kicked him out of her house over by Loneman because she was afraid he would have some accident with the woodstove while drunk and burn the place down. Rex said Le was now staying at Aurelia's.

I was angry at Le because of the way I had acted when he visited me—my behavior had been his fault, somehow—and so put off going over to Aurelia's. The night before I planned to drive back to Missoula, I was sitting in a motel in Custer and I felt a sudden regret that I had not seen him, combined with affection and sentimentality. Instead of heading for home the next day, I went back to the reservation. The morning was sunny and clear, the wind now just a breeze instead of a gale. I drove down the long track across the prairie to Aurelia's house and found her in her yard getting water from the pump. Le came from the house as I drove up. He looked fine and fit, fully recovered from his accident. He wore black stone-washed jeans, a white dress shirt with three buttons on the cuff, low-cut running shoes, and a blue warm-up jacket with the name of a cinematic lighting company on the back in yellow letters. He had gotten the jacket from a movie lighting technician he met in L.A., he said.

I asked how his trip had been. "After we left you it started snowin' a blizzard," he said. "We were driving through that pass with drifts alongside the road three times as high as the car, and it was hairy there for a while. But the weather was good in Seattle, and California had flowers like spring. My friend that was going to pay for my CAT scan wasn't home. Her neighbors told me that she had moved to Eureka, California. So I didn't get the CAT scan done. After Wendy finished some business she had, we drove the southern route through Vegas and Wyoming, back to here."

Le and Aurelia and I talked for a while. Aurelia said she felt bad about Florence kicking Le out—"My poor boy's got to have a place to sleep, oh yes, he does"—and I took out my wallet and gave Le the cash I had left, about sixty dollars. I told Aurelia that I always give Le my extra cash when I'm heading home, and that I had wanted to see him before I left. He walked me back to my car. "How's my little white lady, my *waschichu* girl, Cora?" he asked.

"She's okay. You know, you spilled hot coffee on her," I said.

He looked away. It occurred to me that what I'd said was no news to him, and that he already knew I was angry. I told him to take care of himself, and he replied, "*You* take care of *your*self, too." I said goodbye, and I got in my car and left.

I was in a bad frame of mind. The stories I had recently been reading about Pine Ridge in the local histories and newspapers had left me with a residue of dread. They all seemed to involve suffering and violence and hopes destroyed, and car wrecks, one after the next. I felt guilty for my journalistic interest in Le, and for being a chintzy middle-class white guy. Also, I had gone a while without talking to anybody, and that always makes me feel lonesome and sorry for myself. It's better just to overlook these spells, and I generally do. But later, after I got in the accident, I tried to remember what my mental state had been just before it, in an effort to make sense of why it happened. The one lesson I decided to draw from it is: Don't drive when you're feeling guilty and full of dread.

This trip back, I went from Oglala through the Black Hills, over to Newcastle, Wyoming, and then northwest to the interstate highway from there. The day turned balmy. In the prairie past Newcastle, I saw two bald eagles sporting together high in the blue sky. I took the interstate to Sheridan and spent the night in a motel there. Early the next morning I woke to the sound of someone scraping ice from a car windshield. I loaded up the car and with the door open drove to a video store parking lot and scraped the windows there, so as not to wake anyone up myself. The ice was thick and hard, and the scraper made barely a dent. The windshield wouldn't come clear until the engine had idled long enough to warm up the car. I looked for a place to have breakfast, but nothing seemed to be open, so I got back on the interstate thinking I'd have breakfast in Billings, Montana, a couple of hours away. (Another rule: Don't drive hungry.) I tried to find a weather report on the radio but got only mumblings about light snow delivered by a girl disc jockey with a giggle.

Fine snow driven hard by the wind began to come down just beyond Sheridan. The wind was from the west, and the road lay roughly north and south through open country, so mostly the highway was blown clear. I slowed down through road cuts where it had accumulated; I knew the high, narrow Blazer has a tendency to skid. Interstate 90, which I was on, meets Interstate 94 east of Billings. As I came down into the valley of the Yellowstone River just before the intersection, snow was thick in the air and the road had become a hard-polished white. The westbound lanes of I-90 cross I-94 on a bridge, shrink to a single lane, and merge with westbound I-94 from the right. As I went to merge, a white Ford pickup with its headlights on was in the right-hand lane just where I needed to be. Perhaps because the left-hand lane was all snow while parts of the right-hand lane were clear, the pickup didn't pull over to let me in. We were going the same speed. He didn't slow down and I didn't slow down.

We had approached to just a few feet apart when I impatiently stepped on the gas, in order to speed up and go in front of him. At that moment my car went out of control. I was suddenly skidding at 55 miles an hour backwards in the left-hand lane, then into the center divider, back across the right-hand lane, off the right-hand shoulder, and down the embarkment, with plumes of snow blowing past. I crashed sideways through the freeway fence, snapping the barbed wire like string, rolled completely over, and landed on the passenger side in a ditch by an access road.

The seat belt and shoulder strap had held me tight to the seat. I appeared to be all right; later I discovered I had torn a thumbnail. The windshield was broken and the passenger-side window had shattered, and the inside of the car was full of my stuff—briefcase, maps, tapes— all jumbled up with broken glass and snow. Looking at that made me feel as if I were skidding again. I undid my seat belt, and stood on the passenger-side door, opened the driver's-side door above me, pushed it up, climbed out, and hopped to the ground. The white pickup had stopped by the side of the road and its driver, an onion-headed man in a brown corduroy baseball cap, was standing in the snow looking at me with an expression an alien might meet on someone watching him climb from a spaceship. The man asked me if I was okay and I said yeah. He said a woman had already pulled over and had gone for help. He said he would go and call someone, too, and he drove off.

I walked around for a while in the knee-deep snow looking for places in the distance where there might be a phone. I was in the billboard region, near enough to Billings to justify the billboards but too far to have anything more. All around seemed to be nothing but billboards and snow. In a few minutes a highway patrol car pulled up on the shoulder and a patrolman got out and waited for me to walk up the embankment to him. We sat in his car while he wrote down information from my driver's license and called in the accident on his radio. He was black; I had never seen a black cop on the Plains before. He didn't give me a hard time at all or cite me for the accident. When he had finished with the paperwork he walked down with me to look at the car and said, "Maybe you and me could just roll it back up on its wheels." A closer look revealed that would not be possible.

A guy in a small white car pulled up on the access road and sat there for a while looking at my car. Then he got out—a skinny guy with a sparse beard and two cameras hanging from him on straps. He told me he worked for the *Billings Gazette* and was taking pictures of wrecks caused by the weather. I told him I would rather he not take any pictures of my car. He said, "Well, this is the wreck closest to my house, and I'm afraid if I go out on the interstate I'll get in a wreck myself." He unlimbered the cameras and began to snap. I was careful to stay out of the frame.

The tow truck arrived and the jumpsuited driver hopped out, ebullient with all the calls he was getting on this blizzardy morning. He was delighted to learn that his picture might appear in the newspaper and posed for the photographer at the various stages of winching the car upright and hooking it to the tow bar. I climbed into the cab with him and we drove on the access road toward town. I asked how much the tow would cost and he said $80, cash or check. I had no checks and had given Le most of my cash, so the driver took me on a long detour to a cash machine in the middle of Billings. Then we went to a Sinclair station by the interstate which he said was the only place where I could get work done at this hour on a Sunday morning. The guys at the Sinclair station, young fellows with long hair straggling out from ski caps, looked at the car and at me and said, "You must've been wearing your seat belt!" One of the guys told me that I was in luck, that he was a student at an auto-body-repair school. The next time I looked, he was lying on his back on the driver's seat and kicking hard at the crumpled-in roof with both feet. I went across the street to a place called the Lucky Stiff Casino and had breakfast.

When I got back, the roof had been raised enough that it didn't brush the top of my head when I sat up straight. It was still pretty low-slung, though. The guys had taped a piece of heavy cardboard with a few lug-soled bootprints on it over the broken window, and had also duct-taped the bigger cracks in the windshield, and along the lower edge where it had come loose from the frame. They had replaced the various fluids that had drained out when the car was on its side, and had pushed the smashed-in wheel wells out so that the tires wouldn't rub against them. A blond guy in a red jumpsuit, the most talkative of the crew, said that the car was probably drivable but that the state wouldn't let you drive a wreck on the highway unless you first got permission and a sticker from the highway patrol. I did not want to bother with any red tape; for some reason, I just wanted to get back on the highway and keep going. I paid the guys and thanked them, and to their skeptical farewells I backed out of the service bay and headed for the interstate.

By now the snow was coming down so hard I could see only a short distance ahead, and when semis passed me, I could see almost nothing but the snow they swirled. The road was a dim blowing world in which headlights suddenly appeared in the rearview mirror and red taillights suddenly flew by and disappeared. The tape holding the windshield to the frame quickly came apart, and the windshield hung loose like a drapery, bouncing with every jolt and letting snow in to pile up on the dash. The car made a strange noise at speeds above thirty miles an hour and refused to go much faster than thirty-five. I anticipated the start of a skid in every shimmy and gust of crosswind. Ragged breaks in the snow berm showed where other vehicles had skidded off the road. After about forty-five miles and ninety minutes of this, I pulled off at Columbus, Montana, and went to a Super 8 Motel right by the exit. The motel had a lot of trucks in its parking lot and a long line at the check-in desk. When I finally got to the head of the line, the lady there said she had just a few rooms left. She said there had been a wreck with fatalities on the interstate some miles to the west and the truckers had heard about it on their radios and had decided to quit for the day.

Once I got in my little motel room, the unshakable sensation of skidding really took hold. I was skidding as I paced the narrow piece of carpeting between the bed and the bureau, skidding like mad as I lay on my back in the water in the shallow bathtub. I called people on the phone and told them what had happened, pacing around. I watched the Weather Channel for a while, and finally it occurred to me that these interchangeable weather people massaging satellite photos of the United States with their manicured fingernails might as well be talking about storms on Mars. On the subject of the blizzard happening at that very moment in central Montana, they had nothing to say. I ate dinner at a café and came back to the room and tried to sleep. At about three in the morning I woke up and stood at the window watching the snow fall and the traffic go by on the highway. There were no cars, only occasional trucks, but they seemed to be getting through okay. The snow was falling less hard than before. I packed my suitcase, warmed up the car, and set out again.

This time the going was a little easier, with the traffic not as heavy and the wind not as strong. I turned my emergency flashers on—I hadn't known how to turn them on before—and kept a steady thirty-two miles an hour through the dark windings along the Yellowstone. I got to Livingston, about eighty miles farther, as dawn was breaking. A woman followed me off the highway and flashed her lights, and I pulled over in irritation to find out what she wanted. She said that she had been praying to her angels to get me to stop, because my left rear wheel was wobbling as if it was about to come off. She recommended I go to a Tire-Rama nearby. At the Tire-Rama they told me my left rear axle was bent. They didn't have the part, but called the Tire-Rama in Bozeman, which had it there. I bought new studded snow tires in Livingston with a credit card and then wobbled twenty-six miles over the pass to Bozeman. At the Bozeman Tire-Rama they said they could have the axle fixed by late afternoon.

I walked over to the Bozeman public library and happened on a copy of the play *Eleutheria* by Samuel Beckett at the new-arrivals shelf right by the door, and I spent the day reading it. It is a wild play, in which a shoe gets thrown through a windowpane every few scenes and there are characters named Monsieur Krap and Dr. Piouk. Late in the play a "Chinese torturer" named Tchoutchi climbs onto the stage from the audience and begins to torture the characters to get them to tell him what the play is about. I went back to Tire-Rama at about four and they were still working on the axle, so I looked at magazines in the waiting room. A teenage boy and a teenage girl were sitting there. The girl kept saying, "I can't believe I dyed my hair!" accenting a different word in the sentence with each repetition. Her hair looked like any other teenage girl's to me. I was idling through the newspaper, when suddenly I saw my car. On page 1 of the B section of the *Billings Gazette* was a large full-color photo: my car's intricate underside against the white of a snowscape, the winch cable connecting the capsized vehicle to the tow truck, the happy tow-truck driver in the foreground. I took the page with the photo and hurried back into the Tire-Rama work bays past the CUSTOMERS KEEP OUT signs and showed it to the man working on the axle. When he finally understood what I was talking about, he was unimpressed to be working on a famous car featured on page 1 of the *Gazette*'s B section.

The blizzard hit Pine Ridge, too. Le called my house to make sure I'd gotten back all right; my wife told him I had been in a wreck but was okay, and she didn't know when I would be home. He said he would pray for me. He called again soon after I had finally arrived. "I hear you rolled that car of yours off the highway," he said.

"Yeah, I wrecked the body pretty bad and took out some fence, but I had my seat belt on."

"The eagle feather I gave your son was protecting you and your whole family," he said. "That's why you survived, and nothin' happened to your wife or babies while you were gone. Plus I was prayin' for you, and so was Aurelia and Florence and Norma. She's a sister you haven't met yet, the one that prayed for me in the hospital. I've been in eleven car wrecks myself, and I'm still alive. Some of 'em people died in, some of 'em nobody got hurt at all. The thing about a car wreck, even if you don't get hurt you feel strange in your body for a long time after—you'll be sittin' in a chair and you'll think the chair is about to crash into the wall. A wreck shakes up your nerves in a way that's totally uncalled for. I learned that when I was driving stunt cars in the movies. When I was drivin' those stunt cars I was cool on the outside. Like, before a shoot, I was, 'Hey, let's get it on!'—real unconcerned. But inside I had that strange sensation like I'd been in a wreck, all the time."

We talked a lot more about wrecks and disasters. My being in a wreck had somehow restored a balance between us; the bad feelings of the last month went away, and we could act like friends again.

CHAPTER

10

Then it was summer, and across the reservation locusts sizzled in the cottonwood trees. At the outskirts of Pine Ridge village, in the grove with graffiti spray-painted on their trunks by the picnic area, I napped in my (now-repaired) car. On the windshield, ants investigated the remains of smashed insects, while across the field someone tested the loudspeaker system at the powwow grounds. Dust had fallen so thickly that it coated the weeds and grasses, and it rose in puffs wherever you stepped. An invasion of grasshoppers had arrived on a hot wind. Behind the stores of the village, when the wind gusted, it blew dust and grasshoppers above the buildings in clouds. The hoppers had eaten the green off the sweet clover and left it bare as broomstraw, and had eaten the yellow petals of the sunflowers clear down to the brown center. A man collecting empty cans in a big plastic sack walked across a vacant lot with the cans crinkling in the sack and the grasshoppers rising around his legs in such numbers that they collided with each other in the air. Inside the houses the sound of windblown hoppers against the walls and window screens sometimes became a thudding fusillade.

The powwow grounds and the picnic area where I was napping are on the west side of town. The field that includes them is a hundred acres or more of tribal land bordered on its western edge by the brushy course of White Clay Creek, and past the creek is Pine Ridge High

School. Students from distant parts of the reservation board during the school year in brick dormitory buildings on campus; the main classroom building is a newish structure of glazed brick decorated with geometric patterns in the sacred colors of red, yellow, black, and white. The sound of bouncing basketballs echoes from the school's gymnasium, whose doors are often open when the weather is warm. The amphitheater-style football stadium sits below the school buildings in a hollow of White Clay Creek. During the time of the ghost dance, the dancers often gathered in a big hollow farther up the creek because they liked the way the drumming and singing sounded there.

I have already mentioned the center of town—the intersection of Highways 18 and 407 which people still call "the four-way," and Big Bat's Texaco and the tribal office building and Billy Mills Hall. To the south is the Nebraska state line and the town of White Clay. On a hill just north of the intersection is the old IHS hospital and the tribal senior citizens' home. On the town's east side is the new IHS hospital, with a doorknob-shaped light-blue water tower behind it. A row of new streetlights in Pine Ridge village runs from the hospital along Highways 18 and 407 all the way to the town of White Clay, a connection which appears more than coincidental. Developments of one-story homes on gravel streets follow the creek or stretch across the prairie. People sometimes refer to different developments by name, and to addresses like Crazy Horse Street or Eagle Court, but since the town has no street signs, I usually cannot say for sure which developments or streets they mean.

People in Pine Ridge also talk about places in town that disappeared long ago. They talk about the old golf course—not much in the Pine Ridge landscape of today immediately calls a golf course to mind—or about the Pejuta Tipi, the drugstore that was once downtown. They sometimes mention the bowling alley, the moccasin factory, Gerber's Hotel, the motel. All these establishments have closed down for good, with no successors taking their place. A remembered name that comes up often is the fishhook factory. In 1960, the Wright & McGill Company of Denver, manufacturers of fishing tackle, opened a factory to make snelled hooks in Pine Ridge. A snelled hook is one with a short section of monofilament tied to it; a loop at the monofilament's other end makes the hook easier to attach to a fishing line. No machine satisfactorily ties monofilament in knots that small, so the tying must be done by hand. In the early 1960s Wright & McGill was employing over five hundred people at factories in Pine Ridge and other towns on the reservation. Most of the employees were Oglala women who earned from about $45 to about $140 a week, a real addition to the Pine Ridge economy. In 1968, citing foreign competition and a rise in the minimum wage, the company shut down all of its Pine Ridge operations. Today the packages of most Wright & McGill fishhooks bear the words *Made in the U.S.A.* and a picture of the American flag. On the snelled-hook package, however, it says *Hand tied in Mexico.* Today the snelled hooks are made in the Mexican city of Agua Prieta, just across the Arizona border, where the knots may be more cheaply tied than in Pine Ridge, year after year the poorest place per capita (says the Census Bureau) in the United States.

Many towns in rural America, and especially on the Great Plains, have lost businesses over the last thirty years. Vacant storefronts and boarded-up buildings along a town's main street are a common sight. When the businesses go, usually the people go, too; kids grow up and move to big cities, parents age and enter nursing homes, the few residents who remain drive long distances to do their shopping in superstores, and the town begins to die. Oddly, the village of Pine Ridge fits only part of this pattern. Although it has lost many businesses over the last thirty years, during the same period its population has more than doubled. The U.S. census counted 1,256 residents of Pine Ridge village in 1960 and 2,596 in 1990. The tribe estimates that 28 percent of the people on the reservation are homeless, so it is likely that even more live in the village than the census was able to find. The tribe says that about 20,500 people live on the reservation as a whole.

Meanwhile, the population of almost every town neighboring the reservation has declined. Rushville, Nebraska, had 1,228 people in 1960 and 1,127 in 1990; Gordon, Nebraska, went from 2,223 to 1,803; Hot Springs, South Dakota, from 4,943 to 4,325; Custer, from 2,105 to 1,741. Only Chadron, Nebraska, home of a state college, gained in population. The phenomenon of the dying Western town has been reported often before. But on Indian reservations, despite a lower life expectancy, population figures have been on the rise. If the trend continues, perhaps in a hundred years most of the descendants of the pioneers who settled in the West will have left the still-rural parts of it, and the descendants of the Indians will have increased their numbers to more than they were when the first pioneers arrived.

I walked all over Pine Ridge village that hot, windy summer—along the banks of White Clay Creek, up the hill to the old hospital, across the playing fields behind the high school, across the rolling prairie behind the powwow grounds, to the town limits of White Clay, to the houses under construction by the new hospital. Much of the way I followed footpaths worn into the ground. Many tourists and other wanderers show up in Pine Ridge in the summers, so I felt less conspicuous than I had in the winter and fall. Sometimes, though, local people noticed me; they would wave from their cars and ask, "Didn't I see you walking out by Merrival's this morning?"

In some of the developments, I passed houses with lawns and lawn sprinklers and asphalt driveways and basketball hoops. Some houses had large plastic butterflies, for decoration and luck, on the wall beside the front door. Chain-link fence topped with barbed wire surrounded a development just south of town where entering drivers opened the front gate by inserting a plastic card in a key box. In other parts of town, the houses were a sprawl of neglectedness and decay. I saw partly burned houses, a house in which all the windows had been smashed out and an American flag hung as a curtain in the doorless front door, yards full of car parts and skinny dogs. Gang graffiti—"bL%d$," "Lakeside Posse," "BAB GUZHISH will rock your crotch," "NOMADZ are shit-takin' wannabes"—covered some of the walls. Plastic and paper and aluminum trash strewed the streets, sun-faded and wind-torn plastic bags flapped from the branches of the trees. At a corner I stopped to look at the singed, melted trash conspicuous in an empty lot where a recent fire had burned the vegetation away. From a front stoop, a young woman in a wheelchair watched me through her dark hair. Someplace close by, an unmuffled car engine started with a burst like a brick of firecrackers going off.

The run-down parts of town are usually the ones that news stories and TV documentaries concentrate on. These neighborhoods are used to illustrate poverty, an inescapable fact of the reservation. According to the 1990 U.S. census, Shannon County—the county in South Dakota that includes Pine Ridge village and much of the reservation—has the largest percentage of people living in poverty of any county in the nation: 63.1 percent of Shannon County residents have annual incomes that fall below the national poverty line. Of the ten poorest counties in the United States in 1990, four were on Indian reservations in South Dakota. Shannon County has appeared at or near the bottom in earlier censuses as well. Few reports about Pine Ridge fail to mention that it's the country's poorest place, and the fact usually provides reporters with their opening paragraph: "This is as poor as America gets," the stories sometimes begin.

The stories never mention, just as a point of reference, what the richest county in America might be. After reading this lead for the dozenth time, I began to wonder. It turns out that the richest part of the United States is suburban Washington, D.C. According to the same census, the richest place in America is Falls Church, Virginia (technically a city, but it would be considered part of a county elsewhere). The second-richest place is Alexandria, Virginia, and the third-richest is Arlington County, Virginia. Two other counties among the richest top ten are in the suburban Washington, D.C., area.

Only about three people in ten on Pine Ridge have jobs, and those are mostly with the Bureau of Indian Affairs, the Indian Health Service, or the Oglala tribe. The BIA and the IHS are federal agencies, and much of the money the tribe receives comes from treaty and other payments made by the federal government. The wealth of the suburban D.C. counties is due to their closeness to the capital, with income from government-related businesses such as lobbying, law, and consulting firms. Like the poorest place in the country, the richest places get their money mainly from the federal government.

Perhaps because I often had to follow footpaths to find my way, in Pine Ridge I kept my eyes on the ground. The paths' dust was marked with many tracks—of dogs, of bicycles, of the brand-name-pattern soles of expensive running shoes. Occasionally I saw the parallel prints left by wheelchair wheels. For several days, shag-carpet shreds were everywhere. The carpet had been olive, and olive pieces of it blew across the parking lots and along the road; later I found olive shag-carpet shreds stuck to a piece of electrical tape on the wheel of my car. On the dust-and-gravel lot around Yellow Bird's gas and convenience store, flattened yellow plastic Pennzoil bottles dotted the ground. At the picnic area by the powwow grounds, a litter of bitterroot rinds covered the usual flooring of Budweiser shards. Grasshoppers had chewed irregular holes serrated with tiny grasshopper bite marks into the glossy pages of the March issue of *Glamour* magazine lying by the gate to the Pine Ridge cemetery. Some of what I came upon I put in my pocket and kept: the cover from a gangsta-rap CD (*Uncle Sam's Curse*); a rectangular pink rubber eraser which had been carefully colored in pencil to look like an American flag; a piece of ruled notebook paper on which the sentence "I will not run wild when Mrs. Iron Cloud is away" had been written out in pencil thirty times.

Nineteenth-century travelers sometimes commented on the bones and animal hair and broken tipi poles and other detritus that accumulated in encampments where Indians stayed for any length of time. As in these villages, Pine Ridge has plenty of stuff on the ground. Sometimes I would stop and examine a piece of it as if I were a nineteenth-century traveler and this a strange artifact I'd found. Usually, the artifact closest to hand would be a discarded food package of some kind. I would sit on the ground—unlike in other towns, a person sitting on the ground in Pine Ridge does not draw stares—and read the words on the bottle or can. I had not realized before how many warning labels our packaging now bears. On a plastic A&W root-beer bottle it says, *Caution: Contents Under Pressure. Open With Care.* An aluminum nut-can lid warns, *Caution: Sharp Edges.* A plastic press-on coffee-cup lid announces, *Caution May Be Hot Sip With Care.* On a Berry B. Wild Squeezit drink bottle: *Twist off top with hands only. Do not put in mouth.* On a 20-ounce plastic Dr Pepper soda bottle: *Warning: Contents under pressure. Cap may blow off causing eye or other serious injury. Point away from people, especially while opening.*

As I sat, traffic in Pine Ridge came and went around me. Two boys of elementary-school age zipped by on a gas-powered motor scooter, whooping and bouncing across the prairie at twenty or thirty miles an hour; neither had a helmet on. A pickup truck full of people roared down the highway ahead of a thick trail of exhaust, the half-dozen teenagers perched on the sides of the truck bed flying briefly into the air at every bump. A couple of lanky young men in cowboy hats pulled their truck to the side of the road and hopped out to ask a friend for money, taking no time to remove their seat belts, since they had never had them on. Most passersby in the village seemed to live in a way that ignored the cautionary tone of the messages on the roadside trash.

Every summer Pine Ridge opens out in early August like a road map unfolding, as people begin to arrive for the big tribal powwow. First you see one motor home with an unfamiliar license plate, then you see three, then ten. They have lawn chairs strapped to the back or the roof, and they're emblazoned with brand names like Tioga or Itasca or HitchHiker or Wanderer. Suddenly the village seems enlarged—a spread-out encampment rather than a small town. Here and there cars are pulled off the pavement alongside the road, and people in shorts and carrying cameras or binoculars are stepping through the sagebrush in the fields. A pale bunch of teenagers sits on the curb outside Big Bat's licking ice-cream cones, making a row of white knees. At the cement picnic tables west of town a family of seven—two white-haired oldsters, blond dad, blond mom, and three blond children—carefully lay out seven places for a picnic lunch. Then they sit, hold hands, and all bow their heads in prayer; their extra-long motor home has Utah plates.

At Yellow Bird's store, cars wait in line for the gas pumps. At the traffic light downtown there's sometimes a mini–traffic jam. It's loud; with plenty of partly muffled reservation cars in it, a Pine Ridge traffic jam really throbs. The loudspeakers at the powwow grounds are now on all the time, even though no events have begun and workmen are only setting up there. A guy is talking on the public address system as the spirit moves him, commenting on the goings-on: "Get that sod laid down good and tight, boys. We wouldn't want any of our fancy dancers to trip and mess up their two-thousand-dollar fancy-dance costumes . . . And look who's driving up the road now! It's Charlie-Boy Pourier with the water-sprinkler truck. Good to see you, Charlie—let's see if you can get that pesky Pine Ridge dust to lay down . . ."

Some early arrivals pitch tents and lay out campsites among the trees just west of the powwow grounds. There are two-man and four-man high-tech nylon tents in luminous shades, and old-fashioned canvas wall tents, and several white canvas tipis with pennants of colored cloth hanging from the ends of the tipi poles. People indicate their campsite boundaries with low fences made of wooden stakes connected by twine or strips of yellow plastic tape bearing the words POLICE LINE DO NOT CROSS. Next to many tents are stacks of freshly split firewood logs. The tent neighborhood grows, and soon acquires at least two sketchy streets with many vehicles parked along them. One morning the big tractor-trailer trucks begin to arrive—first the stock trucks with the steers and bucking horses and bulls for the powwow rodeo, and then the long caravan of carnival attractions and rides. The stock trucks park by the rodeo corrals, where the bawling of the animals echoes all around. The carnival trucks assemble in a bunch at another part of the field, sort of like circled wagons. Skinny, muscle-y, bristly-haired carny guys in sleeveless T-shirts get out of the trucks and stretch and smoke and holler remarks at each other. The carny vehicles include three electric generators the size of small boxcars, each with a thick umbilical of cable coming from it. The carny guys begin plugging cables to other cables to yet more cables, until in about an hour the whole carnival encampment is linked to the generators by a web of wires trailing through the dusty grass.

I generally got my breakfast early at Big Bat's, before the morning crowds showed up. The village had a pleasant feeling of expectancy in the cool, just-after-sunup time. One morning as I was staring out the window at the still-empty street and waiting for my Bat's Special Breakfast (two eggs, sausage patty, hash browns, and toast), I noticed Patty Pourier, Bat's wife, sitting two tables away. When my order number was called, I paused by her table, caught her eye, and asked her, "Do you recognize me?" She stared at me for a moment; then the memory of that day when the propane distributorship almost blew up clicked in her eyes. "I thought you looked familiar—we almost died together!" she said. "It's nice to see you here on earth, at Big Bat's, rather than on a cloud someplace in heaven!"

Sometimes when I stopped at Big Bat's I was hugged by a young man whom I'll call Germaine. He seemed to spend a lot of time at Big Bat's sitting at a table or standing just outside waiting for people to hug. As near as I could tell, he hugged only out-of-towners. His hug was unstudied and unhesitant, like a child's. He went right to the person he intended to hug as if magnetized, and during the embrace he rubbed his forehead on the other person's. The first time he hugged me he took me by surprise and his head knocked my hat to the floor. When I tried to disengage myself after a moment, he made a wordless noise of protest. The next time he hugged me he said, happily, "Remember me?" and of course I did. Usually we had conversations. He would say, "Where're you from? Are you married? I'm single. Do you have any children? I like you." Then he would hug me again.

I noticed that the other people Germaine hugged responded in different ways. A number of Pine Ridge's visitors during powwow season come from foreign countries, and occasionally these visitors reacted to Germaine's hugs with a stiffness suggesting that hugging was not a big part of their culture back home. Indeed, many of the people he hugged seemed surprised and even a bit frightened, as I had been myself the first time. I could imagine that in their years of dreaming in Berlin or Paris about the Oglala Sioux of the American West they had not expected to be nearly tackled in Pine Ridge by one of them the minute they stepped out of their rented camper van. But I noticed, too, that almost all the people soon understood the gesture's gentle spirit, and went along.

The sound of foreign languages on the streets of Pine Ridge—a not uncommon sound during powwow time—raises this place to a category of its own among mid-American towns. It reminds you that Pine Ridge village is also the capital of a nation, one that receives emissaries from far away. The fascination many German people, for example, have with the Oglala had seemed merely odd to me until I saw German and other foreigners at the powwow. They were excited, all eyes and ears and electronic gadgetry, and they made what surrounded them seem exciting, too. I reflected that the moment in history when white people and Native Americans first discovered each other was so momentous and fateful and even thrilling for each culture that some of us feel compelled to reenact it again and again. Nor was the powwow's mood of curiosity about the Other limited to just the visitors' side. One evening during powwow week I went for a walk along a dirt road in an out-of-the-way part of the village, and as I came down into a little hollow I met five or six Oglala boys sitting on bicycles. By accident or on purpose they were in a line across the road, blocking it so that I had to stop. Around the road on both sides midsummer foliage screened out all other sights and sounds; we could have been on any creek-bottom road on the Plains. The boys looked at me with unblinking dark eyes. Then the biggest boy, straddling his bicycle and bumping it back and forth between his knees, said to me, "Where did you come from—Europe?"

Most of the time during the week of the powwow I hung out by myself. Le and Floyd John did not seem to be around. Floyd John had left the reservation for Santa Fe or Colorado, depending on which relative I asked. As for Le, all anyone could tell me was that they hadn't seen him. I stopped by Florence's house a couple of times, but no one was there. As I was driving east of Pine Ridge one afternoon, a car came up behind me and blinked its lights and passed, and then arms from the open windows waved me to pull over. I did, and it was Florence and her son Rex and daughter Flora. Florence was on her way to the Porcupine clinic, so sick she looked green. She said she thought Le might be in White Clay, or he might have gone down to Scottsbluff. She said everybody went to the first night of the powwow and I'd surely run into him there. Flora said it was strange that none of us had even seen him walking along the road. I gave them some gas money and went back to Pine Ridge and took a walk on the mown jogging track in the field behind the old IHS hospital. Suddenly from far away I heard a voice shout, *"Hoka hey!"* A figure was waving at me from the road. I went over toward it and soon recognized Le.

His hair was messed up and he had bags under his eyes. He shook my hand. He was carrying his cowboy boots under one arm and wearing a new pair of tassel loafers which he said the Porcupine boys had given him, for reasons he explained to me but I didn't follow. Then he said, "I've been in jail the last five days. The judge just let me go half an hour ago. They picked me up Thursday night driving back from White Clay with my niece Verna Yellow Horse. (She's my niece, but she's only eleven months younger than I am.) We was drinking in White Clay, and then we came back in her car, and I was driving, and they pulled me over for not having my headlights on. I thought I'd hit the dimmer, but I guess I'd turned the lights all the way off. They pulled me out of the car and tried to give me a Breathalyzer test, and I told the tribal cop who was arresting me that he was a guppy-faced immigrant punk and I'd kick his ass for him and put him in the hospital. So they locked me up for drunk and disorderly. They locked Verna up, too. I had to wait to see a judge for a hearing, and the jailer told me I'd be in until after powwow. I said to him, 'No way.' So this morning a judge showed up, and when I went before him he said, 'The famous Mr. Walks Out!' See, he recognized me from your book. He asked me what I was doin' in there, and then he gave me a new trial date and let me go. As I left I said to the jailer, 'I told you so.' They're gonna need the room in the jail during powwow days, anyway."

Le came with me back to the jogging path and we walked a lap together, splashing up grasshoppers at every step. Le said, "They made this path for the people who worked up at the hospital. The doctors and nurses used to walk on it and jog on it for exercise. They was always tryin' to get Indian people to exercise more, for their health and especially so they wouldn't develop diabetes. They didn't persuade too many people, though, so really the only people you ever saw out here were doctors and nurses. Then the hospital moved to the other side of town, and not even doctors came here anymore. We still call this the Path the Doctors Walk On."

At my car I offered to give him a ride to Oglala, where he'd been heading when he called to me. A mile or two from Pine Ridge we passed two women walking along the road. "Hey—that's Verna!" Le said. "They must've just let her out, too." We stopped, and Verna, a heavyset woman with long, tangled hair, got in. Her friend Kay, who was shorter and fatter and had glasses, followed her. They both seemed to be pretty drunk. Verna told me her name several times, and said she had been lucky to be in a cell with Kay, because they were old friends. She told me her age to the month, corroborating Le's story of the difference in their ages. She said, "I'm so stiff from sleeping on that hard cement floor!" She and Le talked in English and in Sioux, apparently comparing notes about their arrest and their appearance before the judge. Verna and Kay got out in Oglala by the post office. Le waited until they had crossed the road, and then he asked me for some money. I gave him a five, which he pocketed without comment. I asked him what he was going to do, and he said, "First I'm going to check my mail, and then I'm going to hitchhike to Oelrichs and buy a gallon of wine." I said I didn't want to go to Oelrichs. I asked if he would be at the powwow tomorrow night and he said yes. We said we'd see each other there. He must've been happy to get out of jail; he smiled broadly and waved as I drove away.

By Wednesday afternoon Pine Ridge was jumping. The rodeo was going on—the "Old Man Events," for cowboys forty-five and older—and the powwow would begin that evening. Wherever you looked, near or in the distance, you saw people, and yet somehow at no single place did they constitute a crowd. Many had dressed up specially for the day's events, even more had not. For a while I just went around checking out what people wore. A group of Oglala veterans who would march in the powwow's grand entry parade stood talking by an olive-drab van with white lettering on its sides listing the names of battles in Vietnam. They had on berets, service patches, medals, and feathers; one guy was in crisp jungle camouflage fatigues, his trousers bloused below the knee into jungle boots of olive nylon and shined black leather. On his head he wore a black baseball cap with a single eagle feather on a leather thong hanging down behind. As I looked at him he nodded back at me and asked if I was a veteran. One of his companions had a clipboard with a list of names; they needed more guys to march in the parade. I said no, I wasn't, and I half-slunk away.

I saw a young woman in dark-purple jeans, silky black blouse, sunglasses, and silver earrings in the shape of baying coyotes, her straight black hair hanging well below her waist and held by a single tie between her shoulder blades; a young man all in denim from his jeans to his sleeveless vest to his oversize Superfly-style denim cap, on which was pinned a large button that read, "I Like A Good Beer Buzz In The Morning"; limping Indian rodeo riders with their identifying numbers still attached to their backs and orthopedic bandages peeking out from their shirts at the wrist or wrapped around the outside of their blue jeans at the knee; a slim young man in a black T-shirt with white lettering that said, "My Heroes Have Always Killed Cowboys"; a one-armed man in a turquoise T-shirt that said "I'm No Wimp"; old Indian men in light-colored Western dress shirts with dark string ties and their hair slicked back; old Indian women in flouncy, many-colored Spanish-style skirts with their hair held in combs and piled up high; little girls in buckskin dresses decorated with elk's teeth; a big, long-haired man wearing a blue-and-white head rag, narrow reptilian sunglasses, a loud Hawaiian shirt unbuttoned over his stomach, and a heavy chrome-silver watch chain looped from his belt to his right front jeans pocket; and a curly-haired man with a drink-ravaged face, a beaded belt that said "Bull Plume," a yellow straw cowboy hat, pegged jeans, and pointy-toed cowboy boots cut off below the ankles so they resembled slippers with high heels. Of course, most people had on the usual shorts-T-shirt-and-sneakers combination of the summer fairgoer, which made the exotic getups look even better.

All the activity—the rodeo, the vehicles and horses, the thousands of strolling feet—stirred up a great dust that rose above the village and hung high in the air. Late in the day as the sun declined, it illuminated the dust and gave the sky a reddish tinge. Pinkish-red light glowed on the western sides of the Pine Ridge water towers. The carnival rides began, and neon tubes in soft shades lit up on the whirling armatures of the Tilt-A-Whirl ride and the Mad Hatter's Tea Party. The carnival's three electric generators roared. Speakers on the façades of the rides played loud rock-and-roll music, and as I stood at a point with speakers on one side and the generators on the other, I decided there wasn't much difference between the two sounds. At sunset storm clouds appeared in the west, and the sky in that direction turned an ominous yellow, and the wind rose. A man named René Shoulders—he had introduced himself to me earlier in the day, not far from the veterans' van, where he, too, had asked if I was a veteran—saw me looking fearfully at the sky. He told me I shouldn't worry. A tornado had been sighted nearby, he said, but the medicine men had prayed and caused the tornado to veer away.

I went into the powwow grounds, passing through a gate in the chain-link fence that surrounded it. Admission was free; among the acts of former tribal chairman Dick Wilson that really irked people back in the seventies was his decision to charge admission to the tribal sun dance. At the center of the powwow grounds, and at the center of the powwow, is an open space about forty steps across where the dancing competitions and other ceremonies and contests are held. A circular structure, poles supporting a roof, encloses this space. The structure includes a raised booth for announcers and officials, with stairs leading to it. Spectators gather under the structure as if at a theater-in-the-round. Some stand or sit on the ground, but most sit on folding lawn chairs they have brought. The best way to observe a powwow is from your own lawn chair, and you may feel a bit unmoored and not-quite-present if you haven't got one. Outside the ring of spectators is a kind of circular promenade lined with booths selling Indian tacos and crafts and lemonade. Many powwow goers occupy this zone, walking round and round.

I did not know for sure what was going on. No program notes had been provided; as at most powwows, events seemed to proceed by spontaneity, with tacit understanding among the main people involved. A tribal official was talking at great length on the loudspeaker, allowing himself many weighty pauses. The spectators remained attentive to the still-empty powwow circle, as if expecting that at any minute something would materialize there. After a while the waiting made me nervous, and I wandered away. When I came back fifteen minutes later, I had just missed the Grand Entry parade. People were refurling flags and folding star quilts and banners. A dozen little girls in jingle dresses ran by, and I saw a young woman with lustrous, yard-long hair who had on a sash proclaiming her this year's powwow queen. Dozens of drum groups, from Pine Ridge and other reservations, had arrived. A group of men in matching ribbon shirts carried a flat drum the size of a truck wheel to a place near the announcer's booth, and a minute later they had set it up and had begun to drum and sing.

The men sat on metal folding chairs in a circle around the drum, hitting it hard with leather-wrapped drumsticks and singing a traditional song in loud, high-pitched unison, above which a single higher voice occasionally rose. Full dark had fallen by now, and the overhead lights had come on, but many corners of the powwow grounds were half-lit or in shadow. Shadows made it hard to see all the singers' faces. In a circle around them, intent white people watched and listened, some holding microphones to catch the sound. The observers' faces were wide-eyed, but the singers, as they leaned into the light and back out of it, had their eyes screwed shut and their mouths wide open in song. Some of the singers held a hand to one ear to plug it, the way musicians in recording studios do. They sang at full voice, from deep inside themselves, all of them hitting each note and word with vehemence and at exactly the same time. The singing, a survival from hundreds of years ago, filled the arena and echoed to the prairie sky.

I walked around in the promenade zone looking among the spectators for Le and for Florence's family, but they weren't there. For a while I kept pace with a man named Rick Weiland, a candidate for Congress from that district, who strolled along introducing himself to people in the crowd. He kept meeting powwow fans who would be small help to him at election time; I heard him say, hiding his vexation, "New Zealand! Wow! There are people here from everywhere!" I saw two other journalist-types like me with notebooks and gave them a wide berth. Suddenly out of the shadows a pair of arms reached to embrace me—it was my friend Germaine. "Remember me?" he asked, rubbing his forehead to mine. After he released me he continued around the circle, hugging every stranger he came upon. Those he hugged hugged him back with powwow enthusiasm, happy that someone had welcomed them. Everyone I saw walking away after a hug from Germaine had a smile.

Elaborately feathered dancers entered the powwow circle for the men's Traditional Dance competition. The crowd of spectators standing behind the rows of lawn chairs grew, and those in back couldn't really see. The view from there reminded me of a crowded exhibition of famous paintings I went to once in a museum in New York City: occasionally a gap in the throng would occur, and through it come a dazzling glimpse of color and form; then the ranks would close and all you could see was the backs of people's heads again. At a less crowded spot I worked my way to the front. The dancers were all going counterclockwise, each dancing as if alone, stepping to the drum music, some crouching down low. All of them had numbers pinned on like those worn by rodeo riders or distance racers; the powwow judges would award cash and other prizes to the best dancers in each category and subcategory. A dancer came right by me. He was a big man, and in his costume—turkey-feather bustle three feet across, feathered anklets, feathered gauntlets, beaded headband, tall roach made of a porcupine tail atop his head—he seemed magnified in every dimension, almost a spirit-being. Then I saw the wristwatch he had on beneath the gauntlet, and the sweat on his temple, and the concentration in his eyes.

Now I wanted to be someplace quiet and empty. I maneuvered through the crowd, went by the taco and lemonade stands, out the gate in the chain-link fence, through the field full of parked cars. The carnival had shut down and the rock-and-roll no longer played, and only one generator still purringly ran. I walked to downtown Pine Ridge, past the tribal building, up the hill to the old hospital, and then onto the open field of the Path the Doctors Walk On. I went half a lap around and sat down. The grass was damp; dew had begun to fall. I could hear the amplified voice of the announcer at the powwow. Then his voice stopped, and the only sound was the singing and drumming. It came through the darkness high and strong and wild as if blown on the wind. It could have been ten voices singing or it could have been a thousand. At moments it sounded like other night noises, coyotes or mosquitoes, or like a sound the land itself might make. I imagined what hearing this would have done to me if I were a young man from Bern, Switzerland (say), traveling the prairie wilderness for the first time in 1843. I knew it would have scared and thrilled me to within an inch of my life.

CHAPTER

11

One morning I wandered into the main tribal building in downtown Pine Ridge and found the door of the circular council room wide open. The Oglala Tribal Council—seventeen members elected from the reservation's nine districts, plus an executive committee of five—meets here. The council room was empty, so I went in. Its roundness and its chairs set in a circle on ascending tiers around an open space at the center gave the room an intimate feel; its lack of windows, low ceiling, and brick walls added the battened-down quality of a war room. A man came in and sat on a chair in the front row and began to look through some papers. He was tall, probably in his fifties, with a butch haircut, a widow's peak, a prominent nose, and dark-rimmed glasses. I expected he would kick me out; but he said hello amiably, as if I were someone with important business there myself. I thought I recognized him from newspaper photographs. I asked, "By any chance, are you Oliver Red Cloud?"

"Oliver's my father. I'm Lyman Red Cloud," he said.

The photographs I remembered had accompanied a news story about a TV movie on the life of Crazy Horse that had aired not long before. The news story said that the Red Cloud family was suing Turner Network Television for the movie's portrayal of their ancestor Chief Red Cloud. I had seen the movie and could understand why the Red

Cloud family was annoyed. I mentioned the lawsuit to Lyman Red Cloud, and he said, "That's right! We're suing TNT and Ted Turner for $100 million for lying about my great-great-grandfather. They made Chief Red Cloud into an evil savage who was trying to kill Crazy Horse practically from the day he was born. If you believed that movie, the Lakota were constantly fighting with each other and trying to kill each other back then. The Turner people told us they'd do right by Red Cloud, but they disgraced his history. That TNT is a bunch of rippers."

"I thought the nude love scene between Crazy Horse and Black Buffalo Woman was especially bad," I said.

"They put in all that nudity just to draw an audience," Lyman Red Cloud said. "The Oglala people didn't walk around naked like that. And they wouldn't be makin' love outdoors where people could see. The Oglala were chaste and careful about their courtship. Crazy Horse would have *never* done that."

I said, "Another thing that was dumb was when the young Crazy Horse went on a vision quest, and his horse stood nearby, and the horse turned at one point and lifted its back foot, and you could see a shiny steel horseshoe."

"You weren't the only one that grabbed that detail, brother," Lyman Red Cloud said. "We were watching the movie on a VCR and we stopped the action right then. There it was—on the right hind foot—a horseshoe! Sioux people didn't have iron shoes on their horses back then. A man like Crazy Horse, he was a spiritual man, he didn't need shoes on his horse. A man like that, his spirituality protected the whole horse."

The council room began to fill up for a meeting, so I left. I was delighted to have met a Red Cloud. The original Red Cloud, in a sense the founder of the Pine Ridge Reservation, was perhaps the most important Indian leader of the nineteenth century. Other Indians would be more famous than he, and would live longer in myth and popular imagination; none would have more influence on the government's Indian policy. Red Cloud was born on the banks of Blue Creek, near where it meets the North Platte River in present western Nebraska, in 1821 or 1822. A meteor that crossed the sky in September 1822 was recorded in a Sioux pictorial calendar of the time, as well as by U.S. soldiers at a fort in Minnesota. According to some sources, Red Cloud's name referred to the meteor's light in the sky at his birth; others say that the name was in the family and had been his father's and his grandfather's. Red Cloud lived to be eighty-seven, feeble and blind and forgotten, and he died at his government-built frame house west of Pine Ridge village. Father Buechel, the Jesuit and lexicographer, recalled that just twelve Indian policemen came to Red Cloud's funeral on a cold winter day in 1909.

As an admirer of Crazy Horse, I at first had contempt for Red Cloud. Red Cloud did not participate in the Battle of the Rosebud or the Little Bighorn, where Crazy Horse won fame; Red Cloud had been at peace with the whites for almost eight years by then. After Crazy Horse surrendered and came in to the agency in 1877, Red Cloud bore tales against him to the authorities, and very likely conspired in his death, out of jealousy. Certainly, the death of the popular warrior removed a threat to Red Cloud's power at the agency. Red Cloud's behavior at that time is the worst that can be said about him, and is hard to forget. But it is also true that Red Cloud's biography tells the bigger story of the Oglala in the second half of the nineteenth century. As the tribe's leading chief for much of that time, he continued to work for his people, and had some successes, under circumstances where failure seemed to be built in. The destruction of the Indian way of life in those years was such that no Indian leader really survived it; Red Cloud almost did. Crazy Horse, who died in his thirties, is a good hero for someone young. As you age and see more of life's complications, you may find sympathy, if not admiration, for Red Cloud.

He was a big man, over six feet tall and two hundred pounds. A correspondent for *Harper's Weekly* who saw him in 1870 described him: "of herculean stature, six and a half feet in height, and large in proportion." An Army wife at Fort Laramie when he came there in the 1860s said he had "a pleasant smile." He grew up in the camp of a chief called Smoke, his mother's brother. His own father, sometimes called Lone Man, died of drink when Red Cloud was a boy. In 1841, taking Smoke's part in a quarrel, Red Cloud shot and killed Smoke's rival, a powerful chief called Bull Bear. The killing added to Red Cloud's reputation but divided the Oglala for decades. Red Cloud told interviewers in later years that he had been in eighty battles. Unfortunately for his national fame, most were with other Indian tribes and occurred before many white men had arrived. The autobiographical narrative which he related to a friend in old age is full of the killings of Pawnee and Shoshone and Omaha, the wiping out of fifty families of Arapahoe, the scalping alive of Crow.

The country at large first heard of Red Cloud after the Civil War. Gold seekers headed for Montana had put a wagon road through the Powder River country, the Sioux's favorite refuge and hunting ground in present eastern Wyoming. Red Cloud, by then the Oglala's most powerful war chief, led a campaign of large and small attacks over several years that ended up closing the trail and destroying the forts the Army had built to protect it. The war, first called the Powder River War, came to be known as Red Cloud's War; he was the only Indian ever to win a war with the United States. In 1868 he signed the Treaty of Fort Laramie, a peace agreement of such generosity to the Indians that the government would soon regret it.

In 1870, Eastern advocates of peace with the Indians brought Red Cloud to Washington and New York City. The trip made Red Cloud a star. He spoke at New York's Cooper Union to an overflow crowd that applauded and cheered after his every translated sentence; the New York *Tribune* called the speech "a triumph." Crowds lined Fifth Avenue to watch him and the other Sioux of the delegation walk by. A newspaper correspondent afterward wrote: "His name has been heralded with electric speed, within a month, to the remotest parts of the civilized world." The trip was, of course, a great encouragement for the policy of peace with the Indians as well. One reason for the enthusiasm of Red Cloud's reception may have been the fascination with the West that appeared in the years after the war. For a country that had been painfully divided, the myth of the West—of the cowboys, of dime-novel gunfighters and heroes, of wide-open spaces, of undefeated Indians like Red Cloud—reimagined America as a place without boundaries, still new and whole.

Red Cloud would make many more trips to the East to meet with the government on his people's behalf. His later middle age was spent in a series of political and policy disputes with Indian agents and officials from Indian Affairs. Not long after the Fort Laramie treaty of 1868, the government had second thoughts about the boundaries it had set for Sioux lands. Specifically, it wanted the Black Hills. There had long been rumors of gold in the Hills; then, in 1874, a treaty-violating Black Hills expedition led by General George Custer reported "gold in the roots of the grass," and a gold rush began. Red Cloud did not like Custer going into the Hills and said so. When a government commission came to his agency in 1875 and tried to get the Sioux to sell the Hills, Red Cloud called the commission offer of $6 million "just a little spit in my mouth." He said that the Black Hills were "the head chief of the land," and suggested $600 million as a more realistic price. The commission concluded that the Indians valued the Hills beyond any price that could be paid. After Custer's death at the Little Bighorn, the United States finally got an opportunity to take the Hills at a bargain. Threatening to cut off the rations of agency Indians, it forced a token number of Sioux to agree to the sale. Red Cloud signed the treaty with reluctance, and later said he hadn't understood what he had signed. Among Lakota today who work for the return of Black Hills land, Red Cloud's agreeing to the sale of the Hills is his most egregious sin.

The main struggle of Red Cloud's leadership period was over the location of the Oglala's permanent home. In five years during the 1870s, the Red Cloud Agency had four different locations. ("Agency" meant the place where the Indian agent lived and tribal business was done; in a larger sense it meant roughly what "reservation" does today.) The first site was on the northern bank of the North Platte River, just downstream from Fort Laramie, where, for strategic reasons having to do with the Oregon Trail and the railroad, the Army did not want the Sioux at all. The next was on the White River in western Nebraska; the Nebraskans had said repeatedly that they did not want the Sioux within their borders. From Nebraska the Sioux were made to move to an agency on the Missouri River in central South Dakota in 1877. They never quite got there, stopping short of the Missouri at a site on the lower White River for about a year, then turning around and moving back to the valley of White Clay Creek just north of the Nebraska line, where Pine Ridge village is today. Each of these new locations involved the uprooting of thousands of people, the construction of new agency buildings, much planning and debate. As I mentioned in Chapter 3, most of the turmoil was the result of the railroad interests' imperatives pushing the Indians around, a fact Red Cloud never seemed to grasp.

Red Cloud spent the last thirty years of his life at the house he shared with his large family about a mile west of Pine Ridge village. The foundations of his house still remain, in a thicket of chokecherry bushes. His later years saw his powers as an Oglala leader and advocate decline. He refused offers to join the Wild West Show and exhibit himself, as Sitting Bull and others did, preferring to keep his dealings with the whites on a dignified level. At various times he worked for better rations, better Indian agents, Catholic missionaries to replace the Episcopalians the government had sent. In an attempt to humiliate him, General George Crook had deposed Red Cloud as chief in 1876; apparently the demotion didn't take, because an Indian agent who hated him and wished for his death tried to depose him again in 1880. Red Cloud's later trips to Washington never equaled the success of the trip in 1870. During the Ghost Dance troubles he was kidnapped by ghost dancers fleeing Pine Ridge after the massacre at Wounded Knee. The Indians who took him fired their guns around him to speed him up, and when he returned home after many days, he found his house and barn had been plundered. In 1898 he unsuccessfully opposed the building of fences on reservation land. In 1894, on a trip to visit hot springs on the Shoshone reservation, Red Cloud was arrested and jailed in Casper, Wyoming—the center of the Platte River country he used to roam—for killing a deer out of season. He used two horses to pay the $66 fine.

When the Oglala had finally settled on upper White Clay Creek, the site that would remain their permanent home, Indian agency officials debated about what to name the agency. Red Cloud had long advocated this site and had mentioned it to the President in person and in a letter. But government officials chose not to name it after him—perhaps to curtail Red Cloud's power, perhaps to avoid associations with the controversies about various sites which had gone before. Someone suggested the agency be called Oglala, but the Indian Commissioner objected that "not one in a hundred can spell Ogalala [sic] correctly." Pine Ridge was the name officialdom decided on. Its generic blandness and vaguely bucolic quality anticipated similar names—the Oak Parks and River Groves and Lake Forests and Chestnut Hills and so on— which would appeal to other planners of real estate across the land. Beneath the reservation's name of Pine Ridge, ineradicable as a watermark, the name of Red Cloud survives.

•   •   •

Most places in Pine Ridge village, if they're named for anyone, are named for people I had never heard of. Sometimes I asked around to find out who these people are or were. Behind the main tribal building, on the other side of a parking lot, is the Moses Two Bulls Tribal Court Building. One afternoon I went in there and asked a lady behind a desk who Moses Two Bulls was. She said he was a respected judge who served on the tribal bench for a long time and died about twenty years ago. She said his daughter, Joan, worked in the tribal enrollment office in the BIA building. I went to the enrollment office and stood in a long line of people with complicated questions, most of which seemed to involve getting their children enrolled. When I finally reached the head of the line, an Indian couple showed up, and the woman at the door naturally took them first. Only after the couple had left and I was waiting there alone did she turn her attention to me.

Joan Two Bulls, who had short hair, glasses, and a pained expression, seemed reluctant to admit even that she was she. I explained that I was writing a book and wanted to know about her father, who I assumed had been a great man in the tribe. She said that she did not think it was right to share information about him with an outsider. She said she would talk to her sisters and see whether they thought she should talk to me or not. If I came back in a month or two, she might be able to talk to me, she said. (I did, but she hadn't changed her mind.) All I was able eventually to learn about Moses Two Bulls was that he had belonged to the Seventh-day Adventist Church, often handed down strict sentences, and wore a hearing aid which he was suspected of turning off when arguments in his courtroom went on too long.

A short walk from the building named for him is the tribal senior citizens' home, known locally as the Cohen Home. Directions to that part of town often refer to it: "Take your second right past the Cohen Home." Its official name is the Felix S. Cohen Retirement Center. Places named after Jews are rare on the Great Plains; finding one on an Indian reservation might seem unlikelier still. One afternoon I entered the gate into the Cohen Home's fenced-in parking lot and grounds, passing five different signs that said intoxicated visitors would be taken to jail and another that warned visitors not to ask residents for money.

The young man at the security desk by the door did not know who Cohen was, though he did know his first name was Felix. He called for the director, and after I told her what I wanted, she let me in. She was Yvonne "Sister" Wilson, a short, vivid woman with dark, curly hair. She had on a turquoise turtleneck top and blue slacks. (Her late husband, Dick Wilson, was the tribal chairman and *casus belli* during the years of the Wounded Knee takeover.) She led me on a tour of the center—through the large living room with its tall windows flecked with BB-shot holes and its many armchairs and ashtrays aligned facing the TV, down the hall lined with paintings of old cowboys sitting around the campfire, into the dining room, where a few residents were playing bingo as a caller read out letters and numbers through a loudly amplified microphone. Yvonne Wilson said the center is for residents still able to care for themselves, and that when they no longer can, they go to a nursing home. Guests sleep two to a room and pay a total cost of about $200 a month, most of which comes from Social Security.

The home was built in 1965, she said. She didn't know who had suggested naming it after Felix S. Cohen, but thought the idea might have been the contractor's. She said that Cohen was a lawyer who did some work for the tribe and might have written the tribal constitution and by-laws back in the 1930s.

Felix S. Cohen, I later learned, was the leading expert on federal Indian law of this century. Indeed, probably no one in the history of the country has known more about the subject than Felix Solomon Cohen. He was born in New York City in 1907. His father, Morris Raphael Cohen, came to America from Russia when he was twelve and eventually became a professor of philosophy at the College of the City of New York (CCNY) in the Bronx. He was a widely renowned philosopher, and the main library at CCNY is named for him. Felix's mother, Mary Ryshpan Cohen, a schoolteacher, tutored Felix at home until he was eight. Felix went to Townsend Harris High School and entered CCNY early, graduating magna cum laude at eighteen. He paid some of his way through college by collecting and trading stamps. After CCNY he went to Harvard, where he received an M.A. in philosophy in 1927 and a Ph.D. in 1929. He got his law degree from Columbia Law School in 1931. By then he was twenty-four.

In that year he married Lucy M. Kramer, a graduate student at Columbia with an M.A. in mathematics whom he had met at a Halloween party when both were eighteen. They would have two daughters. As a young man Felix Cohen wrote many philosophical articles on such subjects as "What Is a Question?" and "The Ethical Basis of Legal Criticism," but he believed that philosophy should engage itself with problems of the real world. To him, the law was where the two met, and he regarded law as the central, all-inclusive institution of civilization. He also believed strongly in ethnic culture—he played the guitar and liked to sing folk songs of different nations—and he envisioned the country's future as a place of many ethnic groups working together and appreciating each other and getting along. His ideology and his learning made him an obvious choice to serve in the New Deal government that took over in Washington in the thirties. John Collier, the new head of Indian Affairs, hired Felix Cohen as an assistant solicitor to draft Indian legislation, and he moved to Washington in 1933.

Federal Indian policy has historically been a crooked path swerving between two extremes: one, the attempt to abolish all Indian tribes, end all treaty obligations, and assimilate Indians into the American mainstream (a policy sometimes called termination); and the other, the attempt to increase tribal sovereignty, encourage traditional Indian culture, and reduce federal and state involvement in the governing of the tribes. Felix Cohen arrived in Washington at the beginning of a big swerve in the second direction. For the previous half century, termination had ruled, with a policy of land allotment designed to make Indians property-owning citizens like everybody else. The legislation Felix Cohen worked on ended allotment, increased tribal landholdings, and strengthened the sovereignty of Indian tribes. It had at its center a deep belief in the curing power of democracy. The Wheeler-Howard Act of 1934, called the Indian Reorganization Act (IRA), gave the tribes many of the powers previously held by the federal government. It also said that tribes could vote on whether they wanted to govern themselves as constitution-style democracies. Disappointing the drafters of the IRA, about a quarter of the tribes voted not to accept the act at all. The Oglala accepted it and adopted a tribal constitution. Felix Cohen did not write it for them, although he may have consulted with them on it, and his department may have given them a model constitution to work from. A generation later, when factional fighting broke out on the reservation in the 1970s over opposition to the elected tribal government, some Oglala traditionalists blamed the changes brought by the IRA. They said that majority-rule democracy was wrong for the tribe, which had previously ruled itself more loosely, with various headmen in charge of different groups and no dissenting group absolutely compelled to go along.

Part of Cohen's work for the government involved a review of all existing federal Indian laws for the Justice Department. From this came the achievement for which Cohen is most remembered, his *Handbook of Federal Indian Law* (1941), which went on to be the standard text on the subject. Cohen left the government for private practice in 1948, but continued his interest in Indian affairs. He believed that "our democracy entrusts the task of maintaining its most precious liberties to those who are despised and oppressed by their fellow men," and Indians were foremost among the oppressed in his mind. He wrote passionate essays about their contributions to the world, represented individual tribes in lawsuits, and traveled widely with his family on the reservations. The Blackfeet tribe of Montana adopted him and gave him the name "Double Runner." He worked for legislation that included Indians among those entitled to Social Security benefits, and he won several lawsuits against states that had not allowed Indians to vote.

In 1953, at the age of forty-six, Felix Cohen died of lung cancer. He had been a vigorous man—he climbed forty of the forty-six Adirondack peaks over 4,000 feet high—and aside from an occasional Parliament cigarette in the evenings, he did not smoke. The notices of his death were filled with eulogy. He was remembered for his scholarship, his selflessness, his integrity, and the "almost saintly qualities" he attained in his later years. John Collier praised him as "an enemy of the drive toward cultural homogeneity, the enforced cultural flatland." Cohen's rabbi said of him, "His words flowed softly like the waters of Siloam out of the sanctuary of his being." Supreme Court Justice Felix Frankfurter, with whom he had studied, said that Felix Cohen carried out his earthly pilgrimage "with high adventure and the gallantry of the wise and the good."

Admirers recalled the poetic sense of harmony that Cohen brought to the work and hobbies he loved—to writing, teaching, tending his vegetable garden, collecting stamps, rooting for the CCNY basketball team. His college was one of the great loves of his life, and he kept up with fellow alumni and stayed in touch with the school. After his death the CCNY alumni magazine printed a memorial to him, along with a poem he had written after he graduated:

> *O City College, castle of the mind,*
> *I could not see your towers in the sun;*
> *I climbed your stairways confident and blind;*
> *The way was pleasant and the way is done.*
> *Within your walls my days of springtime lie . . .*
> *Gray towers melt away into the sky.*

Several places in and near Pine Ridge village are named for athletes. There's the Paul "Dizzy" Trout Field House at the Red Cloud School, named for the Detroit Tigers pitcher who led the American League in wins in 1943. Dizzy Trout was an active member of an Illinois athletic club that raises money for the school; he died at about the time the field house was built, and his friends asked that it be named after him. Billy Mills Hall, the auditorium at the corner of 18 and 407 in downtown Pine Ridge, honors the Oglala runner who won the gold medal in the ten-thousand-meter race in the 1964 Olympics. No other American has ever won a gold in that event. Billy Mills was born and raised in Pine Ridge village, and he trained for the Olympics while in the Marine Corps. He is now a spokesman for a charitable organization and makes motivational speeches and videos. He lives in California.

The Leroy "Sunshine" Janis Memorial Park—the official name of the picnic area by the powwow grounds—is dedicated to a well-known Pine Ridge resident who died of cystic fibrosis in 1984. Sunshine Janis was born in 1927 and grew up in a remote part of the reservation called the Gunnery Range, used back then by the Air Force for target practice. His siblings remember the recurrent sound of gunfire and the shells that would buzz over the house sometimes. Sunshine was a good amateur boxer and fought many bouts when he was in high school. After his junior year he dropped out and joined the Army Airborne. He liked the military and might have made a career of it, but ruined his knee on a jump when another soldier got tangled in his parachute. He came back to Pine Ridge and worked various jobs and was a tribal po-

liceman for a while. In his spare time he organized and coached a boxing club for Pine Ridge kids, and for many years drove the boys to
matches in the big Buick Specials and Ford station wagons he favored.
He stood over six feet tall and weighed 220 pounds. He loved to play
practical jokes and sing funny songs and clown, imitating popular
singers and movie stars. People remember especially how he used to
wear an old black hat, put his false teeth in upside down, and recite the
Pledge of Allegiance in the voice of the actor Gabby Hayes.

Next to the Leroy "Sunshine" Janis Memorial Park is the Delmar
"Fudd" Brewer Memorial Field, where local softball leagues play.
There are a lot of Brewers in Pine Ridge. Someone told me that Delmar's brother Dennis is head of the BIA's highway maintenance shop in
town, and I found him there, in his small office with safety posters on
the walls beside a hangar-sized garage full of dump trucks and road
graders. A crackling shortwave radio on a shelf relayed a conversation
between road crews in an outlying district who were trying to contain a
grass fire. Dennis Brewer is a stocky man with glasses, close-set eyes,
big arms, and a shock of hair across his forehead. He was happy to tell
me about his brother, and asked me to sit down. "There was nine of us
kids," he said. "Six boys and three girls: Dave, Deane, Duane, Dennis,
Delmar, and Rich; and Colleen, Judy, and Doris. We just lost Dave here
about a month ago. He was head of records out at Pine Ridge Hospital.
The other one that died was Delmar. He was born February 23, 1951,
and he died March 14, 1991. I was born in 1948, and he was the
brother closest to me. When we were kids we lived in Rapid City, but
then my dad—he was a construction worker—moved us down here to
Pine Ridge.

"Us boys grew up playing baseball. We lived and died it, we couldn't
wait for spring. A lot of times it was just me and Fudd—everybody
called him that, because of Elmer Fudd, ever since he was a kid. We
played this game we made up, with a flat wooden stick for a bat and one
of those yellow plastic ReaLemon juice bottles for a ball. They're
shaped like a lemon, you know, and you can make 'em do all kinds of
things when you throw 'em. Fudd had a good screwball. I couldn't hit
that sucker, but I had a backup ball, and Fudd couldn't hit that. So it
would be me against him, with our two dogs, Sparky and Duke, in the
outfield. They were Lab-shepherd crosses, and they could really play

ball. Them dogs could catch anything—pop-ups, long flies, line drives—and if the dogs caught it, you were out. We played hour after hour, all summer long. After we'd perfected this game, we got other kids to play it, and I'll tell you, it was a great game, more competitive than baseball.

"Fudd was an all-around good athlete, though. He was about five-nine and 155 pounds, and he had an excellent arm. As soon as he was old enough, he played regular ball: Little League, Pony League, then American Legion ball. He played a lot of positions, but he was best as a pitcher. He always went into a game knowing he was gonna win, and usually he did. Every year he won fifteen or twenty games, and he once struck out twenty-two guys in a game. If he hadn't been sick, he could've played pro ball. His best pitch was his fastball, and he didn't walk many guys. I played, too—I was a catcher. Plus, him and me always played in a fast-pitch softball league, travelin' to games all around here. Some Saturdays or Sundays we'd play a baseball double header in Pine Ridge in the afternoon and then in the evening drive to Rushville or someplace and play a fast-pitch softball game. It was just in the blood, it was fun. In 1987 our team won the state championship in fast-pitch softball.

"We gave Fudd the trophy. He'd had to quit by then. He finally got too sick—he had childhood diabetes and it began to affect his eyesight. It was hard for him to hang it up. He still came with us to the games, supporting and coaching. He lived here in Pine Ridge and worked in the property and supply office at Pine Ridge Hospital. He was real professional about his job; he started there right after high school and stayed right straight through almost until he died. The people at the hospital was the only ones in town that called him Delmar. After his health declined he watched a lot of sports on TV. He had to have a leg amputated, and an arm. He joked about it sometimes. He was just a happy guy who joked a lot and made other people feel good. He was married twice, had a couple of kids. People around town loved Fudd. After he died, G. Wayne Tapio, a tribal councilman, came up with the idea of naming the field after him and the park after Sunshine, and on Labor Day a couple years ago they had the dedication ceremony."

• • •

One afternoon Le and I were driving on Highway 18 in Pine Ridge when I noticed a single-story factory-style building across a weedy field. It had some lettering and a mural of a landscape on the front. A sign by the highway said it was the SuAnne Big Crow Health and Recreation Center, and below that were the words "Happytown, USA." I asked Le if he knew who SuAnne Big Crow was. He said, "She was a basketball star for Pine Ridge High School who helped 'em win the state championship and died in a car wreck a few years back. It was when I was living in New York, though, so that's about all I know."

A day or two later, I drove up to the building and parked in the dirt parking lot out front. Up close, I could see that the mural painted on the building's wall of corrugated steel depicted Sioux country from the Black Hills to the prairie and Pine Ridge. The tops of the letters of "SuAnne" in the center's name were lost in the white clouds over the Hills. A chunk of cinder block propped open the green steel front door. I went in. First to greet me was the smell of hamburgers frying. In the many times I would return, that frying smell would always be there. I would bring it away with me in my clothes and even in the pages of my notebooks, and when I happened to meet it in other places, I would always think of the SuAnne Big Crow Center. I had never much liked hamburgers or their smell before, but now it is a happy and inspiring aroma in my mind.

The entry hall had fluorescent lights above and a banner that said WELCOME TO HAPPYTOWN, USA. The images in the hall were a temporarily confusing combination of Oglala pride and 1950s-revival style. The words for "Boys" and "Girls" on the restroom doors on my left were in Sioux. On a table in a corner was a highly polished pair of brown-and-white saddle shoes. Above them hung the flag of the Oglala nation, and next to the flag was a large framed portrait of a young Elvis Presley—a more Indian-looking Elvis, it seemed to me, with a darker complexion and blacker, straighter hair. Framed photographs of a teenage girl smiling in a basketball warm-up jacket, making a shot in a basketball game, looking serious in a formal dress next to a boy in a tuxedo, gave the place the additional aura of a shrine.

The hall led, on the left, to a café in a big room with a lunch counter and tables and booths. The back end of a 1955 Packard affixed to one wall held potato and macaroni salads in its open trunk. A few late lunch customers were eating burgers at the booths or helping themselves to salad. A loud jukebox played fifties and sixties songs. Old-time Pepsi-Cola memorabilia decorated the walls, along with black-and-white photo portraits of John F. Kennedy and Martin Luther King, and several more portraits of Elvis. Kids of junior high age and younger were hanging out—eating ice-cream cones, playing video games.

At the end of the hallway on the right was a smaller room with glass trophy cases along the walls. The trophies all were from the athletic career of SuAnne Big Crow, the teenage girl in the photos, the person for whom the center was named. I looked at the trophies, I watched a short video playing on a VCR in the room, I read some framed news stories about SuAnne Big Crow, and a sense of discovery came over me. Here was a hero—not a folk hero, a sports hero, a tribal hero, or an American hero, but a combination of all these. I had thought that Oglala heroes existed mostly in the past. But a true Oglala hero appeared in the late 1980s, while the rest of the world was looking the other way, in suffering Pine Ridge, right under everyone's noses: SuAnne Big Crow.

If you ask people nowadays to name a hero, probably they'll say Michael Jordan, or maybe Mother Teresa, or maybe AIDS researcher Dr. Mathilde Krim. In the public sphere, the pickings have become pretty slim. Or else they'll mention someone unknown to the public at large—perhaps a parent, or a dedicated teacher they had in high school. The first kind of hero is admired by millions and exists for us mainly through the newspapers or (most often) on TV; the second kind has dozens or at most hundreds of admirers, and is seldom or never in the news or on TV. Historically, though, the distinction between the two kinds of heroes has been much less clear; that is, in the past a hero to the public at large might also have been someone you knew or knew of from your community—someone you would see on the street now and again, an acquaintance, a friend-of-a-friend. Also, for most of history, the first news of a hero came not through any written or broadcast word but by word of mouth.

For the Oglala, heroes have always been of the first and second kinds simultaneously. Crazy Horse, for example, was just a guy you saw around from time to time, herding his horses, sitting before his lodge, smoking with his friends. And yet he was also . . . *Crazy Horse*: the near-magic warrior, the victor of many battles, the man never wounded once in a fight, the famous destroyer of Custer and the Seventh Cavalry. Our usual experience of heroes today is so divided between the one or the other kind, and so diminished in general, it may be hard to imagine how someone who is both kinds of hero at once can elevate your soul. Imagine that when you were a little kid you thought, as kids often do, that your father was the strongest man in the world; but when you got older, you discovered that in your case your father actually *was* the world's strongest man, and you watched him win the gold medal in weightlifting in the Olympics. Or imagine that an older kid you looked up to when you were in elementary school, instead of fading in luster in the usual way as time went on, not only fulfilled every expectation you had for him but surpassed these with glorious public feats you never dreamed of.

Imagine that the hopeful, innocent, unbounded fantasy you had about someone you really admired when you were a child did not meet the usual puncturing and deflation but simply continued to grow; that you kept it with the same innocence and hope, finding more justification for it every day; that the person you admired, someone as familiar to you as yourself and yet at the same time set apart, took the hope invested in her onward into the larger world without a hitch, increasing her fame and achievements and admirers geographically along the way; and imagine that against odds upon odds she *won*, won at everything important she tried, won so blithely as to hardly show her strength; and that she carried the hope invested in her unstoppably aloft, defying the death and fear in the world. And imagine that as she did this she somehow carried you with her, lifted you, too, above the fear and the death, and gave you and all the people around you someone to be—a self, a freedom, a name. Warfield Moose, Sr., SuAnne's teacher of Lakota studies at Pine Ridge High School, said of her, "She showed us a way to live on the earth." Such was SuAnne's stature and generosity, she was able to do that not only for her Oglala people but for those who knew her and knew of her in the state of South Dakota, and beyond.

Reader, books are long, and I know that even the faithful reader tires. But I hope a few of you are still with me here. As much as I have wanted to tell anything, I want to tell you about SuAnne.

CHAPTER

12

SuAnne Marie Big Crow was born on March 15, 1974, at Pine Ridge
Hospital—the brick building, now no longer a hospital, just uphill from
the four-way intersection in town. Her mother, Leatrice Big Crow,
known as Chick, was twenty-five years old. Chick had two other daughters: Cecelia, called Cee Cee, who was three, and Frances, called Pigeon, who was five. Chick had been born a Big Crow, and grew up in
her grandmother Big Crow's house in Wolf Creek, a little community
about seven miles east of Pine Ridge. Chick had a round, pretty face,
dark eyes, a determined chin, and wiry reddish-brown hair. Her figure
was big-shouldered and trim; she had been a good athlete as a girl. Now
she worked as an administrative assistant for the tribal planning office,
and she was raising her daughters alone with the help of her sisters and
other kin. People knew that Everett "Gabby" Brewer was the father of
the two older girls, but Chick would never say who SuAnne's father was.
If asked, Chick always said she didn't want to talk about it. When
SuAnne got old enough to wonder, people sometimes told her that her
father was Elvis. And sometimes, when SuAnne wore her hair a certain
way with a curl in front, you would have to admit that a resemblance
was there.

   SuAnne's birth came at a dark time on the reservation. The ongoing battle between supporters and opponents of Dick Wilson's tribal government showed no signs of letup, with violence so pervasive and unpredictable that many people were afraid to leave their homes. Just the month before, a nine-year-old boy named Harold Weasel Bear had been shot and seriously wounded as he sat in his father's pickup in White Clay; his father was a Wilson man. Russell Means had campaigned against Wilson for the tribal chairmanship that winter and got more votes than Wilson in the primary. In the runoff election, however, Wilson won, by about two hundred votes out of the more than three thousand votes cast. Means had promised to "destroy" the present system of tribal government if he won, and many people were glad he wouldn't get a chance. He accused Wilson of stealing the election, and the federal Civil Rights Commission later agreed, saying that almost a third of the votes cast seemed to be improper and that the election was "permeated with fraud."

The beatings and stompings and shootings and bombings on the reservation would continue until the killing of the FBI agents the following year, after which a general exhaustion plus the presence of hundreds of FBI investigators brought the violence level down. In those days, if you were on the Pine Ridge Reservation you picked a side, and Chick Big Crow was for Dick Wilson all the way. She still calls Dick Wilson one of the greatest leaders the tribe ever had. Distinctions between those with anti– and pro–Dick Wilson loyalties, between AIM and goon, mean less today than they did then. Before SuAnne's sixteenth birthday, she would have a lot to do with causing those divisions to heal.

As a Big Crow, SuAnne belonged to one of the largest clans—the Lakota word for the extended family group is the *tiospaye*—on Pine Ridge. In the Pine Ridge telephone directory, Big Crow is the fourth-most-common name, behind Brewer, Pourier, and Ecoffey. (This method of figuring is not definitive, of course, since most people on the reservation don't have phones.) Chick Big Crow's mother, Alvina Big Crow, was one of nine children, and Chick had many Big Crow first cousins, as well as many with other last names. Her mother's sister Grace married a Mills; Olympic champion Billy Mills is a first cousin of Chick's. Chick's uncle Jimmy Big Crow married a woman named Marcella who bore him twenty-four children, including nine sets of twins. TV shows sometimes featured Jimmy and Marcella Big Crow and their family, and for a while they were listed in the *Guinness Book of World Records*. Basketball teams at Pine Ridge High School have occasionally been all or mostly Big Crow brothers or sisters and their first cousins.

The name Big Crow comes up rather often in the history of the Sioux. Big Crows are mentioned as headmen, though not as leaders of the first rank like Spotted Tail or Red Cloud. They seem to have been solidly upper-middle-class, if such a description can apply to nineteenth-century Sioux. When Francis Parkman arrived fresh out of Harvard to visit the Oglala in 1846, he stayed in the well-appointed tipi of a man called the Big Crow (Kongra Tonga), who was known for his friendliness to the whites. Parkman described in his book *The Oregon Trail* how the Big Crow sat in his tipi at night telling stories in a darkness suddenly made light by the flaring of a piece of buffalo fat on the fire, and how the Big Crow returned from a buffalo hunt with his arms and moccasins all bloody, and how he particularly vexed his lodger by getting up every midnight to sing a long prayer the spirits had told him to sing. In 1859, this Big Crow or another was killed by Crow Indians on a raiding expedition; the event appears in a Sioux winter count which marks 1859 with a pictograph that translates as "Big Crow was killed." In 1871, a Big Crow is listed among the chiefs who accompanied Red Cloud to a council at Fort Laramie. In 1877, when Crazy Horse fled the Red Cloud Agency to seek refuge at the Spotted Tail Agency, a Brule Sioux named Big Crow confronted him and lectured him, saying that Crazy Horse never listened but that now he must listen and must go with Big Crow to the commanding officer.

Leatrice "Chick" Big Crow does not know for sure whether any of these Big Crows is an ancestor of hers, but she thinks not. She says that her branch of the family descends from Big Crows of the Sans Arc Lakota, a tribe much smaller than the Oglala, who lived on the plains to the north and west. A medicine man has told her that among the Sans Arc long ago lived a chief named Big Crow who was greater than any chief we know of. This chief was also so wise that he never put himself forward and never identified himself to the whites so they could single him out as chief; he knew the jealousy and division this would cause.

For years the chief led the Sans Arc in war and peace, carefully avoiding all notoriety as the tribe prospered and grew strong. After he died, the tribe began to quarrel among themselves and dwindled away. The memory of this chief vanished except among a few, according to the medicine man. After SuAnne died, the medicine man told Chick that she had been the spirit of this great leader come back to reunite the people.

SuAnne grew up with her sisters in her mother's three-bedroom house in Pine Ridge. She was an active child; she sat up on her own while still an infant, and walked at nine months old. From when she was a baby, she wanted to do everything the bigger girls could do. When she was two, she told her mother that she wanted to go to school. She walked with Pigeon and Cee Cee to the school-bus stop in the mornings and often had to be restrained from getting on. Pigeon's memory of SuAnne is of her looking up at her from under the bill of her baseball cap. She was always looking up at her sisters and following them. When they went places around town, she went with them, telling Pigeon, "I'll walk in your footsteps." She played easily with kids much older than she. Chick came home from work one afternoon and found that SuAnne, then only four, had escaped from the babysitter and gotten on a big kid's ten-speed bicycle. Chick saw SuAnne coming down the hill, standing on the crossbar between the pedals and reaching up with her arms at full length to hold the handlebars.

Even today, people talk about what a strict mother Chick Big Crow was. Her daughters always had to be in the house or the yard by the time the streetlights came on. The only after-school activities she let them take part in were the structured and chaperoned kind; unsupervised wanderings and (later) cruising around in cars were out. In an interview when she was a teenager, SuAnne said that she and her sisters had to come up with their own fun, because their mother wouldn't let them socialize outside of school. Pigeon remembers Monopoly games they played that went on for days, and Scrabble marathons, and many games of Clue. In summer they could take picnics to White Clay Creek and spend the day there in the shallows, lying back and seeing different shapes in the clouds. One summer when Pigeon was in summer school the girls had their own school in their basement when she came home in the afternoons, with a full schedule of math and geography and English and so on. They played badminton in their yard and did Tae Kwon Do, and they made up a version of kickball played under the sprinkler on their lawn's wet grass where they could slide for miles. On evenings when their mother bowled at a league in Rushville they held road races with shopping carts on a track they made in the basement; they later said that the shopping carts taught them how to drive. At night, though they were sent to bed early, the three girls would read by flashlight under the covers or by the light from the hall—they liked the Nancy Drew mystery books and the Little House on the Prairie series, and the stories of the Babysitters' Club, and books by Beverly Cleary and Lois Duncan and Judy Blume. They had a little radio they kept under the bed, and when a local station signed off at ten o'clock with the national anthem, they would unharmoniously sing along.

Chick Big Crow was (and is) strongly anti-drug and -alcohol. On the reservation, Chick has belonged for many years to the small but adamant minority who take that stance. When SuAnne was nine years old, she was staying with her godmother on New Year's Eve when the woman's teenaged son came home drunk and shot himself in the chest. The woman was too distraught to do anything, so SuAnne called the ambulance and the police and cared for her until the grown-ups arrived. Perhaps because of this incident, SuAnne became as opposed to drugs and alcohol as her mother was. She gave talks on the subject to school and youth groups, made a video urging her message in a stern and wooden tone, and as a high-schooler traveled to distant cities for conventions of like-minded teens. I once asked Rol Bradford, a Pine Ridge teacher and coach who is also a friend of her family, whether SuAnne's public advocacy on this issue wasn't risky given the prominence of alcohol in the life of the reservation. "You have to understand," Rol Bradford said, "SuAnne didn't *respond* to peer pressure, SuAnne *was* peer pressure. She was the backbone of any group she was in, and she was way wiser than her years. By coming out against drinking, I know, she flat-out saved a lot of kids' lives. In fact, she even had an effect on me. It dawned on me that if a sixteen-year-old girl could have the guts to say these things, then maybe us adults should pay attention, too. I haven't had a drink since the day she died."

• • •

As strongly as Chick forbade certain activities, she encouraged the girls in sports. At one time or another, they did them all—cross-country running and track, volleyball, cheerleading, basketball, softball. Some of the teams were at school and others were sponsored by organizations in town. Chick's sister, Yvonne "Tiny" De Cory, had a cheerleading drill team called the Tiny Tots, a group of girls eight years old and under who performed at local sporting events and gatherings. SuAnne became a featured star for the Tiny Tots when she was three; many in Pine Ridge remember first seeing her or hearing about her then. She began to play on her big sisters' league softball team at about the same time, when the bat was still taller than she was. Coaches would send SuAnne in to pinch-hit, hoping for a walk, and telling her not to swing. Often she swung anyway; once, in a tie game, she swung at the third strike, the catcher dropped it, and several errors later she had rounded the bases for the winning run.

Pine Ridge had a winter basketball league for girls aged seven to eleven, and SuAnne later recalled that she played her first organized game in that league when she was in kindergarten. She had gone with her sisters to a tournament in Rushville when a sudden snowstorm kept some of the players away. The coach, finding himself short-handed, put SuAnne in the game. "It was funny," SuAnne told a basketball magazine, "because all I really knew how to do was play defense, so that's all I did. I not only took the ball away from our opponents, but also from my own teammates!" A coach who watched her play then said, "If you ever saw the movie *Star Wars*—well, you remember the Ewoks? Well, SuAnne was so much smaller than the other kids, she looked like one of those little Ewoks out there runnin' around."

In the West, girls' basketball is a bigger deal than it is elsewhere. High school girls' basketball games in states like South Dakota and Montana draw full-house crowds, and newspapers and college recruiters give nearly the same attention to star players who are girls as they do to stars who are boys. There were many good players on the girls' teams at Pine Ridge High School and at the Red Cloud School when SuAnne was little. SuAnne idolized a star for the Pine Ridge Lady Thorpes named Lolly Steele, who set many records at the school. On a national level, SuAnne's hero was Earvin "Magic" Johnson, of the Los Angeles Lakers pro team. Women's professional basketball did not exist in those years, but men's pro games were reaching a level of popularity to challenge baseball and football. SuAnne had big posters of Magic Johnson on her bedroom walls.

She spent endless hours practicing basketball. When she was in the fifth grade she heard somewhere that to improve your dribbling you should bounce a basketball a thousand times a day with each hand. She followed this daily exercise faithfully on the cement floor of the patio; her mother and sisters got tired of the sound. For variety, she would shoot layups against the gutter and the drainpipe, until they came loose from the house and had to be repaired. She knew that no girl in an official game had ever dunked a basketball—that is, had leaped as high as the rim and stuffed the ball through the hoop from above—and she wanted to be the first in history to do it. To get the feel, she persuaded a younger boy cousin to kneel on all fours under the basket. With a running start, and a leap using the boy's back as a springboard, she could dunk the ball.

Charles Zimiga, who would coach SuAnne in basketball during her high school years, remembered the first time he saw her. He was on the cross-country track on the old golf course coaching the high school boys' cross-country team—a team that later won the state championship—when SuAnne came running by. She was in seventh grade at the time. She practiced cross-country every fall, and ran in amateur meets, and sometimes placed high enough to be invited to tournaments in Boston and California. "The fluidness of her running amazed me, and the strength she had," Zimiga said. "I stood watching her go by and she stopped right in front of me—I'm a high school coach, remember, and she's just a young little girl—and she said, 'What're you lookin' at?' I said, 'A runner.' She would've been a top cross-country runner, but in high school it never did work out, because the season conflicted with basketball. I had heard about her before, but that day on the golf course was the first time I really noticed her."

SuAnne went to elementary school in Wolf Creek, because of her family's connections there. Zimiga and others wanted her to come to Pine Ridge High School so she could play on the basketball team, and finally they persuaded Chick to let her transfer when she was in junior high. By the time SuAnne was in eighth grade, she had grown to five feet, five inches tall ("but she played six foot," Zimiga said); she was long-limbed, well-muscled, and quick. She had high cheekbones, a prominent, arched upper lip that lined up with the basket when she aimed the ball, and short hair that she wore in no particular style. She could have played every game for the varsity when she was in eighth grade, but Coach Zimiga, who took over girls' varsity basketball that year, wanted to keep peace among older players who had waited for their chance to be on the team. He kept SuAnne on the junior varsity during the regular season. The varsity team had a good year, and when it advanced to the district playoffs, Zimiga brought SuAnne up from the JVs for the play-off games. Several times she got into foul trouble; the referees rule strictly in tournament games, and SuAnne was used to a more headlong style of play. She and her cousin Doni De Cory, a 5'10" junior, combined for many long-break baskets, with Doni throwing downcourt passes to SuAnne on the scoring end. In the district play-off against the team from Red Cloud, SuAnne scored thirty-one points. In the regional play-off game, Pine Ridge beat a good Todd County team, but in the state tournament they lost all three games and finished eighth.

Some people who live in the cities and towns near reservations treat their Indian neighbors decently; some don't. In cities like Denver and Minneapolis and Rapid City, police have been known to harass Indian teenagers and rough up Indian drunks and needlessly stop and search Indian cars. Local banks whose deposits include millions in tribal funds sometimes charge Indians higher loan interest rates than they charge whites. Gift shops near reservations sell junky caricature Indian pictures and dolls, and until not long ago, beer coolers had signs on them that said, INDIAN POWER. In a big discount store in a reservation border town, a white clerk observes a lot of Indians waiting at the checkout and remarks, "Oh, they're Indians—they're used to standing in line." Some people in South Dakota hate Indians, unapologetically, and will tell you why; in their voices you can hear a particular American meanness that is centuries old.

When teams from Pine Ridge play non-Indian teams, the question of race is always there. When Pine Ridge is the visiting team, usually their hosts are courteous, and the players and fans have a good time. But Pine Ridge coaches know that occasionally at away games their kids will be insulted, their fans will not feel welcome, the host gym will be dense with hostility, and the referees will call fouls on Indian players every chance they get. Sometimes in a game between Indian and non-Indian teams, the difference in race becomes an important and distracting part of the event.

One place where Pine Ridge teams used to get harassed regularly was in the high school gymnasium in Lead, South Dakota. Lead is a town of about 3,200 northwest of the reservation, in the Black Hills. It is laid out among the mines that are its main industry, and low, wooded mountains hedge it round. The brick high school building is set into a hillside. The school's only gym in those days was small, with tiers of gray-painted concrete on which the spectator benches descended from just below the steel-beamed roof to the very edge of the basketball court—an arrangement that greatly magnified the interior noise.

In the fall of 1988, the Pine Ridge Lady Thorpes went to Lead to play a basketball game. SuAnne was a full member of the team by then. She was a freshman, fourteen years old. Getting ready in the locker room, the Pine Ridge girls could hear the din from the fans. They were yelling fake-Indian war cries, a "woo-woo-woo" sound. The usual plan for the pre-game warm-up was for the visiting team to run onto the court in a line, take a lap or two around the floor, shoot some baskets, and then go to their bench at courtside. After that, the home team would come out and do the same, and then the game would begin. Usually the Thorpes lined up for their entry more or less according to height, which meant that senior Doni De Cory, one of the tallest, went first. As the team waited in the hallway leading from the locker room, the heckling got louder. The Lead fans were yelling epithets like "squaw" and "gut-eater." Some were waving food stamps, a reference to the reservation's receiving federal aid. Others yelled, "Where's the cheese?"—the joke being that if Indians were lining up, it must be to get commodity cheese. The Lead high school band had joined in, with fake-Indian drumming and a fake-Indian tune. Doni De Cory looked out the door and told her teammates, "I can't handle this." SuAnne quickly offered to go first in her place. She was so eager that Doni became suspicious. "Don't embarrass us," Doni told her. SuAnne said, "I won't. I won't embarrass you." Doni gave her the ball, and SuAnne stood first in line.

She came running onto the court dribbling the basketball, with her teammates running behind. On the court, the noise was deafeningly loud. SuAnne went right down the middle; but instead of running a full lap, she suddenly stopped when she got to center court. Her teammates were taken by surprise, and some bumped into one another. Coach Zimiga at the rear of the line did not know why they had stopped. SuAnne turned to Doni De Cory and tossed her the ball. Then she stepped into the jump-ball circle at center court, in front of the Lead fans. She unbuttoned her warm-up jacket, took it off, draped it over her shoulders, and began to do the Lakota shawl dance. SuAnne knew all the traditional dances—she had competed in many powwows as a little girl—and the dance she chose is a young woman's dance, graceful and modest and show-offy all at the same time. "I couldn't believe it—she was powwowin', like, 'get down!' " Doni De Cory recalled. "And then she started to sing." SuAnne began to sing in Lakota, swaying back and forth in the jump-ball circle, doing the shawl dance, using her warm-up jacket for a shawl. The crowd went completely silent. "All that stuff the Lead fans were yelling—it was like she *reversed* it somehow," a teammate said. In the sudden quiet, all you could hear was her Lakota song. SuAnne stood up, dropped her jacket, took the ball from Doni De Cory, and ran a lap around the court dribbling expertly and fast. The fans began to cheer and applaud. She sprinted to the basket, went up in the air, and laid the ball through the hoop, with the fans cheering loudly now. Of course, Pine Ridge went on to win the game.

Because this is one of the coolest and bravest deeds I ever heard of, I want to stop and consider it from a larger perspective that includes the town of Lead, all the Black Hills, and 125 years of history:

Lead, the town, does not get its name from the metal. The lead the name refers to is a mining term for a gold-bearing deposit, or vein, running through surrounding rock. The word, pronounced with a long *e*, is related to the word "lode." During the Black Hills gold rush of the 1870s, prospectors found a rich lead in what would become the town of

Lead. In April 1876, Fred and Moses Manuel staked a claim to a mine they called the Homestake. Their lead led eventually to gold and more gold—a small mountain of gold—whose value may be guessed by the size of the hole its extraction has left in the middle of present-day Lead.

In 1877, a mining engineer from San Francisco named George Hearst came to the Hills, investigated the Manuels' mine, and advised his big-city partners to buy it. The price was $70,000. At the time of Hearst's negotiations, the illegal act of Congress which would take this land from the Sioux had only recently passed. The partners followed Hearst's advice, and the Homestake Mine paid off its purchase price four times over in dividends alone within three years. When George Hearst's only son, William Randolph, was kicked out of Harvard for giving his instructors chamber pots with their names inscribed on the inside, George Hearst suggested that he come West and take over his (George's) share in the Homestake Mine. William Randolph Hearst chose to run the San Francisco *Examiner* instead. His father gave him a blank check to keep it going for two years; gold from Lead helped start the Hearst newspaper empire. Since the Homestake Mine was discovered, it has produced at least $10 billion in gold. It is one of the richest gold mines in the world.

Almost from the moment of the Custer expedition's entry into the Black Hills in 1874, there was no way the Sioux were going to be allowed to keep this land. By 1875, the Dakota Territorial Legislature had already divided the Black Hills land into counties; Custer County, in the southern Hills, was named in that general's honor while he was still alive, and while the land still clearly belonged to the Sioux. Many people in government and elsewhere knew at the time that taking this land was wrong. At first, the Army even made halfhearted attempts to keep the prospectors out. A high-ranking treaty negotiator told President Grant that the Custer expedition was "a violation of the national honor." One of the commissioners who worked on the "agreement" that gave paper legitimacy to the theft said that Custer should not have gone into the Hills in the first place; he and the other commissioners reminded the government that it was making the Sioux homeless and that it owed them protection and care. The taking of the Black Hills proceeded inexorably all the same.

Sioux leaders of Crazy Horse's generation began working to receive fair compensation for the Hills in the early 1900s. The Black Hills claim which the Sioux filed with the U.S. Court of Claims in the 1920s got nowhere. In 1946, the government established the Indian Claims Commission specifically to provide payment for wrongly taken Indian lands, and in 1950 the Sioux filed a claim for the Black Hills with the ICC. After almost twenty-five years of historical research and esoteric legal back-and-forth, the ICC finally ruled that the Sioux were entitled to a payment of $17.5 million plus interest for the taking of the Hills. Further legal maneuvering ensued. In 1980 the Supreme Court affirmed the ruling and awarded the Sioux a total of $106 million. Justice Harry Blackmun, for the majority, wrote: "A more ripe and rank case of dishonorable dealings will never, in all probability, be found in our history"—which was to say officially, and finally, that the Black Hills had been stolen.

By the time of the Supreme Court ruling, however, the Sioux had come to see their identity as linked to the Hills themselves, and the eight tribes involved decided unanimously not to accept the money. They said, "The Black Hills are not for sale." The Sioux now wanted the land back—some or all of it—and trespass damages as well. They especially wanted the Black Hills lands still owned by the federal government. These amount to about 1.3 million acres, a small proportion of what was stolen. At the moment, the chances of the Sioux getting these or any lands in the Black Hills appear remote. The untouched compensation money remains in a federal escrow account, where it, plus other compensation moneys, plus accumulated interest, is now over half a billion dollars.

Inescapably, this history is present when an Oglala team goes to Lead to play a basketball game. It may even explain why the fans in Lead were so mean: fear that you might perhaps be in the wrong can make you ornerier sometimes. In all the accounts of this land grab and its aftermath, and among the many greedy and driven men who had a part, I cannot find evidence of a single act as elegant, as generous, or as transcendent as SuAnne's dance at center court in the gym at Lead.

For the Oglala, what SuAnne did that day almost immediately took on the stature of myth. People from Pine Ridge who witnessed it still describe it in terms of awe and disbelief. Amazement swept through the younger kids when they heard. "I was, like, '*What* did she just do?' " recalled her cousin Angie Big Crow, an eighth-grader at the time. All over the reservation, people told and retold the story of SuAnne at Lead. Any time the subject of SuAnne came up when I was talking to people on Pine Ridge, I would always ask if they had heard about what she did at Lead, and always the answer was a smile and a nod—"Yeah, I was there," or "Yeah, I heard about that." To the unnumbered big and small slights of local racism which the Oglala have known all their lives, SuAnne's exploit made an emphatic reply.

Back in the days when Lakota war parties still fought battles against other tribes and the Army, no deed of war was more honored than the act of counting coup. To count coup means to touch an armed enemy in full possession of his powers with a special stick called a coup stick, or with the hand. The touch is not a blow, and only serves to indicate how close to the enemy you came. As an act of bravery, counting coup was regarded as greater than killing an enemy in single combat, greater than taking a scalp or horses or any prize. Counting coup was an act of al-most abstract courage, of pure playfulness taken to the most daring ex-treme. Very likely, to do it and survive brought an exhilaration to which nothing could compare. In an ancient sense which her Oglala kin could recognize, SuAnne counted coup on the fans of Lead.

And yet this coup was an act not of war but of peace. SuAnne's coup strike was an offering, an invitation. It took the hecklers at the best in-terpretation, as if their silly mocking chants were meant only in good-will. It showed that their fake Indian songs were just that—fake—and that the real thing was better, as real things usually are. We Lakota have been dancing like this for centuries, the dance said; we've been doing the shawl dance since long before you came, before you had gotten on the boat in Glasgow or Bremerhaven, before you stole this land, and we're still doing it today; and isn't it pretty, when you see how it's sup-posed to be done? Because finally what SuAnne proposed was to invite us—us onlookers in the stands, which is the non-Lakota rest of this country—to dance, too. She was in the Lead gym to play, and she in-vited us all to play. The symbol she used to include us was the warm-up jacket. Everyone in America has a warm-up jacket. I've got one, proba-bly so do you, so did (no doubt) many of the fans at Lead. By using the warm-up jacket as a shawl in her impromptu shawl dance, she made Lakota relatives of us all.

"It was funny," Doni De Cory said, "but after that game the relationship between Lead and us was tremendous. When we played Lead
again, the games were really good, and we got to know some of the girls
on the team. Later, when we went to a tournament and Lead was there,
we were hanging out with the Lead girls and eating pizza with them.
We got to know some of their parents, too. What SuAnne did made a
lasting impression and changed the whole situation with us and Lead.
We found out there are some really good people in Lead."

America is a leap of the imagination. From its beginning, people had
only a persistent idea of what a good country should be. The idea involved freedom, equality, justice, and the pursuit of happiness; nowadays most of us probably could not describe it a lot more clearly than
that. The truth is, it always has been a bit of a guess. No one has ever
known for sure whether a country based on such an idea is really possi
ble, but again and again, we have leaped toward the idea and hoped.
What SuAnne Big Crow demonstrated in the Lead high school gym is
that making the leap is the whole point. The idea does not truly live unless it is expressed by an act; the country does not live unless we make
the leap from our tribe or focus group or gated community or demo-
graphic, and land on the shaky platform of that idea of a good country
which all kinds of different people share.

This leap is made in public, and it's made for free. It's not a product
or a service that anyone will pay you for. You do it for reasons unexplainable by economics—for ambition, out of conviction, for the heck
of it, in playfulness, for love. It's done in public spaces, face-to-face,
where anyone is free to go. It's not done on television, on the Internet,
or over the telephone; our electronic systems can only tell us if the leap
made elsewhere has succeeded or failed. The places you'll see it are
high school gyms, city sidewalks, the subway, bus stations, public parks,
parking lots, and wherever people gather during natural disasters. In
those places and others like them, the leaps that continue to invent and
knit the country continue to be made. When the leap fails, it looks like
the L.A. riots, or Sherman's March through Georgia. When it succeeds,
it looks like the New York City Bicentennial Celebration in July 1976,
or the Civil Rights March on Washington in 1963. On that scale,

whether it succeeds or fails, it's always something to see. The leap requires physical presence and physical risk. But the payoff—in terms of dreams realized, of understanding, of people getting along—can be so glorious as to make the risk seem minuscule.

I find all this hopefulness, and more, in SuAnne's dance at center court in the gym in Lead. My high school football coach used to show us films of our previous game every Monday after practice, and whenever he liked a particular play, he would run it over and over again. If I had a film of SuAnne at Lead (as far as I know, no such film or video exists), I would study it in slow motion frame by frame. There's a magic in what she did, along with the promise that public acts of courage are still alive out there somewhere. Mostly, I would run the film of SuAnne again and again for my own braveheart song. I refer to her, as I do to Crazy Horse, for proof that it's a public service to be brave.

chapter 13

Doni De Cory is a big, light-brown woman with vivid dark eyes and big hair. Or, as she puts it, "huge hair." "I had the hugest hair in Pine Ridge High School," she says. Immaculately done, ginger-tinted, and huge, her hair can make most other kinds of hair look bedraggled and not-well-thought-out by comparison. Besides being a basketball star, she was three times South Dakota state champion in the shot put, and an all-American in the event her junior and senior years, and she walks with the grace and control of someone who can do just about anything physical she chooses to do. When Chick Big Crow called her on the phone and told her that I was at the SuAnne Center and that I wanted to talk about SuAnne, Doni De Cory came over right away. She was wearing black pants and a black blazer with a white blouse, her long nails were manicured a light purple shade, and she had on high heels and big silver earrings. In a nondescript shirt and slacks, I felt disrespectfully underdressed.

She had clearly been waiting for someone like me to show up and ask her about SuAnne. She spoke with intensity, in a quiet rush, talking not so much to any one person as to listeners in general. From time to time she elegantly changed how she was sitting, recrossing her legs. "I was three years older than SuAnne, but it didn't seem like it," she said. "Even when she was little it was like we were the same age. SuAnne never hung out with her own age group—she hung with us older girls, and in sports she could keep up with anything we did. She and I were really close and shared everything and talked all the time—almost every day, even after I went away to college. We played on I don't know how many teams together, from when we were kids, and I had so much confidence in her. I always put pressure on her because I always knew she could do it. In basketball, SuAnne and me were one of the best fast-break teams ever to come out of the state. And it didn't matter how far down we'd get in a game, we never gave up. Even when we were forty points down we kept playin' hard, because we had that confidence in each other.

"I just love my tribe to death, and SuAnne felt the same. That was something else in common. We used to talk about all the good that's here, and about how we were gonna come back after college and make this a better place. She was really proud of bein' from Pine Ridge. Anywhere we went, for basketball or volleyball games, or for cheerleading competitions, she would tell people, 'We're from an Indian reservation in the middle of the country, we're from Pine Ridge, South Dakota.' Then sometimes she'd throw back her head and yell, 'We're Oglala Sioooooooooux!'

"SuAnne and me always went out of our comfort zone, wherever we traveled. A lot of times the other girls would just want to stay in the hotel, but we were always outspoken and outgoing and adventurous. When we went to Hawaii to be in the half-time show at the Aloha Bowl—our cheerleading squad won a national cheerleading contest in Rock Springs, Wyoming, that's how we got picked to go—we walked all over the island, it seemed like. We snuck into the Hard Rock Café, we weren't even eighteen years old. We had to rehearse for the half-time show five or six hours a day, and we got to meet the Osmond Brothers singing group. They were the main half-time act, these little, cute boys. We met them at a banquet where there was nothing to eat but stuff like octopus and shark, and afterward SuAnne and me came out of there *starving* for some McDonald's food, and we took off our high heels and walked two miles in our bare feet to the only McDonald's on the island and stood in line for an hour and a half to pay about twice what it costs in South Dakota. SuAnne didn't care, though. She loved McDonald's.

"The woman could *eat*. Four Big Macs and four large fries was nothin' to her. She'd finish all that and then come around to see if you had anything you didn't want to eat that was left over. The seven-dollar meal allowance did not begin to be enough for her. She'd stay at our house sometimes, and she could eat four big platefuls of carbo meals like spaghetti, no problem at all. She could eat a whole commod pie by herself—that's a big casserole made with canned commodity foods like meatball stew. When it came to eating in the school cafeteria, SuAnne could keep up with the guys. She was good at blowing bubble-gum bubbles, too. She'd throw a whole pack of that Hubba Bubba bubble gum in her mouth and blow bubbles one inside the other. She always won the bubble gum–blowing contests at pep rallies.

"One thing I know I helped her with was in how to make herself look good, how to do her makeup and her hair. She was always the center of attention when she walked into a room, but before she was fourteen or fifteen she had never tried to beautify herself. I mean, here she was in high school and didn't even know how to use a curling iron! Before our cheerleading picture one time I made her hair huge like mine, and streaked it with lemon juice and put a whole bunch of mousse in it. After that, when she would get dressed up for something, she would always ask me or Jeanne Horse, our cheerleading coach, how she looked. She was really pretty, and by the time she was elected Homecoming Queen her senior year, she knew it, and she knew how to take advantage of it.

"She was just a big personality, a big person. She cared so much about Pine Ridge. She wanted there to be more opportunities here. Sometimes we talked about how to provide for the tribe's future, for seven generations ahead, the way Chief Red Cloud and them said you should do. She always paid attention to anybody who wanted something from her. No one knows what she went through makin' everybody happy. Anybody who came to her door hungry, she gave 'em something from the cupboard—Chick finally had to tell her to stop givin' their food away. A lot of kids who are grown up now will tell you, 'She used to pump me home on her bicycle'—if she saw a kid walkin' when she was on her bike, she'd tell him to get on behind, and she'd pedal and give him a ride home. She had what she called her giveaway bag in her closet filled with stuff she'd brought back from her team trips, little souvenirs and stuff like that, and any time you went to her house she'd give you something to take with you when you left. Mainly, she helped people open their eyes to the good things that were right in front of them. She saw so much good in life herself. Everything was . . . *revealing* to her. Everything was revealing."

Doni De Cory said a lot more about SuAnne—about her ambition to be an optometrist, about her sadness at the jealousy on the reservation, about her horrible singing voice, about her collection of sweatshirts from many different colleges, about how hard she worked, about how SuAnne and Doni and a boy cousin once beat the best all-guy basketball teams on the reservation during a three-man basketball tournament in the town of Kyle. Doni also talked a lot about when SuAnne died—about the ugly feeling that came over her out of nowhere as she was doing her laundry at the time of the crash, and about the red light on her answering machine jumping out at her after her father had called to tell her the news.

"For some reason, when I think of SuAnne, the first thing that always comes to mind is her hands," Doni said. "I could do an exact description of her hands. There was the lump on her middle finger where she held a pencil, and her calluses from playin' ball, and her fingernails, which she always chewed. She had these real, real low fingernails, probably because you can't have very long fingernails and handle a basketball. Her fingernails were always so low they looked like they hurt."

Many people, I discovered, wanted to talk about SuAnne. All these years after she died she's still on people's minds. Some people dream about her. Many I talked to would recommend others for me to talk to, who would recommend others, and so on. Here's some of what they said:

Rol Bradford, teacher and coach: "When I was coaching boys' basketball at Pine Ridge, SuAnne was my student manager—she did that along with cheerleading—and I used to put her in scrimmages during practice sometimes. When she was playing, unless you looked close, you would never know there was a girl out there. She was just as good as a lot of the boys and better than some, and she could run with 'em perfectly easy, and the level of play didn't go down at all. If anything, it improved. For fun in gym class once in a while we used to play this game called Mob Basketball. It's basketball but with no fouls. Anything goes in Mob Basketball except bitin', kickin', and scratchin'. Well, once SuAnne and I went for a loose ball at the same time and we both got our arms around it, and we're down on the court rollin' around, and she would not let *go*. I could not believe she was so tremendously strong. I'm a rodeo cowboy in the summers, I rassle steers—and I really had to scrap to get that ball away. And I was exhausted when I finally did, too."

Gordon Bergquist, one of the most successful basketball coaches in South Dakota history, whose team SuAnne's team beat in the state finals: "Anytime I ran into SuAnne, she always said hello and talked to me without any hesitation at all. Now, I'm not making generalizations, but Native American kids very rarely do that. I'm an adult, I'm blond, I'm 'Euro,' and . . . well, Indian kids just don't usually go out of their way to talk to me. But when I ran into SuAnne in the Kmart in Watertown one time we visited for quite a while, leaning up against the clothes racks. She was telling me where she was thinking about going to college, how she wanted to do something for her people.

"What impressed me maybe the most about SuAnne was how she could play so hard, right at the top of her intensity, and never show the least bit of impatience or anger. She had such a pleasant disposition, and she didn't want to do anything except have a good time and win. I'll never forget when we played against her in a holiday tournament in Arlington in '91—I never saw a game in which one player dominated so much. She really took us apart. She scored forty-three points against us and Pine Ridge won, 87 to 53. If I hadn't been the opponent I'd've thoroughly enjoyed watching someone play that well. After the game I went over to her and kidded with her—I said, 'Are you gonna graduate pretty soon?' That was the last time I saw SuAnne Big Crow. I think about her more than you would expect to think about a kid you played against a long time ago."

Pigeon Big Crow, sister: "She had a funky laugh, this all-out laugh. There was a knock-knock joke she told for a whole summer—now I can't remember it, it'll come to me—and she'd laugh at it every time she told it, and you'd laugh at her laughin'. But after Magic Johnson got AIDS and there were those jokes about him goin' around, you could *not* say a Magic Johnson joke around her. She loved Magic Johnson and she would not hear a word against him.

"By the time SuAnne was a teenager she was in demand all the time, always with stuff goin' on. And yet somehow she was always there for my kids. If I needed someone to look after 'em, she found the time. Because of SuAnne, I never had to worry about my kids. I came home one time when Lyle was three months old and SuAnne had his legs propped way out and she was tryin' to get him to sit up. I said, 'SuAnne, what're you doin'?' She said, 'I'm trying to create equilibrium.' She got him sitting up, and she got him walking early, too."

Chick Big Crow, mother: "Don't start thinking that SuAnne was only an angel, though. She was mis-*chie*-vous, with a capital M. She was always testing how far she could go, what could and could not be done. She'd always push you. In our neighborhood we had a bootlegger who sold beer and wine from a drive-up window out of his house. The name he went by was Suitcase, and SuAnne used to harass and devil him. She used to yell, 'Hey, Soup-Face!' through the drive-up window at him, which for some reason he absolutely hated. He put SuAnne's name on a list of people he wouldn't allow on his property—SuAnne was blacklisted at Suitcase's along with a couple of the worst deadbeat drunks in town. One time she and another kid set a mattress on fire behind his house."

Yvonne "Tiny" De Cory, aunt: "I let her play on a girls' softball team I coached when she was only five or six years old. She wanted to so bad, I couldn't say no. The helmet couldn't fit her, it was way too big. I'd tell her all I wanted her to do when she went up to bat was draw a walk. I'd say, 'Now, SuAnne, you just stand there at the plate and *don't swing.*' She'd listen to every word I said, lookin' at me with her big raccoon eyes wide. Then she'd go up there—this was a twelve-year-old girl pitching to a six-year-old, remember—and she'd stand there, and first pitch she'd swing away. I'd call time out and bring her over and tell her again, 'Sue, I told you not to swing!' She'd look at me and listen and nod her head and say, 'Yeah, uh-huh, okay.' Then she go back up there and next pitch she'd swing again. Didn't matter what you told her, she was going to swing. She always went in there thinking maybe she'd hit a home run. Even at that young age, she wanted to make a statement with whatever she did. She was going to have her swings."

Jeanne Horse, Pine Ridge High School librarian; former cheerleading coach and sponsor: "I remember one time I went with the squad to a boys' basketball tournament at the Corn Palace in Mitchell, South Dakota, and I was in the ladies' room, and I heard some non-Indian girls in there say, 'SuAnne Big Crow is a cheerleader for Pine Ridge. Let's go watch her.' That cheerleading squad—Doni De Cory, Lisa Carlow, Robin Akers, Kellee Brewer, SuAnne and her sister Cee Cee— they were really achievers. I call it my dream team. I don't even know how many competitions we won, offhand. I was watching a football game at the University of Nebraska at Lincoln one time when Nebraska was the top college football team in the country and I saw their cheerleaders do a pinwheel stunt—bigger kids twirling in a circle at the center and some lighter girls, like spokes, flying out—and I said, 'Oh, let's try that!' We practiced and practiced the pinwheel, and we finally got it to work. Robin and Lisa were our lighter girls, and Doni and SuAnne were in the center, and it was really striking to see these high school kids do such a beautiful job on a difficult, college-level stunt. In cheerleading, I still compare everybody and everything to them."

Dennis Banks, AIM leader: "I was running the limo service in Rapid City when the Pine Ridge cheerleaders went to the Aloha Bowl. Jeanne Horse called me and asked if I'd drive the kids to the airport in my limo and I was happy to do it, door-to-door and for free. It's really exciting to see kids like that pushing and excelling, but with incredible allegiance to each other. For me as an AIM leader it was great the way SuAnne and them were against racial slurs, taking a stand on their own, letting it be known they weren't going to accept it. I became a big fan of Lady

Thorpes basketball and went to a lot of their games, and my daughter, Chubs, became their mascot. She was about five years old at the time. SuAnne and another girl made outfits for her. I truly, truly enjoyed being with the Lady Thorpes. Once just after they won a really close game, SuAnne saw me in the stands and yelled, 'Hey, Banks! How do you feel?' Holy cripes, I was still screaming, I was so excited."

Milo Yellow Hair, tribal vice-chairman: "One of our biggest problems as Oglala people is that we don't know how to take a compliment. If you single someone out for praise, it's a fine line not to embarrass 'em and make 'em uncomfortable with the unwanted publicity. For most of us, bein' a marquee character just is not in our capacity. SuAnne could be comfortable with a lot of attention, but at the same time she always understood that she was just a part of the whole. When she got a compliment, she always held back and allowed the other kids to get credit, too. She might have been the spirit at the center, but she didn't overwhelm you with her ego, she let the other kids rally around. She understood that was the essence of how things should be done."

Chick Big Crow: "She would never let me brag about her. She used to tell me, 'Mom, if you have to do that, I didn't earn it.' "

Wesley Bettelyoun, friend, second cousin; hospital maintenance man: "I grew up in the same neighborhood as SuAnne. She was three years older than me, and she used to bribe me to do stuff for her sometimes. Like, if her mom told her to pick up trash around the yard, SuAnne would tell me that if I did it she would ride bikes with me. A lot of kids liked her and wanted to do stuff with her. So I'd pick up the trash, and then we'd go speedin' around on our banana-seat bikes, racin' and goin' over jumps. Me and Butterball Littlebear, we were the chubby kids in the neighborhood, and she let us follow her around. When she was practicing jump shots or foul shots in the gym, we'd retrieve balls for her. SuAnne got me into sports, taught me about sportsmanship. When she was playin' sports she didn't ever get angry and she didn't ever cry. I played on the same hardball team with her one time and I was pretty little and they weren't putting me in the game, and she faked hurt so that I could play. That was cool of her—she grabbed her arm and fell down, and the coach sent me in for her at first base, and I played a lot after that. But no one besides me knew she wasn't really hurt, because when she really was hurt she didn't ever cry.

"One thing she did for me I'll always remember—I was a freshman at Pine Ridge High School when she was a senior, and back then at Pine Ridge they had this setup where all freshmen had to go through initiation. The way it worked, a senior would pick a freshman to initiate during initiation week, and then the senior would make the freshman do stuff like dress up in dresses (if the freshman was a guy), or wear weird makeup, or bring the senior cookies, or carry his books, or clean out his locker—stuff like that. Well, when SuAnne was a senior she had to pick a freshman to initiate, and I don't know why, but she picked me. And then she didn't make me do nothin'! All the other freshmen were doin' all these dumb initiation things, and I was walkin' around free with nothin' to do at all. Me and SuAnne were just laughin'. It made the other freshmen kind of mad. Pine Ridge outlawed initiations a few years after that.

"SuAnne always told me to be strong, to make my own way, and to look out for my family and friends. She said that if everybody on the rez did that, this place would be a paradise. She always treated people good herself. I never saw her disrespect anybody. She used to say, 'I want to go somewhere to college and then come back here and work.' She's always in my mind. I got pictures of her on the walls all over my room, they're the first thing I see every morning when I get up.

"Of course I loved her. I love her still."

SuAnne's freshman year, the year of her dance at center court at Lead, the Lady Thorpes basketball team beat the team from Winner, South Dakota, in the regional play-offs. In the state tournament, Doni De Cory was sidelined with a sprained ankle, and Pine Ridge lost a key semifinal game and finished fourth. At the end of the season SuAnne promised Coach Zimiga that before she graduated, Pine Ridge would win the state championship. Zimiga thought they had a good chance. Pine Ridge had never won the championship before.

The season for girls' basketball in South Dakota lasts from September until late November. In the winter, SuAnne was a cheerleader for the boys' basketball team, and she played on the girls' volleyball team. In the spring, she ran sprints and relays on the girls' track team. She also paid attention to her studies; like her sisters and Doni De Cory, SuAnne usually got the best grades in her class. That summer she had a job at Big Bat's—thirty to forty hours a week at the register and the deli counter, making $3.85 an hour. In her spare time she ran the cross-country course for endurance and practiced basketball, working out perhaps harder than she ever had. Coach Zimiga found her in the school gym early and late, lifting weights in the weight room or shooting jump shots.

When school started again in the fall of 1989, SuAnne was a sophomore, fifteen years old. Many people in high school sports in South Dakota knew about her by then. They knew, too, that Doni De Cory had graduated. What they didn't know, Zimiga was sure, was how many other good girl basketball players Pine Ridge had. There was Rita Bad Bear, a senior, who at almost six feet was the team's center and leading rebounder; Mary Walking, a junior who had grown up way out in the country where there was nothing to do but practice three-point shots, which had made her an excellent shooter from outside; Dakota "Happy" Big Crow, a skilled ball handler; and Darla Janis, Toni Morton, Jodee Bettelyoun, and Kellee Brewer, versatile athletes who could fill in anywhere. For their part, the girls thought Zimiga was great. He is a slim, quiet man as intense as a migraine, from which he in fact suffers sometimes. His players all called him Charley, or "Char" for short.

A record of this 1989 team exists in videotapes of their games made by friends and family members. The crimson, black, and white of the Pine Ridge game uniforms go well with the girls' dark features. The girls look confident and strong, exchanging high-fives after a score, hanging their heads and breathing hard during a time-out, ambling to the bench and sitting down and wiping the sweat from their faces with a towel as they listen to Coach Zimiga. Each is different from the next—one is tall, one short, one movie-star lovely, one curly-headed, and so on—and one is SuAnne, even in an amateur video clearly the star. But most striking is how solid they appear as a team. At certain moments when they are standing together, their different-looking faces are all lit similarly from within, and they have a constant awareness of one another in their eyes.

Local newspapers covering girls' basketball that year sometimes called her "sophomore sensation SuAnne Big Crow," and she lived up to the billing. In a game against Lemmon, South Dakota, SuAnne scored sixty-seven points, setting a single-game scoring record for the state. Afterward the Lemmon coach asked Zimiga, "How many SuAnnes did you have out there, anyway?" She was averaging over thirty points a game on her way to setting another state record—761 points, the most ever by a player in a single season. Pine Ridge beat Custer, Spearfish, Lead. When the Lady Thorpes played in their home gym, it was always packed. People on the reservation who couldn't get to the games listened to them at home over KILI radio, which broadcast every game live. In mid-November Pine Ridge won an important match-up against their always-strong reservation rivals, the team from Red Cloud Indian School. SuAnne scored thirty-five points in that game.

Late in the season the Lady Thorpes went to Eagle Butte, South Dakota, on the Cheyenne River Indian Reservation, for an all-Indian girls' basketball tournament. Just before it, a medicine man took Chick Big Crow aside and told her that someone was trying to harm SuAnne. He knew this, the medicine man said, because he had seen blue sparks coming off her. He said he could do a ceremony to remove the danger but that it would require twelve medicine men, because there were so many angry spirits around. In the tournament game between Pine Ridge and Little Wound not long after, a Little Wound player ran up behind SuAnne when she was shooting a layup and slammed her into the wall. As SuAnne collapsed to the floor, the girl who had hit her threw her arms into the air in triumph and grinned at the crowd. SuAnne got up slowly, went to the sidelines, and then came back in and made both foul shots. She felt dizzy and had a bump on her head, and Chick took her to a hospital, where she was diagnosed with a mild concussion.

On the strength of their regular-season record (sixteen games won, four lost) and their victory over Red Cloud, Pine Ridge got a spot in the district championship play-off against the Bennett County Lady Warriors, from Martin, South Dakota. SuAnne had recovered enough from her injury to score twenty-eight points in the district game, and the Lady Thorpes won it easily. Next step was the regional play-off in late November against the team from Winner, whom Pine Ridge had met in the regionals the year before. At this level of competition, the referees again clamped down on the Pine Ridge defensive style, and the Lady Thorpes soon got into foul trouble. With the team behind in the fourth quarter, SuAnne fouled out. Rita Bad Bear, another stalwart, had to play gingerly because she was carrying four fouls. Zimiga turned to the players on his bench for reinforcements, and sent in Toni Morton and Jodee Bettelyoun. These girls hadn't played much in the post-season, and they were keyed up and shaking as Zimiga told them what he wanted them to do. On the court they calmed down, and ran a complicated trapping defense so expertly that they turned the game around. Pine Ridge beat Winner in overtime 54–52. SuAnne had seventeen points in the game, but this time Toni Morton and Jodee Bettelyoun were the stars.

By coincidence, the same week that the Lady Thorpes won the regionals, Pine Ridge was once again in the national news. A crew from the NBC *Nightly News* had visited the reservation and interviewed people and shot a lot of footage for a multipart report titled *Tragedy at Pine Ridge*. When people came home the evening of November 20, and when the girls sat down to dinner after basketball practice, the first part of *Tragedy at Pine Ridge* was on TV. NBC anchorman Tom Brokaw announced, "This is Thanksgiving week, of course, but on the Pine Ridge Indian Reservation in South Dakota it's hard to find reason to give thanks, when tragedy is never out of season." There followed pictures of reservation poverty, statistics on unemployment and average yearly income, and interviews about the damage done by alcohol. The reporter, Betty Rollin, said, "The high point of life here, called Carnival Week, is the start of every month when the aid checks come in . . . almost everyone spends some, even all of the money, or barters food or sells cans for alcohol." (Chick Big Crow and her daughters found this surprising; they had never heard of the term "Carnival Week.") The segment ended with Rollin's observation that people here find it hard to leave because the reservation has not equipped them to live anyplace else, and that those who do leave usually come back and "succumb again to the ways of Pine Ridge—idleness and alcohol." The reports that followed over the next two nights were variations on this theme.

The success of the Pine Ridge High School girls' basketball team, the fact that one of its players had set state records that fall, the fact that the team was going to the state tournament—these all escaped the notice of NBC News. Indeed, from the beginning of the report to the end, NBC did not find one good thing to say; the "bleakness" story is a rigorous form, with little room for extraneous details. Undeniably, many sad facts of the reservation can be told with bleakness as the text. But the NBC story irritated people on Pine Ridge no end, especially SuAnne. She talked to anyone who would listen about all the good on the reservation that NBC had overlooked, and about the unfairness of showing only the suffering and apparently hopeless side. She went around saying "Carnival Week!" and *Tragedy at Pine Ridge*! in a derisive snort. Years later she would still complain about how stupid *Tragedy at Pine Ridge* was.

That year the state tournament for class A schools (those with enrollment under four hundred) was held in an arena in Sioux Falls, about 300 miles east of Pine Ridge. People in South Dakota sometimes divide the state into East River and West River when speaking of it; the Missouri River crosses South Dakota from south to north and cuts it more or less in half. East River gets more rain, and its grasses grow higher, and the landscape looks more like green Minnesota than like the tawny short-grass plains of the West. To someone from Pine Ridge, East River places like Sioux Falls can seem very far from home. The Lady Thorpes set out for Sioux Falls and the tournament in their chartered bus on a Wednesday morning with Coach Zimiga, and with Jeanne Horse as chaperone. The bus had a tape player and a TV and VCR. The New Kids on the Block Christmas tape was playing as they pulled out of town, and everybody was in a festive mood. SuAnne was saying, "When we come back with the trophy, then it'll really be 'Carnival Week'!"

They reached the city late in the afternoon and checked into the Holiday Inn in downtown Sioux Falls. Jeanne Horse had a suite and the girls hung out in it, ordering pizza and watching TV. The girls were high and happy, with no apparent fear at all. Zimiga wanted them to get to bed early because their first game was at eleven the next morning, but he saw they were having fun and he wasn't strict with them. He let them stay up a while, and a few went down and swam in the pool. They even got a kick out of the lobby and the elevators; some of the Pine Ridge kids had not spent much time in a high-rise hotel before.

To reach the finals Pine Ridge needed victories in the tournament's first two rounds. On Thursday morning they played the Flandreau Lady Knights, from the Flandreau Indian School just north of Sioux Falls. For this game the stands were mostly empty, the loud contingent of fans from Flandreau outnumbering a small Pine Ridge crowd. Throughout the game Pine Ridge kept building up big leads, but Flandreau kept fighting back. Pine Ridge was ten points ahead at the end of the first half. At the start of the second half, Flandreau pulled to within one. Pine Ridge was ahead by nine in the third quarter when Rita Bad Bear went out with an injury and Flandreau scored four unanswered points. Finally, in the fourth quarter, SuAnne scored thirteen points, giving her a total of thirty-six for the game, a tournament record. Pine Ridge won, 70–55.

In round two on Friday afternoon, Pine Ridge played the Parkston Trojans, a team with two tall sisters named Dawn and Staci Schulz. Zimiga countered their scoring threat by collapsing his defenders around them, but the game stayed close to the end, with Parkston just two points behind in the fourth quarter. A run of fourteen straight points for Pine Ridge then put the game out of reach, and Pine Ridge won, 62–47. SuAnne scored twenty-eight points, Mary Walking hit three three-point shots, and Rita Bad Bear and Darla Janis each scored ten. Both victories had been tougher for the Lady Thorpes than the final scores made it seem.

While Pine Ridge was advancing to the championship, so were the Lady Bulldogs, of Milbank High School. Milbank is a town of about 4,500, ten miles from the Minnesota border in the northeast part of the state. People in Milbank work in the granite quarries, for the coal-fired electric plant, in the cheese factory, or for two small insurance companies. Milbank's streets are tree-lined and quiet, and at noon on a summer day you can hear the sounds of many differents kinds of cuckoo clocks chiming from the well-kept houses. The town's big high school was built in 1978, and as at Pine Ridge High School, the bouncing of basketballs echoes from its gym on idle afternoons. The Milbank girls had won the state championship in 1987, and had been runners-up in 1988. For Milbank's coach, Gordon Bergquist (quoted earlier on the subject of SuAnne), his team's victory in the second round of this tournament had been his hundredth win in five years of coaching girls' basketball at Milbank High.

Pine Ridge met Milbank for the title game Saturday evening in the Sioux Falls Arena at eight o'clock. As it happened, this was the last game of the tournament (which also included bigger schools, in the AA division), because the bigger schools had played earlier in the day. Fans of girls' basketball had heard about SuAnne and they knew how tough Milbank was, and they expected a good contest. The arena was full and highly charged. A large group from Milbank filled a block in the center of the stands on one side. Across the way the Pine Ridge rooters made a smaller group, which was nonetheless impressive when you considered how far they'd had to drive. Chick Big Crow sat close to the aisle; she knew her nervousness would eventually cause her to get up and walk somewhere. As the public-address system announced the names of the Lady Thorpes one by one and the girls ran out from behind a curtain at an end of the arena, they were startled for a moment at the noise and the people in the cavernous hall. None had ever played in front of a crowd this large before. The Lady Thorpes formed two lines and gave each other high-fives with both hands, then gathered around Coach Zimiga for some final words as the Milbank team came out.

Zimiga's strategy for the first half was to try to keep the game close. In the front of his mind was a rule he had learned playing non-Indian schools east of the river: Don't foul. He told the girls to play cautiously, not to press on defense, and to be patient. Somehow beneath his anticipation he felt comfortable and calm. On the Milbank side, Coach Bergquist's plan involved maneuvering his tall girls, Kris White and Jolene Snaza, underneath the basket, where they could get rebounds. Mainly, he wanted to shut down SuAnne. He knew she liked to play close to the basket and he told his players to try to keep her farther outside.

I must imagine this game based on what people who were there told

me, on news stories, and on videotapes made by fans of Milbank or
Pine Ridge. My impressions of it are sort of jumpy, like images in a
hand-held video camera. The slap and squeak of rubber shoe soles on
the floor, the nervous drumming of the ball, the referee's whistle,
and the multiplied noises from people in the stands all crowded together in the brightly lit air above the game. The Pine Ridge girls
looked excited enough to run through walls. The effort it took to follow
their coach's instructions about patience and restraint showed in the
tentativeness of their offense at first, and in the way they sometimes
seemed to recoil from any contact with the Milbank girls. For Milbank's
part, the team moved up and down the floor deliberately and confidently; some of the Milbank players, of course, had been in a championship game before.

The collision of the two coaches' strategies made for a slow-scoring
and stiff first half. Milbank kept Pine Ridge away from the basket, and
Pine Ridge was hesitant to object. SuAnne got almost no close-in
chances. Whenever she took the ball, two or even three Lady Bulldogs
converged on her; she scored only five points the whole first half. Mary
Walking tried several three-point shots, but made none. Milbank's re-
bounding plan worked well, with Jolene Snaza taking the ball off the
boards and sometimes putting in missed shots; in the first quarter alone
she scored eight points. Kris White got eight of her own for the Bulldogs in the second quarter, mostly on offensive rebounds. If it hadn't
been for Rita Bad Bear, Pine Ridge would have ended the first half far
behind. Rita got rebounds and made follow-up shots and short jumpers,
to account for nine points in the half. Her performance was the more
remarkable because she was weak and faint from spells of morning sickness that came and went in waves. She had recently discovered she was
pregnant, but told no one.

When time ran out at the end of the first half, Pine Ridge was behind, 22–18. The Lady Thorpes were dejected; they had not looked
flashy or strong, Milbank had stymied them. They went to their locker
room and lay on the floor, sat in chairs with their heads drooping to
their knees, or perched on stools and stared. Coach Zimiga stood at the
chalkboard and described the more aggressive defense they would use
later in the second half. He did not get mad or holler at them to listen
up. In fact, he was not unhappy with how the first half had gone. His

team had done as he asked—their careful play had kept them from collecting too many fouls, and the score was about as close as he had
hoped it would be. He knew, too, that Milbank would be delighted at
their success against SuAnne, and might get overconfident. He told the
girls that they had played well, that they were definitely still in the
game, and that they could win.

The start of the second half seemed to refute his optimism. Milbank's Kris White got a quick tap-in basket, and on their next possession
Christi Wherry hit a shot from outside. Pine Ridge was now down by
eight. At this point Dakota "Happy" Big Crow decided that since no
one else on her team appeared to be hot, she would take a chance on
her own. Starting far from the basket she drove through Milbank's defenses in a high-speed dribble, changing hands as she did, and scored.
The dazzle of the move was itself a lift to the spirits of Pine Ridge. Next
time Happy got the ball, she took a shot from outside and again hit,
bringing her team back to within four. Christi Wherry then hit a shot,
which was answered by a score from Rita Bad Bear. On the next Milbank possession, SuAnne stole a pass and sprinted away from everybody for an easy layup. Soon after, she hit a twenty-foot jump shot.
Darla Janis, the team's worst foul shooter, then sank two foul shots. The
referees had called Kris White for her fourth foul, and Coach Bergquist
took her out of the game. A foul shot by Darla in the last second of the
third quarter put Pine Ridge ahead, 31–30.

Starting the fourth quarter, SuAnne stole another pass and made the
layup. Now it was Pine Ridge by three. Milbank then got two baskets in
a row, and Rita Bad Bear hit a foul shot to tie, 34–34. On Milbank's
next possession, Mary Walking committed an unnecessary foul, and after the second foul shot had been missed, she let the rebound slip from
her grasp. Milbank grabbed it and put it up and in. Now Milbank was
ahead by three. As the Lady Thorpes went back downcourt, Mary
called to Happy Big Crow to give her the ball. Happy passed it to her,
and Mary pulled up just outside the three-point line to the left of the
basket, aimed, and shot. She had not hit a three-pointer all evening, and
Zimiga said (quietly), *"No Mary no!"* as he saw what she was doing. But
in the next instant the ball went in, and his last "no" became an aston-
ished cheer.

Now Zimiga was sure they could win. He called a time-out and put in his team in a tight pressing defense. The tactic seemed to discomfit Milbank. Both teams traded foul shots, Pine Ridge getting the advantage by two. Now it was Pine Ridge, 40–38. Milbank's ball; another foul followed, the foul shot missed, and two rebound shots went wide. Then Milbank's Ginny Dohrer came up with the ball and fired an awkward, off-balance shot from about twenty feet away. It went in. Score: Pine Ridge 40, Milbank 40.

Eleven seconds now remained in the game. Zimiga took another time-out. The girls stood close around him listening as he explained a last-second play. SuAnne concentrated so closely, was so focused and attuned, her metabolism seemed to be going a hundred miles an hour. She stood almost on her tiptoes, her eyes scanning quickly from him to her teammates and back again; she hardly seemed to breathe. The ref calls time in. He blows his whistle for play to resume. The ball goes to SuAnne. She takes it fast all the way down the court, pulls up short of the basket, jumps, shoots. The ball caroms off the rim. Rita gets a hand on it, slaps it to Darla. There's a scramble, Milbank has it for an instant, loses it; and then, out of the chaos on the floor: order, in the form of SuAnne. She has the ball. She jumps, perfectly gathered, the ball in her hands overhead. Her face lifts toward the basket, her arched upper lip points at the basket above the turned-down O of her mouth, her dark eyes are ardent and wide open and completely seeing. The ball leaves her hand, her hand flops over at the wrist with fingers spread, the ball flies. She watches it go. It hits inside the hoop, at the back. It goes through the net. In the same instant, the final buzzer sounds.

Ginny Dohrer, the Milbank player who tied the game at 40 in the closing seconds, is now Ginny Dohrer Schulte. She lives with her husband, Calvin, and their two small children in Watertown, South Dakota. One evening they kindly agreed to watch their videotape of the game with me on the television in their living room. The video was made from the Milbank side, and at the moment of SuAnne's winning shot its perspective is from high up in the stands and includes the whole court. On the video, SuAnne makes the shot and then turns from the basket and throws her arms in the air. She waits for half a second, looking around to be sure that there are no fouls and that Pine Ridge has really won. When she realizes they have, she flings herself into the air and then leaps and bounds far down the court in ultimate cheerleader style, jack-knifing her head so far back and her heels so far up that they almost touch behind her, throwing her clenched fists out and up, covering the distance in a single bounding burst that hardly seems to touch the ground. She crosses the screen in a streak, like a bold signature written by a lighted pen. If you unfocus your eyes, she blurs into a vibrant beam of light.

The Schultes stopped the VCR and rewound the tape a little and played her victory run again. Calvin Schulte, a Milbank graduate who knew SuAnne only from watching his now-wife play against her, shook his head in quiet amazement as SuAnne leaped and ran. Then he said her name in the affectionate tones you might use about someone you had known your whole life. "SuAnne," Calvin said, shaking his head and smiling. "SuAnne."

The moment Pine Ridge won, a man from arena security came to Coach Zimiga and told him, "Charley, I don't want your people on the floor." Arena management was afraid of the Pine Ridge fans making a disturbance. After hugging in a toppling-over pile at center court, the Lady Thorpes shook hands with their Milbank opponents, then ran to Zimiga and lifted him onto their shoulders. The security guard told them to put him down. "We don't want no demonstrations," he said. "You're not gonna do any of that in here." Along the stands on the Pine Ridge side, security people stood and watched as the fans filed out. On the Milbank side, precautions were not so strict; Milbank fans came onto the court and wandered around and embraced the Milbank players. TV coverage of the scene after the game showed mostly Milbank fans and players consoling each other, with only a few shots of players from the winning team. A half hour or so later, after the arena had emptied out, Zimiga returned with the championship trophy and ran his victory lap around the dimmed court alone.

Outside Pine Ridge's locker room, several newspaper reporters were waiting for SuAnne. She answered their questions, and when they were done she told them, "Don't forget to call your story 'Tragedy at Sioux Falls.'"

Zimiga and Jeanne Horse and some other Pine Ridge people took the girls out to dinner at a Denny's restaurant. They stayed there late, then went back to the hotel. Rol Bradford and SuAnne and some of the other girls grabbed Zimiga to throw him in the hotel pool, giving him time first to remove his billfold and cowboy boots. Both he and the throwers ended up in the water. Everyone then gathered in Jeanne Horse's room and watched the video of him getting thrown in and talked about the game and made phone calls and accepted congratulations from well-wishers who stopped by and talked about the game some more.

Next morning they got on the bus for the long drive back to Pine Ridge. Most of the girls finally slept then. The bus stopped at a McDonald's someplace for a lunch break, and Jeanne Horse and the girls decorated the outside of the bus with streamers and slogans. The whole reservation knew about the victory by that time. In the most remote places, in houses and trailers scattered across the prairie, people had listened to the game on KILI radio, and at the end of it they had thrown open their doors and cheered themselves hoarse into the night. Rosebud Sioux police cars escorted the bus across the Rosebud Reservation. As soon as the bus crossed the eastern edge of the Pine Ridge Reservation at the Bennett County line (still over fifty miles from Pine Ridge village) carloads of fans began to fall into line behind. By the time the bus reached the Wounded Knee turnoff, hundreds of cars were waiting for it. Parents and kids and grandparents stood by the intersection peering east to catch the first glimpse of it. As the bus went by, they waved and cheered and ran to their cars to honk the horns, and then they joined the lengthening train. The cars had their headlights on in the late-autumn twilight, and the line of lights stretched behind the bus for miles. SuAnne and Coach Zimiga were standing by the front door of the bus on the steps looking out the window. At a place in the road where it curved, far into the distance she could see the line of lights following them. She said to Zimiga, "Oh, Char! Oh, Char! Oh, Char!"

Along the road approaching Pine Ridge village people had pulled their cars onto the shoulder on both sides facing perpendicular, and their headlights made a lit-up aisle. Hastily painted welcoming sign-boards lined the route. Horns were honking; pedestrians everywhere caused the bus and its entourage to go slower and slower. By the time the bus reached the four-way intersection in the middle of town, the crowds were too thick for it to move anymore. The sun had just gone down. SuAnne and the others came from the bus to loud cheering, and then several climbed onto the bus roof. They had promised each other that when they got to the four-way they would twirl on the streetlight, but now that they saw it they decided it was too high. A drum group had set up by the intersection and was drumming at top powwow volume as the singers' voices rose in a Lakota victory song. On the roof of the bus, SuAnne and the other girls danced.

People later said that it seemed as if everybody on the reservation was there. "It was the festival of festivals," recalled Dennis Banks, who had flown home early from a conference when he heard about the victory and had joined the procession behind the bus with his limousine. "Those girls *owned* that town," he said. People were carrying SuAnne and Rita and Mary and Darla and the other girls on their shoulders. As the drumbeats sounded, people threw their arms around each other's shoulders and formed a big circle and began a dance called the round dance. People outside the ring danced, too, stepping now this way, now that, shouting and singing. Kids from Pine Ridge High School and their rivals from Red Cloud, political enemies who hadn't spoken to each other in decades, country people who had supported AIM and village guys who had been goons, Dennis Banks and men who in 1973 might have been proud to shoot Dennis Banks—there on the pavement beneath the single streetlight at the four-way, everybody danced.

After a while the crowd went across the street to Billy Mills Hall for speeches and an honoring ceremony. Fans had decorated the hall with crepe paper and posters, and a big banner at one end of the hall proclaimed the words that had become a kind of slogan of the victory: "Tragedy at Sioux Falls!" Folding tables against the walls held trays of food and urns of coffee, and there were big single-layer cakes for each girl on the team, each cake with the player's name written on it in frosting. The drum group sang, tribal officials spoke in praise of the team, and Charles Zimiga said a few words. Light spilled from the doors into the night as people came and went; the crowd was almost more than the hall could comfortably hold. To the girls it seemed as if they had talked to everybody they had ever known. At about ten in the evening people started to go home.

Coach Zimiga lives across the street from the high school. When he awoke the next morning, he could hardly see his house for all the decorations heaped upon it. There were streamers and congratulatory posters and banners and artificial flowers and real flowers and plastic butterflies and wreaths and even a stuffed animal or two—the most thorough job of decorating he had ever seen. In the days after, he and his team got fan letters from all over the state. Grade school classes wrote to them, and little girls from tiny towns like Dupree and Timber Lake, and kids at Indian community colleges. South Dakota governor George Mickelson sent his congratulations, and thanked the team for the reconciliation and understanding they had helped to bring about. For SuAnne Big Crow, the victory meant statewide fame and more. A week or two after girls' basketball season ended, national organizations began to compile their high school all-American teams. The newspaper *USA Today* included SuAnne on its all-American roster, a remarkable honor for a sophomore from a small school in a prairie state. Soon, college recruiters would begin to call. SuAnne and the Lady Thorpes basketball team had made the biggest noise to come out of Pine Ridge in a long time.

CHAPTER

14

Small-town glory is like no other kind. It's so big you can hardly see around it, yet intimate at the same time. When you're fifteen years old, it's as much of glory as you can easily comprehend; praise from faraway strangers seems a bit unreal compared to praise from friends and neighbors you grew up with and run into every day. A small town, and even more a village like Pine Ridge, has for its citizens no very solid boundaries between inside and outside. If you were raised in Pine Ridge you know the inside of lots of houses there, and when you leave your house and walk the village streets you know almost everyone you see outside. Sometimes the warmth of this familiarity can give you an idea of why people decided to live in villages to begin with. And when you're fifteen years old and the people you see in your village greet you not only familiarly but with shouts of praise—well, for a moment then your happiness wraps around you a full three hundred and sixty degrees.

After basketball season, SuAnne's year proceeded like the one before it. Christmas was the usual big production in the Big Crow household, and SuAnne and her friends went around the village looking at the lights and arguing about which house had the best display. In the winter there was volleyball and cheerleading for boys' basketball. That season SuAnne won an individual cheerleading trophy at the boys' all-

Indian basketball tournament. In the spring she ran on the track team. She tended to her schoolwork and worked out in the gym and did errands for her mother on her bicycle just as before. Now, though, SuAnne was really *somebody*. Her school and her town had no bigger star. Little kids copied her, parents paid her to hang out with their kids, old women stopped her in the grocery store to tell her they hoped their grandchildren would grow up to be like her. As is only natural—indeed, as the dark Pine Ridge night follows day—SuAnne acquired rivals, and reservation jealousy began to watch her out of the corner of its eye.

A national Indian organization called Chick that year and said they were putting together the first-ever European tour of a Native American all-star girls' basketball team, to play exhibition games against teams in Finland and Russia. The tour would be that summer, and they wanted SuAnne to join it. Chick was agreeable and SuAnne liked the idea, so to come up with the expense money she and Chick and Pigeon held bake sales and sold raffle tickets and made snacks to sell at local bingo nights. The tribe chipped in some money, and an article in the newspaper brought in a few more donations. By midsummer they had raised enough, and SuAnne had gotten her shots and her passport. Chick drove her to Bismarck, North Dakota, for a few days of practice with the rest of the team. SuAnne later told her that she felt so scared just after she dropped her off that if Chick had come back she would have jumped in the car and gone home. But she stayed, drove with the team to the airport in Minneapolis, and went on to Europe.

Chick had a vision after SuAnne left that made her fear the plane had crashed or something else bad had happened to SuAnne. Both Chick's and SuAnne's misgivings turned out to be partly justified. The Finland leg of the trip went well, but then the team was not allowed to enter Russia, due to visa problems. They had to settle for playing teams in Lithuania; videotape of those games shows SuAnne zipping around the taller and slower Lithuanian girls. In Lithuania SuAnne came down with a stomach illness. On the other side of the globe Chick sensed that SuAnne was sick and prayed her daughter would get back safely. When Chick met the returning team in Mitchell, South Dakota, at the end of the summer she was shocked at SuAnne's appearance. SuAnne had taken on a sickly yellowish color and had lost eleven pounds.

Most likely SuAnne did not know that she was participating in another Native American tradition: since Columbus's time and through the days of the Wild West Shows, Indians have been going to Europe and getting sick there. For Pocahontas and many others, the trip proved fatal. After SuAnne got home she went to several doctors, but none could give her a definite diagnosis. Chick thought it might be a kind of hepatitis. Whatever the ailment was—an unknown virus, travel strangeness, a strong constitution's first intimations of mortality, or some combination of these—it lingered for a long time. SuAnne was tired and couldn't keep food down and some days could hardly move. In a span of two or three months she ended up losing over twenty pounds. She couldn't attend early basketball practice, and during basketball season her junior year she missed more than half the games. To keep up with her schoolwork she went to her classes once or twice a week just to get her assignments, then finished them at home. Her friends and teachers found it strange suddenly not to have her around. Once Jeanne Horse called her to find out how she was doing; she wasn't even sure SuAnne would answer the phone. But SuAnne did, sounding weak. She said she wasn't sure what was wrong with her and hoped to be back in school soon.

By the time SuAnne had recovered enough to return to the team, the Lady Thorpes had lost a lot of games. She played well in several games toward the end of the fall and again was selected for the all–South Dakota team; but this year Red Cloud beat Pine Ridge, and the Lady Thorpes did not advance to the play-offs.

With SuAnne's illness, a certain darkness enters her story. Chick has said that she does not think SuAnne was ever a hundred percent well again. This darkness often lifted, and SuAnne went on to other triumphs; but somehow from then on it was always there. At a distance, one can understand why SuAnne might have been a bit unhappy and confused at this point in her life. After the excitement of the championship had worn off, her fame perhaps became as uncomfortable for her as it was large. People who remember her often talk about how down-to-earth and unassuming SuAnne always was—how she took time for the younger kids who followed her around, how she acted no differently than she ever had, how she hung out with her friends just as before. Perhaps such self-effacement was a strain sometimes. No society is more egalitarian than the Oglala, and SuAnne had encountered one of its contradictions: how can a person always act just like everybody else when, as it happens, she's not?

Until then SuAnne had always been the kid sister, the youngster on the team. With the departure of senior stars like Doni De Cory and Rita Bad Bear, she became the leader looked up to by the younger girls. Perhaps as she got older and observed the Pine Ridge world from the higher vantage point of her fame, she could see just how big were the divisions she had miraculously bridged. Reservation enmities generations old had been set aside in admiration of her; what if people expected her to accomplish this reconciliation again and again? Also, she certainly had heard the old people say that no Pine Ridge basketball star had ever gone on to any big-time success in the sport beyond high school, and that she, SuAnne, would finally be the one. Such pressures might rattle anybody, let alone a sixteen-year-old girl.

As I went around talking to people about SuAnne, I sometimes stopped at Aurelia's house to see my friend Le, or I passed him along the highway and gave him a ride. My interest in SuAnne, when I mentioned it to him, seemed to make him morose and sour. He said a few disparaging things about Chick Big Crow and the SuAnne Big Crow Center, but I paid them little mind. Then one day when I visited him he was about three-quarters' drunk and he quickly cut short my latest revelation about SuAnne. "You know, that SuAnne Big Crow was a big hypocrite," he said. "All that stuff about how she didn't touch drugs or alcohol was a lie. She was a wild kid and she loved to party, and she drank whiskey and smoked marijuana all the time. That whole Big Crow Center is built on a lie." I asked him how he knew this, and he said a niece of his had gone to school with SuAnne and had often told him that she had seen SuAnne partying and that this niece had partied with her herself.

The news depressed me to a standstill. I left Le at Aurelia's house and drove away dejectedly. I didn't know whether to believe him, as I often don't, but I hated to hear him say this all the same. I remained in the dumps for a while. In Pine Ridge one afternoon I happened to run into the niece he had referred to, and I told her what Le had said. She said, "Where does Leonard *get* that stuff? I didn't go to school with SuAnne—I'm five years older than she was—and I never saw her drink or do drugs, and no one ever told me that she did. I didn't even know SuAnne. Why does Leonard say stuff like that about me?"

When SuAnne talked about the reservation, people recall, she sometimes used the metaphor of the basket of crabs. It's a common metaphor on Pine Ridge. She said that the reservation is like a bunch of crabs reaching and struggling to get out of the bottom of a basket, and whenever one of them manages to get a hold and pull himself up the side, the other crabs in their reaching and struggling grab him and pull him back down. The metaphor could apply, no doubt, to many places nearly as poor and lacking in opportunity as Pine Ridge. But somehow it seems even more true here—Oglala society is at once infatuated by and deeply at odds with fame. It creates heroes and tears them down almost simultaneously, as leaders from Red Cloud to Dick Wilson have learned. Perhaps the explanation for this has to do with the Oglala's free-and-equal view of how people are supposed to be, combined with the general distress the culture has undergone. But if the cause is unknowable, the result is usually quite clear: the Pine Ridge Reservation is not a comfortable place to be famous in for longer than a week or two.

The question of where SuAnne would go to college loomed. One of her life's ambitions was to play college basketball at a Division I school. Lots of colleges wanted her, and she had begun to hear from them even before her junior year. As a star athlete and the best student in her class, she qualified for full scholarship assistance at many places. Columbia University in New York City pursued her, offering to fly her and her mother there so she could see the school and meet the coaches. The Air Force Academy, the University of Montana, Penn State, the University of Colorado—sometimes two or three coaches called her house in an evening. SuAnne did most of the negotiating herself. She would put one coach on hold and then talk to the next; she seemed to enjoy bantering with them and asking what they could offer her. Big manila envelopes of promotional material from college sports programs began arriving in the mail. In the end she never actually got around to visiting any faraway schools, though, because the more she thought about it, the less she was sure that she wanted to be so far from home. She often talked on the telephone to Doni De Cory about what she should do. Doni was at Brigham Young University in Utah and feeling homesick herself. Chick inclined toward advising SuAnne to choose a school close by. SuAnne told Coach Zimiga that she couldn't imagine playing basketball where her mother and sisters and friends couldn't always watch her play. She asked him what people would think if she decided to go to college in South Dakota. He said she should not worry about what people thought, she should worry what she thought.

She was seventeen years old and still had not gone out on a date. Evenings when she wasn't at some sport or activity she spent at home, doing schoolwork or playing board games with her family. A group that wanted to stop kids on the reservation from using drugs and alcohol paid for her to go to Chicago and make a video to be shown on local TV. SuAnne had never given a speech to a camera before, and as she argued her anti-drug and -alcohol views, her face appeared rigid and ill at ease, so unlike its vivacity in films where she did not notice she was being watched. For a similar campaign she made a film in which she pretended to be a drunk. This film, which was never finished, shows her sitting on a chunk of rock before the Longhorn Saloon in Scenic swilling on a wine jug (empty) and saying, "I was once state champion!" In an outtake, she nearly falls over and then comes up giggling—the effect is of a death-defying kind of fooling around. Though the trip to Europe the year before must have been scary to remember, she again joined the Native American girls' all-star team the summer after her junior year. This time the team toured Australia and New Zealand, and she did not get sick there.

I know only a few details about the trouble SuAnne got from people on the reservation who didn't like her. Friends say that kids sometimes yelled insults at her and spread rumors and threatened to beat her up, and that two or three large families were very anti-SuAnne. This hostility saddened her; she didn't know what to do about it. Some of the problem seemed to come from the rivalry between the two high schools, Pine Ridge and Red Cloud. Some of her most persistent enemies were Red Cloud girls. In the early fall of SuAnne's senior year, a conflict with Red Cloud kids that had been going on for a while led to a fistfight that ended with several combatants, including SuAnne, in the tribal jail.

The fight started one Thursday evening by the gas pumps at Big Bat's. SuAnne's friend and cousin Angie Big Crow and a Red Cloud girl got into an argument, yelling back and forth, and then suddenly began to fight. They were punching hard and ripping at each other's clothes. Angie ripped off the other girl's shirt and the girl continued to fight just in her bra. Angie stopped fighting for a moment to let her put her shirt back on, and then they went to slugging each other again. Inside the store Chick saw the fight, and she and SuAnne ran to break it up. Other Red Cloud kids piled out of a pickup and started yelling stuff at Chick, and SuAnne went after them, and a general brawl ensued. The tribal police came and got into it, stopping one group of battlers only to have the fighting break out someplace else. The police arrested SuAnne and Angie and the kids they were fighting with and charged them all with disorderly conduct. (Chick later was also charged, with assaulting a minor.) They put the kids in jail, SuAnne and Angie in the same cell. The two had a long wait before their parents could get them out, so to kill time, they ran through their cheerleading cheers.

In the aftermath, nothing came of the fight. All the charges were dropped eventually, and no one had been seriously hurt. Angie Big Crow got a black eye, of which she was very proud the next morning in school. She later came to be on cordial terms with the girl she had fought. The girl told Angie that for such a skinny kid, she fought good. SuAnne showed no ill effects of the brawl when she appeared as her school's Homecoming Queen during half time at the football game a week or two later. She wore a ruffled red dress and a black sequinned top and a tiara in her hair as she stood smiling beside the Homecoming King, Charlie Campos, a longtime friend. Her fight, the only one she ever got into, can be dismissed as the kind of minor scuffle that tribal police deal with often. And yet it has endured as a marker on SuAnne's timeline: The Fight at Big Bat's. Like her illness, in retrospect it takes on the exaggerated darkness of a bad omen. To people for whom she was a hero, the fight was an unscripted event, out of character for SuAnne, one that should never have occurred.

SuAnne played a full season of basketball her senior year and did well. She averaged thirty-nine points a game and again made the all-state team, and Pine Ridge lost only twice. Unhappily, both those losses were to Red Cloud, who beat Pine Ridge by three points in the all-Indian tournament and again by three in the district play-offs. None of the starting players from Pine Ridge's '89 championship team besides SuAnne remained, and the Lady Thorpes no longer had as much depth as Red Cloud. Late in the season the team went to an invitational tournament, where they gave a drubbing to their old foe Milbank as SuAnne scored forty-three points. After that game, as Milbank's Coach Bergquist recalled, he had his last conversation with SuAnne.

Many memories people have of SuAnne her senior year involve "last times." For Christmas that year SuAnne gave presents to everyone she knew. Some of the presents were big and some small, but she made sure to include everyone, even if the present came from the dollar store. She gave her mother a necklace with three gold shoes for pendants, each shoe engraved with the name of her or her sisters and each set with the appropriate birthstone. Toward the end of her Christmas shopping she ran out of money and was hurrying from the house of one friend and another to borrow coupons for last-minute gifts from the grocery store. When people asked her about plans for the future, she often answered vaguely. Her mother asked if she would like a car for graduation, but SuAnne said she didn't think she'd need one. A chance came up for her to go to Spain the following year but she said she would not be going. If later circumstances had been different, remarks like these would have been forgotten.

Just before Christmas SuAnne received a letter from a medicine man who told her that she was a holy person of great importance to the future of her tribe. She told her mother what the letter said, and added that it upset her to think of herself that way. She tore the letter up and threw it out.

That year the Pine Ridge cheerleaders had been invited to take part in another half-time show at a college football bowl game—the Fiesta Bowl, in Tempe, Arizona, over New Year's. After Christmas the girls made the long drive from Pine Ridge in two cars with Jeanne Horse and Wes Whirlwind Horse, a Pine Ridge High School administrator. The traveling was long, the expense money tight, and the group uncongenial, and the trip did not succeed as well as the one a few years before to Hawaii. The kids had no opportunity to sightsee, and rehearsed or stayed in the hotel almost the whole time. In the show they joined a cast of hundreds doing dance routines in the background behind the main star, singer Merrill Osmond. (They thought it strange to be performing again with an Osmond Brother.) The show's theme was "The Year of the Child," and Merrill Osmond surrounded himself on the stage with elementary school kids of many races, including a lot of Indian kids from the Navajo reservation. SuAnne told Jeanne Horse that the way he used the kids, especially the Indian kids, gave her the creeps. On the way to a Fiesta Bowl banquet, SuAnne left one of the memorable images of herself on video. She is walking up some stairs in the hotel wearing a peach-colored silk dress. The camera (held by someone in the Pine Ridge party) is following close behind. All at once SuAnne stops, checks over her shoulder, flips up the back of her dress, and accurately moons the camera. Then she laughs goofily and continues up the stairs.

A teacher at Pine Ridge High School, Harvey Nelson, died unexpectedly of a heart attack that January. He was only in his forties and had been a popular teacher and was well liked in the town. The school held a memorial assembly for him. His death was a shock, and students and teachers talked a lot about it afterward. On the team bus coming back from a volleyball game in Edgemont, South Dakota, SuAnne and the other girls on the volleyball team were remembering him, discussing his death and his funeral. The talk turned to funerals in general, then to imagining what their own funerals would be like. SuAnne said that if she died everyone in town would go to her funeral, and that they'd announce her death on the radio, and that she would have a funeral procession through town that was hundreds of cars long. She wasn't sad as she said this—she seemed to get a kick out of picturing it, as teenagers in particular sometimes do. She said that if she died tomorrow she'd die a virgin and would be buried in a coffin of pure white.

In February, SuAnne and her mother planned to go to Huron, South Dakota, for the Miss Basketball in South Dakota award banquet. The award is the state's most prestigious for girls' basketball, and SuAnne was one of the nominees. The day before the banquet she talked to Doni De Cory on the telephone. She said again how sad she was about the jealousy on the reservation, how tired she was of it. Doni told her that nothing people could say could take away what she'd accomplished. Doni said she thought SuAnne would win the Miss Basketball award. SuAnne said she hoped she could come up with a good acceptance speech if she did. They talked a while longer, told each other they loved each other, and hung up.

SuAnne had her first-ever real date that evening, with a boy named Justin, the quarterback on the Pine Ridge High School football team. SuAnne usually never talked much about boys, but she had been mentioning Justin's name a lot since New Year's. He was a sophomore, two years younger than she. She asked her mother to cook something for her so she could have dinner beforehand; she said, "If he sees how much I eat, he'll never ask me out again." Justin picked her up at six and took her to dinner at Pizza Hut in Chadron, and then to a movie. SuAnne got home about eleven. Her mother was just leaving for her job at the tribal Department of Public Safety. Through a scheduling mix-up at Public Safety, Chick had to work the night shift at the police dispatch desk. She did not want to, knowing that she had to travel the next day, but agreed to relieve a dispatcher who had already put in three shifts straight. SuAnne was excited about her date and about the upcoming banquet, and she couldn't sleep. She called Chick at work; they talked at about two in the morning, and SuAnne didn't get to sleep until after that.

The day was Sunday, February 9, 1992. Chick came home from work, she and SuAnne had breakfast, and they set out on the 300-mile trip to Huron. A friend had told them he could drive them, but at the last minute he called to say that something had come up and he wouldn't be able to. SuAnne and Chick took Pigeon's car, a blue '91 Oldsmobile Cutlass Calais. Chick drove. They headed east from Pine Ridge on Highway 18 for about forty-five miles, then turned onto state Route 73 going north. At the town of Kadoka, Route 73 meets Interstate 90. Chick pulled over in Kadoka at a convenience store with a big statue of a bull out front and went in to get SuAnne a snack of chicken gizzards. SuAnne liked the gizzards at that place and said they always gave you a lot of them. She had been asleep, but when Chick returned she was sitting in the driver's seat. She told her mother she would drive and Chick could sleep now. SuAnne knew Chick was tired after working all night. Chick asked her if she was sure she wasn't too tired and SuAnne said she wasn't.

She turned onto the interstate eastbound. Chick pushed the passenger seat back into its reclining position and began to doze. She woke once or twice to see if SuAnne was getting tired, but SuAnne told her to go back to sleep, she was fine. They passed several exits for small South Dakota towns—Belvidere, Midland, Okaton. The road was straight and monotonous, unenlivened even by the billboards for Wall Drug that pester the westbound lanes. The sky was overcast, the weather calm. She was going about sixty miles an hour. About six miles past the exit for the town of Murdo, on a long, gradual upgrade, she apparently fell asleep. The car went off the road to the right and hit a delineator post. When SuAnne tried to correct the swerve and get back on the pavement, the car rolled over in the right-hand lane, then rolled a second time into the median strip. As per Pine Ridge custom, neither SuAnne nor her mother had her seat belt on. The driver's-side door came open as the car rolled, and SuAnne was flung from it. She landed in the median strip twenty or thirty feet from the upside-down car.

The accident occurred at about 11:40 in the morning. A state highway patrol car reached the scene seven minutes later, and ambulances arrived a few minutes after that. Chick had cuts and other minor injuries, but was conscious. She could hear people saying that she must be in shock, and she wanted to tell them that she wasn't, but somehow she couldn't talk. Paramedics were working on SuAnne. She had severe head injuries and was unconscious. The police told Chick they were taking SuAnne in the first ambulance and that the second one would carry her. Chick agreed to this, not really understanding what they meant. Both ambulances drove to St. Mary's Hospital in Pierre, about forty-five miles away. Doctors at St. Mary's examined SuAnne's injuries, then decided she should be flown immediately by helicopter to a bigger hospital in Sioux Falls. Before they could get her on the helicopter, at 3:35 that afternoon, she died.

I could try to describe the sorrow—the telephones ringing all across the reservation and across the state, the calls that poured in by the hundreds to KILI radio, the people driving disconsolately around Pine

Ridge village and stopping each other and having nothing to say, the weeping of men whom no one had ever seen weep before, the arrival of SuAnne's body in the early-morning hours of Monday at the Pine Ridge funeral parlor, the crowd that was there to meet it, the wake on Tuesday night in the Pine Ridge High School gym, the funeral the next morning, the basketball net Coach Zimiga put in her coffin, the military honors which a contingent of Pine Ridge war veterans awarded her, the farewell salute fired over her grave, and on and on—but knowing SuAnne's dislike for the tragedy-at-Pine-Ridge genre, I hesitate. The truth is, I can hardly bear to imagine it all.

As SuAnne had predicted just a week or two before, the line of cars in her funeral procession stretched for miles. People said there were more cars than had followed the bus into town after the '89 championship game. Also as she had predicted, her coffin was white. The governor of South Dakota sent his condolences, the state legislature held a moment of silence in her honor, and schools and tribal offices in Pine Ridge closed for the day. Lakota singers composed memorial songs, KILI radio played over five hundred requests in her honor. High school teams from the reservation and elsewhere that SuAnne had played against sent representatives. In a town that had seen too many funerals, nobody could recall a funeral as big as hers.

Jeanne Horse said later, "So much happened then, it was like a daze. I remember it in pieces. But I'll never forget that Monday morning, the morning after SuAnne died, when they got all the kids together in the high school gym for an assembly and a memorial. School attendance was almost perfect that day. When I arrived, the gym was already full, and what stays in my mind is the sound I heard as I walked in—the sound of all those kids in the gym crying."

Chick Big Crow never went back to work for the Department of Public Safety. Aside from attending the funeral, she stayed in her house day after day. Family members and friends took turns staying with her, because they did not want her to be by herself. She said little and emotionally more or less shut down. She had been raised a Catholic but could not see much purpose to her faith now. When she thought of it, she also remembered the hostility people harbored for SuAnne at the

Catholic Red Cloud School. Soon after SuAnne's death, medicine men started coming by to visit Chick. One in particular, Chauncy Yellow Horse, told her that the spirits had told him that it would be his job to comfort her. Chauncy Yellow Horse was living in a remote part of the reservation, but he said that she should not give him tobacco or blankets or even gas money, because his reward would come from the spirits.

Chauncy told her that in her grief she would often feel her soul start to slide away. Each time it did that, he said, the spirits would help it to return. He talked a lot about SuAnne, and what her purpose had been, and how her spirit had been with the tribe since a time far in the past. He said there was a purpose to her leaving and to Chick still being here. He took Chick to a traditional honoring ceremony called the Wiping of the Tears, held in a school gym in the little community of Cherry Creek. Chick resisted going and finally did only on impulse and at the last minute. The gym was packed with people, most of whom she didn't know. They sang honoring songs for SuAnne and for her, and they gave her gifts, and the elders whispered words of comfort and advice in her ear. Chick said later that if it hadn't been for Chauncy Yellow Horse she might have lain down and never gotten up again.

She wondered whether it made any sense to stay on in Pine Ridge. When she thought of the sadness here, and of the meanness and jealousy of so many people on the reservation, she considered packing up and moving away. She had no place in particular that she wanted to go—just away. Then one day something happened to change her mind. She tells the story often: "About a week after the funeral I was sitting in my kitchen in the afternoon. I was alone, for a change. I wasn't reading or watching TV or listening to the radio—just sitting there. It got to be late afternoon and darker outside, and I didn't even bother to stand up and turn on the light. Pretty soon it was almost completely dark. I heard someone knock on the door and I didn't care to answer it. The knock came again, and then two girls opened the door and walked in and came over to where I was. I remember what the girls looked like, but I'd never seen them before, and I've never seen them since that day. I had my head down on the kitchen table. I could feel their grief as they gave me a hug, and then they opened up my hand and put something in it. Then they left. After a while I finally got up and turned on the light and looked at the paper in my hand. It was a valentine—Valentine's Day had just passed—and on it were the words 'SuAnne was our hero. We loved her and we love you too.' "

The next day Chick decided what she wanted to do. SuAnne had often talked of an ideal place she called Happytown, where kids could go and hang out and have fun and not get in trouble. As her cousin Angie recalled, "Someday she was going to build Happytown, where nobody would fight or be jealous, where it would be clean, have a mall and lots of places for good fun. She was always making plans for her Happytown." Remembering her vision, Chick decided to build a place like that in Pine Ridge. In a few hours she had written out a statement of mission and a description of the facilities a Happytown would require. She envisioned a sizable space with recreation rooms, video games, a snack bar, trophy room, library, game room, computer room, and offices. When she called Rol Bradford and Jeanne Horse to tell them her idea, it was as if they had just been waiting for her to call. They came over to her house right away to discuss the plans with her. A day or two later her friend Tom Grey brought her a set of blueprints already drawn. Within a month Chick had set up the Visions of SuAnne Big Crow, Inc., as a nonprofit corporation to benefit Native American youth. Its board of directors included AIM people like Dennis Banks, along with former goons—the unexpected Pine Ridge coalition that SuAnne's appeal had helped to bring about.

Chick called tribal councilman G. Wayne Tapio and asked if the tribe had a building it wasn't using. A few days later he called back and said that she could have the old doll factory, a 6,000-square-foot space full of miscellaneous junk and old machinery. The tribe would lease it to her corporation, he said, for a dollar a year. At first a Pine Ridge group contested the claim to the building, but by May, Chick and her friends had it free and clear. They began by cleaning it out. The former factory had made small plastic Indian dolls to sell with the moccasins from another Pine Ridge factory, and there were lots of doll parts lying around, and hundreds of fifty-pound sacks of plastic pellets, and eight three-ton machines for melting the plastic down and molding it. People came with pickups and carted the sacks of pellets to the dump. In a single day a group of volunteers tackled the machines, heaving and skidding them across the floor on slicks of motor oil until they toppled them out the loading-bay doors. The tribe later sold them, and they were hauled away.

All summer, guys with carpentry skills donated their time to the Big Crow Center (as it was now being called), working mostly in the evenings and on weekends, putting up walls and remodeling the inside. People brought casseroles and hot dogs and crockpots full of beans for the workers. There was activity in the building at all hours, and electric saws buzzing at four-thirty in the morning sometimes. For Chick, the enthusiasm and the camaraderie were renewing. By mid-August most of the essential carpentry had been done.

Chick knew that the small donations that had carried the project so far would dwindle eventually and that she could expect no funding from the tribe. To succeed, the center would have to be able to support itself. Since the renovation began, there had always been food at the center; she and her sisters were good cooks; she decided that it made sense for the center to support itself with a restaurant. In those start-up days people joked that all Chick had to do when she needed something was reach up and pull it out of the air. Once, she mentioned in a meeting of the board that the center needed a hot water heater, and when they stepped out in the parking lot a local contractor was unloading a hot water heater for them from the back of his truck. Chick wanted a soda fountain for the restaurant and by chance came across a used one from an old drugstore at a small local auction. The auctioneer was trying to get rid of it and he let her have it for five dollars. Other fortunate purchases produced a counter, stools, tables, a refrigerator, a grill. The center opened the restaurant on September 1, 1992, and sold its first hamburger. The restaurant has remained open six or seven days a week ever since, serving hamburgers, sodas, ice cream, and daily specials like chicken and dumplings or meat loaf or chicken-fried steak or lasagna. In the summer tourist season it does a brisk business at lunch hour. The restaurant provided the essential income to keep the center running during lean times when bills were piling up and the power company was threatening to turn off the electricity.

During that first year a representative of the Boys' and Girls' Clubs of America who was visiting Pine Ridge stopped by the center and looked at the building and the plans. He said that he thought the center would be perfect as a member club in his organization. The center's board of directors liked the idea of a national affiliation, so they applied for a Boys' and Girls' Club charter. The Boys' and Girls' Clubs provide sports and recreation activities for kids six or seven to eighteen years old during vacation months and after school, and most of the clubs are in cities. About a year after applying, the Big Crow Center became the first chartered Boys' and Girls' Club on an Indian reservation. It served a membership of over a hundred kids its first year, and over three hundred kids the next. With mostly volunteer counselors it offered weekday and weekend programs for grade school and high school kids—softball, weightlifting, table tennis, crafts, games, and special events like Halloween hayrides and Christmas sing-alongs. Besides the regular members, many drop-ins came to the center, and it did not turn any well-behaved kid away. Since 1992, the center has served thousands of kids.

Early on, the center set down a strict set of rules for kids on the premises: No fighting, no speaking disrespectfully to peers or counselors, no drugs or alcohol, and no gang colors. The prevailing difficulty of the Pine Ridge surroundings has often slowed the center's progress. Although dues are fifteen dollars a year per member—a modest amount, given what many parents routinely spend on their kids—most parents of kids who attend pay no dues. (The notion that all services should be free runs deep among people on Pine Ridge.) The prohibition against gang colors and the center's unwillingness to be a hang-out spot for any one gang have limited to some extent the teens it can attract, because so many of the kids on Pine Ridge are in gangs. The no-drugs-or-alcohol rule, which also applies to counselors on or off the job, has made finding and keeping counselors and other workers much harder. Sometimes the center has no teen programs scheduled, due to lack of members or of counselors, or both. Teenage kids on Pine Ridge get into scrapes and violence and car wrecks all the time, and the teen suicides common on other reservations also occur far too frequently here. Despite a desire to reach the kids who most need its help, the center often does not succeed.

Yet the Big Crow Center, amazingly, has stayed in operation for seven years now with almost no funding assistance from anywhere. Not many people know that Pine Ridge has in fact produced a number of sound economic ventures in recent years, all of them unusual in that they received little or no help from the federal government or the tribe. Big Bat's Texaco is one; KILI Radio, the locally owned radio station, is another. *Indian Country Today*, an Indian-owned and -staffed newspaper with a national circulation and a reputation for good reporting and commentary out of Rapid City, began as *The Lakota Times* in Pine Ridge. The Big Crow Center, like these enterprises, has survived on its own against the daunting reservation odds.

"I've made many mistakes in what I've done here over the years," Chick Big Crow said to me recently. "I never followed up on a lot of ideas for improvements I had, I didn't acknowledge people who sent me donations, I let important matters slide sometimes. I tried to handle everything myself, from cooking in the restaurant to figuring out our computer system to managing the budget to mowing the softball field. I had a hard time delegating any job. Maybe I was trying to punish myself over guilt at SuAnne's death, maybe I was expressing a grief that I had never dealt with. I don't think I was really fitted to the job of running this place—I guess I had never even liked kids very much before. Looking back now, I see what I would have done differently, and what I'll do differently in the future. I've learned a lot—I've learned more from SuAnne than she did from me. But considering all my failings, I really believe it was the spirituality of this place that's kept it open, not me."

So much is so wrong on Pine Ridge. There's suffering and poverty and violence and alcoholism, and the aura of unstoppability that repeated misfortunes acquire. But beneath all that is something bigger and darker and harder to look at straight on. The only word for it, I'm afraid, is evil. News stories emphasizing the reservation's "bleakness" are actually using this as a circumlocution for that plain, terrible word. For journalistic reasons the news cannot say, "There is evil here." And beyond a doubt there is. A bloody history, bad luck, and deliberate malice have helped it along. Sometimes a sense of it comes over me so strongly that I want to run home to bed—for example, when I walk down the row of almost-new child-size bicycles in a local pawnshop, or when I see a bunch of people the police have recently evicted from White Clay staggering back to it, or when I'm driving on a deserted reservation road at night and there's a large object suddenly up ahead, and I skid to a stop a few feet from it, and it's the hulk of a car so completely incinerated that it has melted the asphalt around it; it's just sitting there with no warning, with no other cars on the scene, empty and destroyed and silent in the middle of nowhere. At such moments a sense of compound evil—that of the human heart, in league with the original darkness of this wild continent—curls around me like shoots of a fast-growing vine.

Good appears most vividly in resistance to its opposite; that's what heroism is about, after all. The more you see of Pine Ridge's bad side, the more you long for evidence of good, and the happier you are when you find it. Great good does exist here, too, in the lives of people who hold fast to it and serve their neighbors without much encouragement or reward, and in the steadfastness of the old Oglala culture that endures. Longing for the good here was what first drew me to SuAnne. You sense the good in the SuAnne Big Crow Center when you walk in the door. Usually the awareness takes a few minutes to register; it's like feeling the sun on your face when your eyes are closed, or suddenly realizing in a smoke-filled room that someone has opened a window somewhere.

Big Bat's Texaco welcomes strangers for commercial reasons, but the Big Crow Center welcomes them for spiritual ones. SuAnne's well-known openness to people in general has provided the model for an openhearted place. All kinds of people come wandering through the center; I often see passersby looking at the trophies and clippings on the walls and asking questions of the staff. Nowhere else in town do you see strangers in a contemplative mood. A life of bravery and generosity and victory and heroism was the founding inspiration here, and if SuAnne's death was a terrible sorrow, it also had the effect of holding the good she represented fixed and unchanged. SuAnne Big Crow, though gone forever, is unmistakably still around. The good of her life sustains this place with a power as intangible as gravity, and as real.

A while ago I visited the site on Interstate 90 where SuAnne and Chick's car accident occurred. I would not have taken the interstate otherwise; I was driving from Pine Ridge to Minneapolis and in no rush for time. The interstate highways that cross the plains do indeed have many monotonous stretches. The Plains were not meant to be seen this way—through a speeding windshield heading east or west—no matter how much the wide-open geography tempts you to think in terms of the farthest horizon and the straightest line. Droning along on the interstate you forget sometimes that you're on the Plains, or on a highway, or anywhere at all.

As I got closer to the crash site, I could easily imagine the danger of falling asleep at the wheel. In this part of the state the prairie is rolling, but the interstate travels a roadbed that is raised above the low places and so stays essentially level all the time. I had the state Department of Transportation accident report with me, and it said that the wreck had been at four-tenths of a mile west of the milepost numbered 200. After I passed the Murdo exit I began to look for the mileposts. The time of the year was June and the hour midday; the heat above the road was hazy with traffic exhaust. I went as slowly as I could get away with as trucks and cars came up behind me and whizzed by. About seven miles past Murdo I spotted the 199 post. Six-tenths of a mile beyond it I saw the fatality marker erected by the state. The right-hand shoulder descends in a long, rather steep grade here, and the fatality marker looked small down at the bottom of it next to the fence that runs along the highway. If I had been in the passing lane I could not have seen the marker at all, nor if I had been on the westbound side. Even going as slowly as I was, in a second it had disappeared behind me.

I understood better now how the accident might have occurred. SuAnne, waking when her drifting car hit the delineator post at the roadside, looked to her right and saw that long and steep decline. She then probably turned the wheel violently to avoid going down it, and the suddenness of her correction caused the car to overturn. As the accident site receded in my rearview, I wondered how I could get back to it. Then I noticed a small dirt lane running just the other side of the highway fence. I turned off the interstate at the next exit, found the lane, and went bumping slowly back along it in the direction I had come. It dead-ended at a little hollow filled with brush. I left the car and walked through tall grass along the highway fence to the fatality marker.

I had never visited a historic site on an interstate highway before. I climbed over the fence and examined the marker. Its grim slogans—X MARKS THE SPOT and DRIVE SAFELY and WHY DIE?—looked new, their lettering still unfaded by the sun. It was, of course, a distance from here to the pavement and median strip, the actual site of the crash. From the marker I walked up the long incline to the shoulder beside the eastbound lanes, where the continuous traffic was going by like a loud, sooty wind. The cars made a humming that expanded in the ear as they passed, and the trucks gave off a rising and falling whine. I walked along the shoulder trying to imagine: The car would have hit the post here, it would have rolled there, it would have ended up there. In a momentary break in the traffic I could almost see it—but then the cars and trucks again came rushing by. Each passing vehicle was like the swoop of an eraser on a blackboard, and millions of them, probably, had gone across this piece of highway since SuAnne died.

Occasionally a passing driver quickly turned his head to look at me. I wasn't hitchhiking, I wasn't walking, and no disabled car waited nearby, so my presence could not be explained. This simply was not a place for a person to be standing around. After a few minutes I walked back down the incline to the fatality marker and sat beside it in the grass out of sight of traffic. When I did, I noticed wildflowers—little megaphone-shaped blossoms of pale lavender on a ground vine, called creeping jenny hereabouts, and a three-petaled flower called spiderwort, with a long stem and long, narrow leaves. The spiderwort flowers were a deep royal blue. I had read that in former times the Sioux crushed spiderwort petals to make a blue jelly-like paint used to color moccasins. Mid-June must be these flowers' peak season; among the roadside grasses, lost hubcaps, and scattered gravel, the spiderwort and creeping jenny grew abundantly.

There are no historic markers by the sides of interstate highways. You find them by two-lane roads, but almost never by any roads that are bigger. Evidently history cannot exist at speeds above 55 miles an hour. Because I knew that no historic marker here would ever tell about SuAnne, I began to compose one in my head:

SUANNE BIG CROW

SuAnne Marie Big Crow, a star basketball player for Pine Ridge High School on the Pine Ridge Indian Reservation, died as a result of a car accident that occurred at this spot on February 9, 1992. Born in Pine Ridge village on March 15, 1974, she was a talented athlete who took up basketball as a young girl.

During her high school career she set two South Dakota high school records and was named to the state all-star team four years in a row. In 1989 she led Pine Ridge to the state Class A championship, scoring the winning basket in the last second of play. Known for her humor, determination, sportsmanship, and generosity, as well as for the quickness and grace of her game, SuAnne carried the pride of her Oglala tribe to basketball courts all around the state, and beyond. She is a daughter this state of South Dakota and this country are proud to claim.

On down the slope, across the corner of a wheatfield, was a grove of cottonwood trees. I climbed back over the highway fence and walked to it. Perhaps because of the rolling topography, I could hardly hear the traffic here. Just a couple of hundred yards away, the twenty-four-hour-a-day noise of the interstate had disappeared into its own dimension. The cottonwoods stood in a grove of eight or ten, all of them healthy and tall, around a small pool of clear water bordered with cattail reeds and dark-gray mud. Herons, ducks, raccoons, and deer had left their tracks in the mud not long before. From the cattails came the chirring song of red-winged blackbirds, a team whose colors no other team will ever improve on. Old crumpled orange-brown leaves covered the ground around the trees, and false morel mushrooms of a nearly identical shade grew in the crotches of the roots. The cottonwoods had appeared a deep green from the highway, but seen from underneath, their leaves were silvery against the blue sky. High above the trees bright white cumulus clouds piled one atop another. They went on and on, altitude upon altitude, getting smaller as they went, like knots on a rope ladder rising out of sight.

CHAPTER

15

Pine Ridge was Pine Ridge still. Its hard times, sadly, seemed to have no end; by phone and occasional visits I kept up with the news. Twelve people died as a result of alcohol-related car accidents on the reservation's roads in 1996, and seven in 1997, and at least five in 1998. Among the victims were a longtime teacher at Wolf Creek School and his grandchild, killed when a drunk driver ran into their car. Someone robbed the Taco John's take-out restaurant in Pine Ridge, and not long after that it burned to the ground. The tribal treasurer caused a commotion by buying a small herd of prize cattle with $200,000 of the tribe's money that people said should have been used to house the homeless. Later he had to resign. Former tribal officials sued current ones for various violations and crimes. The roads deteriorated to such a point that they were causing accidents themselves. In Oglala, some local teenage gang members tortured and killed a neighbor boy; FBI agents came and took them off to jail. Other Pine Ridge teenagers killed themselves. The regional bureau of the Indian Health Service reported that diabetes now affected over 50 percent of the adults on Pine Ridge, and declared the disease an epidemic there.

To make things worse, in June of '99 a tornado hit Oglala. It destroyed 160 buildings in the town and killed one man and left scores of people without homes, living in temporary shelters or camping in tents on the lots where their houses used to be. Government agencies hurried to rebuild or replace the houses and compensate the sufferers. A number of people whose houses the tornado had not touched damaged their houses themselves in the hope of qualifying for aid. In Pine Ridge village a group of protesters including reunited AIM veterans Russell Means and Dennis Banks said the government should pay attention not just to the tornado damage but to the violence done to Indians every day. To dramatize their anger at recent unexplained deaths of tribal members along the reservation's border with Nebraska, they led a march to the town of White Clay, where rioting soon began. People looted a store and set fires in it and threw rocks at fire trucks coming to put them out. The protest leaders promised marches every week until the mystery of the deaths was solved, the killers punished, and the liquor stores in White Clay shut down.

The tornado and the protests put Pine Ridge once again in the national news. Not long after the tornado, President Clinton came to Pine Ridge as part of a trip he was making across the country to draw attention to problems of poverty. He visited a woman who told him she had twenty-eight people living in her shack and trailer home. Outside Pine Ridge High School the President told the Oglala and other tribal leaders in attendance that the federal government would support economic revival in Indian country by providing tax credits for new business development. People were impressed that he had come –no President since F.D.R. had visited an Indian reservation—but no one got too excited about what he had to say.

Meanwhile, the teachers went on teaching, the school buses ran, the tribal casino on the western boundary of the reservation stayed open round the clock, the graduating classes at Oglala Lakota College kept growing, the crowds of summer visitors arrived as always for the sun dances, Big Bat expanded his operation with new stores in Chadron and Hot Springs, the doctors at the hospital kept delivering babies, and the annual August powwow was bigger than the one the year before.

And what of my friend Le?

I did not see much of Le for a while. I guess we were still kind of mad at each other. I know I was exasperated with him. On a couple of trips to the reservation I looked for him but did not find him. One time his sister Florence told me that he was staying over in White Clay, and that she had seen him on the street there so drunk he was blank. Another time Aurelia told me that he had been thrown in jail for disrupting the singing of the National Anthem at the Calico Community powwow. When I heard these reports I figured it was just as well I hadn't run into him. On the few occasions when we did get together he told me stories that were so wild and unverifiable I didn't know what to say. Then he'd repeat them, as if I hadn't appreciated them enough the first time.

Once when I was home Le called me collect and said he was going to tell me a story that he had never told anyone before. Then he went into a long description of a *yuwipi* ceremony his grandfather had held for him as a boy, during which a loud growling and a rank smell came into the cabin as the ceremony was going on, and then the door flew open and a bear walked in and put his paw on Le's chest, imparting to him the bear's power. The story went on from there, but I didn't listen closely, because I had heard it before. I only said, as I often do, "Wow!" In the next breath Le asked me to wire him some money. I told him that I couldn't, that my credit cards were limited out—a lie, but he sounded drunk and strange, and I didn't want to send him anything. He was silent. Then he told me that when I came back to the reservation not to look for him, because he didn't want to see me, and not to go around to see his sisters, either. Then he said that he would be dead in a few weeks and that I would never see him again.

When I was in Oglala a few months later I looked him up anyway. I found him staying at the house of the Porcupine boys, Sam and Gilmore. He greeted me as cheerfully as if our last conversation had not taken place. Though fall had arrived and a cold wind was blowing, he was walking around in just his shirtsleeves. He explained that he had gotten into a fight with some guys on the top of a nearby butte and in the course of the fight had lost his coat. I skeptically drove him to the butte he indicated and up a steep but navigable track to the top. To my surprise we immediately found his reading glasses on the ground and his glasses case and some folded-up prescription papers from his doctor a short distance away. But though we searched all over as Le told me about a UFO that had once landed there, we found no coat. I offered to give him the down coat I was wearing—it was old, and I had another in the car—but when he put it on, the sleeves came up to his elbows.

The next day I went to a clothing store in Chadron and looked through coats by the dozen until I found one I thought might fit him. It was a fleece-lined brown canvas Carhart coat, size 46 tall. I bought it and drove over to Oglala and took it to him at the Porcupines'. He tried it on and it fit exactly. Little in life is as satisfying as buying someone an article of clothing that really fits. After he had zipped it and buttoned it and shrugged the sleeves up and down for a while, he said, "You know, Wendy Cody and them were sayin' that you didn't want to see me that time we visited you, that you were tryin' to get rid of me. They said you never come around because you're not really my friend."

"Well, to be honest, Le, I wasn't very happy to see you that time. But that was mainly because you were drunk. I'm happy to see you otherwise."

"I can understand that. That's cool."

"And no matter what anybody says, I *am* your friend."

Over the following winter he and I talked often on the phone. He was staying at Bluch Fire Thunder's place out by the Oglala dam. He said someone had stolen his firewood, so he was burning old tires in his stove. When he went outside, he said, the chimney with the black smoke pouring from it looked like the smokestack of a train. I wired him money for firewood. In early spring he called with bad news: he had been diagnosed with prostate cancer. "I didn't react at all when the doctor told me," he said. "I just sort of shrugged and said, 'That's the way it goes, it's okay with me.' The doc was surprised; he said, 'You don't seem too upset.' I said, 'No, I'm actually glad. It gives me something to die of besides liver failure.' Those docs were all amazed at me. I had three different docs up there at the IHS hospital. One was a German woman, one was a Puerto Rican guy, and one was a Filipino guy. They had a conference with me, and I asked 'em, 'Tell me something—how come none of you doctors have American names?' They said, 'What do you mean, American names?' I said, 'You know, good American names, like Kills in Sight.' That made 'em laugh."

He said the doctors were sending him up to Rapid City Regional for a prostate biopsy, to be a hundred percent sure. I wired him money for the carfare. He could have been making all this up, but when he called me soon after, the details of the biopsy procedure he described were grisly and convincing. A few weeks after that he called to say he had received the biopsy results: they were negative. He didn't have prostate cancer after all. I shouted for joy.

In the late spring he told me I should come for the sun dance his younger sister Minerva planned to hold near Loneman. In July he announced that he would be one of the chefs at the big feast at the August powwow and that I should come down for that. But with work and family and summer company, I couldn't get away. I didn't have a chance to return to the reservation until that December, about two weeks before Christmas. I had never been to Pine Ridge around Christmas time. I wanted to see Le and Florence and Aurelia; also, Floyd John had just returned from a long stay at an alcohol rehab program in Wisconsin, and I hadn't seen him in almost two years. My wife bought a big ham for Florence and another one for Aurelia, and basketball-star Barbie dolls for Florence's granddaughters, and University of Montana T-shirts for her grandsons. I bought winter gloves for Le and Floyd John, and I supplied my wallet with twenties, always a useful denomination on the rez. The weather cooperated by being strangely warm and windy and clear. I loaded up the car and set out on an almost-hot afternoon.

I have visited the reservation in all seasons and in many personal moods, including foreboding, fear, and gloom. I know that the hopeful, big-sky feeling with which we often invest Western landscapes is at odds with the reality of life on Pine Ridge. And yet, despite the suffering there, again and again when I see the reservation it still looks grand to me. I came down Highway 79 from Rapid City early in the morning, noticing with surprise that this part of 79 had been widened to a more sensible four lanes. No longer did it give the impression that a serious wreck waited just up ahead; it was now well laid out and modern and safe. The eight crosses commemorating the Dismounts Thrice accident, however, still stood beside the road.

The sun had just come over the horizon as I turned off the highway at Hermosa and headed southeast on the two-lane road to Red Shirt Table and the reservation. The sky was a limpid blue, without a cloud. On the low buttes the shadows and the sunlight alternated like braiding, in long, horizontal sweeps. A pheasant stepped from the grass, set his white-ringed neck forward like a gearshift lever, and ran across the road. I passed the bridge over the Cheyenne River, the red-and-white sign with the Oglala flag announcing the boundary of the reservation, the village of Red Shirt. For some miles past Red Shirt the road was smooth and newly paved. Then, as it entered badland country, it got worse. The tribe had evidently torn up the pothole-riddled asphalt from before and simply graded over the rough surface beneath it. The morning sun left blue shadows in the washboard ruts.

Across the White River bridge and ahead on the horizon was the Loneman water tower. Then the elementary school, the tribal building, the intersection of Highway 18, and the wreath in memory of Wanda Kindle. I stopped and got out to look at it. Now it was decorated with Christmas ribbons and greenery, a large plastic snowflake, a white wooden cross, and a long-stemmed artificial red rose. I wanted to drop off the hams, so I swung by Florence's house—no one home. Then I decided to try Aurelia's, and on my way there I passed Le and Floyd John walking along the road. They didn't recognize me until I had pulled over and hit the brakes. I leaned across and opened the passenger door. Floyd John was wearing a black leather jacket, jeans, and cowboy boots. As he climbed into the back seat—accepting, as always, Le's natural right to the front—I asked how he was doing. He said, "How'm I doing? I'm myself, and I'm glad I am. I've got my self back. Been sober for ten months now." Le got in and shook my hand and closed the door. He had on an oil-stained brown down coat, jeans, tennis shoes, and a black felt cowboy hat with a bright red cord for a hatband. To my question, he replied, "Oh, I'm hangin' in there," as unsurprised as usual at seeing me.

I negotiated the long mud driveway to Aurelia's house almost without effort, remembering how challenging I used to find it. Now it seemed easy; I felt comfortable and oddly at home in this place I'd been to so often and thought so often about. Aurelia had left for her volunteer job at the Presbyterian child-care center, so Le led me into her house and we put the ham in her refrigerator. In her kitchen, I was suddenly so glad to see him I gave him a hug. It was kind of an awkward moment, but I think he was pleased. He said, "I'm glad to see you, too, bro." We got back in the car, and I told him and Floyd John that I'd never been to Pine Ridge at Christmas time before, that I'd wanted to see what the season was like here. "Seventy percent of the people on the reservation don't believe in Christmas," Le said. "I don't believe in it myself. It's something the priests wanted us to believe in, but we never did. Christmas ain't nothin' around here."

We were silent for a moment as we headed toward Oglala. Le told me to stop at the post office. As we pulled into the parking lot, Floyd John said, "Do you remember that song 'Grandmaw Got Run Over by a Reindeer'?" He began to sing:

> *"Grandmaw got run over by a reindeer*
> *[something something something] Christmas Eve.*
> *You may say there's no such thing as Santa,*
> *But as for me and Grandpaw, we believe."*

Le introduced me to the new postmaster, a young man named Kelly who asked me if Le was really as famous as he said he was. I said, "Oh, even more." Le checked his mailbox. It contained an eight-page newsprint circular for the Sioux Nation supermarket in Pine Ridge advertising holiday specials on baking supplies, self-basting turkeys, stuffing mix, and dinner rolls. He immediately threw it in the wastebasket, where it joined a growing pile. Floyd John opened his box and found a letter from a woman he knows in Germany and a Christmas card from a pawnshop in Hot Springs, South Dakota, thanking him for his patronage that year.

As it happened, Le and Floyd John had been on their way to another pawnshop that morning—the one in White Clay, where they planned to exchange Le's black felt cowboy hat and Floyd John's Walkman for money with which to buy a part they needed to repair Floyd John's car. Instead of going to White Clay, we now went directly to Pronto Auto Parts in Pine Ridge, where I exchanged two of my twenties for the part Floyd John needed and another part Le said he needed for a car of his and five quarts of transmission fluid. Outside, Le and Floyd John had a conversation in Sioux with an old man with a big nose and striped suspenders. They got back in the car laughing. "That was Raymond Pipe on Head," Le said. "Ray's a Korean War vet, and he's always kiddin' with Floyd John about the Army and him bein' in Vietnam. Just now Ray was sayin', 'I heard they had to discharge you from the service in Vietnam because you were eatin' up all the monkeys and snakes over there.' He told Floyd, 'When you started in on eatin' the *rare* and *endangered* ones, that's when they knew they had to get rid of you.' "

Floyd John's car, a Chevy Celebrity, was parked under the cottonwoods by Aurelia's place. We worked on it there all morning and into the afternoon. Le pointed out that I actually did not do much of the work myself, but I replied that I had watched so closely that I felt as if I had. The car's problem involved the right front axle. This axle, or transaxle, as it's called, connects to the transmission through a seal called the transaxle seal, a rubber-lined metal ring about two inches across which keeps the transmission fluid from leaking out. The Celebrity's transaxle seal had broken, causing a potentially disastrous leak. Le and Floyd John now had to jack up the car, remove the right front tire, remove the transaxle, remove the broken transaxle seal, install the new seal, and then put the transaxle and the wheel back on.

"We just replaced that transaxle a few days ago," Le said. "It give out when we were driving up in Rapid, so we hitched back down here, took a transaxle off a junker we knew about, put it in a rip-stop parachute bag of Floyd's, hitched back up to Rapid, took off the busted one, put in the good one, and drove the car back here. Only thing was, we didn't know that seal was shot, too. We had to keep stopping and putting in new transmission fluid. Between here and Rapid we went through twelve quarts.

"Our cousin Leon Long Soldier helped us with the mechanic work up in Rapid. Leon's pretty good at fixing cars. He had just gotten out of jail the day before. They had him down in Nebraska for vehicular homicide, but then they dropped the charges. What happened was, Leon was coming back from taking his dad to the doctor in Scottsbluff and he was driving really fast up Highway 87 between Rushville and White Clay, and all of a sudden he heard this *bump blam*—he run over something in the road. He thought he'd hit a deer, but when he went back to look he saw it was a man. He checked the guy and the guy was dead. So Leon came on to Pine Ridge and told the police, and they called the Dawes County sheriff in Nebraska, and the sheriff checked it out and found the dead guy, and then he came to Pine Ridge and arrested Leon. Leon was in jail for a few days before the highway patrol investigators went over the accident scene and found out that the guy had also been run over by someone else in the ditch beside the road.

They asked the coroner to determine the time of death, and it turned out the guy had been dead by the time Leon ran over him. I guess someone had run him over in the ditch, and then he had climbed up to the road and finally died there. But it ain't a crime to run over a dead body, so they had to let Leon go."

Floyd John borrowed the screw jack from my Blazer and got to work. He was under the car wrenching and hammering, while Le fetched tools and offered advice. They had to lift up the axle even farther to get some bolts out, and Le found a metal fence post to use as a lever. When it didn't work, he found a four-by-four wooden beam about six feet long, and that did the job. He was telling stories about his bull-riding days, such as the one about the bull nobody had ever ridden before—how he drew the bull in a big rodeo, and how he rode him for the full eight seconds and more, and how he finally jumped off, and how the bull then walked over to Le in front of the whole arena and bent his foreleg and bowed down to him. Le laughed. "I told that story the other day to a young guy and his girlfriend who gave me a ride from Pine Ridge. After I said that the bull bowed down to me, the guy asked, 'Did he *really*?' His girlfriend got mad at him and slugged him on the arm. She said, 'Don't you know Indian bullshit when you hear it?' "

At lunchtime Le went in the house and brought me out a sandwich made of a quarter-inch-thick slice of bologna on white bread with lots of mayonnaise. The sandwich had a few faint thumbprints of oil on it but was tasty anyway. I sat on an upended stove log in the sun and looked at the stuff in the yard—an armchair, a pink plastic bottle in the shape of a baby's shoe, a pile of shingles, an old-fashioned TV antenna, beer cans, a rusting John Deere swather. Across the open field to the east, a flock of pheasants flew low and almost in a straight line. I counted twelve of them. Le took a 12-volt auto battery from the trunk of the Celebrity and sat down cross-legged by it on the ground and began to clean the battery posts with a rag. On his back under the car, Floyd John wrenched and tapped. At the side of the house, Gunner, the dog, growled away at a section of deer ribs Le had thrown her. Two kittens, one yellow and one black, chased each other around. A warm wind blew. For a moment, we might have been sitting in front of a tipi in an Oglala camp along the North Platte River 150 years ago, braiding lariats and making arrows and gazing off across the Plains.

• • •

As usual, I spent the nights in a motel in Chadron, Nebraska. The thirty-two miles from Oglala to Chadron via the back road has become one of my favorite Western drives. The Budweiser cans and bottles and cases that sometimes litter it, and its occasional stretches of broken pavement, make it a road not to daydream on. But being alert helps you appreciate its scenery better, too. For miles its talc-colored track of dusty gravel stretches ahead through unfenced grasslands. I've seen many hawks on phone poles along the road or in the sky, and antelopes grazing, and a coyote loping across a field. The prairie grasses in winter turn a pale ginger-brown just the color of antelopes, and the leafless cottonwoods and willows in the creek bottoms are coyote-fur gray. The big cottonwoods standing here and there by themselves in the fields lose every leaf in winter, and then you can see how contorted their branches really are; they look as if they had decided never to grow leaves again and were tormented by the decision. Once, in the sky just west of the road I saw, two hundred or three hundred feet up, a bald eagle holding almost motionless. The white band of its tail was visible when it turned, and gently turned again. It flew offhandedly, with careless, recreational ease, the way a winged human might fly.

If I didn't take the back road but went the long way via Highways 18 and 385, I would pass the Prairie Wind Casino. The tribe built this casino on the reservation's western edge just thirteen miles from a highway—U.S. 385—which may someday be part of a major interstate running north and south to connect Interstates 80 and 90. If such an interstate is ever built, the tribe hopes it will bring lots of gamblers to this admittedly remote place. Sometimes when I went by Prairie Wind, its lights glowing in the empty Plains darkness reminded me of a military installation, or an oil-drilling rig from the former days of the energy boom. One night, out of curiosity, I stopped at the casino and played the nickel video-poker machines until nearly dawn. Until about midnight the casino was a mixed crowd of Indians and white-haired white people. Rumors of big payouts occasionally ran through the room. The slot machines were chiming their bells and their little signifying noises, with the frequent louder jingling of the *"Ahhh-le-luia!"* sound indicating a jackpot. A country-rock tape played hour after hour until it and the *"Ahhh-le-luia!"* sound chafed the mind.

By three in the morning I had lost twenty or thirty dollars in nickels. Besides me, only two other people were still gambling. Oglala employees in white shirts, black vests, and black bow ties idly dusted the tops of the slot machines. A young security guard hunched on a stool with his hands in his pockets and his heels hooked on a middle rung. At about 4:30 I went out in the parking lot and sat in my car. My hands smelled like coins, and cigarette smoke saturated my clothes. The prairie wind—the actual version—made the light poles shudder and caused shadows to shudder on the gravelly ground. Two reservation dogs came sore-footing along and got up on their hind legs to check the trash barrels by the casino's main entrance. A truck from a uniform and linen supply place pulled up, and the dogs sore-footed away. Beyond the casino's lighted oasis, no lights were visible anywhere.

Also as usual, at the first opportunity I stopped in at the Big Crow Center. What with all the time I'd spent there, Chick Big Crow and I had gotten to know each other and had become friends. I like her a lot, and I like her sisters and her daughters and her nieces. Chick talks in a small, quiet, and reasonable voice that can sometimes really make me laugh. Once she was talking about Dennis Banks and another Indian leader, and she said, in her quiet and reasonable voice, "Dennis Banks is a serious person who really cares about the Native community, but [So-and-so] is apparently just a stark raving lunatic." I laughed at this for about half an hour.

I found Chick sitting at her desk in her office and talking to her sister Mary Iron Cloud. Chick's hair was in a new shag cut with reddish tints and she had on a white blouse and a holly-leaf lapel pin. Someone had given her a talking Christmas tree about a foot and a half high which sometimes threw back its top to reveal a large mouth that said, "Merry Christmas! Ho ho ho!" in a loud mechanical voice. This happened unpredictably, causing everybody to jump. Chick was in a good mood. A friend of the center who works for the Ford Motor Company in Detroit had persuaded his bosses to give the center a brand-new heavy-duty twelve-passenger van, and Chick was due to go to a Ford dealer in Rapid City and pick it up the following day.

Kids and parents and counselors came and went past Chick's open office door as we talked. Two young Mormon men in white shirts and narrow ties who were volunteering leaned in the door to tell Chick good night and that they would see her tomorrow. A hefty Oglala woman marched past, followed closely by a boy and three tall Oglala men, and Chick said, "Would you excuse me for a moment, please?" and hurried after them. A few minutes later the party marched back out, and Chick returned. "That little boy called one of the counselors here a bitch, and the counselor told him he had to leave, and the boy went home and told his family, and they came back here to beat up the counselor. I talked to them in a polite and calm way and explained the rules. Fortunately, they left without a fight. And after all that, I can tell you for sure that the boy will be back here tomorrow."

Chick and Mary Iron Cloud were talking about a cousin, Richard Big Crow, who had just died. They said that they would combine a memorial for him with the graveside memorial they had every Christmas time for SuAnne. Mary Iron Cloud went home. Chick said that she was going out to the cemetery to put up Christmas lights around SuAnne's grave, and asked if I would like to come with her and help. I said sure. We got in her green Pontiac Grand Am and drove east from Pine Ridge about seven miles, then turned off at a dirt road. The cemetery, St. Anne's, is about half a mile down the road, behind a white wooden fence with a gate. We opened the trunk of Chick's car and took out boxes and boxes of Christmas lights. Some were those new icicle lights, the kind with many little white bulbs on strands that hang down from a central line like teeth on a comb. They took a lot of untangling. We plugged strings of lights together and draped them on the cemetery's few small pines and duct-taped them to the sides of SuAnne's headstone and stapled them along the cemetery fence's top rail with a stapling gun. Lots of Big Crows were buried here. We moved gingerly among the graves with our lights and extension cords.

One grave was a mound of fresh earth covered with windblown floral wreaths and bouquets. Chick said that was Richard Big Crow's grave. Something in her and Mary's conversation had made me curious, so I asked, "Was he run over on the road between Rushville and White Clay?"

"Yes, someone beat him up outside a bar in Rushville, and then I think they later ran him over in the ditch beside the road. He was only nineteen years old."

I didn't mention the story Le had told me about his cousin Leon. Still, I thought about the coincidence, and about how entwined with each other people are here. When we had finished hanging all the lights, we plugged them into the main cable leading from a box on the phone pole across the road. They lit up in a widely distributed multitude, brilliant in the twilight. "I think we need more," Chick said after considering them for a while. "It seems to me we had more of them last year."

The red sunset made a black silhouette of the house on the rise to the west, and of the basketball backboard and post beside it. A white horse was grazing along the cemetery fence. Its teeth pulled up a tuft of weeds with a dull snapping noise. Chick crossed her arms and shrugged her jacket more closely around her against the evening breeze. "At least this year it wasn't ten below out here when we put the lights up, the way it's been sometimes. There's been Decembers when we could only do this for a few minutes at a time between spells of warming up in the car. One Christmas Eve I came out here by myself and sat on that little bench by SuAnne's grave, and I fell asleep, and when I woke up it was late at night. I got chilled clear through, and I caught pneumonia, and I was sick for weeks afterward."

I knew that Florence had dialysis treatments on Mondays, Wednesdays, and Fridays, so on a Tuesday morning I went to her house to drop off the Christmas presents and the ham. She was home, making fry bread to take to a church event that evening and minding her grandchildren. Her fifteen-year-old grandson, E.J., had the day off from Red Cloud School because one of his classmates had shot herself and today was the funeral. Florence's five-year-old granddaughter, RaeDawn, was waiting for a van to take her to preschool. Florence cleared some breakfast plates from the kitchen table and made me a place to sit, and she gave me a cup of black coffee. The Sioux word for coffee is *pejuta sapa*, which means black medicine, and most of the coffee I've had on the reservation fits the description. A few sips set my heart pounding.

As Florence worked she told me what she knew about the girl who had shot herself, and she gave me the latest news about her own health and especially about a kidney transplant she might possibly receive from her son Willie, who's in prison. She also talked about her grandfather Woz'aglai, and how much he hated to see people drinking, and how he used to whack her father, Asa, with his cane when Asa came home drunk, and how Woz'aglai used to say, "Don't go near that town of Pine Ridge, it'll get you drunk! All you have to do is stand on the hill over Pine Ridge and breathe that Pine Ridge air, and you'll get drunk!" Meanwhile, she made a lot of fry bread. Fry bread is sort of like a glazed doughnut without the hole in the middle or the sugar glaze. Florence had a big blue plastic tub of dough beside her; first she took a double handful of dough, rolled it flat with a rolling pin on a floured place on the Formica countertop, cut it into trapezoidal pieces about the size of a small paperback, scored each piece in the middle with a knife, and dropped the pieces into an iron skillet full of bubbling lard. After the pieces had been in the skillet for a minute or two, she turned them with a long-handled fork. They puffed up and soon got golden brown on both sides. One at a time she took the pieces out and set them in an enamel colander to drain, and then she took the pieces from the colander and laid them gently one atop another in a big cardboard box. She gave me some fry bread to try. Freshly made fry bread and black coffee is the most delicious breakfast you can have. Fry bread cooked in lard tastes even better than it is bad for you, which is saying a lot.

RaeDawn, a sturdy little girl with quick, dark-brown eyes, came over to me and asked my name. I said, "RaeDawn, when I first saw you, you were just a little baby doing somersaults on the floor."

She said, "I'm five now. I just had my birthday on December 7th."

"You used to run around in those little plastic jellies—remember those green sandals you used to wear?"

"My little brother has those now."

"Well, you sure talk more than you used to. You talk really well, RaeDawn."

"Yes, but John won't let me answer the phone, because he says I get the messages all mixed up."

Florence explained that her son John, RaeDawn's uncle, gets a lot of calls there and doesn't like RaeDawn to answer them and talk so much to everybody, the way she does. Carefully Florence added another layer of fry bread to the cardboard box. I finished my coffee and stood up to leave. Florence went to the living room and returned with a large shopping bag containing a star quilt she and her daughter Flora had made for me. I took a look at the quilt and exclaimed over it and thanked her. It was lavender, with olive and brown and dark purple patterns on it. At the door I could not resist picking up RaeDawn and giving her a hug. I thought how much my own kids would like to play with her, and vice versa. For a mad moment I even thought of asking Florence if I could take her home with me.

Over at Aurelia's house, Le and Floyd John were drinking cups of *pejuta sapa* and sitting on the couch near the barrel stove. Their first attempt to repair the transaxle seal on Floyd John's car had not gone well. They had hammered and hammered at the seal trying to get it in, and in the process they had bent it. Now they were discussing what to do next. The job, they concluded, required an expert, and that expert was Chet Cross Dog. Chet is Florence's oldest son. He lives sometimes in Oglala and sometimes in Seattle, where he works for a big transmission-repair place and makes a thousand dollars or more a week. He has a degree from a transmission-repair school in Texas. Putting this seal in would be no problem for Chet.

First, though, we had to find him. Chet is a man much in demand on Pine Ridge. A skilled mechanic is always a useful person to know there, but a skilled mechanic who also happens to be a relative and who will work cheap or, out of the goodness of his heart, for free, is like an eminent old-time chief. Le and Floyd John had searched for Chet the day before with no success. Now we got in my car and set off to try again. I knew he wasn't at Florence's, so we didn't go there. We checked a couple of places between Oglala and Pine Ridge—no luck. In Pine Ridge Le and Floyd John got out at Pronto Auto Parts to pick up a new seal while I parked across the street at the BIA building and went in to use the restroom (*pejuta sapa*). When I came out Le and Floyd John were hurrying along the street and waving wildly at a passing car. The car pulled over.

Inside it were a young man named Jamie Yellow Horse; his wife, Cissy; their daughter, Julie; a young woman named Cory Spotted Elk; and, at the wheel, Chet. Le brought me over to introduce me. Then the conversation proceeded in Sioux. After a few minutes, Le stood up from the car window and reported, "Chet says he can do it, and he's got time to do it right now. He's only gonna charge us a case of beer." This was good news. We drove to White Clay, I provided the funding, and Jamie and Cissy went into the Jumping Eagle package store for the beer. Chet came over and leaned in the window of my car and took the transaxle seal from Floyd John and turned it this way and that in his hand. Chet is a round-faced man of about forty-five with slightly protruding eyes, a big chest, skinny legs, and a long, long black ponytail. He had on an Oglala Nation baseball cap. He talks very fast. He said, "Oh-yeah-okay-that's-a-seal-on-a-transaxle-intake, I-never-worked-on-one-when-the-tranny-was-still-in-the-car-the-way-yours-is, I-could-tap-it-in-with-two-taps-of-a-hammer-if-the-tranny-was-out-of-the-car-but-I'm-sure-I-can-do-this-anyway . . ." all in about two breaths.

Jamie and Cissy came out of the package store with a shiny new red-white-and-blue case of Budweiser. Twenty minutes later we were piling out of our cars in Aurelia's yard. The beers were broken out and passed around. Chet took a big sip, handed the can to Cory Spotted Elk, and approached the ailing vehicle. The rest of us withdrew a step or two to give him room. Like a magician he produced an object in his right hand: a box cutter. From the yard's scattered miscellany he took an empty cardboard appliance carton, and with a few strokes of the box cutter detached from it a rectangular section. He carefully laid the piece of cardboard on the ground under the car to protect his new shirt—black, with a Native American pattern in neon shades—his immaculate pipe-stem jeans, and his cowboy boots of light brown and shiny green. Then he crawled under the car until only his boots and blue-jean legs could be seen.

The rest of us looked on and talked in expectant tones. Cory Spotted Elk paid no direct attention to what Chet was doing, and yet somehow she seemed to watch him all the time. Le had told me that she was related to the Crows, a local family, and at a moment when I was standing next to her I asked her if she was a Crow. She gave me a level look and said, "Do I look like a Crow?" She had a full-lipped mouth that went all the way across her face, smooth brown hair, smooth brown skin, wire-rim glasses, lavender eye shadow, and hazel eyes. Such wattage turned directly at me caused me to hem and haw self-consciously and turn away. Chet suddenly popped out from under the car. Some inner part not involved in this operation was hanging down on him and bumping him and annoying him. He searched the ground for a moment, found a piece of barbed wire, and clipped a section from it with another tool that came miraculously to his hand. A few more clips trimmed the barbs. Then he dove back under the car and wired the offending part up out of the way.

The seal just would not go in, it seemed. Sounds of frustration rose from under the car. Le and Floyd John leaned in and consulted with Chet, shifting this way and that to see him through the machinery. Aurelia came home from her volunteer job, a scarf tied around her hair and a sack of commodity goods in her arms. She looked at the gathering in her yard, said, "Oh, me . . ." shook her head, and went inside. Tools were called for and then set down. The kittens chased each other up the side of a cottonwood. The little girl, Julie, went around digging in the ground with a screwdriver. Cissy Yellow Horse and Cory Spotted Elk began to shiver from the cold beer and the rising wind. Chet called for something to pound the seal into place. Le and Floyd John produced the six-foot-long wooden beam they had employed before. The beam was thrust into the car through the wheel well. Floyd John held it in position so it wouldn't fall on Chet, Le held it by the middle to keep it level, and Jamie Yellow Horse whacked on the end of the beam with the butt of an ax. *Whack whack whack.* "Hit it again." *Whack whack whack.* "Again." *Whack whack whack.* Long pause. "The goddam seal just fell out," Chet said.

He hopped up from under the car. He said, "I-know-this-is-gonna-work, I-know-I-can-get-the-sumbitch-in." He took a breath and spoke more slowly to us all. "In the tranny shop, sometimes guys'll get scared or lose their confidence when they're workin' on a complicated car like an Infiniti or something. I tell 'em I don't let *nothin'* scare me. My philosophy is, someone with a human mind thought of this machine, so you can use your own human mind to figure it out. The worst mistake you can make is thinking something is more complicated than it is." Then he dove back under the car, the hammering with the beam continued, and in two minutes he hopped up again triumphant, but not letting on. "Just needs a couple taps with a ball-peen," he said. Jamie Yellow Horse went under the car, made the final taps: job done. Chet turned to me. He said, "Well, you watched pretty close. Did you learn anything?" I said, "Yes, I learned that a six-foot-long wooden beam is an important automotive tool."

Chet opened his hand, and a beer appeared in it. He took a long pull, hooked his other hand in his jeans pocket, and strutted around. Cissy Yellow Horse yelled, "Chet, let's go! We're gettin' cold!" Le and Floyd John set about putting the transaxle and the wheel back on. Orrie Morris, their next-door neighbor, came over to help them, making the fifth Indian to work on this car in less than an hour. Le told again his story about the bull who bowed down to him, and Chet said that when he was a boy he used to watch Le ride in rodeos, and he was always amazed Le didn't get killed. Cissy started the car they had come in, and it began to idle with a deep bass throb. Chet opened that car's trunk and took out a jar of GoJo liquid hand cleaner and cleaned his hands carefully, digit by digit, wiping each individually with a rag. To look at him when he had finished, you would not guess he had just been lying on his back under a car. "Well, we'll see you guys later," he said. Then to Le he said, "I'll send you a bill for my services."

"*Tok' sha Paha Sapa*," Le replied and everybody laughed.

("What did you just say?" I asked.)

"That's something Sioux people say all the time," Le told me. " '*Tok' sha Paha Sapa*'—it means, 'I'll pay you when I get my Black Hills money.' "

A lot more stuff happened. Unexpectedly, on this trip I had a great time. Part of the reason probably was that Floyd John's not drinking made it easier and more fun to be with him and Le. We sat around the stove in Aurelia's with cups of *pejuta sapa* talking about one thing and another—Le told stories about how he wrote hit songs for the Jefferson Starship and the Steve Miller Band during his years in California, and he recounted the entire plot of *Hombre,* one of his favorite movies. Floyd John showed me choker necklaces of deerskin and leather belts he was working on. We again went looking for Chet to do some more repairs on various cars. I rode with Le and Floyd John, in Floyd John's car for a change. Sitting in the back seat felt very different from driving. Due to a further problem with the transmission, the car refused to shift out of second gear. I enjoyed watching the Pine Ridge scenery go by at thirty miles an hour.

One evening I went to the cemetery east of Pine Ridge for the memorial service for Richard Big Crow and SuAnne. About thirty-five of us assembled in an open part of the cemetery among the Christmas lights, under the needle-sharp stars. There were two Mennonite volunteers from the Big Crow Center; Rick and Ann Abdoo, the Michigan couple who had arranged for Ford Motors to contribute the van; a Pentecostal preacher and Oglala tribal member named Leon Matthews; Richard Big Crow's family; and other family members, teenagers, little kids, and friends. Tiny De Cory had us stand in a circle holding hands. She said that every circle of people is sacred and unique, because the same people will never stand in this exact same circle again. Leon Matthews gave a speech and led a prayer, and many talked of their love and support for the family of Richard Big Crow. Some people were crying. Occasionally little kids keeping warm in the idling cars honked the car horns, jarringly. Together we sang "Silent Night," but faltered at the second verse because nobody knew it, which caused some giggles.

Then a young man named Peta Catches, son of the famous Oglala medicine man Peter Catches, sang a traditional Lakota memorial song. Its words translated, "Where have you gone, departed ones? We are looking for you, we are not finding you." It was in a minor key, a descending series of notes, powerful and ancient-sounding in the Christmas-light glow on the dark prairie. The woman on my right kept dropping my hand to tend to a young child. I found myself squeezing the hand of the woman on my left harder and harder, and I quickly relaxed my grip so as not to seem weird. But soon I noticed that I was squeezing it hard again.

I knew I was almost done working on this book, and as I drove around the reservation or sat at Aurelia's or the Big Crow Center, I was tempted to draw conclusions. Books about Indians often end with an

analysis of Indian problems and advice from the author about what Indians could do to improve their lot. Certainly, I could imagine the
Oglala's lot improved. I could imagine the tribe growing in numbers
and prospering at new enterprises, at last; I could see them staying put
as the plains around them continue to lose population, and gaining
strength and importance in the region until in a hundred years or so
they regain their long-ago stature as a major power in the middle of the
continent. Maybe young leaders of SuAnne's generation and the ones
that follow will offer the tribe a vision that takes it beyond the hard
times of today. I recalled Angie Big Crow's description of SuAnne's
hoped-for Happytown, "where nobody would fight or be jealous, where
it would be clean, have a mall and lots of places for good fun." There
are worse dreams to work for. As to actual advice to the Oglala, however, I have none. Advice from authors and others—representatives of
the church, or officials in the government—usually has not worked out
too well in the past. Besides, no Oglala has ever asked me.

I do have a suggestion for the rest of us Americans. Back in the
1980s bills were introduced in Congress to return the federal lands in
the Black Hills to the Sioux. One of the bills was sponsored by Senator
Bill Bradley of New Jersey, who learned about the Sioux during a basketball clinic he held on Pine Ridge in his playing days. In 1987
Bradley's land-return bill died in committee, and no similar bill has
been introduced since. That the Black Hills were stolen is a fact on
which the Sioux and the government have been in essential agreement
for almost twenty years. The remaining disagreement is about how to
right the wrong. Perhaps now we could again consider the possibility of
returning some or all of the stolen federal lands.

One morning not long before Christmas it turned cold. An arctic front
arrived at about ten o'clock, and in fifteen minutes deep winter had
taken over the countryside. Snow crossed the ground and sky on winds
like an arctic express, never seeming to light anywhere. Tumbleweeds
invisible before were suddenly dashing before the wind—down dirt
roads, behind houses, along fences, across fields. Empty acres came
alive with the hither-and-thither panic of the tumbleweeds. Dark
clouds hunkered about a hundred feet overhead, blotting out the

tops of buttes and any trace of horizon. After the front's leading edge had passed, the winds decreased; by late afternoon eight inches of new snow had fallen. It was an airy, light powder snow in which each snowflake seemed unimpinged by the varied flakes resting lightly around it. The temperature had fallen to 2 degrees below zero.

As I drove to Oglala from Chadron on the back road the next morning I heard a disc jockey on KILI Radio say, "Okay, you Oglala carboys—it's time for you to get out there and warm up your cars, so your old ladies can get to work!" And indeed, every car I saw at that hour seemed to contain only a vexed-looking woman at the wheel. Black cows topped with snow stood breathing steam in the whitened fields while hawks sat in cottonwoods above, their feathers so fluffed out against the cold they looked like footballs. The dogs, too, looked bulky in their upraised fur, but unlike the other creatures, the dogs seemed to be having a good time, snuffling along in the drifts and checking things out and grinning companionably at passersby.

I could tell by the tire tracks in the snow of Aurelia's driveway that nobody would be home there. I found her neighbor Orrie Morris on a ladder repairing her windows. While unclogging a tube of caulk he told me that Le and Floyd John had gone to the commodities building in Pine Ridge. I drove to Pine Ridge, didn't find them, came back to Oglala, and spotted Le going into the post office. He told me he was on his way to Pine Ridge with some friends. I said I'd be glad to give him a ride, if he wanted. He said, "Sure. I love riding with you." With Le I drove back to Pine Ridge, where he did some business at the tribal building. Then we went to his sister Norma's house, where he gave her her mail; then over to White Clay. Then we drove around for a while. Le was drinking 24-ounce cans of Colt 45 extra malt.

He said, "Aurelia kicked me out of her house this morning. She says I can't stay there no more because I won't give her five hundred dollars. She's really an unpredictable person—she's got a Heckle and Jeckle personality. I'm gonna stay at Verna Yellow Horse's place tonight."

Eventually I drove him to Verna Yellow Horse's house across from the Catholic church in Oglala, and we sat in my car with the engine idling and the heater on. Le told me about police officers he had fought or intimidated (one in Grand Junction, Colorado, in particular), and he went on to revile and defy all immigrants to his country, and he said this was his land, and he said, *"I know who I am!"* He sang some Lakota songs. He said many times that he and I are brothers. He said that there is a deep spiritual bond between us. He took my hand in the "power" handshake—hands clasped upright, palm to palm—and held on to it for a long time. I was a bit uncomfortable, as I sometimes am with him. I disregarded a lot of what he said and reduced it in my mind to about 20 percent face value. But the part about us being brothers I did not discount. By different routes and for different reasons, our affections have ended up in the same place; being called Little Brother means a lot to me. Through the swerves in our relationship it took me years to discover this.

Le got out of the car and then leaned back in through the open door to say a lot more. He said that the part we had bought for his car some days previously needed a special socket in order to be properly installed, and the socket happened to be a rare one, and it cost twenty dollars. I gave him twenty. He said tomorrow we'd go way out in the badlands onto a butte called Cuny Table, and from there we'd drive on a little-known road to a place called the Stronghold, where the ghost dancers hid out after the massacre at Wounded Knee. He told me to give his love to my wife and kids, and said to drive safely, and that I'd find him here at Verna's tomorrow morning.

When I showed up at Verna's the next morning nobody knew anything about him. He hadn't slept there the night before. No one had seen him around. I went to Aurelia's and met Floyd John driving out her driveway. He hadn't seen Le either. He had some suggestions of where he might be, but the directions he gave were complicated and I decided not to look. Floyd John and I talked for a while through our open car windows while our engines idled loudly in the cold. Overnight the temperature had gone down to eighteen below. I could have hung around, but I wanted to start for home. I told Floyd John what a good time I'd had, and I thanked him, and I said that his quitting drinking was a wonderful thing. He said he would make me a choker necklace and send it to me. He checked in his billfold to make sure he still had my address. He said, "God bless you," and I said it back to him. Then he rolled up his window and spun his tires pulling out of the drive, and I started for home down the Red Shirt Table Road.

NOTES

CHAPTER 1

4　A description of the recalcitrance of Powhatan is found in *Linking Arms Together: American Indian Treaty Visions of Law and Peace, 1600–1800,* by Robert A. Williams, Jr. (1996), p. 31. The Englishmen wished Powhatan to come to them at Jamestown to receive his crown, and Powhatan objected, "Your father is to come to me, not I to him."

John Smith, of the Jamestown Colony, was among the party who went to Powhatan's village to present the crown, and he recalled the ceremony in his *Captain John Smith's History of Virginia* (reprinted 1970), p. 69: "But a foul trouble it was to make him kneel to receive his crown; he neither knowing the majesty or meaning of a crown, nor bending of the knee, endured so many persuasions, examples and instructions as tired them all. At last, by leaning on his shoulders, he a little stooped, and three having the crown in their hands put it on his head."

4　Joseph Brant, a graduate of Dartmouth, also translated the Bible into Mohawk. On one of his visits to London he met James Boswell, who became a friend and interviewed him for *The London Magazine.* See *Life of Joseph Brant—Thayendanega,* by William L. Stone (1845), Vol. II, p. 251.

Indians Abroad, 1493–1934, by Carolyn Thomas Foreman (1943), p. 96, says that the famous incident between Brant and the King and Queen took place during a visit Brant made in 1785.

4　There are a number of biographies of Red Cloud. The description of his trip to New York and Washington, D.C., and of his reception and speech in the capital, is in *Red Cloud and the Sioux Problem,* by James C. Olson (1965), pp. 103–5.

4 The Senate select committee went to Standing Rock Reservation in 1883 to investigate grievances there. The committee chairman tried to intimidate Sitting Bull with accusations that he was not a chief: "I do not know any difference between you and the other Indians at this agency." Sitting Bull replied, "I am here by the will of the Great Spirit, and by His will I am a chief. My heart is red and sweet, and I know it is sweet, because whatever passes near me puts out its tongue to me." The senator who told Sitting Bull that he had "no following, no power, no control, and no right to any control," and threatened to throw him into the guardhouse, was John A. Logan of Illinois. The Sioux called him "High Hat," because he wore one. See *Sitting Bull, Champion of the Sioux*, by Stanley Vestal (1957), pp. 241, 247.

5 Many twentieth-century Indian accounts describe the efforts of educators to break Indian students of speaking their native tongues. Among others, see *Sundance: The Robert Sundance Story*, by Robert Sundance with Mark Gaede (1994); *Lame Deer, Seeker of Visions*, by John Fire/Lame Deer and Richard Erdoes (1972); and the somewhat unreliable *Where White Men Fear to Tread: The Autobiography of Russell Means*, by Russell Means with Marvin J. Wolf (1995).

6 The quotation from the account of Amerigo Vespucci appears in "Americanizing the White Man," an essay by Felix S. Cohen collected in his *The Legal Conscience: Selected Papers of Felix S. Cohen*, edited by Lucy Kramer Cohen (1960), p. 324.

6 So widespread was the notion of the Indians' coming extinction that it served (for example) as the justification for the photographs of Indians taken by Edward S. Curtis at the turn of the century. These now-familiar pictures, of Chief Joseph and Geronimo and many other Indians famous and obscure, were done partly to record a race that would soon be gone, as Theodore Roosevelt pointed out in his foreword to Curtis's *The North American Indians: Being a Series of Volumes Picturing and Describing the Indians of the United States, and Alaska* (1907–9).

6 In February of 1891 Bill Nye wrote a column that attempted humor on the subject of the Ghost Dance and the Wounded Knee massacre:

> Standing Horse, who led the ghost dance, wore a United States wagon cover on his arrival, and also threw one corner of it over his departure; but when the dancing began he checked this outer wrap, and was discovered to be dressed lightly in a tiara of dickey bird's feet and a coat of shellac. He danced until utterly worn out and exhausted, when he fell to the ground, and a tidy was thrown over him by an attendant . . .

The column appeared in the Aberdeen (South Dakota) *Saturday Pioneer* of February 8, 1891. The *Saturday Pioneer*'s editor was L. Frank Baum, later the author of the "Wizard of Oz" books for children. Baum hated Indians, and days after Wounded Knee wrote in his editorial column: "The PIONEER has before declared that our only safety depends upon the total extirmination [sic] of the Indians. Having wronged them for centuries we had better, in order to protect our civilization, follow it up by one more wrong and wipe these untamed and untamable creatures from the face of the earth. In this lies future safety for our settlers . . ." Aberdeen *Saturday Pioneer*, January 3, 1891.

7   In 1996 the United Methodist Church apologized for the Sand Creek Massacre— Colonel John M. Chivington, who led the Colorado militiamen who attacked the Cheyenne at Sand Creek, was a Methodist lay preacher.

Laird Cometsevah, of Clinton, Oklahoma, is a spokesman for the descendants of Sand Creek survivors. He is the great-grandson of a survivor named Leg Calf.

7   Stories about the Mohican tribe's successful protest against Wal-Mart appeared in *The New York Times* of January 21, 1996 (XII-WC, 12:5), and February 16, 1996 (B, 6:1).

(The Mohican Tribe, known as the Stockbridge Munsee Community, whose reservation is in Bowler, Wisconsin, say that Fenimore Cooper got his orthography wrong, and that the Indians he had in mind were probably the Mohegans. Uncas was a chief of the Mohegans, not the Mohicans.)

7   Indian population figures come from newspaper articles on the U.S. Census (*The New York Times*, April 25, 1971, 61:2; October 20, 1971, 26:4; November 19, 1992, A, 20:4), and from *Killing the White Man's Indian: Reinventing Native Americans at the End of the Twentieth Century*, by Fergus M. Bordewich (1996), pp. 53–55.

7   Details about the genocidal policies of the state of California in the nineteenth century appeared in news stories in *Indian Country Today*, a nationwide newspaper published out of Rapid City, South Dakota (May 14–21, 1996, p. A6), and in *The New York Times* (May 7, 1996, A, 14:4).

7   The story of the Gnadenhutten massacre is in *A Century of Dishonor: A Sketch of the United States Government's Dealings with Some of the Indian Tribes*, by Helen Hunt Jackson (1881), pp. 317ff.

8   Nancy Bill, injury prevention specialist with the Indian Health Service in Window Rock, Arizona, told me about the high rate of traffic fatalities among the Navajo.

8   The contribution of American Indians to world agriculture is described in Cohen, p. 317. For a more extensive discussion of this subject, see *Indian Givers: How the Indians of the Americas Transformed the World*, by Jack Weatherford (1988), Chapters 4–6.

8   The first Europeans to record a sighting of the potato were Spaniards with the expedition led by Jiménez de Quesada to native villages in the Andes Mountains in what is now Colombia. The year was 1537. By 1590 the potato had appeared in England. See *The Potato: Evolution, Biodiversity, and Genetic Resources*, by J. G. Hawkes (1990), p. 10.

8   Cohen (pp. 321ff.) also describes the seminal contribution of the Iroquois to American democracy and constitutional government.

9   Besides Franklin and Jefferson, a number of others among the Founding Fathers—Adams, Madison, Thomas Paine—expressed admiration for Native Amer-

ican ways of government. A helpful book on the subject is *Indian Roots of American Democracy*, a collection of essays edited by José Barreiro (1992).

9 Cohen (p. 306) mentions the many thinkers of the Enlightenment who were inspired by the example of Indian liberty. Thomas More referred to the letters of Amerigo Vespucci in his *Utopia*, a work read throughout Europe, which incorporated Indian ideas of freedom and equality. See also Weatherford, Chapter 7.

10 General Howard's impatience with the Nez Perce is in Helen Hunt Jackson (p. 129). Her source is Howard's own account, which appeared in a magazine two years after the event. Chief Joseph remembered the encounter differently: he said that Howard "lost his temper, and said 'Shut up! I don't want to hear any more of such talk!' "

For more on the wrongs done to the Nez Perce, see *Let Me Be Free: The Nez Perce Tragedy,* by David Lavender (1992).

11 The preface to the *Lakota-English Dictionary*, by Rev. Eugene Buechel, S.J. (1970), has a concise description of the main tribal divisions among the Sioux.

In *Lame Deer, Seeker of Visions*, John Fire Lame Deer disagrees with recent tradition on the subject of the tribe's name. He says, "Our people don't call themselves Sioux or Dakota. That's white man talk. We call ourselves Ikce Wicasa— the natural humans, the free, wild common people. I am pleased to be called that" (p. 23).

12 For a history of the military campaigns of Chief Pontiac, see *The Conspiracy of Pontiac*, by Francis Parkman (reprinted as a Library of America edition, 1991), one of the classic works of American history. Two useful books on Chief Tecumseh are *Tecumseh and the Quest for Indian Leadership,* by David E. Edmunds (1984), and *God Gave Us This Country: Tekamthi and the First American Civil War,* by Bil Gilbert (1989).

12 For more on Protestant sectarianism in America, see my *Family* (1994), Chapters 3 and 13.

14 An interesting book, *Kill Devil Hill: Discovering the Secret of the Wright Brothers*, by Harry Combs with Martin Caidin (1979), has a photograph of Wilbur Wright flying around the Statue of Liberty in 1909.

14 I learned about new high-yield trees in an article in the Missoula, Montana, *Missoulian:* "Fast-growing Trees Have Power to Save the Planet," by Dennis T. Avery (August 19, 1997, p. A 4).

15 For details on the life of Crazy Horse, see my *Great Plains* (1989), pp. 96ff., and notes. The first full-scale biography of Crazy Horse, Mari Sandoz's *Crazy Horse: The Strange Man of the Oglalas* (1942), though flawed as history, remains a good place to begin when reading about the great Oglala warrior.

In *Red Cloud: Warrior-Statesman of the Lakota Sioux*, by Robert W. Larson (1997), Crazy Horse is described as belonging to the Hunkpatila band of the Oglala (pp. 64, 75). George E. Hyde, in his classic *Red Cloud's Folk: A History of the Oglala Sioux Indians* (1957), says that Crazy Horse belonged to the Bad

Faces (Iteshicha). Some Oglala I have asked about this agree with Hyde. Charlotte Black Elk says he belonged to a band called the Oyukhpe.

17   The shooting of Clyde Bellecourt is mentioned in many accounts of the events at
Wounded Knee and after—e.g., *Wounded Knee II*, by Roland Dewing (1995),
pp. 135–36. The *New York Times* story of the shooting appeared August 28, 1973
(36:5). The paper reported on September 13, 1973 (13:1), that Bellecourt had refused to press charges.

The item about Clyde Bellecourt's daughter working for her Gold Bar, "the
highest achievement in Girl Scouts," was in *Indian Country Today* (April 28 –
May 5, 1997, p. C 7).

18   The firebomb on the subway exploded in the sixth car of a Brooklyn-bound number 4 train at the Fulton Street station in lower Manhattan during afternoon rush
hour on December 21, 1994. The hero who said he was no hero was off-duty
transit cop Denfield S. Otto, a fifty-four-year-old grandfather from Harlem. All
the New York papers of December 22 covered this event.

18   Bil Gilbert's statement about Indians, Greeks, and heroes was in a *Life* magazine
special issue on heroes (May 1997), p. 13.

CHAPTER 2

20   For more on my first meeting with Le War Lance, see my *Great Plains*, Chapter 6.
26   Jim Clark, twice world auto racing champion, died not at Indianapolis but in a
crash of his Lotus Ford racer during a race at Hockenheim, West Germany, on
April 7, 1968.
29   Sources on Indians in movies are: *The BFI Companion to the Western*, edited by
Edward Buscombe (1988); *Movies: The History of an Art and an Institution*, by
Richard Schickel (1964); *Western and Frontier Film and Television Credits
1903–1995*, by Harris M. Lentz III (1996); *American Film Institute Catalogue:
Feature Films 1911–1920*, and *The Only Good Indian . . . The Hollywood Gospel*,
by Ralph E. Friar and Natasha Friar (1972).
30   The Friars' book has the figures on movies about the Apache and the Sioux. The
entry under *The Indian Wars* (Buffalo Bill Cody's movie) in the *American Film
Institute Catalogue* goes into some detail about the making of the film, and about
what happened to it. Apparently it was rather sympathetic to the Indians; this an-
gered officials in Washington, and government pressure caused the film not to be
widely released. Footage from this film was included in a number of films released after Cody's death in 1917.
31   Information about Indians and the Academy Awards appeared in an article about
Indians and Hollywood in *Indian Country Today* (April 4, 1996; p. B 7).

Dan George, a Squamish Indian from the Berard Reserve outside Vancouver,
British Columbia, who was memorable as the old Cheyenne chief in *Little Big
Man,* lost to John Mills in *Ryan's Daughter.* Graham Greene, an Oneida from

Ontario who played a Sioux medicine man in *Dances with Wolves,* lost to Joe Pesci in *Goodfellas.*

(Buffy Sainte-Marie, the lone winner, is a Cree. She is also from Canada.)

CHAPTER 3

35 The George Will column on the subject of sixties' era permissiveness and Jerry Garcia was "About that 'Sixties Idealism' " (*Newsweek,* August 21, 1995, p. 72).

36 As I mention in Chapter 15, this section of Highway 79 has since been widened to four lanes.

36 I learned Indian life-expectancy figures for the north-central Great Plains—North Dakota, South Dakota, and including western Minnesota and eastern Montana—from the offices of the Indian Health Service in Aberdeen, South Dakota. The bulk of the Indian population here is in South Dakota, and the figures are for 1992. In this region Indians of both sexes have a life expectancy of 64.7 years, compared with a U.S. average of 75.8. Life expectancy for males is 60.8 years (U.S. average is 72.3) and for females 69.3 (U.S. average is 79.1).

37 Details about the car accident near Hermosa may be found in the Rapid City *Journal* of June 28, 29, and 30, and July 1 and 2, 1986; and in the Sheridan (Wyoming) *Press,* June 30, 1986.

38–39 For a good depiction of the shrinking of Sioux lands since 1851, see the maps in *Black Hills, White Justice: The Sioux Nation versus the United States, 1775 to the Present,* by Edward Lazarus (1991), pp. xviiff. The resistance of Red Cloud and the Oglala to the idea of moving east to the Missouri is discussed in Olson, Chapters 5–9.

39 By the terms of the Manypenny Agreement, ratified by Congress February 28, 1877, the Sioux received 900,000 acres of grazing land for the 7.3 million acres in the western portion of the Great Sioux Reservation, a tract which included the Black Hills. See Lazarus, p. 91.

39 The U.S. Court of Claims later ruled that only about 10 percent of the required number of Sioux had signed the Manypenny Agreement.

Besides Pine Ridge, the other Sioux reservations within the former lands of the Great Sioux Reservation are the Standing Rock Reservation in North and South Dakota; and the Cheyenne River, Lower Brule, Rosebud, and Yankton Reservations, all in South Dakota. See the map of the Great Sioux Reservation in Lazarus; see also *Discover Indian Reservations USA: A Visitors' Welcome Guide,* edited by Veronica E. Tiller (1992), p. 300.

39 *The Oglala of the Great Sioux Nation* (no author or date), an informational booklet on file in the Rapid City, South Dakota, Public Library, says that the original land base of the Pine Ridge Reservation was 2,786,539 acres. *Oglala Religion,* by William K. Powers (1977), gives almost the same figure, and says that Pine Ridge is 4,353 square miles. Dewing says the original reservation holdings were 2,809,444 acres.

39 Any book that discusses federal Indian policy mentions the Dawes Act. For a good, brief summary of the act and its consequences, see the entry under "Dawes Severalty Act" in *The Reader's Encyclopedia of the American West,* edited by Howard R. Lamar (1998). The entry says Indian lands were to be divided into "160-acre plots for heads of families, eighty acres for single persons over eighteen years of age, and forty acres for minors." (There were no provisions for the unborn.)

40 Dewing says that the loss of tribal lands on the Pine Ridge Reservation was over a million acres—of 2,804,444 acres, only 1,518,261 acres were still under Indian control in 1969 (p. 13). *The Oglala of the Great Sioux Nation* gives the distribution as follows: 2,786,539 acres in all; 835,917 owned by tribe; 24,095 owned by federal government; 930,083 allotted to tribal members (most of which is leased to non-Indian farmers and ranchers); and 996,444 owned by non-Indians.

40 Helen Hunt Jackson's *A Century of Dishonor* favored citizenship for Indians as a guarantee of their rights of property, so often cruelly abused. She wrote: "The utter absence of individual title to particular lands deprives every one among them of the chief incentive to labor and exertion—the very mainspring on which the prosperity of a people depends" (p. 341). Translated into law, this idea led to the Dawes Act, and allotment—an excellent example of good intentions leading to disastrous public policy.

40 The Red Shirt Table Road has been stripped, graded, and resurfaced various times since I first drove it. As of July 1999, it had been somewhat improved.

41 The closest interstate highway to the reservation is I-90, about ninety miles from Pine Ridge village (though closer to the reservation's less-populated northeastern part). The closest freight rail service is at Rushville, Nebraska, about 24 miles south of Pine Ridge village. There is no regular passenger rail service in this part of the Plains.

    Although Pine Ridge residents travel to Rapid City, South Dakota, and other places for errands almost daily, no commercial bus lines serve the reservation.

41 In the mid-nineteenth century the Oglala ranged widely on the Central Plains— to the Powder River country, the Black Hills, and the Platte River country in present western Nebraska. They kept coming back to Fort Laramie, which was ideally located for them. A repeated request of Red Cloud's during negotiations with the government was that the Oglala be allowed to have their agency at Fort Laramie.

41 Many sources describe the government's desire to move the Sioux away from the route of the transcontinental railroad. *Our Indian Wards,* by George W. Manypenny (the official whose name is on the "agreement" by which the Sioux lost the Black Hills), published 1880, quotes the Act of Congress that created the 1867 treaty commission. Its purpose, the act said, was to move the Indians to a place where they would not "interfere with established highways of travel, and the contemplated railroads to the Pacific" (p. 194). On this subject, see also Olson, pp. 60ff., and Larson, pp. 106ff.

    George Hyde (p. 161) says that the peace commissioners thought they were being clever when they gave such generous concessions with the Treaty of 1868:

they were pretending to mollify the Indians as well as the Eastern supporters of peace while simultaneously pursuing the real agenda of moving the Indians away from the railroad. (The government would later regret its generosity when gold was discovered in the Black Hills.)

In 1876 the government had a plan to move the Oglala and other Sioux to Indian Territory (present Oklahoma), but it was thwarted by railroad interests who hoped for land grants there (Manypenny, p. 345). The railroads were indeed the behind-the-scenes power in the early reservation years of the Western Sioux.

42 James Naismith expressed his pleasure at seeing "basketball goals in some out of the way place" in his *Basketball: Its Origin and Development* (1905; reissued 1996), pp. 109–10.

CHAPTER 4

50 The traffic light at the four-way is no longer the only one on the reservation. Since my first visit to Pine Ridge, another has been installed, at an intersection on Highway 18 a short distance east of the four-way.

51 Long-time Pine Ridge resident Ben Irving used to sit by the four-way back in the fifties and tell stories to children and passersby. When Irving was three he went to England with the Wild West Show; the Queen liked the show so much that she kissed him. (See the *Sheridan County Star* of Rushville, Nebraska, August 14, 1958, p. 2.)

51 Baptiste "Big Bat" Pourier, the present Big Bat's ancestor, came West when he was seventeen and worked for the famous fur trader John Reeshaw. He also worked for the Army as a scout. He was an interpreter at the treaty council at Fort Laramie that produced the treaty of 1868, and the Red Cloud School has pictures of him at that council. His Oglala wife was a mixed-blood named Josephine Richards. (My thanks to Patty Pourier for supplying Pourier family data.)

In an interview with Judge Eli S. Ricker (included in the so-called Ricker Tablets, interviews on file in the Nebraska State Historical Society), Baptiste Pourier said that he was in the room with Crazy Horse all night on the night Crazy Horse died (Ricker Collection, series 2, tablet 13, p. 19).

53 The sun-dance controversy occupied the pages of *Indian Country Today* in July, August, and September of 1997. See particularly "The Selling of the Sun Dance: Spiritual Exploitation at Heart of Pine Ridge Controversy," *Indian Country Today*, July 28–August 4, 1997, p. A 1.

54–55 Many of Le's stories are hard to document. The death of Francis Slow Bear, however, was reported in the *Sheridan County Star,* December 8, 1960, p. 1:

PINE RIDGE MAN FREEZES TO DEATH

Funeral services for Francis Slow Bear, 28, of Pine Ridge, who froze to death in last week's blizzard, were held last week in Pine Ridge.

Slow Bear's body was found in an open pasture about 4½ miles northwest of Oglala on Friday. Floyd Clausen, who was herding cattle, found the body.

The dead man had last been seen on Saturday night, November 26, and said he was headed home when friends last saw him. He apparently got trapped in the blizzard of Sunday morning, November 27th.

An autopsy in Rapid City Saturday revealed no evidence of foul play.

57 *In the Spirit of Crazy Horse,* by Peter Matthiessen (1983), is the story of the Pine Ridge wars of the seventies, with emphasis on the shooting of the FBI agents and the capture and trial of Leonard Peltier.

59 The loss of the ancient tanned-hide star maps is mentioned in *Lakota Star Knowledge: Studies in Lakota Stellar Theology,* edited by Ronald Goodman (Rosebud, South Dakota: Sinte Gleska University Press, 1992), p. 18.

59 Books that discuss the Wounded Knee Massacre are too many to list. I recommend Hyde; *The Last Days of the Sioux Nation,* by Robert M. Utley (1963); and *Eyewitness at Wounded Knee,* by Richard E. Jensen, R. Eli Paul, and John E. Carter (1991). The last of these has a good summary of the massacre and events leading to it, as well as a selection of photographs taken at the time.

59 As with most casualty figures in combat, those from Wounded Knee are uncertain. One hundred and forty-six Indians are buried in the mass grave on the hill. Others died elsewhere. Including the Army casualties, the total was probably closer to 250 (see Jensen, Paul, and Carter, p. 20).

60 Among the many books about the Wounded Knee takeover in 1973, I have relied on *Like a Hurricane: The Indian Movement from Alcatraz to Wounded Knee,* by Paul Chaat Smith and Robert Allen Warrior (1996); Dewing; Matthiessen; and *Wounded Knee 1973: A Personal Account,* by Stanley David Lyman (1991).

The takeover was front-page news all over the country. I referred to newspaper accounts from *The Washington Post* and *The New York Times.*

62 The federal marshal, Lloyd Grimm, was wounded on March 26. On April 17, an occupier named Frank Clear or Frank Clearwater was hit during a firefight that followed a drop of supplies from airplanes over the occupiers' compound. He died soon after. On April 27, gunfire killed occupier Lawrence "Buddy" Lamont; his death prompted the occupiers to reach a negotiated solution.

68 David Carradine also says of Le, "I think he was not popular with his tribe because he was an inconsistent, emotional person. Also, he did not submit to the authority of his elders, not in the sense that he did anything bad, but in the sense that he ignored what they told him to do. He was a seeker, and he preferred to do his searching out there in the world." See *Endless Highway* (1995), p. 361.

Stories about the murder of taxicab driver George Aird, and about the arrests and trial that followed it, may be found in the *Los Angeles Times* of October 11, 1974, 1, p. 3; October 17, 1974, 1, p. 3; October 29, 1974, 1, p. 2; June 15, 1977, 2, p. 1; January 25, 1978, 1, p. 3; and May 25, 1978, 1, p. 1. See also *Blood of the Land: The Government and Corporate War against First Nations,* by Rex Weyler (1992), pp. 168–69 and 170–71.

CHAPTER 5

70 Much of the information in this chapter comes from newspaper reports over the last forty years. I will list only some of them.

A good comprehensive reference book on modern Indian reservations is *Discover Indian Reservations USA: A Visitors' Welcome Guide,* edited by Veronica E. Tiller (1992).

70 Before the casino boom, California's Agua Caliente tribe, which owns much of the land in Palm Springs, California, was sometimes referred to as the richest tribe in the United States. The Las Vegas Paiute tribe owns twelve acres of land in downtown Las Vegas.

71 The quarter-acre reservation belongs to the Paugussett Golden Hill, a state-recognized tribe in Connecticut. See *Discover Indian Reservations USA,* p. 92.

72 In February 1999, the federal government agreed to a return of over seven thousand acres of land in southeastern California to the Timbisha Shoshone; the tribe plans to use some of their new reservation for housing and commercial enterprises. See *Indian Country Today,* April 26–May 3, 1999, p. A 2.

74 Helen Hunt Jackson says (*Century of Dishonor,* p. 277) that Davy Crockett, the legendary frontiersman, "spoke warmly" against a bill for the removal of the Cherokee when he was a congressman from Tennessee. *David Crockett: The Man and the Legend,* by James Atkins Shackford (1981, p. 116–17), says that although a speech Crockett allegedly made against the removal was published in a volume of others on the subject, he in fact never made the speech. Crockett was no friend to Indians, Shackford says, and opposed the bill only as part of his larger campaign against President Andrew Jackson, whom he strongly disliked.

76 Historian Francis Parkman detailed the ferocity of the Iroquois with relish in his nine-volume masterwork, *France and England in North America* (1899). He thought the Iroquois were savages, and that to ascribe nobility to them was ridiculous; and yet he sometimes depicted them that way himself ("tall, stalwart figures, limbed like Greek statues"—Vol. IV, Part I, p. 82).

It was Parkman who mentioned Benjamin West's comment on seeing the Apollo Belvedere. See Parkman, *The Oregon Trail* (1849, reprinted 1982), p. 211.

77 The interest Karl Marx and Friedrich Engels had in Lewis Henry Morgan's writings on the Iroquois is mentioned in *Wasi'chu: The Continuing Indian Wars,* by Bruce Johansen and Roberto Maestas (1979), pp. 37–38. See also *The Origin of the Family, Private Property, and the State, in Light of the Researches of Lewis H. Morgan,* by Friedrich Engels (Alec West, trans.; 1884, reprinted 1972).

77 The St. Regis Mohawk Reservation, in upstate New York on the U.S.–Canadian border, includes almost 24,000 acres in both countries, and predates the founding of either. See *Discover Indian Reservations USA,* p. 236.

77 The recent struggle between the Iroquois and the state of New York over the state's attempt to collect sales tax received extensive coverage in *The New York Times.* See in particular its stories of May 9, 12, 19, 20, 21, 23, and 24, 1997.

78 What seemed to nettle Robert Moses most of all about the Tuscarora land-grab controversy was the mention of it in *Apology to the Iroquois,* by Edmund Wilson (1960). Wilson strongly sympathized with the Tuscarora. Moses's pamphlet, *Tuscarora Fiction and Fact: A Reply to the Author of Memoirs of Hecate County,* is an eight-page pamphlet (on file at the New York Public Library) that attempts to rebut Wilson.

80 For an excellent portrait of the violence and alcoholism in towns that border Indian reservations, see *Bordertowns,* by Marc Gaede (1988), a collection of photographs made mostly in Gallup, New Mexico, and Winslow, Arizona. Gaede says, in the note accompanying his photo of the big tank in the Gallup jail, "With dimensions of 4,500 square feet, *Police Magazine* reports it to be the largest jail cell in the United States. It holds 500 people . . . uncomfortably. The heat generated by so many bodies creates a furnace effect, and there is a blast of hot air on approach to the entrance. At first glance, this image usually provokes accusations of injustice. But those interned will go home to their families the following day. Without protective custody, there would be an endless nightly series of beatings, stabbings, muggings, rapes, death by exposure and car accidents."

80 Information about the many fatalities on U.S. 666 from Gallup to the reservation, and about the effort to get streetlights installed, comes from Nancy Bill of the IHS in Window Rock, Arizona; as well as from newspaper accounts (e.g., *Indian Country Today,* April 23–30, 1996, p. C 1).

81 The story of the rise of Indian casinos deserves a book in itself. Beginning in about 1992, newspaper articles about Indian gambling enterprises became so many as to crowd out other news from Indian country. A look at gambling coverage as represented by listings in the indexes of major newspapers in the 1990s shows how the gambling phenomenon grew nationwide. For example, in *The New York Times Index* for 1991, the listings under "Gambling" were about four columns long; in 1993 they were six and a half columns; in 1997 they were nine and a half columns.

82 The involvement of the federal government in the oversight of tribal gambling operations has followed major decisions in the federal courts that gave wider scope to the tribes. In the 1980s, a federal court in Connecticut ruled that the Mashantucket tribe's bingo operations were exempt from state jackpot regulations, and the U.S. Supreme Court ruled that the state of California could not regulate the gambling business of the Cabazon Band of Mission Indians. The IGRA was passed largely as a result of these decisions.

In 1996 the Supreme Court ruled for the state of Florida in a suit brought by the Seminole tribe, saying in effect that if a state refused to negotiate gaming compacts with a tribe under the provisions of the IGRA, the tribe had no recourse, because a state is immune from suit and the federal government cannot take that immunity away. By apparently undercutting the legal basis for the IGRA, this decision left tribal gaming in a legal limbo region, where it has remained.

83 I surmise that much of the gambling boom is related to the aging of the population, corporate downsizing that encourages early retirement, and the transfer of much of the discretionary income in the country to people over sixty-five. Today the average seventy-year-old spends 20 percent more than the average thirty-year-old; the elderly have a median per capita income 67 percent above that of the population as a whole. See *The Future of Capitalism*, by Lester C. Thurow (1996), Chapter 5.

83 Americans legally gambled about $250 billion in 1987 and $638 billion in 1997. Of course, the figure for the total amount gambled would be higher, because much of gambling remains illegal and unreported. (See *The New York Times*, November 8, 1998, IV, 3:1.)

85 The Navajo leader so opposed to casino gambling was tribal chairman Albert Hale. See *Indian Country Today*, May 7–14, 1996, p. C 1.

89 During the bombing of Yugoslavia in the spring of 1999, an eighth F-117-A Nighthawk Stealth fighter was destroyed—shot down by Serb gunners who were apparently firing antiaircraft missiles at it more or less blindly.

90 The Oglala census with the obscene names was published in 1994 by the Nebraska State Historical Society under the title *The Crazy Horse Surrender Ledger*, edited by Thomas R. Buecker and R. Eli Paul. It reproduces photographically the pages of a ledger book in which Army officials kept records of Indians at the Red Cloud Agency, including a list of the Crazy Horse band compiled after they came into the agency in May 1877. The obscene names look especially striking in the careful Victorian handwriting in which they are set down.

91 Red Cloud went in search of Crazy Horse in April 1877, when efforts were under way to get Crazy Horse to surrender. His letter from the field to an Army officer, dictated to a companion who could write:

> A Pril 15, 1877
>
> Sir My Dear I have met some Indians on the road and they say the Indians on bear lodge creek on the 16th april and I thought let you know it and I think I will let you know better after I get to the camp so I sent the young man with this letter he have been to the camp before his name is arme blown off.
>
> RED CLOUD

(Hyde, p. 291)

CHAPTER 6

99 Le was reading Oates's *Abraham Lincoln: The Man Behind the Myth* (1984). For a thorough discussion of Lincoln and the Mankato hangings, see *Lincoln and the Indians: Civil War Policy and Politics*, by David A. Nichols (1978), Chapter 8.

CHAPTER 7

118   The book in which Charlotte Black Elk explains her theory of precession as it relates to the Black Hills is *Lakota Star Knowledge: Studies in Lakota Stellar Theology.* (See note for p. 59 above.) She and Gerald Clifford are no longer married.

124   *Indian Country Today* occasionally does stories about the liquor traffic in White Clay. See "Tribe Wants Bordertown Bars Closed" (November 17–24, 1997, p. C 1) and "White Clay Liquor Problem Still Unresolved" (April 6–13, 1998, p. C 1). Additional information comes from the Nebraska Department of Revenue and the Nebraska Liquor Control Commission.

129   For stories about the Rodriguez shooting, see *Indian Country Today,* January 4, 1996, p. B 9; and August 5–12, 1996, p. B 1.

129   The state traffic accident report describes Wanda Kindle's accident somewhat differently than Le and others did at the time. According to the report, her car was not on the Chadron road but just west of the accident site, at the junction of Highway 18 and BIA 41 (the road to Loneman). Apparently her car had missed a turn and skidded into the ditch. Skid marks on the highway near her body suggested a hit-and-run accident. The driver who hit her was not in a pickup truck but in a Pontiac Lemans. The report says that a police officer found her body eighteen minutes after the accident occurred.

CHAPTER 8

131   Bars and drinking are naturally subjects that come up often in nonfiction accounts of Indian life published in the last fifty years. The bars in this chapter are taken from a number of as-told-to reminiscences and autobiographies.

     A harrowing and interesting book mostly about drinking is *Sundance: The Robert Sundance Story* (see note for p. 5 above). It tells the story of a Sioux, born in 1927, through his many misadventures as an almost-lifelong alcoholic.

     For additional information on this subject and many others, I am indebted to Sundance's brother Pat McLaughlin, past tribal chairman of the Standing Rock Sioux.

132   Robert Sundance spent a lot of time in Casey's Golden Pheasant in Billings, and describes the bar as it was then in some detail.

133   Joseph Mitchell's "The Mohawks in High Steel" appeared in *The New Yorker* of September 17, 1949. It may also be found in his collected works, *Up in the Old Hotel* (1992).

134   Many Los Angeles bars are mentioned in *Where White Men Fear to Tread: The Autobiography of Russell Means.*

138   The connection between Anheuser-Busch breweries and imagery of the Custer battle is examined in "Anheuser-Busch and Custer's Last Stand," by John M. Carroll, an interesting article published in *Greasy Grass,* an annual magazine of the Custer Battlefield Historical & Museum Association (May 1987; p. 25). (My

thanks to Thomas Buecker of the Fort Robinson Museum near Crawford, Nebraska, for calling it to my attention.)

139   The whiskey trader who bemoaned the liquor trade was J. W. Schultz, in his *My Life as an Indian: The Story of a Red Woman and a White Man in the Lodges of the Blackfeet* (1906), p. 95.

140   Frank Fools Crow talked about alcohol and the Oglala in *Fools Crow*, by Thomas E. Mails (1979), pp. 147ff.

In *Sundance: The Robert Sundance Story*, the reformed alcoholic Robert Sundance said, "As long as Indians remain terminally drunk in the gutter, there will be no respect for them . . . American society thinks, 'Why not take their water rights, their mineral rights, their land, why not flood their sacred land with dams? They're just a bunch of goddam drunks.' " (pp. 279–80)

140   Wesley Whiteman's statement on the subject of Buffalo Gap and the sun dance is in *The Last Contrary: The Story of Wesley Whiteman (Black Bear)*, by Warren E. Schwartz (1988), p. 72.

140   Information about the town of Buffalo Gap and surrounding region may be found in these books, all at the public library in Custer, South Dakota: *Our Yesterdays*, by the Eastern Custer County Historical Society (1970); *Custer County History to 1976*, edited by Jessie Y. Sundstrom (1977); *Buffalo Gap: A French Ranch in Dakota*, by Le Baron E. de Mandat-Grancy (1889). See also "Fire Station Latest Addition to Buffalo Gap," in the Rapid City *Journal* (December 1, 1974).

143ff   Dewing, in *Wounded Knee II*, describes the Bad Heart Bull stabbing and its aftermath in detail. Other information about the incident may be found in accounts of Darld Schmitz's trial in the Rapid City *Journal* of April 30, May 1, May 2, and May 3, 1973.

144   Amos Bad Heart Bull (1869–1913) was one of the most gifted Indian ledger-book artists of his day. See *A Pictographic History of the Oglala Sioux*, drawings by Amos Bad Heart Bull, with text by Helen H. Blish (1967).

147   The former district attorney who told me about the film of the Custer riot is Lynn A. Moran of Custer, S.D.

148   I have been unable to find a full text of Sacheen Littlefeather's speech at the Academy Awards. *The New York Times* gave only a general description of what she said, and called the speech "an emotional diatribe." (Later it printed a correction, saying both her demeanor and her statement were restrained.)

148   I followed the post–Wounded Knee careers of Dennis Banks and Russell Means through newspaper reports at the time, and from the account in Means's autobiography.

CHAPTER 9

153   Father Buechel's dictionary, published by the Red Cloud Indian School (605-867-5491), is available from the school's bookstore.

166 The photo of my car was in the *Billings Gazette* of Monday, February 26, 1996, p. B 1.

CHAPTER 10

169 Jan Hardy of the Wright & McGill Co. in Denver is the source for information about the company's operations in Pine Ridge. The hand-tied hooks are now made in Korea as well as in Mexico.

170 Population figures for Pine Ridge and surrounding towns may be found in the *1990 Census of Population and Housing: Population and Housing Unit Counts* (U.S. Department of Commerce, Economics and Statistics Administration, Bureau of the Census).

172 For more on the poverty of Shannon County and the Pine Ridge Reservation, see "Sad Distinction for the Sioux: Homeland Is No. 1 in Poverty," in *The New York Times*, September 20, 1992, I, p. 1:5.

172 *The Washington Post* announced the capital area's dominance of per capita income in an article, "Washington Peerless on List of Richest Areas" (March 1, 1990; E, 1:2).

CHAPTER 11

184 Turner Network Television's *Crazy Horse* first aired on July 7, 1996. *Indian Country Today* reported the objections of Lyman Red Cloud and others to the movie in its issue of July 15–22, 1996, p. A 1.

185 Sources on the life of Red Cloud are the biographies cited (Hyde, Olson, and Larson) and *The Autobiography of Red Cloud*, edited by R. Eli Paul (1997).

Among sources published during Red Cloud's lifetime is an article describing his 1870 visit to New York City in *Harper's Weekly* (June 18, 1870; Vol. XIV, no. 703, p. 385).

186 The serious charge that Red Cloud conspired against the life of Crazy Horse is substantiated most tellingly (to my mind) by the account of William Garnett, interpreter at Fort Robinson; Garnett says that Red Cloud and other chiefs met with an officer at the fort who offered $300 and a fast horse to the man who could kill Crazy Horse. See "Report of William Garnett, Interpreter, to Gen'l H. L. Scott and Major J. McLaughlin," a copy of a typescript, on file at the New York Public Library. (See also my *Great Plains*, Chapter 6 and notes.)

191 Information about the life of Felix S. Cohen may be found in newspaper obituaries; in the introduction to his *The Legal Conscience: Selected Papers of Felix S. Cohen* (See note for p. 6 above); in the *Dictionary of American Biography* (supplement 5, 1951–1955); and in the Felix S. Cohen file in the Morris R. Cohen Library at the College of the City of New York.

Also, I am grateful to Lucy M. Kramer Cohen for kindly answering questions about her late husband which I sent to her by mail.

194 The siblings of Leroy "Sunshine" Janis I interviewed were Aqualynn Janis and Wilbert Janis.

CHAPTER 12

210 The Homestake Mine in Lead maintains a small historical museum; some of the information about the mine comes from there, and from *History of the Homestake Gold Mine*, a pamphlet published by the company.

210 The mining career of George Hearst is described in *The Hearsts: Family and Empire—The Later Years*, by Lindsay Chaney and Michael Cieply (1981). *William Randolph Hearst: His Role in American Progressivism*, by Roy Everett Littlefield III (1980), has details about W. R. Hearst at Harvard (pp. 3–5).

210 Sioux sources put the value of the gold taken from the Homestake Mine at $14 billion (*Indian Country Today*, June 18–25, 1996, p. A 1). The Homestake Mining Co. itself says it has produced 39 million ounces of gold. The price of gold fluctuates, of course. At present prices, which are low, that much gold would be worth about $10 billion.

210 Episcopal Bishop William H. Hare, head of a government commission to investigate problems at the Red Cloud Agency, wrote to President Grant of his displeasure at the planned Custer expedition (Olson, p. 173). Commissioner George W. Manypenny later called the Custer expedition "unlawful"; see Manypenny's *Our Indian Wards*, p. xxix. He and the other commissioners used the opportunity of the report that accompanied the Black Hills "agreement" to lecture the government on the wrongs it had done.

211 The course of the Sioux claim for the Black Hills through the Indian Claims Commission and the courts may be followed in newspaper stories—see *The New York Times* of July 1, 1980, p. 1:6; July 19, 1980, p. 5:1; May 27, 1981, p. 12:1; June 3, 1981, p. 18:5; January 19, 1982, p. 14:3; January 28, 1982, p. 14:6; December 11, 1983, I, p. 28:6; March 11, 1987, I, p. 23:1).

Lazarus (see note for p. 38) provides a good and readable account of the history of this complicated claim.

CHAPTER 13

For details about SuAnne Big Crow's high school basketball career I am indebted to Chick Big Crow, Rol Bradford, Charles Zimiga, Gordon Bergquist, Jeanne Horse, and Yvonne "Tiny" De Cory.

Interviews with members of the 1989 championship team—Rita Bad Bear, Mary Walking, Dakota "Happy" Big Crow, and Angie Big Crow Cournoyer —

also furnished valuable information. Ginny Dohrer Schulte and Coach Bergquist gave the perspective of the Milbank side in the championship game.

Additional facts may be found in the sports coverage of the *Lakota Times* (a reservation newspaper that later became *Indian Country Today*) in its issues of November 21, November 28, and December 5, 1989; and in the Grant County *Review* of Milbank, South Dakota, December 6, 1989.

226 Transcripts of the NBC *Nightly News* report on Pine Ridge that was broadcast on November 20, 21, and 22 of 1989 were obtained from Burrell's Information Services, Livingston, New Jersey.

234 Many people described the celebration in Pine Ridge after the victory. Dennis Banks, Charles Zimiga, Jeanne Horse, and the players on the championship team mentioned above were especially helpful.

CHAPTER 14

As with much of what I know about SuAnne, information in this chapter comes from interviews with her family, coaches, and friends, in particular Doni De Cory, Chick Big Crow, Wesley Bettleyoun, Jeanne Horse, and Charles Zimiga.

247ff For the details of SuAnne's car accident and her funeral I have relied on newspaper accounts (the Chadron [Nebraska] *Record* of February 14, 1992; the Rapid City *Journal,* February 10, 1992, p. 1; the *Lakota Times* [now *Indian Country Today*], February 12, 1992, p. 1; February 19, 1992, B 4–5); interviews with Chick Big Crow; and the South Dakota Department of Transportation accident report.

250 Along with Chick Big Crow, Rol Bradford described for me the early days of setting up the Big Crow Center.

CHAPTER 15

143ff My sources for statistics on alcohol-related vehicle fatalities on the reservation come from *Indian Country Today* (November 25–December 2, 1997, p. C1) and from the South Dakota Department of Transportation booklet, *Motor Vehicle Traffic Accident Summary* (1997, with additional data for 1998).

If one includes accidents involving alcohol not only on the reservation but near it, the figures are higher. *Indian Country Today*, citing the Pine Ridge Office of Environmental Health, reported (July 12–19, 1999, p. A1) that thirty-seven people died on or near the reservation in the preceding three years in alcohol-related crashes.

None of the people I know in Oglala suffered serious damage in the tornado. After the wreckage had been cleared away, much of the village had disappeared and neighborhoods were reduced to streets and driveways leading to nothing. The tribe says that Oglala will soon be rebuilt with two hundred new homes.

The protests in White Clay declined in size in the weeks following the riot, and no further violence occurred. The protesters had given the liquor stores in White Clay a deadline to shut down that came due about a month after the first march; the deadline passed unmarked. One of the store owners said business in White Clay had returned to normal.

President Clinton's visit to Pine Ridge was a major news story of July 8, 1999. See *The New York Times* of that date, p. A 12.

Foreword

YOU ARE ABOUT TO ENTER THE PERSONAL AND PROFES-
sional lives of thirty remarkable educators. The stories they tell
here are as varied as the actors themselves who have played on the
stages of public and private, elementary, middle, and high, wealthy
and impoverished schools around the country. Yet all of these
authors have in common two distinctive qualities: each was once a
beginning school head, and each has chosen to share with us in
writing that turbulent first year.

The language in these sometimes poetic accounts reveals the
delight, the frustration, and above all the ambiguity attendant to
that initial year. The words with which these formative experiences are wrapped move me deeply for they evoke my own unfor-
gettable first year as principal of an inner-city school. Indeed, the
paradoxes and passions that jump out of these pages are generic,
common to everyone's beginning experience as an educator:

> wonderful and wicked
> control and chaos
> hugs and heartaches
> isolation and collegiality
> respected and unloved
> power and powerlessness
> conviction and compromise
> prosecutor and jury
> leadership and luck

pleasure and adversity
confidence and self-doubt
tenacity and vulnerability
firmness and flexibility
work and play
faith and fear
humor and pathos
stability and change
surprise and routinization.

But what shines through these accounts for me, above all, is the profound and often painful learning of the novice school leader. The learning curves of these educators are steep indeed. As one put it, "Nothing could have prepared me for my first year as principal." And another, "But once in the principal's office my true education had just begun."

In the pages that follow, you, too, will learn what each of these school heads learned. You will go where they went and sit with them in their offices that sometimes resemble a courtroom, sometimes a seminar, sometimes a board meeting, and most often a hospital emergency ward.

It is an all too common belief that when a school practitioner speaks, what emerges is a "war story." Indeed, I find many vivid descriptions of practice do resemble war stories. But when these portrayals of practice are accompanied by careful and thoughtful analysis and reflection, as they are here, war stories are transformed into abundant craft knowledge. This collection offers a fine-grained description and analysis of one year in the past—with important lessons for the future. The wisdom of the craft revealed here has much to offer those who aspire to be principals and those who aspire to prepare others for the principalship and, of course, those who are themselves experiencing their first year as head of a school. Whatever stereotypes one holds about school leaders—whether as heroic commander on a white horse or as innocuous manager pushing papers—are likely to be updated, perhaps violated, by these vivid portraits.

I found myself unable to read through this volume continuously. Rather, I find these little vignettes best consumed, like peanuts, a few at a time, allowing plenty of opportunity to savor and chew them over. "Have you got a minute?" are words heard frequently by heads of schools. When I heard them, I never knew what was coming next. If you do have a minute, you are in for an unusual journey in the unexpected world of the beginning school leader. Part of the surprise for me was discovering that I had worked with and

for many of these authors over the years. I think all of us will discover here some unexpected connections with our past.

One of the great paradoxes of school life is that elementary, middle, and high schools are thought to be places that promote the learning of young people. These stories suggest just how much the schoolhouse can be a rich context for the development of educators themselves. Powerful, replenishing learning comes to those who reflect on practice—and to those of us who are privy to their reflections.

Roland S. Barth

Preface

IN SEPTEMBER 1991, SCOTT MCVAY, EXECUTIVE director of the Geraldine R. Dodge Foundation, and I met with the directors of four principals' centers. As Millie Blackman, Michael Gillespie, India Podsen, and Laverne Scott spoke to us about their experiences with principals, I passed Scott a note which said, "What about doing a book called *First Year as Principal?*" Scott smiled, since the idea proceeded naturally from Dodge Foundation support of a prior book, *The First Year of Teaching* (Walker 1991).

The Dodge Foundation had been looking at the role of principal in the complex ecosystem of schools for some time. With long experience in making grants directed to secondary schools and more recently to middle and elementary schools, the foundation was ready to launch a major initiative seeking to promote principals as "instructional leaders," a phrase that is connected to the original role that school leaders played.

Over the last half century, as central office bureaucracy has grown to meet new demands (and created some demands of its own), the job of the principal has changed. Whereas once the "educational buck" might have stopped at the principal's office in all matters relating directly to the classroom, in many schools the role of principal is no longer that of academic catalyst or explorer of new possibilities for teaching and learning. People involved with schools (and certainly many parents) wonder where the leadership is in education because all too often those who have, or

appear to have, the authority and responsibility are not in the school-house itself.

For all the national lament about the quality of schools, there are, of course, some stunning exceptions that give hope for the future. And where these exceptions are found, typically we also find a principal who is a true instructional leader, an educator whose vision stays focused on the full potential of schools and whose eyes betray the joy of learning no matter how persistent the distractions. This book is an effort to let principals share their own stories with those who are considering a career in school leadership and also with the general public—both policymakers and the polity—who need to understand better what school leadership requires.

To find these stories, the foundation advertised nationally, calling for essays that shed light on the "human side" of school leadership especially as it is experienced during that first critical year on the job. Responses came from people who had led every type of school in almost every state (and Canada). Some of these principals were looking back as far as forty years; a few took pen (or rather word processor) in hand literally as they were completing their first year. Each essay was reviewed by five experienced school leaders who took on the difficult task of ranking. This book contains the top thirty essays from that process.

The stories share at least two themes, one of which is the basic realization that the step into the principal's office has a significantly higher rise than the smooth progression of treads preceding it. Here we find career educators who have spent years in the classroom working with students, colleagues, and parents and who by all accounts know the essence of schooling as well as the technical side of how school "keeps." Yet, pulling it all together and providing the vision of where a school ought to go next require a whole new set of skills. Leadership, it appears, is not experienced by the leader in quite the way it is experienced by those being led.

A second theme is the frustration felt by many principals who set out to provide instructional leadership for their schools but soon find themselves in a dozen other roles ranging from traffic cop to plumber, fire fighter to arbitrator. Leadership means knowing what to do when the country is shocked by the assassination of its president, or when it ought to be more shocked by the tragedy of how it treats even one of its children. But it means other things, too—like going through the trash looking for a child's lost dime-store ring, encouraging a bull to leave the school yard, or being on the "gotcha" end of a practical joke cooked up by two playful teachers. The challenge is finding the balance or the variety of balances needed to meet the myriad needs of every

student and every teacher under conditions that are mostly unpredictable and often uncontrollable.

The essays begin with a journal entry from Johanna VanderMolen, who gives us a Vermeer-like peek into the daily life of a first-year principal. They end with a pair of stories written by Joseph and Mark Segar, father and son, each of whom followed his own path to the principal's office. In the middle are twenty-seven others by a fascinating array of educators. These stories pertain only to the people who wrote them. Yet taken together, they tell a broader story that in one way or another has something to say to every school leader and to all who care about schools.

In my work as editor and midwife for this book, I have many people to thank. Cheryl Kimball at Heinemann has been there every step of the way coaxing, guiding, offering good suggestions—always in a gentle way. Her predecessor at Heinemann, Tom Seavey, saw the Dodge Foundation's "Call for Essays" and thought the book was such a good idea that he contacted us to see if we had a publisher. While such an approach makes good business sense for a publisher, the folks at Heinemann care first about schools, and I believe Tom's call had much more to do with good education than good business. Also, Gail Gorman, my assistant at Cambridge College, has done yeoman service keeping all the strands of this project from unraveling.

Roland Barth has been a spiritual guide long before the idea for this book came onto anyone's screen. Not only is he the godfather of perhaps *every* center for principals in the country, but his clear vision about the way schools can and should work has helped many educators. In his Foreword we get to hear his overview of how these stories fit with the insights he has gained from his distinguished career working with principals.

Also, to Scott McVay, the Dodge trustees, and my wonderful colleagues at the foundation, I am deeply grateful for a spirit that is difficult to capture in words. The foundation operates with a level of hope and passion that I have never experienced any other place. It was a joy to spend long days at 163 Madison Avenue and to know the many people whose lives and dreams intersect with the foundation. Scott McVay's Introduction to this volume provides a window into his own personal commitment to education and his faith in people. He was the one who suggested we include Marge Piercy's "To Be of Use" and that we use Lonni Sue Johnson's drawing for the cover. Together they tell quite a story. Although Scott has never held the title "teacher," he is one of the best I ever had.

Finally, I am grateful for the support of my family, especially my wife, Joanne Hoffman, who started her own first year as a school head while this

book was being edited and produced. On many early mornings and late nights, I would hear her worrying over the very same challenges I was reading about in the essays scattered across my desk. Her experience was all the proof I needed to confirm the validity of these stories.

In the end, the purpose of schooling is to make sure that all children have the chance to know themselves and to explore the world with the vision and gifts that are theirs alone. People who want to lead schools know that, and their singular goal, often against great odds, is to serve those children well. For me, the purpose of schools and this book is intensely personal: I wish for my daughter, Katie, and for my stepdaughter, Caitlin, that every school always be as good as its promise. We can tolerate nothing less.

Ronald Thorpe

Among a Company of Pilgrims

EARLY IN THE CENTURY NOW DRAWING TO A CLOSE, George Ade was writing pieces known as fables for a newspaper in the Midwest. He had a great following. Readers were hungry for what he dished up almost daily, and the fables answered a need in people's lives the way a good story or poem might. His fables were more read than Aesop's in those parts.

My favorite is "The Old Fox and the Young Fox." One day Old Fox called in Young Fox to share with him a few hard-won nuggets of truth gleaned from having spent some time in this valley. Young Fox yawned since he knew things the way a sophomore knows things. His eyes glazed over as he tuned out. Yet in that little fable are hints and clues about how to live that don't compete with the Ten Commandments but nonetheless contain some practical stuff.

For instance, one of Old Fox's maxims is, "Never accuse a Man of being Lazy. There is no such thing as Laziness. If a Man does not go about his work with Enthusiasm, it means that he has not yet found . . . the Task that Destiny has set aside for him."

Or, notes the Old Fox, "An Ounce of Prevention is worth a Pound of Cure and costs more. Don't attempt to prevent Trouble or you will lose your eyesight watching so many corners at the same time. Wait until Trouble comes and then consult a Specialist." Or, "If you expect to be a popular After-Dinner Speaker, don't attempt to work at anything else. That is a sufficiently large contract for one brief Existence."

The book you hold in your hands is a first attempt to gather in one place the experience of the first year as a principal. You will read here that prior schooling and experience as a teacher do not fully prepare anyone for that daunting first year, a year that can almost overwhelm the vision of the first day.

But the spirit and generosity of these thirty essays suggest that if teaching is one of the highest callings to which a human being can aspire, then to be the principal teacher or lead learner must be the absolute fulcrum of school reform.

Written from many points on the trajectory of experience, from the vantage point of a retired principal recalling that vivid first year to one who has been one year in the saddle, each essay sheds light on the extraordinary opportunity to be a good principal. Fables abound as do "morals of the fables." Ade suggests, "Even the Elders can give a number of Helpful Hints."

This book is meant for any principal or aspiring principal, but we expect that it will be most closely read by those new at the craft or considering it closely. Their antennae are out, and they may already be dealing with the flywheel of daily events in a large community of children and adults. And they (you) will find instruction and solace in the thoughts of those who are just ahead on the path of instructional leadership.

Who will not read closely Barbara Landis Chase's "The Best News of All" that sees the first year as crucible. As she looks back on the first year, the lessons she came to understand and believe remain valid. So many points jump out, seem honest and helpful, including:

> It is hard for others to comprehend the power of the connection we feel to our schools. I know that this was something I never understood until I walked this ground.

And a thought can animate a school and drive the vision of that learning community:

> My own litmus test for every decision is to ask if it is the right thing for the students: present and future.

At a Celebration of Teaching event in 1992 honoring the County Teachers of the Year in New Jersey, four recipients spoke of breakthrough strategies in teaching. In each case they felt that had they asked permission, it would have been denied, and yet those very ideas were what won them acclaim. As Mary Ann Sinkkonen notes:

> The best advice I received as I was beginning that first year was, "Use your position to say, 'Yes.'"

In Albert Adams's fascinating piece, wherein he met in the early days of his principalship with parents, teachers, students, and alumni, he made a good map of the territory of that school. In identifying the themes that define his school, including challenges that require attention, he notes:

> In many cases it is recurring stories, rather than specific information, which provide the deepest insights.

Here, too, you will find recurring stories, some familiar, others surprisingly fresh, yet speaking to your precise situation. As a principal, new or seasoned, you will see that your triumphs and travails are widely shared. Those of you who had a tough but exhilarating first year will find here others who fared less well.

But, overall, you will be left with the impression that you are among a company of pilgrims on a quest to make vibrant communities of learners. You are learning by doing, swapping stories along the way, and reconfirming at every step the initial tug to teaching that has shaped your lifework.

Scott McVay

Then and Now: Lessons of a New Principal

JOHANNA A. VANDERMOLEN

JOURNAL ENTRY, JUNE 12, 1988

As the sun comes up tomorrow morning I'll hurry across town to finish my first year as an elementary school principal. But sleep does not close my eyes tonight although the stars are out and the evening is late and cool. Before me I see student faces who will move on to middle school, faces that laughed *at* me and *with* me, those who cried when I counseled them, and others who begged me to give them another chance before I called mom or dad to let them know that their child had broken some school rule. I see Jeanne who confided to me that she had been sexually assaulted by a neighbor since attending the third grade, and Carlos who used pictures to communicate because his desire to speak was abruptly taken away by insufferable traumas no child should have to endure. And prideful Joey, who is so rough and tough, always looking for a fight, and who, just as often, has sat in my office and cried for his long-lost father. I'm going to miss them deeply, for they have indeed touched and changed my life.

I have felt sadness, exasperation, challenges, joy, and frustration this year. I have also learned about humankind, forgiveness, hardships, working with people, and building working relationships. My heart has ached and bled, but mostly it sang with jubilation at the love that I saw teachers give to children every day.

These teachers and the parents of the children with whom I have worked have been supportive, challenging, and stimulating. They have also at times been unmoving and difficult.

1

My first job as principal began late one Wednesday evening in February 1988 when I received a phone call from the superintendent requesting that I take an elementary principalship the following Monday morning. As a middle school assistant principal, I had my back pocket stuffed with years of elementary experience, so I agreed. I fumbled my way through the week closing out my current job and on Monday drove across town to my new assignment.

Nothing could have prepared me for my first year as principal. The school I entered was overcrowded and experiencing boundary changes that were opposed by both the teachers and the parents. As a result, the faculty was depressed and the parents were angry.

I knew little about the situation, the anger, or the depression before I became the school's principal. This, in retrospect, was probably my saving grace. I simply accepted the school as a new, exciting experience and assumed that everyone wanted to work together in harmony.

I had believed that when I became a principal I would be a notable instructional leader. This school was so demoralized, however, that at the end of a few weeks I decided to place my job as instructional leader on hold and focus on a more immediate concern: staff and community morale.

Fortunately, this faculty was one of the best with which I had ever worked—energetic, professional, and, as I found out later that year, very enthusiastic. They were a great group of people to whom I was drawn both professionally and personally. We established a tennis club where many faculty members took tennis lessons together (I can freely admit that I was the worst player) and a monthly Literature Club. Many of us repainted the faculty room during that first summer.

JOURNAL ENTRY, JUNE 1993:

It's five years later, and I've just reread my journal from that first year. It makes me sit back, reflect, and smile. Over the course of that year the boundary changes were made and, contrary to the fears of the staff and community, the school continued to be successful, earning the California Distinguished School Award the following year.

I'm still a principal but in a different school and city. In reflection I recognize that many of my current "guiding principles" were initially developed during that first year:

· Choose Your Battles
I learned to prioritize what needed to be done. I had to realize that I could NOT do everything at once and that some problems are just more pressing than others.

- Stay Focused
  I learned to decide what my goals are and then make decisions throughout the year supporting those goals. By staying focused I have found that I can get more done without being scattered in many directions.
- Build Upon the Successes the School Already Has
  I learned that teachers and parents take enormous pride in their school, even if there are problems. By building upon the actual and perceived successes of the school, I have found that changes can be made.
- Keep Things in Perspective
  I learned that friends and mentors are to be cherished, for through discussions with these people the perceived vastness of many problems will diminish.

I now visualize the course of a school as a river with smooth currents and pounding, steep rapids. My school sits upon this river, moving with the flow. Empowered by my "guiding principles," there are rapids that I choose to run and those that are best to circumvent. There are smooth waters that are comfortable, but when the calm continues too long, I can lift my oar, stir the current, and challenge the crew to explore new territory. Most important, I must keep us all flowing toward our main goal—discovering what is in the best interest of our children.

JOHANNA VANDERMOLEN IS THE PRINCIPAL OF THE NORTHWOOD SCHOOL IN NAPA, CALIFORNIA.

The Best News of All

BARBARA LANDIS CHASE

Slowly, I place the thirteenth standard black "Day-At-A-Glance" at the end of the line with its twelve identical partners standing on the bottom bookshelf in my office. My first impulse is to turn away immediately, giving my attention to the crisp, new 1993–94 academic planner sitting at the ready on my desk across the room. But a vague sense of wistfulness holds me back, as it has every year when I have performed this entirely private but somehow momentous ritual. Glancing down this row of silent chroniclers of my years as a school head, I look at the first book and think back to the young woman who had so much to learn in that first year.

I started that year with a bag of tricks and a Pandora's box, not of evils, but of inexperience. On one hand, I was generally, at least as far as I could tell, a candidate with whom people at the school were satisfied. I was young (thirty-five) and energetic. I had, for whatever reason, the confidence that I could do a good job. My husband was enormously supportive. This all-girl school was strong and established; the board savvy and eager to be helpful.

On the other hand, I was deficient in many areas: I had almost no experience in finance or development, writing for publication, or public speaking. Yet I would have to work with a multi-million dollar budget, raise money, write a monthly column for the school newsletter, and speak to countless student assemblies and parent and alumnae meetings. I had not hired, fired, or supervised anyone in my previous experience as teacher and then as director of admission, but in that first year, I would need to make a number of very tough personnel decisions.

4

I can't honestly say I learned everything I know about independent school leadership in that first year; I must have known a little bit going into it. Certainly I have learned a lot since. Even more certainly, I still have much to learn. The first year of any experience is, in many ways, a crucible. You reveal the way you think and understand the world. You set patterns of behavior that henceforth become expectations. You settle pretty substantially the issue of trust.

What did the events of that first year teach me about leadership—a subject heretofore theoretical and secondhand but now so real and so personal? Looking back, I can see that the lessons I came to understand and believe that first year have remained valid for me. The events of subsequent years have fleshed them out, given them new and fascinating faces, but have never changed them. The ambiguity that is a condition of life for school heads means that every rule has its important exception and that embedded in every axiom is the undoing of the axiomatic. Nevertheless, I believe it is important for me to hold to these lessons. I can't say how valid they are for other people in other schools. Maybe what is most important is for each of us to sit down every once in a while and take the time to consider what these lessons are for us. Here are mine:

LESSON 1

You must learn to live with frustration; the multitudinous demands of the job are such that you will constantly disappoint people—including yourself.

This is a job, I am fond of saying, for people with short attention spans. We never do one thing long enough to become bored. That is the good news. The bad news is that we are pulled in so many directions that we rarely feel satisfied that we have truly finished one thing. Just dealing with the mail is daunting. In my first year, I went through the mail every day and sorted out the things I needed to deal with right then and there. I put everything else onto a "reading pile" on a shelf by my desk. At the beginning of the summer, I began going through the pile, and I discovered many things that I really should have done something about earlier: announcements of important professional development opportunities, articles that could have informed talks, and articles I had to turn out. But I simply couldn't deal with all the paper. I've learned to cope with the flood of paper much more expeditiously—yet the reading pile still mounts up as the busy spring accelerates toward graduation. We do see some absolutely fascinating and sometimes very inspiring reading cross our desks: from the latest issue of the *Harvard Education Review* to letters of gratitude from recent or not-so-recent graduates. We are lucky, as school heads, to have

a change of pace in the summer—allowing us to catch up on important and enriching reading.

The mail represents only a small fraction of the time demands. Daily, hourly, minute by minute, we try to meet the needs and expectations of the people who comprise the major constituencies we serve: students, faculty, parents, alumnae, trustees, the community. They each have their own needs and they can't possibly all be met because of time restraints and because the needs of various constituencies are often in conflict. As independent school heads, we are the chief executive officers of small businesses (non-profit though they be), but we are also the head teachers.

Beyond the routine administrative matters, we are called upon to handle, competently, any unusual events. In that first year, I had to hire a new business manager midyear, and then I had to work with that new business manager to cope with the situation when our food service manager quit on very short notice. As I recall, between us we figured out how many loaves of bread and how much peanut butter and jelly we would need to go out and buy, if it came to that. What did any of this have to do with academics? Not much. But at the same time, I was learning to recognize the strengths and weaknesses of each faculty member, the rationale for the science sequence, and the need for a major revision of the advising program.

I learned that the trustees and parents expected me to run the school like a well-run business but also to know them and their children and each faculty member personally and to be accessible in person or by telephone, whether at 7:30 A.M. or 7:30 P.M. I was expected to keep up with the administrative side of things and also to appear at each hockey game, the Upper School performance of "Oklahoma," and parent meetings for every division of the school. The students wanted a headmistress they could feel close to, that is, spend time with, and the development director wanted me to get out on the road to meet the alumnae. Finally, I learned that fulfilling all of these expectations was absolutely impossible and thus, that I would be disappointing people, including myself, all of the time. I also learned that I derived surprising pleasure and real energy from coming into contact with all of these people in so many settings. I almost always felt energized and enthusiastic about what I was doing and the work the school was doing after one of these events. Often, it was pure fun.

LESSON 2

Be willing to do the right thing and then live with the sudden silence in the faculty room when you walk in. And, as a corollary: Learn to reach out to your colleagues.

Ours is often a lonely job. The hard decisions are most often ours to make. You can't please all of the people in any given situation, even if that is precisely what you set out to do, so you might as well try to do the right thing, even if it doesn't win you popularity in the short run. My own litmus test for every decision is to ask if it is the right thing for the students: present and future. They are the only reason we exist. That first year, I discovered that the faculty were permitted to smoke in the lunchroom—a practice I decided should end. At an early faculty meeting, I simply told them they couldn't—by edict or fiat or whatever you might wish to call such an authoritarian move. They accepted it—some, rather reluctantly. Yet, I sensed that I had only a certain number of chips to use up this way. Most decisions were much more participatory.

Doing what is right for students doesn't mean doing just what they would have you do. That first year, I needed to tighten up on rules for dances. It was not a popular move, and the students let me know it. So I learned to accept and live with the feeling of being unloved.

And I learned the important need for political grounding. The board of trustees had better be ready to support you, which means they had better know what you're about and understand and agree with it. Most of all, they had better not be unhappily surprised. It is, after all, the board who hired you, and it is they who have the power to fire you if they don't think you are doing a good job. There were and continue to be too many examples of heads losing their jobs because they have lost the support of the board.

And now for the corollary: I also learned the critical importance of the telephone as lifeline when times get tough and life feels lonely. The only people who completely understand what you are going through are the people who have gone through it themselves: other school heads. I learned to call the colleagues I trust and admire and seek their advice and sympathy. I have never called and been rebuffed. I have never hung up and not felt better.

LESSON 3

Learn from your mistakes; learn to know yourself as other people perceive you. Then try to change the things you can change and live with the things you can't.

I learned this lesson the first time I got back the results of formal evaluations from the board and faculty. They said some very nice things. People seemed to think I was doing a good job—but, of course, not a perfect one.

The most frustrating thing was that it was hard to respond to the negative feedback. Evidently, some people found me *too* efficient and (I'll never

forget this particular phrase) "not the warmest person in the world." At first, I was devastated. *I* knew I was a warm, emotional, *personal* kind of person. The feedback just had to be wrong. But the more I thought and talked about it with people I knew and trusted, the more philosophical I became. It was true that I could become so immersed in an issue or problem that I might seem aloof or distant. This tendency became clear one day as I was walking across campus with something on my mind and suddenly realized that I had passed two people without saying hello. On another occasion, a trustee I looked up to and trusted was kind enough to tell me that, although she knew I didn't do it deliberately, I sometimes rolled my eyes in meetings when things were proceeding too slowly or people were being obtuse. So, I learned there was some truth in the perception.

But I also came to believe, and still do, that women have a particularly difficult time in positions like ours. We are expected to be efficient in our executive duties, and we are also criticized for seeming *too* businesslike, *too* professional. In short, we can't win. I have learned to accept this as a paradox of our current evolving gender attitudes, but I cannot stress enough the importance of seeking and using self-knowledge, informed by an understanding of how others see us. We *must* learn from our mistakes. And our most important mistakes (and, thus our most important opportunities for victories) come in the area of human relations.

LESSON 4

Hire the very best administrators you can find. Then stand back and let them do their jobs. Support them assiduously. Accept the blame for things that go wrong and give them the credit for everything that goes right.

I learned quickly that the people with whom I worked most closely every day were extremely important to me. They needed my ear for listening and my arm for support, and I needed them to make sure things went well. I couldn't possibly do everything myself. I had to be ready to help them solve a tricky personnel problem or talk through a challenging situation with a student. I needed to praise them freely and give them constructive criticism. I needed to support their professional growth and development, even when it meant helping them to move on to another position and thus losing them. I owe this not only to them, but to the profession. In short, I learned that the power I had as head of the school was exponentially enhanced if I shared it with these people. The more I enabled and empowered them, the more got done, the more progress we made.

LESSON 5

Come to understand the nature of your connection with the school as its leader. Learn to use it, but always understand the underlying danger of its power.

I have thought about this paradox so much that I have given it a strange name: "Materfamilias and Jonah's Whale." It is hard for others to comprehend the power of the connection we feel to our schools. I know that this was something I never understood until I walked this ground. We are, whether we want to be or not, in a real sense the mothers or fathers of these school families. When there is crisis, we feel the stress of full responsibility. The bomb threat or fire or lawsuit rests on our shoulders far more heavily than on anyone else's. When there is loss, we grieve and yet must be strong for everyone, just like parents in any family. I learned early how important it is for the leader to be on the scene, visible and strong in these inevitable times of crisis, or celebration, or ritual, or loss—how important it is to say the right things in a moving way, to shepherd the community safely through these passages.

I also began to notice, almost from the beginning, that although this connection was intensely beautiful and meaningful, it was also dangerous. As school heads, we are all tempted to think of and speak of these schools as "ours." Many of us use the personal possessive "my" before "faculty" or "school." We do this at our peril. These are institutions far beyond our illusory power to shape or guide them. Our school was founded a hundred years before I came onto the scene, and it will prevail long after I am gone. My stewardship, although important, was not all-important. Calling the school "my school" would be like Jonah calling the whale that had swallowed him up, carried him for three days and three nights through the sea, "my whale." The institutions we lead carry us to lands we could never have imagined, on a course we chart with limited proficiency.

I came to believe that this sense of connection the leader feels for the institution she leads had better be tempered with a large grain of humility. I came to believe this after seeing several school heads, who had spent years at an institution, forced to leave not on their own terms but terminated, fired, or, as the euphemism has come to be used, "disruptively separated" at great cost to themselves and the school. They and the school were not, after all, one and the same. And that is a good thing, if only we can remember it. We need to be separate from our institutions, not only because it is good for them, but because it is the only way for us to maintain our own mental health. Having what our students would call "a life" (as in "Get one!") is absolutely essential.

I reflect, as I turn from the shelf with my thirteen years lined up on it, that for all its frustrations and riskiness, I cannot think of a job I would rather be doing. What we do as school heads matters—really matters. Working in a place that cares about and educates young people stimulates us, challenges us, gratifies us. That line of thirteen books represents one of the best things about life as a school head: each year we get a fresh chance to start all over again. Each September brings a new opportunity to get on a new footing with all of those myriad constituencies. We get to give another talk at parents' evenings, work with a new senior class, write another Class Day Talk, forge a stronger relationship with each of our colleagues. The best news of all is that we will never do it perfectly, so we have the chance each year to try again to do it a little better.

BARBARA LANDIS CHASE IS HEAD OF SCHOOL AT PHILLIPS ACADEMY IN ANDOVER, MASSACHUSETTS.

There's Nothing As Practical As a Good Theory

SARAH L. LEVINE

This piece is about the confluence of theories, desires, and realities during my first year as head of a small elementary school. With the perspective of subsequent years, it is also about the importance of conviction, tenacity, flexibility, humility, and patience.

When I walked into my office on that steamy July morning, feelings of fear far outweighed the confidence I had exuded during the search process. Certainly I knew a lot about leading schools; I had been sharing the latest research with principals and other school leaders around the country for the last six years in my job at the Harvard Principals' Center. Yet for all the time I had spent in schools and for the many times I stood in front of principals, heads, superintendents, and even state commissioners, I had never actually sat in their chairs or walked in their shoes in the offices and schools where the real and complex issues of school leadership come to rest.

What I brought to the principalship was a set of theories—convictions—about: schools as communities of learners and leaders; writing as a powerful tool for staff development; practice shaped by core values; and adult growth as a fundamental condition for children's development. With all the idealism of a first-year principal tempered by the realities of a mid-life adult, I

11

wanted to share with children, teachers, and parents my convictions and commitments so that together we could bring to life the possibilities and promises that reside within every school.

Soon after my appointment, I learned that for some members of the hiring committee, offering the role of head to someone from a university was a mighty leap of faith. Why would a person want to move from "higher" to "lower" education? Would I be aloof, impractical, or overly academic? Rather than an asset, my affiliation with Harvard was something I needed to overcome. Manifestations of this consideration came from both parents and faculty. During my first weeks, I sent parents an article by a well-known early childhood educator. While I didn't agree with all that the article proposed, I thought the ideas were provocative and might lead to interesting discussion. Immediately, the article and my views became synonymous. Sharing research only fanned the fires for those worried about the new head's overly academic frame of reference.

Determined to make faculty meetings substantive, I spoke to teachers about school culture during opening school meetings, modifying a talk I had given successfully many times before—complete with overheads! "We're not in graduate school," I heard within minutes of completing the presentation. This was neither the first nor final time I was to feel a keen sense of uneasiness when what I believed to be important was not immediately embraced.

I have a firm belief in writing as a tool for staff development. This belief was generated and nurtured at the Principals' Center, and principals who came there for the summer couldn't wait to return to their schools, journals in hand. So what if they later told me it was hard to keep up the practice once the school year began? So what if they could never convince their faculties of the power and importance of writing? It would be a different story for *me* with *my* teachers. Of that I was (almost) certain.

"I'd like to tell you about 'freewriting'," I said enthusiastically at the beginning of a faculty meeting. "Freewriting is putting pen to paper and continuing to write whatever comes to mind without stopping. If you get stuck, just write 'I'm stuck, I'm stuck, I'm stuck' until your next thought comes." During the first year, I asked faculty and staff to bring to every meeting the journals I had given each of them. Before we talked about a complex issue— children and discipline, or faculty evaluation—I asked everyone, myself included, to freewrite about it.

The first few times, everyone wrote. Then some wrote while others stared out toward the playground. "Oh, were we supposed to bring our journals?" asked two teachers almost at the same time. It seems both had left their writing notebooks back in their classrooms. Again that uneasy feeling made its way up

and down my spine. Was this to be another potent theory without practical meaning? Almost always our discussions were enriched by our written reflections. Yet, some teachers felt the writing and talking took time and energy away from the *doing*. Together we are still searching for a comfortable balance.

Establishing core values and creating a common vision—these tenets I *knew* to be as valid in practice as they are in the ivy-covered towers of academe. Convinced of this wisdom, I asked the art teacher to cover the bulletin boards at the school's entrance with these three statements: Everyone Can Learn; Celebrate Diversity; and BDS (our school initials) Means Community. Indisputable values, I thought confidently, and ones that everyone could get behind. Long discussions and debates about the multiple meanings of diversity or the strengths and limits of school as community have since complicated my thinking. Nevertheless I have appreciated and learned from the open and honest interchange that has helped us move toward common ground.

Everyone Can Learn—simple enough, I thought, and certainly beyond question. "What promises are we making when we say everyone can learn?" a veteran teacher asked seriously soon after the brightly colored letters appeared. "Are we saying that the school will find a way to reach every child? What if a child has insurmountable limitations?" At almost the same moment, we recalled a recent legal case where a nearby school was backpedaling from such a claim. Putting core values on a bulletin board in bright letters was clearly easier than defining them, putting them into practice, or defending them.

Finally, I brought to my new school a belief in the importance of adult development as a *prerequisite* for children's growth. Teachers must feel vital and alive about their work in order for students to be engaged in meaningful and sustained learning. To think about schools as communities of learners where everyone—children, teachers, principal, and parents—is learning was a new and not-so-obvious idea for some. After all, elementary and secondary schools are for children and adolescents. Since when did adults factor into the equation?

Commensurate with the high value I place upon adult growth, one of the first things I asked from my board was an allocation of substantial funds for professional development. But finding good substitute teachers is not always easy, and children need consistency in the classroom. What about those times when funds are limited, and hard decisions have to be made about their allocation? Since schools must take account of diverse perspectives, I now hold my thinking about adult growth in a broader context of substitutes, consistency for children, and making hard choices with limited funds. Decisions in practice are not always as simple as theory would make

them seem. Now, when the dailiness of school life dampens my idealism, it is teachers who remind me how important it is for them to grow *so that* their students can learn.

Why share all of this as a reflection on the first year of the principalship? Why not offer a story or vignette that captures a more finite aspect of how I have come to make sense of school leadership? I choose to paint a broader picture for several reasons. Many of the issues I have written about that seemed so new, so hard, and so unsettling during my first year have, with considerable persistence, patience, and a willingness to learn, become "the way we do things around here" at the school. Rather than abnormalities to be questioned, they are norms increasingly valued if still to be explained, examined, and refined.

Not every one of the beliefs or theories I brought with me has proved resilient or even relevant to the particular school culture I inherited and have now helped to shape. But many *have* become meaningful, and others that originated from faculty, staff, parents, and children have contributed to my growth and to the school's collective vision. All along I have been grateful for the theories and perspectives I brought with me and for the views about schools, school leadership, and children's learning that others have contributed to the continuing conversation.

What really happened to me that first year as a principal and every year since is that I have brought my views and theories into the school as clearly and forcefully as I believe them. I also have worked to keep myself open to new ideas, and especially to ideas that are different from mine. Gradually, I am learning to tolerate that uneasy feeling that still runs up and down my spine when I encounter differences and disagreements. But I can't think of a better or more important place to make theory good and practical nor a place where I would rather work and learn.

Most principals will agree that children tend to accept new ideas more quickly than do many adults. At the end of my first year, several fifth graders presented me with a wooden plaque they had been crafting together for months in the shop. Choosing an assembly where the impact of the gift would be most widely evident, they ceremoniously handed me the sign, which reads: HEAD LEARNER. With their help, I hung it near the top of my office door— just to be sure that I, and all the adults who pass by, cannot help but read it!

SARAH L. LEVINE IS HEAD AT THE BELMONT DAY SCHOOL IN BELMONT, MASSACHUSETTS.

Detective, Prosecutor, Judge, and Jury

GORDON A. DONALDSON, JR.

"Just sit down and shut your mouth, Jason! . . . Now, Carol, where were you yesterday fourth period, Ms. Stark has you marked absent? . . . Aw, come on, Carol, you said you were in Clinic *last* week, too. Are you sick or just sick of Civics?" So began another day for me at Ellsworth Junior-Senior High School in Ellsworth, Maine. In 1976, at the age of thirty, I became principal of EJSHS, a school of eight hundred students, grades 7–12.

Each day began with a parade of students who were called to the office for various infractions the previous day. My job was to stand on the "other side" of the office counter, question the twenty to thirty students who had been summoned on the public address system about their infractions, and mete out punishments. It was the linchpin of a system of discipline I inherited. I suspect it had been developed because it beat chasing kids all day and pulling them out of classes to interrogate them. Once I got the hang of it, the system seemed to work well—as long as I ignored some fundamental principles of human decency.

In retrospect, I am embarrassed by the insensitivity I showed toward students. "Sit down and shut your mouth, Jason!" was the only way I could deflect a protesting sixteen-year-old so that I could get to the other twenty students who were waiting "their turn" at the counter (and enjoying Jason's performance at my expense!). Calling Carol's "sickness" into question in public put her on the defensive and allowed me to cut to the chase with a

minimum of dialogue—again because I had so many kids waiting and missing their first-period classes.

The principal's insensitivity, though, came with the system. The role required me to be a modern-day Inquisitor. With ominous voice, I called students to the office over the public address system. They (usually) showed up dutifully, milling around the office door until I summoned each one to the counter. There, each received his or her minute of public grilling from me as I tried to get to "the bottom" of his or her misdemeanor. If time and I permitted, a student could explain his or her "side." At the conclusion, I would declare an end to the "fact-finding" and often issue a punishment to fit the crime. I was detective, prosecutor, judge, *and* jury all in one. And I did it all in one minute per case! I participated in this judicial charade for two years before I had the courage to change it.

Changing it was difficult because this traditional system served some institutional—and some personal—purposes. Public lists of student names boomed through the classrooms of the school serving notice to all that Donaldson was ever-vigilant! Nobody escaped the daily dragnet for class-skippers and transgressors of minor rules. (Of course, major violations were handled instantaneously!) The public grilling at "the counter" added a touch of public shaming to the process: you were presumed guilty by virtue of being called to the office; now you had to defend yourself on this very exposed village green. Finally, Donaldson would announce the punishment, serving notice to all that, yes, discipline was strong at EJSHS.

The system I inherited was, as well, successful in establishing and sustaining my own position as a disciplinarian. As a relatively young principal who was entirely new to such a big school, I knew I had to "earn my spurs" in the eyes of faculty, staff, and community. The "public-ness" of the traditional system for routine discipline put me on display. My remarks to Jason and Carol, uttered with appropriate sternness, said to everyone: "Donaldson's no pushover." The more adept I got at pinning kids down on their stories in a short period of time, the more the students would see that "you can't get away with anything with Donaldson."

But the system was wrong. It *did* work for the institution by nabbing miscreants and helping to maintain order. And it *did* work for me by reinforcing my power as a disciplinarian and my control over the system. But it mistreated kids. And in a way it mistreated me. It violated the basic purpose of a school to help youngsters develop a sense of justice and respect for themselves and for others.

I began to realize this about five months into the job, only after I had made the system work. The school was running fine. Faculty and students

pretty much did what they were supposed to. Major disciplinary events did not disrupt the school but, oddly, the stream of minor violations leading to the morning Inquisition had not diminished. When, I wondered, were these kids going to stop skipping classes and committing other misdemeanors? More to the point, when was I going to be free of this grueling daily regimen? Clearly, what I was doing was not preventing many students from repeating their offenses. My system was not helping students take more responsibility for themselves.

Recognizing this fact, I began to look differently at what I was doing and I began to see how it did not square with why I had become a principal. I was making students' behavioral problems very public and, in so doing, reducing my chances of learning what was *causing* problems. At the counter, my curt, accusatory, and sometimes sarcastic treatment of habitual offenders was publicly shaming them. (And I was convincing myself that they were beyond being shamed!) In my role as the self-appointed detective, prosecutor, judge, and jury, I guaranteed that *students' views and rights of review* had no chance. In short, there was precious little respect for students or for just treatment in the system.

As an educator, these procedures worked against everything I stood for even though they helped establish my credibility as a new principal. I now see this as tragic. Many new principals, particularly in middle and high schools, feel the same pressure to establish discipline and control and, in the process, to convince others of their competence. Students are sacrificed in this process. Their feelings, ideas, and personal circumstances—the motives that often lead to disciplinary incidents—are neither recognized nor honored. They are taught that power, not justice, will decide their fate, and they will go about their lives at school and after they leave school, too, feeling wronged. For some who are habitual offenders, their identities as "bad-asses" will be confirmed each time we call them publicly to the office and they will learn to relish this attention. In the end, few of those students I called to the office, *learned to become self-disciplining young adults* from my treatment of them.

I eventually learned that to be a just disciplinarian, I needed to do the opposite of the system I inherited. Although it made *me* less conspicuous as a disciplinarian and took more time, I sought out individual "miscreants" and had conversations with them about their behavior, their feelings, and their motivations. These happened at all times and in all places in the school—often in the down times before and after school and during lunches. My conversations made plenty of space for student talk; I learned to question better so that kids would come to recognize the choices they were making. In following up with students, I talked more frequently to the teachers who had

"turned them in" and, in the process, involved them more fully in handling their own disciplinary issues. I still meted out punishment, but I did it privately and, more often than not, kids understood their responsibility for the behaviors that led to it.

Most important, I came to see my role not so much as the disciplinarian but as the behavioral counselor. My goal was not primarily to control the school; it was rather to build a just and positive climate and culture among students and adults. I was not just the principal; I was an educator still.

GORDON DONALDSON IS THE DIRECTOR, MAINE ACADEMY FOR SCHOOL LEADERS.

I Probably Am Crazy

MARY BUTTLER

*I*t took almost a week for me to begin to walk on the ground after I was asked to be the principal of Davidson Middle School in San Rafael, California. I soon realized, however, that I had probably gone too far this time, and my ecstasy shifted to terror. I had to be crazy accepting a job with one of the most complex middle schools in Marin County. Did I have the expertise to do the job? Perhaps a more experienced administrator would have been a better choice. This was my first principalship—what if I fell on my face!

My first year began with the need to hire four teachers in August and within days the need to eliminate six class periods due to a low enrollment and a very serious statewide budget crisis that appeared suddenly during September. I had a teacher to evaluate who had unsatisfactory evaluations in the past and lots of written plans for improvement to write and then monitor. In October, one of the new teachers I hired quit to take a job in a high school program with fourteen students in a class rather than the thirty-three students in each of her classes at Davidson. The nightmare continued. A much-needed parcel tax election failed after hours of work by teachers and me. One elementary school in the district wanted to restructure its program to include grades 6–8. The parents at both schools involved the school board, the media, and many parents in their effort. I had regular thoughts of "How many years do I really have to stay as a principal before I can apply for some sort of district job?" I was not sure I would be able to last many years like this!

Then, without warning, things actually got worse. Each and every one of us dreams of being important. One April morning I

picked up the local newspaper and found my picture on the front page of the newspaper—right underneath the full-size, colored picture of a gun taken from one of my students. And during the final days of my first year, when four girls were denied the opportunity to attend the final eighth grade graduation dance, their parents rented a local hotel to host a dance of their own at the same time as the school dance.

I list the above problems for one reason. Each of these situations generated a significant number of phone calls and visits from parents, teachers, and the community. I was responsible for being an instructional leader for my school, but there was no room in my day for instructional leadership. I had to deal with parent calls, meetings of all types, district administrators, school board members, and funding agents for the extensive number of programs.

I was determined to make instructional leadership a priority. To do so meant that I spent many nights and weekends at school doing paperwork. I made parent calls at night if possible. I wanted to be visible on campus and in the classrooms during school hours.

As I write this essay, it is now June. I feel as if I have given up a year of my life to survive my first year as principal. I am exhausted, but I do not regret a minute of it. I am proud of my achievements with curriculum and instruction. I had to sacrifice my personal time to establish and maintain a focus of instructional leadership, but the foundation has been laid. I continue to believe next year will be less work. Curriculum had been neglected the past three years as the task of managing the business of school took every free minute for the former principal. I realize that it is not satisfactory for some to consider giving so much personal time to a school program, especially when it takes away from family, but for me the needs of students are extremely important. I also believe that I need to work alongside teachers to model a student-centered approach. Equal access for all students is critical for any school program and can easily be put aside because there are always vocal parents who want the perfect education for their child at the expense of the entire school. I find it to be most challenging to maintain support programs for students and teachers when the building plant needs continue to grow, and to maintain an educational program of quality for every student at the school when many believe that all children cannot learn.

In a never-ending attempt to self-destruct, I asked teachers to complete an evaluation of my performance during that period. The feedback was definitely worth the risk. There were so many positive comments and a real appreciation for the support I provided to teachers. Parents and students also made me feel valued at the end of my first year. I had no idea the impact I had made on the Davidson school community until the end of my first year.

It was only a short time ago that I wanted to consider applying for any district office job available anywhere. Now I can hardly wait for next year to begin at Davidson. I have many more ideas of how to support students and teachers. I have learned that I can survive almost anything. I want to make a difference, and I probably am crazy.

MARY BUTTLER continues to be principal of DAVIDSON MIDDLE SCHOOL IN SAN RAFAEL, CALIFORNIA.

Principals Must Go Through the Trash

MARK W. LANGE

*T*he 1992–1993 school year was my first as an elementary school principal. I made this fact obvious the first day of July when I stopped by my office. I had left the keys to the school at my home in Lawrence, 150 miles away. I called the secretary, explained what had happened, and she graciously came over to let me in. I mentioned to her this would be the first of many times she would need to bail me out. That prediction was very true. If I could grant one wish to a first-year principal, it would be to have an experienced, competent, cooperative, and patient secretary.

For fourteen years I was an elementary physical education teacher and assistant high school football and track coach. I came to my first year as principal at Lincoln Elementary excited and enthused about the opportunities; I still am. Many of my memories from this past year involve kids. Some brought me pain, some made me mad, and others brought me laughter.

There was the first grade girl still in my office on Friday at four o'clock because mom had not yet picked her up. Mom eventually showed up, with her new husband. She explained they decided to get married and did not expect it to take so long.

I met with her mom the next week to discuss the girl's difficulties at school. She informed me they were moving out of state. She wondered why the girl was withdrawn, why she was struggling. Maybe it has to do with three schools in six months, I wanted to say, or mom getting divorced, remarried, and moving

22

out of state. Just maybe these events contributed to her daughter's difficulties. I still feel guilty for not saying what should have been said.

There was the day three second grade boys came to my office for a visit. One of these boys I knew by name. I began to ask the questions I always asked. "Who has a problem?" "I do," said the first boy. "I do," said the boy on the end. The boy in the middle looked both ways, looked at me, and remained silent. "Who is the only one who can solve this problem?" "I am," said the first boy. "I am," said the boy on the end. The boy in the middle looked both ways, but again remained silent. I asked the last question. "What are you going to do to solve this problem?" The first boy replied, the boy on the end replied, and the boy in the middle looked both ways and looked at me. After a few moments of silence he asked me, "How do these guys know all the answers?" We laughed.

The year affirmed my belief that to lead is to serve. A principal must be willing to ask: what can I do to help you? That simple question is very difficult for some teachers to answer, and some of the answers are very difficult for principals to hear.

The last month of school a second grade girl told me she had dropped two rings in the trash can. I asked her if she had them a long time, "No, I just got them at Wal Mart." I asked if they cost a lot. "No, but I really like them." She looked at me with her blue eyes through red-rimmed glasses. I began digging through the lunch trash, pancakes, sausage, syrup, hash browns, milk cartons, napkins, and other lunch items, piece by piece. After ten minutes of searching we reached the bottom of the trash can. There, lying in a puddle of chocolate milk were two shiny rings. I reached down, picked up the rings, and gave them to the girl as she smiled and said thank you. This moment reminded me that unless we are willing to do the dirty work, we have no right to lead, or expect people to follow.

One mother had been very difficult during the year. There were several times I sat and listened more than I cared to, but there was no doubt she loved her kids and cared about them. The children improved as the year progressed, and during the last week of the school year, the mother stopped by to shake my hand, thank me, and express her pleasure with Lincoln. I treasure that moment. When I ask myself if it is worth all the time, work, and worry, I remember moments such as this and think YES!

MARK LANGE IS THE PRINCIPAL OF LINCOLN ELEMENTARY SCHOOL IN AUGUSTA, KANSAS.

Getting the House in Order

DEBORAH L. HURD

*T*he telephone rang late Friday evening on May 8. It was Father John saying, "The principal's search committee voted unanimously to hire you as principal of St. John's School." The shock and joy that I experienced lasted until Saturday morning when I woke up and realized that I had chosen to do a task that many thought was a losing battle. St. John's was considered a school "at risk." This was the last effort on the part of the diocese to determine if St. John's should remain open. I realized I was invited to make miracles!

The selection of a new principal was a serious and arduous task. The new principal had to turn the school around within a short period of time and prove to the diocese that the school could be a successful venture both academically and financially. I was honored to be selected for this challenge. After ten years serving as assistant principal in a neighboring parish school, I felt the need for a change. I knew the needs of St. John's and felt compelled to give it a try.

I had the opportunity to meet with the parents of St. John's school before school ended in June. At the meeting, I shared with them my belief that parents, school personnel, and the community at large must be actively involved in the education of the children. Parents especially play a unique role and must be involved in all affairs of the school through a strong parent association. The response of the parents was positive.

The halls looked as dreary as some of the local penal institutions. My first task in July was to paint the halls. Fr. John gave me check for $4,000, which I used to purchase paint supplies. I hired

people from my previous school to paint, which they did happily, as a gift to me for my new job. I also was able to have the marble floors stripped, waxed, and buffed. The next task was to create some handbooks for students, parents, and teachers. I did this during the month of July, using models from my former school. In addition, I created a school calendar indicating important dates for school closings, parent meetings, and early dismissals. I was ready for September.

The first week of school was calm and uneventful. Enrollment went to 216, which was twenty-five students more than the previous year. I met with all of the students and went over the handbook with them. I talked about suspensions, rules, and expulsions. Above all I talked about striving for excellence.

I also established an advisory board consisting of university, corporate, and government workers. We had divided the board into three areas: fund development, public relations, and academic development. My focus for the academic team was to help develop the areas of math and science by bringing in professionals to do staff development in these areas. I wanted to develop the technology areas and introduce robotics using Lego Logo Programming. This required finding a computer science teacher who could work part-time on this project. We did accomplish that goal and were able to hire a computer teacher for three full days a week. We also established a partnership between the local public university and St. John's allowing students from the seventh and eighth grades to attend the university for four weeks in the summer for hands-on training in math, science, and computer.

My greatest challenge was with the parents. The first three parent meetings were filled. By winter, there was a turnout of twenty-five to fifty. Some parents felt that I was not sharing with them and was much too secretive with my goals and objectives. They wanted to be included in all of my decisions. So I called a meeting of this group of parents and told them all of the plans that I had in mind. I gave them a game plan and a time line for the work. Although overwhelming, it made them feel part of the team. Actually, I discovered that once I worked out that strategy, my work became less troublesome. I learned how to share the load so I wasn't playing all of the instruments while trying to lead the band.

A strategy that I used for my teachers was to reassign them to new grade levels. Many had been teaching the same grade for years. I wanted everyone to feel and act like a first-year teacher who brings a great deal of enthusiasm and motivation to the students. After observing the teachers in the classroom and how they related to the students, I decided who would be best in other grades. I presented my ideas to the teachers individually and asked each one to think

about it overnight and let me know. Out of eight teachers, I was able to change six. They were all quite excited. To put a clincher on the school year, I had everybody move out of their classrooms. Some teachers had accumulated years of materials and clutter. By moving, they would be forced to clean out their closets. The teachers' attitudes toward their work became more positive.

Sitting in my office on this last day of June and reflecting on my experiences from this past year, I realize that, I have accomplished some things:

1. A Home School Association in place and ready to go in September
2. A working advisory board composed of merchants, corporate people, university people, and people from city government
3. A kindergarten class that will open in the fall for the first time
4. A school yard with an enclosed playground for preschoolers through second grade designed and constructed by the Housing Preservation Department of our city government at no cost to the school
5. A grant of $20,000 from private patrons who will guarantee funding for at least three years to do any project that will increase enrollment
6. The establishment of the position of assistant principal
7. The establishment of the breakfast program and after school program
8. Departmentalized junior high school grades 6–8

Much of the first year had to do with reorganizing space and with setting the tone for the student body, school personnel, parents, and the community at large. Next year, I will focus more on curriculum with the help of the assistant principal, concentrating on math and science and providing some staff development training in these areas. In addition, I hope to be able to offer adult job-training programs by providing space to a community-based organization.

DEBORAH L. HURD IS PRINCIPAL OF ST. GREGORY THE GREAT SCHOOL IN NEW YORK CITY.

Trouble and Triumph: A First-Year Experience

NANCY J. MOONEY

My first year as an elementary school principal was both trouble and triumph. First, there was the thrill of being chosen for the principalship from among a tough crowd of competitors. Having spent a teaching career in special education and diagnostic testing, I was a long shot for the job. No one from the special education staff had ever been given the nod, and I was thrilled beyond belief to be the first. Reality set in quickly. Now that I had the job, I was faced with leading a large inner-city school with the highest minority ratio in the city and some of the poorest families.

With fervor, I planned an opening staff meeting that included all the usual business and some staff development centered on creating a discipline plan for the building. Over the summer I had written a teacher handbook that contained written procedures for most of the normal routines of the school such as lunch-count, attendance, fire drills, and substitute teachers. At the faculty meeting I spent time sharing my expectations and listening to theirs. A building leadership team (BLT) was chosen. They helped plan the inservice for the opening faculty meeting, and we got off to a grand start.

Week One was incredible. On opening day there were more than sixty new enrollments. Parents and students were lined up outside the secretary's office, and a few hours seemed like days before all students were in a classroom. I vowed to have a better system the next year. Then came the district head lice check. The

team of nurses who arrived one morning to check for head lice found eighty cases. Children were sent home and parents notified. That's when I found out that people in poverty don't have telephones. This problem of communication plagued the school throughout my tenure, but the first year I had no backup plan for such a crisis.

Also that first week, I encountered the federal government's euphemism called "free lunch." Truly, it is a worthwhile program for children whose parents cannot provide a hot lunch daily, but there is nothing free about the bureaucracy involved in processing a form for every child. I could not possibly handle the forms during the day, so each night I took home a pile of forms (more than three hundred in all) and slowly checked, approved, signed, and recorded each form. Thank goodness for an understanding and helpful husband, or I would probably still be working on that pile.

Quickly the urgency of developing a schoolwide discipline plan became apparent. Racial tensions were high and fights were commonplace. Students brought pocket knives and razor blades to school and threatened to use them on each other. Fighting seemed the only strategy they knew for solving a dispute. Child abuse and sexual abuse cases came to my door. I quickly became acquainted with the Division of Family Services and knew the hotline numbers from memory. I saw some tough cases that first year and often as many as eight to ten on a single day. By Christmas, my parents thought I was going to have a nervous breakdown, and I was tired beyond belief.

The tide turned about March of that first year. After one particularly exhausting day, I met a staff member after school. He gave me some of the first feedback I had heard all year. It amounted to little more than encouragement to "hang in there." I needed to hear it in the worst way, and slowly I began to pull out of the depths to "fight back" with what I knew about instructional leadership and a philosophy of schooling.

Communication became a watchword. Throughout the year I had published a weekly calendar for staff that included highlights of the week's events. The calendar took on other dimensions. "A Matter of Principal" was a weekly column, actually a paragraph, that was my opportunity to talk about the things I thought were important to the school. I used a weekly quotation and centered my comments on basic notions of teamwork, perseverance, respect, humor, and caring. The calendar complimented anyone on the staff whose performance exemplified the expectations I had set out at the beginning of the year and the values I held for professional conduct. Even announcements of personal celebrations like the success of a faculty member's child or spouse, a special honor, award or recognition, or the selection to serve on a district committee were applauded in the calendar.

The faculty began to meet to make decisions with me regarding problems and concerns in the school. At first, the creating of a shared vision was awkward because some faculty were unsure of what role they should and could play in deciding the fate of several hundred children and themselves. The basis for mutual trust and respect was laid that first year, a foundation that grew and flourished all the years I was privileged to work with those fine teachers.

There are many more stories of that first year, some wonderful and some wicked. I learned to cope with pressures I never knew existed in the world, and I learned to love a group of children as valuable and important natural resources. Over my seven-year tenure as principal, the discipline plan changed, the fights decreased, and the weapons disappeared. Communication remained of critical importance as well as shared decision making, teamwork, and the creation of a vision of what a grand school can be. I made a lot of mistakes that first year and I worked harder than I have ever worked before or since, but I wouldn't trade that year of frontline experience for any other. Mistakes and all, I made a difference and that was my goal all along.

NANCY MOONEY IS THE SUPERVISOR OF LANGUAGE ARTS IN THE ST. JOSEPH, MISSOURI, SCHOOL DISTRICT.

A Paradoxical Opportunity

SISTER MARIA JUDE

What lies behind us and what lies before us are tiny matters compared to what lies within us.

—William Morrow

*I*t was a small, all-girl, Catholic parish, inner-city high school, located just minutes from the center of Boston, with a student body composed of many cultures— Haitian, Afro-American, Caucasian, Vietnamese, Cambodian, Hispanic, American Indian, Asian, and Portuguese. It was this ethnic and racial diversity that made the school so special to the administration, the faculty, and the students.

In June 1991, I was asked to become "acting principal" of this parish high school, a school where I had been for five years— two years as full-time classroom teacher and three years as vice-principal. I wasn't totally sure how to act as a principal, but I was willing to give it my all. There was no doubt in my mind and heart that it was a right decision even though I had no idea what was to come.

My roles as principal were as diversified as the school. But in each of them, the goal was to encourage young women to grow and develop spiritually, intellectually, culturally, and emotionally as total and unique individuals.

Little did I know that this was to be my first and final performance as principal of this particular high school. In mid-November of my first year, I was told to inform the faculty, staff, parents, and students that the school would close its doors in June, after sixty-nine years of educating young women. This announcement stirred in me an uncomfortable sense of déjà vu since I had been vice-principal of a school that closed under similar circumstances six years earlier in New York.

What I learned from my New York experience and what I had gained from my experiences and challenges while in Boston only made me realize more deeply that in the middle of every difficulty lies opportunity. My opportunity this year was that even though I could not direct the wind, I could adjust the sails and take the ship as far as we could go in the short time we had. I have come to believe that God has a purpose in mind for everything that happens in our lives, and whether we accept it or understand it, He knows what is best for us. I was not going to allow this announcement to diminish a whole school year even though we were living out a paradox—keeping a school alive while at the same time closing its doors. Every journey, no matter how short, has opportunities.

The year was a singular experience, something not many people are asked to live through. It was a time for giving and being truly called to lead.

Since "all eyes" were on the new and "closing" principal—who she is, what she attends to, or what she appreciates or seems to appreciate—it was important to me to be sure that people knew what I valued and how those values related to the long-established SCHOOL CULTURE. My office was located in a very advantageous place near the main office where most of the traffic was, and it was set up so that it didn't welcome only those who were "in trouble." I tried to make sure that I was always on an "up," that I had a sense of humor despite all the frustrations confronting us, that I could be informal as well as formal, that I was approachable, and that I cared very much for each and every individual.

Because I was involved in academics, sports, and extracurricular activities, it wasn't hard for me to convince others that school should be fun and interesting—like a "family,"a community of caring adults and students working together cooperatively—and that I valued a well-rounded person. I also made time to be a constant presence in the school, to be highly visible by visiting classes, working and visiting in the cafeteria in the morning and at lunchtime, and visiting with faculty and students between classes. It was also important to me to learn each and every student's name and background as best I could.

As I stood at the podium in the sanctuary of the parish church on May 21, just before presenting each member of the Class of 1992 with her diploma and knowing that it was my final curtain call, I shared these thoughts with the entire cast—the faculty and staff, the parents, the students, the Class of 1992, and all our friends:

> I thank each of you for what you have added to the spirit of our school. For without you, respect for and understanding of our many different cultures would have been lacking in every way. It has been a pleasure for me to wake up each morning and know I was going to spend my day with you. I couldn't think of any other place I would have liked to have spent my energies and my days—you are my energizers.
>
> You have a lot of potential, commitment, understanding, and love. You are the future and the future is yours; I depend on you, make a difference. Do not worry or fret about what you leave behind. Take with you the lessons you have learned and the ideals and values that you have added to your individual person. Continue to have faith in yourselves, faith in your abilities, faith in your dreams, and faith in your responsibilities.
>
> The time for moving on is now, creating new relationships,
> new challenges,
> new memories.

One of the questions frequently asked of me throughout the year was "If you had known in July 1991 what you'd be asked to do, would you have taken on the role, responsibility, and challenge of being principal?" My answer was always a very humble and unequivocal *"YES."*

SISTER MARIA JUDE IS VICE-PRINCIPAL FOR ACADEMIC AFFAIRS AT BISHOP FEEHAN HIGH SCHOOL IN ATTLEBORO, MASSACHUSETTS.

The Tip of the Iceberg

DAVID H. WRIGHT

*E*veryone knows that the largest part of an iceberg is below the surface of the water. Well, life's experiences can be like that too. What is visible may seem very manageable and not very intimidating. Looming below the surface, however, is an enormous amount of mass that will not easily give in to any kind of force. This is how I found the principalship.

Finally, it happened! That phone call that puts a knot in your stomach and causes your once-confident voice to shake and sound very much like an adolescent with overactive hormones. I was being offered a position as elementary principal. At that moment I was feeling every emotion that can be described. The master plan was working! I was going to accept. Iceberg sighted!

At the first opportunity, I gathered the family around the map, and while pointing to the town I shared the news. The children ran crying to their rooms, and my wife cried all over the map. The iceberg was getting bigger.

The day finally arrived when I officially reported to school. The elementary handbook had been approved and sent off to the printers; the secretary was busy preparing attendance records and class lists, taking inventory of new materials, assembling first-day packets for teachers and students, and completing a million other tasks that are traditionally done at the beginning of the school year. I was busy being briefed by the superintendent about procedures, board policy, supervision of the special education and Chapter 1 programs and the day-to-day operations of the school. After the first week I was completely exhausted, which really

scared me because the staff and students wouldn't be in school for another three weeks. The full extent of the iceberg's mass was strongly suspected.

That first week of school finally arrived, and as with any new marriage everyone was nervous, very forgiving, tolerant, and understanding. Knowing that all situations don't last forever, I still wanted this wonderful rapport to last the entire school year. Who was I kidding! What I didn't realize was that from the very beginning I was considered by the older staff members (with a zillion years of experience in the very same building) as a "nice boy" who meant well. I was a "nice boy" until I started suggesting some subtle changes in the day-to-day routine, and I then became the bad boy on the block. The iceberg's depth below the surface was at fifteen fathoms.

"Didn't you know you were interfering with tradition?" "The teachers have never done it that way before!" "That's not the way we do things around here!" These battle cries rang through the building *and the universe*. It was October and the honeymoon was over. The *entire* mass of the iceberg above and below the surface was finally realized.

Now was the time for some reflective thought and analysis. I operated on the premise of "we is smarter than me." I had scheduled regular staff meetings for the purpose of information sharing, group problem solving, and decision-making sessions. After trying hard to keep staff members involved, still there were complaints and dissatisfaction, and I was frustrated.

When situations get too overwhelming with "principal stuff," my secretary can find me with the kindergarten students laughing, playing, and just plain getting excited about being in school. I get more pleasure going into the kindergarten room to learn how to color all over again with such wise and learned six-year-olds than anywhere else in the building. I enjoy visits by the students to the office to work on class assignments, talk about the school day, or just discuss a favorite project. Whenever the frustrations get too great, I return to the children and the teaching to remind myself what this business is all about.

I survived the first year with only a dent in the rudder and minor damage to the bridge.

DAVID WRIGHT IS THE ELEMENTARY PRINCIPAL OF THE ALBION PUBLIC SCHOOLS IN ALBION, NEBRASKA.

Up the Hawsepipe

THOMAS EISMEIER

There is an expression in the Merchant Marine that describes officers who are former deckhands or engine room wipers and rose to licensed rank not by going to college—not by graduating from one of the seven maritime academies—but by passing examinations after learning on the job. Such people are said to come up the hawsepipe.

—John McPhee, *Looking for a Ship*

After about fifteen years teaching underprivileged kids in Chicago, overprivileged kids in Brooklyn, and plain country kids in Vermont, I came "up the pipe" to become the teaching principal at a small, rural elementary school. I had begun my teaching career with little more preparation than the proverbial good intentions. By the time I became interested in administration, I had a realistic idea of how schools worked—or didn't work—and an idealistic determination to improve them.

Teaching principals in Vermont are not required to hold an administrative license, but having come up the anchor chain, I decided to take the courses to earn a license. My performance on the job, moreover, proved to be a series of personal quizzes, tests, exams, and institutional trials that lent depth and meaning to the professional title of principal.

New principals seem to have a natural tendency to try to please every-body and do everything. When aided and abetted by parents, teachers, and school board members, this tendency can become harmful to a principal's health. As the school's first "real" administrator, I think I suffered more than most from the I'll-do-it-myself syndrome.

I realized early on that I had to set strict guidelines about my availabil-ity as a principal. I sent a letter home asking parents to call me either before 7:30 or after 11:30 A.M., when my classroom responsibilities ended; otherwise they could leave a message with the secretary. I made it clear to teaching staff that I did not want to be interrupted in the classroom for anything less than a natural disaster. In the meantime, word spread swiftly that a new and highly paid person was available at the school to listen to complaints, sympathize with real or imagined grievances, and tend to chores that nobody else wanted to do. Parents appeared at my classroom door demanding immediate satis-faction to their problems. Kids from other classes streamed into my room bearing notes that read either that they had been bad or that a toilet was clogged. There wasn't much to do except put out the fires as they flared up and hope that the small crises would subside. Eventually, people realized that I was not on call twenty-four hours a day, and the teaching part of my sched-ule settled into a pleasant and productive routine.

I was just as strict about maintaining my administrative role as I was about preserving the integrity of my daily teaching time. Outside the class-room I metamorphosed into the principal. The fifth/sixth graders in my classroom were surprisingly adaptive to this shift in roles when I visited them with their "other" teacher in the afternoons. Some of the younger students, whose classes I visited every day, were shocked to hear from older siblings that the principal—the man in the tie—was also a teacher.

Leaving the classroom responsibilities behind for the day, I was ready for the morning's accumulation of mail, notes, phone calls, and kids and adults waiting to see me. I dealt with the demands as best I could, sometimes comparing the whole operation to a triage in a M*A*S*H unit. Somehow, though, at the end of the day, no matter how long I stayed, not everything was completed. I lugged home a briefcase weighted both with kids' assignments and with administrative forms and letters. I worked evenings; I worked week-ends. I even hired a substitute for myself so that I could spend at least one full day observing and recording the school's established rhythms and routines inside and out.

While responding to people's immediate needs I also invested consider-able time and effort in organizing schedules, systems, and procedures to make the school less dependent on me personally. For example, because we

were in mild crisis when I first arrived, I practically force-fed a Glasser-based discipline model to the staff and parents. We used staff meeting and inservice time to discuss kids' behavior and how to respond without reflexively sending them to the office to be scolded by the principal. I knew we were making progress when parents began asking for more information so that they could try using time-out and planning techniques at home.

My first year at West Fairlee was rich, varied, challenging, and difficult. The job description for the administrative half of my position included:

- Lighting the pilot on the hot water heater when the janitor wasn't around— and wondering why I always seemed to be wearing light-colored clothes on these occasions
- Directing a backhoe late at night after part of the septic system failed and no one could remember exactly where it was buried
- Calling substitutes at 6:00 A.M. and repeating to myself that teachers and staff members didn't get sick on purpose
- Developing budgets and then cutting them
- Supervising and evaluating the staff while trying not to run afoul of union rules
- Meeting the superintendent periodically for a reality check
- Putting the tether ball back up when the rope broke
- Officiating kids' soccer games
- Participating on the district's administrative team with all the clout of a small third world country on the UN Security Council
- Reminding angry kids not to yell or use four-letter words
- Reminding angry parents not to yell or use four-letter words
- Reminding myself that I might be making a difference

Looking back at that first year now that I am a full-time principal in another, larger school, I did not realize how difficult it was until I stopped doing it.

THOMAS EISMEIER IS THE PRINCIPAL AT MORETOWN ELEMENTARY SCHOOL IN MORETOWN, VERMONT.

The Lessons Learned

IRA E. BOGOTCH

*I*f I had known then, what I know now . . . ah, there's the rub. Today, as a professor of educational leadership at the University of New Orleans, I study and write about beginning principals. But, of course, what I do today didn't matter when I first started being a principal. What mattered then was that I had a job to do, an overwhelming job, for which few are ever ready when they begin.

Thoughts about my first faculty meeting, my first parent-teacher night, my first accreditation report . . . everything was my first! . . . all merge together. I remember how faculty meetings changed from being primarily social and business meetings to becoming real professional development conferences led by teachers; how teachers learned to communicate with parents about what teachers did in class and how that related to the overall purposes of the school curriculum; and how the school's earning of accreditation turned on outrageous luck.

In 1988–89, I assumed the principalship of a private, sectarian elementary school that had a long-standing reputation for the caring and nurturing of children but was also known for its weak academics. The goal, impressed upon me by the school's board, was to improve curriculum and instruction without disrupting the positive climate for teachers and students. It was obvious that the teachers enjoyed teaching at this school and that they believed in their students' potential for academic achievement. Their job satisfaction, however, did not translate into effective teaching. Although most of the teachers expressed some degree of criticism of the school's textbooks, the curriculum-in-use was the textbooks

themselves coupled with teacher's editions and commercial, supplementary materials. Too many of the daily classroom activities were limited to the chronology of textbooks and the suggestions of the editors.

Here were talented teachers who were not using their talents effectively, and who, despite their congeniality did not work together as cohesive and collegial faculty in planning and implementing a balanced or articulated curriculum. On these issues, their message to me was quite clear: unless I was going to make curricular decisions the textbooks would have to suffice. They were not going to make such decisions.

Thus, I began a process aimed at changing attitudes, building teacher self-confidence, rediscovering or learning skills, and implementing a better academic program. The process was essentially inductive: we (1) held weekly lunchtime staff meetings to discuss the findings from effective school and effective teaching literatures, (2) informally visited each other's classrooms, (3) promoted and shared new ideas seen in and out of the classrooms, (4) scheduled one formal classroom observation based on teaching behaviors associated with effectiveness (e.g., time on task, monitoring student performance, and classroom management), and (5) collaborated in designing self-evaluation projects based on classroom observations that were shared with the rest of the staff.

While this emphasis on academics resulted in some notable changes during that first year, the overall goal of identifying the principles upon which to build the curriculum was not attained. Teachers were still teaching material independent of what others had done previously and with no real idea of how student knowledge progresses through grade school. Progress within any one classroom did not influence changes throughout the school. Moreover, without any unifying principles as a school curriculum framework, some of the positive steps taken during year one to advance the academic program did not see the light of day in year two.

Somewhat frustrated by the lack of teacher self-directedness, I wrote a grade-by-grade sequence based on some general learning principles upon which we could all agree, such as self-esteem, technical student proficiency, global literacy, tolerance, and self-awareness. The sequenced topics were not a curriculum, but rather consensual views within which to explore grade-level metaphors— school as family theatre, being successful by apprenticing, discovering and caring for what's around us, taking a cross-country trip, and going around the world in 180 school days.

Despite the groundwork laid in consensus building and collegiality, the changes suggested by the ambiguous metaphorical themes created, for a

while, a decline in faculty morale. Most of the teachers urged me privately to clarify the meaning of these metaphors as they related to specific grade-level curriculum and teaching assignments. I had hoped that over time and without my direction, some of the teachers would start to move away from their textbook-driven curriculum, and their teaching would become more child-focused, skill-oriented, and creative.

Some teachers began to explore materials and give substance and meaning to the sequenced metaphors—all for the next school year. Another sign that attitudes were changing was that as a faculty we were able to implement other new and significant programmatic improvements without a great deal of turmoil. For example, new grading standards were clarified, and a more rigorous standardized test was adopted that reflected greater confidence in ourselves.

As a first-year principal, I also had the experience of going through an accreditation visit. Amidst the extra pressure of this close scrutiny, the leader of the visiting team asked us to hold a fire drill. The bells rang and the children dutifully exited the building, moving quickly to their assigned places across the street. One of my responsibilities as principal was to check the student bathrooms before I left to make sure every child was safely outside. In my eagerness to join the students and teachers, I almost decided to skip that step, but at the last moment I changed my mind. And lucky for me I did. The boys' room was empty, but standing in one of the girls' room stalls like an inspector general was the leader of the accreditation team waiting to see how thorough I was. He smiled, and the two of us walked out of the building together.

What lessons can be learned from these experiences? Clearly, the private school context permitted me and the faculty far greater choice about the content of curriculum. Yet, the dynamic social processes are essentially the same for teachers within all schools.

LESSON ONE

If I were to begin anew, I would start with the program adopted during year two, that is, working with teachers to define the school's philosophy of education and to develop a schoolwide consensus on the principles of learning. To improve schools, teachers and administrators as well as parents need to have answers to the why's of their behaviors if improvement is going to occur. Philosophy precedes curricular development and instructional methods, not vice versa.

LESSON TWO

Restructuring an ongoing school program takes more time than creating new programs. The institution's history regarding the way things have been done previously is important for restructuring. Leadership needs to emphasize academics and to create an environment that supports change. There are certainly quicker paths to change, but restructuring is more than a one- or even two-year effort. Even when the innovation is considered successful, it does not insure its institutional continuation.

LESSON THREE

No instructional leader has unilateral power. Such leadership is a matter of mutual dependency. Teachers' commitment and effort appear to count most in determining continued progress of a newly created program. Leadership can try to create meaningful incentives in terms of people's career choices. But the willingness to act over time rests with teachers.

LESSON FOUR

The demands and realities of our jobs as teachers and school administrators are not structured to permit sufficient reflection or time to adjust to the dynamics of change. Good teachers and administrators are overworked. School leaders need to make time for teachers and themselves by first taking away some of the present responsibilities before adding new work.

LESSON FIVE

Our jobs in education are never finished or fully realized. Restructuring requires sustained direction and commitment, regardless of personnel changes.

LESSON SIX

Hope for your share of outrageous good luck.

As a professor, I am now helping others to engage in the never-ending work of educating others. I keep rewriting the script I follow in my classes, constantly seeking to improve. The only script I can't rewrite or correct is the one I lived as a beginning principal.

IRA E. BOGOTCH IS ASSISTANT PROFESSOR IN EDUCATIONAL LEADERSHIP AT THE UNIVERSITY OF NEW ORLEANS.

The Year of Living Dangerously

THOMAS A. DRAZDOWSKI

*A*s we entered the music classroom, there was Jimmy standing on a chair, swinging his arms in rhythm to gain momentum for his flight, all the while looking menacingly down at the teacher. Below him was a row of four guitars, all neatly arranged at equal distances and soon to be victims of a lethal game of guitar hop frog. Sister Dominica calmly but firmly directed Jimmy to come down safely from his perch, deflecting his vulgarities with a matter-of-factness that de-escalated the situation and my own strong urge to pummel the offender for saying such nasty things to a nun. As the anger started to dissipate from Jimmy's body, he slowly stood erect, glanced one more time at the teacher, then jumped from the chair, skillfully missing the first guitar. He headed out the door and toward my office. As I silently followed behind, I began to wonder what I had gotten myself into. It was only the first twenty minutes of my first day in my first job as a principal, and already I had found that there was much my professors forgot to teach me in graduate school. My true education had just begun.

The setting for my first year as principal was a small private secondary school that had been established by an order of nuns to serve children who had been labeled socially and emotionally disturbed. The students came to the school from around the state, mostly referred to us by their former school districts, child welfare agencies, or the juvenile courts. Out of one hundred plus students, approximately sixty females were residents of the school as well,

giving them a chance to escape from some bad home environments while allowing them to concentrate on school studies and to receive professional counseling. The teachers, all certified in their content areas as well as special education, were assigned from the local state intermediate unit. Having been hired by the good sisters, I was expected to walk the delicate balance between the private and the public sector and help develop a school that was consistent with the total-treatment milieu. Despite Jimmy, or maybe because of him, I knew that first day I would like this place. Much more than "traditional" education was going on here. Whole lives were being transformed. Shortly my own would be added to the list.

As I reviewed the long inventory of duties on my job description, many seemed to fit with my expectations for the role of principal, such as providing leadership in improving classroom instruction and professional development of staff, designing and improving the curriculum, preparing the school budget, and maintaining communications with the state board of private academic schools. Because this was a small school and virtually a one-person office, the list also included making the schedule of classes, providing academic and career counseling, maintaining an effective system of student record-keeping and the effective execution of administrative details, such as receiving supplies, doing inventories, answering correspondence, distributing school mail, and assigning lockers. The list covered three pages with thirty such items. I would need a very big closet to store all the hats I was expected to wear. Most principals do.

The items that would consume most of my school day, however, appeared at the end of the list: maintain satisfactory principal-student informal relationships, order, and discipline. Sister Dominica had the title of "crisis intervention specialist" and would assist me in this area. All teachers had access to a telephone, and when a lid was about to blow, my office would get a call. These kids needed lots of extra TLC, and finding the balance between hug and hardnose was a continual challenge for me. But Sister was a wonderful teacher, and the experienced staff were willing to share their collective expertise.

As with any school, I quickly found that the teachers were its strength and soul. Each performed heroic efforts each day, tempering all actions with care and compassion. The ways of the good sisters seemed to rub off on whomever they came in contact with. There was Ted, the science teacher, whose garden and greenhouse cultivated so much more than just fresh produce for the school kitchen. Jill, the math teacher, whose dry humor and unflappable nature gave kids a sense of security in facing both the subject matter and the perils of life. Greg, the beloved art teacher, whose classes gave

the kids a creative outlet for a host of pent-up emotions. Each member of the twelve-person faculty brought special talents to bear, sharing not only knowledge but humanness, helping to make the journey a reward in itself.

And of course, there were the kids. Jimmy, the guitar lover, who had a hair-trigger temper and had already blown through several schools and foster homes. Gloria, who after losing her mother in a fire, survived on the streets of a major city by living with "cousins" until a child welfare agency finally tracked her down. Margaret, who slept each night cuddling a baseball bat, used in her dreams to protect her from a frightening past. Many of the kids had suffered physical and/or sexual abuse and needed a safe environment in order to have a chance. Several had been arrested for prostitution, others for involvement with drugs. Mark had taken part in an armed robbery. Jake had accidentally shot and killed his brother while playing with a gun. A nation at risk indeed. Our students were a collection of derailed lives looking for guidance and direction, all brought together by fate and circumstance to this very special school.

That first year of twelve-hour days passed quickly. There were setbacks and failures but also many of the so-called "small victories" that continue to compel us forward. As a principal, as faculty, and as students, we faced each day and grew and learned together. Six of our twelve graduating seniors that year were accepted into post-secondary schools. All returned to the mainstream of life to continue the daily struggle but with a newfound confidence and perspective on life that only a loving environment can provide.

My educational career continues to take many turns, from teaching in the Alaskan bush (yes, the show *Northern Exposure* was my life!) to getting my doctorate and becoming a teacher of teachers. Challenges all, but challenges met with the wisdom gained from that first year as a principal. I've had a new compass to guide my life. As Frost so aptly pointed out, the road less traveled by has made all the difference. For anyone approaching that first year as principal, my advice is to look forward to this opportunity to be transformed.

THOMAS A. DRAZDOWSKI IS A FACULTY MEMBER IN THE EDUCATION DEPARTMENT AT KING'S COLLEGE.

Tale of the First Year

MARY ANN SINKKONEN

*W*ho, me? A principal? That was a recurring thought that first year. A confessor, confidante, facilitator, humorist, director, teacher, parent, and friend. That's who I was. Prepared or not, I had the job.

The pace of a principalship is fast. A principal makes split-second decisions, and with practice over time, hopes they are thoughtful. The following description is aimed toward moving the reader into the environment of the principalship. Feel what it's like and wonder, would you want the job?

A snapshot of a day:

7:30 A.M. I find that during the night someone squirted glue into all the exterior door locks. The custodian, who arrived at 7:00 A.M. has called the maintenance department. The doors have been deglued but I check them to be sure. All are OK.

7:50 A.M. A phone call from the sub desk. The secretary will be absent and there is no sub for the day. I close the school library and reassign the clerk to the office. She had subbed in that capacity before. This makes sense to me but not to the head librarian.

8:00 A.M. A parent walks into the office and announces that he would like to speak to the principal. I respond. There is a problem. As a high school and collegiate basketball player, he is concerned because all of our hoops are netless. How can a decent game of "B" ball be played with a netless hoop? I listen and share with him the reality of outdoor courts and community use during non-school hours. I recount the almost perpetual replacement of nets that

occurs when nets are installed on outdoor hoops. Practicality is not an acceptable reason for him, and he assures me the matter will be taken up with someone at the district level.

8:25 A.M. A teacher reminds me to come by the classroom at 9:15 to enjoy the fifth grade performance of their Civil War play.

8:27 A.M. Art docent arrives and notices that the portfolio for her presentation today (five classrooms) has not arrived from the previous week's school. I make phone calls to see if we can locate the material. Her first appointment is at 8:45 A.M.

8:35 A.M. I am on my way to pick up the portfolio at another school.

8:30 A.M. While I am on the road, the school bell rings to start the day.

8:50 A.M. The portfolio is in the hands of the docent and she walks to the first class of the day, just five minutes late. The head librarian is waiting for me. The issue is reassigning the library clerk to the office without asking the head librarian. I describe my responsibility and let it be known that in the best interest of the school, I would do it again. Case disagreeably closed.

9:00 A.M. The custodian walks in. "There is a guy practicing his golf swing on the back field." I suggest that he ask the fellow to leave since the grounds are closed during school hours. "The guy has a Doberman with him and I'm not getting near the dog." I look around and not seeing any other person to approach the golfer, I walk out to the field. The golfer is cooperative. The dog is quiet and obedient. The field is cleared of golfer and dog.

9:15 A.M. The fifth grade play. What a joy! The students have written the script from the point of view of eyewitnesses. Their dialogue takes the form of letters to various persons. Their grasp of key ideas, emotions, politics, geography, etc., is impressive. Parents in attendance are awed by the depth of understanding.

10:05 A.M. On my way back to the office, I meet four sixth grade students who are putting up the ancestor chart on the window of the multiuse room. We have been studying heritage as a theme across the school. This class has volunteered to collate all of the information and to chart the ancestry of all of our students.

10:15 A.M. A third grade classroom for a formal teacher observation. Solve the problem: "With the materials provided, build a shelter for a family lost in the forest." There are criteria, parameters outlined in the instructions to the groups. At the planning conference, the teacher has asked that I note the clarity

of his directions with regard to the nature of any student questions about the task. He also would like feedback about the students' on-task behavior.

11:15 A.M.   Back in the office, I begin to reflect on the teacher observation. A parent has called to express concern about my decision to continue past practice regarding "no dances" for sixth graders. I return the call.

11:45 A.M.   A half hour later I return to the observation but am diverted by a yard supervisor. "There is no water running in the drinking fountains or faucets." I ask the secretary to call the water district and see what's happening. We are about to dismiss 570 students for lunch. We are told that due to construction a few blocks away, all water has been turned off for the next half hour. I decide that we need to alert all students that restrooms, fountains, and sinks are off limits until 12:15. Only emergencies should come to the office restroom. The yard supervisors and I lock student restrooms.

12:15 P.M.   Water is turned on again. There is the anticipated rush to the restrooms. I'm helping with traffic to the restrooms and drinking fountains.

1:00 P.M. The after-lunch roundup, cleanup and investigation. This is the daily routine, the after-lunch recess report from the yard supervisors. Today, only one incident. A fourth grader was roughed up by a sixth grader because the fourth grader had pushed his way onto the sixth grade basketball court and would not take "no" for an answer when told to go to the fourth grade court.

1:15 P.M.   I try to eat lunch. As I open the brown bag, I hear our secretary say, "I think you better talk with our principal." When I hear those words I know that she has tried everything and this could take a while. The person I see is a parent who is concerned with the school dress code. "Why can't the girls wear shorts to school?" This discussion is just the beginning of what materializes into a major parent/student conflict over a period of several months and culminates in a survey and a change in the "Shorts Rule."

1:30 P.M.   I'm back to the lunch bag, when I realize it is time for me to go to a classroom where I have been invited to see weekly art centers. Close the lunch bag.

2:00 P.M.   The early arrival students, (we have an early/late schedule for grades 1–3) are dismissed. We are short one bus supervisor so I stand bus duty for twenty minutes.

2:20 P.M.   I notice I am hungry and that I haven't been to the restroom since I left home at 7:00 A.M. I head for the restroom but I am distracted by the

sounds of the fifth grade chorus in the multiuse room. This session is sometimes difficult for the music teacher, and I decide to stop in. The little cherubs, those fifth graders, need a few glances from me to focus on "Oh What a Beautiful Morning."

2:25 P.M.   Yes, the restroom is on my way back to the office.

2:30 P.M.   While I was on campus, four phone messages came in. I note that one of them is from the superintendent. I make that call and learn that our school has been selected for a visit from our local state congressman next week. We discuss the details, and I begin to consider a schedule.

2:45 P.M.   The lunch bag is looking tired. I'm thinking that tomorrow's lunch will be better. I'm not really hungry anyway.

3:00 P.M.   Dismissal. Again, I'm on bus duty.

3:15 P.M.   I begin to read the day's mail. I jot down appointments for meetings. I attend to paperwork related to the earlier teacher observation.

3:30 P.M.   Teachers begin to drop in. The most frequently used phrase is "Got a minute?" The conversations center around: What about this or that field trip? What about this or that student? What about this or that parent? What about this or that teaching strategy?

4:30 P.M.   Back to paperwork: observation, budgets, weekly community newsletter, staff bulletin, notes to teachers, thank-you letters, express mail to district personnel.

6:00 P.M.   Walk to the parking lot. One day of this school year has passed.

Why would anyone do this job? Are we all crazy? For me the job was the hardest job I have ever had and the most rewarding. The school community is like a big classroom. I loved classroom teaching, and I loved the principalship. After fifteen years of classroom teaching, then three years in staff development, the principalship was a logical step for me.

Looking back on that first year, here's what helped me most:

· keeping a journal so I could write, reread, and reflect
· listening, being a sounding board so people could discover that the solutions were within themselves
· having a friend with whom I could role play and who could help me better prepare to face awkward situations
· asking questions

- tending to the obvious like repainting the staff room, repairing broken window blinds, replacing chalkboards
- talking socially with the staff in the lunchroom
- recognizing and celebrating successes

If there was anything routine it was being everywhere: in classrooms, out on the yard, in the library, the computer lab, in the special education classrooms.

The best advice I received as I was beginning that first year was, "Use your position to say, 'Yes'."

MARY ANN SINKKONEN IS THE COORDINATOR OF CATEGORICAL PROGRAMS FOR THE NOVATO UNIFIED SCHOOL DISTRICT IN CALIFORNIA.

Wings: My First Year as a Principal

ELAINE M. PACE

*T*he anticipated phone call echoed in my ears, "Congratulations, Elaine! We'd like to offer you the position of elementary school principal in Parsippany." "Yes!" I shouted inwardly, while outwardly I replied quite professionally, "Why, thank you. I'm thrilled. I have a few questions, but I'd be delighted to accept."

Acceptance. Another challenge. Reach for the stars, I had always believed, and you'll fly far higher than if you reach for something on a level with yourself. I reached.

I always liked Disraeli's words, "We are not creatures of circumstance; we are creators of circumstance." Here was my opportunity to be a creator. Truthfully it was "community" I wanted to create. I had been a director of staff development previously, working out of the central office. While I had had an opportunity to touch lives indirectly by designing programs and training teachers, I remained Queen for a Day in that former job. I yearned for the opportunity to become more a part of what I created.

Not until later when I read Roland Barth's wonderful book, *Improving Schools from Within,* did I begin to grapple with the meaning of "the school as community." I learned at the Harvard Principals' Center just how affective the principal's job was. I had led communities of children, but a community of adults presented a different challenge. My acquaintance with the work of Drs. Judith Arin-Krupp and Sarah Levine was invaluable in helping me understand the stages of adult development and the concept of the

50

adult learner. The 1990 U.S. Department of Education monograph, *The Principal's Role in Shaping School Culture,* defined my new role succinctly. I would shape school culture as a symbol . . . a potter . . . a poet . . . an actor . . . and a healer. It was as simple as that! All jest aside, that monograph was a treasure. Then, once I learned to create the culture, I would need to learn the valuable skill of how to "reframe" it according to Drs. Lee Bolman and Terry Deal. But I'm getting ahead of myself. Back to the first year of principalship.

"Well begun is half done," Aristotle proclaimed. I made a good beginning. The "agreeables" joined my camp right away; the "wait and sees" within a year. With the help of a perceptive and faithful secretary and a small cadre of reassuring staff members, I managed to maintain relatively open communication with the "skeptics."

The P.T.A. was another matter. An overly zealous group of novice parents met my initial efforts with consternation. Accustomed to unchecked power in the wake of a former absentee principal, this small but vocal group of parent leaders challenged my every effort to steer the starship Littleton back onto course. When I increased security so that strangers would no longer be able to enter the school at all hours, I was accused of not welcoming parents. When I formed a collaborative advisory council of parents, teachers, and school leaders, I was accused of trying to subvert the power of the P.T.A. This problem required a long-range view. Veteran principal colleagues convinced me that I should rise above the fray, remain open and collaborative, and gradually nurture my own followers. That took nearly two years, but the rewards were worth every step in the struggle and every iota of self-discipline required of me. In my third year as principal, I bravely hired the president of the P.T.A. as one of my staff members.

When I was a staff developer, I remember learning about attribution theory. Attribution theory says that some things happen purely out of luck, some out of innate ability, some out of task difficulty, and some out of effort. That memory culled from my repertoire helped me grapple with the predictably unpredictable in my first year of principalship. Principals are generally people who enjoy control. Attribution theory helped me to understand what I could and could not control, a valuable lesson in that first year. Most of us become principals because we are willing to expend the effort to control well. The challenge is how to share that control with our staff, our colleagues, and our community. I learned to beware first impressions. One colleague whom I had thought would be my best friend turned out to be relentlessly competitive. I was determined in easing myself out of that yoke. A teacher's camaraderie, in another case, proved to be self-serving and not committed to fostering a

wholesome, trusting culture in our building. We should invite others into our "inner circle" judiciously. We want our friends, not our foes, in there with us. Sharing control is paramount for a good principal, but sharing is an art not developed fully in the first year of principalship. It is the reward, in the long term, for a job well done. It makes the job a lot less lonely, too!

There are surely certain events that unexpectedly engineer hours, sometimes days and weeks, of our time, forcing the postponement of even our most routine tasks. I think of my first six weeks as principal and of the bus driver who wrapped one of our school buses around a tree en route home one afternoon. The driver, sufficiently relaxed from the alcohol in his body, escaped unharmed. That accident occurred less than five minutes after our last elementary school child had alighted from the bus.

Attribution theory also says that outcomes are often determined by innate ability that surely directs the progress we may or may not make as principals. I dealt with a middle-class, suburban neighborhood where many parents took pride in an elitism of holding P.T.A. offices, sponsoring their own school board candidate, running soccer and Little League, Girl Scouts, Boy Scouts, Cubs, Daisies, and enough fund-raisers to contribute approximately $15,000 per year to our school. The innate ability was surely here. This culture may sound ideal, but, despite its assets, it makes the school a hard place for a principal to be a hero. What could I do to make a real difference in this place?

Task difficulty is the third component of attribution theory. How difficult is this task of being a principal? On many days it seems insurmountable, even in the best of schools. Because we have chosen, as one scholar says, "to take abuse for a living," there's only one way to deal with the difficulty of our task—simplify, simplify, simplify. We can only deal effectively with one or two issues at a time. Prioritizing was very important for me. Having already tried to be a super mom, a super teacher, a super wife, a super principal, and a super person, I realize that I can't do it all and still be super! I've become better at delegating and focusing all my energies on only one to two things at a time. Then I turn my back and go home. The work never fails to greet me the next morning.

Finally comes effort. Effort we can control. I'd venture to guess that most principals comprise a premium group of overachievers. After all, most of us became principals because we were successful teachers. If we weren't such overachievers, we'd still be teaching—a profession most of us loved!

When I was a college senior, I devoured the poetry of T.S. Eliot. One of my favorite quotes continues to live with me as I venture on the journey of

principalship. In "Little Gidding," the fourth of Eliot's *Four Quartets*, he writes:

> We shall not cease from exploration.
> And the end of all our exploring
> Will be to arrive where we started
> And know the place for the first time.

The hope of our exploring is that as principals we discover how to shape the cultures of our schools knowingly, with compassion, and, most important, with wisdom!

ELAINE PACE IS THE PRINCIPAL OF THE LITTLETON SCHOOL IN PARSIPPANY, NEW JERSEY.

Lives of a Rural Principal

EDWARD ROBERT WILKENS

*I*n the days before public kindergarten became popular, Mrs. Smithson's private, half-day preschool prepared me reasonably well for life as an elementary school student. I entered first grade in 1959, moderately socialized and equipped with reading and math readiness.

Two years ago, after nineteen years as a student, I reentered elementary school. This time as a principal. And this time, despite an array of academic credentials garnered since 1959, I was probably no better prepared than Mrs. Smithson had made me for first grade.

I did have a B.A. in English literature and an M.Ed. focused on administration and planning, with courses such as Public School Finance 344, School Law 312, Curriculum Concepts and Development 377, and Organizational Leadership 308 behind me. The courses were interesting and necessary. Actually, only some of the courses were interesting—but, according to the state certification board, all were necessary.

Surely no people on the state certification board were thinking about a rural elementary school when they determined the standards. If they had, they would have included three areas that can be broadly catalogued as Mechanics, Nature, and People.

During my first two years as principal of a small, rural elementary school I encountered a spectrum of situations, problems, and emergencies, none of which was even peripherally considered during my graduate training for this job. That is no one's fault; it is simply not possible to anticipate, much less gain practice necessary

to cope with, such aspects of the principalship as backed-up sewer lines, lost teeth, a wandering bull, a parent with a clumsy left hook, and the People's Republic of China.

ENCOUNTER WITH A BUS

Of mechanics, nature, and people, the area that I am least comfortable with and knowledgeable about is mechanics. Yet, one snowy, windy morning a bus driver thought it essential that I join him in inspecting the cracked leaf springs on a bus. We went to the lot, and he slid under the bus. I was content to crouch gingerly alongside and peer under the vehicle, avoiding the oiled and muddied slush as much as possible. Not satisfied with such a cursory investigation, the driver urged me under the bus with him. He wanted me to be as informed as he, so I ignored the fact that I was wearing my best suit for a meeting later that day at the state department, and I crawled—as much as possible on toes and fingertips—under the bus to the damage site to frown and shake my head knowingly at the cracked springs.

Since that morning I have grown even more familiar with our buses. I have delivered gas, transported damaged heater coils, ridden in, helped jump-start, and driven the buses enough to satisfy any latent curiosity I may have had about their mechanical psyches.

STEMMING THE TIDE

If I am not an accomplished mechanic, I am even less a plumber, but I have gained the sensitivity no longer to question why plumbers get $25 per hour. At the end of an otherwise uneventful day, I met with a substitute teacher to ask about her experience with the class, thank her, and say good night. Just before leaving, she turned and said, "Oh, by the way, you should probably check the class bathroom. We had a few problems this morning."

She left, and I checked. The morning's "few problems" had grown to a tide of sewage. Second graders are not ecologically minded, as evidenced by their wanton use of toilet paper. Fortunately, there is an inch-high threshold leading to the bathroom, and the water had not yet crested that dike. The custodian, who is also a bus driver, was unavailable. Besides, I reminded myself, I am the principal. I should deal with all aspects of this school. But where does he keep that plunger?

Eventually, armed with the plunger, mop and bucket, and knee-high barn boots, I waded in and stemmed the tide. When the regular second grade

teacher returned she never learned of the problem, for there was no evidence of my valiant efforts. But the custodian did ask if I knew why his barn boots were so filthy.

My assumption in the plumbing incident that "I should fix it because I'm the principal" has been echoed several times since—increasingly by others, decreasingly by me. On one such occasion the cook blustered into my office, wringing her hands about the meat sauce and the noodles and water on the floor and the funny spitting noise and the meat is all thawed and the government says we can't refreeze it and we have all that surplus cheese to use somehow and it's already 9:15—and would I please fix it right away? It did not matter to her that my desk was littered with files, computer printouts, adding machine tape, and budget requests. I went with her not because I understood the problem, but because she so obviously had one.

Actually, she had four. The steam pressure cooker was 1) not regulating itself, 2) getting threateningly hot, 3) leaking scalding water, and 4) making that funny spitting noise.

Initially she pleaded with me to "fix it before something happens." Though the problems looked and sounded worse than they actually proved, I was not ready to correct them myself, and promised to call a repairman. That did not satisfy her. Since appealing to my principalship had failed, she shifted to challenging my gender. "You're a man; fix it!"

DE NATURAE NATURA

Contrary to her assumptions, neither my profession nor my gender proves sufficient to solve all problems, especially when those problems stem from mechanical or other nonhuman sources. Mechanical problems are usually frustrating, never amusing at the time, and rarely fascinating. On the other hand, problems presented by nature are only occasionally frustrating, often amusing, and always fascinating.

Despite being a native Vermonter and having spent years hunting and fishing, I still find it singularly fulfilling to drive the fifteen minutes to school and enjoy the beginning day. Blue jays cross the road in front of my car at the same place and time each day. Cows head out to pasture. And four times in two years I have stopped the car to watch deer forage.

This may all sound rather idyllic, and it is—usually. But one spring morning a recess aide came to me to report that a cow was loose on school property. Since cows graze on adjacent meadows constantly, such trespass was not particularly noteworthy. But this aide was new, so I went with her as assurance.

The cow, however, proved to be a bull. And it was surrounded by 107 kindergarten through fourth graders, most of whom thought the whole scene quite funny. The bull obviously did not. I immediately herded the children back into the school and then set about herding the bull back to his pasture.

Not until after forty-five futile minutes of alternate pursuit and flight on my part did several staff members, trying to stifle their laughter, enlighten me that one does not herd a bull—especially an irritated bull. While performing endless, inconclusive minuets with the bull, I actually considered brandishing my jacket like a matador's cape to entice him through the gate. Fortunately for my then unestablished public image, I rejected the temptation to play El Cordobes to imaginary Oles! Also, fortunately for me, when the seventh graders came out for phys ed, the girl who owned the bull sauntered over, called his name, and guided him home. I thanked her, slung my cape over my shoulder, and tried to retire from the field of honor as inconspicuously as possible.

IN SEARCH OF TEETH

A less threatening natural phenomenon had me on my hands and knees on the playground, searching for a first grader's two lost teeth. They were the first teeth the child had lost, and she was heartbroken. My assurances that the Tooth Fairy was as omniscient as Santa Claus and would know what had happened even without dental evidence, did nothing to stop her tears. But my assurance that I would find her teeth worked wonders. She did not know that I caution staff members not to promise what they may not be able to deliver.

I felt a bit like an archaeologist must feel at a dig. I gently brushed sand and spread blades of grass. Five marbles, two algebra quizzes, a ring, and a chocolate chip cookie later, I found one of her teeth. One out of two was good enough for me, and I made such a show of returning it to her that one satisfied her also.

ON BEING DIPLOMATIC

Dealing with mechanical and natural disasters requires knowledge and action. Dealing with people usually requires the addition of diplomacy. During the past two years I have practiced personal diplomacy, self-defense diplomacy, and international diplomacy.

My personal diplomacy and tact are particularly tested when I counsel junior high students about sexuality. Eighth graders tend not to be as aware of or concerned about social propriety as adults, especially as it relates to "PDA"—the students' term for public display of affection. More than once I have tried to explain diplomatically and tactfully why entwined bodies at

lunchtime do not mix appropriately with hot turkey sandwiches, peas, and chocolate pudding. I have tried to caution about the embarrassing, expensive, and painful consequences when two sets of braces lock in a kiss. The lovers may only become convinced that I have never been in love, but the diplomacy usually works—for a while.

One less humorous incident illustrates that even with people, knowledge and action may be the only recourse. Especially action.

As is probably the case with most principals, I have had at least one student whose behavior has been repeatedly disruptive, antisocial, and occasionally dangerous. Our discipline system involves parents as much as they are able and willing to cooperate, but one father had bucked me and the system constantly. One morning, in response to what had become a series of discipline notices, this father roared into our school parking lot via the exit, screeched to a halt in the bus loading zone, and stomped into my office demanding to see me.

I gave him time to calm down by feigning a phone call, but when I finally bade good-bye to the receiver and rose to greet him, he only became more angry. I tried to interject reason and diplomacy between his epithets and threats of everything from lawsuits to my pending need for plastic surgery. Frustrated by his failure to persuade me of the justice of his cause, the man swung his fist at my face. He missed. Before he left the building I called the police to notify them that I had been publicly threatened with personal and property injury.

At the time, this seemed to me a case where diplomacy and reason had failed completely. The next time I saw the man, however, the first thing he did was apologize for his words and actions that day.

Diplomacy on a scale more familiar to Dr. Kissinger was expected at a Halloween Party. In addition to supervising the planned extras of Halloween parties and upper-grade sports physicals, I was asked to host a group of female physicians from the People's Republic of China on the first such tour of the United States. These upper-echelon policymakers were particularly interested in rural medical service delivery systems, and would be in Vermont on Halloween. Since we had scheduled regional doctors, nurses, and interns for our school clinic that day, we were asked to serve as a whistle-stop on the Chinese tour.

It was exhilarating and humbling to consider the political and historical significance of that visit. And except for temporary confusion and panic when we had a 50 percent power failure just one hour before their scheduled arrival, the day was a joy. We spoke through interpreters and smiled a lot. The doctors seemed as interested in our school system as in our medical services,

and enjoyed themselves immensely during a visit to the first grade classroom. The most difficult concept I discussed with these women had nothing to do with education or medicine. I tried vainly to explain why the children and even some teachers were dressed like Bugs Bunny, Casper the Friendly Ghost, Spider Man, Wonder Woman, and Darth Vader. In lieu of resolving that cultural dilemma, we smiled even more, posed for pictures, thanked each other, and waved good-bye.

Within fifteen minutes of their departure the business of our school day resumed. Athletes stripped to their underwear and stood on cold scales. Darth Vader and Wonder Woman worked on math at the computer. Sixth graders had a library period. And I sat in my office for a few minutes, marveling at the fascination of this job.

In my office now are two photographs that exemplify my feelings about being a principal. Though the technical and academic skills for this position come from School Finance 344, Curriculum Concepts and Development 377, and the like, the emotion comes from living it. That is the truest and most valuable training available.

One of those pictures is of five Chinese women and me. It is posed. We are dressed in our respective uniforms: suit and tie for me, blue smock-jackets and pants for the Chinese. The other photograph, also of me, is candid. I am surrounded by second graders, and in addition to my uniform I am sporting foot-tall, pink, construction-paper bunny ears and whiskers.

The key to this job is that the man in both pictures is happy.

EDWARD ROBERT WILKENS IS EMPLOYED BY NORTHEAST REGIONAL RESOURCE CENTER AND IS ENROLLED IN A DOCTORAL PROGRAM AT THE UNIVERSITY OF VERMONT.

Survival First

BARBARA L. SKIPPER

On a hot, August day four years ago I walked across the driveway of Randolph High School. Walking toward me was "Mr. Johnson," the principal, carrying a cardboard box. As we approached each other I recognized several familiar items protruding from the top of the open box. There were the pictures of his cherished wife and daughter and the box with his initials on top that usually sat on his large walnut desk. The look on his face was one of apprehension, and his eyes looked sadder than usual. Sensing that something out of the ordinary was happening, I asked, "Is there something that I need to know?" He quietly said that he had been board-approved the night before to be principal of another high school nearby. It was no secret that he and our new superintendent did not see eye-to-eye, but I still did not expect this announcement. He looked back at the school one more time and continued walking toward his car, leaving me standing in the hot sun.

I was the counselor for this secondary campus, a position I had held only one year. Mr. Johnson and I had grown close and worked well together, and I suddenly felt abandoned. I immediately headed for the superintendent's office, which was on the high school campus. I went straight to the superintendent's door without waiting for his secretary to announce me. He looked at me and said, "Do you want to be a principal?" Part of me said, "Yes!" while another part of me screamed, "NO! Not under these circumstances!" The superintendent continued talking and said that he had already contacted the five school board members who would support his recommendation of me as principal. I suddenly

realized that in reality it was done. I could never have imagined the roller-coaster ride that had just begun!

I entered the principal's office, which seemed barren. The hunting and fishing pictures that were still on the wall I always thought belonged to Mr. Johnson, and now I realized they belonged to an earlier principal. I left and went to my office and sat down. The registrar walked in and said, "What about registration and the master schedule?" I looked blankly back at her. She continued, "Tomorrow we will register new students and we have the master schedule to finish!" A feeling of terror instantly permeated every inch of me. I had never done a master schedule! I had visions of the first day of school with hundreds of students who had no place to go! I called the superintendent on the telephone. I told him that the master schedule needed to be completed, and I had no experience in that area. He said, "I've never done one either, but I'm sure you'll figure it out!" I truly panicked at this point.

The first lesson I learned was that the secretaries, clerks, and registrars were invaluable in "figuring out" those things that I did not know how to do. Often they needed someone to make decisions while they actually made the master schedule, registered new students, calculated attendance, and produced grade cards. Many decisions could be made with common sense and logic, relying on my previous experiences as a teacher or counselor. Sometimes simply saying, "How has this been handled before?" elicited the needed information. Since I was the only secondary principal in the district, I found that secondary principals in other districts were willing to help. In addition, the local state educational agency that provided the master scheduling, registration, and attendance software was willing to send consultants to help. It was comforting when I realized that I was truly not alone and that I did not have to know all of the answers.

In the first year there was one particularly humorous incident although the humor escaped me at the time. The event happened the first day of school. (My nightmare was coming true.) The campus had a new attendance secretary who was also responsible for assigning student lockers. She assigned students to lockers 1–300 by last name A to Z. Make sense? We thought so until half the students mutinied and ended up in my office. It seems that the TRADITION of the school was that SENIOR lockers were ALWAYS together in the English classroom hall, JUNIOR lockers were ALWAYS together in the history classroom hall, SOPHOMORE lockers were ALWAYS in the math and science classroom hall, and the FRESHMEN lockers were ALWAYS in the unpopular locker bay across from the library. I went to the hall to assess the damage and found unhappy juniors and seniors pushing and shoving

their way into the locker bay to get to their lockers. They were physically too big for the narrow locker aisle and seemed to almost wedge themselves into the space. This would never work!

The second lesson that I learned was not to underestimate the ability of the students or the importance of tradition. I called the student council officers together and enlisted their help. They came up with a plan to have all students take their books to their first period class. At the end of the class, each student would put his or her books into a newly assigned locker in the proper hallway. I had my doubts about whether or not it would work but "Voila," and it was done.

I completed the year fairly successfully except for my bout with mononucleosis (great timing!) and forgetting to give tickets to the ticket takers at a football game (Post-it notes worked fine). Probably the most important lesson I learned was to keep a sense of humor! Instructional leadership took a backseat to survival that year.

BARBARA SKIPPER IS THE ASSISTANT SUPERINTENDENT IN UVALDE, TEXAS.

A Difference Runs Through Us

JAMES A. BAILEY

*A*s I sat in the darkened movie house, the line I had just heard rang in my ears so loudly I thought I would become deaf: "Why is it the ones who need the most help won't take it?" The meaning of that line rang out to me as an affirmation for my first year as principal with amazing clarity and certainty. The movie, *A River Runs Through It* continued, but I turned to the pressing matter of James.

The challenge of educating our diverse population today presents a daunting opportunity, but those of us who choose this calling are often unprepared for the difficulties that diversity poses for us. Especially challenging for me my first year was a young boy, James, and the inner struggle that I fought all year between trying to accept differences in students and pushing them toward a narrow definition of what we in school call "success."

The story of James is familiar to those of us in education: low grades, antisocial behavior, unmarried mother, poor family life, public assistance for existence. All you have to do is change the face and the name and you have the classic "at-risk" student, a label of expectation for many.

James had been in and out of our school many times when I arrived as a first year principal armed with my inner belief that all children can and will learn given the right motivation and opportunities. Unfortunately for James we never did find what it took to bring him into our vision of community. The first few months as a fifth grader, James slowly stopped working and began to get into

more and more trouble. One day he was hitting people in line in the back as hard as he could; the next he was refusing to do any work; the next he was using vulgar language. Everything that his teacher and I tried seemed to push him further away from norms of acceptable behavior. According to his mother, everything could be worked out with a firmer hand. Later, on the advice of the school psychologist, we tried a softer, more humane approach letting James focus on personal issues ahead of school issues. But by mid-November, James had driven himself away from all of his classmates, had been sent to see me twenty times, and had not done anything in class in a month.

Our next step was, of course, to refer him to special education—burdening him with yet another label. Now he was not only at-risk, defiant, lazy, and a troublemaker, in our wisdom we now stuck him with the label of an emotionally disturbed eleven-year-old as if the label would cure the problem.

At first, our plan to self-contain James for most of the day worked. He connected with our special education teacher whose classroom was not so full of other people and rules. He could study what he wanted as long as he was earning time for playing the drums in the band and for computer time. He could even lounge in a beanbag to read if he wanted.

Unfortunately our optimism was premature. Within two weeks, James was back to his same behaviors—failing to work, sleeping in class, fighting—and his absences once again pronounced his hatred for school. When questioned about his absences, his mother always retorted, "Well, he's not learning that much anyway."

The moment of truth came when James was sent to see me after a fight on the playground and a bad day in class. Having worked with James in and out of class all year, I knew that using anger and power tactics would not work, yet I, like everybody else, reached my breaking point that day. When I gave James the choice of leaving until he could straighten out, he ran out of the building in a moment of brief freedom realizing, of course, that at eleven years of age he could never truly be free in an educational system based more on standardization than individuality.

Eventually, James was placed in an adolescent psychiatric ward where nothing was found to be wrong. When he returned to us, he was put back into the regular classroom on a strict behavioral plan. James left us for good in late April after an emotional outburst when he told me he could not go back into any classroom again. He called his social worker and within a few minutes his mother ran into school. Instead of consoling him, she yanked him up by the hair and took him back to the psychiatric ward. Like the rest of us, she was acting in frustration and looking for answers outside of herself.

In the end, James's mother approached us with a home schooling plan to prepare James for sixth grade. She promised that he would study and learn and be a better kid next year because there would be a different set of teachers and this was just one of those years. I never got too optimistic as I would drive by his house day after day hoping to see him reading, talking with another adult or building something in his front yard. In fact, all I ever saw was James sitting on the curb tossing pebbles into the stream of water floating by in the gutter probably wishing he could go where the water took him.

Rewatching the end of *A River Runs Through It* months later, I am reminded that as a beginning principal the ideals of human life and happiness far exceed the narrow need to succeed academically. Acceptance and acknowledgment of people's differences is the first and only step toward the larger end: learning to live. One of the ending quotes from the movie is, "In the end all things converge, and a river runs through it." If this movie had been about James, the end quote might have been, "In the end we all converge to one ideal, but a river of difference runs through us."

JAMES A. BAILEY IS THE PRINCIPAL AT DARRELL SMITH HIGH SCHOOL IN STERLING, COLORADO.

The Chocolate Milk Compromise

ANITA PAGE

I wasn't their first choice. In fact, I was their fourth choice. In late August, I received a phone call from the superintendent of a rural school district where I had interviewed in the spring. Their first and second choices had declined the job offer; an interim arrangement with a teacher in the school had fallen through. Would I come in for another interview?

If I knew then what I know now after twelve years as a school principal, I would have picked up my bag and run in the opposite direction after that meeting with him. The superintendent was very frank. The school had had a new principal every two or three years. My immediate predecessor had been pressured to leave by the school committee, and the teacher who offered to serve in the interim was not welcomed by the other teachers. After the meeting, he offered me the position and I took it without knowing any better.

School opened without me because I had to meet a deadline on my dissertation proposal. At the first meeting with the teachers, it was clear that they saw me as a bird of passage. After all, they had lived through many principals. All of the teachers had been at the school more than ten years.

It was a unique school. Its funding was high because of the taxes from a nuclear power plant in the town, and the town itself was the most prosperous in a poor county. Three-quarters of its students were tuitioned in from the next town, the poorest one in

the county. All students received free lunches, classes did not exceed sixteen in number, and the school owned enough cross-country skis to equip every single student.

I was on my own in a rural district twenty-five miles from the district office. So if any emergency happened, I had to deal with it on the spot. The previous principal had left me no background information or suggestions. I spent the first few weeks trying to inform myself by reading two years of school committee minutes, and every other piece of paper I could lay my hands on. Essentially, I left the teachers alone.

I had not come well prepared for the principalship. I had been a drama teacher, an arts coordinator, and had become certified at a time when only one supervision course was required. What stood me in good stead was my theatre directing experience where I learned how to work with groups and how to develop talent. And I was good at improvising.

What I did not understand then is that there are certain elements of a school culture—the sacred cows—that must not be changed without great care, if at all. The kitchen of the school was one such element. The school committee took pride in the fact that they could afford to give free lunches to all children and had a cook who made delicious desserts served with chocolate milk. She played a central, nurturing role in the school. The lunches were a symbol of abundance in an area of scarcity. I frankly was concerned about the amount of sugar being consumed during the day (including morning snacks), and by the end of my first month I declared that we would serve only white milk. If I had said we would do a sun dance around the school every morning, I could not have stirred up a greater fuss. I ended up with a compromise: we would alternate white and chocolate milk. What I learned from that experience was the necessity to examine the role that certain practices play in a school. If you feel they need to be changed for educational or health reasons, you need to find a substitute for the symbolic role that that practice has served.

I learned that communicating with parents is also a learned art. A number of the parents did not understand some of the progressive practices of the school, such as not correcting every spelling error in the first draft of a child's writing, because they were different from their own schooling experiences. When parents came in to ask about spelling in students' first drafts, I was quick to launch into a defense of what we were doing. After some counterproductive parent meetings, I learned that a number of these people were not protesting what we were doing but wanted a chance to express their confusion about what we were doing. What they wanted more than anything else was an opportunity to make their perceptions known. In that year, I learned

that good communication with parents means not only informing them of what you are doing, but also listening to them and keeping the door open.

Some of the staff and some of the community members were more understanding of my goals in education than others. I had no central office staff nearby or fellow principals to turn to. So I did turn to certain staff and certain community members for support. I learned, however, that you must seek that kind of support with discretion. I generated some resentment among staff and community members who felt they weren't in "my camp." Although a principal must find support in the school, she is ultimately the principal of the entire community and needs to project that primary responsibility.

After four years, I left that position for a larger school in a college town, definitely with a feeling of goodwill and a sense of accomplishment. That first year was a crash course in school change, parent relations, and diplomacy. It only took four years in my new position to get a salad bar introduced in the cafeteria!

ANITA PAGE IS THE PRINCIPAL OF MOSIER ELEMENTARY SCHOOL IN SOUTH HADLEY, MASSACHUSETTTS.

Worth the Sacrifice

JANE C. SHIPP

As I look back on my first year as the head of an independent school, I would characterize it as one of ups and downs to a degree unusual in my experience. Several crises occurred that would have been more than challenging for an old pro, crises which (for legal reasons) I cannot describe even after three years. There were other extremes as well: mood swings ranging from unexpected joy in accomplishments to discouragement over problems that seemed insoluble. There were occasions when I practically broke my arm patting myself on the back, and others when I felt certain I was in the wrong profession. And these two sentiments would occur in the same twenty-four hour period, leaving me slightly schizophrenic.

I marvel now that I had the energy to sustain my momentum through that first year. When I think of the organizational changes that I put into place while trying to get to know at least a thousand new people, making my way in a new community, earning the respect of a hundred employees of the school, and attending to the myriad daily details that are routine for all of us, I don't know how I did it, and I wonder whether I could do it again.

On second thought, I know that I was able to do it because of the support I was lucky enough to find from so many individuals and groups of people in the school community. I was blessed with an exceptionally good president of the board of trustees who gave me just the right amount of support and advice and provided just the right amount of autonomy for me. The faculty and staff were eager for a new era and did not block any of the changes that I needed to make. Indeed, they gave me wholehearted support as I

69

plunged into deep water. Nevertheless, I came to learn in that first year the price I pay for maintaining an appropriate level of comfort and civility in the interactions over which I preside. I am collaborative and democratic to a fault, which is a time-consuming modus operandi. Because I believe so completely in the value of an inclusive process of decision making, I don't feel successful merely having made a decision; I feel successful only when I have persuaded others to engage themselves in the outcome of that decision. Such an expectation for success is draining.

It also became clear to me that I am not able to keep my hands out of the details of running a school. I like to choose the color of the paint; I want to do all the teacher evaluations; I try to know all five hundred children's names; I attend faculty and trustee committee meetings and parent association meetings. The list is long. This approach is probably not sensible for the long term, and it undoubtedly accounts for the unreasonable hours that I spend at school and the board's fear that I will "burn out." I know I should change these habits, but I face the fact that my compulsiveness is not only an integral part of my personality, but also responsible to some degree for whatever success I've had. Now as I begin year number four and a capital campaign looms ahead, I know I won't be able to continue this level of involvement. Learning to delegate more effectively will be a major challenge.

I was startled that first year, and have continued to be surprised, by the degree of affection that I have received from all sides. Without it I would not function as well, and I continue to be grateful that it happens. I doubt that I could work for any length of time in an adversarial environment, although many school heads do. I learned early on that it is an immense joy to structure situations so that everybody comes out winning. When I can make that happen, I'm elated. I have a high tolerance for eccentricity and even for cantankerous behavior, as long as it serves the common good and ultimately benefits the children. Given the culture of my school, it is fortunate that I have this tolerance. It is a trick and a half to maintain one's own integrity and the integrity of one's vision for the school in such a culture, but with patience and care it can be done—and what a glorious feeling when it all comes together!

I remember many accomplishments from my first year: putting into place a fair and open salary system; establishing a preliminary faculty evaluation procedure; setting up a structure of faculty and staff committees to participate in decision making; preparing the school's first curriculum guide for parents; organizing the process for developing a strategic plan; reworking the progress report forms and procedure; rebuilding a sense of trust on the part of parents in the school and its mission. I often pondered, during that time and afterward, the right and wrong use of power in a position such as mine.

Heads have power, no doubt about it, though not as much as most people think. It was a shock to me to realize how much of the job is reactive. It seems to me I have mended more than my share of fences that should not have been broken in the first place. Particularly in the beginning, I felt as if I were constantly reacting to other people's stimuli, which is apt to leave one feeling ever so slightly out of control!

I remind myself, when I need to, that the power we heads have is the power to do good; that is why people like us take on headships. In addition, I have been sustained always by the conviction that the work I do is important work, the most important work in the world. When I'm particularly tired or discouraged, I ask myself whether it's work that is worth sacrificing such a huge amount of one's personal life for: I also wonder about the ego of someone who answers that question, as I do: "Yes! What I can accomplish here is worth the cost." Nevertheless, I said that at the end of my first year and I still say it. I know that I am privileged to have an opportunity as rich as that of heading a school. Now if only I can raise salaries, keep the budget balanced, reach the annual fund goal, take care of deferred maintenance, help the board stay appropriately engaged, maintain faculty morale, hear parents' concerns, and be sure the students learn what they should—then I will sleep well at night.

JANE C. SHIPP IS THE HEADMISTRESS OF THE RENBROOK SCHOOL IN WEST HARTFORD, CONNECTICUT.

Entry: The Door to Effective Headship

ALBERT M. ADAMS

I have had the good fortune to experience *two* first years as a school head—the first as I began my five-year tenure at the Cambridge School of Weston, and the second, when I arrived at Lick-Wilmerding in 1988. As I approached each of these "new beginnings," well-intentioned friends offered conventional advice: "Enjoy the honeymoon." "Spend the first year listening." Others, in contradiction, intoned, "Think of the first hundred days of the presidency; put yourself on the map early with dramatic initiatives."

While these exhortations contained elements of wisdom, I instinctively knew that any, taken literally, was bad advice. My instincts were confirmed when, six months before moving to Weston, I was introduced to Barry Jentz and the book, *Entry*, which he coauthored with his partner, Joan Wofford. Written primarily for public school superintendents and principals, *Entry* suggests a fresh and dynamic process for assuming leadership at a new school—namely to enter, in equal measures, as anthropologist and proactive leader. It offers a practical solution to the conundrum with which a head of school struggles: how to start, and particularly, how to balance the need to listen and learn with the need to assert strong leadership.

An underlying premise of *Entry* is that I, as the arriving head, am entering my new school with respect—that is, without preconceptions or pet prescriptions for what the school ought to become. Another is that it is not *my* school; instead my role is that of leader

and steward for one important chapter in the school's evolution, with connection, continuity, and change being the threads that stitch together past, present, and future. Another premise predates, but seems to anticipate, Peter Senge's notion of the "learning organization," with *inquiry, reflection, and growth* being at the center of the enterprise. *Entry* also allows me, as the new head, to incorporate Lee Bolman's and Terry Deal's four "frames" through which to view an organization. Specifically, it provides the discipline to assure that I look equally through the structural, human resource, political, and symbolic lenses. Further, the very act of modeling my respect for the community and my commitment to honest inquiry is a symbolic statement that can define my entire tenure at the school.

When I started as head at Lick-Wilmerding, my public commitment was to spend an hour to an hour and a half with each board member and administrator prior to September, and with each faculty member before Thanksgiving. In addition, I would do the same with representative samples of parents, students and alumni/ae—mostly individually, but sometimes in small groups.

My introductory letter to the various constituencies included my reasons for undertaking this formal entry process, the timetable for feedback/validation sessions (late fall), a projection of planning steps, and the list of questions that would form the backbone of the semi-structured interview format I would use in our upcoming conversations. My letter spoke of the special opportunity I wanted to seize to fill in the portrait of Lick which I was painting in my mind. It went on to say that, "I want to take advantage of this transitional moment—to capture the freshness of early insights, to appreciate the various angles of vision and to understand the issues which define Lick's hopes and challenges for the future."

Beyond communicating to the entire community what kinds of inquiries I would make in the interviews, inclusion of the questions with the introductory letter allowed interviewees to prepare answers, if they chose. Many, in fact, came with pages of notes, and a few even submitted well-developed papers. In addition to several inquiries about personal stories and points of connection with Lick, I also posed questions such as:

- What are the key issues facing Lick today? Why is each important? Can you rank these issues in priority order?
- What qualities do you most want to see preserved at Lick-Wilmerding?
- What networks of people are typically interested in influencing decision making? What do the members of these networks have in

common? How do they differ?

· Describe a moment when the school was in conflict. How did the conflict arise? What people or groups played roles in it? How? How was the problem resolved? Might it have been handled differently?

· Describe a difficult decision you have had to make (as a board member). Why was it important? How did you reach your decision? What did others think? Would you, in retrospect, have done anything differently?

The public nature of the plan was, in itself, a powerful statement to the community about how I intended to do business. In addition to signaling an open and inclusive leadership style, my questions reflected the seriousness, breadth, and depth that would characterize my initial inquiries, as well as my ongoing approach to leadership at Lick.

Certainly one immediate and pragmatic result of announcing my *Entry* intentions was that every "key player" was assured of equal access to "my ear." This notion of establishing a "level playing field" right from the start has paid significant dividends throughout these five years. On the more personal, less political side, nothing convinces people of your genuine interest in them better than focused, uninterrupted one-on-one time. Amazingly, I can think of a dozen examples from the academic year just past when one colleague or another made reference to our initial conversation five years ago! The impact of those first six months not only set the stage for our work together, but has endured in dramatic and surprising ways.

The explicit purpose of *Entry* is to identify prevalent themes that define the school of today, including any major challenges that require attention. In many cases it is recurring stories, rather than specific information, that provide the deepest insights. In addition, the new head also begins to learn about the personal and political forces at play as he/she begins to fashion strategies for moving the school forward.

The real power of *Entry* is that it puts the new head in a position to say, in effect, to each constituency: "Here is what you (in the aggregate, since all individual perspectives are confidential) have told me. Did I get it right? Given these insights and perspectives, here is how I believe we should proceed." The resulting opportunity to refer continually to "what you have told me" and "my understanding of how you view it" allows the head to enjoy many of the benefits of being a consultant—that is, to take the high road, while also being the most central participant.

A magical moment in my entry to Lick came in late August of that first summer when the board joined us for a working session at our faculty retreat.

The goal was to write individually, then in small groups, and last as a whole group, a one-paragraph mission statement for the school. Having achieved that, we pushed to the next level of distilling the essence of the "ideal Lick" into short metaphorical banners or mottoes. The central issues and descriptive languages which emerged came directly out of the first two months of *Entry* interviews! What is more, those foundations: "EDUCATION FOR THE HEAD, HEART, HANDS," "PRIVATE SCHOOL WITH PUBLIC PURPOSE," "CAN-DO CONFIDENCE" have resonated with every constituency, including alums from sixty and seventy years ago, with whom I have met over these five years. They also became the central elements of the strategic plan and financial long-range plan which we developed over the next two years. In a very literal way the issues, ideas, and language that bubbled up in the entry process have become Lick-Wilmerding's anchor—the summation of past virtues, present achievements, and future dreams.

A final premise underlying the theory of *Entry* is that it represents the beginning of a systematic, ongoing planning process. Thus, at the end of my first year at Lick, with *Entry* wrapped in tidy bows, we had Susan Stone, a strategic planner, facilitate the beginning of a full review of the school's goals, rationales, and implementation steps for all twelve components of an independent school. The process which followed unfolded over the next eight months, and we published a twenty-four page document which included a financial long-range plan, with five-year projections.

These steps are relevant in the context of *Entry* because the fundamental building blocks surfaced and were crystallized in those first six months: quality of program (top salaries and benefits), full integration of the technical arts (shops) into the rigorous college prep curriculum, access, and affordability (to assure that students of color and students paying "flexible tuition" represent at least a third of the school). They became a credo of sorts—a regular expression and affirmation of our shared values. As such, they serve as both prod and measuring stick, and their enduring effectiveness derives from the knowledge that they truly have their roots in the soul of the whole community.

ALBERT ADAMS IS THE HEADMASTER AT LICK-WILMERDING HIGH SCHOOL IN SAN FRANCISCO, CALIFORNIA.

Baptism by Fire

JUDITH T. HORNBECK

*Y*ou have heard of baptism by fire? Well, consider a baptism that included fire, floods, contaminated water, a bomb threat, and an asbestos removal accident requiring total evacuation of the school. Not only was my desire to become a principal severely tested, but my very faith itself!

I left a position as the assistant principal of a middle school in a neighboring county to assume the principalship of a K–5 school, housing approximately six hundred students. I assumed my duties midyear with the knowledge that the school was undergoing extensive remodeling, including many areas of new construction. During my intensive interview sessions, I was also made aware of the school community's desire for a strong, visionary leader, who would be called upon to solve the school's multiple problems as quickly as possible. Interestingly enough, ownership of a magic wand was never mentioned as a job requirement!

My first two days passed in a deceptively calm manner. I met more than sixty staff members and started playing the name game! I visited classrooms, was interviewed by members of the press, and was feeling pretty pleased with myself. Then . . . Day 3 arrived. An innocent holiday door decorating contest spawned my first calamity. One of the kindergarten teachers had used angels as part of the holiday decorations. Heaven Forbid! After solving the "angel flap" dilemma and drying the teacher's tears, I was propelled rapidly into Day 5, which opened with a bus accident. Although no one was seriously injured, the entire community was shaken by the event that received extensive press coverage. (Not exactly the headlines I had hoped for!)

An eternal optimist, I started Week 2 with a clean slate. My bliss, however, was short-lived. Friday afternoon, I was called home to check on a potential furnace fire. Shortly after I left, a fire erupted in a transformer on the school roof! There was no structural damage and no injuries, but I could sense the first tremors of faltering faith.

Several weeks sped by as I adjusted to my new environment. Always an early bird, I arrived early and stayed late, often working twelve- or fourteen-hour days. I began to flex my leadership muscles as teachers began coming to me with educational problems and concerns. Ah, the lull before the storm.

After a particularly heavy winter rainstorm, I arrived at school early one Monday to find the front section of the auditorium under three feet of water! The construction workers had blocked the egress for the storm drains. The superintendent arrived to take a look, and the problem was "fixed." Imagine my surprise when the entire scenario was repeated again, this time on a Saturday morning—I just happened to stop by the school because I was concerned by the heavy downpour. Needless to say, this time the problem was permanently fixed.

During this entire time period, I had become extremely popular with the construction crew, the job foreman, the clerk of the works, and the school engineer. Actually, they tried to hide when they saw me coming! Renovation of a school with the students still present is difficult at best, and despite these problems, I really did have a good rapport with the construction crew.

Spring finally arrived only to bring additional water woes. We survived two separate incidents with impure water, one due to the presence of E-coli bacteria, the other resulting from rust and sediment contamination. The entire school drank bottled water from water coolers placed strategically around the school.

Time for another full-scale evacuation! I received a bomb threat through our in-school postal system, WEE DELIVER. The police were called and the building was dutifully searched and pronounced "safe." Students patiently filed back into the building and resumed their day. One teacher mentioned the real possibility that the school was "jinxed!" (I have received several four-leaf clovers as presents!)

Everyone is familiar with the old saying, "Save the best for last." I will never forget the feeling I had the day the engineer came to my office to tell me that a construction worker had accidentally disturbed some floor tiles that could contain asbestos. I determined that we needed not only to evacuate immediately, but that we needed to send the children home until scientific tests could be completed. Again, I was a media star. Three local television stations

arrived, all clamoring for an interview. I received the "all-clear" sign that night, and we returned to school the next day.

Throughout my first year as principal, I received overwhelming support from staff, parents, and students. I found that there is a special spirit of enthusiastic cooperation in school that cannot be duplicated anywhere else. Although I received numerous gifts at the end of the year, none could compare to the words of thanks I received from my staff for guiding them through a most difficult and trying year. . . . Now, where did I put that magic wand?

JUDITH HORNBECK IS THE PRINCIPAL OF T. C. WALKER ELEMENTARY SCHOOL IN GLOUCESTER, VIRGINIA.

Adversity: It's Our Reward?

JOHN R. KELLY

*E*ven though my first year as principal was thirteen years ago, many of the days during that year stand out vividly in my memory. It was a year that taught me an incredible amount about schools, their organization, and the politics of organizations.

The advertisements for the principal position were published in late July. I was aware that the town of Leduc had established its own Catholic school district the previous year. My wife had a passing acquaintance with one of the newly elected trustees, and, knowing that I was a teacher, he would occasionally pass on information to her about the problems they were having in establishing their district. When I saw the ad, I figured I would throw in an application for the position.

I was only thirty at the time. The six years teaching experience I had gave me a sense that administration might be a possibility. Somehow the thought of being in charge of a school appealed to me. At any rate, in July of 1990, I assembled my resumé and sent it off.

Within a week, I got a call. I met with an area superintendent for Edmonton Catholic Schools who had taken on the position in Leduc as sort of a lend-lease arrangement. He explained to me that the board hoped to begin operations in September with a bus load of students coming into Edmonton (approximately 20 km) while awaiting the construction of the board's first school, which was slated to open the following September. The board, he claimed, wanted to get things rolling slowly so that the school opening

could be smooth. They had already hired a teacher for the kindergarten program (which was to be run in the church basement in Leduc) and another teacher for the middle grades. Classroom space was secured for us, he claimed, in an underused elementary school in Edmonton.

It all sounded great to me. With the wide-eyed enthusiasm of a true rookie, I expounded on my theories of education, discipline, and religion. He must have been impressed, because two days later I got a call to meet with the board the next week for a formal interview.

When that evening came around, I had a chance to shake hands with the other applicant on his way out. He was about fifteen years older than I and was introduced as Doctor somebody. I figured the game was over. I was just being brought in to fill out the slate. With nothing to lose, I let the trustees (one gentleman was away on holidays) have both barrels. We joked, talked, planned, and dreamed together. For over an hour and a half, all the world seemed to stand still as we envisioned the future successes of the yet to be named, yet to be built, yet to be opened school.

Lo and behold, the next morning I got the phone call. The board loved me. Would I take the job? The answer was an immediate affirmative. Monday would be my starting day. After all, we only had two weeks to go before school was supposed to open and there would certainly be a lot to do.

So many things happened in rapid succession during those last two weeks of August that my head still spins. In no particular order, they were:

- No, we would not bus the kids into Edmonton after all. Instead, portable classrooms would be located on our school site, supposedly within the first month of the school year.
- Yes, the parents in town loved the idea of no busing to the city, so twice as many students registered as had been expected.
- The trustee who was away on holidays came back and was aghast that the board had hired a principal without his opinion being considered. Over the next ten months, he was to be a personal thorn in my side. This was despite the fact that a) we shared the same last name, and b) he was a teacher with the city district.
- At the first regularly scheduled board meeting after my appointment, the secretary-treasurer (also on loan from the city district) stormed out of the room and resigned because of my namesake's antics.
- I was authorized to hire another teacher to meet our rapidly expanding enrollment. When I interviewed the first applicant for the job, she broke down in tears, explaining that she just found out that she was pregnant, and her wedding was only a week away. I figured that she

was honest and had courage, so I hired her.

- The board decided to name the school Notre Dame. Also, while we waited for the portables to be moved from the city, we contracted to use Sunday school facilities of the local Pentecostal church. They were far below school standards, but they would only be for a few weeks, we were assured.

- My staff and I had to begin the task of assembling a school overnight from scratch. Since we were the only school in the district, there was no one to lean on for help. Our students were coming out of the town's public school system, so colleagues in the system were understandably cool toward us. We had no supplies, no textbooks, no furniture, no curriculum guides, no forms to fill out, and no policy manual for operations.

Somehow, in those two weeks, we put together a school. The day after Labor Day students arrived, all fresh and clean, ready for a new experience in a new school system. We opened with ninety students in grades one through six and another twenty-five in kindergarten. The board was elated. Things were under way. Our problems had just begun.

Running an elementary school out of Sunday-school rooms in the basement of a church would have been fine if it was just for a month. The promise of portables was not as easy as it seemed. We were not able to move in until the week before Christmas. Every Friday, we had to put all our belongings away in a storage room and move the chairs, tables, and walls back to their original position. Each Monday, we had to do the reverse.

The euphoria of opening a new school quickly turned into the routine of any September. Along toward the end of the month, one of the staff inquired, "When do we get paid?" This brought on a wonderful exercise in innovation. No one had thought about how payroll was to be set up, what procedures were to be followed, or which wage scale we were to follow (each school district in the province negotiates independently with its own board). With the help of our provincial teachers' association, a contract settlement was reached with our board.

With no central office, a superintendent for only two days a month, and a rather unique group of school trustees, school operations were a challenge and a joy. We wrote school policy as things happened. It was both a principal's dream and nightmare.

Our students were generally not the scholars from the other school district, so we had to set up a resource room program. I got to interview and hire the teacher. Unfortunately, the Provincial Department of Education decided,

a month after we had hired her, that her credentials from New Zealand did not qualify her to teach in Alberta. We went on a two-year appeal process to have one of the most talented teachers I have ever encountered keep her job.

We also hired and fired substitute teachers and janitors. We had our first maternity leave and an intervention by the Social Services Department on a child neglect case. Throughout everything, an excellent staff and supportive parents kept the school operating. The new building was begun in February. Our enrollments increased monthly. I made my share of rookie mistakes but had successes, too. Things were sailing along fine until late April. Then, the crisis came.

During the course of the school year my namesake on the board had been causing all sorts of problems. Being a teacher himself (you can sit as a trustee in Alberta if you do not teach in the district, but only reside there), he figured that he knew education pretty well. He was close to retirement age and had emigrated from Scotland only ten years before. As human beings go, he was the most disagreeable individual I have ever met.

Our number projections for September showed us having nearly three hundred students. The superintendent and I estimated that we would need at least a dozen new staff members. His instructions to me were simple: solicit applications, interview candidates, and come to the board with a proposed staff list. I did as I was instructed. It was a wonderful part of the job to talk with teachers about building a school district together. My trustee friend, however, did not think it was proper procedure for a young principal to make hiring decisions and forward them directly to the board.

In late April, at a private board meeting, the superintendent and my trustee friend squared off in a shouting match. They hurled accusations back and forth like snowballs. After one particularly fierce volley, the superintendent slammed his briefcase shut, said he had another meeting in the city, and stormed out of the room, leaving me alone with five trustees and a recommended staff list. Somehow I got out of the meeting alive.

The next morning, I was summoned to the superintendent's office in Edmonton to discuss our next course of action. He informed me that he was going to offer a letter of resignation and wondered if I was going to do the same. His logic was simple: The chairman of the board would have a choice of us or one of his trustees. Which direction did he want the school district to take? I was looking down the barrel of a loaded gun. I needed the job, the superintendent was merely on loan. Summoning up all the courage I could muster, I wrote a letter too. Together, we presented them to the chairman and waited. By midnight we were informed that three trustees had resigned and by-election papers would be issued the next morning to fill the vacancies. We had won.

The year ended with sunshine, final exams, and class trips. Our new building was being built before our very eyes. Everyone had a collective sense that we had survived a rather unique first year. The school operates today with a strong spirit of community togetherness. Although I left after the third year, some of my founding staff are still teaching there and still tell the stories from that first year. Adversity is often its own reward.

JOHN KELLY TEACHES AT ST. ALBERT HIGH SCHOOL IN ST. ALBERT, ALBERTA.

The Leap Year of 1992

MARK KAVARSKY

I was fortunate that it was a leap year. I was hired in February 1992 as the interim acting principal of Salome Urena de Henriquez Intermediate School 218 in the Washington Heights–Inwood section of upper Manhattan. IS 218 was scheduled to open on March 2, 1992. Therefore, I had just one month to make a vision into a reality. Leap year provided me with a much-needed extra day.

The challenges before me were formidable. IS 218 was the first of many new schools planned by the New York City School Construction Authority in District Six. The middle school was the first new school under construction in more than twenty years for a neighborhood struggling with the city's most overcrowded schools, a large population of poor, first-generation immigrant families, many young people at risk of dropping out of school, and not enough assistance from the city's large service providers. It was also a community with a drive to succeed. Members of the community were determined to help their children despite the absence of medical, dental, and health services and a strong presence of drugs. Recognizing the urgent need for services, the concept of a "community school" was developed.

The community school would be an integral part of the community and contain all of the health and welfare services of a large social service agency under the roof of IS 218. It would serve as a focal point to which children and their parents could turn for both education and all those social services they sorely needed.

84

Suddenly and without warning, the role of the principal evolved from the educational leader of a school to the facilitator of the community school. At the same time, the work of the principalship evolved from a seven-hour and twenty-minute workday into a six-days-a-week, fifteen-hours-a-day, year-round schedule.

What was proposed was not just to use the school from 3:00 to 10:00 P.M. every day, but to work side by side with the parents, health agencies, and community-based organizations to ensure that children had every chance to succeed. Consequently, the construction of the school had to be modified to accommodate such a concept. I worked tirelessly with the School Construction Authority, not only to complete their construction in a timely fashion for the March opening, but also to make adjustments in the original blueprints to create a family resource room, a parenting resource room, a medical and dental services room, and a health and social services room. Hours of meetings ensued as medical and health service agencies as well as the local community-based organizations met with me to collaborate on plans for the opening of IS 218. Fortunately, the Children's Aid Society joined the collaboration to provide medical, dental, and health services to the community. The expertise and resources of C.A.S. made a dream into a reality by June of 1992. Even Mercy College joined the collaboration to offer degree-bound credit and continuing education courses to the mothers and fathers of our children both in the day and in the evening at IS 218.

The recruitment of staff was only partially completed by February 1992. District Six had completed an agreement with the union stating that one-third of the staff would be acquired through a seniority application plan outside of District Six, and one-third of the staff would be acquired through principal's choice. In reality, few teachers could obtain easy approval in the month of February (middle of the school year) from either their district and/or principal to transfer to a new school.

Moreover, I had difficulty convincing teachers with experience to transfer to a school district notorious for overcrowded and decaying facilities. My repeated attempts to recruit a quality work force were especially frustrating as I spent long hours on the telephone each night trying to convince the large pool of excellent teachers to take a risk. The more I spoke of a "community school" concept, however, the less favorable was the reaction of my colleagues. It became obvious to me that the majority of teachers would rather remain in a known setting despite the adversities, than transfer to an unknown setting that could potentially make their professional dreams come true. I would remember this lesson as I planned the organizational structure of the school.

One week before the opening of the school, the administrators, teachers, paraprofessionals, aides, and parent volunteers were in place. The Children's Aid Society and C.B.O.'s were hard at work soliciting funding for their services. Endless hours of cabinet meetings helped to formulate a mission statement for the school. IS 218 would soon become Salome Urena Middle Academies (SUMA). In 1991, I had earned my Ed.D. from Fordham University by studying the most successful middle schools in and around the metropolitan New York City area. I was convinced that an inner-city school could obtain positive results by utilizing a middle school philosophy.

Consequently, IS 218 with a student population of twelve hundred students was transformed into four sub-schools (academies) with a population of approximately three hundred students. Each academy would be self-autonomous with teams of teachers making decisions to meet the needs of the teachers, parents, and children that they governed. An opportunity to collaborate and reflect on decisions was provided for each team with the intent to create a professional working environment. Staff development was emphasized with before, during, and after school workshops on middle school philosophy, discipline with dignity, advisories, curriculum development, theme infusion, flexible scheduling, and interdisciplinary planning. We offered brainstorming and consensus-building courses and encouraged people to take risks.

My last task was to develop a school climate that recognized the characteristics of the middle school child. Dramatic changes in the physical, emotional, and cognitive growth of early adolescents warranted an instructional program that facilitated the new capacity to think in more abstract and complex ways. Teams of teachers began to plan interdisciplinary themes that encouraged children to work cooperatively and on long-term projects using a hierarchy of critical thinking skills.

Because the middle school child has an increased sense of self and an enhanced capacity for intimate relationships with both adults and peers, an advisory program was established in which every child has an adult mentor and a small group of classmates to turn to in times of need. The overall effect of educating the "whole child" has been the community's acceptance of the school as a caring home and safe haven. Not surprisingly, nearly 50 percent of our children voluntarily remain in our extended day programs rather than return to their mean streets.

The result of the efforts of many individuals at SUMA speaks for itself. In a few short months, SUMA staff have already received invitations to speak at local, state, and national forums on such varied topics as community youth service for the middle school child and the integration of the "community

school" concept and curriculum. A thirty-minute documentary on SUMA titled "Three O'Clock and Beyond" has been broadcast by PBS. The children of SUMA have been featured on the cover of *Middle School Years* and written about in many local and national newspapers and journals. The parents and the community have forged a compact with their "community school" that has set a model for schools of the twenty-first century.

Upon reflection, I have never worked harder in my life than I have worked in my first year as a principal. Nevertheless, I look forward to future leap years with the knowledge that I will once again have a much-needed extra day.

MARK KAVARSKY IS PRINCIPAL AT INTERMEDIATE SCHOOL 218 IN NEW YORK CITY.

Not Quite a Noble Example

SCOTT D. THOMSON

Suddenly, it struck my consciousness with the force of a tidal wave. On the first day of school, as students streamed from the initial back-to-school group orientation and headed for the classrooms, I realized there was nothing I could do now that would make a difference. As principal, I was supposed to be leading, to be in charge, but already events had streaked beyond my control.

Yes, I had been on the job and "in control" for two months, meeting with faculty and arranging for September's opening activities. I felt confident that school would begin smoothly. But, as the students moved from the bleachers, my confidence was overwhelmed by a sense of vulnerability. The events of the balance of the day, and to a large degree of the entire year, were beyond my direct control. School had begun to move forward to its rendezvous with June, and I was simply a ghost conductor, my baton hidden from most of the players most of the time. If teachers and students chose to mangle the composition, I feared, then it would be clear evidence of the incompetence of the new principal. My fate as a principal, therefore, depended in large measure on the wisdom and experience and goodwill of others in the school, and on my ability to shape these attributes in a program beneficial to all on campus. This job of leadership was more complicated than I had envisioned.

I walked back to my office with assistant principals Bill Hutchinson and Phyllis Leveen, sat down at the desk, and stared at the appointment calendar. It was blank, offering mute evidence of my expendability. The train was moving, and nobody wanted to talk to the engineer.

Then I glanced again at the calendar, dated Monday, September 14, 1964, and knew that I would be all right. Printed on the bottom of the page was Bert Estabrook's observation that "One needs common sense to succeed, and a sense of humor to be happy." Assuredly I have these qualities, I thought, and so, feeling better, turned the calendar to Tuesday. Four appointments and a meeting had been printed neatly by my secretary. Perhaps I could be useful after all.

Nine and a half months and 180 school days later brought graduation for the seniors of Cubberley High School. Some observers contend that graduation ceremonies are for parents and not for the students who would settle for a simple diploma. Actually, graduation is for new principals, as well. It provides visible affirmation for the principal of the significance of the job, and it offers personal assurances of worth seldom found in other occupations.

Whatever else happens during that first year, the successes and the defeats and the inconsequentials, graduation stands firm as the closing gate. It also is the preeminent public ritual in American culture, a summit experience for parents and families. Graduation offers discernible evidence of a continuing national rebirth generationally, intellectually, socially, and economically. It provides the keystone of continuity for the American culture as expressed in the late twentieth century. The family continues, the occupations flourish, and the community and nation grow. Without schooling and its capstone ceremony over which principals preside, the national welfare would erode.

At these graduation ceremonies, new as well as veteran principals are the visible, front-stage symbols of the entire event. They represent the faculty and its work and the achievements of students. And they affirm that the young people crossing the stage may now be called adults. Symbolically, this is major league, with the principal standing at its center. For the first-year principal, this is heady stuff, nourishing the spirit beyond whatever bruises and doubts remain from the mistakes of inexperience. Yes, graduation is for principals as well as for parents.

I have kept the appointment calendar from my first year as principal and find the initial entries enlightening in retrospect. The first contacts in July are a diverse lot: a meeting with the superintendent, a Rotary Club luncheon, conferences with the assistant principals and the P.T.A. president, interviews with teacher candidates for a late vacancy, and a briefing from the chair of our tech prep committee, a program again popular in the 1990s.

Then the teachers with agendas drifted in, one by one. First came Dave Buck, the drama teacher who wanted to gauge my interest in the arts. Then two department chairs appeared seeking redress for budget decisions made

earlier. They were followed by Gypsy Laurence, the social studies aide with work-load concerns; by Sylvia Hoyt, a liberal English teacher who thought the curriculum restrictive; and by Dottie Bradshaw, another English teacher with whom my wife and I shared mutual friends. Soon thereafter arrived a reporter from the Palo Alto *Times* and the director of buildings and grounds for the school district with the veiled message that his staff, and not the building custodians, were to conduct all maintenance.

As a new principal, confident that my progressive ideas about improving instruction and delegating major responsibilities to teachers would be received warmly, I began to understand that my agenda for the school was only one of many. Furthermore, some agendas had long roots leading back for years, confirming that teachers possess long memories that are activated when new principals appear. Clearly, if my agenda was to gain broad support, then I must show consideration for these problems. Contrary to the view that new principals enjoy a honeymoon of six months in which to act, I believe that old hurts and issues should be addressed early as they arise, if only to listen and discuss. Then teachers will be motivated to support the principal's program. A proper courtship must precede the honeymoon if the marriage is going to work in the long run.

The question of expectations faces all principals. How do your expectations for teachers and students square with those of the school culture? Is the school driven to excel by tradition or by the professionalism of key teachers, or is morale flat with little sign of group standards? Do students feel they should live up to the reputation of the school, or are students disengaged from school affairs?

As a new principal I found that a few key faculty tend to determine expectations for their colleagues and students. This "culture" then tends to define the way things are done around the school. The power of informal organization, however, does not diminish the principal's leadership responsibility to improve the school. It is wise to understand the current culture before proposing surgery and then to act with W. Somerset Maugham's advice in your ear: "It's a funny thing about life; if you refuse to accept anything but the best, you very often get it."

The culture of Cubberley High School was driven by an interesting mix of people and focused on the personal as well as the academic development of students. Its culmination was expressed by the presentation of "Senior Bowls" at graduation, engraved large silver bowls awarded by the faculty to six students who most personified the values of academic achievement *and* service to the school. Its mentors included the English chair and an English teacher, two counselors, the science chair, the math chair, a biology teacher, and the industrial technology chair.

Lying beneath the exalted horizons of most graduate courses are the job skills that enable new principals to succeed. Here are a few that worked for me:

1. Organize the school week by publishing for teachers every Friday afternoon the events of the next week, day by day. Include commendations and announcements. This document places everyone on the same page in a busy school.

2. Meet occasionally with the secretarial and custodial staff. They know some things about the school missed by teachers, and their work deserves recognition. One of the best heads at Cubberley was Tim Mellor, the chief custodian.

3. Close down the public address system when classes are in session.

4. Take your share of the dirty work; good example goes a long way.

5. Make the school look good; people will respond and gain pride. My first visible act as principal was to remove the vending machines in the entry foyer and replace them with art.

6. Develop new programs with teachers to improve instruction. Always have something going based on research to replace the status quo. Work with the departments most ready, and the others will come along. Incremental change tends to be more successful and lasting than dramatic, schoolwide initiatives that quickly lose steam.

At the end of my first year as principal, the day following graduation, I was exhausted but feeling affirmed. I had made my share of mistakes: misread a couple of teachers, pushed an unready department too hard to change, was too tough with some students and too easy with others, did not handle a parent conference well, and could have taken dozens of initiatives that time simply did not allow. But, on balance, the 180 days and 90 nights spent on school business had gone reasonably well for a novice principal.

The desk calendar, now a bit shopworn, falls open to Monday, June 21. The quotation at the bottom of the page reads, "We can finish nothing in this life: but we make a beginning, and bequeath a noble example." Not a bad thought for a new principal in June, even for one who was not quite a noble example.

SCOTT THOMSON IS WITH THE NATIONAL POLICY BOARD FOR EDUCATIONAL ADMINISTRATION IN FAIRFAX, VIRGINIA.

Compromises

THEODORE R. SIZER

"Can you lend me a quarter?"

The stringy, smirking kid stood in front of his dormitory, addressing me as I climbed out of my car. It was May 1972. The headmaster-elect, I was making my once-a-week visit to Andover, still juggling the duties of a Harvard deanship with trying to figure out what this residential high school might be all about.

Cheeky? Yes. He had obviously been put up to this little request. His friends were visible at the dormitory windows, giggling. My predecessor was seen by many of the kids as aloof and formal, particularly during the last months as he was dying of cancer. No one would try to cadge a quarter off him.

So, what about this new guy, thirty-nine years old and only distantly a practicing school person? The kids must have sensed my awkwardness in the assemblies where I had first met them. They did not really know that I had not worked among adolescents since 1958, and then in an Australian grammar school, but they acutely sensed my rawness.

"Sure." I fumbled in my pocket and, mercifully, found a quarter. "Will I get it back?"

"Ummm." Laughter. "Of course. . . ." He took off. The dormitory windows dribbled guffaws. I felt like a turkey.

So much of my first year was like that. There was much to do of an administrative nature, both pushing ahead with good initiatives already resting on the faculty's agenda, merging the school (then for males only) with an adjacent school for young women, coping with putting together two wary faculties, calming a board of trustees still reeling from all the embarrassing newnesses foisted

upon them by the 1960s. While none of this with adults was always easy, it was familiar stuff. I had coped with that and worse as a Harvard dean during the sixties. It was the cheeky kids that made me nervous.

One minute they were naughty Tom Sawyers hornswoggling a naive new headmaster, the next, hard headed student newspaper editors with carefully wrought opinions on demonstrably important matters. They did very dumb things, from constantly losing their books to taking LSD, and yet they pulled off smart things, not only in BC Calculus but also beyond, as when the seniors, largely drawn from the football team, quietly negotiated with their counterparts at the local high school a privately but firmly enforced smothering of rough teenaged rowdiness that had cropped up in the neighborhood.

They couldn't follow a simple and logical argument in history class one minute, and they saw deeply into a comparable matter the next. Many claimed that they knew that they were really in love and that sleeping with that freshman girl was an oh-so-adult expression of lifetime fidelity, and at the next moment they could deeply fathom the fear of a newcomer to the school from a foreign place (an American inner city or another country, for example) and subtly intuit what collective nurturing and befriending of that fresh arrival must be summoned.

Dumb and smart. Thoughtful and thoughtless. Narcissistic and empathic. All at once. Even in the same fifteen minutes.

By contrast, the graduate students in education that I had been teaching for over a decade were a dull lot, often too predictable. Adolescents? How do you school a person who is a boy one minute and a man the next, a girl at 9:00 A.M. and a woman at noon?

Collectively, the faculty members, veteran, skilled, and committed though they were, gave no help at all.

"We have to have rules at this school and we must consistently enforce them. The students have to learn that the world is a demanding place, that there are some things that are nonnegotiable. To waffle on standards is to hurt the youngsters. For us to fail as certain adults is to let this school drift into chaos. We must be clear. The rules must be clear. We know what these kids need. They want us to be firm. They learn from pushing against us. . . ."

"Our job is to get these kids to make good decisions on their own. They need practice at that. If we tell them what to do and when to study all the time, if we order their lives for them, we do them a disservice. We must stop incarcerating them in enforced dependency, we the rule-delivering jailers, they the cowed inmates. They'll revolt. Indeed, they already are in revolt, in this school at least, in a sneaky, remarkably polite sort of way. And they are

not all alike and don't want to be treated alike. They deserve to take, they have to take more responsibility. . . ."

"There is a core of knowledge that every young person must know."

"Students should have some say in what they study. If they don't they will just go through the motions, mindlessly dishing back to us what we have dished out to them. They should be considered apprentices in learning, not vessels into which we pour our knowledge."

"How in God's name does a student who doesn't know anything know what he wants to study?"

"They're old enough to be left alone with their lives. For their own sakes we have got to get off their backs. Give them some respect, some privacy, for heaven's sake!"

"They are children. When they are at school, we must act in loco parentis. They can't be trusted, and every day they demonstrate that truth for all of us to see."

"Good grief, kids all over the world take responsibility. Read history. Adolescents have made a difference when they have been expected to make a difference in their lives. We are putting diapers on these young grown-ups."

"Where have you been? Do you know what some of the kids did over last weekend? Come off it. These youngsters aren't Joan of Arc. You just want to pretend they are to get yourself off the hot seat of telling them there are some standards around here."

So, the new headmaster wondered, how do you write the student handbook? Where do you draw the line? How do you cope with a student body drawn from many cultural quarters, where what is a crucial (if substantively trivial) symbol for one person (wearing a baseball cap all the time, for example) is an offense for another ("Don't wear your hat in the house"). How do you tell young people to be violent on the hockey rink ("Kill, Kill, Hate, Hate, Murder, Murder, Mutilate" from the cheerleaders) and to be nonviolent everywhere else? How do you talk of the sweetness of chastity and still gather around and support the girl who becomes pregnant?

Aren't there rules in this world? Or is everything spongily relative, the world rudderless? Can adults ever avoid the ubiquitous adolescent charge of hypocrisy? Can't we all depend on anything? If not, how, for Pete's sake, do you run a decent and happy and constructive school?

I was surprised during those first months at Andover to find the students more at ease with these ambiguities than were the faculty, but in time I learned better. They just faked at it more, probably because they did not know that their confusion wasn't just their own personal confusion. There is no more wisdom coming out of the mouths of adolescent babes than clarity on

these matters emerging from a solemn faculty meeting. The hard fact, I soon learned, was that there would never be sharply etched answers, that, paradoxically, all of the questions being asked and answers given were, to some degree, correct.

In our culture, adolescence is, for better or worse, a deliberately gray area, a zone of inescapable ambiguity. The best teachers want their students both to develop habits of decent, informed, and thoughtful behavior and not to hurt themselves, indeed even be happy. The youngsters are groping, wanting at the same time autonomy and respect from their elders. Most of the world, however, is for them new, and their autonomous decisions are, not surprisingly, often dumb ones. The less respect the young people sense, the more grotesque is their pushing against their elders, from being merely cheeky to evolving into gangs that make sure that none are "dissed" without retribution.

As a result, high school is a seesaw, requiring here, giving choice there, being clear here, being deliberately reserved and ambiguous there. It is a place for kids trying out, being both girls and women, boys and men. It is tough for them and tough for their teachers (and their parents). It is never dull, and it is often scary, for young and old.

School is about making endless, wise compromises. There is no Rule, no Predictability. Adolescence denies that. But there is clarity sometimes, direction sometimes, freedom sometimes, empathy and caring and patience always. I learned that during my first year.

No, I never got that quarter back. In my confusion I had forgotten, of course, to ask the cadger his name.

THEODORE R. SIZER TEACHES AT BROWN UNIVERSITY IN RHODE ISLAND. HE IS THE DIRECTOR OF THE ANNENBERG INSTITUTE FOR SCHOOL REFORM AND CHAIRMAN OF THE COALITION OF ESSENTIAL SCHOOLS.

The Monk in the Schoolhouse

BRUCE A. SEGALL

My wife, Dorothea, and I were born and raised in the New York metropolitan area. When I received the appointment as principal of Alfred-Almond Junior-Senior High School, it was with great joy but a bit of anxiety. Almond is a small rural town in upstate New York, beautiful but culturally very different from what Dorothea and I were accustomed to. Alfred, on the other hand, is a university town with cultural and athletic opportunities that made our adjustment to the area much easier.

I vividly remember that first day, sitting by the tennis courts in front of the school and having this feeling of calm and peace come over me. It was as if someone had taken me and let some of the air out of my balloon. I could feel the slower pace of life. This same experience occurred again later that day when I got ready to leave for my temporary home. It was 5:00 P.M. I remember getting that awful feeling urbanites get at "rush hour." I would surely get caught right in the middle of it. I dashed out of school and drove quickly down the road. As I moved up the ramp to Route 17, I looked around and, to my amazement, there was not a car in sight. Needless to say, it was a very pleasant ride home that evening and every evening thereafter.

THE TEACHERS

What made my first year so memorable were the teachers. They were an extraordinary group of dedicated professionals who took an idealistic young principal under their wings. The friendships and relationships built up over the years are still very much a part

of my life. I remember Jan, a dedicated English teacher who would never be out of class because her lessons were so individualized that it took two to three pages of instructions for each class. She spent hours correcting papers and preparing lessons. She and her husband became lifelong friends to Dorothea and me. She helped me see each student as an individual with unique needs.

Mike was a very special person. The room lit up when he walked in. Caring and charismatic, he reminded me that as I was leading the troops through the wilderness, he was killing the snakes and alligators. He was a social studies teacher who helped me start an alternative program for high-risk kids. Many years later he would die of cancer. I still miss him.

Bob was my jock-friend. We loved to play basketball together and talk about administration. He became the assistant principal in a neighboring school. One day Bob and Mike handed in a discipline referral on a fictitious student named, "Barney Rubble" and signed Jan's name. Every day for a week I called "Barney" over the P.A. system. Finally, on the fifth day I got on the P.A. and said that if Barney Rubble did not report to the office he would be in serious trouble. A few minutes later Mike and Bob came laughing into my office. I had been accepted into the culture of the school. Everything would work out.

One of the most moving expressions of the relationships that were being built up with the teachers was the presence of so many of them and their spouses when I bought a house and moved into the district. More than half the staff helped me move twice, once to a temporary home and finally to my permanent residence. I will always remember their kindness in providing the labor and food at this important time in my life.

COSLOS

Coslos was a family restaurant down the road from the school. Every so often we would have a T.G.I.F. get-together after school. I believed strongly in building a foundation of trust among the teachers. I also strongly believed in building community. Social affairs can be very important in that total process and enhance the quality of the work we do. Shortly before he died, Mike told me that Coslos had more to do with my success than anything else. Some of my staff didn't agree with everything I was doing, but at least they could sit down with me in an informal setting and share their thoughts and aspirations. Coslos went a long way in helping to build a community of educators with a common mission.

A SOCCER GAME/THE SITDOWN

Two of the biggest challenges I had to face as a new principal were in the area of discipline. The first dealt with a soccer game early in the fall. Our team had a number of incidents of unsportsmanlike conduct. At one point there were some actual fights. I had become increasingly alarmed at the behavior of the student-athletes, and the fighting was the last straw. After speaking privately with the coach and athletic director, I called an assembly of the entire school and announced my decision. I was suspending the entire team from competition for one game and would not permit them to play again until they proved to me and the coach that they were ready to play the game properly. Shortly after the assembly, the captains and the coach came to me to say they had learned their lesson and were ready to play the game in a sportsmanlike manner.

The second challenge came unexpectedly. Alfred-Almond did not have a written student handbook. I had always been a strong proponent of such a document because it clearly lays out the rules and the consequences. I spent time with the staff drafting the rules and had them typed up and printed in manual form. I called an assembly for the student body and explained the need for a handbook and rules. As the students left the assembly, I noticed that many were walking rather slowly. I left the room for a few minutes and when I returned, there were about one hundred students still there engaged in a "sitdown." They said they objected to the handbook and were not going to classes. I had to think fast, so I told them they had five minutes to get to class or they would be suspended, but I also said that I would be happy to meet with any individual or his/her representative during lunch, study period, or after school. Gradually, all the students returned to their classes. Several students did show up, and we discussed their concerns. Each year thereafter the student council reviewed the handbook before it was printed.

THE DREAMS

I am an idealist. I always have been and I hopefully always will be. I dream about the perfect school, and that first year I had several dreams.

The first had to do with the notion of authority. From my theological studies I was aware of the concept of the "Primus Inter Pares" or the "First Among Equals." Although this was only my first year in public administration, I felt that the idea of a lone chief on top of bureaucratic order was dissatisfying and unproductive. I wanted my staff to know that, like them, I too was an educator. I wanted to help them in any way I could to become better educators. I substituted frequently, lectured occasionally, and wanted to teach periodically, which I did a few years later. I tried to use memos,

announcements, and assemblies as learning experiences. Although a teacher, I had responsibilities beyond the individual classroom and therefore, I had to be the "first" among teachers. As the principal educator I wanted to provide the instructional, ethical, and dynamic leadership that was necessary to make our school absolutely first rate.

My second dream had to do with building a real community of educators. I needed to lay a foundation of trust so that real change could take place. I needed to *model* this trust and establish relationships in such a way that we could say with sincerity and integrity that "we are a community of educators bound together by a common purpose."

My third dream was to work toward a comprehensive evaluation program that would involve a multiplicity of perceptions on observable teacher behavior. Evaluation programs are usually limited because they involve only the perceptions of the supervisor, however competent he/she may be. I wanted to enlarge on this by including self, peer, and student evaluations along with the supervisory ones. With this kind of information matrix, we could begin to focus on our strengths and improve on our weaknesses.

THE MONASTERY

Before I began my career in education, I was a Marianist Brother for six years. The Marianists were a teaching order of Brothers and Sisters. During those years I developed a prayer life that became essential to me as a person and especially as I began my career as a high school principal. Less than an hour from my school was Mount Savior Monastery that I had come to know before my appointment. After my appointment it became my oasis. Several times a year I had the need to journey there—discovering in silence and solitude ways to cope with the pressures, trials, and tribulations of my profession. Long, silent walks and journal writings about my life and profession became critical life supports for me that first year and are still, seventeen years later. When I moved back downstate after eight years, I looked first for another monastery within an hour's drive. Behind my desk on the wall in my office is a picture which I asked my sister-in-law to draw for me. The picture shows a man walking down from the mountain into a classroom full of children. The title of the picture is, "The Monk in the Schoolhouse."

MY FAMILY

In addition to my prayer life, my family has always been instrumental in my ability to cope with the stress of my job. One cannot overestimate the value of a happy home life. Having a loving wife and wonderful children to come

home to every evening puts a job and a profession into proper focus. Learning how to be a good husband to Dorothea and a father to Ken, Christiane, and later to Brad has been tremendously fulfilling. While I certainly recognize and accept the variety of roles a woman can play in modern life, I can honestly say that having Dorothea as wife, friend, and fellow parent was absolutely essential to my initial success as a principal.

Equally essential were those moments each evening and on weekends as I watched and played with my children. As I flip through years of memories, I can still see them playing with the pots and pans in the kitchen that first year at Alfred-Almond.

BRUCE SEGALL IS THE PRINCIPAL AT MAHWAH HIGH SCHOOL IN MAHWAH, NEW JERSEY.

The Time I Spend

PATRICIA McRAE

I did not move up through the system in the lighthouse district in which I now work. I came from Alaska where I had been a teacher and then principal/teacher in small (some might say minuscule) rural Alaskan towns for nine years. I moved from teaching and principaling in a school of thirty-five students K–12, to Jackson Park Elementary, a school of 450 students on the Olympic Peninsula in Washington. The staff at my new school surpasses the number of students and parents combined at my previous school. There was a larger population of caribou in Cantwell, Alaska, than humans; and worries about children's safety as they got off the school bus focused on grizzly bears in the area as opposed to child snatchers or drive-by shootings. But whether in a big school or small, in the bush of Alaska or on the outskirts of a metropolis, the principal functions as the person who ensures the children's safety and security, the person who keeps the goals, beliefs, and vision of the school community dynamic, and the person who sets the tone for leadership and learning. The biggest differences I have faced have been more in the amount of time spent on individual tasks than in their content.

Of all I have dealt with this year, time has been the challenge with which I have struggled the most. When payday comes I find that I think more about the time it will take me to go to the bank and deposit the money than I think about the sum of money itself. Because I have always loved my work and have felt my schools were a second home, I spend much time at them.

Up north my children and my husband and I all worked and learned at the same school. Now that we are mainstream Americans, we all go our separate ways every morning in two different cars and two different school buses to get to four different schools. We arrive at home in four different vehicles at four different times every afternoon. I am invariably the last one to arrive.

Evening meetings are frequent for me, and I leave our home after eating only to return after my family has gone to sleep. In Alaska I worked sixty to seventy hours a week, but the majority of weekend hours were spent on classroom projects or all-school field trips to "town." (Town was Fairbanks or Anchorage, two hundred miles either way.) These days the majority of my after school hours aren't spent on field trips or bulletin boards. They are spent on survival. As a full-time principal in a school of 450, there are no all-school field trips, a reality I find very frustrating since "town" is here. I want to take ALL 450 kids to a play at the theatre, but to do so would cost more than our school budget for supplies. My office usually looks as though a tornado has hit the area and meeting deadlines for the numerous tasks that go along with this job has been one of my challenges. In Alaska my school employed four other full-time staff members besides myself, and I was married to one of them. I knew when a fellow staff member had a hangnail or a poor night's sleep. When I began at Jackson Park last August, I was positive that I would be able to talk with every staff member every day and that I would visit every classroom every day. I have found that such a goal is not practical. Ensuring time for communication while doing an adequate job of management is the balance I am still trying to achieve. Having an "open door" when a parent, staff member, or student needs me will always take first place, but that doesn't replace the accountability for paperwork, meetings, and deadlines.

Late hours, a messy office, and the lack of all-school field trips aside, I love this confounding job. I love it when I am at the mall or the grocery store and one of my Jackson Park Patriots sees me and whispers in an excited voice, "Mom! It's the PRINCIPAL!" These occasions remind me of the enormous responsibility I have in living up to my students' expectations. I was immensely gratified the other day as I walked through a sixth grade classroom and one of the students (whose mother I have had to call about less than pleasant matters many times) said, "Ms. McRae, my mother likes to talk to you on the phone!" The feeling is mutual. Everything about us, our lives, and our experiences are different, yet we have found that we have a lot in common. This relationship is what enables us to work together for her child's success.

In my first year as an elementary principal, I have attempted to be a person who can share the thoughts I have about the strengths of this school community, and I have tried to model my belief in the power of listening, caring,

and learning. My staff has supported me, and I feel great about that. I truly believe that the children who attend Jackson Park School couldn't ask for a better place to grow and become what they hope to be. And neither could I, but the clock is still running.

PATRICIA MCRAE IS PRINCIPAL AT JACKSON PARK ELEMENTARY SCHOOL IN BREMERTON, WASHINGTON.

The First Hundred Days

JOSEPH C. SEGAR

*I*t was 1963, for me the first of twenty-six years at Shady Hill. As a rookie school head I had a lot to learn and, although none of us was aware of it, the country was on the verge of a series of catastrophic events. Approaching the little grey cottages of Shady Hill's campus early that July morning I wasn't at all sure the search committee had found the right man. Would I have something special to offer this unique and distinguished school? How would I measure up in Cambridge, the "Athens of the Western World"?

I felt that my first task was to begin to understand the people who made the school function. In July there was little activity . . . a small summer school for academic enrichment supplied the only students and faculty. The skeleton office staff and the groundspeople were busy with all those jobs schools have to complete before Labor Day. I sent a general invitation for teachers and staff to come see me, and many did. My opening ploy in those conversations was, "What do you think I need to know about you and where you fit in at Shady Hill?" And my final question, as the discussion concluded was, " What advice do you have for me?" Those talks with staff were immensely useful to me, and I believe they laid strong foundations for our work on behalf of children. I discovered the generosity of Shady Hill people and their pride in the school; each talk helped me enormously, and soon I was developing some insights about what should happen next. By mid-August I had begun to know the faculty and staff, some of the overseers, and a few students and parents.

Two unscheduled visits I recall with special pleasure. The first came from grinning Eddie Pratt, then headmaster of the neighboring Browne and Nichols School, who strolled across his playing fields to introduce himself and offer his help.

The second was from a very tall man with craggy features who had to duck his head as he entered my office one afternoon. He seemed familiar, and I thought I should know him, but he didn't give his name. He knew who I was, and it soon became clear that he was a school parent because he talked about his sons and his hopes for them. Our conversation rambled; he was cordial, tremendously well-informed and somewhat opinionated. I enjoyed the visit and as he rose to leave I realized . . . belatedly . . . that he was John Kenneth Galbraith.

The parents were an impressive lot and, for a first-year school head, sometimes intimidating. I learned quickly that these people did not come to Shady Hill wearing their laurels or their titles: they came as mothers and fathers, with all the hopes, all the fears that any parent brings to her or his child's school. What they wanted was the best possible experience for their son or daughter. And since they had a close, working relationship with schools and schooling, they were apt to be more understanding, more tolerant than many. It was sometimes difficult to convince teachers that they were the experts when they sat down with a parent in the classroom after school to have a conference about a student's progress. No matter how distinguished, the parents came to school to learn from the teacher.

Opening faculty meetings, the first day of school, the first overseers' meeting, the first all-school assembly, the new parents dinner, even the first fire drill . . . it was all unfamiliar territory for me, and I moved through those early weeks in something of a fog, trying hard to be a leader, not forgetting that I was very much a learner. I tried to honor the resolutions I'd made during the summer. "Think before you decide." "Be a listener." "Remember everyone's name." "Know the faculty by Halloween and the students by Thanksgiving." "Keep a diary." "Don't get bogged down in fragments; look for the big picture." "Visit classes regularly." "Write appreciative notes; be lavish with praise and stingy with criticism."

But things happened. A teacher wanted to introduce a major new element into the curriculum. Immediately. (Not yet. I need to know whether quality is being sacrificed.) A parent wanted her daughter excused from sports to ride because she was destined to be an Olympic equestrienne. (No. Part of the value of sports for children at this age is participating in a joint endeavor.) The student council wanted to install a soft drink vending

machine. (No. Distracting, unhealthy, trash-producing.) I wanted to keep my door open, to be available, but I was frequently being interrupted. I was inefficient and I seldom got out of the office to visit classes or go to games. My vision of myself as the benevolent headmaster was fading.

And then, on November 22, in Dallas, optimism was caught in the cross hairs of an assassin's rifle. That Friday and throughout the weekend that followed, the dreadful events were played and replayed on the television screens of every home in America. Shady Hill students—the eldest was only fourteen—were frightened. They had seen the effect of these events on the adults in their lives, and they needed to know that someone would take care of them, that their world would not disintegrate.

The first thing on Monday morning, I called most of the students and their teachers to the Hall. We talked, we sat silent, we listened to each other's reactions, we cried. I stood in the midst of that crowd, trying to be the understanding, reassuring figure everyone wanted. Could I explain the unexplainable? Could I make sense from senseless violence? Certainly not. But something needed to be said, and I tried. Afterward, a teacher slipped onto the piano bench and began softly to play, and we all sang, softly at first and then with the increasing strength we gathered from each other . . . "Mine eyes have seen the glory of the coming of the Lord . . . " Then, as if it had been rehearsed, each class silently followed its teacher out of the Hall.

It was then, in those forty minutes, that I felt I was going to become the leader of the school. Not when I proposed a new system of marking to the faculty. Not when I suggested to the overseers that we build a new field house. Not when I hosted the new parents dinner for the first time. But that day, just before Thanksgiving, in the third month of my first year, with the same lump in my throat, the same questions in my mind, the same ache in my heart that everyone had, I learned what it meant to be a school head.

JOSEPH SEGAR LIVES AND WORKS IN BARNSTABLE, MASSACHUSETTS.

Hopeful to Hectic

MARK WARREN SEGAR

*E*veryone knew who I was, of course. The teachers, students, parents, and custodial and office staffs all greeted me by name that first day. I remember a sense of imbalance welling up, a kind of professional vertigo as I looked at all those welcoming, wondering faces with names not yet securely attached.

I was sure that most of them wanted me to succeed; certain, too, that some of them had special interests to guard, maybe even axes to grind, and that they would be anxious to know where I stood on a whole host of issues facing the school and its community. All those projected hopes, unvoiced but no less real, piled high on the in-basket of expectations and emotions that met me as I began this new and different work.

I had come to The Common School from state government, from the governor's staff where I'd worked on state policy for education and youth services. I'd been eager to get away from state politics for some time. I wanted to work with real families again, with individual children instead of statistical populations and groups. Politicians constantly wondering about the extent of their minimal obligations to children had strained my commitment to child advocacy and early education. The opportunity to lead a small, experimental school was timely, a chance to move away from questions like "What can we afford?" toward "What's the best we might do?"

And besides, the governor I devotedly worked for had lost his reelection bid and then died suddenly while still in office. His successor seemed an unlikely patron for the liberal likes of me.

My political past followed me from the State House to the schoolhouse. Who was I to head this school, to lead this faculty? What values would a veteran of the political trenches bring—and project—in the hitherto untainted role of school leader? I hadn't been a teacher in years, and I'd never taught long division.

So I'd planned carefully for that first opening day. I would be outside to greet all the arriving students and parents. I would spend the bulk of the morning in classrooms. I would be out with my sneakers on for recess. I would be visible, engaged, observing, welcoming, offering a hand.

Things went from hopeful to hectic in a hurry. First my wife called to say that her car was dead in our driveway. She was late for work. Our boys (already bearing the ignominious weight of having Dad for a principal) were late for their first day, and I would have to drive home and pick up everyone. School opened without me, essentially. (No doubt some thought I was isolated in my office already.)

By the time I got back there were other problems. A toilet had backed up. No custodian was available. Did I know where the plunger was? On it went through the day to faculty meeting, where my bumbling efforts to ingratiate myself with humor met with puzzled (not even bemused) silence. It was a rocky start.

I thought the first few months should be a time for observation, for gathering ideas, for listening to opinions, for constructing a set of ideas about challenges and priorities for the future. Others immediately thought otherwise. When would I move from being a facilitator to being a leader? How soon could my ideas for curriculum be implemented? Any luck yet on new sources of funding?

I kept responding and reacting, eager to solve, to soothe, to please. It took me a while to figure out that I wouldn't be able to work this way for long. Or that if I did, I'd never accomplish anything significant or coherent. I needed help.

Sometimes I think that people who become principals aren't very good at asking for help. We tend to be the types who, when confronted with a problem, respond with "I'll tackle it," or "I'll get right on it," or—if we've made a little progress—"You're right about that. Let's work on it together." We want to get things done. We have faith in our own ideas and abilities. We like to get right to work. A worthy attitude, but not necessarily always what's needed. And untenable when the demands pile up, as they did so quickly for me.

So I called my father and another principal and spilled all sorts of concerns and questions into the phone, hoping for good answers from these wise

and experienced leaders. The similarity of their responses was startling. Neither of them had answers to offer. Instead they had questions. Question after question in response to mine, probing for details about the culture of my school, about the nature of the particular challenges I faced, about my own tentative ideas and strategies for next steps.

Suddenly in the midst of those phone calls, the connections began to form clearly in my mind—between a belief in questions as the essential units of learning and a commitment to leadership as something other than coming up with all the solutions by myself. Reflecting on all the questions my interrogators had for me, I thought back to how much of my own schooling and training had emphasized answers, had stressed getting it right alone. I thought about my own school's philosophical commitment to discovery learning and collaborative problem solving for students. I even dredged up from college studies the memory of Lao Tze's wisdom (already invoked, of course, by Roland Barth and many other experienced principals, as I would come to learn) that of a great leader the people will all say, "We did this ourselves."

Awash in realization and reverie, I finished the calls as politely as I could, already feeling the press of unmanageable expectations beginning to lift. A way of working successfully and sustainably at this still wonderful job was beginning to take shape. It has served me well, and I remain grateful to those model question askers from my first year.

MARK WARREN SEGAR IS HEAD OF WAYNFLEET SCHOOL IN PORTLAND, MAINE.

The first year as
principal : real world

Contents

vii

To Be of Use

The people I love the best
jump into work head first
without dallying in the shallows
and swim off with sure strokes almost out of sight.
They seem to become natives of that element,
the black sleek heads of seals
bouncing like half-submerged balls.

I love people who harness themselves, an ox to a heavy cart,
who pull like water buffalo, with massive patience,
who strain in the mud and the muck to move things forward,
who do what has to be done, again and again.

I want to be with people who submerge
in a task, who go into the fields to harvest
and work in a row and pass the bags along,
who are not parlor generals and field deserters
and move in a common rhythm
when the food must come in or the fire be put out.

The work of the world is common as mud.
Botched, it smears the hands, crumbles to dust.
But the thing worth doing well done
has a shape that satisfies, clean and evident.
Greek amphoras for wine or oil,
Hopi vases that held corn, are put in museums
but you know they were made to be used.
The pitcher cries for water to carry
and a person for work that is real.

Marge Piercy

Heinemann
A division of Reed Elsevier Inc.
361 Hanover St.
Portsmouth, NH 03801-3912
Offices and agents throughout the world

Every effort has been made to contact the copyright holders for permission to reprint borrowed material where necessary. We regret any oversights that may have occurred and would be happy to rectify them in future printings of this work.

The editor and publisher wish to thank those who have generously given permission to reprint borrowed material:

"To Be of Use" from *Circles on the Water* by Marge Piercy. Copyright © 1982 by Marge Piercy. Reprinted by permission of Alfred A. Knopf Inc.

Lives of a Rural Principal, by Edward D. Wilkens, was originally published in *Principal.* NAESP, May 1983.

Library of Congress Cataloging-in-Publication Data
The first year as principal : real world stories from America's
 principals / edited by Ronald Thorpe.
        p.   cm.
    ISBN 0-435-08128-4 (alk. paper). — ISBN 0-435-08127-6 (pbk.)
      1. School principals—United States.   2. School management and
 organization—United States.   I. Thorpe, Ronald.
    LB2831.92.F57   1995
    371.2′012′0973—dc20   95-22960
                                                                                 CIP

Editor: Cheryl Kimball
Production: J.B. Tranchemontagne
Cover design: Jenny Jensen Greenleaf

Printed in the United States of America on acid-free paper
99 98 97 96 95 VB 1 2 3 4 5 6 7 8 9

The First Year as Principal

Real World Stories from America's Principals

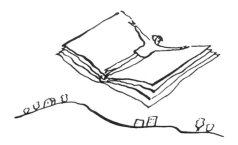

Edited by
Ronald Thorpe

HEINEMANN
PORTSMOUTH, NH

The First Year as Principal

Everything looked as she'd left it: minimal, cheap furnishings — nothing big enough for an adult to hide behind — empty counters and tabletop, no ornaments or artwork. Sterile. She knew that even with the avocado-and-mustard-vinyl flooring and the popcorn ceiling, it still looked a little like a laboratory.

Maybe the smell was what made it feel like a lab. The room was so scrupulously sanitary, an intruder would probably attribute the pool-supply-store scent to cleaning chemicals. But only if he got inside without triggering her security system. If he triggered the system, he wouldn't have time to register many details about the room.

The rest of the house was just a small bedroom and bathroom, set in a straight line from the front door to the far wall, nothing in the way to trip her. She turned the light off, saving herself the walk back.

She stumbled through the only door into her bedroom, sleepwalking through the routine. Enough light made it through the mini-blinds — red neon from the gas station across the street — that she left the lamp off. First, she rearranged two of the long feather pillows on top of the double mattress that took up most of the space in the room into the vague shape of a human body. Then the Ziploc bags full of Halloween costume blood were stuffed into the pillowcases; close up, the blood wasn't very convincing, but the Ziplocs were for an attacker who broke the window, pushed the blinds aside, and shot from that vantage point. He wouldn't be able to detect the difference in the neon half-light. Next, the head—the mask she'd used was another after-Halloween-sale acquisition, a parody of some political also-ran that had fairly realistic skin coloring. She'd stuffed it to roughly match the size of her own head and sewn a cheap brunette wig into place. Most important, a tiny wire, threaded up between the mattress and box spring, was hidden in the strands of nylon. A matching wire pierced through the pillow the head rested on. She yanked the sheet up, then the blanket, patted it all into shape, then twisted together the frayed ends of the two wires. It was a very tenuous joining. If she touched the head even lightly or jostled the pillow body a bit, the wires would slip silently apart.

She stood back and gave the decoy a once-over through half-closed eyes. It wasn't her best work, but it *did* look like someone was asleep in the bed. Even if an intruder didn't believe it was Chris, he would still have to neutralize the sleeping body before he went on to search for her.

Too tired to change into her pajamas, she just stepped out of her loose jeans. It was enough. She grabbed the fourth pillow and pulled her sleeping bag out from under the bed; they felt bulkier and heavier than usual. She dragged them into the compact bathroom, dumped them in the tub, and did the bare minimum of ablutions. No face-washing tonight, just cleaning the teeth.

The gun and the gas mask were both under the sink, hidden beneath a stack of towels. She pulled the mask over her head and tightened the straps, then clapped her palm over the filter port and inhaled through her nose to check the seal. The mask suctioned to her face just fine. It always did, but she never let familiarity or exhaustion make her skip the safety routine. She moved the gun into the wall-mounted soap dish within easy reach above the bathtub. She didn't love the gun — she was a decent shot compared with a totally untrained civilian, but not in the same class as a professional. She needed the option, though; someday her enemies were going to figure her system out, and the people coming for her would be in gas masks, too.

Honestly, she was surprised her shtick had saved her this long.

With an unopened chemical-absorption canister tucked under her bra strap, she shuffled the two steps back into the bedroom. She knelt beside the floor vent on the right side of the bed she'd never used. The vent cover grille probably wasn't as dusty as it should be, the grille's top screws were only halfway in, and the bottom screws were missing altogether, but she was sure no one looking through the window would notice these details or understand what they meant if he did;

Sherlock Holmes was about the only person she *wasn't* worried would make an attempt on her life.

She loosened the top screws and removed the grille. A few things would be immediately obvious to anyone who looked inside the vent. One, the back of the vent was sealed off, so it was no longer functional. Two, the large white bucket and the big battery pack probably didn't belong down there. She pried the lid off the bucket and was immediately greeted by the same chemical smell that infused the front room, so familiar she barely noted it.

She reached into the darkness behind the bucket and pulled out, first, a small, awkward contraption with a coil, metal arms, and thin wires, then a glass ampoule about the size of her finger, and, finally, a rubber cleaning glove. She positioned the solenoid — the device she'd scavenged from a discarded washing machine — so that the arms extending from it were half submerged in the colorless liquid inside the bucket. She blinked hard twice, trying to force herself into alertness; this was the delicate part. She put the glove on her right hand, then pulled the canister free from her bra strap and held it ready in her left. With the gloved hand, she carefully inserted the ampoule into the grooves she'd drilled into the metal arms for this purpose. The ampoule rested just under the surface of the acid, the white powder inside it inert and harmless. However, if the current running through the wires that were attached so tenuously atop the bed were to be interrupted, the pulse would snap the solenoid shut, and the glass would shatter. The white powder would turn into a gas that was neither inert nor harmless.

It was essentially the same arrangement that she had in the front room; the wiring was just simpler here. This trap was set only while she slept.

She replaced the glove and the vent cover and then, with a feeling that was not quite buoyant enough to be called relief, lurched back to the bathroom. The door, like the vent, might have tipped off someone as detail oriented as Mr. Holmes—the soft rubber liners around all the edges were definitely not standard. They wouldn't entirely seal the bathroom off from the bedroom, but they would give her more time.

She half fell into the tub, a slow-motion collapse onto the puffy sleeping bag. It had taken her a while to get used to sleeping in the mask, but now she didn't even think about it as she gratefully closed her eyes.

She shimmied herself into the down-and-nylon cocoon, squirming till the hard square of her iPad was nestled against the small of her back. It was plugged into an extension cord that got power from the front-room wiring. If the power fluctuated along that line, the iPad would vibrate. She knew from experience that it was enough to wake her, even as tired as she was tonight. She also knew that she could have the canister—still in her left hand, hugged tight against her chest like a child's teddy bear—unsealed and screwed into place on the gas mask in less than three seconds, despite being half awake, in the dark, and holding her breath. She'd practiced so many times, and then she'd proved herself during the three emergencies that had not been practice. She'd survived. Her system worked.

Exhausted as she was, she had to let her mind tick over the evils of her day before it would let her be unconscious. It felt horrible—like phantom-limb pain, not connected to any actual piece of her body, just *there* anyway—knowing they'd found her again. She wasn't satisfied with her e-mail response, either. She'd come up with the plan too impulsively to be sure of it. And it required her to act more quickly than she'd like.

She knew the theory—sometimes, if you ran headlong at the guy holding the gun, you could catch him off guard. Flight was always her favorite move, but she didn't see a way out of the alternative this time. Maybe tomorrow, after her tired brain had rebooted.

Surrounded by her web, she slept.

CHAPTER 2

As she sat waiting for Carston to show, she thought about the other times the department had tried to kill her.

Barnaby — Dr. Joseph Barnaby, her mentor, the last friend she'd known — had prepared her for the first attempt. But even with all his foresight, planning, and deep-rooted paranoia, it was just dumb luck in the form of an extra cup of black coffee that had saved her life.

She hadn't been sleeping well. She'd worked with Barnaby for six years at that point, and a little more than halfway through that time, he'd told her his suspicions. At first she hadn't wanted to believe he could be right. They were only doing their job as directed, and doing it well. *You can't think of this as a long-term situation,* he'd insisted, though he'd been in the same division for seventeen years. *People like us, people who have to know things that no one wants us to know, eventually we become inconvenient. You don't have to do anything wrong. You can be perfectly trustworthy. They're the ones you can't trust.*

So much for working for the good guys.

His suspicions had become more specific, then shifted into planning, which had evolved into physical preparation. Barnaby had been a big believer in preparation, not that it had done him any good in the end.

The stress had begun to escalate in those last months as the date for the exodus approached, and, unsurprisingly, she'd had trouble sleeping. That particular April morning it had taken two cups of coffee rather than the usual one to get her brain going. Add that extra cup to the smaller-than-average bladder in her smaller-than-average body, and you ended up with a doctor running to the can, too rushed to even log out, rather than sitting at her desk. And that's where she had been when the killing gas filtered through the vents into the lab. Barnaby had been exactly where he was supposed to be.

His screams had been his final gift to her, his last warning.

They both had been sure that when the blow came, it wouldn't happen at the lab. Messy that way. Dead bodies usually raised a few eyebrows, and smart murderers tried to keep that kind of evidence as far removed from themselves as possible. They didn't strike when the victim was in their own living room.

She should have known never to underestimate the arrogance of the people who wanted her dead. They didn't worry about the law. They were too cozy with the people who made those laws. She also should have respected the power of pure stupidity to take a smart person completely by surprise.

The next three times had been more straightforward. Professional contractors, she assumed, given that they'd each worked alone. Only men so far, though a woman was always a possibility in the future. One man had tried to shoot her, one to stab her, and one to brain her with a crowbar. None of these tries had been effective because the violence had happened to pillows. And then her assailants had died.

The invisible but very caustic gas had silently flooded the small room — it took about two and a half seconds once the connection between the wires was broken. After that, the assassin was left with a life expectancy of approximately five seconds, depending on his height and weight. It would not have been a pleasant five seconds.

Her bathtub mixture was not the same thing they'd used for Barnaby, but it was close enough. It was the simplest way she knew to kill someone so swiftly and so painfully. And it was a renewable resource, unlike many of her weapons. All she needed was a good stock of peaches and a pool-supply store. Nothing that required restricted access or even a mailing address, nothing that her pursuers could track.

It really pissed her off that they'd managed to find her again.

She'd been furious since waking yesterday and had only gotten angrier as the hours passed while she made her preparations.

She had forced herself to nap and then drove all the next night in a suitable car, rented using a very weak ID for one Taylor Golding and a recently obtained credit card in the same name. Early this morning, she'd arrived in the city she least wanted to be in, and that had turned her anger up to the next level. She'd returned the car to a Hertz near Ronald Reagan National Airport, then walked across the street to another company and rented a new one with District of Columbia plates.

Six months ago, she would have done things differently. Gathered her belongings from the small house she was renting, sold her current vehicle on Craigslist, purchased a new one for cash from some private citizen who didn't keep records, and then driven aimlessly for a few days until she found a medium-size city-town that looked right. There she'd start the process of staying alive all over again.

But now there was that stupid, twisted hope that Carston was telling the truth. A very anemic hope. It probably wouldn't have been enough motivation on its own. There was something else—a small but irritating worry that she had neglected a responsibility.

Barnaby had saved her life. Again and again. Every time she survived another assassination attempt, it was because he had warned her, had educated her, had made her ready.

If Carston was lying to her—which she was 97 percent sure he was—and arranging an ambush, then everything he'd said was a lie. Including the part about her being needed. And if they didn't need her, that meant they'd found someone else to do the job, someone as good as she had been.

They might have replaced her a long time ago, might have assassinated a whole line of employees for all she knew, but she doubted it. While the department had money and access, the one thing it had in short supply was personnel. It took time to locate, cultivate, and train an asset like Barnaby or herself. People with those kinds of skills didn't grow in test tubes.

She'd had Barnaby to save her. Who was going to save the dumb kid they'd recruited after her? The newcomer would be brilliant, just as she had been, but he or she would be blind to the most important element. Forget *serving your country*, forget *saving innocent lives*, forget the *state-of-the-art facilities* and the *groundbreaking science*, and the *unlimited budget*. Forget the seven-figure salary. How about not being murdered? No doubt the person now holding her old position had no idea that his or her survival was even in question.

She wished she had a way to warn that individual. Even if she couldn't spend all the time Barnaby had devoted to helping her. Even if it could be only one conversation: *This is how they reward people like us. Get ready.*

But that wasn't an option.

The morning was spent on more preparations. She checked into the Brayscott, a small boutique hotel, under the name Casey Wilson. The ID she used wasn't much more convincing than Taylor Golding's, but two of the phone lines were ringing as she registered, and the busy desk clerk wasn't paying close attention. There were rooms available this early, the clerk told her, but Casey would have to pay for an extra day, as check-in did not begin till three. Casey agreed to this stipulation without complaint. The clerk seemed relieved. She smiled at Casey, really looking at her for the first time. Casey controlled her flinch. It didn't matter if this girl remembered Casey's face; Casey would make herself memorable enough in the next half hour.

Casey used androgynous names on purpose. It was one of the strategies she'd gleaned from the case files Barnaby had fed her, something the real spies did, but it was also common sense, something the fiction writers had figured out as well. The logic was that if people were searching this hotel for a woman, they would start with the clearly female names in the register, like Jennifer and Cathy. It might take them another round to get to the Caseys and the Terrys and the Drews. Any time she could buy for herself was good. An extra minute might save her life.

Casey shook her head at the eager bellman who stepped toward her offering his services and wheeled her single piece of luggage behind her to the elevator. She kept her face turned away from the camera over the control panel. Once inside the room, she opened the bag and removed a large briefcase and a zipper-top black tote. Other than these two things, her suitcase was empty.

She took off the blazer that made her thin gray sweater and plain black pants look professional and hung it up. The sweater was pinned in the back to make it formfitting. She removed the pins and let the sweater bag around her, changing her into someone a little smaller, maybe a bit younger. She removed her lipstick and rubbed off most of her eye makeup, then checked the effect in the large mirror over the dresser. Younger, vulnerable; the baggy sweater suggested that she was hiding in it. She thought it would do.

If she'd been going to see a female hotel manager, she would have played it slightly differently, perhaps tried to add some fake bruises with blue and black eye shadow, but the name on the card at the desk downstairs was William Green, and she didn't think she would need to put in the extra time.

It wasn't a perfect plan, and that bothered her. She would have liked to have another week just to review all the possible repercussions. But it was the best option she could set in motion with the time she'd had. It was probably overly elaborate, but it was too late to rethink it now.

She called the desk and asked for Mr. Green. She was connected quickly.

"This is William Green—how can I help you?"

The voice was hearty and overly warm. She immediately had the mental image of a walrus of a man, bushy mustache included.

"Um, yes, I hope I'm not bothering you..."

"No, of course not, Ms. Wilson. I'm here to help in any way I can."

"I do need help, but it might sound a little odd... It's hard to explain."

"Don't worry, miss, I'm sure I can be of assistance." He sounded extremely confident. It made her wonder what kinds of odd requests he had fielded before.

"Oh, dear," she dithered. "This might be easier in person?" She made it into a question.

"Of course, Ms. Wilson. Fortunately, I will be available in fifteen minutes. My office is on the first floor, just around the corner from the front desk. Will that suit?"

Fluttery and relieved: "Yes, thank you *so* much."

She put the bags in the closet and carefully counted out the bills she needed from the stash in the large briefcase. She slipped this into her pockets, then waited thirteen minutes. She took the stairs to avoid the elevator cameras.

As Mr. Green ushered her into his windowless office, she was amused to see that her mental image had not been that far off. No mustache — no hair at all except for the barest hint of white eyebrows — but in all other ways very walrus-y.

It wasn't hard to play frightened, and halfway into her tale of her abusive ex-boyfriend who'd stolen the family heirlooms, she knew she had him. He bristled in a very male way, looking as if he wanted to rant about the sort of monsters who hit little women, but he mostly held his peace aside from several *Tut-tut, we'll take good care of you, you're safe here* kinds of assurances. He probably would have helped her without the generous tip she gave him, but it certainly didn't hurt. He swore to tell only the members of the staff who were part of her plan, and she thanked him warmly. He wished her well and offered to bring the police in, if that would help. Casey confessed with great sadness how ineffective the police and the restraining orders had been for her in the past. She implied that she could handle this alone as long as she had the help of a big, strong man like Mr. Green.

He was flattered, and he hurried out to get everything ready.

It wasn't the only time she'd played this card. Barnaby had suggested it initially, when their escape plan had reached the fine-tuning stage. At first she had bristled at the idea, offended in some obscure way, but Barnaby was always practical. She was small and female; in a lot of people's heads, that would always make her the underdog. Why not use this assumption to her advantage? Play the victim to keep from being one.

Casey went back to her room and changed into the clothes she'd kept inside the briefcase, trading her sweater for a tight, black V-neck tee and adding a thick black belt with intricately braided leatherwork. Everything she took off had to fit back into the briefcase, because she was leaving the suitcase and she wouldn't be returning to this hotel.

She was already armed; she never went out without taking some precautions. But now she moved to the high-alert version of her personal protection, arming herself to the literal teeth — or to the tooth, really; she inserted a fake crown full of something much less painful than cyanide but just as deadly. It was the oldest trick in the book for a reason: It worked. And sometimes the last move you had was permanently extracting yourself from the hands of your enemies.

The big black tote bag had two ornamental wooden

pieces at the apex of the shoulder strap. Inside the tote was her special jewelry in little padded boxes.

Every piece was one of a kind and irreplaceable. She would never again have the access to acquire ornamental tools like these, so she was very careful with her treasures.

Three rings—one rose gold, one yellow gold, one silver. They all had small barbs hidden under clever little twisting hatches. The color of the metal indicated which substance coated the barb. Very straightforward, probably expected from her.

Next, the earrings, which she always handled with delicate care. She wouldn't risk wearing them for this part of the journey; she would wait until she was closer to her target. Once they were in, she had to move her head very deliberately. They looked like simple glass globes, but the glass was so thin that a high note could shatter it, especially as the little spheres were already under pressure from the inside. If anyone grabbed her by the neck or head, the glass would burst with a quiet pop. She would hold her breath—which she could do for a minute fifteen, easy—and close her eyes if possible. Her attacker would not know to do that.

Around her neck went a largish silver locket. It was very conspicuous and would command the attention of anyone who knew who she truly was. There was nothing deadly about it, though; it was just a distraction from the real dangers. Inside was a photo of a pretty little girl with fluffy, straw-colored hair. The child's full name was handwritten on the back of the picture; it looked like something a mother or an aunt would wear. However, this particular girl was Carston's only grandchild. Hopefully, if it was too late for Casey, the person who found her body would be a real cop who, due to the lack of identification, would be forced to dig into this evidence and bring her murder around to the doorstep where it ultimately belonged. It probably wouldn't really hurt Carston, but it might make things inconvenient for him, might make him feel threatened or worry that she'd released other information elsewhere.

Because she knew enough about hidden disasters and classified horrors to do much more than inconvenience Carston. But even now, three years past her first death sentence, she hadn't grown comfortable with the idea of treason or the very real possibility of causing a panic. There was no way to foresee the potential damage of her revelations, the harm they might cause to innocent citizens. So she'd settled for just making Carston *think* that she had done something so reckless; maybe the worry would give him an aneurysm. A pretty little locket filled with drippings of revenge to make losing the game more palatable.

The cord the locket was attached to, however, *was* deadly. It had the tensile strength of airline cable in proportion to its size and was easily strong enough to garrote a person. The cord closed with a magnet rather than a clasp; she had no desire to be lassoed with her own weapon. The wooden embellishments on her tote's shoulder strap had slots where the ends of the cords fit; once the cord was in place, the wooden pieces became handles. Physical force wasn't her first choice, but it would be unexpected. It gave her an advantage to be ready.

Inside the intricate patterns of her black leather belt were hidden several spring-loaded syringes. She could pull them individually or flip a mechanism that would expose all the sharp ends at once if an attacker pressed her close to his body. The mix of the different substances would not blend well in his system.

Scalpel blades with taped edges were tucked into her pockets.

Standard shoe knives, one that popped forward, one to the rear.

Two cans labeled PEPPER SPRAY in her bag—one containing the real thing, the other with something more permanently debilitating.

A pretty perfume bottle that released gas, not liquid.

What looked like a tube of ChapStick in her pocket.

And several other fun options, just in case. Plus the little things she'd brought for the unlikely outcome—success. A bright yellow, lemon-shaped squeeze bottle, matches, a travel-size fire extinguisher. And cash, plenty of it. She stuck a key card in the tote; she wouldn't come back to this hotel, but if things went well, someone else would.

She had to move carefully when she was in full armor like this, but she'd practiced enough that she was confident in her walk. It was comforting to know that if anyone caused her to move less carefully, he'd be the worse for it.

She left the hotel, nodding to the clerk who had checked her in, a briefcase in one hand and the black tote over her arm. She got into her car and drove to a crowded park near the middle of the city. She left the car in an adjacent strip mall's lot on the north side and walked into the park.

She was quite familiar with this park. There was a bathroom near the southeast corner that she headed into now. As she'd expected, midmorning on a school day, it was empty. Out of the briefcase came another set of clothes. There was also a rolled-up backpack and some more accessories. She changed her clothes, put her previous outfit in the briefcase, and then shoved it and the tote into the large backpack.

When she walked out of the bathroom, she was no longer immediately recognizable as a *she*. She slouched away toward the south end of the park, loose-kneed, concentrating on keeping her hips from swaying and giving her away. Though it didn't appear that anyone was looking, it was always smarter to act like someone was.

The park started to fill up when lunchtime approached, as she'd known it would. No one paid attention to the androgynous kid sitting on a bench in the shade furiously texting on a smartphone. No one came close enough to see that the phone wasn't on.

Across the street from the bench was Carston's favorite lunch spot. It was not the meeting place she'd suggested. She was also five days early.

Behind the men's sunglasses, her eyes scanned the sidewalks. This might not work. Maybe Carston had changed his habits. Habits were, after all, dangerous things. Like the expectation of safety.

She'd sifted through the advice that both the factual accounts and the novels had given on disguises, always focusing on the commonsense stuff. Don't slap on a platinum wig and high heels just because you're a short brunette. Don't think *opposite;* think *inconspicuous.* Think about what attracts attention—like blondes and stilettos—and avoid it. Play to your strengths. Sometimes what you believe makes you unattractive can keep you alive.

Back in the normal days, she'd resented her boyish frame. Now she used it. If you put on a baggy jersey and a pair of well-worn jeans a size too big, any eyes looking for *woman* might slide right over *boy.* Her hair was short as a boy's and easy to hide under a ball cap, and layered socks inside a pair of too-large Reeboks gave her that puppy-pawed look of the average teenage male. Someone who really looked at her face might notice some discrepancies. But why would anyone look? The park was filling with people of all ages and sexes. She did not stand out, and no one hunting for her would expect her to be here. She hadn't been back to DC since the department's first attempt to murder her.

This wasn't her forte—leaving her web, hunting. But it was, at least, something she'd put some thought into beforehand. Most of what she did in an average day took only a small part of her attention and intelligence. The rest of her mind was always working through possibilities, imagining scenarios. It made her slightly more confident now. She was working from a mental map that had been many months in the creation.

Carston had not changed his habits. At exactly 12:15 he sat down at a metal bistro table in front of his café. He'd picked the one that was angled so he could be completely covered by the umbrella's shade, as she'd expected. Carston had once been a redhead. He didn't have much of the hair anymore, but he still had the complexion.

The waitress waved to him, nodded toward the pad of paper in her hand, then went back inside. So he had a usual order. Another habit that could get you killed.

If Casey had wanted Carston dead, she could have managed it without his ever knowing she had been here.

She got up, shoved the phone in her pocket, and slung her backpack onto one shoulder.

The sidewalk led behind a rise and some trees. Carston couldn't see her here. It was time for another costume. Her posture changed. The hat came off. She shrugged out of the jersey she'd layered over the T-shirt. She tightened the belt and rolled up the bottom inches of the jeans, turning them into a boyfriend-cut look. The Reeboks came off and traded places with the slip-on ballet–slash–athletic shoes from the backpack. She did all this casually, as if she were hot and just stripping down a bit. The weather made it believable. Bystanders might have been surprised to see a girl under the masculine clothing, but she doubted this moment would linger in anyone's memory. There were too many more extreme styles on display in the park today. The sunshine always did bring out the freaks in DC.

Her tote went over her shoulder again. She dropped the backpack behind an out-of-the-way tree while no one was looking. If someone found it, there was nothing inside that she couldn't live without.

Decently certain that no one could see her, she added a wig and then, finally, carefully, she threaded her earrings into place.

She could have confronted Carston in her boyish garb, but why give up any secrets? Why let him connect her to her surveillance? If he'd even noticed the boy, that is. She might need to be a boy again soon, so she would not waste the persona now. And she could have saved some time by wearing the costume from the hotel, but if she'd made no changes to her appearance, the image of her captured by the closed-circuit security cameras at the hotel could be easily linked to the footage from any public or private cameras picking her up now. By spending extra time on her appearance, she'd broken as many links as she could; if someone was trying to find the boy, or the businesswoman, or the casual park visitor she was now, he would have a complicated trail to follow.

It was cooler in her female outfit. She let the light breeze dry the sweat that had been building up under the nylon jersey and then walked out to the street.

She came at him from behind, taking the same path he had just a few minutes earlier. His food had arrived—a chicken parm—and he seemed to be totally absorbed in consuming it. But she knew Carston was better than she was at appearing to be something he was not.

She dropped into the seat across from him with no fanfare. His mouth was full of sandwich when he looked up.

She knew that he was a good actor. She assumed he

would bury his true reaction and display the emotion he wished before she could catch sight of the first. Because he didn't look surprised at all, she assumed she'd taken him completely unawares. If he *had* been expecting her, he would have acted like her sudden appearance had shocked him. But this, the steady gaze across the table, the unwidened eyes, the methodical chewing—this was him controlling his surprise. She was almost 80 percent sure.

She didn't say anything. She just met his expressionless gaze while he finished masticating his bite of sandwich.

"I guess it would be too easy to just meet as planned," he said.

"Too easy for your sniper, sure." She said the words lightly, using the same volume he had. Anyone overhearing would think the words a joke. But the two other lunch groups were talking and laughing loudly; the people passing by on the sidewalk listened to earphones and telephones. No one cared what she was saying except Carston.

"That was never me, Juliana. You must know that."

It was her turn to act unsurprised. It had been so long since anyone had addressed her by her real name, it sounded like a stranger's. After the initial jolt, she felt a small wave of pleasure. It was good that her name sounded foreign to her. That meant she was doing it right.

His eyes flitted to her obvious wig—it was actually quite similar to her real hair, but now he would suspect she was hiding something very different. Then he forced his eyes back to hers. He waited for a response for another moment, but when she didn't speak he continued, choosing his words carefully.

"The, er, parties who decided you should...retire have...fallen into disfavor. It was never a popular decision to begin with, and now those of us who were always in disagreement are no longer ruled by those parties."

It could be true. It probably wasn't.

He answered the skepticism in her eyes. "Have you had any...unpleasant disturbances in the past nine months?"

"And here I was thinking that I'd just gotten better at playing hide-and-seek than you."

"It's over, Julie. Might has been overcome by right."

"I love happy endings." Heavy sarcasm.

He winced, hurt by the sarcasm. Or pretending to be.

"Not so happy as all that," he said slowly. "A happy ending would mean I wouldn't have contacted you. You would have been left alone for the rest of your life. And it would have been a long one, as much as that was in our power."

She nodded as if she agreed, as if she believed. In the old days, she'd always assumed Carston was exactly what he appeared to be. He had been the face of the good guys for a long time. It was almost fun now in a strange way, like a game, to try to decipher what each word actually meant.

Except then there was the tiny voice that asked, *What if there is no game? What if this is true . . . if I could be free?*

"You were the best, Juliana."

"Dr. Barnaby was the best."

"I know you don't want to hear this, but he never had your talent."

"Thank you."

He raised his eyebrows.

"Not for the compliment," she explained. "Thank you for not trying to tell me his death was an accident." All of this still in the lighthearted tone.

"It was a poor choice motivated by paranoia and disloyalty. A person who will sell out his partner always sees the partner as plotting in exactly the same way. Dishonest people don't believe honest people exist."

She kept her face stony while he spoke.

Never, in three years of constant running, had she ever spilled a single secret that she'd been privy to. Never once had she given her pursuers any reason to think her a traitor. Even as they tried to kill her, she had remained faithful. And that hadn't mattered to her department, not at all.

Not much did matter to them. She was distracted for a moment by the memory of how close she had been to what she was looking for, the place she might have reached by now on her most pressing avenue of research and creation if she hadn't been interrupted. That project had not mattered to them, either, apparently.

"But the egg is on those disloyal faces now," Carston continued. "Because we never found anyone as good as you. Hell, we never found anyone half as good as Barnaby. It amazes me how people can forget that true talent is a limited commodity."

He waited, clearly hoping she would speak, hoping she would ask something, betray some sign of interest. She just stared at him politely, the way someone would look at the stranger ringing her up at a register.

He sighed and then leaned in, suddenly intent. "We have a problem. We need the kind of answers only you can give us. We don't have anyone else who can do this job. And we can't screw this one up."

"*You*, not *we*," she said simply.

"I know you better than that, Juliana. You care about the innocents."

"I used to. You could say that part of me was murdered."

Carston winced again.

"Juliana, I'm sorry. I've always been sorry. I tried to stop them. I was so relieved when you slipped through their fingers. *Every* time you slipped through their fingers."

She couldn't help but be impressed he was admitting all of it. No denials, no excuses. None of the *It was just an unfortunate accident at the lab* kind of thing she had been expecting. No *It wasn't us; it was enemies of the state.* No stories, just acknowledgment.

"And now everyone is sorry." His voice dropped and she had to listen hard to make out his words. "Because we don't have you, and people are going to die, Juliana. Thousands of people. Hundreds of thousands."

He waited this time while she thought it over. It took her a few minutes to examine all the possible angles.

She spoke quietly too, now, but made sure there was no interest or emotion in her voice. Just stating obvious facts to move the conversation forward. "You know someone who has vital information."

Carston nodded.

"You can't take him or her out, because that would let others know that you are aware of them. Which would expedite whatever course of action you would prefer not to happen."

Another nod.

"We're talking about the bad stuff here, yes?"

A sigh.

Nothing worked the department up like terrorism.

She'd been recruited before the emotional dust had entirely settled around the hole where the Twin Towers used to stand. Preventing terrorism had always been the main component of her job—the best justification for it. The threat of terrorism had also been manipulated, turned and twisted, till by the end she'd lost a lot of faith in the idea that she was actually doing the work of a patriot.

"And a large device," she said, not a question. The biggest bogeyman was always this—that at some point, someone who truly hated the United States would get his or her hands on something nuclear. That was the dark shadow that hid her profession from the eyes of the world, that made her so indispensable, no matter how much Joe Citizen wanted to think she didn't exist.

And it *had* happened—more than once. People like her had kept those situations from turning into massive human tragedies. It was a trade-off. Small-scale horror versus wholesale slaughter.

Carston shook his head and suddenly his pale eyes were haunted. She couldn't help but shudder a little internally as she realized it was door number two. There were only ever two fears that big.

It's biological. She didn't say the words out loud, just mouthed them.

Carston's bleak expression was her answer.

She looked down for a moment, sorting through

all of his responses and reducing them to two columns, two lists of possibilities in her head. Column one: Carston was a talented liar who was saying things he thought would motivate her to visit a place where people were better prepared to dispose of Juliana Fortis forever. He was thinking quickly on his feet, pushing her most sensitive buttons.

Column two: Someone had a biological weapon of mass destruction, and the powers that be didn't know where it was or when it would be used. But they knew someone who did.

Vanity carried some weight, shifting the balance slightly. She knew she was good. It was true that they probably hadn't found someone better.

Still, she would put her money on column one.

"Jules, I don't want you dead," he said quietly, guessing her train of thought. "I wouldn't have contacted you if that were the case. I wouldn't *want* to meet with you. Because I am certain you have at least six ways to kill me on your person right now, and every reason in the world to use one of them."

"You really think I would come with only six?" she asked.

He frowned nervously for a second, then decided to laugh. "You make my point for me. I don't have a death wish, Jules. I'm on the level."

He eyed the locket around her neck, and she suppressed a smile.

She returned to her light voice. "I would prefer it if you called me Dr. Fortis. I think we're past the point of nicknames."

He made a hurt face. "I'm not asking you to forgive me. I should have done more."

She nodded, though again, she wasn't agreeing with him, she was just moving the conversation along.

"I am asking you to help me. No, not me. To help the innocent people who are going to die if you don't."

"If they die, it's not on me."

"I know, Ju—Doctor. I know. It will be on me. But who's to blame won't really matter to them. They'll be dead."

She held his gaze. She wouldn't be the one to blink.

His expression shifted to something darker. "Would you like to hear what it will do to them?"

"No."

"It might be too much even for *your* stomach."

"I doubt it. But it doesn't really matter. What *might* happen is secondary."

"I'd like to know what is more important than hundreds of thousands of American lives."

"It's going to sound horribly selfish, but breathing in and out has sort of trumped everything else for me."

"You can't help us if you're dead," Carston said bluntly. "The lesson has been learned. This won't be the last time we'll need you. We won't make the same mistake again."

She hated to buy into this, but the balance was shifting even more. What Carston was saying *did* make sense. She was certainly no stranger to policy changes. What if it was all true? She could play cold, but Carston knew her well. She would have a difficult time living with a disaster of this magnitude if she thought there was any chance she could have done something. That was how, in the beginning, they'd roped her into possibly the worst profession in the entire world.

"I don't suppose you have the files on you," she said.

CHAPTER 3

Tonight, her name was Alex.

She'd needed to put a little distance between herself and DC, and she'd ended up in a small motel just north of Philadelphia. It was one of half a dozen that lined the interstate on the way out of the city. It would take any tracker a while to search all of them, even if he first somehow narrowed down her position to this part of town. She'd left no trail to even get a hunter to Pennsylvania. Regardless, she'd be sleeping in the bathtub tonight as usual.

There was no table in the small room, so she had all the files laid out on the bed. Just looking at them exhausted her. It had not been a simple matter of having Carston FedEx them somewhere.

The information was ready, Carston had told her. He'd been hopeful that she would meet with him, and he would have brought the files with him if he'd been expecting her. She insisted on hard copies, and he agreed. She gave him the delivery instructions.

The difficulty was breaking the connection on both ends.

For example, she couldn't just have Carston dump the files into a trash can and hire someone to pick them up for her—it was too easy for people to keep an eye on that trash can. The watchers would see the person who picked the files up and then follow that person. That person could take the files to a separate drop spot before she came near them, but the eyes would already be there. Somewhere along the line, the package had to be out of the observers' sight long enough for her to perform a complex little shell game.

So Carston had, as instructed, left a box for her at the front desk of the Brayscott Hotel. Mr. Green was ready. He thought Carston was a friend who had stolen back those family heirlooms from the violent ex, who was surely following him. Mr. Green had given her the code so she could remotely watch the hotel's video surveillance feed from an Internet café miles away. Just because she hadn't seen people following Carston didn't mean they weren't there, but he appeared to simply deliver the box and walk away. The manager did a good job of following all her instructions, most likely because he knew she was watching. The box went into the service elevator and down to the laundry, where it was transferred to a maid's cart, delivered to her room, and then put into her inconspicuous black suitcase by the bike messenger to whom she'd given the key card and five hundred dollars. The bike messenger had taken a circuitous route, following the instructions she'd given him over a cheap prepaid phone that she'd already disposed of, and eventually dropped the box with a confused salesperson at the copy store across the street from the café.

Hopefully, the watchers were still back at the hotel, waiting for her to walk through the front door. Probably they were smarter, but even if there were ten watchers, there wouldn't have been enough to follow every stranger who walked out of the hotel. If one had attached himself to her messenger, he would have had a hard time keeping up. She could only cross her fingers that no one was watching now.

She'd had to move fast. That next hour was the most dangerous part of her plan.

Of course, she'd known there would be some kind of tracking device hidden in the materials. She'd told Carston she would scan for a trick like this, but perhaps he'd guessed that she didn't have the tech to do that. As quickly as possible, she made a set of colored duplicates. It took fifteen minutes, much too long. The duplicates went into the suitcase, and the originals into a paper bag that the girl at the counter gave her. She left the box in the garbage there.

The clock was really against her now. She'd climbed

in a cab and had the driver head toward a rougher part of DC while she looked for the first place that would give her the privacy she needed. She didn't have time to be picky, and she ended up having the cabbie wait for her at the end of an unsavory alley. It was the kind of behavior he would definitely remember, but there was no help for it. They could be watching her already. She hurried to the bottom of the dead-end alley — what a place to be caught! — stepped behind a dumpster, and cleared a spot on the broken asphalt with her foot.

The sound of movement behind her made her jump and spin around, her hand on the thick black belt at her waist, her fingers automatically seeking the thin syringe hidden farthest to the left.

Across the alley, a dazed-looking man on a bed of cardboard and rags was watching her with a mesmerized expression, but he said nothing and made no move to either leave or approach. She didn't have time to think about what he would see. Keeping the homeless man in her peripheral vision, she turned her focus to the bag of original documents. She pulled her lemon-shaped squeeze bottle out of her handbag and squirted it into the paper bag. The smell of gasoline saturated the air around her. The man's expression didn't change. Then she lit the match.

She watched the burn carefully, the fire extinguisher in her hands now in case the flames started to spread. The homeless man seemed bored by this part. He turned his back to her.

She waited until every scrap was ash before she doused the flame. She didn't know what was in the files yet, but it would assuredly be very sensitive. She had never worked on a project that wasn't. She rubbed the toe of her shoe across the black and gray powder, grinding it into the pavement. There wasn't a fragment left, she was sure. She tossed a five to the man on the cardboard before she ran back to the cab.

From there it was a series of cabs, two rides on the Metro, and a few blocks on foot. She couldn't be sure that she'd lost them. She could only do her best and be ready. Another cab landed her in Alexandria, where she rented a third car on a third brand-new credit card.

And now she was outside of Philly in this cheap hotel room, a heavily perfumed deodorizer warring with the smell of stale cigarette smoke, staring at the neat stacks of paper laid out on the bed.

The subject's name was Daniel Nebecker Beach.

He was twenty-nine. Fair-skinned, tall, medium build, medium ash-brown hair with longish waves — the length surprised her, for some reason, perhaps because she so often dealt with military men. Hazel eyes. He was born in Alexandria to Alan Geoffrey Beach and Tina Anne Beach née Nebecker. One sibling, Kevin, eighteen months older. His family had lived in Maryland for most of his childhood, except for a brief stretch in Richmond, Virginia, where he had gone to high school for two years. Daniel had attended Towson University and majored in secondary education with a minor in English. The year after graduation, he'd lost both parents in a car accident. The driver that had hit them was killed as well; his blood alcohol concentration had been .21. Five months after the funeral, Daniel's brother was convicted on drug charges—manufacturing methamphetamine and dealing to minors—and sent to serve a nine-year sentence with the Wisconsin Department of Corrections. Daniel had married a year later, then gotten a divorce two years after that; the ex had remarried almost as soon as the rushed divorce was final, and she'd produced a child with the new husband—a lawyer—six months after the wedding. Not terribly hard to read between the lines on that one. During that same year, the brother died in a prison fight. A very long rough patch.

Daniel currently taught history and English at a high school in what most people would consider the wrong part of DC. He also coached girls' volleyball and oversaw the student council. He'd won Teacher of the Year—a student-voted award—twice in a row. For the past three years, since the divorce, Daniel had spent his summers working with Habitat for Humanity, first in Hidalgo, Mexico, then in El Minya, Egypt.

The third summer, he'd split his time between the two.

No pictures of the deceased parents or brother. There was one of the ex — a formal wedding portrait of the two of them together. She was dark-haired and striking, the focal point of the photograph. He seemed almost like an afterthought behind her, though his wide grin was more genuine than the expression on her carefully arranged features.

Alex would have liked the file to be more filled out, but she knew that, with her detail-oriented nature, she sometimes expected too much of less obsessive analysts.

On the surface, Daniel was totally clean. Decent family (the self-destructive cycle that had led to the brother's death was easy enough to understand in light of the parents' crash). The victim in the divorce (not uncommon for the spouse of a crusading teacher to realize that the salary would not support a lavish lifestyle). Favorite of the underprivileged kids. Altruist in his free time.

The file didn't state what had first caught the government's attention, but once they'd scratched that surface, the dark came seeping out.

It seemed to have begun in Mexico. They hadn't been watching him then, so it was only the bank numbers that told the story. The forensic accountants had put together a well-documented history. First, his own bank balance, which had sat at just a couple of hundred dollars after the divorce, was suddenly plus ten grand. And then a few weeks later, another ten. By the end of the summer, it was sixty total. He went back to work in the States, and the sixty grand disappeared. Maybe a down payment for a condo, a fancy car? No, nothing visible, nothing on the record. The next year, while he was in Egypt, there were no sudden increases in his finances. Had it been gambling? An inheritance?

That alone wasn't enough to catch anyone's attention without some kind of a tip-off, but she couldn't locate the catalyst in the file. Even with an explicit tip, someone in the accounting department had to have been putting in overtime or else was very, very bored, because despite the lack of urgency, the financial analyst had hunted down that original sixty thousand dollars like a bloodhound with his nose to the ground. Eventually he found it—in a new bank account in the Caymans. Along with another hundred thousand.

At this point, Daniel's name was put on a list. Not a CIA or FBI or NSA list—an IRS list. Not even a high-priority list at that. His name wasn't very near the top; he was just someone to look into.

She wondered for a moment how his brother's death had affected him. It looked like he had logged some fairly consistent visits to the brother, his only family left. Wife runs out, brother dies. Seemed like a decent recipe for pushing someone deeper into his bad choices.

The money kept growing, and it was in no way consistent with what a drug mule or even a dealer might make. Neither job was so well compensated.

Then the money started to move and became harder to trace, but it added up to about ten million dollars in Daniel Beach's name bouncing around from the Caribbean to Switzerland to China and back again. Maybe he was a front, with someone using his name to hide assets, but as a general rule, the bad guys didn't like to put those kinds of funds into the hands of unwitting schoolteachers.

What could he be doing to earn it?

Of course they were watching his associations at this point, and it paid off quickly. Someone named Enrique de la Fuentes showed up in a grainy black-and-white photo taken by the security camera in the parking lot of Daniel Beach's motel in Mexico City.

She'd been out of the game for a few years, and this name didn't mean anything to her. Even if she had still been with the department, it probably wouldn't have been a part of her usual caseload. She had done some occasional work on the cartel problem, but drugs never got the red lights flashing and the sirens screaming the way potential wars and terrorism did.

De la Fuentes was a drug lord, and drug lords—

even the scrappy, upwardly mobile kind—rarely got any attention from her department. Generally the U.S. government didn't much care if drug lords killed each other, and usually those drug wars had very little impact on the life of an average American citizen. Drug dealers didn't want to kill their customers. That wasn't good for business.

She had never in all her years, even with the high-security clearance that was a necessary part of her job, heard of a drug lord with an interest in weapons of mass destruction. Of course, if there was a profit to be made, you couldn't count anyone out.

Profiting from the sale of was quite a different kettle from *unleashing,* though.

De la Fuentes had acquired a medium-size Colombian outfit in a hostile (to put it mildly) takeover in the mid-1990s and then made several attempts to establish a base of operations just south of the Arizona border. Each time, he'd been repelled by the nearby cartel that straddled the border between Texas and Mexico. He'd become impatient and started looking for more and more unorthodox methods to dispose of his enemies. And then he'd found an ally.

She sucked in a breath through her teeth.

This was a name she knew—knew and loathed. Being attacked from the outside was horrific enough. She felt the deepest revulsion for the kind of person who was born to the freedom and privilege of a democratic nation and then used that very privilege and freedom to attack its source.

This domestic-terrorist ring had several names. The department called them the Serpent, thanks to a tattoo that one of their late chiefs had possessed—and the line from *King Lear*. She'd been instrumental in shutting down a few of their larger conspiracies, but the one they'd accomplished still gave her the occasional nightmare. The file didn't say who had made the first contact, only that an accord had been reached. If de la Fuentes did his part, he would receive enough money, men, and arms to take out the larger cartel. And the terrorists would get what they wanted— destabilization of the American nation, horror, destruction, and all the press they'd ever dreamed of.

It was bad.

Because what was better for destabilization than a deadly, laboratory-created influenza virus? Especially one you could control.

She could tell when the narrative shifted from the analysts' point of view to the spies'. Much clearer pictures.

The spies were calling it TCX-1 (no notation in the files on what the letters stood for, and even with her rather specialized background in medicine, she had no idea). The government was aware that the TCX-1 superflu existed, but they thought they'd eradicated it during a black ops raid in North Africa. The lab was destroyed, the responsible parties apprehended (and executed, for the most part). TCX-1 hadn't been heard of again.

Until it showed up in Mexico a few months ago, along with a supply of the lifesaving vaccine, already incorporated into a new designer drug.

She was starting to get a headache, the kind that was extremely localized. It was a hot needle stabbing directly behind her left eye. She'd slept a few hours after checking in and before diving into the files, but it hadn't been enough. She made the short walk to her toiletry bag beside the sink, grabbed four Motrin, and swallowed them dry. She realized two seconds later that her stomach was totally empty, and the Motrin would no doubt burn a hole through the bottom as soon as it hit. In her bag she always had a stash of protein bars, and she quickly gnawed her way through one as she returned to her reading.

The terrorists knew they were always being watched, so what they'd given de la Fuentes was information. De la Fuentes would have to provide the manpower—preferably innocuous, unremarkable manpower.

Enter the schoolteacher.

From what the best analytical minds could piece together, Daniel Beach, all-around good guy, had gone to Egypt and acquired TCX-1 for a hungry, unstable drug lord. And he was clearly still part of the plot. From the evidence available, it appeared he would be the one dispersing TCX-1 on American soil.

The inhalable designer drug containing the vaccine was already in circulation; valued customers would never be in danger, and perhaps this was a second part of the plot. Even the most unstable drug lord had to be pragmatic where money was concerned. So maybe noncustomers would learn just where salvation waited—and that would create a whole new desperate clientele. Daniel Beach was no doubt immune by now. It wasn't a difficult job to circulate the virus; it would be as simple as wiping an infected swab across a surface that was regularly handled—a doorknob, a countertop, a keyboard. The virus was engineered to spread like the proverbial wildfire—he wouldn't even need to expose that many people. Just a few in Los Angeles, a few in Phoenix, a few in Albuquerque, a few in San Antonio. Daniel already had hotel reservations in each of these cities. He was due to embark on his deadly journey—ostensibly to visit more Habitat for Humanity sites as a preparation for next fall's school field trip—in three weeks.

The Serpent and de la Fuentes were attempting to orchestrate the most debilitating attack that had ever been perpetrated on American soil. And if it was true that de la Fuentes already had the weaponized virus and the vaccine, they had an excellent chance of success.

Carston hadn't been kidding. What she'd originally thought had been an act to play to her sympathies now appeared to be an amazing demonstration of self-control. Of all the potential disasters that had crossed her desk — back when she'd had a desk — this was one of the very worst, and she'd seen some bad things. There had even been one other biological weapon with the potential to do this kind of damage, but that one had never made it out of the lab. This was a feasible plan already in progress. And it wasn't hundreds of thousands of people dying they were talking about here — it would be closer to a million, maybe more, before the CDC could get control of the situation. Carston had known she would discover that fact. He'd deliberately downplayed the disaster so that it would sound more realistic. Sometimes the truth was worse than fiction.

The stakes were higher than she'd expected. This knowledge made it harder for her to justify her own little low-stakes game. Was the tight focus on saving her own life even defensible in the face of this kind of horror? She'd held a hard line in her conversation with Carston, but if there was any chance this story was more than a trap, did she have any choice but to try to stop it?

If Daniel Beach disappeared, de la Fuentes would know someone was onto him. Odds were, he would act sooner than he'd planned, ahead of schedule. Daniel had to talk, and he had to talk quickly. And then he had to go back to regular life, be seen, and keep the megalomaniac drug lord calm until the good guys could take him out.

In the beginning, it was standard operating procedure for Alex's subjects to be released into the wild for a short time. This was a major part of her specialty; Alex was the best at retrieving information without damaging the subject. (Before Alex, Barnaby had been the best and only man for the job.) The CIA, the NSA, and most similar government sections had their own teams for interrogating subjects who were slated for disposal after the information was acquired. Over time, as she proved more successful than even the best of the other teams, Alex had gotten a lot busier. Though the other sections would rather have stayed insular, kept the information with their own people, the results spoke for themselves.

She sighed and refocused on the now. Eleven pictures of Daniel Beach lay in a row across the pillows at the head of the bed. It was hard to reconcile the two sides of the coin. In the early pictures he looked like a Boy Scout, his softly waving hair somehow projecting innocence and pure intentions. But though it was obviously the same face in the spies' photos, everything was different. The hair was always hidden under hoods or ball caps (one of her own frequent disguises); the posture was more aggressive; the expressions were cold and professional. She'd worked on professionals. It took time. Possibly more than one weekend. She looked at the two matching but contradictory faces again and wondered briefly if Daniel had an actual psychiatric disorder or if it was a progression she was looking at, and the innocent no longer existed at all.

Not that it mattered — yet.

The headache felt like it was searing a hole through the inside of her eyeball. She knew it wasn't the hours of reading that had caused it. No, the decision looming in front of her was the source of the pain.

She gathered up all the files and stuffed them into a suitcase. The decimation of the population of the American Southwest would have to take a backseat for a few hours.

She was in a different car than she'd started out with that morning. Before checking into the motel, she'd returned the rental in Baltimore, then taken a cab to York, Pennsylvania. The cabbie dropped her a few minutes' walk from the house where a man surnamed Stubbins was selling his three-year-old Tercel, as advertised on Craigslist. She'd paid cash and used the name Cory Howard, then driven to Philly in her new ride. It was a trail that *could* be followed, but it would be very hard to do.

She drove several miles away from her motel, then chose a little dive that seemed to be doing brisk business. That was desirable for two reasons. One, she would be less memorable in a crowd. Two, the food was probably edible.

The dining area was packed, so she ate at the small bar. The wall behind the bar was mirrored; she could watch the door and front windows without turning around. It was a good perch. She had a greasy burger, onion rings, and a chocolate malt. All were delicious. While she ate, she turned off her brain. She'd gotten pretty good at that over the last nine years; she could compartmentalize almost anything. And while she focused on the food and watched the people around her, the headache subsided to a dull throb. Over the course of the meal, the Motrin finally won and the pain dissolved completely. She ordered a piece of pie for dessert—pecan—though she was completely stuffed and could only pick at it. She was stalling. Once the meal was over, she'd have to make a decision.

The headache was waiting for her in the car, as she'd known it would be, though it was not as sharp as before. She drove randomly down the quiet residential streets, where anyone following her would be obvious. The little suburb was dark and empty. After a few minutes she wandered closer toward the city.

There were still two columns of possibilities in her head.

The first column, that Carston had been lying in order to lure her to her death, was beginning to seem more and more unlikely. Still, she had to stay alert. This whole story could be fiction. All the evidence and coordinating departments and separate analysts with their differing writing styles and the photographs from around the world—it could be a very detailed, elaborate setup. Not a foolproof one, either, since they had no way of knowing she wouldn't just walk away from it.

But why would Carston have all this info prepared if he'd hoped to get her to a prearranged meeting? They could have killed her easily there without all this window dressing. A ream of blank paper was all you would need if you expected your mark's brains to be on the pavement before she could open the briefcase. How quickly could this kind of thing be thrown together? She'd given him no time to manufacture it on the spot with her early arrival. Who was Daniel Beach in this scenario? One of their own? Or an unsuspecting civilian Photoshopped into the exotic scenes? They had to know she would be able to verify some of this information.

They'd offered her a plan of action in the final file. In five days' time, with or without her, they would pick him up during his regular Saturday-morning run. No one would miss him until school began again Monday. If anyone did happen to look for him, it might appear that he'd taken a little holiday. If she agreed to help, she would have two days to get the information they needed, then she would be free to go. They hoped she would consent to keep in some form of contact. An emergency e-mail address, a social network site, the classifieds even.

If she didn't agree to the job, they would do their best without her. But trying to leave the informant physically unmarked would be slow...too slow. Failure was hard to contemplate.

She almost salivated at the thought of all the goodies waiting for her back at the lab. Things she could never get her hands on out here in the real world. Her DNA sequencer and polymerase chain reactor. The already fabricated antibodies she could stuff her pockets with if the invitation was on the up-and-up. Of course, if Carston was for real, she wouldn't need to steal those things anymore.

She tried to imagine sleeping in a bed again. Not carrying a pharmacy's worth of toxins on her body at all times. Using the same name every day. Making contact with other human beings in a way that left nobody dead.

Don't count on it, she told herself. *Don't let it go to your head and impair your judgment. Don't let hope make you stupid.*

As pleasant as some of her imaginings were, she hit a wall when she tried to visualize the steps she would need to take to make them happen. It was impossible to see herself walking back through the shiny steel

doors into the place where Barnaby had died screaming. Her mind totally refused to construct the image.

The lives of a million people were a heavy weight,
but still an abstract idea in many ways. She didn't feel
like anything could push her hard enough to get her
through those doors.

She would have to go around them, so to speak.

Only five days.

She had so much work to do.

CHAPTER 4

This operation was murdering her nest egg.

That thought kept circling in the back of her brain. If she lived through the next week, and nothing changed in regard to her working relationship with the department, she was going to have serious financial issues. It wasn't cheap changing lives on a triannual basis.

Just acquiring disposable funds in the first place had been a major procedure. She'd had money—the salary had certainly been a factor in her choice to do the job in the beginning, and earlier than that, she'd inherited a decent insurance payout when her mother had died. But when you work for powerful paranoids who probably note it in your file when you switch toothpaste brands, you can't just withdraw all your money and put it in a shoe box under the bed. If they weren't planning to do anything to you before, you might have just given them a motive. If they were, you just made them decide to accelerate their plans. You could try withdrawing all your money on the way out of town, but that limited your ability to pay for any advance preparations.

Like so much of it had been, it was Barnaby's scheme. He'd kept her in the dark about the details to protect the friend or friends who helped him set it up.

In the cafeteria located a few floors up from the lab, she and Barnaby had let themselves be heard talking about a promising investment situation. Well, Barnaby had called it promising and worked to convince her of it. There was nothing remarkable about the conversation; various versions of it were probably taking place by watercoolers in several normal offices at the same moment. She played being convinced, and Barnaby loudly promised to set it up. She wired money to an investment firm—or a company that sounded very like an investment firm. A few days later, that money was deposited—minus a 5 percent "commission" to compensate those friends for their time and risk—in a bank in Tulsa, Oklahoma, in the name of Fredericka Noble. She received notification of this new account in an unmarked envelope placed in a copy of *Extranodal Lymphomas* at the county library. An Oklahoma driver's license for Fredericka Noble, with her own picture on it, was also in the envelope.

She didn't know where Barnaby's drop was. She

didn't know what his new name was going to be. She'd wanted them to leave together—the vast aloneness of running was already part of her nightmares then—but he had thought that unwise. They'd both be safer separated.

More investments, more little envelopes. A few more accounts were created for Freddie, but there were also accounts and IDs for Ellis Grant in California and Shea Marlow in Oregon. All three identities were strong creations that would hold up under scrutiny. Freddie had been blown the first time the department found her, but this only made her more careful. Ellis and Shea were still safe. They were her prized possessions and she used them carefully and sparingly so as not to contaminate them by any association with Dr. Juliana Fortis.

She'd also started buying jewelry—the good stuff, and the smaller the better. Canary diamonds that looked to her eyes like nothing more than yellow sapphires but that cost ten times as much as their clear counterparts. Thick gold chains; heavy solid-gold pendants. Several loose gems she pretended to be planning to set. She knew all along that she would never get back half of what she paid, but jewelry could be carried easily and later converted to cash under the radar.

From a pay phone, Freddie Noble rented a small cabin just outside Tulsa, using a new credit card that would be paid from the Tulsa bank account. The cabin came with a sweet older landlord who sounded happy to bring in the boxes she mailed there — boxes full of the many things she would need when she walked away from her life as Juliana Fortis, everything from towels and pillows to her unset jewels to reflux condensers and boiling flasks — and collected his rent without commenting on her absence. She left a veiled hint here and there that she was planning to leave a bad relationship; it was enough for the landlord. She ordered supplies from library computers, giving an e-mail address she never accessed on her laptop at home.

She did everything she could to be ready, and then she waited for Barnaby to give the signal. In the end, he did let her know that it was time to run, but not the way they'd planned it.

That money, so carefully hoarded for so long, was now flowing through her fingers like she was some entitled trust-fund brat. One big spree in hopes of gaining her unlikely freedom, she promised herself. She had a few tricks for making real money, but they were dangerous, involving risks she could ill afford but would have no choice but to take.

People needed medical professionals who would break the rules. Some just wanted a doctor who knew how to oversee the administration of a treatment that was not approved by the FDA, something they'd picked up in Russia or Brazil. And some people needed bullets removed but didn't want it done in a hospital, where the police would be notified.

She'd maintained a floating presence on the web. A few clients had contacted her at her last e-mail address, which was now defunct. She'd have to get back on the boards that knew her and try to get in touch with some contacts without leaving any new trails. It would be hard; if the department had found the e-mails, they probably knew about the rest. At least her clients understood. Much of the work she did for them ranged from quasi-legal to totally criminal, and they would not be surprised by occasional disappearances and new names.

Of course, working on the dark side of the law added other dangers to her already overloaded plate. Like the midlevel Mafia boss who found her services very convenient and thought she should set herself up permanently in Illinois. She'd tried to explain her carefully composed cover story to Joey Giancardi without compromising herself—after all, if there was money to be made by the sale of information, the Mob wasn't exactly known for its loyalty to outsiders—but he was insistent, to put it mildly. He assured her that with his protection, she would never be vulnerable. In the end, she'd had to destroy that identity, a fairly well-developed life as Charlie Peterson, and run. Possibly there were members of the Family looking for her, too, now. It wasn't something she lost sleep over. When it came to manpower and resources, the Mob couldn't touch the American government.

And maybe the Mob didn't have time to waste on her anyway. There were lots of doctors in the world, all of them human and most of them corruptible. Now, if he'd known her real specialty, Joey G would have put up more of a fight to keep her.

At least Joey G had been good for changing her jewels into cash. And the crash course in trauma medicine couldn't hurt. Another perk of working in the underground: no one got too upset about your low batting average. Death was expected, and malpractice insurance wasn't necessary.

Whenever she thought of Joey G, she also remembered Carlo Aggi. Not a friend, not really, but something close. He'd been her contact, the most constant presence in her life then. Though he was stereotypically thuggish in appearance, he'd always been sweet to her—treated her like a kid sister. So it had hurt more than the others when she hadn't been able to do anything for Carlo. A bullet had lodged in his left ventricle. It was too late for Carlo long before they'd brought his body to her, but Joey G had still been hopeful; Charlie had done good work for him in the past. He was philosophical when Charlie had pronounced Carlo dead on arrival. *Carlo was the best. Well, you win some, you lose some.* And then a shrug.

She didn't like to think about Carlo.

She would have preferred a few more weeks to think about other things—to fine-tune her scheme, consider her vulnerabilities, get the physical preparations perfect—but Carston's plan gave her a deadline. She'd had to divide her limited time between surveillance and organizing a workspace, so neither had been perfectly done.

It was likely that they'd be watching her in case she tried to make a move without them. After her early visit to Carston, they would be anticipating it. But what choice did she have? Report for work as expected?

She'd seen enough to bet that Daniel would follow the same pattern today as he had the past three. Something about his almost identical outfits—similar jeans, button-down shirt, casual sport coat, all featuring only minor differences in hues—made her suspect that he was a creature of habit in his public life. After school, he would stay past the final bell to talk to students and work on his lesson plan for the next day. Then, with several folders and his laptop in a backpack over his left shoulder, he would head out, waving to the secretary as he passed. He would walk six blocks and get on the subway at Congress Heights around six, just as the commuting mayhem was at its worst. He had a straight shot up the Green Line to Columbia Heights, where his tiny studio apartment was located. Once there, he would eat a frozen dinner and grade papers. He went to bed around ten, never turning the TV on as far as she'd seen. It was harder to follow what happened in the morning—he had rattan shades that were basically translucent when lit from inside, but opaque in the morning sun. He hit the street at five for a morning run, returned an hour later, then left again after another thirty minutes, headed for the subway station three blocks away, longish curly hair still wet from his shower.

Two mornings ago, she'd followed his exercise route as best she could from a safe distance. He held a strong, fast pace—obviously an experienced runner. As she watched, she found herself wishing that she had more time to run. She didn't love running the way others seemed to—she always felt so exposed on the side of a road, no car to escape in—but it was important. She was never going to be stronger than the person they sent after her. With her short legs, she wouldn't be faster, either, and there was no martial art she could learn that would give her an advantage over a professional killer. But endurance—that could save her life. If her tricks could get her past the crisis moment, she had to be able to keep going longer than the killer could keep chasing. What a way to die—winded, muscles quitting, crippled by her own lack of preparation. She didn't want to go out that way. So she ran as often as she could and did the exercises she could manage inside her small homes. She promised herself that when this operation was over, she would find a good place to jog—one with plenty of escape routes and hidey-holes.

But his running route—like the apartment and the school—was too obvious a place to make her move. The easiest way to do this would be to grab him off the street as he was finishing his run, worn out and unfocused, but the bad guys would know this too. They would be prepared for her. The same was true for the walking portion of his journey to school. So it had to be the Metro. They would know the Metro was another possible option, but they couldn't cover every line, every stop, while also watching each leg of his commute.

There were cameras everywhere, but there was only so much she could do about that. When it was over, her enemies would have a million clear shots of what her face looked like now, three years later. Not much change, in her opinion, but they would still, no doubt, update her file. That was all they would be able to do, though. Her former position with the department had given her enough familiarity with the mechanics of snatching a target off the street to know that the difficulties were a lot greater than the average espionage TV series would lead one to believe. The purpose of the Metro cameras was to help catch a suspect *after* the crime. There was no way they'd have the resources and manpower to act on the coverage in real time. So all the cameras could tell them was where she *had* been, not where she *would* be, and without that information, the footage was useless. All the usual discoveries the tapes could help with — who she was, where she'd gotten her information, what her motive was — were things they already knew.

In any case, she couldn't think of a less risky option.

Today her name was Jesse. She went with a professional look — her black suit with the V-neck black tee underneath and of course the leather belt. She had another, more realistic wig; this one chin-length and lighter, a mousy blond-brown color. She held this back with a simple black headband and added glasses with thin metal rims that didn't make it look like she was hiding but still subtly disguised the shape of her cheekbones and forehead. Her face was symmetrical with small features; nothing stood out. She knew that as a general rule, people overlooked her. But she also knew she wasn't so generic-looking that someone specifically searching would fail to recognize her. She would keep her head down whenever she could.

She brought a briefcase rather than her tote; the wooden details from her shoulder strap snapped into place on the handle of the briefcase. It was lined with metal, heavy even when empty, and could easily be used as a bludgeon if necessary. The locket, the rings, but not the earrings. She would have to do a bit of manhandling, and the earrings wouldn't be safe. The shoe knives, the scalpel blades, the ChapStick, the various sprays...almost full armor. Today it didn't make her feel more confident. This part of the plan was far outside her comfort zone. Kidnapping wasn't something she'd ever imagined needing to do. In the past three years, she hadn't thought of a scenario that didn't boil down to either kill or escape.

Jesse yawned as she drove through the dark streets. She'd not been getting enough sleep, nor was sleep going to figure largely in the next few days. She had a few substances that would keep her awake, but the crash could be delayed for only seventy-two hours at most. She would need to be hidden very well when that crash came. She hoped it wouldn't be necessary to use them.

There were plenty of spaces available in the economy parking lot at Ronald Reagan. She pulled into one near the shuttle bus stop, where most people would want to park, and waited for the bus to arrive. She knew this airport better than any other. She felt a long-missing sense of comfort kick in—the comfort of familiar surroundings. Two other passengers showed up before the shuttle, both of them with luggage and tired faces. They ignored her. She rode the bus to terminal three, then doubled back on the pedestrian bridge to the Metro stop. This route took her about fifteen minutes at a brisk walk. Nice thing about airports—everyone walked fast.

She'd debated wearing boots with wedge heels, going for a different height, but then decided she would be walking—and possibly running, if things went badly—too much today. She wore the dark flats that were half sneaker.

As she joined the crowd heading down to the Metro platform, she tried to keep her face hidden as much as possible from the ceiling cameras. Using her peripheral vision, she searched for a likely group to join. Jesse was sure that the watchers would be looking for a lone woman. A larger group—any group—was a better disguise than makeup or a wig.

There were several clusters of people heading to the tracks with her as the first wave of rush hour began to crowd the escalators. She chose a trio, two men and one woman, all in dark business suits and carrying briefcases. The woman had shiny blond hair and was a good nine inches taller than Jesse in her high-heeled, pointy-toed pumps. Jesse edged her way around a few other parties until she was somewhat hidden between the woman and the wall behind them. Any eyes examining the new quartet would naturally be drawn to the tall blonde. Unless those eyes were specifically looking for Juliana Fortis.

Jesse's quartet moved purposefully through the crowd, claiming a spot near the edge of the platform to wait. None of the others in the group seemed aware of the small woman moving in tandem with them.

There were too many close-packed bodies for her proximity to be noticeable.

The train raced into view, whipping past and then jerking to an abrupt stop. Jesse's group hesitated, looking for a less crowded car. She contemplated abandoning them, but the blonde was impatient, too, and she forced her way into the negative space of the third car they considered. Jesse pushed in close behind the woman she'd been following, her body pressed against both the blonde and another, larger woman behind her. She would be all but invisible between them, uncomfortable as the position might be.

They rode the Yellow Line up to the Chinatown station. There she left the trio and joined a new couple, two women who could have been secretaries or librarians in their buttoned-up blouses and cat-framed eyeglasses. They rode the Green Line together up to the Shaw-Howard station, Jesse's head cocked in the direction of the shorter brunette, pretending to be absorbed in a story about last weekend's wedding reception that hadn't included an open bar, of all the nerve. Mid-story, she left the secretaries on the train and melted into the crowd exiting the Metro. She did a quick U-turn through the densely packed ladies' room and then joined the crowd heading down to the tracks for the next train. Timing would be everything now. She wouldn't be able to hide inside the herd.

The shrill wail of the approaching train had Jesse's

heart bouncing up into her throat. She braced herself; it felt like she was a sprinter crouched at the blocks, waiting for the gun to fire. Then she shuddered at the metaphor in her head—it was only too possible that a gun was actually about to fire, but this one would have real bullets and wouldn't be aimed at the sky.

The train shrieked to a stop, and she was on the move.

Jesse power-walked down the line of cars, elbowing through the flow of passengers as the doors whooshed open. Scanning as fast as she could, she searched for the tall frame with the floppy hair. There were so many bodies ducking past her, blocking her view. She tried to put a mental X through every head that didn't match. Was she moving too quickly? Not quickly enough? The train was leaving by the time she got to the last car, and she couldn't be positive he wasn't on it, but she didn't think he was. By her calculations of his last two arrivals, he was most likely on the next train. She bit her lip as the doors closed. If she'd blown this one, she'd have to try again on his next trip. She didn't want to have to do that. The closer the time got to Carston's plan being put into action, the more dangerous this would be.

Rather than linger in plain sight, she continued briskly toward the exit.

She did another circuit through the restroom, wasting a little time pretending to check the makeup she wasn't wearing. After counting to ninety in her head, she rejoined the stream of commuters on their way to the tracks.

It was even more crowded now. Jesse chose a spot close to a group of suited men at the far end of the platform and tried to blend in with the black fabric of their jackets. The men were talking about stocks and trades, things that seemed so far from Jesse's life that they might as well have been science fiction. The next train was announced and she got ready to walk and scan again. She stepped around the traders and examined the first car as it came to a stop.

Moving fast, Jesse's eyes ran through the next car. *Woman, woman, old man, too short, too fat, too dark, no hair, woman, woman, kid, blond...* The next car—

It was like he was helping her, like he was on her side. He was right beside the window, looking out, standing tall, with the wavy hair very much in evidence.

Jesse gave the rest of the occupants a quick once-over as she walked toward the open doors. Many business types—any one of them could have been hired by the department. But there were no obvious tells, no extra-wide shoulders that didn't quite fit into normal-size suit coats, no earpieces, no bulges under the jackets, no eye contact between riders. No one wore sunglasses.

This is the part, she thought to herself, *where they try to bag us both and haul us back to the lab. Unless this is a setup, in which case Daniel and his innocent curly hair will be one of them. He might be the one to shoot me. Or stab me. Or they'll try to get me off the train to shoot me somewhere in private. Or they'll knock me out and throw me on the tracks.*

But if the story is all true, they'll want us both alive. They'll probably try something similar to what I'm about to do to Daniel. Then they'll cart me off to the lab and my odds of ever walking out again are...less than encouraging.

A thousand other bad endings raced through her head as the doors closed behind them. She walked quickly to stand beside Daniel, sharing the same pole for balance, her fingers close below his paler, much longer fingers. Her heart felt like someone was squeezing it in a tight fist; it got more painful in direct proportion to her proximity to the target. He didn't seem to notice her, still staring out the window with a far-away look, a look that didn't change as they pulled into the darkness of the tunnel and he could see only reflections from inside the car. Nobody in the car made any move toward them.

She couldn't see any of the other guy in Daniel Beach, the one she'd seen pictures of in Mexico and Egypt, the one who hid his hair and moved with aggressive assurance. The abstracted man next to her could have been an Old World poet. He must be an incredible actor...or was it possible that he was legitimately psychotic, suffering from dissociative identity disorder? She didn't know what to do with that.

Jesse tensed as they neared the Chinatown stop. The train lurched into the station, and she had to grip the pole tighter to keep from swinging into Daniel Beach.

Three people, two suits and one skirt, exited the train, but none of them looked at Jesse. They all hurried past, moving like they were late for work. Two more men got into the car. One caught Jesse's attention — a big man, built like a professional athlete, wearing a hoodie and sweatpants. He had both hands in the front pouch of the hoodie, and unless his hands were the size of shoe boxes, he was carrying something in them. He didn't look at Jesse as he passed her, just went to the back corner of the car and grabbed an overhead strap. She kept him in the corner of her eye in the reflection, but he didn't seem interested in either herself or the target.

Daniel Beach hadn't moved. He was so absorbed in his distant thoughts that she found herself relaxing beside him, as if he were the one person on the train she didn't have to guard against. Which was foolish. Even if this wasn't a trap, even if he was exactly who she'd been told he was, this man was still planning to become a mass murderer in the very near future.

The athlete pulled a boxy pair of headphones out of his sweatshirt's big pocket and covered his ears with them. The cord led back down to the pocket. Probably to his phone, but maybe not.

She decided to make the next stop a test.

As the doors opened, she bent down as if to fix the nonexistent cuff on her pants, then straightened suddenly and took a step toward the door.

No one reacted. The athlete in the headphones had his eyes closed. People got on, people got off, but no one looked at her, and nobody moved to block her exit or suddenly brought up a hand with a jacket awkwardly draped over it.

If her enemies knew what she was doing, they were letting her do it her way.

Did that mean it was real or that they just wanted her to believe it was for now? Trying to think around their circles made her head hurt. She grabbed the pole again as the train started moving.

"Not your stop?"

She looked up, and Daniel Beach was smiling down at her — the perfectly sweet, guileless smile that belonged to the school's most popular teacher, to the Habitat for Humanity crusader.

"Um, no." She blinked, her thoughts scrambling. What would a normal commuter say? "I, uh, just forgot where I was for a minute. The stations all start to blur together."

"Hold on. The weekend is only eight or nine hours away."

He smiled again, a kind smile. She was more than uncomfortable with the idea of socializing with her subject, but there was a strange—possibly counterfeit—normality about Daniel that made it easier for her to assume the role she needed to play: Friendly commuter. Ordinary person.

She snorted a dark little laugh at his observation. Her workweek was just beginning. "That would be exciting if I got weekends off."

He laughed and then sighed. "That's tough. Law?"

"Medicine."

"Even worse. Do they ever let you out for good behavior?"

"Very rarely. It's okay. I'm not much for wild parties anyway."

"I'm too old for them myself," he admitted. "A fact I usually remember around ten o'clock every night."

She smiled politely as he laughed, and tried to keep her eyes from looking crazed. It felt both creepy and dangerous to be fraternizing with her next job. She never had any interactions with her subjects beforehand. She couldn't afford to look at him as a person. She would have to see only the monster—the potential million dead—so she could remain impassive.

"Though I do enjoy the occasional quiet dinner out," he was saying.

"Mm," she murmured distractedly. It sounded like an agreement, she realized.

"Hi," he said. "My name is Daniel."

In her surprise, she forgot what her name was supposed to be. He held out his hand and she shook it, tremendously aware of the weight of her poisoned ring.

"Hi, Daniel."

"Hi..." He raised his eyebrows.

"Um, Alex." Whoops, that was a few names back. Oh, well.

"Nice to meet you, Alex. Look, I never do this—ever. But... well, why not? Can I give you my number? Maybe we could have that quiet dinner sometime?"

She stared at him in blank shock. He was hitting on her. A man was hitting on her. No, not a man. A soon-to-be mass murderer working for a psychotic drug czar.

Or an agent trying to distract her?

"Did I scare you? I swear I'm harmless."

"Er, no, I just... well, no one has ever asked me out on a train before." That was nothing but the plain truth. In fact, no one at all had asked her out for years. "I'm at a loss." Also true.

"Here, this is what I'll do. I'll write my name and number down on this piece of paper and I'll give it to you, and when you get to your stop, you can throw it in the next trash can you see, because littering is wrong, and immediately forget all about me. Very little inconvenience to you—just that extra few seconds with the trash can."

He smiled while he spoke, but his eyes were down, focused on writing his information on the back of a receipt with a no. 2 pencil.

"That's very considerate of you. I appreciate it."

He looked up, still smiling. "Or you don't have to throw it away. You could also use it to call me and then spend a few hours talking to me while I buy you food."

The monotone voice overhead announced the Penn Quarter station and she was relieved. Because she was starting to feel sad. Yes, she was going to have a night out with Daniel Beach, but neither of them was going to enjoy it very much.

There could be no room for sadness. So many innocent dead. Dead children, dead mothers and fathers. Good people who had never hurt anyone.

"It's a dilemma," she answered quietly.

The train stopped again, and she pretended to be jostled by the man exiting behind her. The appropriate needle was already in her hand. She reached out as if to steady herself with the pole and grabbed Daniel's hand in a move designed to look accidental. He jerked in surprise, and she held on tight like she was trying to keep her balance.

"Ouch. Sorry, I shocked you," she said. She released him and let the tiny syringe slide out of her palm into her blazer's pocket. Sleight of hand was something she'd practiced a lot.

"No worries. You okay? That guy really knocked you."

"Yes, I'm fine, thank you."

The car started moving again, and she watched as Daniel's face quickly lost its color.

"Hey, are *you* okay?" she asked. "You look a little pale."

"Um, I...what?"

He glanced around, confused.

"You look like you're going to pass out. Excuse me," she said to the woman in the seat beside them. "Can my friend sit? He's not feeling well."

The woman rolled her enormous brown eyes and then looked studiously in the other direction.

"No," Daniel said. "Don't...bother about me. I'm..."

"Daniel?" she asked.

He was swaying a little now, his face dead white.

"Give me your hand, Daniel."

Looking bemused, he held out his hand. She gripped his wrist, moving her lips in an obvious way as she looked at her watch and pretended to count to herself.

"Medicine," he muttered. "You're a doctor."

This part was closer to the scripted version, and it made her more comfortable. "Yes, and I'm not pleased with your condition. You're getting off at the next stop with me. We're going to get you some air."

"Can't. School . . . can't be late."

"I'll write you a note. Don't argue with me, I know what I'm doing."

"'Kay. Alex."

L'Enfant Plaza was one of the biggest and most chaotic stations on the line. When the door opened, Alex put her arm around Daniel's waist and led him out. He draped one arm over her shoulder for support. This didn't surprise her. The tryptamine she'd injected him with made people disoriented, acquiescent, and quite friendly. He would follow her lead as long as she didn't push him too hard. The drug was distantly related to a class of barbiturates that laypeople called truth serum and that had a few effects similar to Ecstasy; both were good for breaking down inhibitions and inducing cooperation. She liked this particular synthesis because of the confusion. Daniel would feel incapable of decision making and therefore would do whatever she told him to until it wore off—or unless she asked him to do something that really pushed against the walls of his comfort zone.

This was easier than she'd hoped, thanks to the unexpected tête-à-tête. She'd planned to stick him, then play the old *Is there a doctor in the house? Why, yes, I happen to be a doctor!* routine to get him to go with her initially. It would have worked, but he would not have been this docile.

"Okay, Daniel, how are you feeling? Can you breathe?"

"Sure. Breathing's good."

She walked quickly with him. This drug rarely made anyone sick, but there were always exceptions. She glanced up to check his color. He was still pale but his lips hadn't taken on the greenish hue that would presage nausea.

"Do you feel sick to your stomach?" she asked.

"No. No, I'm fine..."

"I'm afraid you're not. I'm going to take you to work with me, if that's okay. I want to make sure this isn't serious."

"Okay...no. I have school?"

He was keeping pace with her easily despite his disorientation. His legs were about twice as long as hers.

"We'll tell them what's happening. You have a number for the school?"

"Yes, Stacey—in the office."

"We'll call her while we walk."

This would slow them down, but there was no help for it; she had to allay his concern so he would stay docile.

"Good idea." He nodded, then pulled an old Black-Berry out of his pocket and fumbled with the buttons.

She took it gently from his hand. "What's the last name for Stacey?"

"It's under 'Front desk.'"

"I see it. Okay, I'll dial for you. Here, tell Stacey you're sick. You're going to the doctor."

He took the phone obediently, then waited for Stacey to answer.

"Hello," he said. "Stacey. I'm Daniel. Yes, Mr. Beach. Not feeling so good, going to see Dr. Alex. Sorry. Hate to dump this on you. Sorry, thanks. Yes, get better, for sure."

She flinched a little when he used her name, but that was just habit. It didn't matter. She wouldn't be Alex again for a while, that was all.

It was a risk, taking him out of school. Something de la Fuentes might notice if he was keeping close tabs on his messenger of death. But surely he would not raise the alarm to critical over one missed Friday. When Daniel showed up intact Monday morning, the drug lord would be reassured.

She took the phone from Daniel and pocketed it.

"I'll hold this for you, okay? You look unsteady and I don't want you to lose it."

"Okay." He looked around again and frowned at the giant concrete ceiling arcing overhead. "Where are we going?"

"My office, remember? We're going to get on this train now." She didn't see any faces from the other train in this car. If they were following, they were doing it from a distance. "Look, here's a seat. You can rest." She helped him settle, surreptitiously dropping his phone by her foot and then nudging it farther under the seat with her shoe.

Tracking a cell phone was the very easiest way to find someone without having to do any work. Cell phones were a trap she'd always avoided. It was like volunteering to tag yourself for the enemy.

Well, she also didn't really have anyone to call.

"Thanks," Daniel said. He still had one arm around her, though now, with him sitting and her standing, it was at her waist. He stared up at her dizzily and then added, "I like your face."

"Oh. Um, thank you."

"I like it a lot."

The woman sitting next to Daniel looked over at Alex and examined her face. *Great.*

The woman seemed unimpressed.

Daniel leaned his forehead against her hip and closed his eyes. The proximity was disconcerting on a few different levels, but also oddly comforting. It had been a long time since any human being had touched her with affection, even if this affection had come out of a test tube. Regardless, she couldn't let him fall asleep yet.

"What do you teach, Daniel?"

He angled his face up, his cheek still resting on her hip.

"Mostly English. That's my favorite."

"Really? I was horrible at all the humanities. I liked science best."

He made a face. "Science!"

She heard the woman beside him mutter, "Drunk," to her other neighbor.

"Shouldn't have told you I was a teacher." He sighed heavily.

"Why not?"

"Women don't like that. Randall says, 'Never volunteer the information.'" The way he said the words made it clear he was quoting this Randall verbatim.

"But teaching is a noble profession. Educating the future doctors and scientists of the world."

He looked up at her sadly. "There's no money in it."

"Not every woman is so mercenary. Randall is dating the wrong type."

"My wife liked money. Ex-wife."

"I'm sorry to hear that."

He sighed again and closed his eyes. "It broke my heart."

Another twinge of pity. Of sadness. He would never say these things, she knew, if he weren't high on her Ecstasy–truth serum hybrid. He was speaking more clearly now; the drug wasn't wearing off, his mind was just adapting to working around it.

She patted his cheek and made her voice cheery. "If she was that easily bought, she probably isn't worth crying over."

His eyes opened again. They were a very gentle hazel, an even mix of green and soft gray. She tried to picture them intense—fitting under the baseball cap of the self-assured man meeting with de la Fuentes in the photos—and failed.

She didn't know what she would do if he actually had dissociative identity disorder. She'd never worked with that before.

"You're right," he said. "I know you are. I need to see her for what she really was, not what I imagined she was."

"Exactly. We build up these ideas of people, create the one we want to be with, and then try to keep the real person inside the false mold. It doesn't always work out well."

Gibberish. She had no idea what she was saying. She'd been in one semiserious relationship in her whole life, and it hadn't lasted long. School had been prioritized before the guy, just like work had been prioritized before everything else for six years. Like how she now prioritized breathing over everything else. She had a problem with obsessiveness.

"Alex?"

"Yes?"

"Am I dying?"

She smiled reassuringly. "No. If I thought you were dying, I would have called an ambulance. You'll be fine. I just want to double-check."

"Okay. Will I have to have blood taken?"

"Maybe."

He sighed. "Needles make me nervous."

"It will be fine."

She didn't like that this bothered her—lying to him. But there was something about his simple trust, the way he seemed to ascribe the best motives to everything she did . . . She had to snap out of it.

"Thank you, Alex. Really."

"Just doing my job." Not a lie.

"Do you think you'll call me?" he asked hopefully.

"Daniel, we're definitely going to spend an evening together," she promised. If he hadn't been drugged, he would have heard the edge in her voice and seen the ice in her eyes.

CHAPTER 5

The rest went almost too smoothly...did that mean something? Her paranoia level was already so high, it was hard to say if this new worry elevated it or not.

He got into the cab at the Rosslyn station without protest. She knew how he felt—she and Barnaby had tried out most of the nonlethal preparations to have some concrete experience with what they could do. This one was like dreaming a pleasant dream, where problems and worries were for someone else to figure out, and all one needed was a hand to hold and a nudge in the right direction. In their notes they'd nicknamed it *Follow the Leader,* though it had a more impressive name on the official reports.

It was a relaxing trip, and if it weren't for the fact that she desperately needed her inhibitions, even back then, she might have indulged again.

She got him talking about the volleyball team he coached—he'd asked if he'd be back at school in time for practice—and he spent the entire cab ride telling her about the girls until she felt she knew all their names and their strengths on the court by heart. The cabbie paid no attention, humming along to some song too low for her to make out.

Daniel seemed mostly oblivious to the travel, but at a particularly long red light, he looked up and frowned.

"Your office is far away."

"Yes, it is," she agreed. "It's a hell of a commute."

"Where do you live?"

"Bethesda."

"That's a nice place. Columbia Heights is not so nice. My part of it, at least."

The cab started moving again. She was pleased; the plan was going very well. Even if they'd clocked her getting on and off the last train, they'd be hard-pressed to keep track of one cab in a sea of identical cabs twisting together through rush hour. Preparation felt like a magic spell sometimes. Like you could force events into the shape you wanted just by planning them *thoroughly* enough.

Daniel wasn't as talkative now. This was the second phase of the drug's action, and he would be getting more tired. She needed him to stay awake just a little bit longer.

"Why did you give me your number?" she asked when his lids started to droop.

He smiled dreamily. "I've never done that before."

"Me either."

"I'll probably be embarrassed about it later."

"Not if I call you, though, right?"

"Maybe. I don't know, it was out of character."

"So why did you do it?"

His soft eyes never left hers. "I like your face."

"You mentioned that."

"I really wanted to see it again. That made me brave."

She frowned, guilt pulsing.

"Does that sound weird?" He seemed worried.

"No, it sounds very sweet. Not many men would tell a woman something like that."

He blinked owlishly. "I wouldn't usually. Too... cowardly."

"You seem pretty brave to me."

"I feel different. I think it's you. I felt different as soon as I saw you smile."

As soon as I roofied you, she amended in her head.

"Well, that's quite a compliment," she said. "And here we go, can you get up?"

"Sure. This is the airport."

"Yes, that's where my car is."

His brow furrowed, then cleared. "Did you just get back from a trip?"

"I just got into town, yes."

"I go on trips sometimes. I like to go to Mexico."

She glanced up sharply. He was staring ahead, watching where he was walking. There was no sign of distress on his face. If she pushed him toward a secret, anything that was a pressure point, his docility would turn to suspicion. He might latch on to another stranger as his leader and try to escape. He might get agitated and call attention to her.

"What do you like about Mexico?" she asked carefully.

"The weather is hot and dry. I enjoy that. I've never lived in a really hot place, but I think I would like it. I get burned, though. I've never been able to tan. You look like you've spent some time in the sun."

"No, just born this way." She got her coloring from her absentee father. Genetic testing had informed her that he was a mix of many things, predominantly Korean, Hispanic, and Welsh. She'd always wondered what he'd looked like. The combination with her mother's Scottish background had created in her an oddly ordinary face—she could have been from almost anywhere.

"That must be nice. I have to use sunblock, a *lot* of sunblock. Or I peel. It's disgusting. I shouldn't tell you that."

She laughed. "I promise to forget it. What else do you like?"

"Working with my hands. I help build houses. Not in a skilled way; I just hammer where they tell me to. But the people are so kind and generous. I love that part."

It was all very convincing, and she felt a thrill of fear. How could he stick to the story so well, so effortlessly, with the chemicals moving through his system right now? Unless he'd built up a resistance somehow. Unless her department had created an antidote, unless they'd prepped him and he was playing her. The goose bumps stood up on the back of her neck. It didn't have to be the department that had prepared him. It could be his interactions with de la Fuentes. Who knew what kind of results strange drugs interacting with her own would have? She touched her tongue to the false cap on her back tooth. The department would have just killed her if that were the goal. De la Fuentes would probably want to punish her for attempting to interrupt his plans. But how would he know in advance? How could Daniel have made her as an opposing agent so quickly? She didn't even actually work for anyone anymore.

Stick to the plan, she told herself. *Get him in the car and you're in the clear. Sort of.*

"I like the houses there, too," he was saying. "You never close the windows, just let the air blow through. Some don't even have glass. It's a lot nicer than Columbia Heights, I can tell you. Maybe not nicer than Bethesda. I bet doctors live in nice houses."

"Not me. Boring vanilla apartment. I don't spend much time there, so it doesn't matter."

He nodded sagely. "You're out saving lives."

"Well, not really. I'm not an ER doctor or anything."

"You're saving *my* life." Wide gray-green eyes, total trust. She knew that if this behavior was genuine, it was the drug talking. But it still made her uneasy.

She could only keep playing her role.

"I'm just checking up on you. You're not dying." That much was true. The boys back at the department might have ended up killing this man. At least she could spare him that. Though...after she prevented the catastrophe, Daniel Beach would never see the outside of a prison cell again. Which made her feel...

A million dead. Innocent tiny babies. Sweet elderly grandmas. The First Horseman of the Apocalypse on a white steed.

"Oh, a bus too," he said mildly.

"This one takes us to my car. Then you won't have to walk anymore."

"I don't mind. I like walking with you." He smiled down at her and his feet tangled on his way up the steps. She steadied him before he could fall, then maneuvered him into the closest seat on the mostly empty bus.

"Do you like foreign films?" he asked, apropos of nothing.

"Um, some of them, I guess."

"There's a good theater at the university. Maybe if the dinner goes well, we could try some subtitles the next time."

"I'll make a deal with you," she said. "If you still like me after one evening together, I will definitely see a movie I can't understand with you."

He smiled, his lids drooping. "I'll still like you."

This was totally ridiculous. There should have been some way to direct this conversation away from *flirting*. Why was she the one feeling like the monster here? Okay, she *was* a monster, but she'd come to terms with that, mostly, and she knew she was the kind of monster that needed to exist for the sake of the common good. In some ways, she was like a normal physician—she had to cause pain to save lives. Like cutting off a gangrenous limb to save the rest of the body, just disassociated. Pain here, savior elsewhere. And elsewhere was much more deserving of the save.

Rationalizing, as she always had, so that she could live with herself. She never outright lied to herself, though. She knew she didn't exist in some moral gray area; she existed entirely in the black. But the only thing worse than Alex doing her job well was someone else doing it badly. Or no one doing it at all.

But even if she fully embraced the label *monster*, she was never the kind of monster who killed innocent people. She wasn't even going to kill this very guilty one . . . who was still looking up at her from under his long curls with big hazel puppy-dog eyes.

Dead babies, she chanted to herself. *Dead babies, dead babies, dead babies.*

She'd never wanted to be a spy or work undercover, but now she saw that she was also emotionally unsuited for the job. Apparently she had too much gratuitous sympathy floating around inside her body, which was more than ironic. This is why you never talked to your subject before you *talked* to him.

"Okay, Daniel, off we go. Can you stand up?"

"Mm-hmm. Oh, here, let me take your bag."

He lifted a hand weakly toward her briefcase.

"I got it." Though in truth her fingers were pins and needles around the handle. "You need to focus on your balance right now."

"I'm really tired."

"I know, look, my car is right there. The silver one."

"There are a lot of silver ones."

Exactly the point. "It's right here. Okay, let's put you in the back so you can lie down. Why don't you take off your coat, I don't want you to get too warm. And the shoes, there we go." Less for her to manage later. "Bend your knees up so your legs will fit. Perfect."

He had his head pillowed on the backpack now, which surely wasn't that comfortable, but he was past caring.

"You're so nice, Alex," he murmured, his eyes closed now. "You're the nicest woman I ever met."

"I think you're nice, too, Daniel," she admitted.

"Thanks," he half articulated, and then he was asleep.

Quickly, she pulled the beige throw out of the trunk. It was the same color as the seats. She covered him with it. She pulled a syringe from her bag and inserted it into a vein in his ankle, hunching her body so it blocked any outside view of what she was doing. *Follow the Leader* would wear off in an hour or so, and she needed him to sleep longer than that.

Not an agent, she decided. An agent might have played along with her kidnap drug, but he would never have let himself get knocked out like this. Just a mass murderer for hire, then.

· · ·

THE TEMPORARY LAB she had created was in rural West Virginia. She'd rented a nice little farmhouse with a milking barn that had been a very long time without cows. The exterior of the barn was a white composite siding that matched the house; inside, the walls and ceiling were lined in aluminum. The floors were sealed concrete with conveniently spaced drains. There was a little bunk room in the back; it had been advertised as extra space for visiting guests, *delightfully rustic.* She was sure there were many naive travelers who would find the rusticity charming, but all she cared about was that the electricity and water were hooked up and running. The farmhouse and barn were situated in the middle of a 240-acre apple orchard, which was in turn surrounded by more acres of farmland. The closest neighbor was over a mile away. The owners of this orchard were making money during the off-season by renting out the space to city dwellers who wanted to pretend they were roughing it.

It was very expensive. She frowned every time she thought about the price, but it couldn't be helped. She needed a secluded facility with a usable space.

She'd been working nights to get everything ready. During the day she had followed Daniel from a good distance, then caught up on what sleep she could in the car during school hours. She was completely exhausted at the moment, but she still had a lot to do before her workday was over.

First stop, a minor freeway exit more than an hour out of the city. A narrow dirt road that looked as if no one had used it in a decade took her deeper into the trees. It must have led somewhere, but she didn't drive far enough to see where. She stopped under a thick patch of shade, cut the engine, and went to work.

If Daniel was employed by the department or, more likely, one of the organizations that worked closely with it—the CIA, a few military sections, some other black ops floaters that, like the department, didn't have official names—he would have an electronic tracker on him. Just like she'd once had. Absently, she rubbed her finger across the small raised scar on the nape of her neck, covered by her short hair. They liked to tag the head. If only one part of a body could be recovered, the head was best for identification purposes.

She opened the back passenger-side door and knelt on the damp ground beside Daniel's head. She started with the place both she and Barnaby had been tagged, brushing her fingers lightly along his skin, then again, pressing harder. Nothing. She'd seen a few foreign subjects whose trackers had been freshly removed from behind their ears, so she checked there next. Then she ran her fingers through his hair, probing the scalp for any bumps or hard spots that shouldn't be there. His curls were very soft and smelled nice, citrusy. Not that she cared about his hair, but at least she didn't have to put her hands into some greasy, malodorous nest. She appreciated that.

Now for the heavy lifting. If it was de la Fuentes keeping tabs on this man, the tracker would probably be external. She threw the shoes into the woods beside the road first—they seemed the most likely culprit of his clothes; lots of men would wear the same pair every day. Then she stripped off his shirt, grateful for the button-down, though it was still hard to get it out from under the weight of his body. She didn't bother trying to get the undershirt over his head; she pulled a blade from her pocket, untaped it, and cut the fabric into three easily removable pieces. She scanned his chest—no suspicious scars or lumps. The skin on his torso was fairer than his arms; he had a faint farmer's tan, no doubt from building houses in Mexico with a T-shirt on. Or from acquiring superviruses in Egypt—also very sunny.

He had what she thought of as sports muscles rather than gym muscles. No hard-cut edges, just a nice smooth alignment that showed he was active without being obsessive.

Rolling him onto his stomach was hard, and he fell into the foot space, draped over the hump between seats. He had two light scars on his left shoulder blade, parallel and even in length. She explored them carefully, prodding the skin all around, but she couldn't feel anything besides the normal fibrous, hypertrophic tissue that should be there.

It didn't take her long to realize she should have removed his jeans before rolling him over. She had to climb on top of his awkwardly positioned form and reach both arms around his torso to get the button fly open. So very thankful that he was not wearing skinny jeans, she then climbed out the other passenger-side door and yanked the pants off over his feet. She was unsurprised to see that he wore boxers rather than briefs. It fit his clothing profile. She stripped the boxers off, then the socks, and then she grabbed up the rest of the clothes, walked them a few feet off the road, and stuffed them behind a fallen log. She made another trip for the backpack. The laptop would be a very good hiding place for any electronic device someone wanted him to carry around unknowingly.

This wasn't the first time she'd had to strip a target down herself. In the laboratory environment, she'd had people who prepped a subject for her—Barnaby called them the underlings—but she hadn't always been in the lab, and during her first field trip to Herat, Afghanistan, she'd learned to be deeply grateful to the underlings. Stripping down a man who hadn't bathed in months was not pleasant—especially when she didn't have a shower available for herself afterward. At least Daniel was clean. She was the only one working up a sweat today.

She found the screwdriver in the trunk and quickly changed the DC license plate for one she'd pulled off a similar car in a West Virginia scrap yard.

Just to be thorough, she did a cursory examination of the backs of his legs, the bottom of his feet, and his hands. She'd never seen a tracker on the extremities, probably because extremities sometimes got cut off to make a point. She didn't see any scars. She also didn't see any calluses that suggested he trained with guns or used them frequently. He had soft teacher hands, with just a few hard spots that spoke of blisters from inexperienced labor.

She tried to roll him back up onto the seat but quickly realized it was a vain effort. It wasn't a comfortable sleeping position, but he wouldn't wake up regardless. He would be sore later. Though it was completely ridiculous to even think of that.

As she repositioned the blanket and tucked it around his body as best she could, she was constructing a story about him from the documents she'd read and the evidence in front of her.

She believed Daniel Beach was mostly the man she saw now, the pleasant all-around good guy. The attraction for the avaricious ex was understandable. He was probably easy to fall in love with. After some time had passed, enough time for the ex to take love for granted, she would have been able to shift her focus to the things she didn't have—the nice apartment, the big ring, the cars. She probably missed this side of Daniel now, the grass always being greener and whatnot.

But there was also darkness in Daniel, buried deep, perhaps born from the pain and unfairness of losing his parents, aggravated by his wife's betrayal, and then ignited by the loss of his final family member. That darkness would not surface easily. He would compartmentalize it, keep it away from this gentle life, pack it into the dark spaces where it fit. No wonder he could speak of Mexico so blithely. He would have two Mexicos: the happy one the teacher loved, and the dangerous one the monster thrived in. They probably weren't anything close to the same place in his head.

Not a true psychotic, she hoped. Just a fractured man who didn't want to give up the person he thought of as himself but who needed the release the darkness gave him.

She felt comfortable with this assessment, and it changed her plan a little. There was a great deal of performance to what she did. For some subjects, the very clinical and emotionless persona worked best—white coat, surgical mask, and shiny stainless steel; for others, it was the threat of the crazed sadist (though Barnaby was always more successful with that play; he had the face and hair for it—unruly spikes of white, I've-just-been-electrocuted hair). Every situation was slightly different—some feared the darkness, some the light. She'd been planning to go clinical—it was the most comfortable role in her wheelhouse—but she decided now that Daniel would need to be surrounded by darkness to let that side come to the surface. And Dark Daniel was the one she needed to talk to.

She did a little evasive driving on the way in. If someone had been tracking Daniel's clothes or possessions, she didn't want that person coming along any farther on this trip.

She considered the possibilities again for the millionth time. Column one, this was a very elaborate trap. Column two, this was for real and a million lives were on the line. Not to mention her own.

During her long drive, the balance finally shifted

to rest solidly on one side. This wasn't a government agent in her car, she was sure of that. And if he was an innocent citizen, picked at random to draw her out, then they'd already missed their best opportunities to bag her. There hadn't been one attack, not one attempt to follow her ... that she'd seen.

. She thought of the mountains of incriminating information on Daniel Beach, and she couldn't help herself. She was a believer. So she'd better get to work saving lives.

She pulled into the farmhouse drive around eleven, dead tired and starving but 95 percent sure that there was no trail that could lead either the department or de la Fuentes to her doorstep. She looked the house over quickly, checking to see if anyone had broken in (and died, as he or she would have upon opening the door), and then, after disarming her safeguards, she drove the car into the barn. As soon as she'd pulled the barn door shut and reset the "alarm," she went to work getting Daniel prepped.

All the other tasks were done. She'd bought timers from a Home Depot in Philly and plugged lamps into them in several rooms of the farmhouse; like a traveler leaving for a few weeks, she made certain that the place looked occupied. A radio was plugged into one of the timers, so there would be noise, too. The house was good bait. Most people would clear that before progressing to the dark barn.

The barn would stay dark. She'd constructed a kind of tent in the middle of the barn space that would hide light and muffle sound, while also keeping Daniel completely ignorant of his surroundings. The rectangular structure was about seven feet high, ten feet wide, and fifteen feet long. It was constructed of PVC pipe, black tarps, and bungee cords, and lined inside with two layers of egg foam duct-taped into place. Rough, yes, but more functional than a cave, and she'd handled that in the past.

In the center of the tent was an oversize metal slab with black accordion legs that could be adjusted for height. It had been on display in the barn—for authenticity, no doubt—and was some kind of veterinarian's operating table. It was bigger than she needed—this vet had been dealing with cows, not kittens—but still quite a find. It was one of the items that had pushed her over the edge into renting this extortionate tourist trap. There was another metal-topped table that she'd set up as a desk with her computer, the monitors, and a tray of things that would hopefully only be props. The IV pole was next to the head of the table, a bag of saline already hanging. A wheeled metal cart from the kitchen was positioned beside the pole; a mass of tiny but ominous-looking syringes were lined up in easy view on a stainless-steel tray. There was a gas mask and a pressure cuff on the wire rack below the syringes.

And of course, the restraints she'd bought on eBay, prison-medical-facility grade, which she'd chained into place through holes she'd laboriously drilled into the stainless-steel slab. No one was escaping from those restraints without outside help. And that helper might need a blowtorch.

She'd left herself two exits, just openings in the tarp like the partings in a curtain. Outside the tent she had a cot, her sleeping bag, a hot plate, a small refrigerator, and all the other things she would need. There was a little three-piece bathroom attached to the bunkhouse, but it was too far away for her to sleep in, and there was no tub anyway, just a shower. She'd have to forgo her usual arrangements this weekend.

She used movers' straps to haul Daniel's inert form out of the car and onto a refrigerator dolly, bumping his head a few times in the process. *Probably* not hard enough to cause a concussion. Then she wheeled him to the table, set it to its lowest height, and rolled him onto it. He was still deeply under. She positioned him on his back, arms and legs extended about forty-five degrees from his body, then raised the table. One by one, she locked the restraints into place. He would not be moving out of this pose for a while. The IV was next; luckily he was fairly well hydrated, or maybe he just had really great veins. She got the line placed easily and started the drip. She added a parenteral nutrition bag next to the saline. This was all the sustenance he would get for the next three days, if it took that long. He'd be hungry, but his mind would be sharp when she wanted it to be. She put the pulse oximeter on his toe—he'd be able to pull it off a finger—and the dry electrodes on his back, one under each lung, to monitor his respiration. A quick swipe of the electric thermometer across his forehead told her that his current temperature was normal.

She wasn't as practiced with the bladder catheter, but it was a fairly simple procedure and he wasn't in any state to protest if she did something wrong. There would be enough cleaning up without urine to deal with, too.

Thinking of that, she placed the absorbent, plastic-lined squares—made for house-training puppies—on the floor all around the operating table. There would definitely be vomit if they needed to go past phase one. Whether there would be blood depended on how he responded to her normal methods. At least she had working plumbing here.

It was turning chilly in the barn, so she covered him with the blanket. She needed him to stay under for a while longer, and cold against his bare skin wouldn't help with that. After a moment of hesitation, she got one of the pillows off a bunk-room bed, brought it back, and placed it under his head. *It's just because I don't want him to wake up,* she assured herself. *Not because he looked uncomfortable.*

She inserted a small syringe into the IV port and gave him another dose of the sleeping agent. He should be good for at least four hours.

Daniel's unconscious face was unsettling. Too... peaceful somehow. She couldn't remember ever having seen an alignment of features that was so intrinsically innocent. It was hard to imagine that kind of peace and innocence even existing in the same world that she did. For a moment she worried again that she was dealing with a mental flaw beyond any of her previous experience. Then again, if de la Fuentes had been looking for someone who others would instinctively trust, this was exactly the kind of face he would have wanted. It might explain why the drug lord had chosen the schoolteacher in the first place.

She slipped the gas mask over his mouth and nose and screwed a canister onto it. If her safety precautions killed Daniel, she couldn't get the information she needed.

She did a final patrol around the perimeter. Through the windows, she could see that all the correct lights were on in the farmhouse. In the dead stillness of the night, she thought she could hear the faint strains of Top 40 pop.

Once she was sure that every point of ingress was secured, she ate a protein bar, brushed her teeth in the little bathroom, set her alarm for three, touched her gun under the cot, hugged her canister to her chest, and then sank into the folds of her sleeping bag. Her body was already asleep, and her brain wasn't far behind. She just had time to slip on her own gas mask before she was totally unconscious.

CHAPTER 6

By three thirty in the morning, she was up, dressed, and fed, still exhausted but ready to start. Daniel slept on, oblivious and peaceful. He would feel well rested when he woke up, but disoriented. He would have no idea what time or even what day it was. Discomfort was an important tool in her line of work.

She took his pillow and blanket away, acknowledging the regret this made her feel. But this was important; regardless of training, every subject felt great discomfort being naked and helpless in front of the enemy. Regret would be the last feeling she would allow herself for a few days. She closed off the rest. It had been more than three years, but she could feel things shutting down inside of her. Her body remembered how to do this. She knew she had the strength she would need.

Her hair was still wet from the quick color job, and the makeup felt thick on her face, though she wore very little, really. She didn't know how to do anything complicated, so she'd just smeared on dark shadow, thick mascara, and oxblood-red lipstick. She hadn't planned to adjust her hair color this soon, but black hair and the camouflage on her face were part of the new strategy. The white lab jacket and pale blue scrubs she'd brought lay crisply folded in her bag. Instead, she was in the tight black shirt again with black jeans. It was a good thing the farmhouse had a washer and dryer. The shirt was going to need a wash soon. Well, it needed one yesterday, actually.

It was strange how a little colored powder and grease could change an observer's perception of you. She checked herself in the bathroom mirror and was pleased by how hard her face looked, how cold. She ran a comb through her hair, slicking it straight back, then walked through the barn to her interrogation room.

She'd set up floodlights that hung from the PVC structure overhead, but she left them off now, just turning on two portable work lights that stood waist-high. The black duct tape and gray egg foam looked the same color in the shadows. The air temperature had dropped as the night progressed. There were goose bumps on the subject's arms and stomach. She ran the thermometer across his forehead again. Still within the normal range.

Finally, she turned on her computer and set up the protocols. It would go to screen saver after twenty minutes of inactivity. On the other side of her computer was a small black box with a keypad on top and a tiny red light on the side, but she ignored that now and went to work.

There was a feeling that struggled to break through to the surface as she injected the IV port with the chemical that would bring the subject around, but she suppressed it easily. Daniel Beach had two sides, and so did she. She was her other self now, the one the department called the Chemist, and the Chemist was a machine. Pitiless and relentless. *Her* monster was free now.

Hopefully his would come out to play.

The new drug trickled into his veins, and his breathing became less even. One long-fingered hand fisted and pulled against the restraint. Although he was still mostly unconscious, a frown touched his features as he tried to roll onto his side. His knees twisted, tugging against the fetters on his ankles, and suddenly his eyes flew open.

She stood quietly at the head of the table and watched him panic; his breathing spiked, his heart rate increased, his body thrashed against his bonds. He stared wildly into the darkness, trying to understand where he was, to find something familiar. He stopped suddenly, tense and listening.

"Hello?" he whispered.

She stood still, waiting for the right moment.

For ten minutes, he alternated between wildly yanking against the restraints and trying to listen around the harsh noise of his breathing.

"Help!" he finally called out loudly. "Is anyone there?"

"Hello, Daniel," she answered in a quiet voice.

His head jerked back, stretching his throat, as he looked for where the voice was coming from. It wasn't the instinct of a professional soldier, she noted, to expose the throat that way.

"Who's there? Who is that?"

"It doesn't really matter who I am, Daniel."

"Where am I?"

"Also not relevant."

"What do you *want?*" he half shouted.

"There you go—you got it. *That's* the question that matters."

She walked around the table so he could focus on her, though she was still lit from behind and her face would be mostly shadows.

"I don't have anything," he protested. "No money, no drugs. I can't help you."

"I don't want things, Daniel. I want—no, I *need* information. And the only way you're getting out of here is if you give it to me."

"I don't know anything—nothing important! Please—"

"Stop it," she snapped loudly, and he sucked in a shocked breath.

"Are you listening to me now, Daniel? This part is really crucial."

He nodded, blinking fast.

"I have to have this information. There is no other option. And if I have to, Daniel, I will hurt you until you tell me what I need to know. I will hurt you badly. I don't necessarily *want* to do this, but it doesn't bother me to do it, either. I'm telling you this so that you can decide now, before I begin. Tell me what I want to know, and I will free you. It's that simple. I promise I will not harm you. It will save me time and yourself a lot of suffering. I know you don't want to tell me, but please realize that you *are* going to tell me anyway. It may take a while, but eventually you won't be able to stop yourself. Everyone breaks. So make the easy choice now. You'll be sorry if you don't. Do you understand?"

She had given this same speech to many, many subjects in her career, and it was usually quite effective. About 40 percent of the time, this was when the subject would start confessing. Not often *finish* confessing, of course, and there was always some exploratory work to do, but there was a decent chance the first admission of guilt and some partial information might be surrendered now. The statistic varied depending on who she was giving the speech to; roughly half the time with most military men, the first divulgence would happen before any pain was administered. Only 5 to 10 percent of the actual spies would say anything without some physical distress. Same numbers for religious zealots. For the low-level toadies, the speech worked 100 percent of the time. The man in charge had never once confessed a single detail without pain.

She really hoped Daniel was just a glorified toady.

He stared back at her while she spoke, his face frozen in fear. But then, as she was concluding, confusion narrowed his eyes and pulled his brows together. It wasn't an expression she'd expected.

"Do you understand me, Daniel?"

His voice bewildered: "Alex? Alex, is that you?"

This was exactly why one didn't make contact with a mark beforehand. Now she was off script.

"Of course that's not my real name, Daniel. You know that."

"What?"

"My name isn't Alex."

"But...you're a doctor. You helped me."

"I am not that kind of doctor, Daniel. And I didn't help you. I drugged you and I kidnapped you."

His face was sober. "You were kind to me."

She had to control a sigh.

"I did what I had to do to get you here. Now, I need you to focus, Daniel. I need you to answer my question. Are you going to tell me what I want to know?"

She saw doubt in his expression again. Disbelief that she would actually hurt him, that this was really happening.

"I'll tell you anything you want to know. But like I said, I don't know anything important. I don't have any bank account numbers or, I don't know, treasure maps or anything. Certainly not anything worth all this."

He tried to gesture with his trussed hand. Looking at himself as he did, he seemed to realize for the first time that he was naked. His skin flushed—face, neck, and a line down the center of his chest—and he pulled automatically against the restraints as if trying to cover himself. His breathing and heart rate started spiking again.

Nudity; whether black ops agents or just low-level terrorist gofers, they all hated it.

"I don't want a treasure map. I'm not doing this for personal gain, Daniel. I'm doing this to protect innocent lives. Let's talk about that."

"I don't understand. How can I help with that? Why wouldn't I want to?"

She didn't like the way this was going. The ones who clung to the claim of ignorance and innocence often took longer to break than the ones who owned their guilt but were determined not to sell out their government, or their jihad, or their comrades.

She walked to the desk and picked up the first picture. It was one of the very clear surveillance shots of de la Fuentes, a close-up.

"Let's start with this man," she said, holding the photo at his eye level and using one of the work lights as a spot.

Perfectly blank, absolutely no reaction. A bad sign.

"Who is that?"

She allowed her sigh to be audible this time.

"You're making the wrong choice, Daniel. Please think about what you're doing."

"But I don't know who that is!"

She fixed him with a resigned stare.

"I'm being completely honest, Alex. I don't know that man."

She sighed again. "Then I suppose we'll get started."

The disbelief was there again. She'd never dealt with that in an interrogation before. All the others who'd been on her table had known what they were there for. She'd faced terror and pleading and, occasionally, stoic defiance, but never this strange, trusting, almost-challenge: *You won't hurt me.*

"Um, is this some kind of fetish fantasy thing?" he asked in a low voice, somehow finding a way to sound embarrassed despite the bizarreness of his circumstances. "I don't really know the rules for that stuff..."

She turned away to hide an inappropriate smile. *Get a grip,* she ordered herself. Trying to keep the movement smooth, as if she'd meant to walk away at that exact moment, she went to her desk. She clicked one key on her computer, keeping it awake. Then she picked up the prop tray. It was heavy, and some of the props clanked against each other as she moved it. She brought the tray to his side, rested the edge of it beside the syringes, and angled the light so the metallic implements shone brightly.

"I'm sorry you find this confusing," she said in an even voice. "I am in deadly earnest, I assure you. I want you to look at my tools."

He did, and his eyes grew very wide. She watched for some hint of the other side to break through, the Dark Daniel, but there was nothing. His eyes were somehow still gentle even in abject fear. Innocent. Lines spoken by Hitchcock's Norman Bates flashed through her head. *I think I must have one of those faces you can't help believing.*

She shuddered, but he didn't notice, his eyes fixed on her props.

"I don't have to use these very often," she told him, touching the pliers lightly, then stroking her finger along the extra-large scalpel. "They call me in when they would like to have the subject left more or less... intact." She brushed the bolt cutters on the hard syllable of the last word. "But I don't really need these tools anyway." She flicked her fingernail against the canister of the welding torch, producing a high-pitched pinging sound. "Can you guess why?"

He didn't respond, frozen in horror. He was starting to see now. Yes, this was real.

Only Dark Daniel must already have known that. So why wasn't he surfacing? Did he think she could be fooled? Or that his charm on the train had melted her weak, womanly heart?

"I'll tell you why," she said in a voice so low it was almost a whisper. She leaned in conspiratorially and held her face in a sweet, regretful half smile that didn't touch her eyes. "Because what I do hurts...*so... much...worse.*"

His eyes looked like they were going to bug out of his head. This, at least, was a familiar reaction.

She took the tray away, letting his focus move naturally to the long line of syringes left behind, glinting in the light.

"The first time will last only ten minutes," she told him, still facing away as she set the tools back on the desk. She spun around. "But it will feel like a lot longer. This will just be a taste — you could look at it as a warning shot. When it's done, we'll try talking again."

She picked up the syringe on the far end of the tray, pushed the plunger till a drop of liquid dewed at the top, then flicked it away theatrically like a nurse in a movie.

"Please?" he whispered. "Please, I don't know what this is about. I can't help you. I swear I would if I could."

"You will," she promised, and she stabbed the needle into his left triceps brachii.

The reaction was nearly instantaneous. His left arm spasmed and jerked against the restraint. While he stared in horror at his convulsing muscles, she quietly picked up another syringe and crossed to his right side. He saw her approach.

"Alex, please!" he yelled.

She ignored him and his attempt to somehow evade her, as if he were strong enough to rip free of his cuffs, and injected this dose of lactic acid into his right quad. His knee wrenched flat, the muscles pulling his foot off the table. He gasped, and then groaned.

She moved deliberately, not in any hurry, but not slowly, either. Another syringe. His left arm was already too incapacitated for him to try to resist her. This time she injected the acid into his left biceps brachii. Immediately, the opposing triceps muscle group began tearing against the biceps, battling for contraction dominance.

The air burst out of his mouth like he'd just been punched in the gut, but she knew the pain was much, much worse than any blow.

One more injection, this time into his right biceps femoris. The same ripping struggle that was happening in his arm started in his leg. And the screaming started with it.

She went to stand by his head, watching dispassionately while the tendons in his neck strained into white ropes. When he opened his mouth to scream again, she shoved a gag in. If he bit off his tongue, he wouldn't be able to tell her anything.

She walked slowly to her desk chair while his muffled shrieks were absorbed into the double layer of foam, sat down, and crossed her legs. She looked at the monitors—everything elevated but nothing in the danger zone. A healthy body could experience a lot more pain than most people would think before its important organs were really in any serious peril. She brushed the touch pad on her computer, keeping the screen brightly lit. Then she pulled her wristwatch out of her pocket and laid it across her knee. This was mostly for theatrics; she could have watched the clock on her computer or the monitors just as easily.

She faced him while she waited, her face composed and the silver watch bright against her black clothing. Subjects tended to find this disconcerting—that she could watch her handiwork so dispassionately. So she stared at him, expression polite, an audience member at a mediocre play, while his body thrashed and distorted on the table and his screams choked past the gag. Sometimes his eyes were on her, pleading and agonized, and other times they whirled crazily around the room.

Ten minutes could be a very long time. His muscles started to spasm independently of each other, some locking into knots and others seeming to want to jerk themselves off the bone. Sweat ran off his face, darkening his hair. The skin over his cheekbones looked ready to split. The screams lowered in pitch, turned hoarse, sounding more like an animal's than a man's.

Six more minutes.

And these weren't even the good drugs.

Anyone who was sick enough to want to could duplicate the pain she was inflicting now. The acid she was using wasn't a controlled substance; it was fairly easy to acquire online, even if one happened to be on the run from the dark underbelly of the U.S. government. Back in her interrogating prime, when she had her beautiful lab and her beautiful budget, her sequencer and her reactor, she'd been able to create some truly unique and ultra-specific preparations.

The Chemist really wasn't the proper code name for her at all. However, the Molecular Biologist was probably too big a mouthful. Barnaby had been the chemistry expert, and the things he'd taught her had kept her alive after she'd lost her lab; she had become her code name in the end. But in the beginning, it had been her theoretical research with monoclonal antibodies that had brought her to the department's attention. It was a shame she couldn't risk taking Daniel to the lab. This operation would have produced results much more quickly.

And she'd been *so close* to actually removing pain from the equation. That had been her Holy Grail, though no one else seemed eager for it. She was sure that if she'd been working in the lab for the past three years instead of running for her life, by now she would have created the key that would unlock whatever one needed from the human mind. No torture, no horror. Just quick answers, given pleasantly, and then an equally pleasant trip to either a cell or the execution wall.

They should have let her work.

Still four minutes to go.

She and Barnaby had discussed different strategies for dealing with these periods of the interrogation. Barnaby had told himself stories. He would remember the fairy tales from his childhood and think of modern versions or alternative endings or what would happen if the characters switched places. He'd said some of the ideas he came up with were pretty good, and when he had time he was going to write them down. She, however, felt like she was wasting time if she wasn't doing something practical. She would plan things. In the beginning, she planned new versions of the monoclonal antibody that would control brain response and block neural receptors. Later, she planned her life on the run, thinking of everything that could possibly go wrong, every worst-case scenario, and what she could do to keep herself from falling into each trap. Then how to escape the trap halfway in. Then after it was sprung. She tried to envision every possibility.

Barnaby said she needed to take a mental break now and then. Have some fun, or what was the point of living?

Just living, she had decided. Just living was all she asked. And so she put in the mental effort needed to make that possible.

Today she thought about the next step. Tonight, tomorrow night, or, heaven help him, the night after that, Daniel was going to tell her everything. Everyone broke. It was just a simple fact that a human being could resist pain for only so long. Some people could deal better with one kind or another, but that meant she would just switch to another type of pain. At some point, if he didn't talk, she would roll Daniel onto his stomach— so he wouldn't choke on his own vomit—and administer what she called the green needle, though the serum was actually clear, just like all the others. If that didn't work, she'd try one of the hallucinogens. There was always a new way to feel pain. The body had so many different ways to experience stimuli.

Once she had what she needed, she would stop his pain, put him under, and then e-mail Carston from this IP address and tell him everything she'd learned. Then she would drive away and keep going for a very long time. Maybe Carston and company wouldn't come after her. Maybe they would. And she might never know, because she would most likely keep hiding until she died—hopefully of natural causes.

Before nine minutes were over, the dose started to wear off. It was different for everyone, and Daniel was on the larger side. His screams turned to groans as his body slowly melted into a pile of exhausted flesh on the table, and then he was quiet. She removed the gag and he gasped for air. He stared at her with awed horror for one long moment, and then he started to cry.

"I'll give you a few minutes," she said. "Collect your thoughts."

She left through the exit he couldn't see, then sat quietly on the cot and listened to him choke back his sobs.

Crying was normal, and usually it boded well. But it was obvious that this crying was Daniel the Teacher. There was still no sign of Dark Daniel, not one knowing glance or defensive tic. What would reach him? If this was truly dissociative identity disorder, could she *force* an appearance of the personality she wanted? She needed an actual shrink on her team today. If she'd gone docilely into the lab as they'd wanted, they probably would have been able to find her one almost the moment she asked. Well, there was nothing she could do about it now.

She quietly ate a soft breakfast bar while she waited for his breathing to even out, and then she ate a second.

She washed it down with a box of apple juice out of the minifridge.

When she reentered the tent, Daniel was gazing despairingly at the egg-foam ceiling. She walked quietly to the computer and touched a key.

"I'm sorry you had to go through that, Daniel."

He hadn't heard her enter. He cringed as far away from the sound of her voice as he could.

"Let's not do it again, okay?" she said. She settled back into her chair. "I want to go home, too." Kind of a lie, but also mostly true, if impossible. "And, though you might not believe me, I'm not actually a sadist. I don't enjoy watching you suffer. I just don't have another choice. I'm not going to let all those people die."

His voice was raw. "I don't... know what... you're talking about."

"You'd be surprised how many people say that— and keep saying it for round after round of what you just went through, and worse! And then on the tenth round for one, on the seventeenth for another, suddenly the truth comes pouring out. And I get to tell the good guys where to find the warhead or the chemical bomb or the disease agent. And people stay alive, Daniel."

"I haven't killed anyone," he rasped.

"But you're planning to, and I'm going to change your mind."

"I would never do that."

She sighed. "This is going to take a long time, isn't it?"

"I can't tell you anything I don't know. You've got the wrong person."

"I've heard that one a lot, too," she said lightly, but it touched a nerve. If she couldn't get the other Daniel to appear, then wasn't she truly torturing the wrong person?

She made a snap decision to go off script again, though she was out of her depth when it came to mental illness.

"Daniel, do you ever have blackouts?"

A long pause. "What?"

"Have you, for example, woken up somewhere and not known how you got there? Has anyone ever told you that you did or said something that you can't remember doing or saying?"

"Um. No. Well, today. I mean, that's what you're saying, right? That I'm planning to do something awful, but I don't know what it is?"

"Have you ever been diagnosed with dissociative identity disorder?"

"No! Alex, *I'm* not the crazy person in this room."

That didn't help at all.

"Tell me about Egypt."

He turned his head toward her. His expression made the words he was thinking as clear as if he'd spoken them out loud: *Are you kidding me, lady?*

She just waited.

He sighed a pained little gasp. "Well, Egypt has one of the longest histories of any modern civilization. There is evidence that Egyptians were living along the Nile as early as the tenth millennium BC. By about 6000 BC—"

"That's hilarious, Daniel. Can we be serious now?"

"I don't know what you want! Are you testing to see if I'm really a history teacher? I can't even tell!"

She could hear the strength coming back into his voice. The nice thing about her drugs was that they wore off quickly. She could have a focused conversation between rounds. And she'd found that the subjects had a greater fear of pain when they weren't feeling any. The high-ups and deep-downs seemed to speed things along.

She touched a key on her computer.

"Tell me about your trip to Egypt."

"I have never been to Egypt."

"You didn't go there with Habitat for Humanity two years ago?"

"No. I've been in Mexico for the past three summers."

"You do know people keep track of these things, right? That your passport number is logged into a computer and there's a record of where you've gone?"

"Which is why you should know I was in Mexico!"

"Where you met Enrique de la Fuentes."

"Who?"

She blinked her eyes slowly, her face very bored.

"Hold on," he said, staring up like an explanation might be posted on the ceiling. "I know that name. It was on the news a while ago...with those DEA officers that went missing. He's a drug dealer, right?"

She held up the picture of de la Fuentes again.

"That's him?"

She nodded.

"Why do you think I know him?"

She answered slowly. "Because I also have pictures of you together. And because he's given you ten million dollars in the past three years."

His mouth dropped open and the word came out as a gasp. "Wha...ut?"

"Ten million dollars, in your name, scattered around the Cayman Islands and Swiss banks."

He stared at her for another second, and then anger suddenly twisted his face, and his voice turned harsh. "If I've got ten million dollars, then why do I live in a roach-infested walk-up studio in Columbia Heights? Why are we using the same patched volleyball uniforms that the school's had since 1973? Why do I ride the Metro while my ex-wife's new husband drives around town in a Mercedes? And why am I getting *rickets* from eating a steady diet of ramen?"

She let him vent. The desire to talk was a small step in the right direction. Unfortunately, this angry

Daniel was still the schoolteacher version, just not a very happy schoolteacher.

"Wait a minute—what do you mean you have pictures of me with the drug guy?"

She walked to her desk and pulled the appropriate photo.

"In El Minya, Egypt, with de la Fuentes," she announced as she held the photo in front of his face.

Finally, a reaction.

His head jerked back; his eyes narrowed, then opened wide. She could almost watch his thoughts move as they ran through his brain and settled in his face. He was analyzing what he was looking at and making a plan.

Still no sign of the other Daniel, but at least he seemed to recognize that other part of himself.

"Do you want to tell me about Egypt *now*, Daniel?"

Tight lips. "I've never been there. That's not me."

"I don't believe you." She sighed. "Which is really too bad, because we've got to move this party along."

The fear came back, fast and hard.

"Alex, please, I swear that isn't me. Please don't."

"This is my job, Daniel. I have to find out how to save those people."

All the reticence disappeared. "I don't want to hurt anyone. I want you to save them, too."

It was harder not to believe his sincerity now.

"That picture meant something to you."

He shook his head once, expression closing up. "It wasn't me."

She had to admit, she was more than a little fascinated. This was really something new. How she wished she had Barnaby to consult! Oh well, she was on the clock. She didn't have time for wishing. She stacked the syringes one by one onto her left palm. Eight this time.

He stared at her with terror and...sadness. He started to say something, but no sound came out. She paused with the first needle ready in her right hand.

"Daniel, if you want to say something, do it quick."

Dejected. "It won't help."

She waited another second, and he looked straight at her.

"It's just your face," he said. "It's the same as before...exactly the same."

She flinched, then pivoted and moved up the table to stand beside his head. He tried to strain away from her, but that just better exposed his sternocleidomastoid. Usually she'd save this particular muscle for later in the interrogation; it was one of the very most painful things she could do to a subject under her current limitations. But she wanted to leave quickly, so she stabbed the needle into the side of his neck and pushed the plunger down. Without really looking at him, she replaced the gag as soon as his mouth opened. Then, dropping the other syringes, she escaped the room.

CHAPTER 7

She was rusty, that was all. It *had* been three years. That's why she was feeling things. That's why this subject was affecting her. It was nothing except her having been out of the game so long. She could still get her groove back.

She entered the room once during this session to keep the computer alive but didn't stay to watch. She came back only after the dose was waning, about fifteen minutes later.

He lay there gasping again, but this time he didn't cry, though she knew the pain had been much worse than before. Blood from his chafed skin now stained all the restraints and dripped onto the table. She might need to paralyze him for the next round so his injuries didn't get any worse. That was a frightening feeling, too; it might help.

He started to shiver. She actually turned toward the

exit one millisecond before she realized that she was heading out to get him a blanket. What was wrong with her?

Focus.

"Do you have anything to say?" she asked gently when his breathing was more even.

His answer came out in exhausted, breathy gasps. "It's not me. Swear. I'm not—planning—anything. Don't know the drug guy. Wish I could help. Really, really, really—wish I could help. Really."

"Hmm. You're showing some resistance to this method, so maybe we'll try something new."

"Re...sistance?" he croaked in disbelief. "You think...I'm resist...ing?"

"Honestly, I'm a little worried about messing up your head with hallucinogens—seems like there's already enough trouble up there." She tapped her fingers against his sweaty scalp as she spoke. "Maybe we have no choice but to try old-school..." She continued to absently tap his head as she glanced at the tray of tools on her desk. "Are you squeamish?"

"Why. Is this—happening to me." Totally rhetorical, he wasn't looking for an answer to his broken whisper. She gave him one anyway.

"Because this is exactly what happens when you plan to release a lethal influenza virus in four American states, potentially killing a *million* citizens. The government takes exception to that kind of behavior. And they send me to make you talk."

His eyes focused on her, horror suddenly overtaken by shock.

"What. The. *Actual. Hell!*"

"Yes, it's horrific and appalling and evil, I know."

"Alex, really, this is nuts! I think you have a problem."

She got in his face. "My problem is that you aren't telling me where the virus is. Do you have it already? Is it with de la Fuentes still? When's the drop? Where is it?"

"This is insane. *You're* insane!"

"I'd probably enjoy life a lot more if that were true. But I'm beginning to think they sent the wrong doctor. We *need* the doctor for crazies here. I don't know how to get the other Daniel to show up!"

"Other Daniel?"

"The one I can see in these pictures!"

She whirled and grabbed a handful from the desk, jabbing the computer once angrily in passing.

"Look," she said, shoving them toward his face, peeling off one after the other and dropping them to the floor. "It's your body"—she smacked one photo against his shoulder before letting it fall—"your face, see? But not the right expression. There's someone else looking out of your eyes, Daniel, and I'm not sure if you're aware of him or not."

But there it was again, the recognition. He was aware of *something*.

"Look, for right now, I'd settle for you just telling me what you see in this picture." She held up the top photo, Other Daniel skulking in the back door of a Mexican bar.

He looked at her, torn.

"I can't...explain it...it doesn't make any sense."

"You see something I don't. What is it?"

"He..." Daniel tried to shake his head, but it barely moved, his muscles were so fatigued. "He looks like..."

"Like you."

"No," he whispered. "I mean, yes, of course he looks like me, but I can see the differences."

The way he said it. *Of course he looks like me.* The transparent honesty again, but something still withheld...

"Daniel, do you know who this is?" A real question this time, not snark, not rhetoric. She wasn't playing psychiatrist—badly—now. She felt for the first time since the interrogation started that she was actually onto something.

"It can't be," he breathed, closing his eyes less out of exhaustion and more to block out the picture, she thought. "It's impossible."

She leaned forward. "Tell me," she murmured.

He opened his eyes and stared at her searchingly. "You're sure? He's going to *kill* people?"

So natural, his use of the third person.

"Hundreds of thousands of people, Daniel," she promised, earnest as he was. She used the third person, too: "He's got access to a deadly virus and he's going to spread it for a psychopathic drug lord. He already has hotel reservations—in your name. He's doing this in three weeks."

A whisper. "I don't believe it."

"I don't want to either. This virus...it's a bad one, Daniel. It's going to kill a lot more people than a bomb. There'll be no way to control how it spreads."

"But *how* could he do this? *Why?*"

At this point, she was nearly 65 percent convinced that they were not talking about one of Daniel's multiple personalities.

"It's too late for that. All that matters now is stopping him. Who is he, Daniel? Help me save those innocent people."

A different kind of agony twisted his features. She'd seen this before. With another subject, she would know that his desire to be loyal was warring with his desire to avoid more torture. With Daniel, she rather thought the war was between loyalty and wanting to do the right thing.

In the perfect stillness of the night, as she waited for his answer, through the weak sound barrier of the foam, she clearly heard a small prop plane overhead. Very close overhead.

Daniel looked up.

Time slowed down while she analyzed.

Daniel didn't look surprised or relieved. The noise did not seem to signal rescue or attack to him. He just noticed it the way someone might notice a car alarm going off. Not relevant to himself, but distracting from the moment.

It felt like she was moving in slow motion as she jumped up and raced to the desk for the syringe she needed.

"You don't have to do that, Alex," Daniel said, resigned. "I'll tell you."

"Shh," she whispered, leaning over his head while she injected the drug—into the IV port this time. "I'm just putting you to sleep for now." She patted his cheek. "No pain, I promise."

Understanding lit his eyes as he connected the sound to her behavior. "Are we in danger?" he whispered back.

We. Huh. Another interesting pronoun choice. She'd never had a subject anything like this before.

"I don't know if *you* are," she said as his eyes drooped closed. "But I sure as hell am."

There was a heavy concussion, not immediately outside the barn but too close for her liking.

She put the gas mask securely on his face, then donned hers and screwed in the canister. This time was no drill. She glanced at her computer—she had about ten minutes left there. She wasn't sure it was enough, so she tapped the space bar. Then she jabbed a button on the little black box, and the light on the side started blinking rapidly. Almost as a reflex, she covered Daniel with the blanket again.

She shut the lights off, so the room was lit only by the white gleam of her computer screen, and exited the tent. Inside the barn, everything was black. She searched, hands out in front of her, until she found the bag beside her cot and, with years of practice guiding her, blindly put on all of her easily accessible armor. She shoved the gun into the front of her belt. She took a syringe from her bag, jabbed it into her thigh, and depressed the plunger. Ready as she could make herself, she crept into the back corner of the tent and hid where she knew the darkest shadow would be if someone came in with a flashlight. She pulled out the gun, removed the safety, and gripped it with both hands. Then she put her ear to the seam of the tent and listened, waiting for someone to open the door or a window into the barn, and die.

While she waited through the slow seconds, her mind raced through more analysis.

This wasn't a big operation coming for her. No way any extraction team or elimination team worth its salt would announce its arrival with a noisy plane. There were better ways, quieter ways. And if it was a big, SWAT-style team sent after her without any briefing, just busting their way in by sheer might, they would have come in a copter. The plane had sounded very small—a three-seater at most, but probably two-.

If a lone assassin was coming for her again, as had always been the case in the past, she didn't know what this guy thought he was doing. Why would he give himself away? The noisy plane was the move of someone who was lacking resources and in a very big hurry, someone to whom time was much more important than stealth.

Who was it? Not de la Fuentes.

First of all, a small prop plane didn't seem like a drug lord's MO. She imagined that with de la Fuentes, there would be a fleet of black SUVs and a bunch of thugs with machine guns.

Second, she had a gut feeling about this one.

No, she wasn't a lie detector. Good liars, professional liars, could fool anyone, human or machine. Her job had never been about guessing the truth from the subject's shifty eyes or tangled contradictions. Her job was breaking down the subject until there was nothing left but compliant flesh and one story. She wasn't the best because she could separate the truth from the lie; she was the best because she had a natural affinity for the capabilities of the human body and was a genius with a beaker. She knew exactly what a body could handle and exactly how to push it to that point.

So gut feelings were not her forte, and she couldn't remember the last time she'd really felt something like this.

She believed Daniel was telling the truth. That's why this exercise with Daniel had bothered her so much — because he wasn't lying. It wasn't going to be de la Fuentes coming after him. No one was coming after Daniel, because he wasn't anything more than what he said he was — an English teacher, a history teacher, a volleyball coach. Whoever was coming was coming for her.

Why now? Had the department been tracking her all day and only just discovered her? Were they trying to save Daniel's life, having realized too late that he wasn't the guy?

No way. They would have known that before they set her up. They had access to too much information to be fooled in this. The file wasn't entirely make-believe, but it *was* manipulated. They had *wanted* her to get the wrong person.

For a moment she felt a wave of nausea. She'd tortured an innocent man. She put that away quickly. Time for regret later, if she didn't die now.

The columns reversed again. Elaborate trap, not real crisis. Though she did believe the situation with de la Fuentes was genuine, she no longer believed it was quite so urgent as she'd been told. *Time* was the easiest small change to make to a file; the tight deadline was a distortion. Low stakes again—just her own life to save. And Daniel's, too, if she could.

She tried to shake the thought—it felt almost like an omen—that her stakes had somehow doubled. She didn't need the extra burden.

Maybe someone else—that brilliant and unsuspecting kid who had taken her place at the department— was working on the real terrorist now. Maybe they didn't think she still had the ability to get what they wanted. But why bring her in at all, then? Maybe the terrorist was dead, and they wanted a fall guy. Maybe they'd discovered this doppelgänger weeks ago and held him in reserve. Get the Chemist to make somebody confess to *something,* and tie a bow on a bad situation?

That wouldn't explain the visitor, though.

It had to be near five in the morning. Maybe it was just a farmer who liked to start the day early and knew the area so well that he didn't mind flying without radar through a bunch of tall trees in the pitch-black night and then enjoyed a good crash landing for the adrenaline kick...

She could hear Daniel's breath rasp through the gas mask's filter. She wondered if she had done the right thing putting him under. He was just so...exposed. Helpless. The department had already exhibited exactly how much concern they had for Daniel Beach's well-being. And she'd left him trussed and defenseless in the middle of the room, a fish in a barrel, a sitting duck. She owed him better than that. But her first reaction had been to neutralize him. It wouldn't have been safe to free him, she knew. Of course he would have attacked her, tried to exact revenge. If it came to brute strength, he'd have the advantage. And she didn't want to have to poison him or shoot him. At least this way, his death wouldn't be on her hands.

She still felt guilty, his vulnerable presence in the darkness worrying at the edges of her mind like sandpaper against cotton, pulling threads of concentration away from her.

Too late for second thoughts.

She heard the faint sound of movement outside. The barn was surrounded by bushes with stiff, rustling leaves. Someone was in them now, looking into the windows. What if he just let loose with an Uzi through the side of the barn? He obviously wasn't worried about noise.

Should she lower the table, get Daniel down in case the tent was sprayed with bullets? She had oiled the accordion base well, but she wasn't positive it wouldn't squeak.

She scuttled over to the table and cranked it lower as fast as she could. It did make some low, bass groans, but she didn't think they would carry outside the barn, especially through the foam barrier. She scooted back to her corner and listened again.

More rustling. He was at another window, on the other side of the barn. Her booby trap's wires were inconspicuous, but not invisible. Hopefully he was only looking for a target inside. Had he gone to the house first? Why hadn't he gone in?

Sounds outside another window.

Just open it, she thought to herself. *Just crawl inside.*

A sound she didn't understand—a hissing, followed by a heavy clank from above. Then a *thump, thump, thump* so loud that the barn seemed to shake. Her first thought was small explosives, and she hunkered down into a protective position automatically, but in the next second she realized it wasn't *that* loud, it was just the contrast with the silence before. There was no sound of anything breaking—no glass shattering or metal tearing. Was the reverberation enough to break the connections around the windows or door? She didn't think so.

Then she realized the thumps against the wall were moving *up,* just as they stopped. Above her.

Major hitch—he was coming through the roof.

She was on her feet in a second, one eye to the seam in the tent. It was still too dark to see anything. Above her, the sound of a welding torch. Her intruder had one, too.

All her preparation was falling apart. She glanced back once at Daniel. His gas mask was on. He would be fine. Then she darted out into the larger space of the barn, bent low with her hands stretched out in front of her to find the objects in her way, and moved as quickly as she could toward the faint moonlight filtering through the closest window. There were milking stalls to maneuver around, but she thought she remembered the clearest route. She broke into the open space between the tent and the stalls, half running, and one hand found the milking apparatus. She dodged that and reached out for the window—

Something tremendously hard and heavy threw her to the ground face-first, knocking the wind out of her and pinning her to the floor. The gun flew away into the darkness. Her head thudded resoundingly against the concrete. Bright pops of light skittered across her eyes.

Someone grabbed her wrists and pulled her arms behind her, then wrenched them higher until she guessed her shoulders were close to dislocating. A grunt escaped her lungs as the new position forced the air out. Her thumbs quickly twisted the rings on her left and right hands, exposing the barbs.

"What's this?" a man's voice said directly above her—generic American accent. He changed his grip so he was holding both her wrists in one hand. With the other, he yanked off her gas mask. "So maybe not a suicide bomber after all," he mused. "Let me guess, those hot wires aren't connected to charges, are they?"

She squirmed under him, twisting her wrists, trying to get her rings in contact with his skin.

"Stop that," he ordered. He clocked the back of her head with something hard—probably the gas mask—and her face smacked the floor. She felt her lip split, and tasted blood.

She braced for it. In such close quarters, it would probably be a blade across her carotid artery. Or a wire around her throat. She hoped for the blade. She wouldn't feel the slice as pain—not with the specially designed dextroamphetamine she had racing through her veins right now—but she'd probably feel the strangulation.

"Get up."

The weight lifted off her back and she was drawn up by her wrists. She got her feet under her as quickly as possible to take the pressure off her shoulder joints. She needed to keep her arms usable.

He stood behind her, but she could tell by where his breathing came from that he was tall. He pulled her wrists until she was on her tiptoes, struggling to maintain contact with the floor.

"Okay, shorty, now you're going to do something for me."

She didn't have the training to beat him in a fight, and she didn't have the strength to wrest herself free. She could only try to make use of the options she'd prepared.

She let her weight sag precariously against her stressed shoulders for one second as she kicked the toe of her left shoe down with enough pressure to pop the stiletto blade out of the heel (the front-facing blade was in her right shoe). Then she slashed awkwardly back toward where his legs had to be. He jumped out of the way, loosening his grip enough for her to rip free and spin around, her left hand flying out for an open-handed slap. He was too tall; she missed his face, and her barb scraped against something hard on his chest—body armor. She danced backward, away from the blow she could hear coming but could not see, her hands extended, trying to make contact with unprotected skin.

Something cut her legs out from under her. She hit the ground and rolled away, but he was on top of her at once. He grabbed her hair and bounced her face against the concrete again. Her nose popped and blood flooded her lips and chin.

He bent down to speak directly in her ear. "Playtime is over, honey."

She tried to head-butt him. The back of her head connected with something, but not a face—uneven spires, metallic...

Night-vision goggles. No wonder he'd been able to control the fight so well.

He slapped the back of her head.

If only she'd put her earrings on.

"Seriously, stop it. Look, I'm going to get off you. I can see you, and you can't see me. I've got a gun, and I will shoot you in the kneecap if you try one more stupid trick, okay?"

While he was talking, he reached back with one hand and ripped her shoes off, one after the other. He didn't check her pockets, so she still had the scalpel blades and the needles in her belt. He jumped off her. She heard him move away and click the safety off his gun.

"What do you ... want me to do?" she asked in her best frightened-little-girl voice. The split lip helped. She imagined her face was a sight. It was going to hurt like hell when the drugs wore off.

"Disarm your booby traps and open the door."

"I'll need" — sniff, sniff — "the light on."

"No problem. I'm switching my night-vision goggles for your gas mask anyway."

She dropped her head, hoping to hide her expression. Once he had the mask on, 90 percent of her defenses were rendered obsolete.

She limped — too theatrical? — to the panel by the door and turned the light on. She couldn't think of any other option right now. He hadn't killed her immediately; that meant he wasn't under direct orders from the department. He must have an agenda here. She had to figure out what it was he wanted and then keep it from him long enough to gain the advantage.

The bad news was that if he needed the door open, it was probably not just to have an easy escape route. It meant he had backup, which didn't help her odds. *Or Daniel's,* a voice in her head added. Like she needed more pressure. But Daniel was here because of her. She felt responsible for him. She owed him.

When she turned, blinking against the brilliance of the overhead lights, the man was twenty feet from where she stood. He had to be six foot three or four, and the skin on his neck and jaw was definitely white, but that was all she could be sure about. His body was covered with a black one-piece suit—almost like a wet suit, but rough, with jutting plates of Kevlar. Torso, arms, and legs all armored. He looked pretty muscular, but some of that could be the Kevlar. He wore heavy all-terrain boots, also black, and a black watch cap on his head. His face was hidden by her gas mask. Over one shoulder was slung an assault rifle— a McMillan .50-caliber sniper. She'd done her homework; it wasn't hard to become an expert on just about anything when you spent all your free time studying. Knowing gun makes and models could tell her a lot about an assailant, or any suspicious man on the street who might be planning to become an assailant. This assailant had more than one gun; a high-standard HDS was holstered on his hip, and a SIG Sauer P220 was in his right hand, pointed at her knee. *Right-handed,* she noted. She had no doubt he could hit her kneecap from this distance. Given that particular rifle, she figured, he could probably hit her wherever he wanted from however far away he wanted to.

He reminded her of Batman, but without the cape. Also, she thought she remembered something about Batman not ever using guns. Though if he did, assuming taste and skill, he would probably choose these.

If she couldn't get this assassin out of the gas mask, it wouldn't matter how many super-soldier friends were waiting for him outside. He would have no trouble killing her once he had what he wanted.

"Disarm your leads."

She feigned a brief dizzy spell as she limped over to the barn door, trying to get as much time for thinking as possible. Who would want her alive? Was he a kind of bounty hunter? Did he think he could sell her back to the department? If they'd put out a contract on her, she was sure that all they would have asked for was her head. So a blackmailer–slash–bounty hunter? *I have what you want, but I'll release it alive, back into the wild, unless you double the reward.* Smart. The department would definitely pay.

That was the best guess she could come up with by the time she was to the back edge of the door.

The system wasn't complicated. There were three sets of leads for each area of ingress. The first was outside in the bushes to the left of the barn door, hidden under a thin layer of dirt. Then there was the trigger line that ran across the seam where the door opened, connected loosely enough to pull apart with the slightest breach. The third was the safety, tucked under the wood paneling beside the door; its exposed wires were separated by an inch of space. The current was only stable if at least two of the connections were linked. She wondered if she should make the process look more convoluted than it actually was, but then decided there was no point. All he'd have to do was examine the setup for a few seconds to understand it.

She wrapped the ends of the third lead tightly together and then stood back.

"It's . . . off." She made her voice crack in the middle of the words. Hopefully he would buy that he'd knocked the fight out of her.

"If you would do the honors?" he suggested.

She gimped her way to the other side of the door and then pulled it back, her eyes already on the spot in the darkness where she assumed the dark heads of his companions would be. There was nothing but the farmhouse in the distance. And then her eyes dropped, and she froze.

"What is *that?*" she whispered.

It wasn't actually a question for him, it was just shock breaking through her façade.

"That," he answered in a tone that could only be described as obnoxiously smug, "is one hundred and twenty pounds of muscles, claws, and teeth."

He must have made some kind of signal—she didn't see it, her eyes were locked on his "backup"—because the animal darted forward to his side. It looked like a German shepherd, a very big one, but it didn't have the coloring she associated with Alsatians. This one was pure black. Could it be a wolf?

"Einstein," he said to the animal. It looked up, alert. He pointed to her, and his next word was obviously a command. "Control!"

The dog—wolf?—rushed her with its hackles rising. She backed up until the barn door was against her spine, her hands in the air. The dog braced itself, snout just inches from her stomach, its muzzle pulled back to expose long, sharp white fangs. A low, rumbling growl began deep in its throat.

Intimidate would have been a better name for the command.

She thought about trying to get one of her barbs into the dog's skin but doubted they were long enough to make it past its thick fur. And it wasn't like the thing was going to sit there and let her pet it.

The Batman wannabe relaxed a bit, or she thought he did. It was hard to be positive about what his muscles were doing under the armor.

"All right, now that we've broken the ice, let's talk."

She waited.

"Where is Daniel Beach?"

She could feel the shock on her face even as she

tried to suppress it. All her theories whirled around again and turned upside down.

"Answer me!"

She didn't know what to say. Did the department want Daniel dead first? Make sure the loose ends were all tied up neatly? She thought of Daniel, exposed and unconscious in the center of the tent—not exactly a strong hiding place—and felt sick.

Batman stalked angrily toward her. The dog reacted, moving to the side to allow the man through even as its snarl grew in volume. The man shoved the barrel of his SIG Sauer under her jaw roughly, knocking her head against the barn door.

"If he's dead," the man hissed, "you're going to wish you were, too. I'll make you *beg* me to kill you."

She almost snorted. This thug would probably hit her a few times—maybe, if he had any creativity, he would cut her up a bit—and then he'd shoot her. He had no idea how to generate and maintain real pain.

But his threats did tell her something—he apparently wanted Daniel alive. So they had that one thing in common.

Resistance was counterproductive at this point anyway. She needed him to think she was out of the game. She needed him to relax his guard. And she needed to get back to her computer.

"Daniel is in the tent." She pointed with her chin, keeping her hands raised. "He's fine."

Batman seemed to consider this for a moment.

"Okay, ladies first. Einstein," he barked. "Herd." He pointed to the tent.

The dog barked in response, and moved around to her side. It poked her thigh with its nose, then nipped her.

"Ow!" she complained, jumping away. The dog got behind her and poked her again.

"Just walk, slow and steady, to your tent thing, and he won't hurt you."

She really didn't like the dog behind her, but she kept her pace to the injured hobble she'd been faking. She glanced back at the animal to see what it was doing.

"Don't worry," Batman said, amused. "People don't taste very good. He doesn't *want* to eat you. He'll only do that if I tell him to."

She ignored the taunt and moved slowly to the curtained access point.

"Hold that open so I can see in," he instructed.

The tarp was stiff with the layers of egg foam. She rolled it back as far as she could. It was mostly black inside. Her computer screen glowed white in the darkness, the monitors dull green. Because she knew the shapes, she could make out Daniel under the blanket, just a foot off the ground, his chest rising and falling evenly.

There was a long moment of silence.

"Do you want...me to turn on...the lights?" she asked.

"Hold it there."

She felt him come up behind her and then the cold circle of the gun barrel pressing into the nape of her neck, just at her hairline.

"What's this?" he murmured.

She held perfectly still while his gloved fingers touched the skin next to the gun. At first she was confused, but then she realized he had noticed the scar there.

"Huh," he grunted, and his hand dropped. "Okay, where is the switch?"

"On the desk."

"Where is the desk?"

"About ten feet in, on the right side. Where you can see the computer screen."

Would he take off the gas mask and put on the goggles again?

The pressure of the gun disappeared. She felt him move back from her, though the dog's nose was still pressed against her butt.

A slithering noise hissed across the floor. She looked down and watched the thick black cord for the closest work light whip past her foot. She heard the bang when it fell over but no crunch of glass.

He dragged the light past her, then flipped the switch. For a fraction of a second she allowed herself to hope that he'd broken the light, but then it flickered to life.

"Control," he commanded the dog. The snarling started again, and she held herself very still.

Aiming the light in front of him, he stepped into the tent. She watched the wide beam sweep the walls, then settle on the form in the middle.

He moved into the room, sliding into a sinuous gait that was totally silent. Obviously a man of many skills. He walked around the body on the floor, checking the corners and probably looking for weapons before he focused on Daniel. He crouched, removed the blanket, examined the bloody restraints and the IV, followed the sensors to the monitors, and then watched those for a moment. He put the light down, angling it at the ceiling to get the widest spread of illumination. Finally, he reached down, carefully removed the gas mask from Daniel's face, and set it on the floor.

"Danny," she heard him whisper.

CHAPTER 8

Batman ripped the black glove off his right hand and pressed two fingers to Daniel's carotid. He bent down to listen to Daniel's breathing. She examined her attacker's hand—pale skin, fingers so long they almost looked like they had an extra joint. They looked...familiar.

Batman shook Daniel's shoulder lightly and asked, louder, "Danny?"

"He's sedated," she volunteered.

His face jerked up toward her, and though she couldn't see it, she could feel his glare. Suddenly he was on his feet, launching himself at her. He grabbed her arms and yanked them over her head again as he shoved his masked face into hers.

"What did you do to him?" he shouted.

Her concern for Daniel's safety evaporated. *Danny* was going to be just fine. The one she needed to worry about was herself.

"There is nothing wrong with him," she said calmly, dropping the injured-damsel routine. "He'll wake up from the sedation in about two hours, feeling fine. I can bring him around sooner if you want."

"Not likely," he growled.

They had a staring contest for a few seconds, one she wasn't sure if she'd won or lost. She could see only her own face in the reflective mask.

"Okay," he said. "Let's get you situated."

In a smooth move, he had her hands behind her back, wrists held tight in his gloveless right hand, probably holding the gun in his left. He marched her into the room, toward the folding chair by the desk, and she went along docilely. The dog's hot, heavy breath was close, following right behind.

She was almost 70 percent sure she could twist her hand into a position that would put the left barbed ring against his skin, but she didn't try. It was a risk, but she wanted Batman alive. There was a large hole in her picture of what was going on, and Batman would have at least some of the answers she needed. She carefully nudged the covers over the barbs again.

She didn't resist as he sat her—none too gently—in the chair. He pulled her hands in front of her and zip-tied them together.

"I feel like you're the kind of person whose hands I want to keep an eye on," he muttered as he bent down to secure her ankles to the chair legs. All the while, the dog's face was directly in front of her own, eyes unblinking. A few drips of warm drool fell onto her sleeve and soaked through. *Gross.*

He zip-tied her elbows to the chair back and stood up, towering over her now, dark and menacing. The long, silenced barrel of his HDS was just a few inches from her forehead.

"The switch for the overhead lights is right there." She jerked her chin toward the power strip on the back edge of the desk. Two standard outdoor extension cords were plugged into it.

He stared in that direction, and she imagined he was eyeing the switches warily.

"Look, anything that can kill you is going to kill me first," she pointed out.

He grunted and then leaned away and punched the power button.

The lights flared overhead.

Suddenly the tent looked less threatening. With all the medical equipment, it could have been a medic's tent in a war zone. Except for the torture implements on the tray, of course. She saw his face orient toward them now.

"Props," she explained.

She felt the glare again. He whipped a look back at Daniel, naked and clearly intact on the table. His focus swung back to her.

"What's the flashing light?" he demanded, gesturing to the little black box with the keypad.

"It's telling me the door is unarmed," she lied evenly. In fact, the box wasn't hooked up to anything. It was just a nice red herring to distract from the real trap.

He nodded, accepting that, then leaned over to look at her computer. There were no open documents, no files on the desktop. Her background was just a pale geometric design, little white squares on a faintly darker gray field.

"Where are the keys?" He jerked his head toward Daniel.

"Taped to the bottom of the desk."

He seemed to be eyeing her again through the mask.

She willed herself to look calm and compliant. *Take it off, take it off, take it off,* she prayed silently.

He kicked her chair over.

She held her neck tight as her left arm and thigh smashed into the ground with bruising force. She was just able to keep her head from hitting the concrete again. She wasn't sure if she was already concussed, and she really needed her brain working right.

He grabbed the back of the chair and yanked her upright. In his right hand he held the keys.

"That wasn't necessary," she said.

"Einstein, control."

Growling in her face, more drool on her chest.

Batman turned away and quickly unlocked Daniel's shackles.

"What's in the IV?"

"Saline in the top one, nutrients in the lower."

"Really." Sarcastic. "What happens if I pull the tubing out?"

"He'll need a drink when he wakes up. But don't use the water bottles on the left side of the minifridge outside the tent. Those are poisoned."

He turned, pulling the mask off his head so he could glare at her more effectively, yanking the sweaty watch cap off at the same time.

Yessssssssss!

She kept the relief off her face as he dropped the mask on the floor.

"You've changed your tactics," he noted sourly, running his free hand through his short, damp hair. "Or are the ones on the right really the poisoned bottles?"

She looked up at him calmly. "I thought you were someone else."

And then she really *looked* at him.

She didn't have the resources to keep her face from reacting now. All the theories spun around again, and a bunch of things fell into place.

He smirked, realizing what she was seeing.

So many clues she'd missed.

The pictures that *were* Daniel but at the same time *weren't*.

The holes in the file on Daniel's history, the missing photos.

Time, dates, *birth dates*—the easiest small changes to make if you wanted to hide something.

Daniel's strange reluctance to believe what he was seeing when he looked at the spy images.

His struggles with loyalty.

Those long, long fingers.

"Other Daniel," she whispered.

The smirk vanished. "Huh?"

She blew out a breath and rolled her eyes—she couldn't help it. It was all too much like one of her mom's ridiculous soap operas. She remembered the frustration of every holiday she and her mother had spent together, the afternoons lost to the incredibly slow-moving, implausible dramas. No one was ever really dead; everyone came back. And then there were the twins. Always with the twins.

Batman actually didn't look that much like Daniel, as far as identical twins went. Daniel's features were refined, his aspect gentle. Batman was all hard angles and tightly gripped expressions. His hazel eyes seemed darker, maybe just because his brows were pulled down, putting them in shadow. His hair had the same color and curl but was cropped close, the way she would expect in an agent. Judging from his thicker

neck, she would guess Batman had the gym muscula-
ture to Daniel's sports build. Not immensely bulky or
he wouldn't have been able to pass for his brother in
the pictures. Just harder, more defined.

"Kevin Beach," she said in a flat voice. "You're
alive."

He sat on the edge of her desk. As her eyes followed
him, she didn't let them rest for even a second on her
computer's clock right by his elbow.

"Who were you expecting?"

"There were a few options. All of whom would
want both me and your brother dead." She shook her
head. "I can't believe I fell for this."

"For what?"

"Daniel's never even met de la Fuentes, has he? It
was always you."

His face, which had begun to relax, was suddenly
guarded again. "What?"

She nodded to the photographs scattered on the
floor. He seemed to notice them for the first time. He
leaned over to examine one, then bent down to grab
it. Then the one underneath, and the next. He crumpled them in his fist.

"Where did you get these?"

"Compliments of a small department working for
the American government—entirely off the books. I
used to be in their employ. They asked me to
freelance."

His face contorted in outrage. "This is highly classified!"

"You wouldn't believe my clearance level."

Back in her face, he grabbed the front of her T-shirt and lifted her and the chair a few inches off the ground. "Who are you?"

She kept herself calm. "I'll tell you everything I know. I got played and I'm about as happy about it as you."

He set her down. She wanted to count in her head, mark the time, but she was afraid he would notice her distraction. He stood over her, arms folded.

"What's your name?"

She spoke as slowly as she thought she could get away with. "It used to be Dr. Juliana Fortis, but there's a death certificate with that name now." She watched his face to see if any of this information meant something to him; it didn't, as far as she could tell. "I operated under the direction of the department—it doesn't have another name. It doesn't exist officially. They worked with the CIA and some other black ops programs. Interrogation specialists."

He sat back down on the edge of the desk.

"Three years ago, someone decided to dissolve the department's two key assets. Namely, me and my mentor, Dr. Joseph Barnaby." Still no recognition. "I don't know why, although we had access to incredibly sensitive information, and I'm guessing something we knew was the motive. They murdered Dr. Barnaby and tried to murder me. I've been running ever since. They've found me four times. Three times they tried to have me assassinated. The last time, they apologized."

His eyes were narrowed, evaluating.

"They told me they had a problem, and they needed me. They gave me a stack of files on the de la Fuentes situation and named your brother as his collaborator. They said that in three weeks Daniel would be spreading the supervirus across the American Southwest. They told me I had three days to find out where the virus was and how to stop de la Fuentes from implementing his plan."

He was shaking his head now.

"They told you that much?" he asked in disbelief.

"Counterterrorism was always the main component of my job. I know where all the warheads and the dirty bombs are buried."

He pursed his lips, making a decision. "Well, since you already know the details, I guess it's not a huge breach of policy for me to tell you that I shut down the de la Fuentes situation six months ago. De la Fuentes's death is not common knowledge. What's left of the cartel is keeping this quiet so they don't appear vulnerable to the competition."

She was surprised at the relief she felt. The weight of knowing that so many people were doomed to painful execution had been heavier than she'd realized.

"Yes," she breathed. "That makes sense."

The department wasn't *that* cold-blooded, apparently. They'd used a nightmare catastrophe to motivate her, but they weren't messing around with civilians still in danger.

"And the Serpent?"

He looked at her blankly.

"Sorry, department nickname. The domestic terrorists?"

"My associates bagged two of the three ringleaders and took out the entire southern chapter. No survivors."

She smiled tightly.

"You're an interrogator," he said in a suddenly icy voice. "A torturer."

She lifted her chin. "Yes."

"And you tortured my brother for information he didn't have."

"Yes. The very initial phases, at least."

He backhanded her. Her head snapped to the side; the chair bobbled, and he shoved it down with one foot.

"You're going to pay for that," he promised.

She worked her jaw for a second to see if anything was broken. When she was satisfied that nothing was seriously compromised, she responded. "I'm not positive," she said, "but I think that's why they did this to him. Why they fed me this whole elaborate story."

Through his teeth. "What reason?"

"They haven't had the greatest success in killing me. I guess they thought you would get the job done."

He clenched his jaw.

"What I don't understand, though," she continued, "is why they didn't just *ask* you to do it. Or order you, I suppose. Unless... you're no longer with the CIA?" she guessed.

The gun had been the giveaway. From her research, she was pretty certain that the HDS was the gun most commonly carried by CIA agents.

"If you didn't know about me, how do you know where I work?" he demanded.

About halfway through his question, she saw the bright white rectangle in her peripheral vision go black. Trying to be inconspicuous, she sucked in the deepest breath through her nose she could manage.

"Answer me," he growled, raising his hand again.

She just stared at him, not breathing.

He hesitated, brow furrowed, then his eyes went wide. He dove for the mask on the floor.

He was out before he hit the ground.

Another thump—the dog collapsed into a puddle of fur beside her chair.

Under testing circumstances, she'd once held her breath for one minute and forty-two seconds, but she'd never been able to repeat the feat. Usually she ran out of air at about one fifteen, still way above average—lung capacity had become a priority in her life. This time, of course, she hadn't been able to hyperventilate beforehand. But she wouldn't need a full minute.

She hopped her chair over to Batman's inert form and pushed herself forward, bracing her knees against his back. With her hands secured in front of her, it was easy...ish. Kevin Beach had left Daniel's gas mask on the floor; she hooked it with one finger and then tilted the chair back until all four legs were on the ground. She leaned her face as close to her hands as she could and slipped the mask over her head, pressing the rubber rim tight to her face to create a seal. She blew out her air in a big whoosh, clearing the chamber, and then took a hesitant breath.

If some of the chemical had lingered, she figured she still would have been okay. She'd built up a decent resistance and would not have been out as long as the others. But it was especially nice to have such a big head start.

She scooted to the desk and rubbed the zip tie around her wrists against the edge of the scalpel on her props tray. It popped quickly against the pressure she was generating. It was easy work to slice the rest of the ties, and then she was free.

First things first. She reset the screen saver on

her computer to come on after fifteen minutes of inactivity.

She couldn't lift Batman, sprawled facedown on the floor beside his brother, but his arms and legs were close enough to Daniel's that she could use the restraints that had been around Daniel's left wrist and left ankle to secure Kevin's. He'd thrown the key carelessly on the table by Daniel's side; she pocketed it.

She didn't resecure Daniel. Maybe it was a mistake, but she'd already done so much to him, it just felt unfair. And underneath it all, she wasn't afraid of him. Another potential mistake.

She stripped Batman of his guns and removed the cartridges and firing pins from the rifle and the HDS. She put the safety on the SIG Sauer and tucked it into the back of her belt. She liked it — it looked more serious than her PPK. She went out to the barn stalls to find her PPK and then shoved it in beside the SIG Sauer. She was more familiar with her own. Better to keep it handy, too.

She found her shoes, stashed the other guns, and then grabbed the movers' straps on her way back into the tent. The dog was too heavy to move easily, so she wrapped the straps around it and hauled it back to the bunk room. At first she simply closed the door and walked away — dogs didn't have opposable thumbs. A moment later, though, she changed her mind. The dog's name *was* Einstein; who knew what it was capable of? She looked for something to drag in front of the door. Most of the heavy machinery was bolted down. After a few seconds of thought, she walked around to the silver sedan. It just fit between the tent and the stalls. She pulled it right up to the bunk-room door, wedged the front bumper tight against the wood, and then put it in park. She threw the parking brake on for good measure.

She closed the barn door and rearmed it. A quick look outside told her that it was almost dawn.

Back to Other Daniel. The Batsuit was a chore to remove. The fabric between the Kevlar panels was thick and ribbed with fine cables, almost like gristle. She snapped two blades on it before finally quitting at his waist. She settled for peeling back the top half and patting down his legs, which didn't have as much Kevlar to disguise them. She found a knife holstered in the small of his back and one shoved into each boot. She pulled his socks off. He was missing the pinkie toe on his left foot, but he had no other weapons that she could find. Not that he'd need any if he got his hands on her again. His whole body was roped with lean, hard bands of muscle. His back was a mess of scars—some from bullets, some blades, and one bad burn—with one more telling scar under the edge of his hairline. He'd removed his tracker, too. Definitely no longer with the CIA. A defector? A double agent?

But how had he found his brother?

She remembered the droning of the noisy prop plane, the booming thud of the improvised crash landing—someone in a hurry, she'd thought. Someone for whom time was the biggest problem.

She turned to look at Daniel; it seemed another examination was in order. She'd done a more thorough job going over his back, so she looked closely now at his stomach, groin, and thighs. Something she should have done before, but she'd misread the situation badly.

It was the idea of time—the hurried way Batman had arrived and attacked—that pointed her toward what she was looking for. An ordinary tracker would indicate only where the subject was, and Daniel wasn't really that far from home, not far enough to cause his dead brother to panic and run in guns blazing. So this tracker must monitor something more than just location, and it would have to be placed in the right spot.

She wanted to kick herself when she saw it—the little red tail of a scar sticking out from the edge of the tape she had used to secure the catheter tube against his leg. She pulled the tape now—always better to do that when the subject was still under anyway—and then removed the catheter. He'd be getting up soon.

The scar was tiny, with nothing raised under the skin. She figured the device must be more deeply implanted, next to the femoral artery, no doubt. When his blood pressure had gone crazy with the first round of interrogation, or maybe even from his fear when he'd first woken up, it must have tipped off his brother. And whoever else was monitoring him. The tracker would have to come out.

She had enough time before he woke up, so she got her first-aid kit. After snapping on some gloves, she numbed the site and sterilized the scalpel—good thing she hadn't broken all of them on the Batsuit. She scrubbed the skin with iodine, then made a quick, neat incision on top of the old one, though a bit longer. She didn't have forceps or tweezers, so she just poked around carefully with one finger on the inside and one on the outside. When she found the device— a little capsule about the size of a throat lozenge—she was able to pressure it out fairly easily.

She cleaned up the site and then superglued the edges together.

After that, she treated the raw skin on his wrists and ankles, cleaning and bandaging everything. Finally, she put the blanket over him and got him the pillow.

The capsule she left to cool on the steel table. To anyone watching the tracker on a monitor, it would appear that Daniel Beach had just died. She had a feeling that his death wouldn't bother anyone in the department. She had a better sense of the other side's plan now, and she was pretty sure it wasn't all about her.

She exited the tent to attend to her own face, first wiping off the blood and then trying to determine the extent of the damage. The lip was swollen, and the tear needed a stitch; she applied a drop of superglue. Her cheek was missing a few layers of skin and she was going to have a matched set of very pronounced black eyes. Her nose was swollen and crooked, so she took advantage of her current painless state to push it back into shape as well as she could.

The pain would return fairly soon, though she'd given herself the maximum dose of the drug she'd privately named *Survive*. It wasn't meant to work long term; it was just for making it through an attack like the one she'd just endured. Kind of like the adrenaline her body naturally generated, just much more powerful, and with some opiates to block the pain. *Survive* wasn't on the books; her list of duties had not included creating *anti*-torture concoctions, but she'd thought it might be something she'd need someday, and she'd been right. This wasn't the first time she'd used it—she'd overreacted to those earlier assassination attempts—but it *was* the first time she'd actually suffered through a decent beating with *Survive* in her system. She was pleased with its performance.

She didn't have anything to stabilize her nose with, so she would have to try to be more careful with her face for a while. Luckily she was a back sleeper.

The face was going to be a problem. A big problem.

She couldn't exactly walk into a grocery store right now and escape notice.

When she had done everything she could think of to do, she lay on the cot for ten minutes, just gathering her strength — or what was left of it. The drug still made her feel strong, but she knew she'd sustained some damage. There would be repercussions to deal with. She needed time to rest and heal — time no one was going to give her.

CHAPTER 9

She decided to wake Daniel up. Once Batman came around—which he probably would in about fifteen minutes or so—the conversation was not going to be very genteel. She wanted a chance to explain—and apologize—before the shrieking and the death threats started.

She reset the protocols on the computer.

The chemical mixture in the air had long since dispersed, so she didn't need the gas mask inside the tent anymore. She grabbed the other mask, then tucked both sets of straps through her belt, keeping them close.

She pulled Daniel's IV first. She didn't want him tethered to anything at all when he woke up. He'd had enough of that. His veins were still looking good. It was easy to inject the solution into the antecubital fossa of his other elbow. She sat on the edge of the table, lowered so that it nearly rested on the floor. She wrapped her arms around her knees and waited.

He came to slowly, blinking against the overhead lights. He raised one hand to shade his eyes, then awareness hit. He stared at his hand—free, bandaged—and then his eyes darted around the bright room.

"Alex?" he asked quietly.

"Right here."

He turned toward her gingerly, moving his legs under the blanket, checking to see if he was still bound.

"What is happening now?" he asked cautiously, his eyes still struggling to focus.

"I believe you. And I'm very sorry for what I did to you."

She watched him process that. Carefully, he raised himself up on one elbow, then clutched at the blanket, realizing again that he was naked. It was funny how nonmedical people reacted to that; physicians were fairly relaxed about nudity in general. She felt exactly the same about nudity as any other doctor, but he wouldn't assume that. She should have put on her lab coat.

"You do believe me?" he asked.

"Yes. I know you're not the person I thought you were. I was...misled."

He sat up a little farther, moving warily, waiting for something to hurt. He should feel fine, though—just tired from the muscle spasms. And his upper thigh would be a little sore when the local wore off.

"I—" he started, and then froze. *"What happened to your face?"*

"It's a long story. Can I say something before I get into it?"

His expression was full of concern. For her? No, that couldn't be right.

"Okay," he agreed hesitantly.

"Look, Daniel, what I told you before was true. I don't like hurting people. I didn't like hurting you. I only do that when I think the other option is much more horrible. I have never in my life done this before—hurt a totally innocent person. Never. Not every person I've been asked to interrogate was as depraved as the rest, but all of them were at least part of the plot. I've long since realized that my old bosses will stoop to almost anything, but I still can't believe that they set me up to interrogate someone entirely guiltless."

He thought about it for a few seconds.

"Are you asking me to forgive you?"

"No, I'm not asking for that. I would never ask for that. But I wanted you to know. I never would have hurt you if I hadn't truly believed it would save lives. I am so sorry."

"And what about the drug dealer? The virus?" he asked anxiously.

She frowned. "I've received some new information. Apparently, de la Fuentes was taken care of."

"No one is going to die?"

"Not because of a weaponized virus spread by a drug czar, no."

"So that's good, right?"

She sighed. "Yeah, I guess that's the silver lining of what happened here."

"Now will you tell me what happened to your face? Did you have an accident?" Again with the concern.

"No. My injures are related to that new information I mentioned." She wasn't sure how to break it to him.

Sudden indignation. His shoulders tensed. "Somebody *did* that to you—on purpose? For hurting me?"

His mind certainly didn't work like somcone in her line of business. Things that would be obvious to anyone who had ever worked on any facet of a mission were totally foreign to him.

"Essentially," she answered.

"Let me talk to him," he insisted. "I believe you, too. I know you didn't want to do it. You were trying to help."

"That's not really the issue. Um, Daniel, you know when I was showing you those pictures before and you recognized the person in them but you didn't want to tell me who it was?"

His face closed up. He nodded.

"You can relax. I'm not asking you to confess anything; this isn't a trick. I didn't know you had a twin. They covered that up in the file so I wouldn't—"

"No, but it wasn't Kevin," he interrupted. "That's what I didn't understand. It looked just like him, but it's impossible. Kevin is dead. He died in prison last year. I don't know who it could be unless we were actually triplets, and I think Mom might have noticed that..."

He trailed off, watching her expression change.

"What?" he asked.

"I'm not sure how to tell you this."

"Tell me what?"

She hesitated for a moment, then stood up and walked around the table. His eyes tracked her, then he sat up, bunching the blanket carefully around his waist. She stopped and looked down. His eyes followed hers.

Kevin Beach's face was turned toward the table where Daniel sat. It was curious how much more he looked like Daniel when he was unconscious, all the tension in his expression erased.

"Kevin," Daniel whispered, face going white, then flushing bright red.

"Did you know your brother worked for the CIA?" she asked quietly.

He looked up, aghast. "No, no, he was in prison.

He'd been dealing drugs." He shook his head. "Things got bad after our parents died. Kev went off the deep end. He self-destructed. I mean, after West Point—"

"*West Point?*"

"Yes," he said, face blank. Obviously the significance was lost on him. "Before the drugs, he was a different person. Graduated near the top of his class. He was accepted to Ranger school…" Daniel trailed off, assessing her frown.

Of course. Alex suppressed a sigh, upset with herself for not worrying more about the file's gaps in information, for not taking the time to find a faraway library where she could have safely searched all Daniel's family connections.

Daniel looked down at his brother again. "He's not dead now, is he?"

"Just sleeping. He'll wake up in a few minutes."

Daniel's brow furrowed. "What is he *wearing?*"

"Some kind of military armored suit, I guess. Not my specialty."

"The CIA," he whispered.

"Black ops, I would imagine. Your brother didn't self-destruct, he just switched divisions. That's why he was involved with the drug lord."

His wide eyes turned sober. "He was helping the drug lord with the virus?" he whispered.

"No. Shutting him down, actually. We're basically

on the same side, though you wouldn't know it to look at us." She nudged his supine form with her toe.

Daniel's head whipped back up to hers. "Did Kevin do that to your face?" Funny, but he sounded more upset about that than the idea that his brother was a murderous criminal.

"Yes, and I did this to him." Another nudge.

"But he's going to wake up?"

Alex nodded. She was a little conflicted about Batman waking up. It wasn't going to be pretty. And Daniel was being so nice about everything, about her. That would probably change once his brother started talking.

He smiled just a little, staring at his brother's exposed back. "So you won?"

She laughed. "Temporarily."

"He's a *lot* bigger than you are."

"I would say I was smarter, but I made some pretty huge mistakes in my security here. I think I was just luckier this time."

Daniel started to get to his feet, then paused. "Are my clothes around here anywhere?"

"Sorry, no. I thought there might be tracking devices in them. I had to cut them off you and ditch them."

He blushed again, all the way down to that small spot on his chest. He cleared his throat. "Why would someone track *me?*"

"Well, at the time, I thought the drug lord might be monitoring you. Or that you were a trap, and my department would use you to track *me*. Which is a little bit closer to the truth, actually."

He frowned. "I am so confused."

She gave him the bullet-points version as succinctly as possible. While she was talking, he got to his feet, wrapping the blanket around his waist like an oversize towel, and started pacing back and forth in front of his brother's body.

"They tried to kill you *four* times?" he asked when she was finished.

"Five now, I think," she said, looking pointedly at Batman.

"I can't believe Kevin is alive." He sighed. He folded his long legs under the blanket and settled to the floor beside his brother's head. "I can't believe he lied to me. I can't believe he let me think he was a criminal...I can't believe he let me think he *died*...I can't believe how many times I visited him—do you know how *long* it takes to drive from DC to Milwaukee?"

He stared in silence at his brother. She let him have a moment. She couldn't imagine how she would feel if Barnaby walked back into her life without warning. How did you process something like that?

"When he wakes up," Daniel murmured gently, "I'm going to punch him in the throat."

Well, that was one way to process it.

"Why did you handcuff him?" Daniel wondered.

"Because as soon as he's conscious, he's going to try to kill me."

Wide eyes again. *"What?"*

"It's not hard to understand. All he knew when he came through the roof was that someone was hurting you. He let me live only because he wasn't sure if you were really okay. For example, maybe I would have to give you an antidote or something. I'm pretty sure if I hadn't gotten the upper hand for a second, the minute you woke up, he would have shot me."

She could see Daniel didn't believe her. He shook his head, eyebrows pulling down, upset. A thatch of curls flopped onto his forehead, still a little damp with sweat. It was amazing how short a time had actually passed, but everything had changed. And she needed a new plan.

Was it safe to go back to her most recent home, the place she'd been living when Carston had contacted her? It would certainly be easiest. There was food there, and no one would have to see her face for as long as it took to look normal again. She didn't think she'd compromised the house...

But then what? How much of her nest egg had she blown through for this stupid trap? How long would she be able to keep going on what she had?

Carston knew about her online presence, so it

would be a risk to go looking for a real job on the Internet. The department didn't have to know where she was to tie her hands.

Something touched her leg and she jumped. It was just Daniel's hand.

"I didn't mean to scare you, sorry."

"Don't apologize."

"You just look so worried. Don't. I can talk to Kevin."

She smiled humorlessly. "Thanks, but I'm not worrying about Lazarus at the moment."

"You're worried about your department."

She turned away, walked to her computer, and rested her hand against the space bar. Hopefully it didn't appear deliberate.

"Yeah," she said without looking at him. "You could say that."

Out of the corner of her eye, she saw a short hitch in Kevin's breathing before it evened out again. Good thing she'd moved away. She definitely didn't want to be within reach now.

"Is there...I don't know...is there anything I can do to help?" Daniel asked seriously.

She stared at him, surprised to feel actual tears pricking her eyes.

"I don't think I deserve your help, Daniel."

He made an exasperated noise in the back of his throat.

"And, really," she continued, "you've got enough problems of your own."

It was clear he hadn't thought through the long-term implications of what had happened.

"What do you mean?"

"You're a target now, too. You've just learned a lot of things that you're not supposed to know. If you go home, if you go back to your normal life, they'll end it."

"Not...go...back?"

He was totally stunned. Pity welled up inside her. Again she remembered how far away his kind of life was from hers. He probably thought he could fix everything by hiring a lawyer or writing to his congressman.

"But Alex, I *have* to go back. My team is in the championship tournament!"

She couldn't help it. She started laughing, and the pricking tears turned into real drops. She saw his expression and waved her hand in apology.

"Sorry," she said, gasping. "It's not funny at all. I'm sorry. I think my painkillers are beginning to wear off."

He got quickly to his feet. "Do you need something? Aspirin?"

"No, I'm good. I just have to come down from the high."

He walked over and rested one hand lightly on her

arm. She felt the sting, the bruising there just beginning to grow sensitive. It was going to be a very rough day.

"Are you sure?" he asked. "Can't I get you something?"

"*Why* are you being so nice to me?"

He looked at her in surprise. "Oh. I guess I see your point."

Finally, she thought. She'd been starting to worry that maybe the drug she'd used to kidnap him—*Follow the Leader*—had some permanent neurological effects they'd missed in the trials.

"Look," she said. "After I have a little chat with Kevin, I'll get my stuff together, and then I'll give you the key so you can unlock your brother once I'm in my car."

"But where will you go? What about your injuries?"

"You're being nice again, Daniel."

"Sorry."

She laughed once more. The sound hitched on the end, like a sob.

"Seriously, though," he said, "you don't have to leave right away. You look like you could use some sleep and some medical attention."

"Not on the agenda." She eased herself into the desk chair, hoping he couldn't see just how stiff and weary she felt.

"I wish we could talk some more, Alex. I don't

know what I'm supposed to do now. If you really mean it, that I can't go back...I don't even know how to begin to think about that."

"I do mean it. And I'm sorry. But I think your brother can probably fill you in on the details. I imagine he's better at hiding than I am."

He looked at his brother—wearing half of a Batsuit—doubtfully. "You think?"

"Don't you agree, Kevin?" she asked. She was fairly sure he'd been awake for at least a few minutes.

Daniel fell to his blanketed knees next to his brother. "Kev?"

Slowly, with a sigh, Kevin turned his head to look at his brother. "Hey, Danny."

Daniel leaned in and embraced him awkwardly. Kevin patted Daniel's arm with his free hand.

"Why, Kev, why?" Daniel asked, his voice muffled in Kevin's hair.

"Trying to keep you safe, kid. Safe from people like that—" And he added several quite unflattering descriptions of her; she knew all the individual words, but the combinations were fairly unusual.

Daniel jerked away and cuffed Kevin's head.

"Don't talk like that."

"Are you kidding me? That psychopath *tortured* you."

"Not for very long. And she only did it because—"

"Are you *defending* that—" More creativity.

Daniel smacked him again. Not hard, but Kevin wasn't in a mood to play. He grabbed Daniel's hand and twisted it into an unpleasant position. He got his right knee pulled up under his body and tried to yank away from the table. The locked wheels whined against the floor as the metal slab shifted a few inches.

Her eyes widened. The table had to weigh at least four hundred pounds. She scooted her chair back.

Daniel wrestled with his free hand, trying to break his brother's hold.

"I'll gas you again if you don't let go of him," she promised Kevin. "The bad news is, the chemical I'm using does have a few negative side effects. It kills only a small percentage of your brain cells with each use, but it adds up over time."

Kevin dropped Daniel's hand, glared once at her, and then focused on his brother.

"Danny, listen to me," he hissed. "You're bigger than her. Get the keys and get me out of these—" Suddenly his face froze, went beet red, and the vessels in his forehead pulsed in time with his words. *Where is my dog?*" he shouted at her. The table squealed another inch across the floor.

"Sleeping in the back room." She had to work to keep her voice even. "It weighs less than you; the gas will take longer to wear off."

Daniel was rubbing his wrist and looking confused. "Dog?"

"If he's not one hundred percent—" Kevin threatened.

"Your dog will be fine. Now, I need to ask you a few questions."

Daniel looked up at her, wild-eyed. "What?"

She glanced at him and shook her head. "Not like that. Just a normal exchange of information." She turned back to Kevin. "Can we talk calmly for just a few minutes, please? Then I'll get out of your hair."

"In your dreams, psycho. We've got unfinished business."

She raised her eyebrows over her blooming black eyes. "Can we talk for a few minutes before I put you into a medically induced coma, then?"

"Why would I do anything for you?"

"Because your brother's safety is involved, and I can tell that's something that matters to you."

"You're the one who pulled Danny into this—"

"That's not entirely accurate. This is as much about you as it is about me, Kevin Beach."

He glowered at her. "I already don't like you, lady. You really don't want to make that feeling stronger."

"Relax, black ops. Hear me out."

Daniel's eyes were flashing back and forth like he was a spectator at a tennis match.

Kevin glared.

"The CIA thinks you're dead?" she asked.

He grunted.

"I'll take that as a yes."

"Yeah, that's a yes, you —"

Daniel backhanded the top of Kevin's head and then scooted out of the way as Kevin made a grab for him. Then Kevin refocused on her.

"And I'm going to keep it that way. I'm retired."

She nodded, considering. She opened a blank document on her computer and typed a line of random medical terms.

"What are you typing?"

"Notes. Typing helps me think." Actually, she was sure he would notice if she kept "accidentally" touching the computer to keep it awake, and she might need that trap again today.

"So what does it matter? I died. Danny shouldn't be a target anymore."

"I was a target?" Daniel asked.

Kevin propped himself up on his right elbow and leaned toward his brother. "I worked deep undercover, kid. Anyone who connected me to you would have used you as leverage. It's one of the downsides of the job. That's why I went through the whole prison charade. As long as on paper Kevin Beach was away, the bad guys wouldn't know about you. I haven't been Kevin in a long time."

"But when I visited —"

"The Agency hooked me up with the warden. When you were on your way, if I could, I'd fly in and do the meeting. If I was unavailable—"

"That's why you were in isolation. Or they said you were. Not for fighting."

"Yep."

"I can't believe you lied to my face for so many years."

"It was the only thing I could do to keep you safe."

"What about maybe picking a different job?"

She broke in when the vessels in Kevin's head started to swell again. "Um, could we put the reunion drama on hold for the moment? I think I've got it pieced together. Listen, please. And you'll tell me if I'm wrong, I'm sure."

Two nearly identical faces regarded her with nearly opposite expressions.

"Okay," she continued. "So, Kevin, you faked your death—after the de la Fuentes job, right?" Kevin didn't respond in any way, so she went on. "That was six months ago, you said. I can only conclude that the Agency was concerned about the lack of a body—"

"Oh, there was a body."

"Then they were concerned about the inconsistencies with that body," she snapped. "And they thought of a plan to draw you out, just in case."

He frowned. He knew his former bosses, just like she knew hers.

"Daniel's your weak spot—like you said, their leverage against you. They know this. They decide to take him, see what happens. But they know what you're capable of, and no one wants to be the one left holding the bag if you do turn up alive."

"But—" Kevin started to say. He stopped himself, probably realizing whatever argument he'd been about to make wouldn't hold up.

"You're a problem for the CIA. I'm a problem for my department. At the top, the people involved in both our former workplaces are pretty tight. So they offer me a deal: 'Do a job for us, and we'll call off the hunt.' They must have had it worked out pretty solidly before they contacted me. Fixed the files, got ready to feed me the crisis story I can't turn my back on. None of them make a move on me because they've already sacrificed three assets trying and they don't want any more losses. They knew I'd come in prepared for anything like that. But, if you were *really* good, maybe I wouldn't be prepared enough for you."

Kevin's face had changed while she was working it out. "And either way," he concluded, "one problem gets solved."

"It's elaborate. Sounds more like your agency than mine, if I had to guess."

"Yeah, it does sound like them, actually," he agreed grudgingly.

"So they put us together like two scorpions in a

jar and shake it up," she said. "One way or another, they get a win on the books. Maybe, if they're really, really lucky, we take each other out. Or at least weaken the winner. No chance of any losses on their side."

And they *had* weakened her—reduced her assets and damaged her physically. A partial success for them.

"And it doesn't bother them that my brother is also stuck in the jar," he said furiously. "Only he's an ant, not a scorpion. They just throw him into the mix, don't even care that he's completely defenseless."

"Hey," Daniel protested.

"No offense, Danny, but you're about as dangerous as hand-knitted socks."

Daniel opened his mouth to respond, but a loud whine from the bunk room interrupted. The whine was quickly followed by angry snarls and a few sharp barks, then a strident clawing at the wooden door.

She was glad she'd gone the extra mile in securing the wolf.

"He's upset," Kevin accused.

"The dog is fine. There's a toilet back there, it won't even get dehydrated."

Kevin just raised his eyebrows, not as concerned about the animal as she would have expected. The clawing and snarling didn't let up.

"You really brought a dog?" Daniel asked.

"More of a partner." He looked at her. "Well, what now? Their plan failed."

"Narrowly."

He grinned. "We could go another round."

"As much as I would dearly love to inject a few things into *your* system, I'd rather not give them the satisfaction."

"Fair enough."

The dog was scratching and growling in an unbroken stream through all of this. It was getting on her nerves.

"I do have a plan."

Kevin rolled his eyes. "I bet you always have a plan, don't you, shorty?"

She regarded him with flat eyes. "I can't rely on muscle, so I rely on brains. It appears you have the opposite problem."

He laughed derisively.

"Um, Kev," Daniel interjected. "I'd like to point out that you *are* chained up on the floor."

"Shut up, Danny."

"Please, boys, if I could get one more second of your time?" She waited till they looked at her. "Here's the plan: I write an e-mail to my ex-boss. I tell him I got the truth, the real truth, and both of you are out of the picture. I really don't appreciate the manipulation. If he tries to contact me in any way again, I'm making a personal visit to his kitchen pantry."

"You claim the win?" Kevin asked in a disbelieving voice. "Please!"

"Chained on the floor," Daniel murmured under his breath.

"It's a gift," she snapped back. "You get to be dead again. No one is looking for either of you."

Kevin's cynical expression dissolved. For a second, the twin thing was a lot more evident.

The sound of the dog was like a howling wood chipper in the next room. She hadn't really planned to stick around for her security deposit, but it clearly was not an option now.

"Why would you do that for us?" Kevin asked.

"I'm doing it for Daniel. I owe him. I should have been smarter. I shouldn't have taken the bait."

It was all so completely obvious now: How easily she'd slipped through their surveillance—because there hadn't been any. How simple it had been to snatch Daniel—because no one was trying to stop her. The heavy-handed way they'd given her a deadline with plenty of time for her to act. It was embarrassing.

"Then what happens to you?" Daniel asked quietly. She almost had to read his lips over the noise of the dog.

"I haven't decided yet."

She had learned a few things from this exercise in gullibility, maybe things they didn't want her to know.

There weren't going to be any helicopters or elimi-nation teams. Carston—the one name she could be absolutely certain of at this point—and whoever else wanted her dead had sent only the occasional lone assassin because that was all they had. Her enemies had been driven to this wild collaboration, and she knew it wasn't because the department didn't have the resources. It could only be because she wasn't common knowledge. And Carston—and whoever his confederates were—couldn't afford to have her become so.

She'd assumed, when she'd seen the obituary for Juliana Fortis and read about the cremation, that everyone involved was in on the scam. But what if it was just a few key people? What if Carston had prom-ised his superiors that the job would be done and then was afraid to admit he'd missed on the first swat?

Or—revolutionary idea—what if most people at the department thought it *was* a lab accident? That she and Barnaby had mixed the wrong test tubes and punched out together? What if Carston's superiors *hadn't* wanted her dead? What if only those few key individuals had wanted that, and now they had to keep their attempts to finish the job under the radar? That would change everything.

It played. It fit with the facts.

It made her feel stronger.

The ones who had arranged her death had been

afraid of what she knew, but they had never been afraid of *her*. Maybe it was time for that to change.

There was a sudden earsplitting noise—an explosive fragmenting of wood. And then the enraged snarling got a lot closer.

CHAPTER 10

It took her one second to realize what had happened, and by that time the rabid wolf was bounding into the tent.

There was still a little bit of extra adrenaline in her system, apparently. She was on top of the desk before the animal was all the way inside, and her nervous system, not satisfied with that distance, launched her toward the PVC framework overhead before she had time to realize what she was doing. She caught hold with both hands, flipped her legs up and crossed her ankles around the pipe, then wrapped her elbows tightly around as well. She turned her head to the side to see that the creature was right below her, big paws on the desk as it strained to get its teeth into her. One paw mashed down on the keyboard, which was too bad. A little gassing would help a lot right now, and she already had both masks.

The dog snarled and slavered under her while she tried to maintain her hold. She'd used the heavy-duty five-inch-diameter, class 200 pipe, but it was still shaking from her sudden attachment to it. She was sure it would bear her weight...unless someone attacked the base. Hopefully Kevin wouldn't think of that.

Kevin started laughing. She could imagine how she looked.

"Who's chained to the floor now?" he asked.

"Still you," Daniel muttered.

At the sound of his master's voice, the dog gave a little whine and looked around. It dropped off the desk and went to examine Kevin, with one parting growl in her direction. Kevin patted its face while the dog leaned down to lick him, still whining anxiously.

"I'm okay, buddy. I'm good."

"He looks just like Einstein," Daniel said, wonder in his tone. The dog looked up, on guard at the sound of a new voice.

Kevin patted Daniel's foot. "Good boy, he's cool. He's cool." It sounded like another command.

And sure enough, dropping the whine, the huge beast went to Daniel with its tail wagging furiously. Daniel stroked the gigantic head like that was the most natural thing in the world.

"That's Einstein the Third," Kevin explained.

Daniel scratched his fingers through the thick coat appreciatively. "He's beautiful."

Her arms were getting tired. She tried to readjust while still watching, and the dog bounded right back to the desk, snarling again.

"Any hope of your calling the dog off?" she asked, trying to keep her voice composed.

"Possibly. If you throw me the keys."

"And if I give you the keys, you won't kill me?"

"I already said I'd call the dog off. Don't get greedy."

"I think I'll just stay up here, then, until the gas knocks you all out. Daniel's probably got enough brain cells to spare."

"See, I think I'll be okay. Because even though Einstein can't reach you, Daniel *can*. And if the gas hits you after he relieves you of those masks...well, the unconscious fall to the floor won't kill you, obviously, but it won't do you any favors."

"Why would I do that?" Daniel asked.

"What?" Kevin demanded.

"She's on our side, Kev."

"Whoa there. Are you insane? There are two very different sides here, kid. Your brother is on one, and the sadist who tortured you is on the other. Which side are you on?"

"The side of reason, I guess."

"Good," Kevin grunted.

"Um, that's not your side, Kev."

"*What?*"

"Calm down. Listen, let me broker a truce here."

"I can't believe you aren't reaching up there to throttle her yourself."

"She was only doing what you would have done in her place. Be honest—if you knew some stranger was going to kill millions of people and you needed to find out how to stop him, what would you do?"

"Find another solution. Like I *did*. Listen to me, Danny—you're out of your league here. I know people like her. They're sick. They get some twisted high off other people's pain. They're like venomous snakes; you can't turn your back on them."

"She isn't like that. And what's the big deal to you, anyway? *I'm* the one who got tortured. What do you even know about that?"

Kevin just stared at him, deadpan, for one moment, then pointed with his secured left hand to his secured left foot. He wiggled his four toes.

It took a few seconds for comprehension to hit, and then Daniel sucked in a horrified gasp.

"Amateurs," she scoffed from the ceiling.

"I don't know," Kevin said coolly. "They seemed pretty good to me."

"Did they get what they were after?"

He made a disbelieving noise in the back of his throat. "Are you kidding?"

She raised one eyebrow. "Like I said."

"And you could have made me talk?"

Her lips pulled into a bleak smile. "Oh, *yes*."

Out of the corner of her eye, she saw Daniel shudder convulsively.

The dog was quiet now but still alert underneath her. It seemed unsure of the situation, with its master talking so calmly to its target.

"Hey, I know who you are," Kevin said suddenly. "Yeah, the girl. I heard rumors about you. Exaggerations. They said you'd never had a miss. You were batting a thousand."

"Not an exaggeration."

His expression was skeptical. "You worked with the old guy, the Mad Scientist, they called him. The Agency called you the Oleander. Honestly, I didn't put it together at first because I heard you both died in some lab accident. And also, I always imagined the Oleander was pretty."

Daniel started to say something, but she interrupted.

"Oleander? That's just awful."

"Huh?"

"A flower?" she growled to herself. "That's so *passive*. A poison doesn't do the poisoning, it's just an inert agent."

"What did your unit call you?"

"The Chemist. And Dr. Barnaby was not a mad scientist. He was a genius."

"Tomato, tomahto," Kevin said.

"Back to the truce I was speaking of," Daniel interjected. The way he looked at her hands and arms, she thought he might have guessed how much they were hurting her. "Alex will give me the keys, and Kevin, you will call off Einstein. When I think everything is under control, I'll let you out. Alex, do you trust me?"

He looked up at her with his wide, clear hazel eyes while Kevin spluttered in inarticulate fury.

"The keys are in the left front pocket of my jeans. I'd hand them to you, but if I loosen my hands, I'll fall."

"Be careful, she'll stab you!"

Daniel didn't even seem to have heard his brother's warning. When he climbed onto the chair, his head was actually higher up than hers. He had to stoop, his head pressed against the foam roof. He put one hand under her back, supporting some of her weight, while he fished gently in her pocket for the key.

"I'm sorry my brother is so socially inept," he whispered. "He's always been that way."

"Don't you apologize for me, you moron!" Kevin yelled.

Daniel smiled at her, then took the key and stepped down. She was actually in agreement with Kevin. How could Daniel be like this with her? Where was the totally natural resentment? Where was the human desire for retribution?

"I've got the keys, Kev. Do you have a lead for the dog?"

"A *lead?* Einstein doesn't need a leash!"

"What's your suggestion, then?"

Kevin glared at him balefully. "Fine. I'd rather kill her myself anyway." He whistled at the dog. "At ease, Einstein."

The dog, who had followed Daniel anxiously as he approached Alex, now went calmly to its master's head and sat down, his tongue lolling out in what appeared to be a smile. A very toothy smile.

"Let me out."

"Ladies first." Daniel climbed up on the chair again and offered her his hand. "Need some help?"

"Er, I think I've got it." She dropped her legs toward the desk, her arms extending as she tried to touch down with her toes. How had she gotten up here? Her tired hands started to slip.

"Here you go." Daniel caught her by the waist as she fell and set her carefully on her feet, one on the desk, the other with a clang in the middle of the prop tray. His blanket skirt loosened; he quickly grabbed the fabric and tightened it.

"I can't believe this," Kevin muttered.

Alex stood cautiously, watching the dog.

"If he tries anything," Daniel murmured to her, "I'll distract him. Dogs love me."

"Einstein isn't stupid," Kevin growled.

"Let's not find out. Now your turn." He climbed down from the chair and crouched beside Kevin.

Alex slithered off the desk as quietly as she could, one hand reaching out for the keyboard. The dog didn't respond; it was watching Daniel release its master. She opened the system preferences. Screen saver wasn't the only way to release the sleeping gas, and she still had both masks.

But she knew that would just make things difficult. She would have to trust that Daniel could handle Kevin for now. She eased herself into the chair.

Daniel had started with the ankle and it was going slowly — he was keeping one hand on his blanket.

"Just give it to me, I'll do it," Kevin said.

"Be patient."

Kevin huffed loudly.

The key turned and Kevin was immediately on his feet, crouching beside his tethered arm. He snatched the key from Daniel's hand and had his wrist free in less than a second. He stood tall, stretching his neck and rolling his back muscles. The torso pieces of his Batsuit hung down like an avant-garde skirt. The dog kept still at his feet. Kevin turned to Alex.

"Where are my guns?"

"Backseat of the car."

Kevin stalked out of the tent without another word, the dog at his heels.

"Don't open any doors or windows!" she called after him. "Everything's armed again."

"Is the car booby-trapped?" he called back.

"No."

A second later. "Where are the magazines? Hey, where are the firing pins?!"

"Pins in the fridge, bullets in the toilet."

"Oh, come on!"

"Sorry."

"I want my SIG Sauer back."

She frowned and didn't answer. She got up stiffly. She might as well disarm the traps. It was time to go.

Daniel was standing in the middle of the tent, staring down at the silver table; he had one hand wrapped around the IV pole as if for support. He seemed to be in a daze. She went hesitantly to stand beside him.

"Are you going to be okay?" she asked.

"I have no idea. I can't understand what I'm supposed to do next."

"Your brother will have a plan. He's been living somewhere, he'll have a place for you."

He looked down at her. "Is it hard?"

"What?"

"Running? Hiding?"

She opened her mouth to say something soothing, then thought better of it. "Yeah, it's pretty hard. You get used to it. The worst part is the loneliness, and you won't have to deal with that. So that's one minor plus." She kept to herself the thought that loneliness might be a better companion than Kevin Beach.

"Are *you* lonely a lot?"

She tried to laugh it off. "Only when I'm not scared. So, no, not too often."

"Have you decided yet what you're going to do next?"

"No...The face is a problem. I can't walk around like this. People will remember me, and that's not safe. I'll have to hide somewhere until the swelling goes down and the bruises fade enough to cover with makeup."

"*Where* do you hide? I don't understand how this works."

"I may have to camp out for a while. I've got a bunch of subsistence food and plenty of water—by the way, don't drink the water in the fridge without checking with me first, the left side is poisoned. Anyway, I may just find someplace remote and sleep in the car until I've recuperated enough."

He blinked a couple of times, probably thrown by the poison thing.

"Maybe we can do something about *your* problem with conspicuousness," she said more lightly, touching his blanket with one finger. "I think there might be some clothes up at the house. I doubt they'll fit you, but they're better than what you've got."

A wave of relief passed over his face. "I know it's a small thing, but I think that would actually help quite a bit."

"Okay. Let me go turn off the lethal-gas trap."

· · ·

IN THE END, she did surrender the SIG Sauer, although with some regret. She liked its weight. She'd have to find her own.

The farmhouse owners' belongings were stashed in the attic, in a set of dressers from six or seven decades back. The man was obviously a lot shorter and wider than Daniel. She left Daniel to sort that out while she went back to the barn to pack up the car.

Kevin was there when she entered, tightly rolling a big swath of black fabric into a manageable armload; it took her a moment to realize the fabric was a parachute. She kept her distance as he worked, but the truce felt solid. For some reason, Daniel had put himself between her and his brother's animosity. Neither she nor Kevin understood *why* he was doing it, but Kevin cared too much about Daniel to violate his trust today. Not when he was still reeling over years of lies.

Or that's what she told herself to muster up the courage needed to walk past the dog to her car.

She was an old hand at packing, and it didn't take her very long. When she'd come out to meet Carston, she'd stowed her things and dismantled the security at the rental house, just in case she didn't make it back. (One of her nightmares was that the department would get her while she was out, and then some innocent, unsuspecting landlord would enter the premises and die.) She'd stashed everything outside DC, then come back for it when she'd started setting up for Project Interrogate the Schoolteacher. Now she fitted it all into the worn black duffels—the pressurized canisters, the miles of lead wires, the battery packs, the rubber-encased vials of components, the syringes, the goggles, the heavy gloves, her pillow, and her sleeping bag. She packed her props and some of the new things she'd picked up. The restraints were a good find, and the cot was decently comfortable and folded down into a small rectangle. She put her computer in its case, grabbed the little black box that was just a red herring, like her locket, pulled down the long cables, and rolled up the extension cords. She was going to have to leave the lights, which was a bummer. They hadn't been cheap. She dismantled the tent, leaving just a pile of meaningless foam and PVC pipe, and shoved the table back to where she'd found it. There wasn't anything to do about the holes she'd drilled.

She could only hope that she'd obfuscated things enough that the owners would only be confused and angry at the destruction rather than suspicious that something nefarious had happened here. There was a chance they'd report their destructive tenant to the authorities, but local police wouldn't be able to construe anything from the mess either. As long as certain words didn't go into the report, there was no reason for anyone in the government to notice. She was sure there were Airbnb stories of destruction much more interesting than this one.

She shook her head at the door to the bunk room. The dog had chewed or clawed a hole two feet high and a foot wide right through the center of the solid wood door. At least it had only jumped over the car rather than eating it on its way out.

She was finished loading the trunk when Daniel came back in.

"Nice capris," Kevin commented, winding the cable of his grappling hook into a neat coil. Alex wondered if he'd climbed back up onto the roof to retrieve it and, if he had, how she'd missed that.

It was true that Daniel's pants made it only half-way down his shins. The cotton shirt was a few sizes wide, and the sleeves were probably too short as well — he had them rolled to the elbows.

"If only I had half a wet suit." Daniel sighed. "Then I would feel ready to face the world."

Kevin grunted. "I'd have a whole wet suit if the psycho wasn't such a perv."

"Don't flatter yourself, I was looking for weapons."

Daniel watched her close the trunk.

"Are you leaving?"

"Yes. I need to get somewhere safe so I can sleep." She imagined she looked haggard enough that the explanation was a little redundant.

"I was thinking…" Daniel said, and then hesitated.

Kevin looked up from his rifle, alerted by Daniel's tone.

"What were you thinking?" Kevin asked suspiciously.

"Well, I was thinking about the scorpions in the jar. Alex said there were only two outcomes—one kills the other, or both die. And I imagine that the people who wanted to kill you thought the same thing."

"So?" Kevin said.

"So, there was a third option," she said, guessing the direction Daniel was headed. "The scorpions walk away. They won't be expecting that. That's what will make you safe, Daniel."

"But there's a fourth option, too," Daniel answered. "That's what I've been thinking about."

Kevin cocked his head. He clearly didn't get it. She did, just before Daniel said the words out loud.

"What if the scorpions joined forces?"

She pursed her lips, then relaxed them when that pulled at the split.

Kevin groaned. "Stop messing around, Danny."

"I'm serious. They'd never expect that. And then we're twice as safe, because we've got both dangerous creatures on the same team."

"Not happening."

She walked closer to him. "It's a clever idea, Daniel, but I think some of the personnel issues might be too big to overcome."

"Kev's not so bad. You'll get used to him."

"*I'm* not bad?" Kevin snorted, peering through his sights.

Daniel looked straight at her. "You're thinking about going back, aren't you? What you said about visiting the pantry."

Insightful for a civilian.

"I'm considering it."

Kevin was giving them his full attention now. "Counterstrike?"

"It might work," she said. "There's a pattern . . . and after looking at it, I think that maybe not so many people know about me. That's why they're going to such lengths to have a fifty-fifty chance at taking me out. I think I'm a secret, so if I can get rid of the people in on that secret . . . well, then nobody's looking for me anymore."

"Does that hold true for me?" Kevin wanted to know. "If they're relying on this to get to me, do you think I might be a secret, too?"

"It's logical."

"How will you know who's in on it?"

"If I could be in DC when I send my little note to Carston, I could watch to see who he goes running to. If it's really a secret, they won't be able to do it in the office."

"They'll know you're close — the IP will give you away."

"Maybe we could work together in a limited way.

One of you could send the e-mail for me from a distance."

"What's your experience in surveillance?" Kevin demanded abruptly.

"Er...I've had a lot of practice in the last few years—"

"Do you have any *formal* training?"

"I'm a scientist, not a field agent."

He nodded. "I'll do it."

She shook her head. "You're dead again, remember? You and Daniel get to disappear now. Don't look a gift horse in the mouth."

"That's a stupid saying. If the Trojans *had* looked in the horse's mouth, they might have won that war."

"Forget the saying. I'm trying to make things up to Daniel."

Daniel was quietly watching the back-and-forth again.

"Look, Oleander, I *have* had training. A lot. *No one* is going to catch me watching and I will see more than you will. I have a place to stash Daniel where he'll be totally safe, so that's not an issue. And if you're right, and this Carston guy goes running to his coconspirators, he'll show me who in the Agency thought this up. I'll see who put Danny in danger to get to me. Then I can clean up my problem and you can clean up yours."

She thought it through, trying to be objective. It

was hard to keep her dislike for Daniel's brother from coloring her analysis. That dislike wasn't fair. Wouldn't she have felt the same way as Kevin if it were her sibling shackled to a table? Done the same things, insofar as she was capable?

But she still really wished she could inject him with something agonizing, just once.

"First of all, don't call me Oleander," she said.

He smirked.

"Second, I see what you're saying. But how do we coordinate? I've got to go under for a while." She pointed to her face.

"You owe her for that," Daniel said. "If you have a safe place for me, maybe she should go there, too. At least until her injuries have healed."

"I don't owe her anything—except maybe another punch in the face," Kevin growled. Daniel bridled and took a step toward his brother; Kevin held up his hands in an *I surrender* motion and sighed. "But we're going to want to move quick, so that might be the easiest arrangement. Besides, then she can give us a ride. The plane's a loss—I had to bail out on the way down. I had us hiking out of here."

Daniel opened his eyes wide in disbelief. Kevin laughed at his expression, then turned to her with a smile. He looked at the dog, then back to her, and his smile got bigger. "I think I might enjoy having you at the ranch, Oleander."

She gritted her teeth. If Kevin had a safe house, that would solve a lot of her problems. And she could spike his food with a violent laxative before she left.

"Her name is Alex," Daniel corrected. "I mean, I know it's not, but that's what she goes by." He looked at her. "Alex is okay, right?"

"It's as good as any other name. I'll stick with it for now." She looked at Kevin. "You and the dog are in the back."

CHAPTER 11

Once upon a time, when she was a young girl named Juliana, Alex used to fantasize about family road trips.

She and her mother had always flown on the few vacations they took—if duty visits to ancient grandparents in Little Rock actually qualified as *vacations*. Her mother, Judy, didn't like to drive long distances; it made her nervous. Judy had often said that far more people were killed in car accidents than in plane crashes, though she was a white-knuckle flyer, too. Juliana had grown up unfazed by the dangers associated with travel, or germs, or rodents, or tight spaces, or any of the many other things that upset Judy. By default, she had to be the levelheaded one.

Like most only children, Juliana thought siblings would be the cure to the loneliness of her long afternoons doing homework at the kitchen table while she waited for Judy to get home from the dentist's office she managed. Juliana looked forward to college and dormitories and roommates as a dream of companionship. Except, when she got there, she found that her life of relative solitude and adult responsibility had rendered her unsuited to cohabitation with normal eighteen-year-olds. So the sibling fantasy took a beating, and by her junior year she had her own small studio apartment.

The fantasy about a big, warm family road trip, however, had survived. Until today.

To be fair, she would probably have been in a better mood if her entire body hadn't felt like one huge, throbbing bruise. Also, she *had* instigated the first argument, though quite unintentionally.

When she drove across the county line, she'd rolled the window down and tossed out the small tracker she'd removed from Daniel's leg. She hadn't wanted to carry it with her for long, just in case, but she also didn't want to leave it right in the middle of her last base of operations. She thought she'd removed most of the evidence, but one could never be sure. Whenever she could muddy the trail, she took the time to do so.

In the rearview mirror, she saw Kevin sit forward.

He'd been able to retrieve a backpack he'd thrown from the plane when he jumped; now he and Daniel looked fairly normal in jeans and long-sleeved

T-shirts — one black, one gray — and Kevin had two new handguns.

"What was that?" Kevin asked.

"Daniel's tracker."

"What?" Kevin and Daniel said together.

They spoke over each other.

"I *did* have a tracker?" Daniel asked.

"What did you do that for?" Kevin demanded.

The dog looked up at Kevin's tone but then seemed to decide everything was fine and stuck his face out the window again.

She turned to Daniel first, looking up at him from under the ball cap that was supposed to be keeping her mangled face in shadow. "How did you think your brother found you?"

"He tracked me? But . . . where was it?"

"Sore spot on your inner right thigh. Keep the incision clean, try not to let it get infected."

"Do you know what a pain it was to get that in place?" Kevin grumbled.

"If you can track it, so can someone else. I didn't want to take chances with our position."

Daniel turned around in the passenger seat to stare at his brother. "How did you . . . How could I not know about this?"

"Do you remember, about two years after the tramp left you, a hot leggy blonde at that bar you go to when you're depressed, what's it called . . ."

"Lou's. How do you even know about that? I never told you...wait, did you have me *followed?*"

"I was worried about you after the tramp—"

"Her name is Lainey."

"Whatever. I never liked her for you."

"When did you ever like a girl for me? As far as I can recall, you only ever liked girls who wanted you. You took it as an insult if someone preferred me."

"The point is, you weren't yourself. But having you followed was unrelated to the—"

"*Who* followed me?"

"It was just for a few months."

"Who?"

"Some buddies of mine—not in the Agency. A few cops I had a relationship with, a PI for a little while."

"What were they looking for?"

"Just making sure you were okay, that you weren't going to jump off a bridge or anything."

"I can't believe you. Of all the—wait a minute. The blonde? You mean that girl, what was her name, Kate? The one who bought me a drink and...she was a spy?"

She saw Kevin grinning in the rearview mirror.

"No, she was actually a hooker. Kate isn't her real name."

"Apparently no one on the entire planet besides me uses his or her real name. I am living in a world of lies. I don't even know Alex's given name."

"Juliana," she said at the same time Kevin did. They cast irritated looks at each other.

"*He* knew?" Daniel asked her, offended.

"It came up while you were unconscious. It's the name I was given at birth, but it's really not me anymore. It doesn't mean much to me. I'm Alex for now."

Daniel frowned, not entirely mollified.

"Anyway," Kevin went on in the tone of someone who was telling a joke he really enjoyed, "the blonde was supposed to get you back to your place, but you told her that your divorce wasn't finalized yet and it *didn't feel right*." Kevin laughed raucously. "I couldn't believe it when I heard. But it was so *you*. I don't even know why I was surprised."

"Hilarious. But I don't see how that little exchange got a tracking device into my leg."

"It didn't. I just really like that story. Anyway, that's what was such a pain. The hooker was easy to set up. And if you'd taken her home, having the tracker placed would have been enjoyable for you, at least. Getting you into your GP's office was a lot more work. But eventually I got a temp in the front office to call you in for checkup. When you got there, you saw one of the new partners. A guy you'd never seen before."

Daniel's mouth popped open in disbelief. "He told me *I had a tumor!*"

"A *benign* tumor. Which he took out right there in the office with a local anesthetic and immediately assured you was nothing. He didn't even charge you. Don't make it into a bigger thing than it was."

"Are you serious? How could you—" Daniel was shouting at full volume now. "How do you *justify* these things to yourself? All these years you've been manipulating me! Treating me like some laboratory animal who exists for your own amusement!"

"Hardly, Danny. I've been putting myself out trying to keep you safe. The Agency wanted me to play dead from the very start, but I couldn't do that to you, not after Mom and Dad. So I made a lot of promises and spent all my free weekends flying to Milwaukee to be a criminal."

Daniel's voice was calmer when he answered. "I *drove*. And was all that really necessary?"

"Ask the poison girl. These kinds of jobs aren't for family people."

Daniel looked at her. "Is that true?"

"Yes. They like to recruit orphans—preferably only children. Like your brother told you before, relationships give the bad guys leverage."

His tone mellowed further. "Are you an orphan?"

"I'm not sure. Never met my father. He could still be alive somewhere."

"But your mother..."

"Uterine cancer. I was nineteen."

"I'm sorry."

She nodded.

There was a brief, very pleasurable moment of silence. Alex held her breath and prayed for it to last.

"When I did finally let you think I was dead..." Kevin began.

Alex turned the radio on and started searching through stations. Kevin did not get the hint. Daniel just stared through the windshield.

"...I was just starting with Enrique de la Fuentes. I could tell in the first few days that it was going to get out of hand. I knew what he'd done to the families of his enemies. It was time to set you free."

"Free yourself from the visitation charade, you mean," Daniel muttered.

Alex found a classical station and turned it up so she could hear it over Kevin's voice.

"That's when I put the tracker in. I needed to know you were okay. No one was watching you anymore, just me."

Daniel grunted in disbelief.

The music's volume was making Alex's head hurt more. She turned it down again.

"It ended...badly with the Agency. The plan was to wait until things died down and I was forgotten, then get the face fixed. Eventually, I was coming back for you, kid. You wouldn't have recognized me at first, but I wasn't going to leave you thinking you were alone your whole life."

Daniel stared straight ahead. She wondered if he

believed what his brother was saying. He was staggering under the weight of so many different kinds of betrayal.

"What happened with the Agency?" Alex asked. She really didn't want to get involved with this conversation, but it didn't look like Daniel was going to pursue it. Before joining this unlikely alliance, it hadn't mattered much to her one way or the other how Kevin had left the CIA. Now this information was important. It affected her, too.

"When the job with the virus was done, and de la Fuentes was out of the picture, the Agency wanted to pull me back in, but there were still some loose ends that bugged me. I wanted to nail it all down. It wouldn't have taken too much longer and I was in a very unique position of power with the cartel. It was also a good opportunity to influence what happened there—who took over, what their agenda might be— while also getting solid information on the new structure. I couldn't believe the Agency was calling me in. I refused to leave. I thought I had explained myself clearly, but...I guess they didn't believe me. They must have thought I'd gone rogue, that I'd flipped and was choosing the cartel. It still makes no sense to me." He shook his head. "I thought they knew me better."

"What did they do?" Daniel asked.

"They burned me. Ratted me out as an agent, told people I'd killed de la Fuentes. And those people came for revenge."

"And got that revenge, as far as the CIA knew," she guessed.

"Exactly."

"Did you kill him?" Daniel asked. "De la Fuentes?"

"Part of the job."

"Have you killed a lot of people?"

"Do you really want to know?"

Daniel waited silently, not looking back.

"Okay. Fine. I've killed around, oh, forty-five people, maybe more. I can't be sure about the number—you don't always have time to check for a pulse. Do you understand why I had to keep you separated from my life?"

Daniel looked at Alex now. "Have you ever killed anyone?"

"Three times."

"Three . . . oh! The people your company sent after you?"

"Yes."

"Don't act like that makes her better than me," Kevin interjected, angry.

"I wasn't—" Daniel started to say.

It was Kevin's turn to shout. "Ask her how many people she tortured before you. Ask her how long for each of them. How many hours—how many days? I just shoot people. Clean and fast. I would never do what she does. To anyone, especially not an innocent civilian like—"

"Shut up," Daniel snapped. "Just stop talking. Don't make this about her. Whatever pain she caused me, remember, you caused me more. It hurt more, and it lasted for much, much longer. You say you had a good reason. So did she. She didn't know she'd been lied to, that she'd been manipulated. I know how *that* feels."

"As if she's just some blameless bystander here."

"I said *shut up!*" Daniel bellowed the last two words at a deafening decibel.

Alex cringed. The dog whined, pulling its face inside and staring at its master.

"Easy," Kevin said, maybe to the dog.

Daniel noticed her reaction.

"Are you okay?"

"Actually, on top of a lot of other uncomfortable injuries, I've got a splitting headache."

"I'm sorry."

"Don't worry about it."

"You look like you're going to crash — figuratively and literally. Want me to drive? You could try to get a nap."

She thought about that for a minute. She'd always had to do things on her own, but that was okay, because then she knew they were done right. She didn't have someone to take turns driving with, but that was also okay, because then she didn't have to trust someone. Trust was a killer.

Still, she knew her limits. There was something so luxurious about the idea of being able to sleep and travel at the same time.

And she did trust Daniel not to hurt her, not to betray her. Knowing it could be a huge mistake, she still trusted him.

"Thank you," she said. "That would be really nice. I'll pull over at the next exit."

The words sounded odd to her as they came out of her mouth. Like something someone would say on television, lines from one actor to another. But she supposed this was how normal human interactions generally sounded. She just didn't have a lot of those in her life.

The silence was lovely for the two miles it took to get to the next exit. The peace made her even sleepier. Her eyelids were already doing the involuntary slow blink as she pulled off onto the dirt shoulder.

No one spoke while they made the exchange. Kevin's head lolled back on his seat, eyes closed. Daniel touched her shoulder lightly as he passed her.

Tired as she was, she didn't fall asleep immediately. At first she thought it was the weirdness of having the car moving beneath her; her body assumed from long habit that she would be the one at the wheel and knew sleep was not allowed. She peeked at Daniel a few times from under her hat, just as reassurance. He knew how to drive a car. It was okay to relax. Sure, the seat was uncomfortable, but not much worse than her usual nighttime setup. She'd taught herself to get rest where she could. But her head felt . . . too unrestrained. As soon as she realized this, she knew it was the gas mask she was missing. It had become part of her sleep ritual.

Understanding the problem helped. She pulled her baseball cap farther down over her sore face and told herself to relax. She'd strung no wires today. No poison gas threatened. Everything was okay, she promised herself.

·   ·   ·

IT WAS DARK when she woke up. She felt stiff, incredibly sore, and hungry. She also really had to pee. She wished she could have stayed asleep longer and thus avoided all of these unpleasant feelings, but the brothers were arguing again. She'd been out for a long time, she knew, so she couldn't blame them for forgetting her, but she wished they hadn't been arguing about *her* when she awakened.

"... but she *isn't* pretty," Kevin was saying as she began to surface.

"You don't even know what she looks like," Daniel replied angrily. "You mauled her face before you had a chance to introduce yourself."

"It ain't just about the face, kid. She's built like a skinny ten-year-old boy."

"You are the reason why women think all men are dogs. Also, the term is *sylphid*."

"You read too many books."

"You don't read enough."

"I call it how it is."

"You have limited perception."

"Hey, it's okay," Alex interrupted. There was no graceful way into this conversation, but she didn't want to pretend to be asleep. "No offense taken."

She pulled the hat off her face and wiped away the drool that had leaked from her damaged lip.

"Sorry," Daniel muttered.

"Don't worry about it. I needed to wake up."

"No, I mean *him*."

"Your brother's low opinion of my charms is its own special kind of compliment."

Daniel laughed. "Good point."

Kevin snorted.

Alex stretched, and then groaned. "Let me guess. When you pictured the Mad Scientist's female partner, the mysterious Oleander, you saw a blonde, right?" She glanced at his face—suddenly rigid. "Yes, definitely a blonde. Large breasts, long tan legs, full lips, and huge blue doe eyes? Did I get it all? Or was there a French accent, too?"

Kevin didn't respond. She glanced back at him; he stared out the window as if he weren't listening to her.

"Got it in one." She laughed.

"He was always a fan of the obvious," Daniel said.

"I never saw one of those on the job," Alex told Daniel. "I'm not saying such a creature wouldn't have the brains necessary, but really, why spend decades buried in unglamorous research when there are so many other options?"

"I've seen girls like that on the job," Kevin muttered.

"Sure, agents," Alex allowed. "That's a sexy job. Exciting. But trust me, lab coats really aren't that figure-flattering, despite the slutty Halloween-costume version."

Kevin went back to looking out the window.

"How are you feeling?" Daniel asked.

"Ouch."

"Oh. Sorry."

She shrugged. "We should find a place to pause. I'm not going to be able to eat in a restaurant without someone calling the cops on you two. We'll have to get a motel somewhere, and then somebody's going to have to go out for groceries."

"Room service not an option?" Daniel wondered.

"Those types of hotels notice when you pay cash," Kevin explained before she could. "Sorry, bro. We'll have to rough it for a night."

"Have you been driving all day?" she asked.

"No, Kev and I switched out a couple of times."

"I can't believe I slept through all of that."

"I think you needed it."

"Yeah, I guess I've been burning the candle at both ends for too long."

"So little time," Kevin muttered, "so many people to torture."

"True story," she agreed lightly, just to annoy him.

Daniel laughed.

Daniel seemed so kind and gentle—more so than anyone she'd ever known—but he was definitely weird. Possibly unstable.

They found a small place on the outskirts of Little Rock. Alex thought she ought to recognize the city just a bit, but nothing reminded her of her childhood visits to the grandparents. Maybe the city had grown too much in the years since she'd been here. Maybe she was just in the wrong part. Somewhere nearby, her mother and her grandparents were buried. She wondered if that should make her feel something. But the place didn't really matter. She was no closer to them for being closer to the remains of their genetic material.

Kevin insisted on making the arrangements at the front desk. It was probably for the best that Kevin took the lead now; Alex was out of commission, thanks to her face, and even if she had looked fine, he was still the expert. She knew only what she'd learned through theoretical research and a couple of years of trial and error. Kevin had been taught so much more, and he'd proved it all in the field. Daniel wasn't even an option. Oh, his face was fine, but his instincts were all wrong.

Case in point, the way he argued when he saw that Kevin had gotten them only one room. It hadn't occurred to him that a hotel clerk would be more likely to remember a man who came in alone yet paid cash for two rooms. And when Kevin parked three doors down from their actual room, Daniel didn't understand why. Misdirection, they explained, but it was foreign to everything Daniel had ever known, every habit he'd formed. He thought like a normal person who'd never had anything to hide. There was a lot he was going to have to learn.

He even asked if they should get permission before they brought the dog into the room.

It had only one bed, but Alex had been asleep for twelve hours straight, so she was happy to be the lookout. Kevin went out for a half hour and came back with cellophane-wrapped sandwiches, sodas, and a large bag of dog food. Alex scarfed her sandwich down, and then chased it with a handful of Motrin. Einstein ate just as enthusiastically as she had, straight from the bag, but Daniel and Kevin were more relaxed about the food. Apparently, she'd missed a couple of stops at the drive-through, too.

A quick assessment of herself in the scratched bathroom mirror was not encouraging. Her nose was swollen to twice its normal size, red and bulbous. On the plus side, odds were it would heal up differently than it began, thus changing her appearance a little. Maybe not as aesthetically pleasing a result as she would get from plastic surgery, but probably less painful on the whole, or at least faster. Her black eyes were an impressive contradiction to their name, boasting a rainbow of colors from jaundice yellow to bilious green to sickly purple. Her split lip puffed out from either side of the scabby fissure like flesh balloons, and she hadn't even known you could develop bruises *inside* your mouth. There was one stroke of luck: she still had all her teeth. Getting a bridge would have been tricky.

It was going to be a while before she could do *anything*. She really hoped Kevin's safe house lived up to the name. It worried her to be headed into the unknown. She hadn't prepared anything, and that was 100 percent unnerving.

She showered and brushed her teeth—a more painful ordeal than usual—and slipped into her black leggings and a clean white tee. She'd reached the limits of her wardrobe. Hopefully the safe house had a washing machine.

Daniel was asleep when she came back out, stretched out on his stomach with one hand under the pillow and one arm falling over the edge of the bed, long fingers brushing the faded carpet. His sleeping face was really something else—like before, when he was unconscious, his innocence and serenity didn't seem to belong in the same world that she did.

Kevin wasn't in the room and neither was the dog. Though she assumed the dog had needs, she couldn't bring her alert level down from orange-red until they'd returned.

Kevin didn't acknowledge her, but the dog sniffed her once as it passed. Kevin lay down flat on his back, his arms at his sides, and immediately closed his eyes. He didn't move again for six hours. The dog jumped onto the end of the bed and curled up with its tail over Daniel's legs and its head pillowed on Kevin's feet.

Alex sat in the only chair—the carpet was just too questionable for her to lie on the floor—and bent over her laptop, surfing the news. She wasn't sure when Daniel's disappearance would be noticed or if it would be broadcast when it was. Probably not. Grown men wandered off all the time. For example, her father. That sort of thing was too common to make waves unless there was some sensational detail—like dismembered body parts in his apartment.

There was also no story yet about the crash of a single-prop plane in West Virginia—no fatalities or injured found, still trying to locate the owner—but she doubted the news would merit more than just a note in a local online paper. When it did surface, there would be nothing in the report that would catch anyone's attention in DC.

She exhausted her search for information that might endanger them. It seemed that, for now, they were in the clear on that front, at least. What was Carston thinking right at this moment? What was he planning? She wasn't due to deliver Daniel until Monday before school, and it was still only Saturday — well, almost Sunday. The department knew she wasn't going to crack Daniel — he had nothing to spill. They had to know she would eventually learn of the identical twin's existence. They must have been pretty sure of Kevin's status in the land of the living. They had expected him to be drawn out into the open early in the game, and they'd been right about that. The only thing they hadn't foreseen was that the torturer and the assassin might have a conversation.

It would never have shaken out this way without Daniel's interference. He'd been a ploy for them, just a pawn moved into peril to lure the more critical players into the center of the board. They never would have guessed that he'd be a catalyst for change.

She planned to hold true to her side of the bargain — she would take the role of victor (though that was really the losing role) and let Daniel and Kevin be dead. Dead *again*, in Kevin's case. But oh, how she wished that she could be the one to die. Wouldn't it be easy for the department to believe that someone like Kevin Beach — who'd toppled a cartel — had succeeded where they had failed? Wouldn't it make sense for them to stop looking then? What would it be like to disappear, but this time with no one searching for her?

She sighed. Fantasies only made it harder; there was no point indulging in them. The men were both pretty well under, she was sure, so she dug into her bag and pulled out the pressurized canister she'd selected earlier. She had only the two gas masks, so nothing deadly tonight, just the airborne sleeping agent she'd had hooked up to her computer yesterday. It was enough. It would let her control the outcome if some-one discovered them.

After she'd strung the leads—only a double line; she wouldn't have to arm or disarm from outside the room tonight—she settled back into her chair. She glanced at the twins. Both were deep, peaceful sleep-ers. She wondered if that was a healthy habit for a spy. Maybe Kevin actually trusted her—enough to sound the alarm at the very least, and maybe even to deal with a problem without killing them all. She and the brothers were strange bedfellows indeed.

How odd it was, watching over them. It felt wrong, and she'd expected that. But it also felt good, satisfy-ing some need she'd never known was there, and *that* she *hadn't* expected.

She spent some time thinking about her analysis of the situation, searching for flaws in her theory, but the more she looked at it, the more it made sense. Even the

woeful lack of evolution in her would-be-assassins—
by the third try, *someone* should have been aware of her
system and changed the approach—made sense in
this light. There had never been any *operation,* just
expendable individuals sent after her with little or no
briefing. She thought through every conjecture two or
three times and felt more confident than ever that she
finally understood the ones hunting her.

And then she was bored.

What she wanted to do was log on to the website of
Columbia University's pathology program and read
the latest doctoral dissertations, but it wasn't safe to
do that while the department was actively trying to
locate her, which she was certain they were. The
department couldn't trace *every* connection anyone
made to her old interests, but this one might be too
obvious. With a sigh, she put in earbuds, opened up
YouTube, and started watching a tutorial about field-
stripping a rifle. It probably wasn't anything she'd ever
need to know, but it couldn't hurt.

Kevin woke up at five thirty on the dot. He just sat
up, as alert as if someone had flipped a switch to turn
him on. He patted the dog once and headed toward
the door. It took him only a second to notice the gas
mask she was wearing and jerk to a stop. The dog, right
on his heels, paused too and pointed its nose in her
direction, looking for whatever had upset its master.

"Give me a sec," Alex said.

She got awkwardly to her feet, still aching and sore—whether more or less than at the beginning of the night, she couldn't tell—and walked stiffly to the door to undo her security precautions.

"I didn't say you could do that," Kevin said.

She didn't look at him. "I didn't ask for your permission."

He grunted.

It took her only a few seconds to clear his path. She removed her mask and used it to gesture to the door.

"Knock yourself out."

"Knock *you* out," she thought she heard him mutter as he passed her, but it was too low for her to be sure. The dog followed him, tail swishing so fast it blurred. She imagined the guy at the front desk probably wasn't paying any attention at this hour, but she still thought Kevin was pressing their luck a little. A screaming match with the management wasn't going to help them stay incognito.

She rummaged through the food Kevin had bought last night. The remaining sandwiches weren't as appetizing as they had been eight hours ago, but there was a box of cherry Pop-Tarts she'd missed before. She was working her way through the second pastry in the sleeve when Kevin and the dog came back.

"You want to catch a few hours?" he asked her.

"If you don't mind driving, I can sleep in the car again. Better to get where we're going."

He nodded once, then went to the bed and lightly kicked his brother.

Daniel moaned and rolled onto his back, covering his head with a pillow.

"Is that necessary?" she asked.

"Like you said, better to get going. Danny's always had a problem with the snooze button."

Kevin yanked the pillow off Daniel's head.

"Let's go, kid."

Daniel blinked owlishly for a few seconds, and then she watched his face change as the memories hit, as he realized where he was and why. It hurt to see the peace of his dreams crumble into the devastation of his new waking reality. His eyes darted around the room until he found her. She tried to make her expression reassuring, but the damage done to her face would probably trump any arrangement of her features. She searched for something to say, something that would make the world a little less dark and scary for him.

"Pop-Tart?" she offered.

He blinked again. "Um, okay."

CHAPTER 12

Alex did not approve of the safe house.

They'd reached it late in the afternoon. She'd kept her nap to just four hours during the drive. She didn't want to be on a nocturnal schedule forever. So she'd been awake as they turned off the highway onto a two-lane surface road, then to an even smaller road, until finally they were on a one-lane dirt *path*—calling it a road was too complimentary.

Sure it was hard to find, but once you did...well, there was only one way out. She never would have chosen to live backed into a corner like this.

"Relax, killer," Kevin told her when she complained. "No one is looking for us out here."

"We should have switched plates."

"Took care of it while you were snoring."

"You weren't actually snoring," Daniel said quietly. He was driving now, while Kevin directed. "But it is true that we stopped at a junkyard and stole a few license plates."

"So we're trapped out here on a dead-end lane while Mr. Smith goes to Washington," she muttered.

"It's secure," Kevin snapped in a tone that was clearly intended to close the discussion. "So don't go stringing your death traps through my house."

She didn't answer. She would do what she wanted when he was gone.

At least his setup was far away from neighbors; they drove for at least fifteen minutes down the dirt path without seeing any evidence of other human beings. That would keep the collateral damage low if for some reason she felt the need to burn everything to the ground.

They arrived at a tall gate flanked by a heavy-duty chain-link fence with a crowning line of spiraled razor wire. The fence ran so far off into the distance to both the right and the left that she couldn't see where it turned or ended. Beside the gate, there was a very serious-looking NO TRESPASSING sign with an additional notice below that read ENTER AT YOUR OWN RISK; OWNERS ARE NOT LIABLE FOR INJURIES OR HARM THAT MAY RESULT FROM TRESPASSING.

"Subtle," she said.

"It gets the job done," Kevin responded. He pulled a key fob from his pocket and clicked a button. The gate swung open, and Daniel drove through.

She should have expected that his safe house would be so obvious.

After a few more miles, the house came into view like a mirage, its dull gray second story hovering on a light haze over the dry yellow grass. Here and there, a few dark, scrubby trees studded the grassland with some texture. Over it all, the washed-out blue sky stretched to infinity.

She'd never been totally comfortable with the Great Plains. She'd been a city girl for too long. This felt so exposed, so... unanchored. Like a strong wind could just erase everything in sight. Which probably did happen around these parts, biannually. She really hoped it wasn't tornado season.

The rest of the house was revealed as they topped a low rise in the mostly flat road. It was large but dilapidated, two stories high with a rickety porch wrapped around half the ground floor. The coarse, dead grass ended about twenty yards from the house, replaced by sand-colored gravel that covered the dirt up to the cracked lattice that attempted to camouflage the foundation. The only breaks in the monotone vegetation were the house, the stunted trees, the reddish scar of the dirt lane, and then several indistinct shapes that were in motion, roving along the edges of the road. She'd seen a lot of cows on the way in, but these animals looked too small to be cows. They did seem to be furry, ranging in color from black to brown to white to a combination of all three.

The shapes started to converge on the car, moving a lot faster than cows.

Einstein's tail began wagging so ferociously that it sounded like a small helicopter in the backseat.

"What is this place, Kev?"

"My retirement plan."

The animals reached the car—half a dozen dogs of various sizes. *Fantastic,* Alex thought. One could have been Einstein's twin. Another was gargantuan, looking like it was more closely related to equines than canines. She recognized a Doberman, two Rottweilers, and a traditionally colored German shepherd.

On the approach, the dogs had been totally silent and aggressive in their posture, but as soon as they saw Einstein, all the tails started wagging and they shared in a raucous chorus of barks.

"I train dogs for placement as guard dogs— commercial and private ownership. I also sell a few to families who just want a really well-behaved animal."

"How do you keep this under the radar?" she wanted to know.

"You can drive, Danny, they'll get out of the way," Kevin instructed.

Daniel had come to a stop when the dogs surrounded the car. Now he eased carefully forward and, as promised, the dogs moved to flank them and follow them in. Kevin then addressed Alex. "Nothing is in my name. No one ever sees my face. I have a partner for that."

As he spoke, she saw a figure walk out onto the porch—a large man wearing a cowboy hat. She couldn't make out any other details from this distance.

"Everybody knows the dog ranch is out here. Nobody bothers with us. It has no connection to my past life," Kevin was saying, but she wasn't paying much attention. Her eyes were riveted on the man waiting at the top of the porch stairs.

Kevin noticed her preoccupation. "What, Arnie? He's good people. I trust him with my life."

She frowned at that expression. Daniel was looking at her, too. He started to slow.

"Is there a problem, Alex?" he asked in a low voice.

She heard Kevin's teeth grind behind her. It was obvious how much he hated the way Daniel turned to her for guidance.

"It's just…" She frowned, then gestured to Daniel and his brother. "*This* is already a lot for me. The two of you. I don't know how to trust even you, let alone *another* person. Who only *this* one vouches for." She pointed at Kevin and he scowled.

"Well, that's just tough, shorty," Kevin answered. "Because this is your best option, and the guy I vouch for is part of the deal. If you want to execute this plan of yours, you'll have to suck it up."

"It will be okay," Daniel reassured her. He put his right hand lightly over her left.

Stupid how something like that could make you feel better. It wasn't like Daniel comprehended even the most basic elements of the danger they were in. But still, her heartbeat decelerated a tiny bit, and her right hand—unconsciously clenched around the door handle—relaxed.

Daniel drove slowly; the dogs kept up with them pretty easily until they stopped on the gravel. She was able to get a better look at the man waiting for them.

Arnie was a tall, heavyset man, part Latino, maybe part Native American. He could have been forty-five, but he could have been ten years older, too. His face was lined, but it looked like the kind of leathering that was due to wind and sun rather than age. His hair, which hung several inches below the hat, was salt-and-pepper gray. He stared at them without any emotion as they stopped, though there was no way he could have expected a third passenger, even if Kevin had told him about Daniel.

Einstein exploded out of the car as soon as Kevin cracked the door open and immediately set to sniffing and being sniffed. Daniel and Kevin climbed out almost as quickly, eager to stretch their long legs. Alex was more hesitant. There were a lot of dogs, and the brown-spotted horse-dog looked to be taller on all fours than she was standing. They seemed to be occupied with one another at the moment, but who knew how they would react to her?

"Don't be such a coward, Oleander," Kevin called.

Most of the dogs had converged on him now, nearly forcing him to the ground with the combined weight of their greeting.

Daniel came around the car and opened the door for her, then offered his hand. She sighed, irritated, and got out on her own. Her shoes crunched on the gravel, but the dogs didn't seem to notice her.

"Arnie," Kevin called over the sound of the happy dogs. "This is my brother, Danny. He'll be staying here. And, um, a temporary...guest, I suppose. Don't know what else to call her. But *guest* seems kind of over-positive, if you know what I mean."

"Your hospitality takes my breath away," Alex murmured.

Daniel laughed, then climbed the stairs in two quick steps. He offered his hand to the stone-faced man, who didn't look as tall standing next to Daniel, and they shook.

"Nice to meet you, Arnie. My brother's told me nothing at all about you, so I look forward to getting to know you better."

"Ditto, Danny," Arnie said. His voice was a rumbly baritone that sounded as if it wasn't used often enough to keep it running smoothly.

"And that's Alex. Don't listen to my brother; she's staying as long as she wants."

Arnie looked at her, focusing now. She waited for a

reaction to the mess of her face, but he just regarded her coolly.

"A pleasure," she said.

He nodded.

"You can move your stuff inside," Kevin told them. He tried to walk toward the stairs, but the dogs were weaving around his legs at high speed. "Hey, bone-heads! *Attention!*"

Like a small platoon of soldiers, the dogs immediately backed off a few paces, formed an actual line, and froze with their ears up.

"That's better. At ease."

The dogs sat down in unison, tongues lolling out in sharp-fanged smiles.

Kevin joined them at the door.

"Like I said, you can grab your stuff. Danny, there's a room for you at the top of the stairs on the right. As for you..." He looked down at Alex. "Well, I guess the room at the other end of the hall will work. I wasn't expecting extra company, so it's not fitted up as a bedroom."

"I've got a cot."

"I don't have any stuff," Daniel said, and though she listened for it, she didn't hear any sadness in the words; he was putting up a good front. "Do you need help with yours, Alex?"

She shook her head. "I'll only take a few things in. The rest I'll stash somewhere outside the fence."

Daniel raised his eyebrows in confusion, but Kevin was nodding.

"I've had to run out in the middle of the night before," she explained to Daniel, pitching her voice low, though Arnie could probably still hear. She had no idea how much he knew about Kevin's old job. "Sometimes it's not so easy to get back to pick up your things."

Daniel's brow creased. Some of the sadness she'd been expecting before flickered across his expression. This was a world not many people entered on purpose.

"You don't need to worry about that here," Kevin said. "We're secure."

Kevin was one of those people who *had* chosen this life, which made his every judgment suspect to her.

"Better to keep in practice," she insisted.

Kevin shrugged. "If that's what you want, I know a place that might work."

· · ·

THE HOUSE WAS quite a bit nicer on the inside than the outside. She'd expected moldy wallpaper, 1970s oak paneling, sagging couches, linoleum, and Formica. While there was still an attempt at a rustic theme, the fixtures were new and state of the art. There were even granite countertops on the kitchen island under the elk-horn chandelier.

"Wow," Daniel murmured.

"But how many contractors were inside this place?" she muttered to herself. Too many witnesses.

Kevin heard, though she hadn't meant him to. "None, actually. Arnie used to be in construction. We got all the materials from across the state line and did the work ourselves. Well, mostly Arnie did it. Satisfied?"

Alex pursed her balloon lips.

"How did you two meet?" Daniel asked Arnie politely.

She really ought to study Daniel, Alex thought, practice his ways of interacting. *This* was how to act like a normal person. Either she'd never really known how or she'd forgotten completely. She had her lines down for waitressing, for cubicle jobs; she knew how to respond in a work environment in the least memorable way. She knew how to talk to patients when she was doing her illicit doctor gig. Before that, she'd learned the best ways to pull answers from a subject. But outside of the prescribed roles, she always avoided contact.

It was Kevin who answered Daniel's question. "Arnie was in a little trouble that related tangentially to a project I was working on a while back. He wanted out, and he gave me some very valuable information in exchange for my killing him."

The silent Arnie grinned widely.

"We hit it off," Kevin continued, "and kept in

touch. When I decided to start preparing for retirement, I contacted him. Our needs and interests aligned perfectly."

"Match made in heaven," Alex said in a sweet voice. *Great, so people might be looking for* him, *too,* she didn't add aloud.

Kevin and Daniel went to the downstairs master to gather a wardrobe for Daniel and outfit him with toiletries. Alex showed herself upstairs, easily locating the small room Kevin had offered her. It would work. He was using it for storage right now, but there was enough space for her cot and personal things. One of the large plastic storage bins would make a decent substitute for a desktop. The bathroom was down the hall; it connected to both the hallway and what would be Daniel's bedroom.

It had been a very long time since she'd shared a bathroom. At least this one was bigger and posher than she was used to.

The brothers were still busy when she went back to the car to sort through her stuff. There were three dogs on the porch; one she was pretty sure was Einstein, one huge black Rottweiler, and a reddish-brown, sad-faced dog with floppy ears who reminded her of the dog whose leg gets broken at the end of *Lady and the Tramp.* So that probably meant he was a hound dog or a bloodhound or something—she wasn't sure which was which.

The Rottweiler and the hound started toward her with more interest than menace, but it was enough for her to take a huge step back toward the door. Einstein raised his head and gave a low, cough-like bark, and the other two stopped. They sat down where they were, like they had when Kevin had given them the at-ease command.

She wasn't sure if Einstein actually had the authority to give the other dogs orders—did dogs recognize rank?—so she moved cautiously along the porch, waiting for them to attack. They held their relaxed positions, just watching her curiously. As she passed, the hound's tail thumped loudly against the wooden slats of the floor, and she had the odd impression that he was playing up the sad eyes in anticipation of being petted. She hoped he wasn't too disappointed that she wasn't brave enough to try it.

She dug through her things wedged in the trunk, pulling together an emergency kit and fitting it into a backpack; this she would keep with her at all times. She took most of her dirty clothes to wash inside— hopefully there was a washing machine—but left the businessy stuff with the other bags in the trunk. She had to have at least one set of clothes with her off-property stash. She'd run out one memorable night— after assassin two was gassed trying to cut her throat—in just her underwear and had to steal a neighbor's coveralls out of the back of his work van.

She'd learned that lesson. And to always sleep in pajamas that could double as daytime clothes.

Even with the cot, it was an easy load to take up
the stairs. She went back for one of the duffel bags,
this one containing her basic lab gear. She shouldn't
waste the downtime when she could be prepping. As
she passed the master bedroom, she heard squabbling,
and the sound made her happy to be out of the way of
it.

The lab setup was a quick process after so much
practice. One of her glass flasks was chipped, but it
looked like it was still usable. She pieced her rotary
evaporator together and then laid out a few condensers and two stainless-steel vessels. She'd used almost
all of her *Survive*, and the way this week was going,
she would probably need more. She had plenty of
D-phenylalanine, but she was disappointed when she
checked on her opioid store. Less than she'd thought.
Not enough to synthesize more *Survive*, and she had
only one dose left.

She was still scowling at her lack of supplies when
she heard Kevin calling up the stairs.

"Hey, Oleander. Ticktock."

By the time she got through the front door, Kevin
was already in the sedan, Daniel in the passenger seat.
When Kevin spotted her hesitating on the porch, he
held the horn down for one annoyingly long blast. She
walked as slowly as possible to the car and climbed

into the backseat with a frown—dog hair was going to get all over her.

They drove along the same slender dirt lane out through the gate and a few miles farther before turning onto an even less pronounced road that headed in a mostly westerly direction. This road was nothing more than two tire tracks worn into the grass. They followed it for about six or seven miles, she guessed. For the first few miles, she caught glimpses of the ranch's fence line, but after that, they were too far west for her to see it anymore.

"Is this your land, too?"

"Yes, after passing through a few other names. This parcel is owned by a corporation that is not affiliated in any way with the parcel the ranch is on. I do know how to do this, you know."

"Of course."

The landscape started to change on her right. The yellow-white grass cut off at a strangely even border and beyond that, the ground turned to level, bare red dirt. When they started to wind back to the north toward that border, she was surprised to see that the red dirt was actually a riverbank. The water was the same color as the red bank, and it moved smoothly west, without rapids or obstacles. It was about forty feet across at the widest point she could see. She watched the flow of the water as they drove roughly parallel to it, fascinated by its existence here in the middle of the dry grassland. For all its smooth progress, the river seemed to be moving fairly quickly.

There was no fence this time. A crumbling-down barn, grayed by the sun, sat about fifty yards from the road, looking as if it had reached the end of its very long life and was only waiting for the right weather system to put it out of its misery. She'd seen hundreds just like it on their quick tour through Arkansas and Oklahoma.

It was nowhere near as nice as her milking barn.

Kevin turned toward it, driving right through the grass now; she couldn't see any official road or pathway.

She waited in the running car while he jumped out to unlock the massive antique padlock and swing the doors open. Outside, in the brilliant light of the open, cloudless sky, it was impossible to see anything inside the murky interior. He was back quickly to drive the car into the darkness.

This time, the inside matched the outside's promise. Dim light filtered through the slats of the barn to illuminate piles of corroded farm equipment, most of a rusted tractor, the shells of a few ancient cars, and a massive stack of dusty hay in the back, half covered with a tarp. Nothing worth stealing, or even examining more closely. If anyone bothered to break in here, the only valuable thing he would find was shade.

When the engine cut off, she thought she could

just make out the rush of the river. They couldn't be more than a couple hundred yards away from it.

"This will work," she said. "I'll stick my stuff in a corner and you can use this car when you head back."

"Roger that."

She piled her four rectangular duffels into a shadowy crevice, partially hidden behind a stack of spiderwebbed firewood. The webs were dusty.

Kevin was rummaging near a pile of blackened metal — maybe parts for another tractor — and came back with a tattered old tarp, which he spread over her bags.

"Nice touch," she approved.

"It's all in the presentation."

"I guess you haven't gotten around to fixing this place up yet," Daniel commented, one hand on the closest car shell.

"I kind of like it how it is," Kevin said. "Let me give you a tour. Just in case you need something while I'm gone. Which you won't. But still."

She nodded thoughtfully. "Overpreparation is the key to success. It's kind of my mantra."

"Then you'll love this," Kevin said.

He walked to the half-tractor and bent down to fiddle with the lug nuts in the center of the huge flat tire.

"There's a keypad behind this hubcap." He spoke directly to Daniel. "The code is our birthday. Not too original, but I wanted you to be able to remember it easily. Same combination for the lock on the outside door."

A second later, the entire front face of the tire swung outward—it wasn't made of rubber, it was something stiffer and lighter, and it moved on hinges. Inside, an arsenal.

"Oh, *yes*," she breathed. "Batcave."

She immediately spotted a SIG Saucr that matchcd the gun she'd briefly stolen from him. He really didn't need two.

Kevin gave her a puzzled look. "Batman doesn't use guns."

"Whatever."

Daniel was examining the hinges on the hidden door. "This is very clever. Did Arnie make it?"

"No, I did, thanks."

"I didn't know you were handy. And when did you have the chance to do this, what with toppling cartels and all that?"

"Downtime between jobs. I can't sit still or I go crazy."

He closed up the fake tire and then gestured to the car shell near where Daniel had been standing before. "Lift the top of the battery and type in the same code. That one's rifles, the next is rocket launchers and grenades."

Daniel laughed, then caught his brother's expression. "Wait, really?"

"She likes preparation; I like to be extremely well armed. Okay, now, this one I couldn't hide so well, and anyway, it's the kind of thing I might need quickly."

Kevin walked around the side of the massive hay tower, and they followed. The tarp hung to the ground on this side. She was pretty confident she knew at least the category of what he was hiding here, and sure enough, he lifted the tarp to reveal a cozy garage behind the hay with a very large vehicle wedged inside. From the way he stood, it was obviously his pride and joy.

"There's a truck back at the ranch that blends in, but *this* is here in case of emergencies."

Daniel made a small noise like a hiccup. Alex glanced at him and realized he was trying not to laugh. She got the joke immediately.

They had both dealt with DC traffic for years, though he more recently. And despite the congestion and tight parking options that were more suited for a Vespa than a medium-size sedan, there was always that one guy trying to shove his gigantic compensation-mobile into a parallel slot. As if anyone needed a Hummer anywhere, let alone in the city. You might as well just get a vanity plate that read D-BAG and be done with it.

When Daniel saw her mouth twitch, he lost his own control. Suddenly he was snorting with laughter.

It was an awkward, infectious *heh-heh-snort-heh-heh* that was much funnier than the military monster truck. She started chortling along, surprised at how out of control the laughter felt almost immediately. She hadn't laughed big like this in so long; she'd forgotten how it grabbed your whole body and wouldn't let go.

Daniel had one hand on the hay while he bent over, the other hand on his side like he had a stitch. It was the funniest thing she'd ever seen.

"What?" Kevin demanded. *"What?"*

Daniel tried to calm himself to answer, but then a sudden burst of giggles from Alex derailed him, and he guffawed again, gasping for air between outbursts.

"This is a state-of-the-art assault vehicle," Kevin complained, half shouting to be heard over their frenzied hilarity. "It has solid rubber tires and missile-proof glass. There are panels through the whole body that a tank can't crush. This thing could save your life."

He was just making it worse. Tears streamed down both their faces. Alex's lip was protesting and her cheeks ached. Daniel was hiccupping for real now, unable to straighten up.

Kevin threw up his hands in disgust and stomped away from them.

They busted up again.

Finally, several long minutes after Kevin had disappeared, Alex started to be able to breathe. Daniel's laughter was trailing off as well, though he was still holding his side. She could sympathize; she had a cramp, too. Oddly exhausted, she sat down on the hay-strewn floor and put her head between her knees, working to even out her breathing. After a second, she felt Daniel settle next to her. His hand came to rest lightly on her back.

"Ah, I needed that." He sighed. "It was starting to feel like nothing would ever be really funny again."

"I can't remember the last time I laughed like that. My stomach *hurts*."

"Mine too." And then he laughed another *heh-heh-heh*.

"Don't start," she begged.

"Sorry, I'll try. I might be a little hysterical."

"Huh. Maybe we should slap each other."

He laughed another burst, and she couldn't help but giggle.

"Stop," she moaned.

"Should we talk about sad things?" he wondered.

"Like living a life of isolation and fear, hunted every minute of the day?" she suggested.

It felt like the murky barn got even darker, and she immediately regretted speaking. Even if it hurt, it had felt so nice to laugh.

"That's a good one," Daniel said quietly. "How about letting down all the people who count on you?"

"Doesn't really apply for me, but it's definitely a depressing idea. Though in your case, I doubt anyone will look at it that way. They'll probably think you've been murdered. Everyone will be heartbroken and they'll leave flowers and candles in front of the school marquee."

"Do you think they will?"

"Sure. There will probably even be teddy bears."

"Maybe. Or maybe no one will miss me. Maybe they'll say, 'Finally, we got rid of that joker and now we can hire a real history teacher. The girls' volleyball team might actually have a chance with him out of the way. You know what? Let's just find a chimp to do his job and put his salary into the retirement fund.'"

She nodded with false gravity. "You could be right."

He smiled, then was serious again. "Did anyone burn candles for you?"

"There wasn't really anyone left to care. If Barnaby had been the one to survive, he might have lit a candle for me. I did a few times for him, in cathedrals. I'm not Catholic, but I couldn't figure out another place where I could do it inconspicuously. I know Barnaby's not around to care, but I needed something. Closure, mourning, whatever."

A pause. "Did you love him?"

"Yes. Aside from my work—and you've seen how warm and cuddly *that* was—he was all I had."

Daniel nodded. "Well, I don't feel like laughing anymore."

"We probably needed the release. Now we can get back to our regularly scheduled depression."

"Sounds lovely."

"Hey, Moe and Curly," Kevin called from outside the barn. "Are you ready to get back to work, or do you want to giggle like schoolgirls a little while longer?"

"Um, giggle, I guess?" Daniel called back.

She couldn't help it—she snickered.

Daniel put his hand gently over her bruised mouth. "None of that, now. We'd better go see what work there is to do."

CHAPTER 13

Kevin kept a firing range set up behind the barn, facing the river. Alex eyed it suspiciously, but she had to concede that random gunshots were probably less likely to arouse attention in rural Texas than anywhere else in the world.

"When's the last time you picked up a gun?" he asked Daniel.

"Hmm... with Dad, I guess."

"Seriously?" Kevin heaved a sigh. "Well, I suppose all we can do is hope you remember *something.*"

He'd brought out an array of weapons and laid them on a hay bale. Other hay bales, each stacked to a man's height and wearing printed black silhouettes, were arranged at varying distances from their position. Some were so far off she could barely make them out.

"We could start with the handguns, but what I'd like is to try you on some rifles. The best way to stay safe is to be shooting from very, very far away. I'd rather keep you out of the close-up stuff if I can."

"These don't look like any rifles I've ever used," Daniel said.

"They're snipers. This one"—he patted the McMillan he wore slung across his back—"has the record for the longest distance kill at over one mile."

Daniel's eyes widened in disbelief. "How do you even know who you want to kill from that far away?"

"Spotters, but don't worry about that. You don't need to learn that kind of distance. I just want you to be able to sit in a perch and pick people off if it comes to that."

"I don't know if I could actually shoot a person."

It was Kevin's turn to look disbelieving. "You'd better figure that out. Because if you don't shoot, the person coming sure as hell won't hesitate to take advantage."

Daniel seemed about to argue, but Kevin waved the mini-conflict away. "Look, let's just see if you can remember how to shoot a gun."

After Kevin reviewed the basics, it was evident that Daniel did remember plenty. He took to the rifle with much more instinctive ease than Alex had ever felt with firearms. He was clearly a natural, while she never had been.

After enough rounds were fired for her to get over the fear of all the noise, she lifted the SIG Sauer.

"Hey, do you mind if I try this out on the closer targets?"

"Sure," Kevin said, not looking up from his brother's sight line. "Join the party."

The SIG was heavier than her PPK and had a more substantial kick, but in a way that felt good. Powerful. It took her a few rounds to get used to the sight, but then she was about as accurate with it as she was with her own gun. She thought that with time, she would get better. Maybe she'd be able to get in some consistent practice while she was here. It wasn't the kind of thing she usually got to indulge in.

When Kevin put an end to the shooting instruction, the sun was almost all the way down. It colored all the yellow grass deep red, as if it were actually touching down on the horizon and setting all the dried brush ablaze.

Reluctantly, she put the SIG away with the other guns. It wasn't as if she didn't know the code. She might do some stocking up when Kevin's *party* was over.

"Well, Danny, it's good to see you've still got it... and that my talent isn't just a fluke. Mom and Dad passed us some solid genes," Kevin said when they were heading back to the house.

"For target practice. I still don't think I could do what you do."

Kevin snorted. "Things change when someone is trying to kill you."

Daniel looked out his side window, clearly unconvinced.

"Okay." Kevin sighed. "Think of it this way. Imagine someone you want to protect—Mom, for example—is standing behind you. Some new recruits need to visualize in order to get themselves in the right frame of mind."

"That doesn't really fit with shooting from a sniper's perch," Daniel pointed out.

"Then picture Mom getting stuffed into the trunk of a car by the guy in your crosshairs. Use your imagination."

Daniel was done. "Fine, fine."

She could tell he still wasn't persuaded, but she had to agree with Kevin on this one topic. When someone came for you, your survival instincts kicked in. In a him-or-you situation, you always chose yourself. Daniel wouldn't know how that felt until the hunters caught up with him. She hoped he'd never have to learn the feeling.

Well, Kevin would do what he could, and so would she. Maybe together they could make the world a safer place for Daniel Beach.

Back at the ranch, the tour continued. Kevin took them to a sleek modern outbuilding, invisible from the front of the house and full of dogs.

Each animal had a climate-controlled stall and access to its own private outdoor run. Kevin explained the exercise schedule to Daniel, which dogs were already spoken for and which were ready to be listed, training him for his future life at the ranch, she assumed. Daniel seemed to love it, petting all the dogs and learning their names. The dogs adored the attention—and asked for it; she wished she could turn down the volume of the barks and whines. The dogs who ran loose were apparently graduates of the program; these followed Kevin on the rounds.

Alex suspected Kevin had let her tag along just to make her uncomfortable. The horse-size spotted one—a Great Dane, she learned—was constantly on her heels, and she was sure the dog hadn't decided to do that on his own. Kevin must have given some unseen command. She could feel the giant's breath on the nape of her neck, and guessed there were probably flecks of saliva on the back of her shirt. The hound dog was tailing her, too, but she thought he might have chosen the assignment for himself. He was still milking those sad eyes every time Alex glanced at him. The other graduates circled Daniel and Kevin, except for Einstein, who stuck close to Kevin only and seemed to take troop inspections very seriously.

They passed stalls with German shepherds, Dobermans, Rottweilers, and several other working-group dogs she didn't know names for. Alex kept to the middle of the long pathway between kennels and didn't touch anything. Always best to minimize the number of fingerprints for wiping down later.

There were two small hound puppies sharing a stall, and Kevin mentioned to Daniel that they were Lola's offspring, gesturing to the bloodhound tailing Alex.

"Oh, Lola, huh? Sorry," Alex murmured, too low for the men to hear. "I shouldn't have assumed."

Lola appeared to know she was being addressed. She stared up at Alex hopefully, and her tail pounded against Alex's leg. Alex leaned down quickly to pat her on the head.

Kevin made a disgusted sound and she straightened up to see him staring at her.

"Lola likes *everyone*," Kevin said to Daniel. "Great nose, poor taste. I'm trying to breed out the lack of discrimination while keeping the olfactory genius."

Daniel shook his head. "Enough already."

"I'm not kidding. I expect better instincts from these animals."

Alex squatted to scrub her fingers along Lola's sides like she'd seen Daniel do, knowing it would drive Kevin crazy. Lola immediately rolled over, offering her belly. Abruptly, the giant dog lay down on Alex's other side, and she was nearly positive he was also looking hopeful. She carefully patted his shoulder with one hand, and he didn't bite it off. His tail beat the ground twice. She took that as encouragement and scratched behind his ears.

"C'mon, Khan, not you, too!"

Both Alex and the Great Dane ignored him. She twisted down so that she was sitting cross-legged with both dogs in view and her back to the brothers. If she was going to be surrounded by furry killing machines, she might as well have a few of them on her side.

Lola licked the back of her hand. It was disgusting, but also kind of sweet.

"Looks like Alex has a fan," Daniel said.

"Whatever. Over here is where we keep the chow. Arnie picks it up every other week in Lawton. We've got most of what we need for..."

The rest of what Kevin said was lost in the yips and grumbles of the dogs left behind.

She stroked the dogs for a few minutes more, not sure how they would take it when she quit. Finally, she rose cautiously to her feet. Both Lola and Khan were quickly on all fours and seemed totally happy to follow her as she walked back to the house. They escorted her right to the door and then made themselves comfortable on the porch.

"Good girl, good boy," she said as she went inside.

Kevin had probably meant to intimidate her, but she liked the way it felt as if the dogs were actually looking out for her, rather than keeping an eye on her. She supposed it was what they were trained for. It was a comfortable feeling. If she had a different lifestyle, it might be nice to add a dog. Except she didn't know where she would get a dog-size gas mask.

Arnie was on the couch in the great room, parked in front of a flat-screen TV that was mounted on the opposite wall. He had a microwave dinner in his lap to which he was assiduously applying himself; he didn't react to her entrance.

The smell of the food—macaroni and Salisbury steak—had her mouth watering. Not a four-star meal, but she was *really* hungry.

"Um, do you mind if I help myself to some food?" she asked.

Arnie grunted without looking away from the baseball game. She hoped it was an affirmative, because she was already en route to the fridge.

The refrigerator—an impressive, double-wide stainless-steel affair—was crushingly bare. Condiments, a few sports drinks, and a supersize jar of pickles. It also needed to be cleaned. She checked the freezer drawer and there found pay dirt: it was stuffed full of dinners like the one Arnie was eating. She heated a cheese pizza in the microwave and ate it on a bar stool scooted up to the island. Arnie seemed completely oblivious to her presence the entire time.

If you *had* to add another person into the equation, Arnie wasn't half bad, really.

She heard the men coming back, so she headed

upstairs. They'd all been forced into close quarters on the ride here, but now that there were rooms to retire to, it was possible to give one another some space. She knew Daniel and his brother had a lot to sort through, and there was no reason she needed to hear any of it.

There wasn't a ton to do in her storage room. She refilled her little acid syringes, though she couldn't think of a scenario where she would need them here. She could have worked on harvesting the kernels out of her peach pits, but she'd left them in the barn. It wasn't worth taking the chance to try to connect to the Internet, just in case she was going to be here for a while, and she didn't have any reading material. There was one project she'd been thinking about, but part of her violently rejected the idea of writing any of it down. Though national security hadn't exactly been her friend for a while, she still wasn't going to put the public in danger. Writing her memoirs was not an option.

But she needed to think it all through in an organized way. Maybe if she just wrote some key words to help her remember?

She was sure of one fact: Something she'd overheard in the six years she'd worked with Dr. Barnaby had been the reason for the lab attack and for every assassination attempt that had followed. If she could pinpoint the information involved, she would have a much better idea of who was behind the murder agenda.

The problem was that she'd heard a lot of things, and all of it was insanely sensitive.

She started to make a list. She created a code, designating the biggest issues, the nuclear ones, as A1 through A4. Four big bombs that had been controlled during her tenure. Those were the most serious projects she'd worked on. It would have to have been something of the gravest nature to merit destroying her section.

She hoped. If it was some petty whim by a cheating admiral who thought he might have been mentioned in an investigation, she had no chance of ever figuring it out.

T1 through T49 were all the non-nuclear terrorist actions she could remember. There were minor plans—ones that hadn't come to much—that were slipping through her memory, she knew. The major plans, T1 through T17, ranged from biological attacks to economic destabilization to importing suicide bombers.

She was trying to come up with a system to help her keep all of the different actions separate (the first letter of the city of origin plus the first letter of the target city? Would that differentiate the events enough? Would she forget the meaning of her notations? But listing the full place-names was too much information to commit to writing) when she heard Kevin calling for her.

"Hey, Oleander! Where are you hiding?"

She snapped her computer shut and walked to the top of the stairs.

"Did you need something?"

He came around the corner and looked up at her. Both of them held their position, keeping the length of the stairs between them.

"Just a heads-up. I'm taking off. I left a phone with Daniel. I'll call when I'm ready for you to send the e-mail."

"Prepaid disposable?"

"This ain't my first rodeo, sister."

"Well, good luck, I guess."

"Don't turn my house into some death lab while I'm gone."

Too late. She suppressed a grin. "I'll try to rein myself in."

"This is probably it. I'd say it was a pleasure..."

She smiled. "But we've always been so honest with each other. Why start lying now?"

He smiled in return, then was suddenly serious. "You'll keep an eye on him?"

She was slightly taken aback by the request. That Kevin would entrust his brother to her this way. And even more shocked by her own response.

"Of course," she promised immediately. It was disturbing to realize how sincere her answer was, and how involuntary. Of course she would keep Daniel safe to the best of her ability. It wasn't even a question. She remembered again the strange feeling that had first surfaced in the dark of her torture tent—her premonition that the stakes had doubled from one life to two.

Part of her wondered when she would be free from this feeling of responsibility. Maybe this was always how someone felt after interrogating an innocent person. Or maybe it only happened when that person was as…what was the right word? *Honest? Virtuous? Wholesome?* Someone as *good* as Daniel.

He grunted, then turned his back and headed toward the main room of the house. She couldn't see him anymore, but she could still hear him.

"Danny, c'mere. We've got one more thing we need to do."

Curious—and procrastinating; the catalog of nightmares past was beginning to give her a headache—she walked quietly down the stairs to see what was happening. She knew Kevin well enough to be sure he wasn't calling Daniel over for a heartfelt good-bye, complete with hugs and snuggles.

The front room was empty—Arnie had cleared out—but she could hear voices through the screen door. She went out to the porch, where Lola was waiting for her. She absently scratched the dog's head while she took in the scene, lit by the porch lamps and the headlights of the sedan.

Einstein, Khan, and the Rottweiler were all lined up at attention in front of Kevin. He looked to be addressing them while Daniel watched.

Kevin started with his star pupil. "Come, Einstein."

The dog stepped forward. Kevin turned his body to point at Daniel. "That's your honey, Einstein. *Honey*."

Einstein ran to Daniel, tail wagging, and commenced sniffing up and down his legs. From Daniel's expression, he was just as confused as Alex was.

"Okay," Kevin said to the other dogs. "Khan, Gunther, *watch*."

He turned back to Einstein and Daniel, dropping into a wrestler's crouch and approaching slowly.

"I'm gonna get your honey," he taunted the dog in a growly voice.

Einstein wheeled around and put himself between Daniel and Kevin's advance. The hackles rose at least six inches off the top of his shoulders, and a menacing snarl slid from between his suddenly exposed fangs. The demon dog she'd first met was back.

Kevin feinted to the right, and Einstein blocked him. He dove left toward Daniel and the dog launched himself at his master, taking him down with a solid-sounding thud. In the same second, Einstein had his jaws wrapped around Kevin's neck. It would have been a frightening picture if it weren't for the smile on Kevin's face.

"Good boy! Smart boy!"

"Kill! Kill!" Alex whispered under her breath.

Einstein released and jumped back, tail wagging again. He pranced a few steps back and forward, ready to play another game.

"Okay, Khan, your turn."

Once again, Kevin identified Daniel as the Great Dane's *honey* and then made as if to attack. Einstein stayed with Khan; supervising, Alex imagined. The big dog simply shoved one massive paw against Kevin's chest as he attacked and toppled him backward. Khan used the same paw to pin him to the ground while Einstein moved in for the jugular.

"Kill!" she said again, louder.

Kevin heard this time and shot her a look that clearly said: *If I weren't in the middle of teaching these dogs something very important, I would have them tear you to shreds.*

Khan sat out the next round, while Einstein supervised again. The barrel-chested Rottweiler took Kevin down even harder than Einstein had. She heard the breath crush out of his chest; that *had* to hurt. She smiled.

"Do you mind if I ask what all that was about?" Daniel asked as Kevin heaved himself to his feet and started brushing the dirt off his dark jeans and black T-shirt.

"It's a command behavior I created for personal-protection dogs. These three dogs will guard you with their lives from here on out. They'll also probably be under your feet a lot."

"Why *honey?*"

"It's just a word. But, to be honest, I was mostly picturing it being used for women and children..."

"Thanks," Daniel retorted.

"Oh, relax. You know I don't mean it that way. Think of a better command and we'll use it with the next generation."

There was an awkward pause. Kevin looked at the car, then back to his brother.

"Look, you're safe here. But stay close to the dogs anyway. And the poison lady. She's tough. Just don't eat anything she tries to feed you."

"I'm sure we'll be fine."

"If anything happens, give Einstein this command." He held out a little piece of paper, about the size of a business card. Daniel took it and stuck it in his pocket without looking at it. Alex thought it was odd that Kevin wouldn't say it out loud. Or maybe he just wrote it down because he didn't trust Daniel's memory.

Kevin looked now as if a hug was actually on his mind, despite what she'd imagined before, but then Daniel's posture stiffened slightly, and Kevin turned away. He kept talking as he walked to the sedan.

"We'll talk more when I get back. Keep the phone on you. I'll call when things are set."

"Be careful."

"Wilco."

Kevin got in the car and revved the engine. He put his right hand on the back of the passenger headrest and watched out the rear window as he maneuvered the car to face the road. He didn't look at his brother again. Then the red taillights were fading into the distance.

A weight seemed to lift off Alex's chest with his leaving.

Daniel watched the car for a minute, the loyal three all sitting close to his feet. Then he turned and walked thoughtfully up the porch steps. The dogs moved with him. Kevin hadn't been kidding about them staying underfoot. Daniel was lucky Khan kept to the rear or he wouldn't have been able to see where he was going.

He stopped next to Alex and turned to face the same way she did, both of them staring out into the featureless black night. The dogs arranged themselves around their feet. Lola got muscled out by the Rottweiler and whined once in protest. Daniel gripped the porch railing in both hands, holding tight like he was expecting a shift in gravity.

"Is it bad that I'm relieved he's gone?" Daniel asked. "He's just...a lot, you know? I can't process everything with him always *talking*."

His right hand relaxed its hold, then moved to rest on the small of her back in an almost automatic manner, like he hadn't consciously decided to place it there.

The way he was always touching her reminded Alex of the experiments she and Barnaby had done years back with sensory deprivation tanks. It was an effective means of getting someone to talk without leaving any marks, but on the whole, it took too much time to be the best option.

Anyone who went into the tank, though, no matter his level of resistance, had the same reaction when he was let out: he craved physical contact like a drug fix. She thought of one memorable experience with an army corporal—a volunteer they worked with in the initial testing phase—and the very long and some-what inappropriate hug she'd received upon his exit. They'd had to have security peel him off her.

Daniel must feel a lot like that soldier. For days he'd been completely out of touch with anything he considered to be normal life. He would need the reas-surance that another warm, breathing human being was there next to him.

Of course, this diagnosis also applied to herself; she'd been out of touch with normal life for much lon-ger than Daniel had. While that meant she was used to the lack, it also meant that she'd been starved of human contact for a very long time. Maybe this was why she felt so improbably comforted whenever he touched her.

"I don't think it's a bad thing," she answered him. "It's natural that you'd need space to deal with all of this."

He laughed once, a darker sound than his earlier fit of hysteria. "Except that I don't need space from anyone but him." He sighed. "Kev has always been like that, even when we were kids. Has to be in charge, has to have the spotlight."

"Funny traits for a spy."

"I guess he's figured out a way to suppress those instincts when he's working—and then it all comes surging out when he's not."

"I wouldn't know anything about it. Only child."

"Lucky, lucky you." He sighed again.

"He's probably not so bad." Why was she defending Kevin? she wondered. Just trying to cheer Daniel up, maybe. "If you weren't stuck in this very extreme situation, he'd be easier to deal with."

"That's fair. I should try to be fair. I guess I'm just...angry. So angry. I know he didn't mean to do it, but *his* life choices have suddenly destroyed all of *mine*. That's so...*Kevin*."

"It takes a while to accept what has happened to you," Alex said slowly. "You'll probably stay angry, but it gets easier. Most of the time, I forget how angry I am. It's different for me, though. It was people I didn't know very well who did this to me. It wasn't my family."

"But your enemies actually tried to kill you. That's worse; don't even try to compare what happened to you to what's happening to me. Kevin never meant to hurt me. It's just hard, you know? I feel like I've died, but I have to keep on living anyway. I don't know how."

She patted his left hand on the rail, remembering how that had made her feel better in the car. The skin over his knuckles was stretched tight.

"You'll learn, like I did. It turns into a routine. The life you had before gets...dimmer. And you get philosophical. I mean, disasters happen to people all the time. What's the difference between this and having your nation overrun by guerrilla warfare, right? Or your town destroyed by a tsunami? Everything changes, and nothing is as safe as it was. Only that safety was always just an illusion anyway...Sorry, that might just be the world's crappiest pep talk."

He laughed. "Not the *very* crappiest. I do feel infinitesimally better."

"Well, then I guess my job here is done."

"How did you get started with all this?" The question rolled out lightly, as if it were a simple thing.

She hesitated. "What do you mean?"

"Why did you choose this...profession? Before they tried to kill you, I mean. Were you in the military? Did you volunteer?"

Again, the questions were spoken lightly, like he was inquiring how she had become a financial planner or an interior decorator. The very lack of emotion was its own tell. He kept his face forward, staring out into the darkness.

She didn't evade this time. She would want to know this, too, if fate had saddled her with one of her peers as a companion. It was something she'd asked Barnaby in the early days of their association. His answer wasn't much different from hers.

"I never actually chose it," she explained slowly. "And no, I wasn't military. I was in medical school when they approached me. I'd first been interested in pathology, but then I shifted focus. I was deep into a particular vein of research—you could call it a kind of chemical mind control, I guess. There weren't many people doing precisely what I was doing, and there were a lot of roadblocks in my way—funding, tools, test subjects ... well, most of it came down to funding. The professors I was working under didn't even fully understand my research, so I didn't have a lot of help.

"These mysterious government officials showed up and offered me an opportunity. They picked up the tab for my massive student loans. I got to finish my schooling while focusing my research toward my new handlers' goals. When I graduated, I went to work in their lab, where every technology I could dream of was at my disposal and money was never an object.

"It was obvious what they had me creating. They didn't lie to me. I was aware of the work I was contributing to, but it sounded noble, the way they described it. I was helping my country..."

He waited, still staring ahead.

"I didn't think I would be the one who would actually *use* my creations on a subject. I thought I would just be supplying the tools they needed..." She shook her head back and forth slowly. "It didn't work like that, though. The antibodies I'd created were too specialized—the doctor who administered them had to understand how they worked. So that left exactly one person."

The hand on the small of her back didn't move—it was too still, frozen in place.

"The only person ever inside the interrogation room with me, besides the subject, was Barnaby. At first, he handled the questioning. He frightened me in the beginning, but he turned out to be such a gentle person... We were mostly in the lab, creating and developing. Actual interrogations made up only about five percent of my job." She took a deep breath. "But often, when there was a crisis at hand, they needed to be running multiple interrogations simultaneously; speed was always critical. I had to be able to work alone. I didn't want to do it, but I understood why it needed to be that way.

"It wasn't as difficult as I'd thought it would be.

The hard part was realizing how good I was at it. That scared me. It's never really stopped scaring me." Barnaby was the only one she'd confessed this to. He'd told her not to worry; she was just one of those people who were good at anything they tried. An overachiever.

Alex cleared the sudden lump out of her throat. "But I got results. I saved a lot of lives. And I never killed anyone—not while I was working for the government." Now she stared out into the darkness, too. She didn't want to see his reaction. "I've always wondered if that was enough to make me less than a monster."

She was fairly certain, though, that the answer was no.

"Hmmm…" It was just a low, lingering sound in the back of his throat.

She kept staring at the dark nothing in front of her. She'd never tried to explain this choice—the line of dominoes that had made her what she was—to another human being. She didn't think she'd done a very good job.

And then he quietly chuckled.

Now she turned to stare up at him in disbelief.

His lips were puckered in an unwilling half smile. "I was braced for something really disturbing, but that all sounded a lot more reasonable than I expected."

Her brows pulled together. He found her story *reasonable?*

His stomach growled. He laughed again, and the tension of the moment seemed to vanish with the sound.

"Did Kevin not feed you?" she asked. "This is a help-yourself kind of place, I guess."

"I could use some food," he agreed.

She led him to the freezer, trying to hide her surprise that he seemed to be treating her no differently than before. It had felt dangerous, speaking all of that out loud. But then, she supposed he already knew the worst of it, having learned it in the cruelest way possible. Her explanation was really nothing after that.

Hungry Daniel might have been, but he wasn't too thrilled by the available supplies. He unenthusiastically chose a pizza, as she had, grumbling about Kevin's deficiencies in the kitchen, which seemed to be long-standing, from what she heard. The conversation rolled easily, like she was just an ordinary person to him.

"I don't know where he gets all that manic energy," Daniel said. "Eating nothing but this."

"Arnie can't be much of a cook, either. Where'd he go, anyway?"

"He hit the sack before Kev left. Early riser, I infer. I think his room is back that way." Daniel gestured in the opposite direction from the stairs.

"Does he seem a little strange to you?"

"What, with the mute thing? I figure that's just the glue in his relationship with Kevin. You have to be able to stomach listening to someone else talk nonstop if you're going to be friends with Kev. No room for your own words."

She snorted.

"There was ice cream under the pizza. You want some?" he asked.

She did, so the search began for silverware and bowls. Daniel did locate an ice cream scooper and soupspoons, but they had to put the ice cream into coffee mugs. As she watched him ladle the ice cream out of the carton, something occurred to her.

"Are you left-handed?"

"Er, yes."

"Oh. I thought Kevin was right-handed, but if you're identical twins, doesn't that mean —"

"Usually," Daniel said, passing her the first mug. The ice cream was plain vanilla, not her first choice, but she was happy to have any kind of sugar right now. "We're a special case, actually. We're called mirror-image twins. About twenty percent of identical twins—the ones where the egg splits late, they think—develop as opposites. So our faces aren't exactly the same unless you look at one as a reflection. It doesn't mean much, for Kevin especially." He savored his first bite of ice cream, then smiled. "I, on the other hand, will run into a problem if I ever need an organ transplant. All of my insides are reversed, so it's very complicated to replace certain things unless they find an organ from another reversed twin who also just happens to be a genetic match. In other words, I better hope I never need a new liver." He took another bite.

"It would make a lot more sense to me if it was Kevin who had everything backward."

They laughed together, but it was much gentler than it had been earlier in the day. Apparently they'd gotten the hysteria out of their systems.

"What does the paper say—the one with the command for the dog?"

Daniel pulled the card from his jeans pocket, glanced at it, and then handed it to her.

It read, in all caps, ESCAPE PROTOCOL.

"Do you think something bad happens if we say it out loud?" she wondered.

"I suppose it's possible. I'll believe anything after seeing his secret lair."

"Kevin really needs to hire someone to come up with better names for his commands. He's not very good at that part."

"I guess that could be my job now." Daniel sighed. "I *do* like dogs. It might be fun."

"It's still kind of teaching, right?"

"If Kev lets me do any." Daniel scowled. "I wonder if he sees me just mucking out stalls? I wouldn't put it past him." And then he sighed again. "At least the students all appear to be pretty bright. Do you think I could teach them to play volleyball?"

"Well...actually, yeah. They don't seem to have many limitations."

"I guess it won't be so bad. Right?"

"Right," she said confidently. And then mentally called herself a liar.

CHAPTER 14

When Alex woke up, the first issue was the soreness. Unconsciousness had given her a break from the pain, and that period of relief, though welcome, made the awakening to reality worse.

The room was pitch-black. She assumed there was a window somewhere behind the boxes, but it must be covered with a blackout shade. Kevin wouldn't want too many lighted windows at night. Better to keep the house looking only partially inhabited. As far as any locals knew, Arnie was the sole occupant.

She rolled out of the cot, groaning when her left shoulder and hip hit the wooden edge, and then felt her way to the light switch. She'd cleared a wide path from the cot to the door so that she wouldn't add to her injuries fumbling around in the dark. Once the light was on, she disarmed the leads and then removed her gas mask. Given that there were people here that she didn't want to kill, she'd used a pressurized canister of knockout gas.

The hall was empty, the bathroom door open. There was one damp towel hanging on the rack, so Daniel must already be awake. That was no surprise. She'd been up pretty late with her memory list, despairing, even as she continued typing, at the probability of recalling in a week's time what any of her cryptic notes stood for. As she worked through it, she noted plenty of secrets worth killing over, but none specific to her or Barnaby. There would have been other victims if any of those particular secrets were the root problem. From what she'd been able to track in the news, her death and Barnaby's had not been followed by any other names she recognized. Nothing public, anyway.

While she shampooed her hair, she thought about how she could narrow down the time frame. She usually did her best creative thinking in the shower.

Barnaby had always been paranoid, but he hadn't started *acting* on that paranoia until two years before his death. She remembered that initial conversation, the first time she'd realized she was in actual danger. It had been late fall—around Thanksgiving. If that was not a random change, if there had been some sort of catalyst, maybe Barnaby had been reacting to the case that was the issue. She couldn't be sure of the timing, but she was fairly positive about the interrogations that had taken place *after* that change—in her memory, they were all riddled through with the new stress and distraction. So those could be ruled out. And she knew all the cases from her first year easily, when everything had been horrifically new and awkward; those could be set aside as well. It still left her three years of work to sort through and two of the nuclear scares, but she was happy to have even the slightest measure of containment.

She appreciated the fluffy towels the bathroom was stocked with. Kevin apparently enjoyed his creature comforts. Or maybe it was Arnie who liked things plush. Whoever it was had also stocked the bathroom with all the toiletries a hotel would provide, only in full-size bottles. There had been shampoo and conditioner in the shower. Toothpaste, lotion, and mouthwash were all set out on the counter. Nice touch.

She took a swipe at the mirror with the towel and quickly confirmed that she was still unfit to be seen. The black eyes were mostly a sickly green color now, with some of the darker purple in the inside corners. Her lip was starting to deflate, but that only made the superglue more obvious. The bruises on her cheeks were just barely beginning to yellow around the edges.

She sighed. It would be at least a week before her face could go out in public, even in makeup.

After dressing in her least dirty clothes, Alex gathered the rest, balled them up inside a T-shirt as an improvised laundry bag, and set off in search of the facilities. It was empty and quiet downstairs. She could hear barking in the distance. Daniel and Arnie must be out dealing with the animals.

She found the spacious laundry room tucked away behind the kitchen. She noted the back door — always good to be familiar with the exits — and the large plastic attachment to the bottom half of it. It took her a minute to realize it was a doggie door — a huge doggie door, big enough to let Khan in. She hadn't seen any dogs in the house so far, but it must not always be off-limits. She started her load, then went to find breakfast.

The cupboards weren't much more helpful than the refrigerator had been. Half were full of cans of dog food, and the other half mostly empty. There was some coffee left in the pot on the counter, thank goodness. She also found a stash of Pop-Tarts, which she pilfered. Apparently Kevin and Arnie cared less about food than they did about towels. She found a mug from a Boy Scout camp circa 1983, chipped and faded. The time frame didn't fit either of the men who lived here — must be a secondhand acquisition. It worked just fine, regardless. When she was done, she loaded the mug in the stainless-steel dishwasher and then went to see what was on the day's agenda.

Lola and Khan were on the front porch, along with the Rottweiler whose name she couldn't remember.

They all got up like they'd been waiting for her and followed as she headed out to the barn. She patted Lola a few times as they walked; it seemed like the polite thing to do.

North of the modern outbuilding was a big run full of animals, Arnie in the center of them all, calling out commands to the frolicking dogs. It didn't look like many of them were listening to him, but a few played teacher's pet. She couldn't see Daniel anywhere. She wandered into the outbuilding, went down the length of it to where the supply room was. Kevin and Arnie stocked the place much better for the dogs than for themselves. Daniel wasn't there, either.

She meandered out to the edge of the practice yard, not sure what else to do. It was odd; she was used to being alone all the time. But now Daniel wasn't around to check on, and suddenly she was at loose ends.

Arnie, of course, paid zero attention to her as she came up to the fence and hooked her fingers through the links. She watched him work with a young German shepherd—still all oversize paws and floppy ears—long past the point when her own patience would have run out. Lola's two pups came over to press their bodies against the fence and beg for licks from their mother. She obliged a few times, then yelped at them, a funny sound that made Alex think of her own mother reminding her to study after dinner. Sure enough, the two half-grown puppies ambled back toward the man with the treats.

Maybe Daniel had returned to the practice range. Kevin had said there was a truck around here, but she'd seen no sign of it. She wished Daniel had waited for her. She wanted to play with the SIG some more. And, honestly, she could use some exercise with her PPK, too. Her life had never depended on her aim in the past, but it very well might in the future. She didn't want to waste the unexpected opportunity to improve her skills.

She watched Arnie with the young dogs for another half hour. Finally, she interrupted, more out of boredom than any driving need to know.

"Hey," she called over the dog sounds. "Um, Arnie?"

He looked up, his face betraying no interest.

"Did Daniel take the truck over to the range? What time did he leave?"

He nodded, then shrugged. She tried to guess at a translation, but quickly gave up. She would have to keep the questions simpler.

"He took the truck?" she verified.

Arnie was focused on the dogs again, but she did get an answer. "Guess so. Wasn't there the last time I went to the barn."

"How far is it to the range?" she asked. It had seemed too long a distance to walk, but she might as well ask.

"'Bout five miles, as the crow flies."

Not as far as she'd thought. Daniel was a runner—couldn't he have left the truck? Well, she could use a run herself, but he'd probably be on his way back before she could get there.

"And you don't know what time he left?"

"Didn't see him. It was before nine, though."

It had been more than an hour. Doubtless he'd return soon. She'd wait her turn.

It was good that Daniel was taking an interest in the practice. Maybe some of what she and Kevin had been trying to tell him had sunk in a little. She didn't actually want him to have to live in fear, but it was the best option. Fear would keep him alive.

She waved her thanks to Arnie, then headed back to the house to finish the laundry, furry entourage in tow.

An hour later, she was in clean clothes for the first time in several days, and it felt fantastic. She put the outfit she'd been wearing in the washing machine, happy at the thought of having her whole wardrobe smelling nice again. She put in another thirty minutes on her memory project; at least she remembered her notations twelve hours later. She was trying to do things chronologically as best she could, though her numbering system was based on severity. It might have made things more confusing than they should be, but she didn't want to reorganize it all now.

This morning she worked terrorist events number fifteen and three—an attempted subway bombing and a stolen biological weapon—trying to think of any names that had come up in context. The terrorist and Russian profiteers on number fifteen had been dealt with, so it was probably nothing to do with them. She noted it down anyway. *NY* was too obvious an abbreviation, so she used *MB* for Manhattan–Bronx; the 1 train had been the target. *TT* for the faction behind it, *KV* for Kalasha Valleys, *VR* for the Russian who sold them the materials. A few outsiders who had aided and abetted: *RP, FD, BB.*

Number three had a few loose ends, as she remembered, but those had been turned over to the CIA. She looked at her letters: *J, I-P* for Jammu, India, on the border of Pakistan. *TP;* the Tacoma Plague, they'd called it. It had been developed by a known terrorist cell from the notes of an American scientist, lifted from a lab near Seattle. The splinter cell, *FA,* was involved in events T10 and T13 as well. The department had still been helping the CIA procure information about the remnants of the cell back when she'd been "fired." She wondered if the CIA had ever shut it down completely. Kevin had been busy enough in Mexico that he probably couldn't give her the answer. She noted down initials for a few connected names. *DH* was the American scientist the formula was stolen from, and *OM* was a member of the terrorist cell whom she'd interrogated. She thought there was another American involved somehow—not a participant in the event. Or had that name been related to number four? She only remembered the name was short, clipped-sounding...did it start with a *P?*

She'd never been allowed to keep any notes, of course, so there was nothing to refer back to. It was frustrating. Enough so that she gave up and decided to look for lunch. The Pop-Tart hadn't exactly been filling.

As she walked into the great room, she could hear the low rumble of an engine pulling up outside, then the grinding sound of heavy tires on the gravel. Finally.

Habit had her checking out the door to make sure it was Daniel. Just as she peeked out, the engine noise cut off. A dusty white older-model Toyota truck with an equally aged and dusty camper shell was parked where they'd left the sedan last night, and Daniel was getting out of the driver's seat. Einstein jumped out the car door after him.

Even as she was admiring the vehicle's ordinary exterior—perfect for blending in—a slow creeping sensation started to inch up her back, raising bumps on her skin as it moved. She froze, wide eyes darting around like a startled rabbit trying to suss out the direction danger was coming from. What had her subconscious noticed that she had not?

She zeroed in on the paper bag cradled in Daniel's left arm. As she watched, he pulled the front seat forward and grabbed another bag. Einstein danced happily around his legs. Khan and the Rottweiler ran down the porch steps to join in.

She felt the blood drain out of her face, leaving a dizzy sensation behind.

And then the second of shock passed, and she was in motion. She charged after the dogs, feeling the blood pulse back into her bruised cheeks.

"Hey, Alex," Daniel called cheerfully. "There are a few more bags in the back, if you're feeling—" He stopped abruptly when he processed her expression. "What's happened? Kevin—"

"Where did you go?" She spit the words through her teeth.

He blinked once. "I just ran out to that town we passed on our way in. Childress."

Her hands balled into fists.

"I took the dog," he offered. "Nothing happened."

She pressed one fist to her mouth, winced, and tried to calm herself. It wasn't his fault. He just didn't understand. She and Kevin should have advised him better. It was her own misstep for assuming some of that guidance had happened while she'd been asleep in the car. But if Kevin hadn't been prepping Daniel for his new life, then what *had* they been talking about for all those hours?

"Did anyone see y—of course they did. You bought things. How many people saw you?"

He blinked again. "Did I do something wrong?"

"You went into town?" A deep voice rumbled behind her.

Daniel shifted his gaze to a point over her head. "Yeah—I mean, you guys were pretty short on groceries. I just wanted to get some nonfrozen stuff, you know? You seemed busy…"

She turned to look at Arnie. His face was impassive, but she knew it well enough now to see little breaks in the façade—stress marks around his eyes, one slightly more prominent vein in his forehead.

"Do you have a way to contact Kevin?" she asked him.

"You mean Joe?"

"Probably. Daniel's brother."

"Nope."

"What did I do?" Daniel asked pleadingly.

She sighed as she turned back to him. "Do you remember when Kevin said that no one around here had ever seen his face? Well…now they have."

Daniel's color started to ebb as he processed that. "But…I used a fake name. I—I said I was just passing through."

"How many people did you talk to?"

"Just the cashier at the grocery store and the one at the—"

"How many places did you go into?"

"Three…"

She and Arnie exchanged a glance—horrified on her part, more inscrutable on his.

"Kevin left me money for things I might need—I assumed he meant stuff like eggs and milk," Daniel offered.

"He meant fake IDs," Alex snapped.

The rest of Daniel's color vanished, and his mouth fell open.

They stared at him for a long moment.

Daniel took a deep breath, visibly centering himself.

"Okay," he said. "I screwed up. Can we take the groceries in before you tell me how bad? It only adds waste to my mistake if the perishables spoil in the truck."

Lips pressed into a tight line—ignoring the irritating glob of superglue—Alex nodded once and went around to the back of the truck to help unload. She saw all the bags inside the camper and felt the blood behind her bruises again.

Of course, on top of going into the closest town, he would have bought enough food to feed an army. And if there was any other thing that would make him more memorable, he'd probably done that, too.

In ominous silence, Alex and Arnie brought all the bags in and put them on the counter. Daniel worked back and forth between the cupboards and the fridge, sorting each item into the right spot. Alex might have thought that he wasn't taking this seriously enough except for the fact that his color kept changing; though his expression was steady, his cheeks and neck would suddenly flush, and then he'd go white again.

The cooling-off period was probably a good idea. It gave Alex a chance to think everything through and be realistic about the danger posed. She'd been about ready to steal Arnie's truck and disappear, but she knew that would be overreacting. Sometimes overreactions saved your life; sometimes they just put you in more danger. She had to remember her face; running now would only cause her more problems.

Daniel placed the last item—some kind of leafy green vegetable—in the fridge and shut the door. He didn't turn, just stood there with his head slightly bowed toward the stainless steel.

"How bad?" he asked quietly.

She looked at Arnie. He didn't seem inclined to speak.

"Tell me you paid cash," she began.

"Yes."

"Well, that's something, at least."

"But not everything," Daniel guessed.

"No. Childress is a very small town."

"Just over six thousand people," Arnie rumbled.

It was worse than she'd thought; she knew of high schools with bigger student bodies.

"So a stranger in town is memorable," she said. "You would have been noticed."

Daniel turned to her. His face was composed, but his eyes were troubled.

"Yes, I can see that," he agreed.

"You were in Arnie's truck, with Arnie's dog," Alex said. "Someone could connect you back to Arnie."

"Einstein stayed in the truck," Daniel said. "I don't think anyone was watching me get in or out."

"There're a hundred similar trucks in town. Five that are the exact same color, year, and model; two of those have campers," Arnie said, not to Daniel, but to Alex. "Half the people there would have a dog with them."

"That's helpful," she told Arnie. "You guys did good here."

"How much does this affect you?" Daniel asked him.

Arnie shrugged. "No way to know. People forget stuff pretty quick when they've got no real reason to remember. We lie low, it'll probably come to nothing."

"Anyway, what's done is done," Alex mused. "We'll just have to be extra careful."

"Kevin's going to be furious." Daniel sighed.

"When *isn't* he furious?" Alex asked, and Arnie actually laughed out one brief chuckle. "Anyway, it's his own fault for not explaining anything to you. A mistake I'm not going to repeat." She gestured toward the couch.

Arnie nodded to himself, then clumped out the front door, back to his work. Kevin had picked a good partner. She found herself wishing that Arnie were Daniel's brother rather than Kevin. Arnie was so much easier to deal with.

"How about I make lunch while you lecture?" Daniel offered. "I'm suffering extreme hunger pangs. I don't know what Arnie survives on around here."

"Sure," she said. She grabbed a bar stool and planted herself.

"I did honestly think that I was helping," Daniel murmured as he went back to the fridge.

"I know, Daniel, I know. And I'm hungry, too," she conceded.

"I'll ask first next time," he promised.

She sighed. "That's a start."

•   •   •

THOUGH SHE DIDN'T want to admit it, the large sandwich Daniel made for her did a lot to mellow her perspective on the incident. She gave him the basics while they ate — there'd be time for more detail when they had a specific task ahead of them — and he listened attentively.

"I don't know how to see the world that way," he confessed. "It all seems so paranoid."

"Yes! Paranoia is exactly what we're shooting for. Paranoia is good."

"That's a little contradictory to how they teach it in the real world, but I'll work on flipping my perspective. I know I can do this much—I will check with you on everything from now on. Before I *breathe*."

"You'll start to get it. It becomes habit after a while. But don't think of what you used to know as the *real* world. The things that happen in *this* world are a whole lot more real, and a whole lot more permanent. It's primitive—survival instincts. I know you have them; you were born with them. You just have to tap into that part of yourself."

"I have to think like the hunted." He tried to keep his face positive, but she could see how much the idea devastated him.

"Yes. You *are* the hunted. And so am I. And so is your brother. And hell, so is Arnie, apparently. It's a very popular state of being around here."

"But you," he said slowly, "and my brother, and probably even Arnie, are still predators. I'm just prey."

She shook her head. "I started out as prey. I learned. You've got advantages I never had. You share an exact genetic code with your brother, the apex predator. I saw you down at the range—once those instincts kick in, you'll be plenty able to take care of yourself."

"You're just saying that to make me feel better."

"I'm saying that because I'm jealous. If I could be tall, and strong, and a natural shot, it would change this game I'm playing."

"If I could be smart and paranoid, I wouldn't have put us at risk."

She smiled. "There's no comparison. You have the ability to learn; I'll never be able to grow any taller."

He grinned back. "But you're so much stealthier the way you are."

"Ugh," she groaned. "Let's go do something productive and shoot up some hay bales."

"Okay, but I have to be back by"—he glanced at the clock on the range—"six o'clock at the latest."

Alex was confused. "Is your favorite TV show on or something?"

"No. I owe you dinner, and it's not like I can take you out on the town." He smiled apologetically. "That's one of the reasons, beyond starvation, I went shopping."

"Um..."

"I asked you to dinner. You don't remember?"

"Oh, I remember. I just think we're probably quits on anything you might have offered before I kidnapped you."

"I won't feel right if I don't make good. Anyway, someone has to cook, and I'm not half bad at it. I already know that Kevin and Arnie are useless in that department."

Alex sighed. "I'm probably just as bad."

"So it's settled. Now let's go improve our aim."

·   ·   ·

DANIEL PICKED THINGS up so quickly, it was no wonder Kevin had been recruited. While they practiced, Daniel told Alex about Kevin's prowess at sports and his particular gift for shooting. Apparently the boys and their father had taken part in many competitions, and Kevin had almost always come away with the first-place trophy.

"I made the mistake of beating him once, when we were nine. *Not* worth it. From then on, I went along to keep Dad happy, but I didn't really compete. I found my own interests, things that Kevin didn't want to bother with. Like books. Community involvement. Distance running. Culinary classes. Girl stuff, as he frequently informed me."

Alex loaded a new magazine. They were really burning through Kevin's ammo, but she didn't much care. He could afford new ammo.

She'd done a thorough search of the barn today and found a few of his cash hoards. It looked like some of the drug money had come home with him. As a general rule, she avoided stealing unless she'd run out of other options, but she was very tempted now to grab as much as she could carry. After all, it was partially Kevin's fault she was so much poorer than she had been last month.

"I wonder what would have happened to me if I'd had a sibling who was better at chemistry and biology in high school?" she asked. "Would I have given it up? Become an accountant?"

She took a shot, then smiled. Right in the heart.

"Maybe you're more competitive than I am. Maybe you would have fought it out for the crown."

He leaned casually into his shooting position and fired a round at a bale a hundred yards farther away than hers.

She fired again. "Maybe I would be happier as an accountant."

Daniel sighed. "You're probably right. I was pretty happy as a teacher. Not a glamorous career, but the mundane can be quite satisfying. In fact, being ordinary in general is highly underrated."

"I wouldn't know. But it sounds nice."

"You were never ordinary." It wasn't a question.

"No," she agreed. "Not really. Unfortunate, as it turned out." Always too smart for her own good, though it had taken her a while to see things that way. She shot her target in the head twice in quick succession.

Daniel straightened up and leaned the long rifle against his shoulder. Einstein got to his feet and stretched out his back. "Well, I had my few areas where I transcended the mundane," he said, and Alex could tell from his tone that he was purposely lightening the mood. "And lucky you," he continued, "tonight you get to see me work in my favorite field."

Alex set the SIG down and stretched, much like the dog had. Her muscles got stiff more quickly with her injuries. She wasn't moving the way she usually did; she was favoring the damaged parts of her body. She needed to force herself to use her limbs equally.

"Sounds exciting. And I'm hungry, so I really hope the field you're talking about is the kitchen."

"It is, indeed. Shall we?" He made a sweeping gesture with his free hand toward the truck.

"As soon as we clean up our toys."

·   ·   ·

DANIEL DID SEEM very at home, humming as he diced things and sprinkled spices on things and put other things into saucepans. Of course, she couldn't help but notice that a lot of the tools appeared to be brand-new and hadn't been in the cupboards when she'd dug through them earlier. She would hold off on the lecture about how people who were just passing through town rarely bought things for their kitchens. It was starting to smell kind of amazing and she didn't want to jinx anything.

She sat sideways on the sofa, her legs curled up under her, watching the news and Daniel at the same time. Nothing interesting on TV—just a lot of local stuff and a little bit about the primaries, which were still about nine months away. The whole election process was irritating to Alex. She would probably have to stop watching the news altogether when the real campaigning started. As someone who knew better than most the kind of darkness that went on behind the scenes and how little any of the important decisions had to do with the figurehead spokesperson the people elected, it was hard for her to care much about left or right.

Arnie had eaten another frozen dinner and retired around seven thirty, as seemed to be his habit. Alex had tried to convince him that a home-cooked meal was worth waiting for, but he hadn't even bothered responding to her coaxing. She was surprised that Daniel didn't give it a try, but maybe he was concentrating too hard on the food to notice. She offered to help once or twice only to be told in no uncertain terms that all she was allowed to do was eat.

Daniel grumbled to himself as he set out the unmatched plates, random silverware, and coffee mugs. She would have to remind him that he wasn't to go off on another shopping spree for monogrammed china. He moved all the food to the table, and she got up eagerly, famished and driven half wild by the various fragrances wafting through the room. He held a chair out for her, which reminded her of things she'd seen in old movies. Was this what normal people did? She wasn't sure, but she didn't think so. At least, not in the places she went out to eat.

With a flourish, he pulled out a lighter and lit a blue-and-pink-polka-dotted candle shaped like the number 1 that he'd stuck into a bread roll.

"This was the closest I could find to a taper," he explained as he saw her expression. "And this was the best I could do for wine," he continued, gesturing to the bottle that sat open beside her coffee mug. The words on the label were all unfamiliar to her. "It's the choicest vintage the United Supermarket carries."

He made as if to pour, and she automatically covered the top of her mug with her hand.

"I don't drink."

He hesitated, then poured a small amount for himself. "I got some apple juice this morning. Or I could get you some water?"

"Juice would be great."

He got up and headed for the fridge. "Can I ask? AA or a religious preference?"

"Safety. I haven't touched anything that might cloud my perception in four years."

He returned and poured her a mugful of juice before sitting opposite her. His face was carefully nonchalant.

"Didn't you start running just three years ago?"

"Yes. But once it really sank in that someone might try to kill me at any moment, it was hard to think about much else. I couldn't afford to be distracted. I could miss something. I did miss something, I guess.

If I'd really been on my toes, Barnaby might still be alive. We shouldn't have waited."

"You don't feel safe here?"

She looked up at him, surprised by the question. The answer was so obvious. "No."

"Because I was stupid this morning?"

She shook her head. "No, not at all. I never feel safe anywhere."

She heard how blasé the words sounded, the way the words *of course* seemed to be embedded in her answer, and watched his face fall a little in response.

"Hey, but I probably have PTSD. It doesn't have to be like that. I'm sure another person could handle things better."

He raised one eyebrow. "Yes, Kevin seems completely normal."

They laughed again. She hadn't laughed this much in the past three years put together.

He lifted his fork. "Shall we?"

CHAPTER 15

No, I'm not exaggerating. I am fairly certain this is the best meal I've ever eaten in my entire life. Granted, I'm generally a fast-food girl, so I'm not a very sophisticated judge, but I also mean what I say."

"Well, that's a lovely compliment. Thank you."

"What is this again?" She poked her fork at the dessert on her plate, wishing she had a tiny bit more space in her stomach. She'd eaten herself nearly sick, but still she craved just one more bite.

"Bananas Foster butter cake."

"I *mean*..." She went for it, ignoring her stomach and savoring a small forkful. "Where did you learn to do this?"

"I took a few culinary courses in college. I watch a lot of the Food Network on the weekends, and I practice when I can afford to."

"Time amazingly well spent. I think you might have missed your calling, though."

"I worked in a few restaurants back in the day. It wasn't conducive to a social life. When I was dating my ex...well, she wasn't a big fan of the schedule. My day job gave us more time together."

"Not everyone would make the sacrifice."

"It wasn't one, really. Working with the kids always felt most important. I loved it. And it wasn't like I couldn't cook at home. So I got both for a while."

"Then you stopped?"

He sighed. "Well, when Lainey left...I didn't want to fight. I let her have whatever she wanted."

Alex could easily picture how that had worked. She'd seen Daniel's postdivorce bank account. "She cleaned you out."

"Pretty much. Hence the ramen diet."

"That is a crime." She looked longingly at what was left of the butter cake.

"Life," he said. "You've had your share of heart-break."

"Honestly, though it all went down with a little too much terror and tragedy, I was ready to quit anyway. It was never what I wanted to do with my life; it's just what I was really good at." She shrugged. "The job took a toll."

"I can't even begin to imagine. But I meant... romantically."

She stared at him, uncomprehending. "Romantically?"

"Well, as you said, it ended in tragedy."

"My life, sure. But...?"

"I just figured, from the way you talk about him, it must have been devastating to lose...Dr. Barnaby the way you did. You never said what his first name was?"

"It was Joseph. But I always called him Barnaby."

She took a sip of her juice.

"And were you in love with him...from the very beginning?"

Her shocked gasp pulled a mouthful of juice into her lungs, and she spluttered and choked. Daniel jumped up and pounded her on the back while she tried to regain control of her breathing. After a minute, she waved him off.

"I'm okay," she coughed out. "Sit."

He stayed by her, one hand half extended. "Are you sure?"

"Just. Caught by surprise. *With Barnaby?*"

"I thought you said yesterday..."

She took a deep breath, then coughed one more time. "That I loved him." She shuddered. "Sorry, I'm just having some seriously squicky incest reflexes right now. Barnaby was like my father. He was a good father—the only one I ever knew. It was really hard knowing how he died, and I miss him like hell. So, yes, definitely devastating. But not like that."

Daniel returned slowly to his seat. He thought for a moment, and then he asked, "Who else did you have to cut ties with when you disappeared?"

She could imagine the long array of faces parading through his mind right now. "That part wasn't so hard for me. It sounds pretty pathetic, but Barnaby was my only real friend. My work was my entire life, and I wasn't allowed to talk about my work to anyone besides Barnaby. I lived a very isolated existence. There were others around...for example, the underlings who prepped subjects. They knew what was happening in a general sense but had none of the classified details about the information we were trying to retrieve. And, well, they were terrified of me. They knew what my job was. So we didn't chat much. There were a few lab assistants who performed a variety of duties outside the action rooms, but they *didn't* know what we were doing and I had to be careful not to say anything to tip them off. Occasionally, people from the different agencies visited individually to monitor a particular interrogation, but I had very little contact with them except to receive instructions about the angles I should cover. Mostly they watched from behind one-way glass, and Carston gave me the information. I used to think Carston was sort of my friend, but he *did* just try to kill me...So I can't compare it to what you're losing. Obviously, I didn't have that much of a life to lose. Even before I was recruited...I guess I just don't bond with other humans like a normal person. Like I said, pathetic."

He smiled at her. "I haven't noticed any deficiencies."

"Um, thanks. Well, it's getting late. Let me help clear this all up."

"Sure." He stood and stretched, then started stacking plates. She had to move quickly to grab a few things before he had efficiently made off with all of it. "But the night is still young," he continued, "and I'm going to have to bring up the other half of our deal now."

"Huh?"

He laughed. His hands were full so she pulled the dishwasher open. She filled in the bottom rack while he did the top and put the bigger pieces in the sink. The chore moved quickly with both of them working in easy tandem.

"You don't remember? It's only been a few days, really. I'll admit, it does seem a lot longer. It could be weeks."

"I have no idea what you're talking about."

He closed the dishwasher and then leaned back against the counter, folding his arms. She waited.

"Think back. Before things got…strange. You promised that if I still liked you after we had dinner together…"

He looked at her with raised eyebrows, waiting for her to fill in the blank.

Oh. He was talking about their conversation on the train. She was shocked he could refer to it so lightly. That was the last moment his life had been normal. The last moment before everything had been stolen from him. And though she hadn't been the architect of that theft, she'd been the hand they used.

"Um. Something about a foreign film theater at the university near you, right?"

"Yes—well, but I didn't mean for you to be *quite* so specific. The university theater is not exactly convenient right now. However..." He opened the cupboard behind him, reached up, and pulled something off the highest shelf. He turned back to her with a huge grin and presented a DVD case. The faded cover had a picture of a beautiful woman in a red dress and a dark, wide-brimmed hat.

"Ta-da!" he said.

"Where on earth did you get that?"

His smile got a little smaller. "Second store I went to. Thrift store. I got very lucky. This is actually a great movie." He assessed her face. "I can read your thoughts. You're thinking, *Is there any place this idiot didn't go? We'll be dead by sunrise.*"

"Not in so many words. And we'd be disappearing into the night in Arnie's stolen truck right now if I thought it was that bad."

"Still, while I'm very, very sorry for my rash behavior, I'm also quite happy I was able to find this gem. You'll love it."

She shook her head—not disagreeing, just wondering how things had gotten so odd in her life. One wrong move and suddenly she was committed to reading subtitles with the most kind and...*uncorrupted* person she'd ever met.

He stepped toward her. "You can't say no. You made a bargain and I intend to hold you to it."

"I'll do it, I'll do it. You just have to explain why exactly it is that you still like me," she said, finishing more glumly than she'd begun.

"I think I can do that."

He took another step forward, backing her against the island. He put his hands on the edge of the counter behind her, one on either side, and as he leaned forward, she could smell the clean, citrusy scent of his hair. He was so close, she could see that he must have shaved recently—his jaw was smooth and there was the hint of razor burn just under his chin.

Daniel's proximity confused her, but it didn't frighten her the way it would have with just about any other person on the planet. He wasn't dangerous to her, she knew that. She didn't understand what he was doing, though, even when he slowly lowered his face toward hers, his eyes starting to close. It never occurred to her that he was about to kiss her until his half-open lips were just a breath away from hers.

That realization startled her. It startled her a lot. And when she was startled, she had ingrained reactions that manifested without her conscious approval.

She ducked under his arm, spinning free. She dashed several feet away, then spun back to face the source of the alarm, sliding into a half crouch. Her hands were automatically at her waist, looking for the belt she wasn't wearing.

As she took in Daniel's horrified expression, Alex realized that her reaction would have fit better if he'd pulled a knife and held it to her throat. She straightened up and dropped her hands, her face burning.

"Uh, sorry. Sorry! You, um, caught me off guard."

Daniel's horror shifted into disbelief. "Wow. I didn't think I was moving that fast, but maybe I should reevaluate."

"I just…I'm sorry, what *was* that?"

A shade of impatience crossed his expression. "Well, I was about to kiss you."

"That's what it looked like, but…*why?* I mean, kiss *me?* I don't…I don't understand."

He shook his head and turned to lean back against the island. "Huh. I really thought we were on the same page, but now I kind of feel like I'm speaking English as a second language. What did *you* think was going on here? With the dinner date? And the sad little candle?" He gestured to the table.

He walked toward her then, and she forced herself

not to back away. Confusion aside, she knew her wild overreaction had been rude. She didn't want to hurt his feelings. Even if he was a crazy person.

"Surely..." He sighed. "*Surely* you've been aware of how often I just...touch you." He was close enough at that point to reach out one hand and brush his knuckles along her arm in demonstration. "On the planet I come from, that kind of thing signifies romantic interest." He leaned toward her again, his eyes narrowed. "Please tell me, what does it mean on yours?"

She took a deep breath. "Daniel, what you're processing now is a kind of sensory deprivation reaction," she explained. "It's something I've seen before, in the lab..."

His eyes widened; he backed out of her space. His expression was totally flummoxed.

"This is a valid response to what you've experienced, and it's actually a very mild response, under the circumstances," she continued. "You're doing remarkably well. Many people would have had a complete nervous breakdown by this point. This emotional reaction might seem similar to something you've experienced before, but I can assure you that what you're feeling right now is not romantic interest."

He regained his composure as she explained, but he didn't seem enlightened or reassured by her diagnosis. His eyebrows lowered and his lips tucked in at the corners like he was annoyed.

"And you're sure you know my feelings better than I do because..."

"As I said, I've seen something like this before in the lab."

"'Something like this'?" he quoted back at her. "I imagine you saw many things in your lab, but I'm also sure that I'm still the best qualified to know when I'm experiencing romantic interest." He *sounded* angry, but he was smiling and he was moving closer while he spoke. "So if your only argument is anecdotal..."

"That's not my only argument," she began slowly, unwillingly. These weren't the easiest words to say. "I may have been...absorbed by my work, but I wasn't totally oblivious. I know what men see when they look at me, the ones who know what I am...like you do. And I understand that reaction. I don't disagree with it. Your brother's animosity—that is a normal, rational response. I've seen it many times before—fear, loathing, an eagerness to assert physical dominance. I am the bogeyman in a very dark and scary world. I frighten people who aren't afraid of anything else, not even death. I can take everything they pride themselves on away from them; I can make them betray everything they hold sacred. I am the monster they see in their nightmares." It was a version of herself she'd come to accept, but not without some pain.

She wasn't unaware that outsiders, people who didn't know her, saw her as a woman rather than a demon. When she needed to, she could make use of her ability to appear delicate and feminine, as she had with the walrus-y hotel manager. It was no different from her ability to look like a boy. Both were deceptions. But even those outsiders who saw her as a female didn't look at her with... *desire*. She wasn't that girl, and that was okay. She'd been born with her own gifts, and you didn't get everything.

He waited patiently while she spoke, his expression neutral. She didn't think he was reacting to her words strongly enough.

"Do you understand what I'm saying?" she asked. "I am intrinsically incompatible with being an object of romantic interest."

"I understand you. I just don't agree."

"I don't understand how you of all people can disagree."

"First, but not entirely to the point, I'm not afraid of you."

She exhaled impatiently. "Why not?"

"Because, now that you know who I am, I am in no danger from you, and I never will be unless I change into the kind of person who should be."

Her lips screwed into a half-pursed frown. He was right... but that wasn't really the issue.

"Second, still tangential, I think you've been spending all your time with the wrong kind of man. A hazard of your particular work, I'd imagine."

"Maybe. But what is the main point you're dancing around?"

He got into her personal space again. "How I feel. How you feel."

She held her ground. "And how can you be sure what you're feeling? You're in the middle of the most traumatic experience of your life. You've just lost your whole world. All that's left is a brother you don't completely trust, your kidnapper-slash-torturer, and Arnie. So it was probably fifty-fifty on whether you'd attach yourself to me or to Arnie. This is pretty basic Stockholm syndrome stuff, Daniel. I'm the only human female in your life—there aren't any other options. Think about it rationally; think about how inappropriate the timing is. You can't trust feelings born in the midst of severe physical and mental anguish."

"I might consider that, except for one thing."

"And what's that?"

"I wanted you before you were the only human female in my life."

This threw her, and he took advantage, placing both his hands lightly on her shoulders. The warmth from his palms made her realize that she'd been cold without recognizing it. She shivered.

"Remember when I told you that I'd never asked a woman out on a train before? That was kind of an understatement. On average, it takes me about three weeks of fairly regular interaction—along with an embarrassing amount of encouragement from the girl—before I work up the nerve to ask someone to go for a casual coffee. But from the second I saw your face, I was willing to leap miles outside my comfort zone to make sure I saw it again."

She shook her head. "Daniel, I roofied you. You were high on a chemical compound with manifestations similar to Ecstasy."

"Not then, I wasn't. I remember. I felt the difference before and after you 'shocked' me. That was when things got confusing. And before the drug, I was already in neck-deep. I was trying to figure out how I was going to get off at your stop without looking like a stalker."

She had no answer. His physical proximity was becoming disorienting. He still held her loosely, bending in slightly so that his face was closer to hers.

It wasn't until this moment that she began to really consider his words. She'd written off everything he'd said and done since the kidnapping as aftershocks from the trauma. She'd analyzed him like a subject, always separating herself from the equation. Because none of it was *about* her. And all of it was within normal parameters for what he'd been through.

She tried to remember the last time a man had looked at her this way, and she came up empty.

For the past three years, every person she'd met, male or female, had been a potential source of danger.

For the six years before that, as she'd just excruciatingly explained, she'd been anathema to every man she'd interacted with. Which took her all the way back to college and medical school and the few brief relationships that had never included much romance. She was a scientist first, even then, and the men she'd formed attachments to had been the same. Their relationships were born from massive amounts of time logged in together and very specific interests that 99.99 percent of the populace couldn't begin to grasp. Each time, they'd settled for each other by default. No wonder it had never amounted to much.

And none of them had ever worn this expression. Wonder and fascination mixed with something electric as he gazed at her face...her battered, swollen face. For the first time, she felt mortified about her mangled appearance for an entirely vain reason. Her hands had been hanging limply at her sides. Now she raised one and covered as much as she could, hiding like a child.

"I've put some thought into this," he said, and she could hear the smile in his voice. "I know what I'm saying."

She just shook her head.

"Of course, all of that is moot if you don't feel a similar way. I've been a little overconfident tonight." He paused. "Given that we haven't been speaking the same language at all, have we? I've been misreading you."

He paused again like he was waiting for an answer, but she had no idea what to say.

"What do you see when you look at me?" he asked.

She lowered her hand an inch and glanced up at him, at the same perplexingly honest face she'd been trying to understand from the beginning. What kind of a question was that? There were too many answers.

"I don't know how to respond to that."

His eyes narrowed for a moment, considering. She wished he would take a step back so that she could think more clearly. Then he seemed to brace himself, squaring his shoulders for some kind of blow.

"Might as well get everything out in the open. Answer this instead: What's the very worst thing you see when you look at me?"

The honest answer popped out before she could think it through. "A liability."

She saw how harshly the word landed. Now he gave her the space she'd just wished for, and she regretted it. Why was the room so cold?

He nodded to himself as he backed away.

"That's fair, that's completely fair. I'm an idiot, clearly. I can't forget I've put you in danger. Also, the fact that—"

"No!" She took a hesitant step toward him, anxious to be clear. "That's not what I meant."

"You don't have to be kind. I know I'm useless

in all this." He gestured vaguely toward the door, toward the world outside that was trying to kill them both.

"You're not. Being a normal person is not a bad thing. You'll learn all the rest. I was talking about… leverage." She couldn't help herself—his expression was just so openly devastated. She took another step toward him and grabbed one of his big, warm hands with both of her little icy ones. It made her feel better when the word *leverage* replaced the pain in his eyes with confusion. She hurried to explain. "You remember what Kevin and I were saying about leverage? About how you're the leverage the Agency needed to get him to expose himself?"

"Yes, that makes me feel *so* much better than useless."

"Let me finish." She took a deep breath. "They've never had anything on me. Barnaby was my only family. I didn't have some sister with a couple of kids and a house in the suburbs that the department could threaten to blow up. There was no one I cared about. Lonely, yes, but I was also free. It was only myself I had to keep alive."

She watched him think through the words, trying to sort out her meaning. She fumbled for a concrete example.

"See, if… if they had you," she explained slowly, "if they grabbed you somehow… I would have to come after you." It was so true it frightened her. She didn't understand why it was true, but that didn't change the fact.

His eyes widened and seemed to freeze that way.

"And they'd win, you know," she said apologetically. "They'd kill us both. But that doesn't mean I wouldn't have to try. See?" She shrugged. "Liability."

He opened his mouth to speak, then shut it again. He paced to the sink, then back to stand right in front of her.

"Why would you come after me? Guilt?"

"Some," she admitted.

"But it wasn't you who involved me, not really. They didn't choose me because of you."

"I know — that's why I said *some*. Maybe thirty-three percent."

He smiled a tiny bit, like she'd said something funny. "And the other sixty-seven percent?"

"Another thirty-three percent... justice? That's not the right word. But someone like you... you deserve more than this. You're a better person than any of them. It's not right that someone like you should have to be a part of this world. It's an evil waste."

She hadn't meant to be quite so vehement. She could tell she'd only confused him again. He didn't realize how unusual he was. He didn't belong down here in the filth of the trenches. Something about him was just... pure.

"And the last thirty-four?" he asked after a moment of thought.

"I don't *know*." She groaned.

She didn't know why or how he had become a central figure in her life. She didn't know why she automatically assumed he would be there in the future when that made no sense at all. She didn't know why, when his brother had asked her to keep an eye on him, her answer had been so earnest and so . . . *compulsory*.

Daniel was waiting for more. She spread her hands helplessly. She didn't know what else to say.

He smiled a little. "Well, *liability* doesn't seem such an awful word as it did before."

"It does to me."

"You know if they came for you, I would do what I could to stand in their way. So you're a liability for me, too."

"I wouldn't want you to do that."

"Because we'd both end up dead."

"Yes, we would! If they come for me, you *run*."

He laughed. "Agree to disagree."

"Daniel—"

"Let me tell you what else I see when I look at you."

Her shoulders hunched automatically. "Tell me the worst thing you see."

He sighed, then reached out to gently lay his fingertips along her cheekbone. "These bruises. They break my heart. But, in a really twisted and wrong way, I'm sort of grateful for them. How shameful is that?"

"Grateful?"

"Well, if my idiot bully of a brother hadn't beaten you up, you would have disappeared, and I would have had no way to ever find you again. Because of your injuries, you needed our help. You stayed with me."

His expression when he said the last four words was very unsettling. Or maybe it was his fingers lingering on her skin.

"Now can I tell you what else I see?"

She stared at him warily.

"I see a woman who is more... *real* than any other woman I've ever met. You make every other person I've known seem insubstantial, somehow incomplete. Like shadows and illusions. I loved my wife, or rather — as you so insightfully pointed out while I was high — I loved my idea of who she was. I truly did. But she was never as *there* to me as you are. I've never been drawn to someone the way I am to you, and I have been from the very first moment I met you. It's like the difference between... between *reading* about gravity and then falling for the first time."

They stared at each other for what felt like hours but could have been minutes or even seconds. His hand, at first just touching her cheekbone with the very tips of his fingers, slowly relaxed down until his palm was cradling her jaw. His thumb brushed across her lower lip with a pressure so light, she wasn't totally sure she hadn't imagined it.

"This is entirely irrational on every level," she whispered.

"Don't kill me, please?"

She might have nodded.

He put his other hand on her face — so softly that despite her bruises there was no hint of pain. It was just live current, like the way a plasma globe must feel from the inside.

She started to remind herself, as his lips pressed gently against hers, that she was not thirteen years old and this was not her first kiss, so really...then his hands moved into her hair and held her mouth more firmly against his, his lips opened, and she couldn't even finish the thought. She couldn't think how the words were supposed to string together.

She gasped — just a tiny puff of breath — and he pulled his face an inch back, still holding her head secure in his long hands.

"Did I hurt you?"

She couldn't remember how to say *Just keep kissing me,* so instead she stretched up on her tiptoes to throw her arms around his neck and pull him closer. He was not unwilling to comply.

He must have felt the drag in her arms, or his back was protesting the considerable difference in their heights; he grabbed her waist and swung her up onto the island counter, never breaking the contact between their lips. Reflexively, her legs wrapped around his hips at the same time that his arms pulled tight around her torso, so their bodies were warmly fused together. Her fingers twisted themselves into his hair, and she was finally able to admit to herself that she had always been attracted to these unruly curls, that she'd secretly enjoyed running her fingers through them while he was unconscious in a way that was totally unprofessional.

There was something honest and so *Daniel* about the kiss, as if his personality—along with his scent and taste—was a part of the electricity humming back and forth between them. She started to understand what he'd been saying before, about how she was real to him. He was something new to her, an entirely new experience. It *was* like her first kiss, because no kiss had ever been so vivid, so much stronger than her own analytical mind. She didn't have to think.

It felt amazing not to think.

Everything was just kissing Daniel, like there had never been another purpose for breathing in and out.

He kissed her throat, her temple, the top of her head. He cradled her face against his neck and sighed.

"It feels like I've been waiting a century to do that. It's like time has lost all continuity. Every second with you outweighs days of life before I met you."

"This shouldn't be so easy." Once he'd stopped kissing her, she could think again. She wished she didn't have to.

He tilted her chin up. "What do you mean?"

"Shouldn't there be some…awkwardness? Noses bumping, all that. I mean, it's been a while for me, but that's how I remember it."

He kissed her nose. "Normally, yes. But this hasn't been a normal thing in any facet."

"I don't understand how this could happen. The odds are astronomically against it. You were just the random bait they put in a trap for me. And then, coincidentally, you just happen to be exactly…" She didn't know how to finish.

"Exactly what I want," he said, and he leaned in to kiss her again. He pulled back too soon. "I'll admit," he continued, "it's not a bet I would have taken."

"Your chances at winning the lottery would be better."

"Do you believe in fate?"

"Of course not."

He laughed at her scornful tone. "I guess karma is out, too, then?"

"Neither of those things is real."

"Can you prove that?"

"Well, not conclusively, no. But no one can prove they are real, either."

"Then you'll just have to accept that this is the

world's most unlikely coincidence. I, however, think there is some balance in the universe. We've both been treated unfairly. Maybe this is our balance."

"It's irrational—"

He cut her off, his lips making her forget instantly what she had been about to say. He kissed along the skin of her cheekbone till he got to her ear.

"Rationality is overrated," he whispered.

Then his mouth was moving with hers again, and she couldn't help but agree. This was better than logic.

"You're not off the hook for *Indochine*," he murmured.

"Huh?"

"The movie. I endangered our lives to acquire it, the least you can do is—"

This time, she didn't let him finish.

"Tomorrow," he said when they came up for air.

"Tomorrow," she agreed.

CHAPTER 16

Alex woke up the next day feeling both full of anticipation and also very, very stupid.

Honestly, it was like she couldn't complete a solid paragraph of thought without going back to some piece of Daniel's face, or the texture of his hands, or the way his breath felt against her throat. And of course, that was where the feeling of anticipation was coming from.

But there were so many practical matters that simply had to be considered. Last night, or rather this morning, by the time he'd kissed her good night for the hundredth time at the top of the stairs, she'd been too exhausted to think through any of it. She'd barely had the energy to arm her defenses and slip on her gas mask before she passed out.

It was probably a good thing; she'd been too addled then to grasp exactly what madness she'd just embarked on. Even now, it was hard to focus on anything but the fact that Daniel was probably awake somewhere. She was impatient to see him again, and yet also a little frightened. What if the crazy swell of emotion that had felt so natural and irresistible last night had evaporated? What if they were suddenly strangers again, with nothing to say?

That might be easier than if the feeling continued.

Today or tomorrow, or perhaps the next day, Kevin was going to call—

Ugh, Kevin. She could just imagine his reaction to recent developments.

She shook her head. That was irrelevant. Because today or tomorrow, Kevin was going to call and then she would send the e-mail that would make the rats scurry. Kevin would compile a list of names. He would go after his rats, and if she didn't act simultaneously, her rats would go to ground once they realized the danger. So she would have to leave Daniel here and embark on her retaliatory strike, knowing full well that there was a good chance she wouldn't be coming back. How would she explain that? How long did she have? Two days, at most? What truly hideous timing.

It didn't feel right to go into the day anticipating all the hours together with Daniel. It was dishonest. He'd heard the plan, but she was positive he hadn't thought it through enough to realize what it meant. So soon, she'd be leaving him here alone. Their time would be much better spent training him in the art of hiding. Some more shooting-range practice wouldn't hurt, either.

The feeling of anticipation turned to a sinking dread as her thoughts wound to a conclusion. Her behavior last night had been irresponsible. If she'd had any idea of what Daniel was thinking, she might have been able to work all this through before it had gotten out of hand. She might have been able to keep the appropriate distance between them. But she'd been taken completely by surprise.

Trying to understand a normal person was not her forte. Though, truly, someone who found the real Alex attractive was not a normal person at all.

She heard barking outside — it sounded like the dogs were coming back from the barn. She wondered if it was still morning or already afternoon.

She grabbed a set of clean clothes, disarmed the door, and snuck to the bathroom. She didn't want to see Daniel until her teeth were brushed. Which was stupid. She couldn't be allowed to kiss him again. That wouldn't be kind to either of them.

The hall was dark, the bathroom empty. The door to Daniel's room was open and the room beyond was empty, too. She ran through her ablutions quickly, trying not to spend too long at the mirror, wishing her face were further along the road to healing. Her lips were worse than yesterday, swollen again, but that was her own fault. The superglue had fallen off in her sleep and the darker welt down the center of her bottom lip showed some promise of changing the shape of her mouth permanently.

She heard the TV on as she came down the stairs. When she walked into the big front room, she saw Daniel bending over the console beneath the flat-screen. The front door was open, a warm breeze blowing in through the screen. It ruffled the curls on the back of his head

He was grumbling to himself. "*Why* does anyone need five different input options?" He ran a hand through the hair that was falling into his eyes. "It's a DVD. I'm not trying to launch the space shuttle."

His Danielness stopped her where she stood, and a wave of cowardice made her want to turn around and sneak back upstairs. How would she tell him the things she needed to say? The thought of making him unhappy was suddenly more repugnant than she had been prepared for.

Lola yelped from outside the front door, looking hopefully through the screen at her. Daniel spun around and when he caught sight of Alex, a huge grin lit his face. He was across the room in four long strides, and then he lifted her up in an exuberant bear hug.

"You're up," he said excitedly. "Are you hungry? I've got everything for omelets."

"No," she said, trying to extricate herself. At the same time, her stomach growled.

He put her down and stared at her with raised eyebrows.

"I mean yes," she admitted. "But first can we talk for a second, please?"

He sighed. "I thought you might wake in an analytical mood. Just one thing before you start..."

She wanted to duck away. The guilt was very strong. But it wasn't as strong as her need to kiss him back. She didn't know if she would get another chance. It was a very gentle kiss, soft and slow. He'd noticed the condition of her lips.

When he broke away—him, not her; it was like she had no self-control at all—it was her turn to sigh.

He let his arms fall but took her hand as he led her to the couch. Little zings of electricity buzzed up her arm, and she silently castigated herself for being such a sucker. So what if this was the first time he'd held her hand? She had to get a grip.

Lola yelped again, hopefully, when she saw Alex nearing the door. Alex shot her one apologetic look. Khan and Einstein were both curled up on the porch behind her, Khan creating a massive boulder of fur.

Daniel grabbed the remote out of his way, muting the TV before dropping it onto the ground. He pulled her down next to him, keeping her hand. He was still smiling.

"Let me guess. You think we are being unwise," he said.

"Well...yes."

"Because it's impossible that we could really be compatible, given the genesis of our relationship. I'll concede it wasn't exactly a Hollywood meet-cute."

"It's not that." She looked down at his hand. It entirely engulfed hers.

Maybe she was wrong. Maybe this whole retribution scheme was poorly thought out. There was nothing to stop her from running again. She could make back the money she'd lost. She could go to Chicago, work things out with Joey Giancardi, be a Mob doctor again. Maybe, given what she now knew about the plan to eliminate her, the Family could actually offer her some protection.

Or she could just work a counter at a backwoods diner and live without the extras—like tryptamines and opioids and booby traps. Who knew how long the IDs she already had might last if she kept her head down?

"Alex?" he asked.

"I'm just thinking about the future."

"Our long-term compatibility?" he guessed.

"No, not long term. I was thinking about what happens tonight. Or tomorrow." She finally looked up at him. His soft gray-green eyes were just a little confused, not troubled. Yet.

"Your brother will call soon."

He made a face. "Wow. I hadn't thought about that." He shuddered. "I guess it's better to mention this casually over the phone—by the way, Kev, I've fallen in love with Alex—than in person, right?"

She disapproved entirely of the tingles that snapped through her nervous system when he made his facetious practice announcement. That wasn't a word to bandy around casually. He shouldn't have used it. But still, the tingles.

"That's not the part I was worrying about. You remember the plan."

"Once he's in position, we send the e-mail. He watches who reacts. Then we meet up with him and..." He trailed off, his brow suddenly furrowing. "Then you both are going to—what's the phrase?—*take them out*, right? That's going to be very danger-ous, isn't it? Couldn't we just let Kevin handle things alone? It seems like he probably wouldn't mind. I get the sense he liked his job."

"That wasn't our deal. And, Daniel..."

"What?" His voice was harder now, with an edge. He was beginning to understand.

"Neither Kevin nor I will be able to...well, perform at our best if the leverage they have against us is in the same place the bad guys are."

There was almost a physical weight to the meaning of her words as they dropped, an aftershock in the silence that followed.

He stared at her, unblinking, for a long moment. She waited.

"Are you joking?" he finally asked. His voice wasn't much more than a whisper. "Do you think I'm really going to let you leave me here to twiddle my thumbs while you risk your life?"

"No. And yes, you are."

"Alex..."

"I know how to take care of myself."

"I know that, but...I just can't wrap my mind around it. How will I stand it? Waiting here, not knowing? Alex, I'm serious!"

His voice turned impatient at the end. She wasn't looking at him; she was staring straight ahead at the television.

"Alex?"

"Turn up the volume. *Now.*"

He glanced at the TV, froze for one brief second, then jumped up and fumbled on the floor for the remote. He jammed a few wrong keys before the newscaster's voice thundered through the surround-sound speakers.

"—missing since last Thursday, when police believe he was abducted from the high school where he teaches. A substantial reward is being offered for information leading to his recovery. If you've seen this man, please call the number below."

On the large screen, Daniel's face was blown up to four times its actual size. It was a snapshot rather than an official portrait from the yearbook. He was outside somewhere sunny, smiling widely, his hair tousled and damp from sweat. His arms were stretched over the shoulders of two shorter people whose faces were cropped out of the image. It was a very good picture of him, both attractive and engaging; he looked like the kind of person you would want to help. An 800 number was printed in bright red across the bottom of the screen.

The picture disappeared, replaced by a handsomely aging anchorman and a much younger, perky blond anchorwoman.

"That's a shame, Bryan. Let's hope they get him back home to his family soon. Now we'll take a look at the weather with Marceline. How are things looking for the rest of the week, Marcie?"

The picture moved to a sultry brunette standing in front of a digital map of the entire country.

"This is national news," Alex whispered. Her mind started working through the scenarios.

Daniel muted the sound.

"The school must have called the police," Daniel said.

She just looked at him.

"What?"

"Daniel, do you know how many people go missing every day?"

"Oh... their pictures don't all end up on the news, do they?"

"Especially not full-grown men who've only been missing a few days." She got up and started pacing. "They're trying to flush you out. What does that mean? Where are they going with this? Do they think Kevin killed me? Or do they think I figured out the truth and took off with you? Why would they think I'd take you with me? It has to be about Kevin. It *is* his face, too. They must think I lost. Right? This news spot would be easier for the CIA to arrange than for my department. Of course, if they're working together..."

"Will Kevin see this?" Daniel worried. "He's right there in DC."

"Kevin's not showing his face, regardless."

She paced for another minute, then went to sit with Daniel again. She curled her legs under her and took his hand.

"Daniel, who did you talk to yesterday?"

His color heightened. "I told you. I didn't speak to anyone but the people at the counter."

"I know, but who were they? Male, female, old, young?"

"Um, the checker at the grocery store was a guy, older, maybe fifty, Hispanic."

"Was the store busy?"

"A little. He was the only checker. There were three people in line behind me."

"That's good."

"The dollar store was small. It was just me. But the woman at the counter had a TV on—she was watching a game show. She didn't look up much."

"How old was she?"

"Older than the first guy. White hair. Why? Older people watch more news, don't they?"

She shrugged. "Possibly. The third?"

"Just graduated, I guess. I remember wondering if school was out before I realized she worked there."

Her stomach felt suddenly heavier. "A young girl? And she was friendly—very friendly." It wasn't a question.

"Yes. How did you know?"

She sighed. "Daniel, you're an attractive man."

"I'm ordinary, at best. And I'm a decade too old for a girl that age," he protested.

"Old enough to be intriguing. Look, it doesn't matter. We'll do the few things we can. You stop shaving as of now, and we lie not just low, but *flat*. Aside from that, all we can do is hope the girl's not a news watcher. And that they don't run any pieces on whatever social media kids are using right now."

"Would they?"

"If they think of it. They're throwing Hail Marys."

He dropped his head into his free hand. "I'm so sorry."

"It's okay. We've all made mistakes on this little endeavor."

"You haven't. You're trying to make me feel better."

"I've made several major errors in the past few weeks."

He looked up, disbelieving.

"One, I didn't just ignore Carston's e-mail in the first place. Two, I fell for the trap. Three, I missed your tracker. Four, I didn't arm the ceiling in the barn. And then Kevin made the mistake of taking off his gas mask...I guess that's the only one I can think of for him, except for not having transport out. Bummer, I guess he wins that round."

"Well, he also did something wrong in the beginning or the CIA would have bought that he was dead."

"Good point. Thanks."

"Arnie, though," he said sadly. "Arnie's still batting a thousand."

"Don't you just hate those insufferable perfectionists?"

Daniel laughed. "So much." The humor left his face. "But I don't think you made so many mistakes. I mean, I guess when it comes to what's best for you, yes. But for me... Well, I'm glad you fell for it."

She gave him a sardonic look. "That's taking romance a little too far, don't you think?" She wished she could completely excise the memory of their first night together, with a scalpel if necessary. She wished those images weren't so clear and sharp in her mind—

the tendons standing out in his neck, the sound of his muffled screams. She shuddered, wondering how long it would take until they faded.

"I'm serious. If it wasn't you, they would have sent someone else for me. And if that person had gotten the best of Kevin, whoever it was would have killed me right then, wouldn't he?"

She looked into his earnest eyes, and then shuddered again. "You're right."

He stared back for a long moment, then sighed. "So what do we do now?"

Alex frowned. "Well, our options are limited. My face still isn't ready for scrutiny. But it's now better than yours. So we can stay here and keep our heads down, or we could go north. I have a place. It's not as fancy as this one or as well protected. I don't have a Batcave." The jealousy in her voice on the last line was unconcealed.

"So you think it's safer here?"

"It depends. I'd like to get Arnie's thoughts about the town before we decide. Kevin's take wouldn't hurt, either. Hopefully he'll call soon. The plans have changed a little. I think he's going to get his wish. He gets to be the victor after all."

· · ·

THE DAY DRAGGED. Alex didn't want to leave the television. It didn't change things much, knowing how many times they aired the piece and how many outlets picked it up, but she still had to watch. Arnie took the new situation with the stoicism she expected, only the tightening of his eyes betraying his worry.

Alex wanted to send Arnie to the Batcave with a list of everything she needed. She'd love to have the SIG for herself, plus extra ammo, and for Daniel the sawed-off shotgun that she'd seen in Kevin's stash. A sniper rifle wasn't as helpful in close quarters as a shotgun would be. It could incapacitate multiple attackers with one load of buckshot.

She also wanted to hunt for gas masks—she couldn't wire up the house if she didn't have a third for Arnie. She doubted Kevin would have overlooked such an obvious safety feature, but then again, maybe it was obvious only to someone like her. In his world, Kevin probably only worried about bullets and bombs.

But though she wanted these things badly, it might already be too late for preparations. If the flirtatious checker had called after the first broadcast—which could have aired earlier in the day than the one they'd seen, or even the day before—it would take a certain amount of time for their enemies to begin the search. Someone had to get here, then ask questions around town, and finally start investigating possible leads. But then, if that someone had good luck, the surveillance would begin. And she had no way of knowing if it already had.

Even though she and Daniel were staying inside with the windows covered, someone could be watching Arnie right now. If Arnie took a field trip to the Batcave, the watcher would follow. At that point, they might as well put up a banner that read CONGRATU-LATIONS, YOU'VE FOUND THE RIGHT PLACE! HELP YOURSELF TO A FEW ROCKET LAUNCHERS!

They could do nothing that might give away the existence of the Batcave.

Her most essential defenses were in easy reach, everything of importance loaded into her backpack— neatly Ziplocked by category—for a quick retreat. She had Arnie move the truck to the back of the house, close enough to Arnie's bedroom window that they could be in the front cab with one well-hidden step.

She wished Kevin would call or that he'd trusted them enough to give Daniel the number to his own burner phone, in case of emergency. There might be additional safeties he'd built into the place that Arnie wasn't aware of.

Daniel made dinner for the three of them, and though it wasn't as high-spirited an affair as the previous night's, it was still delicious. She told him to slow down with his stock of ingredients. It might be a while before shopping was on the agenda again, even for Arnie.

It surprised her how unaware Daniel seemed to be of Arnie's presence — well, not unaware, exactly, just unaffected. Not that he was rude to Arnie or ignored him, but Daniel made no effort to hide his new closeness with Alex in front of him. Twice he took her hand; once he kissed the top of her head as he passed with the dishes. Arnie, unsurprisingly, showed no reaction to Daniel's exhibition, but she couldn't help but wonder what he thought of it.

Arnie told them he had the dogs on rotation to run the perimeter fence — all six miles of it — while it was light out, the time when scouts would be watching through binoculars. If anyone was perched close enough to watch the house, the dogs would alert him. After that announcement, he went to bed early, keeping his normal routine. Alex and Daniel stayed up to watch the evening news.

He curled around her on the sofa so naturally that it didn't feel out of the ordinary at all. She couldn't remember feeling so physically comfortable with anyone in all her life. Even her mother had been a brittle hugger, someone who rarely expressed affection, in words or actions. Alex's closeness with Barnaby was verbal, never physical. So she thought that she should feel awkward and embarrassed with her legs draped across another person's lap, her head cradled against that person's shoulder while his arms were wrapped around her, but she felt only oddly relaxed. As if his proximity somehow removed a portion of the stress from the situation.

The Daniel piece played again, but it ran later in the program than before, and she could tell the night anchor was bored by the story. The Agency might be able to force this bit into the news for a short time, but they couldn't keep the networks from reacting to what a nonstory it was. Of course, there was the obvious second act.

"I should probably warn you...if you haven't thought of it already," she said.

He tried to sound glib, but she could hear the wariness. "I'm sure I haven't."

"Well, if this story doesn't get results quickly, they'll have to up the ante to keep the press working for them."

"What does that mean, up the ante?"

She leaned back so she could see his face, her nose wrinkling in distaste at what she had to say. "They'll make the story more salacious somehow. Say you're suspected of a crime. Invent a student who you abducted or abused. Something along those lines, probably. They could be more creative, though."

His eyes shifted from her face back to the television screen, though the announcer had moved on to early primary predictions. He flushed, then went pale. She let him take his time with the idea. She could imagine how hard it would be for a good man to realize he was about to become a villain.

"There's nothing I can do about it," he said quietly. It was not quite a question.

"No."

"At least my parents aren't around to see it. Maybe...I don't think *all* my friends will believe it."

"I wouldn't," she agreed.

He smiled down at her. "At one point in the not too distant past, you thought I was going to murder a couple million people."

"I didn't know you then."

"True."

When the late news was done, they engaged in a more subdued good-night, then she began the cleanup. They might have to leave quickly. She dismantled and stowed her lab, then changed into leggings and a black T-shirt—things she would be comfortable in if tonight was the night they had to run.

She knew she was tired, but her brain couldn't seem to slow down. She didn't want to miss anything else. Daniel might be right—perhaps her first big mistakes were actually good things in that they might have saved his life. But she couldn't afford any more errors. It wasn't just her own life at stake now. She sighed to herself. There were benefits to having a liability, but the load was definitely much heavier.

A quiet knock interrupted her thoughts.

"Don't open the door," she cautioned quickly, jerking upright. The cot rocked underneath her.

After a short pause, Daniel asked, "Are you wearing a gas mask?"

"Yes."

"I thought so. Your voice sounds muffled."

Another pause.

"Is your security system terribly difficult to disarm?" he wondered.

"Give me a minute."

It took less than that to secure the live wires. She pushed her mask back onto the top of her head and opened the door. He was leaning against the frame. She couldn't see him perfectly in the darkness, but she thought he looked tired...and sad.

"You're very worried," he inferred, reaching to touch her mask lightly.

"Actually, I always sleep with this. It feels weird if I don't have it on. Is something wrong?"

"More than everything? No. I was just...lonely. I couldn't sleep. I wanted to be with you." He hesitated. "Can I come in?"

"Um, okay." She took a step back, switching the light on.

He looked around, a new expression taking over. "*This* is the room Kevin gave you? Why didn't you say something? You should have my room!"

"I'm fine here," she assured him. "I'm not much for beds, anyway. It's safer to sleep light."

"I don't know what to say. I can't sleep in a king-size bed knowing you're stuck in a storage box."

"Really, I like it."

He gave her a doubtful look, which turned suddenly sheepish. "I was going to invite myself in, but there's barely room for you."

"We could shift some crates..."

"I have a better idea. Come with me." He offered his hand.

She took it without considering what she was doing. He pulled her down the dark hall, past the bathroom door, to his own room. The only light came from a small lamp on the bedside table.

It was a very nice room, more in line with Kevin's usual aesthetic than her own storage space. There was a massive bed in the middle of the room, covered in a white comforter, with a rustic four-poster frame made of artfully unfinished logs. A gold blanket that matched the tone of the wood was draped over the foot of the bed.

"You see?" he said. "There's no way I could sleep in here again after seeing your sad situation. I'd feel like a horrible excuse for a man."

"Well, I'm not trading. I already have my room wired."

They stood awkwardly in the doorway for a moment.

"I didn't really have anything specific in mind to talk about. I just wanted to be where you were."

"It's okay. I wasn't sleeping, either."

"Let's not sleep together," he said, then he flushed and laughed embarrassedly. "That didn't sound right at all." He pulled her hand again, toward the big bed. "Look, I promise to be a perfect gentleman," he said. "I'll just feel less anxious if I can see you."

She climbed up on the thick white comforter next to him, laughing with him at his awkwardness and wondering privately if she *wanted* him to be a perfect gentleman. She reminded herself sternly that this was not the appropriate time for those kinds of thoughts. Maybe someday in the future when their lives weren't in danger. If that day ever came.

He took her hand but otherwise gave her space. They both lay back on the stacks of feather pillows. He put his free hand behind his head and looked over at her.

"Yes, see, this is better."

And it was. It didn't make sense—she was out of her secured room and farther from her other weapons— but, paradoxically, she felt safer.

"Yes," she agreed. She slipped the gas mask off her head and laid it beside her.

"Your hand is cold."

Before she could respond, he sat up and grabbed the blanket from the foot of the bed. He shook it out, then settled it over them. When he lay back, he was closer to her. His shoulder touched hers, and his arm lay over hers as he took her hand again.

Why was she so vividly aware of things that, in the grand scheme of survival, didn't really matter?

"Thanks," she said.

"Don't take this the wrong way—I mean it as the highest compliment and not as a slight to your company—but I think I might actually be able to sleep with you here."

"I know what you mean. It's been a long day."

"Yes," he agreed fervently. "Are you comfortable?"

"I am. Don't take *this* the wrong way, but I might put my mask back on at some point. It's just a weird sleep habit."

He smiled. "Like hugging a teddy bear."

"Exactly like that, only not adorable."

He rolled toward her and leaned his forehead against her temple. She could feel his eyelashes brush against her cheek as he closed his eyes. His right arm snaked around her waist.

"*I* think you're adorable," he breathed. His voice sounded like he was already half asleep. "And terrifyingly lethal, too, of course." He yawned.

"Very sweet," she said, but she wasn't sure if he heard her. He was breathing so evenly she thought he might already be out.

She waited a few moments and then, carefully, she reached up with her free hand to touch his curls. They were so soft. Her fingers traced his features, totally calm in unconsciousness. It was that same innocent, serene face that had never belonged in her world. She didn't think she'd ever seen anything quite so beautiful.

She fell asleep like that, with her hand tucked possessively around the nape of his neck, the gas mask forgotten behind her back.

CHAPTER 17

Kevin didn't call.

Daniel didn't seem to think this was odd, but Alex thought she detected some extra strain in Arnie's shoulders.

It was too long.

As she'd understood things, Kevin only had to get into a position from which he could follow the one person they knew for certain was involved—Carston. He could have made the drive to DC in two days, even taking it easy. She'd told him exactly where to find her old boss once he was there. It was only a few hours' work, at most. If Carston wasn't where he was supposed to be, Kevin should have called. What was he doing?

Or had something happened to him? How long should she wait before suggesting that possibility to Daniel?

The new worry added to her paranoia. She strung an extra lead outside the door to her room so that it could be armed while she was in another part of the house. It was so frustrating, not being able to wire the whole first floor. Just one gas mask short.

On the plus side, every hour hidden helped her face. Under low-wattage lighting and with a lot of makeup, she might be able to escape notice for three or even four seconds.

The wait was an odd mix of boredom, stress, and the strangest kind of happiness. Doomed happiness, happiness with a deadline, but that didn't make it less...all-encompassing. She should be in a very dark place right now, the pulsing beat of the hunt filling her ears, but she found herself smiling as a default expression. It didn't help that Daniel was just as inappropriately giddy as she was. They talked about it the next afternoon while watching the news.

Alex had snuck Lola inside when Arnie left to go train with the other animals—she felt bad that they had to keep the door closed on the dogs; it seemed rude—and Einstein and Khan had come with her. Which made the room awkwardly full of dog. She hoped Arnie wouldn't be upset. The dogs must come in sometimes or there wouldn't be the doggie door in the laundry room. She didn't know if the dogs were usually kept outside as part of their training or as an early alarm system or because Arnie had allergies—

though if it was the last option, he'd chosen the wrong lifestyle.

Lola parked her floppy jowls and ears on Alex's thigh, where there would shortly be a drool situation, Alex was sure. Einstein jumped right up on the couch beside Daniel, tail waving enthusiastically at the rule breaking. Khan turned himself into a long ottoman in front of the couch. After the program's dull opening story—focused on politics, naturally, as if there weren't almost a year to go before anything actually happened—Daniel stretched his long legs out across Khan's back. Khan didn't seem to mind. Alex stroked Lola's ears, and Lola's tail thumped against the floor.

It all felt comfortable and *familiar,* though she'd never been in a position like this in her entire life. She'd never been so closely surrounded by living things— touching them, hearing their breathing—let alone holding hands with a man who thought she was ador- able...and lethal. That he could know her full story and still be able to look at her the way he did...

Her eyes moved automatically to his face while the thought ran through her mind, and she found him looking at her, too. He smiled his wide, bright grin— the two days' stubble making him look unexpectedly rugged—and she smiled back without thinking about it. All kinds of bubbly emotions percolated through her chest, and she realized it was probably the best feeling she'd ever known.

She sighed, then groaned.

He glanced at the TV, looking for a reason, but it was just a commercial. "What is it?"

"I feel goofy," she admitted. "Stupid. Bubbly. Why does everything seem so positive? I can't string logical thoughts together. I try to worry, and I end up smiling. I might be losing my mind, and I don't care about that nearly as much as I should. I want to punch myself, but my face is finally just starting to heal."

Daniel laughed. "That's one of the drawbacks of falling in love, I think."

Stomach tingles again. "Is that what you think we're doing?"

"Feels like it to me."

She frowned. "I don't have any comparisons. What if I'm actually going insane?"

"You are most definitely sane."

"But I don't believe people can fall in love so quickly." Truthfully, she didn't entirely believe in *love*, romantic love, at all. Chemical responses, sure; sexual attraction, yes. Compatibility, yes. Friendship. Loyalty and responsibility. But *love* just seemed a little too much of a fairy tale.

"I . . . well, I never used to. I mean, I always believed in *attraction* at first sight. I've experienced that. And that's definitely a part of what's happening for me now." He grinned again. "But love at first sight? Just fantasy, I was sure."

"Of course it is."

"Except..."

"There's no except, Daniel."

"Except that something happened to me on that train, something totally outside of my experience or ability to explain."

She didn't know what to say. She glanced at the TV just as the newscast's ending theme began to play.

That caught Daniel's attention, too. "Did we miss it?"

"No, it didn't run."

"And that's not a good thing," he assumed, an edge creeping into his voice.

"I can think of a couple different things it could mean. One, they pushed the story out, and when it didn't get results, they had to let it die. Two, the story is about to change."

Daniel's shoulders squared defensively. "How soon do you think we'll see the next version?"

"Very soon, if that's what's happening."

There was a third possibility, but she wasn't ready to say it aloud. The story would definitely disappear if they'd gotten what they needed from it. If they had Kevin now.

She thought she understood enough about Kevin's character to be fairly certain that he wouldn't give them up easily. He was smart enough to go with the most believable version of the story if the department caught him: He'd been too late to save Daniel, and—after killing the Oleander—he'd gone to DC for revenge. He'd be able to stick to that story for a while...she hoped. She didn't know who they had doing interrogations now. If that person was any good—well, eventually Kevin would tell the truth. As much as she wasn't Kevin's biggest fan, she felt sick for him now.

Of course, he could have been prepared for capture, the way she would have been. He could be dead already.

Batcave or no Batcave, if Kevin didn't call by midnight, it would be time to leave. She could feel when she was pushing her luck.

Well, all the happy feelings had subsided. At least that was a sign that she wasn't totally crazy. Yet.

They shooed the dogs out onto the porch before Arnie was due to come back, though the animal smell would probably give them away regardless. Daniel started a meat sauce for spaghetti, and she helped with the simple parts—opening cans, measuring spices. It was effortless and companionable working side by side, like they'd been doing this for years. Was that the feeling Daniel was talking about? The strange ease of their togetherness? Though she didn't believe his theory, she had to admit to herself that she had no explanation of her own.

Daniel hummed as he worked, a familiar-sounding

tune that she couldn't place at first. She caught herself humming along a few minutes later. Without seeming to realize he was doing it, Daniel started to sing the words.

" 'Guilty feet have got no rhythm,' " he sang.

"Isn't that song older than you are?" she asked after a moment.

He seemed surprised. "Oh, was I singing that out loud? Sorry, I tend to do that when I cook if I don't keep a strict hold on myself."

"How do you even know the words?"

"I'll have you know that to this day, 'Careless Whisper' remains a very popular song on the karaoke circuit. I kill it on eighties night."

"You're into karaoke?"

"Hey, who says schoolteachers don't know how to party?" He stepped away from the stove, sauce-covered spoon still in his right hand, and pulled her into a loose embrace with his left. He danced her once around a small circle, pressing his rough cheek against hers, while singing, " 'Pain is *ah-all* you'll find...' " Then he turned back to the stove, dancing in place while he sang cheerfully about how he was never going to dance again.

Don't be an idiot, her mind told her as the goofy smile stretched across her face again.

Shut up, her body responded.

Daniel didn't have a voice that belonged on the air,

but it was a pleasant, light tenor, and he made up for any deficiencies with his enthusiasm. By the time they heard the dogs greet Arnie at the door, they were in the middle of a passionate duet of "Total Eclipse of the Heart." Alex quit singing immediately, her face flushing, but Daniel seemed oblivious both to her cowardice and to Arnie's entrance.

" 'I really need you tonight!' " he belted out as Arnie came through the door, shaking his head. It made Alex wonder if Kevin was ever any fun or if it was just business all the time when he and Arnie were here alone.

Arnie didn't comment, just shut the screen door behind him, letting the fresh warm air mix with the smells of garlic, onion, and tomato. Now that it was dark outside and light inside, she'd have to make sure he closed the exterior door before she or Daniel went into the part of the room that would be visible to anyone watching.

"Anything from the dogs?" she asked Arnie.

"Nope. You would have heard them if they'd found anything."

She frowned. "The story didn't run."

Alex and Arnie exchanged a look. Arnie's eyes cut to Daniel's back, then returned to her. She knew what he was asking, and she shook her head no. No, she hadn't talked to Daniel about Kevin and what his silence could mean. Arnie's eyes did that subtle tightening thing that seemed to be his only physical tell for stress.

For Arnie's sake, they'd have to get out as soon as possible. If anyone connected Daniel and Alex to this house, it would put Arnie in danger. She hoped he would understand about the truck.

Dinner was subdued. Even Daniel seemed to catch the mood. She decided she would tell him her fears about Kevin as soon as they were alone. It would be nice to allow him one more night of decent sleep, but they should probably leave before first light.

After they were finished—and not a noodle had survived; Arnie would miss this part of having houseguests, at least—she helped clear while Arnie went to turn on the news. The story lineup was repetitively familiar. She felt like she could recite along with the anchorwoman word for word. Arnie hadn't already watched three rounds today; he settled into the couch.

Alex rinsed the plates and handed them to Daniel to load. One of the dogs whined through the screen door; probably Lola. Alex hoped she hadn't spoiled them too much this afternoon. She'd never thought she was a dog person, but she realized she was going to miss the warm and friendly inclusion of the pack. Maybe someday—if Kevin was somehow still alive and well and the plan was operable after all—she might get herself a dog. If all the happy thoughts were

real, maybe Kevin would even sell her Lola. It probably wasn't a practical —

A low, fast *thud* interrupted her thoughts — it was a
sound that didn't belong. Even as her eyes were moving toward Daniel, looking for a dropped utensil or a
slammed cupboard that would explain the noise, her
mind was leaping ahead. Before her body had
realigned with her brain, a huge baying cry erupted
from the porch, along with a vicious growling. Another
thud, quieter beside the hullabaloo of the dogs, and
the baying broke off into a shocked and pained yelp.

She tackled Daniel to the ground while he was still
turning toward the door. He outweighed her by a lot,
but he was off balance and went down easy.

"Shhh," she hissed fiercely in his ear, then she
crawled over him to the edge of the island and peered
around. She couldn't see Arnie. She looked at the
screen door — a small round hole was torn through
the center of the top panel. She tried to listen over the
sound of the dogs and the TV, but she couldn't hear
any sound from where Arnie should be.

It had to be a distance shot or the dogs would have
seen it coming.

"Arnie!" she hoarsely whisper-shouted.

There was no response.

She slithered to the dining-room table, where her
backpack was propped against the leg of the chair
she'd used. She ripped her PPK out of its Ziploc bag,

then slid it across the floor to Daniel. She needed both hands.

Daniel snagged the gun when it was halfway to the island and leaned around the edge. He hadn't practiced with a handgun, but at this distance that wouldn't matter terribly much.

She shoved her rings on and flung the belt around her waist.

Daniel was on his feet in a fraction of a second, bracing his elbows on top of the counter. He didn't look at all conflicted about his ability to fire. She scuttled to the nearby wall where the dining room jutted out from the great room. As she moved, she saw a hand shoving the handle down — but it wasn't a hand. It was a black furry paw.

So Kevin had chosen not to go with the standard round doorknob for more reasons than aesthetics.

She breathed again as Einstein burst into the room, Khan and the Rottweiler close on his heels. She could hear Lola panting pained cries outside, and her teeth ground together.

While the dogs congregated silently around Daniel, forming a furry shield, she got her fighting shoes on and shoved the garrote wire into one pocket, the wooden handles into the other.

"Give the command," she whispered to Daniel.

The shooter would be running in now, though he would have to be on the lookout for the dogs. If he had the option, he'd switch the distance rifle for something that made bigger holes. Dogs like these would keep coming through a lot of hurt.

"Escape protocol?" Daniel whispered uncertainly.

Einstein's ears quivered. He gave a quiet cough of a bark, then trotted to the far end of the kitchen and whined.

"Follow him," Alex instructed Daniel. She darted across the space between the wall and the island, keeping herself in a low crouch.

Daniel started to straighten, but before she could say anything, Einstein hurtled over and caught Daniel's hand in his mouth. He yanked Daniel back to the ground.

"Keep low," she translated in a whisper.

Einstein led them toward the laundry room, as Alex had expected, with Khan and the Rottweiler bringing up the rear. As she ducked from the great room to the darkened hallway, she tried to see Arnie. She could see only one hand at first, unmoving, but then she spied splatter against the far wall. It was obvious that there was brain matter mixed in with the blood. So there was no point in trying to drag him with them. It was too late for Arnie. And the shooter was obviously a marksman. The good news just kept coming.

Alex was surprised when Einstein stopped short of the laundry room and pawed at a closet in the hall.

Daniel pulled the door open, and Einstein jumped past him and tugged at something inside. Alex crept closer just as a weighty pile of fur fell out on top of her.

"What is this?" Daniel breathed in her ear.

She felt her way through the pile. "I think it's a fur coat—but there's something else. It's too heavy..." She ran her hands quickly over the coat, along the sleeves; there was something stiff and rectangular under the fur. She stuck her hand inside the sleeve, trying to understand what she was examining. Finally, her fingers made sense of it. She wasn't sure she would have put it together if she hadn't recently cut Kevin out of a Batsuit.

Einstein pulled another dense bulk of fur down on them.

"They're lined in Kevlar," she whispered.

"We should put them on."

Alex struggled into hers as she worked through it in her head. The Kevlar made sense, but why the cumbersome fur? Had Kevin trained the dogs during cold weather? Was this just preparation for the elements? Did it even get that cold here? But as she yanked up the arms—too long, of course—to free her hands, she saw how Daniel's coat was blending into Einstein's fur so that she couldn't see where one stopped and the other began. Camouflage.

The coat even had a Kevlar-lined hood, which she

pulled over her head. Now she and Daniel were just two more furry shapes in the darkness.

Einstein went directly through the doggie door at the far end of the laundry room, and Daniel went right after. She could feel Khan's heat close behind her. She got through the door and saw Einstein pulling Daniel back down as he tried to rise into a crouch.

"Crawl," she explained.

It was frustratingly slow; the coat got heavier and hotter with every foot she gained, and the gravel was like knifepoints under her palms and knees. Once they got onto the stubbly grass, it was a little less painful, but she was so impatient with the pace that she barely noticed. She worried, as Einstein led them toward the outbuilding where the dogs lived, that he was trying to take them to the truck that she'd instructed Arnie to move. But the truck wasn't such a great escape. The shooter might be holding his position, just waiting for someone to try to drive out on the only road. Or this could be a new variation, where the shooter had friends to sweep the house and flush his victims out while he waited.

She could hear the restive dogs penned in the outbuilding ahead, none of them happy with what was happening. They'd made it three-fourths of the way when another sharp *thud* kicked a cloud of dirt into her face. Einstein barked sharply, and Alex heard one of the dogs behind her thunder off from their little pack, growling in a low bass. The heavy sound of his paws combined with his compact stride made her sure it must be the Rottweiler. Another *thud,* farther out, but the growling didn't change tempo. She heard something, maybe a muffled curse, and then a hail of bullets rattled out from what was most definitely *not* a sniper rifle. Her muscles tensed, even as she crawled as quickly as she could in Daniel's wake, waiting for the inevitable sound of the Rottweiler's yelps. The sound didn't come, but the growling vanished. Tears pricked her eyes.

Khan moved into position at her side — the shooter's side — and she saw Einstein was providing the same protection to Daniel. Kevin had said the dogs would give their lives for Daniel, and they were proving it. It would probably irk Kevin to know they were doing the same for her.

Kevin. Well, the odds were now better that he was alive. The news broadcasts hadn't cut off because the Agency had found Kevin but because they'd successfully located Daniel.

They made the outbuilding. She crawled gratefully into the obscuring dark. The dogs inside were whining and barking anxiously. Fighting the heavy mass of the lined coat, she struggled to her feet, still bent over but able to move faster. Daniel copied her, keeping an eye on Einstein to see if he would insist they get back down. Einstein wasn't paying attention to Daniel at the moment, though. Both he and Khan were doing a stuttering race down the line of kennels, stopping at each door and then bounding to the next. At first she wasn't sure if she was supposed to run, too, but then she realized what they were doing. The closest kennels swung open, then the following set. Kevin had taught his prize pupils how to open the kennels from the outside.

The freed dogs were immediately silent. The first pair was a matched set of standard German shepherds. The two dogs raced out the barn door, heading north. Before they were out of sight, three Rottweilers sprinted past her toward the south. A lone Doberman followed, then a quartet of German shepherds, each group heading in a different direction. The dogs started flooding out of the building so quickly that she lost count entirely. Easily more than thirty animals, though some of them were still very young. Part of her wanted to cheer, *Tear 'em up, boys!* while the other part wanted to tell them, *Be careful!* She saw Lola's pups run past, and her eyes teared again.

In the dark night, someone shouted in panic. Gunfire, then screaming. A tight, mirthless smile stretched her lips.

But it wasn't entirely good news. She heard shots from another direction. Definitely multiple attackers.

"Gun?" she whispered to Daniel. He nodded and pulled it out from the waist of his jeans. He offered it to her. She shook her head. She'd just wanted to know he hadn't dropped it. She was dripping sweat inside the thick fur. She pushed back the hood and wiped her forearm across her forehead.

"What now?" he murmured. "Are we supposed to wait here?"

She was just about to say that as an *escape,* this didn't quite answer, when Einstein was back, tugging Daniel down again. She got on her hands and knees and followed as Einstein led them out the door they'd come in. Khan was still there, bringing up the rear again. This time Einstein led them due north, though she didn't know of any additional structure that way. It was probably going to be a long crawl, she realized, and her hands were already deeply scratched from the dry stalks of grass. She tried to protect her palms with the cuffs of the coat's sleeves, but that part wasn't lined, so it only helped a little. At least there were too many furry shapes in the night for a shooter to bother with four that weren't attacking. She looked back toward the house in the distance. She didn't see any new lights on. They hadn't started clearing the house yet. The dog sounds continued, faraway growling, the baying of Lola's pups, and random staccato barks.

She lost track of time, only aware of the amount of sweat she was producing, the rasping sound of her panting, the fact that they'd been going slightly uphill the whole way and now Daniel was slowing some, and that her palms were being pierced again and again, despite the coat. But she didn't think they'd gone very far when Daniel gasped quietly and stopped. She crawled up beside him.

It was the fence. They'd reached the northern boundary of the ranch. She looked for Einstein, wondering what they were supposed to do next, and then she realized that Einstein was already on the other side. He looked at her, then pointed his nose down to the bottom edge of the fence. She felt her way along the place he indicated and found that the earth dropped away from the line of chain link; what she'd thought was a shadow was actually a narrow gorge of dark rock. The space was easily big enough for her to slip through. She felt Daniel grab her ankle, using her for guidance. After they were both through, she turned to watch Khan struggle his way into the gorge. She winced, knowing the bottom edge of the chain link must be gouging into his skin. He didn't make any audible complaint.

They came out on top of a shallow, rocky ravine. It had been invisible from the house, hidden in the lee of the slight rise of land; she'd never guessed that there was any end to the flat plains stretching north toward Oklahoma. Einstein was already scrambling down the rocks. It looked like he might be on a faint, narrow path. Khan nudged her from behind.

"Let's go," she whispered.

She lifted herself into a low crouch and, when Einstein didn't object, started carefully down the slope. She could feel Daniel following closely. There did appear to be a path, though it could have been a game trail, too. There was a new sound in the darkness, a gentle whooshing that it took her a few seconds to place. She hadn't realized the river came so close to the house.

It was only about fifteen feet to the bottom of the ravine, and when they reached it, Alex felt it was safe to straighten up. The water coursed quietly past them in the dark. She thought she could make out the far side; the river was much narrower here than it was by the barn. Einstein was yanking at something under a ledge, a place where the water had cut away the bank, leaving an overhanging shelf of stone. She went to help and was thrilled to see that it was a small rowboat. She thought she understood the protocol now.

"I will never say another bad word about your brother," she muttered rashly as she helped tow the boat from its hiding place. If Kevin was still alive— and if she and Daniel lived through the night—she would no doubt break that promise, but for now she was filled with gratitude.

Daniel caught the other side of the boat and pushed. They had it in the water in seconds, the eddies swirling around their calves. Her coat trailed so much lower to the ground than his that the bottom edge was already in the river. The fur soaked up the water, getting heavier with each step. The current ran faster than the smooth surface implied, and they had their hands full hanging on to the boat while the dogs jumped in. Khan's weight lowered the stern of the boat dangerously close to the rippling water, so they both piled into the prow next to Einstein; first Alex while Daniel held the boat, and then he leaped in next to her. The boat took off like an arrow shot from a bow.

She threw off the hot, heavy coat. She'd never be able to swim in it, if that became necessary. Daniel followed suit quickly, whether because he'd thought of the same danger or just because he trusted her to do the right thing.

The strong current pushed them swiftly westward. Alex had to assume that this was part of the plan; Kevin hadn't left any oars. About ten minutes later, the water began to slow as it widened out around a broad bend. Her eyes had adjusted enough for her to make out what she thought was the far edge of the water. The current was pushing them toward the south bank—the same bank they'd started off from. Einstein was anxious in the prow, his ears pointed sharply upward, his muscles stretched taut. She wasn't sure what he was watching for, but when they'd passed some invisible boundary, he suddenly launched from the boat and into the water. It was deep enough that he had to swim, but she couldn't guess how far beneath his churning legs the bottom lay. He looked back at them and yelped.

Realizing it was probably a good idea to get out before Khan did, Alex jumped just a second later. The cool water closed briefly over her head before she surged back to the surface. She heard two splashes behind her — first a small one, then a huge one that sent a wave rolling over her head again. Khan swam past her, the water foaming white around his legs, and found his footing just a second before her toes scuffed against the sandy bottom. She turned to see Daniel fighting with the current as he tried to drag the wooden boat toward the bank. She knew she couldn't help him if she was in too deep, so she waded downriver and met him when he reached the shallows. She grabbed the prow, and he pulled from the middle, his hand wrapped around the bench. It didn't take long to get to the shore, where the dogs were shaking themselves off. They lugged the boat ten feet out of the water, then Daniel dropped it and looked at his hands. She did the same; the rough wood hadn't been kind to her already torn palms. They were bleeding freely now, drops of red trickling from the tips of her fingers.

Daniel wiped his right hand against his jeans, leaving a bloody streak, then reached back into the boat and retrieved the gun and something smaller — a phone; it must have been Kevin's. Daniel had had the good sense to keep both out of the water — impressive, given the shock and pressure they were both under. Luckily everything in her backpack was carefully Ziplocked.

She examined his face quickly. He didn't *look* like he was going to break down, but there might not be much warning.

Daniel grabbed the coats and held them awkwardly bundled in both arms. She was about to tell him to leave them, but then she realized that there was going to be a murder investigation in the near future. Better to hide what evidence they could.

"Put them in the river — the boat, too," she whispered. "We don't want anyone to find either."

Without hesitation, he hurried back to the edge of the water and dropped the coats into the current. Heavy as they were, it didn't take long for them to saturate and disappear under the surface. Alex started shoving the boat, and Daniel joined her, pulling it downhill. In seconds, it was racing off across the dark water. She knew it was marked with their blood and prints, but hopefully it would travel far enough tonight that no one would connect it with Kevin's house in the morning. The boat looked old and weathered, certainly not valuable. Perhaps the people who found it would consider it trash and treat it accordingly.

Alex imagined Kevin and Einstein on the red water

in the daylight, running the route for practice. They must have tried it many times. Kevin would probably be upset about her losing his boat, regardless of the value.

She and Daniel turned back toward land together. The barn was easy to see, the only tall shape in the flat darkness. As they ran toward it, a solid square being suddenly reared up. Alex startled, expecting the dogs to react. Then her eyes made sense of the shape—it was one of the firing-range haystacks. She took a deep breath to settle herself and ran on.

They reached the barn and then raced around to the front doors. Daniel's longer legs got him there first, and he already had the lock free when she caught up to him. He yanked the door out of the way, waited for her and the dogs to get inside, then shut it behind them.

It was pitch-black.

"Gimme a sec," Daniel whispered.

She could barely hear his movement over the sound of her own heartbeat and the panting of the dogs. There was a tinny creak, and then a quiet metallic groan. A faint green light glowed to her right. She could just make out Daniel's shape—his hand lit up as he touched a glowing keypad. Suddenly, brighter white light burst through a long line beside him. As he yanked the crevice open and more light flooded the space, she saw what he was doing. He was at one of the old cars on blocks. He'd opened the fake battery, entered his birthday code, and the false engine had opened. It was the stash of rifles, illuminated from the inside.

"Put some of those in the Humvee," she whispered to Daniel. The low volume was probably unnecessary, but she couldn't make herself speak louder.

The light was enough to brighten a space about fifteen feet around him in every direction. The two dogs stood by the door, facing out as if expecting intruders, waiting and panting.

Alex sprinted to her duffels and threw off the old tarp. She unzipped the side of the bottom bag and grabbed a pair of latex gloves. She pulled them over her bleeding hands. She took a second pair and stuffed them halfway into her front jeans pocket.

When she turned, Daniel had already moved on to the hollow tractor tire. He had two rifles slung over his back, and cradled in his arm were two Glocks and the shotgun she'd been wishing for. As she watched, he reached for the SIG Sauer he'd seen her practice with. He might be new to her world, but his instincts seemed up to the task.

It took her two trips to get her bags into the vehicle hidden behind the hay bales. On the first trip, she gave Daniel the gloves as they passed each other. He put them on without asking for an explanation. She was happy to see the Humvee's interior lights had been disengaged. After her stuff was in, she loaded the grenades but chose to leave the rocket launchers behind — she wasn't sure she could figure out how to use them without blowing herself up.

"The cash?" Daniel asked when she passed him.

"Yes, all of it."

He moved quickly in response, and for one crazy second she had a sense of déjà vu. They worked well together — just like doing dishes.

There was a supply of Kevlar. She put a vest on and tightened the straps as far as they would go, but it still hung a little loose. It wasn't unbearably heavy, so she guessed it had ceramic plates. She pulled another for Daniel. There were a couple of Batman wet suits, but they were too big for her and would probably take too long for Daniel to struggle into. She smiled when she found two thick baseball caps. She'd heard about these but thought only the Secret Service used them. She stuck one on her head and took the other to Daniel along with the vest.

He put both on silently, his face determined and pale. She wondered how long he could hold it together. Hopefully, the natural adrenaline would last until they got out of this.

She strapped a long, thin blade to her thigh, wrapped a holster belt under her usual leather utility, then slung another over her shoulders. She went to the back of the Humvee. She took one of the Glocks and put it on her right hip. She put the SIG under one arm and her PPK under the other. Then she holstered the sawed-off shotgun on her left hip.

"Ammo?"

He nodded. He'd left his favorite rifle slung over one shoulder. She jerked her chin toward it.

"Keep that on you, and take a handgun, too."

He picked up the other Glock and gripped it in his gloved hand.

"We need to wipe down everything you touched."

Before she was finished speaking, he was in motion. He grabbed the tarp that had hidden her bags and tore off two long strips. He threw her one and went out to the lock, Einstein shadowing him. She started on the first car he'd opened. It didn't take them long to get everything. There was blood on the pieces of tarp, so she stuffed them into the back of the Humvee, too.

She stopped to listen for a moment. Nothing but four nervous animals breathing.

"Where do we go now?" Daniel asked. His voice was strained and more inflectionless than usual, but he sounded in control. "Your place up north?"

She knew her expression was hard—and possibly frightening—as she told him, "Not yet."

CHAPTER 18

"You're going back," he said in a hollow whisper.

She nodded.

"Do you think Arnie might still be—"

"No. He's dead."

Daniel's body swayed ever so slightly in reaction to the cold certainty of her words. "Then shouldn't we be running? You told me if they come for us, we run."

He was right, and it was also her nature to run.

She wondered if this was the feeling those mothers had—the ones you read about in the news who lifted the minivan off their child. Desperate, terrified, but also as powerful as a superhero.

Alex had her way of doing things: plan, plan, plan, plan for every possibility, and then, when disaster hit, execute the plan that was the best fit. She did not do spur-of-the-moment. She did not do instinct. She did not do fight; she did flight.

But she didn't just have herself to protect tonight. She had a minivan to lift.

There was no plan, only instinct.

Her instinct was that a serious attack was happening, a well-coordinated one organized by people who had more intel than they should have. She and Daniel could run, but who knew what else the hunters had set up? There could be another trap.

If she could find out who they were and what they knew, her escape with Daniel had a much better chance of success.

Finding things out was her specialty, after all.

Attacking was not, but that just meant it would not be expected. Hell, she was more than a little surprised herself.

The hunters didn't know about the Batcave, or they would have been waiting for her here. They didn't know about the resources she had access to.

If she thought this through at all, she would probably change her mind. But she was high on her own adrenaline now, and trying to make the smart choices. Not just the ones that would save them tonight, but that would save them tomorrow and the next day. She couldn't make the right choices if she didn't have the right information.

"Running would probably be safest in the short term," she answered.

"Then?"

"I haven't had this chance before — to interrogate

one of the assassins sent for me. The more I know about who they are, the safer we'll be in the future."

A second passed.

"You're not leaving me behind," he stated evenly.

"No, I need your help. But only on one condition."

He nodded.

"You have to do *exactly* what I say. I don't care if you like it or not."

"I can do that."

"You have to stay in the car."

His head jerked back just a little, then his lips tightened.

"Exactly what I say," she repeated.

He nodded again, not pleased. She was not convinced he meant it.

"I'll need you to cover me," she explained, "and the Humvee is the best place for that. You can't watch my back if someone shoots you. Okay. This is going to get ugly. Can you handle that?"

"I've handled ugly."

"Not like this." She paused for a second. "My best guess is that these guys think they're here for Kevin and you. There's a chance I'm already dead, as far as the people who matter are concerned. That means I have to do things differently than I usually would. I can do only those things that Kevin could do. It's going to be old school, and we won't be able to leave any survivors."

He swallowed, but nodded once more.

"All right, take the night-vision goggles, you're driving."

She truly wished he didn't have to see what was coming—to see her the way she was going to have to be—but there was no help for it now.

As they drove carefully through the barn door, the dogs silent in the back of the Humvee except for some heavy breathing, she could feel herself changing, getting ready. It was going to be both ugly and very, very messy. That was, if they didn't get her first.

She pulled a small syringe from a bag in her pack. Her last, but then, if she didn't use it now, she might not live to need it another night.

"Do you trust me?" she asked him.

"Yes." The way he said it gave unusual weight to the simple affirmative.

"I've got only this one dose left, so we're going to have to share a needle, like junkies. My blood's clean, I promise."

She stabbed herself in the leg and depressed the plunger a little less than halfway. Daniel was bigger than she was.

"What is it?" he asked nervously.

She'd forgotten. He didn't like needles. "A synthesis of dextroamphetamine and an opioid—kind of like...adrenaline and painkillers. It will help you keep going if you get shot." *Anywhere but the head or heart,* she didn't add.

He nodded, and then very carefully kept his eyes forward as she stabbed him through his jeans and into his thigh. He didn't wince. She pushed the rest of the solution into his body. It was enough to last for thirty minutes at most.

"How well can you see?"

"Surprisingly well."

"Can we go faster?"

He stepped on the gas as his answer.

"When you're in place," she instructed, "get in the backseat and crack open these little side windows. Shoot anything human that isn't me. I shouldn't be hard to pick out—I'll be a lot smaller than anyone else you'll see."

His lips tightened again.

"You stay in here no matter what, you got that?"

He nodded.

"Are you going to have a problem shooting these people?"

"No." He said it forcefully, then clenched his teeth.

"Good. Anything goes wrong—your gun jams, someone gets into the Humvee somehow, whatever, you throw a grenade out the window. That's the signal that you need help. Do you know how to use a grenade?"

"What's your signal?"

"Huh?"

"If you need my help, what's your signal?"

"My signal is *stay in the car, Daniel*. The grenade?"

"I think so," he grumbled.

"This might take a little while, so don't get antsy. I won't start an interrogation until I have everything secured. Oh, pull the goggles off before you throw a grenade, or close your eyes. Look out for flares—they'll blind you."

"Got it."

Suddenly, a phone rang.

Daniel jumped a foot, hitting his head on the low ceiling.

"The hell?" Alex shouted.

"It's Kevin's phone," Daniel said, patting his vest frantically with his right hand. He dug the phone out of a snap pocket meant for ammo. She took it from him as he fumbled with it.

An unfamiliar number glowed on the display. She jabbed the answer button.

"Danny?" Kevin barked in her ear.

"Rotten timing, Beach! He'll call you back!"

"Put him on, you—"

She hung up and powered the phone off.

"Stay focused. You can call him back when we're finished."

"No problem."

Well, Kevin was alive. She supposed that was good news. Except someone was going to have to tell him his retirement arrangements were gone and his friend was dead.

"What are you going to do?" Daniel asked. "Tell me the plan so I know what to watch for."

"You're going to ram through the gate, if they closed it. That will get their attention. We'll tweak the plan if there are more than four waiting. You accelerate up to the house, then turn right so that your side of the vehicle is exposed. Four or less, you slow down, but don't stop. I'll slide out. Hopefully, they'll stay focused on you. Keep going a few yards, then stop driving and start shooting. I'll hit them from the side. You shoot to kill. I will try to get someone down that I can still talk to. I'm hoping that somebody is passed out in my room upstairs, too. I'll take Einstein to keep the other dogs off me. Khan stays with you. If they hole up in the house, I'll get back in and we'll come in through the wall."

"I can see the gate. It's open."

"Punch it up to the house."

He accelerated.

"Lights!" he told her in the same moment she saw them. Headlights coming up the road toward them, moving closer fast.

"Goggles off! New plan. Hit them. Hard. Roll right over them if you can. Brace yourself, don't lose control of the car."

She grabbed the dash with one hand, her seat with the other. Daniel shoved the goggles to his forehead and floored the gas pedal. She wished there was a way to secure the dogs. They were going to feel this.

The other car didn't react to their charge until the last second, like maybe its occupants had been watching behind them rather than out front. Or maybe, with the headlights and running lights off and the matte-black paint, the Humvee was mostly invisible in the night.

It was a midsize SUV, white. Once he saw them, the driver veered off to Alex's right. Daniel jerked the wheel right and the Humvee plowed into the passenger side of the SUV with a deafening shriek of tearing metal and the explosive pop of safety glass crumpling. The dogs flew forward; a shower of metallic clanks and jangles sounded while Khan's body crashed heavily into the back of both the driver's and the passenger's seats. Alex's head whipped forward but missed the dashboard by inches when the seat belt yanked her back. The SUV flew a few feet away, tottered on two wheels for a second, then smashed, driver-side-first, into the ground. The passenger-side headlight burst with another explosion of glass. Khan and Einstein whimpered, falling back to the floor.

"Again!" she yelled.

Daniel slammed the front of the Humvee into the undercarriage of the SUV. Metal protested and squealed. The SUV slid across the flat yard like it weighed no more than a cardboard box. She could see they weren't going to be able to roll it. There was nothing to push it against, just the endless grass.

"Cover me." She snagged the goggles off his head. "Use the nightscope on the rifle. Einstein, come!"

Alex didn't wait for a response. She was out of the Humvee before it was totally stopped. Einstein's toenails scrabbled against the back of her wet jeans as he hurried to join her. She had to move fast, before the men in the car could recover from the impact. Before they could get their automatic weapons back into play.

She ran straight for the windshield, Glock held tight in both hands. She was better with the SIG Sauer, but this was going to be extremely close up and she would probably want to ditch the gun afterward.

Everything was incredibly clear through the lenses, bright green with vibrant contrasts. The driver-side headlight was still on but buried in the ground so it emitted only a low hazy glow in the dust they'd churned up. The windshield frame was entirely empty, and she could see two men in the front seats, two deflated airbags from the initial impact hanging across the hood. The driver was a bloody mess, the top of his head pressing tight against the side-door frame, his thick neck bent at an impossible angle. She could see one eye open, staring sightlessly at her. He looked young, early twenties, with ruddy skin, light hair, and the kind of over-built anatomy that screamed *steroids*. He *might* have been an agent, except the rest of his look was wrong. His hair was about eight inches long and there was an ostentatious diamond stud in the one earlobe she could see. She would bet he was hired muscle. He didn't look like he'd been a decision maker.

The passenger was moving, his head wobbling confusedly as if he were just coming around. He was older than the other, maybe midthirties, and swarthy, with a thick three-day growth on his cheeks, burly through the middle in the way that men who lifted the really heavy weights sometimes were. She'd bet he was a bull on his feet. He was wearing a well-fitting shiny suit that seemed inappropriate for this kind of operation but rang a few bells for her. Still strapped in his seat, he was right about at her eye level. She approached swiftly and jammed the barrel of her gun into his forehead, glancing down to see what his hands were doing. They were currently empty and limp.

"Are you in charge?" she demanded.

"Huh?" he moaned.

"Who is your boss?"

"Accident. We've been in an accident, Officer," he told her, blinking into the dark. His eyes seemed to be moving just slightly out of sync with each other.

She modified her approach, pulling the gun back and softening her voice. "Help is coming. I need to know how many of you there are."

"Uh, six…"

That meant there were four more, possibly heading out toward the sound of the crash right now. At least the dogs were beginning to congregate around her, all of them on silent mode thanks to Einstein's presence. She wondered if they would have remembered her if she were alone.

"Sir?" she asked, trying to imagine how a cop would speak to someone in a car accident. "Where are the others?"

"Hitchhikers," he said, his rolling eyes starting to move more purposefully. "The others are hitchhikers. We picked up four men and dropped them off here. Then there were dogs—crazy dogs attacking us. I thought they were going to chew through the tires."

He was gaining more control, spinning the story carefully. He made a fist, then released it. She raised the gun again and kept her eyes on his hands.

"Were these . . . hitchhikers hurt in the attack?"

"I think so. I think maybe two of them. The others went in the house."

So hopefully there were only two others. But was this the guy in charge? The age was right; however, she'd picked up a few things during her time in Chicago. In an orchestrated hit, usually the guys left in the car were lower on the totem pole. The driver was secondary. The star of the show would be the one the contract was made with. The one with the skills.

"I think I need a doctor," he complained.

"An ambulance is on the way."

The light from the SUV's one surviving headlight was almost entirely blocked by thick grass and settling dirt, but there was enough that his eyes were beginning to adjust. She saw them widen when he abruptly realized there was a gun in his face.

He made a grab inside his jacket. She fired a round into his right shoulder; she didn't want to aim for the hand and take the chance of the bullet passing through and into a vital organ. She wasn't done with him yet.

He screamed, and his right arm jerked out in a pained spasm, flinging blood across her neck and chin. The gun he'd been reaching for slipped from his fingers, dropped onto his dead companion's face, then bounced out of the car and against her shoe. She knew it wouldn't be his only weapon, so she aimed down and shot him through the palm of his left hand.

He howled again and struggled against the seat belt as if he were trying to hurl himself through the empty windshield frame at her. Something was wrong with his legs — he couldn't get the purchase he was looking for.

The action had roused the dogs, who were all snarling now. Einstein launched himself at the passenger side of the car, which was currently the top side. Bracing his paws against the frame of the missing window, he stretched his neck into the SUV and locked his massive jaws around the man's right shoulder — the one she'd just shot.

"Get it off me! Get it off me!" the man shrieked in abject terror.

She took advantage of his total distraction to grab the gun at her foot. It was a cheap .38, safety off.

"Einstein, control!" Alex ordered as she straightened. It was the only command she remembered besides *escape protocol* and *at ease,* and *control* seemed closest to what she wanted. Einstein let go of the shoulder but kept his teeth right in the man's face, slavering spots of bloody saliva onto his skin.

"Who are you?" the man screamed.

"I'm the person who is going to have this animal chew your face off if you don't tell me what I want to know in the next thirty seconds."

"Keep it away!"

"Who's in charge?"

"Hector! He brought us in!"

"Where is he?"

"In the house! He went in and didn't come out. Angel went in after him and didn't come out. The dogs were going to rip the doors off the car! We bailed!"

"Who was on the sniper rifle? Hector?"

Einstein snapped his teeth inches from the terrified man's nose.

"Yes! Yes!"

She'd never thought of using animals in an interrogation, but Einstein was an unexpectedly effective asset.

"Hector was going to make the hit?"

"Yes!"

"Who was the target?"

"I don't know! We're just supposed to drive and shoot anyone who tried to leave."

"Einstein, *get him!*" It wasn't the best improv; Einstein's eyes cut over to her, clearly confused. It didn't matter to the man in the SUV.

"No, no!" he screamed. "I swear! Hector didn't tell us. Those Puerto Rican hitters don't tell outsiders anything!"

"How did you find this place?"

"Hector gave us the addresses!"

Plural? "More than one?"

"There were three houses on the list! We did the first one earlier. Hector said it was the wrong place!"

"What did you do there?"

"Hector went in. Five minutes later, he came out. Told us to move on to the next."

"That's all you know?"

"Yes! Yes! Everything!"

She shot him in the head twice with his own gun.

There was a countdown running in her mind. She had no idea how long it had actually taken to release the dogs, float downstream, and load the Humvee. She didn't know when Hector had entered the house or how long it had taken him to get to her room. What she did know was that the pressurized canister of gas she'd left armed there would continue to quietly exude the chemicals it was packed with for about fifteen minutes after someone opened the door. Once the contents ran out, she had maybe thirty minutes more—dependent on the size of the person involved—before the quarry was back on his feet. It was going to be close.

She jumped into the Humvee, holding the door open so Einstein could climb over her. She threw the goggles back to Daniel, getting only one glimpse of his face before she was blind again. All she could see was that his expression was tense.

"Get us to the house. Same plan as before if anyone comes out. Stop far enough back that you can see the sides of the house; watch for someone coming around."

"The dogs will let me know if they see something."

"Right," she agreed. The advantages of the pack were more extensive than she could have anticipated.

She removed her PPK and holstered the Glock in its place. She stuck the .38 in her belt, shoved the PPK into the bag at her feet, then dug through that bag, pulling the things she needed by feel. She switched the bulletproof hat for the gas mask, quickly tightened it into place over her mouth and nose, screwed in the filter, then grabbed two more pressurized canisters, zip ties, thin tactical gloves, and her earring box; she stowed them in the pockets of her vest. She extracted the heavy bolt cutters last and stuck them through the belt by the empty holster, one handle inside, one out. Though the cutters were compact for their abilities, the handles still reached nearly to her knee. They would impede her movement a little, but if things went the way she wanted, she would need them.

She didn't have time to think about what Daniel might be processing right now—how he might feel about her killing a helpless man.

The house came into view, all the visible windows downstairs lit. The windows upstairs were blacked out too well for her to be able to tell if the lights were on or not.

"Do you see anyone?"

"A body—over there." Daniel pointed toward the outbuilding.

"We need to make sure he's dead." There were still three men unaccounted for. The fewer breathing, the better her chances.

"I'm pretty sure he is. It looks like he's...in more than one piece." His voice sounded a little hollow.

Hers didn't. "Good."

She couldn't see anyone near the house. They weren't dumb enough to run out and see what was going on, apparently. No silhouettes appeared in the windows. Surely they would have shut off the lights if they were going to shoot from one of them. Maybe upstairs...the windows were so completely covered that she couldn't even tell exactly where they were. Or the blackout treatments had been pulled back and someone was watching from a darkened room.

"Can you see the upstairs windows?"

"They all look covered," Daniel told her.

"Okay, start slowing. Two seconds after we're out, stop and get ready to shoot."

He nodded. "Got it."

"Einstein, come here. Get ready."

Daniel angled the car so that his side was facing into the lights of the house. She hoped she would be invisible on the dark side of the vehicle. She opened the door and slid down toward the slowly moving grass below. She tried to re-create the move she'd seen in a hundred movies: she fell to her knees, then rolled onto her side as Einstein leaped over her. She was sure she'd done it wrong, but she wouldn't know *how* wrong until the *Survive* wore off.

She'd forgotten to tell Daniel to close the door and lock everything down, but it was common sense and he seemed to be thinking quickly tonight. Maybe it was genetics again — he was wired for this kind of situation, just like his brother. Anyway, if someone tried to get into the car, Khan would be waiting. She could imagine what it would feel like if someone who'd already been harried by dozens of attack dogs came face to face with Khan on higher ground in the dark. There was no way this wouldn't affect his aim and reaction time.

Even though she had gloves on, crawling across the gravel would have been excruciating if she hadn't drugged herself up. As she hurried away from the Humvee, she heard the rush of her pack's paws approaching in the dry brush—not just Einstein, but the dozens of other survivors. She'd never had backup like this before. A sniper above would have trouble separating her from the mass.

She moved into a crouch next to the porch. The Humvee was stopped now. She heard the door slam. A low whimper, quite near her head, made her freeze. The quiet whine happened again. It wasn't a human sound.

She heaved herself up onto the porch, rolled under the banister, and then stayed down, lower than the windows. Lola was there, curled up in the far corner. Alex knew that even injured, Lola would sound the alarm if someone else were close by. She crawled to the dog, her gloved hands slipping against a trail of blood. Lola raised her head half an inch, and her tail lifted for one limp wag.

"It's going to be okay, Lola. I'm coming right back. You hold on, all right?" She caressed the dog's ears once, and Lola panted softly.

Einstein waited in the shadows by the door. Alex crawled to him.

"Stay with Lola, Einstein."

She couldn't interpret the look he gave her. Hopefully he understood. She had to go in alone this time.

If she got through this night alive, she was going to track down a gas mask made for dogs.

Alex crouched beside the door and carefully inserted her earrings. They were out of place—delicate and fussy—next to the rest of her serious gear, but she didn't have time to be worried about appearances and this could very well get physical. She grabbed the bigger canister from the front pocket of her vest, twisted the top off, pulled the door open, and threw it inside.

There was no reaction. No shout or sound of footsteps retreating as the gas filled the room. She waited two seconds, then half stood and ran crouched through the doorway with the Glock in her right hand and the shotgun in her left. She would be clumsy with her left hand, but you didn't need good aim with a gun like this, not in close quarters.

She didn't bother searching the first floor. If someone tried to come after her in the next five minutes and he didn't have a gas mask, he'd be down quick. She played it out in her head as she moved to the stairs. Hector had come inside, searching for Daniel or Kevin or both of them. Because he'd come in alone, she suspected he'd been looking for only two people. With Arnie down, he'd think it was one on one. Still, he must have been very confident in his abilities to go in solo.

He would have had to check all the rooms downstairs. Then he would have tried the doors upstairs.

She was halfway up the steps now. The mist spilling from the canister below was heavy; it wasn't climbing with her. Looking up, she could see that Daniel's door was open, as was the bathroom's. Light spilled down from the far right. That could only be her storage room.

She holstered the shotgun, crept to the top, put her elbows on the first step down, and leaned around the edge of the banister.

A man was down in the hallway, dressed in rugged black pants and combat boots. His head and shoulders rested on another set of legs, coming out of her room, these in similar pants but wearing black sneakers rather than boots.

Hector would be the one on the floor in her room, if the man in the suit had described events correctly. He would have opened the door, flipped on the light, and dropped. After a few minutes, Angel would have come looking to see if he needed help, seen his legs, and slid along the wall with gun in hand until the gas overpowered him.

She had no idea how long they'd been down.

So far, the man in the suit had been pretty honest with her. It made her feel safe enough to holster the Glock and get started. First, she took the gun she found in the first man's hands and tossed it over the railing to the floor below. There was another gun tucked into the back of his pants — that went over the railing, too. She didn't have time for a better search.

She wished she could inject him with something that would keep him quiet, but unlike the gas, which would disappear from his system in the next half hour, the longer-term sedation would linger in his bloodstream and be a dead giveaway to anyone who suspected she might be here. She zip-tied his hands behind his back and then zip-tied his ankles together.

Hector was smaller than Angel, who looked similar to the dead blond in the SUV except for his coloring; both Hector and Angel were dark-haired, as she'd expected from the suit guy's description. Hector was no more than medium height and lean, fit, but not in a way that would stand out on the street. He was clean-shaven and his skin was unmarked, at least the parts she could see; he wore a long-sleeved black athletic shirt. Angel had tattoos on three of his fingers and one on the side of his neck. Hector was smarter. If you were going to do wet work for a living, it was better to blend in, avoid features that any witness could easily describe to the police sketch artist.

A huge suppressed Magnum lay inches from Hector's right hand. The sniper rifle was holstered across his back. She pulled the magazine from the rifle, took the massive handgun, and carried them back to the hallway to dump them over the stair railing. She heard them thud against the hard wood below; one of them made a metallic *chink* when it hit the previously discarded weapons.

She turned back to secure Hector.

The body lying in her storage room was gone.

She ripped the shotgun out of its holster and pressed her back against the wall beside the door. There was no sound. He would have to come through the door. When he did, she would shoot him. Even the most experienced assassin would be incapacitated with his legs blown off.

When the movement came, it was not through the door. Angel began to writhe, moaning in Spanish. In the split second that Alex was distracted, a shadow peeled off from Angel's body and flew straight at her, knocking the shotgun from her hands and sending them both crashing toward the ground. She braced for the impact even while wrestling with the hands that were trying to strip the gun from her waist. His hands were stronger than hers, but then the crash came, and with it the shattering of tiny glass bulbs.

She could feel the scalding gas sear her neck, the exposed skin around the base of her mask, and she knew she would probably look sunburned there for a few hours, but her eyes and lungs were protected.

Her attacker was not prepared. He choked, his hands flying of their own accord to his throat, his blinded eyes. She whirled, .38 already drawn, and shot, aiming for his kneecap. She hit him in the left thigh instead.

He crumpled to that side and rolled into Angel,

who was thrashing in earnest now, straining to pop the zip ties from his wrists. They were heavy-duty restraints, but he was a strong man.

She couldn't handle them both. She was going to have to make a choice. Quickly.

Angel's head was the closest thing to her. She fired twice into the top of it. He went limp.

Hector was gasping and scrubbing at his eyes at the same time as he was trying to roll away from her toward the stairs. She sprinted after him, hugging the wall to avoid his reach. He wasn't in control enough to make a grab for her yet. She pulled the bolt cutters from her waist and clubbed the back of his head. His convulsing jerked to a stop.

This was all going to be a wasted effort if she'd killed him, but she had to secure him before she could even check for a pulse.

To be safe, she put an additional bullet through his left kneecap, then threw the .38 over the banister to the floor below. It had only one bullet left anyway. She used another zip tie to attach his uninjured right leg to the railing at the ankle and the knee, then his right arm at the wrist and the elbow. He wouldn't be able to do much with his left leg. For lack of a better option, she zip-tied his left hand to Angel's big black boot. Angel's inert form had to weigh two seventy, at least. It was better than nothing. She touched Hector's wrist, marginally satisfied to locate a steady pulse. He was alive; whether or not his brain function was preserved, she would have to wait to see.

She decided to double the cables, just in case. While she was tightening the second tie around Angel's boot, she heard the change in Hector's breathing as he came to. He didn't cry out, though he had to be in tremendous pain. That wasn't a good thing. She'd interrogated other hardened soldiers with good control over their reactions to pain. It took a long time to break them.

But those men had loyalty to their companions or their missions. She was confident this was a hit for hire. Hector would owe nothing to the people who'd given him the job.

She scooted a few feet away with the Glock gripped tight in her hands, watching to see how well her containment system would perform. It was too dark. She got up and backed toward the bathroom doorway, keeping her eyes on the figure on the ground. She felt behind her until she found the light switch and flipped it on.

Hector's face was turned toward her; his dark eyes, although still tearing, were intensely focused. His face showed no evidence of the pain he was in. It was a disconcerting gaze, though his face was in other ways one of the most ordinary she had ever seen. His features were even and nondescript. He wasn't attractive, but he wasn't ugly, either. It was the kind of face that would be extremely hard to pick out of a lineup.

"Why haven't you killed me?" he asked, his voice hoarse from the chemicals. Other than that, his voice was unremarkable. He had no accent at all. He could have been a network news anchor—no hint of where he came from in his inflections.

"I want to know who hired you." Her voice rasped through the mask, slightly distorted. It sounded a little less human. She hoped that would throw him.

He nodded once, as if to himself. She saw minute shifts in his hands as he tested his bonds.

"Why would I tell you anything?" He didn't say it angrily or as a challenge. He just sounded curious.

"Do you have any idea who I am?"

He didn't answer, his face neutral.

"That's the first reason why you should tell me what you know—because whoever sent you out here didn't give you the information you needed to be successful. They didn't prepare you for what you were facing. You don't owe them anything."

"I don't owe *you* anything," he pointed out, still in a polite, conversational voice. His fingers stretched downward, trying to reach the zip tie.

"No, you don't. But if you don't talk to me, I'll hurt you. That's the second reason."

He weighed that. "And the third reason . . . if I talk, you'll let me live."

"Would you believe me if I promised you that?"

"Hmm." He sighed. He thought for a moment and

then asked, "But how will you know whether to believe what I tell you?"

"I know most of it. I just want you to fill in a few details."

"I'm afraid I can't help you much. I have a manager; he works as the middleman. I never saw the person who paid for this."

"Just tell me what your manager told you."

He considered that, then twitched his shoulders as if to shrug. "I don't like your offer. I think you could do better."

"Then I'll have to persuade you."

CHAPTER 19

He watched with a poker face as she stuck the Glock in its holster and retrieved the bolt cutters from the floor by Angel's leg.

She'd considered bringing the welding iron. Fire could be more painful than almost anything else, and many people had related phobias. But Hector was a professional. She didn't have the time to break him down with pain; his resistance would be too high. What would frighten him more than agony would be losing his physical edge. If he didn't have a trigger finger, he couldn't do his job. She'd start with something less vital to him, but he would be able to see the inevitable coming. If he could survive tonight, he would want to do it with functional hands. So he would have to talk to delay her.

Hector's left hand was most convenient. As she fit the metal blades around his pinkie finger, he curled the rest into a fist and fought harder against the ties. She kept a tight hold on the handles, knowing what she would be thinking in his position—if he could get control of the cutters, he would have a chance to free himself. Sure enough, he tried to kick out with his left leg, despite the excruciating pain it must have caused him. She dodged the blow, moved a few feet higher, then refit the cutters to the base of his folded finger.

These were made for cutting through rebar, and she kept the blades sharp. It didn't take too much muscle on her part to snap those blades together.

She watched his reaction. He thrashed against the ties ineffectually. His face turned dark red and the vessels pulsed in his forehead. He gasped and panted, but he didn't scream.

"Sometimes people don't think I'm serious," she told him. "It's good to get that misconception out of the way."

Right now, Hector would be thinking about the amount of time that could pass before it was too late to reattach a finger. He could live without a pinkie, but he needed his hands, and he must know she wasn't going to stop there.

She would emphasize her point.

She snagged the warm, bloody finger off the floor and backed to the bathroom, keeping her eyes on him as he writhed in his bonds; even the best zip ties weren't foolproof. She made sure he was watching as she dropped the finger into the toilet and flushed. Now he knew that she wasn't going to leave him options. Hopefully it would encourage him to give her what she wanted quickly.

"Hector," she told him as he stared, gritting his teeth, fighting to control the pain. "Don't be stupid. It's not going to hurt you to tell me what I want to know. It *is* going to hurt you if you don't. Your trigger fingers are next, then the rest of them. This is what I do, and I can keep it up for as long as I need to. Don't you see? They sent you after the wrong people, Hector. They told you nothing about what you were up against. They just *handed* you to me. Why protect them?"

"You're going after them next?" he grunted through his teeth.

"Of course."

His eyes were full of venom and hatred. She'd seen the look before, but in the past, she'd viewed it from a much better protected position. If he somehow got his hands on her, if their roles were reversed, she would do what she had to in order to die immediately.

"I didn't come for you," he spit out unwillingly. "I was sent for a man. I was given a picture. I was told there would be a second man, but that the second would be easy. The first would be hard. I never saw that one."

"When were you hired?"

"Last night."

"Then you rounded up some extra help and came in today," she guessed. "From where?"

"Miami."

"How did you know where to come?"

"They gave me three addresses. This was the second try."

"I guess I don't need to ask what happened at the first place."

His seething fury twisted into a ghoulish smile. "They were old. A man and a woman. They didn't fit the description, but I was paid well. It doesn't hurt to be thorough, and all it cost me was two bullets."

She nodded. He could see nothing of her expression behind the gas mask, but she kept her features smooth out of habit.

"How far away was the other house?"

"Fifteen minutes south of the little town."

"Where did the addresses come from?"

"No one told me that. I didn't ask."

She hefted the bolt cutters. "No guesses?"

"The other place was nothing like this. I saw nothing in common."

It could be a lie, but it would make more sense for it to be the truth. Why would Carston or whoever was calling the shots at the Agency need to give the hit man more than this location?

She puzzled over it for a moment, trying to think of another avenue to explore. Her eyes never left his hands. What kinds of things might link Arnie's home to random others? What similarity would generate a list of otherwise unconnected addresses?

With a sinking feeling, she thought of a possibility. One she did not like much.

"What kind of car was in the driveway of the first place?"

He seemed surprised by her question. "An old truck."

"White?"

"With a black camper."

Her jaw clenched.

So they'd gotten a very good look at Arnie's truck—the one he'd said had two perfect matches around town. They must have gotten Daniel on camera or they wouldn't be so certain of the make and model. Daniel would have had to drive down the main drag, passing the bank; that was probably how they'd done it. Why bother questioning the girl who called in about the missing teacher? Just take the CC camera footage from town and get something solid, then call the DMV. They didn't get everything—if the plates had been clear, that couple across town wouldn't be dead. But they knew Daniel was alive because Kevin wouldn't have made that mistake. Also, even in a grainy black-and-white video, Daniel didn't look exactly like Kevin if you knew what to look for.

She needed Arnie's truck. She needed it badly. It was inconspicuous. They couldn't exactly roll through town in the Batmobile and escape notice. Where was she going to get another vehicle out here?

She took a step back, feeling tired. She'd had a good resting place, but now the hunt was on again. It didn't even matter that, most likely, the bad guys thought she was dead. Because they knew Daniel was alive.

Liability.

Hector's right hand was busy. He was scratching at the zip tie with the tips of his fingers, almost dislocating his wrist in the process. It didn't look like he was trying to break it or even get to the locking tab. What was he doing? She reached for the Glock; it would probably be safest to put a round through that hand—

A single, concussive shot exploded in the silence, much louder than she would have expected it to sound from outside the house. Daniel—

Her eyes had darted to the direction of the shot though she knew better. In the fourth of a second it took her to recall them while simultaneously ripping her Glock from the holster, Hector's fingers found what they were searching for. He extracted a five-inch serrated blade from the cuff of his sleeve. It sawed across the taut zip tie with a twanging snap. The same motion turned into a cast. She fired into his central mass as the blade flew at her face. She tried to dodge while she kept shooting, ignoring the sudden pressure that wasn't quite pain as it slashed across her jaw— wasn't pain yet, but would be soon, when the drug wore off. She could feel the heat of the blood coating her neck as she continued firing into Hector's chest until the clip was empty.

Hector lay still, his open eyes still pointed in her direction, but no longer focused.

Moving in swift, jerky bursts, she wiped down the Glock and threw it over the banister, wiped and holstered the cutters, and retrieved her shotgun from the end of the hall, trying to concentrate on what to do next. She didn't know what was waiting for her outside. As she crept down the stairs, her fingers worked quickly to make sense of the new damage. The assassin's blade had just missed her carotid artery, hitting the bottom corner of her jaw and slicing halfway through her earlobe. The loose piece dangled against her neck. *Beautiful.*

She fished the remains of her left earring from the damaged lobe—just the hook was left, with a few tiny fragments of thin glass still stuck in the twist of wire— then removed the right. She stowed them in a pocket on the tactical vest. It would be unwise to leave such evidence behind. Even something so small could tip her enemies off, give them a reason to believe she was alive.

On the ground floor, she spared a second to take one quick look at Arnie. His face was turned to the floor. She could see only what was left of the back of his head. It was obvious that he hadn't suffered, but that was weak comfort.

She'd planned to gather evidence on her way out, but she wasn't sure she had time for that now. The dogs were quiet—did that mean everything was okay?

Well, after the volley of shots upstairs, it wasn't like anyone outside was unaware of her presence. She sidled over to the door and crouched beside it, lower, she thought, than anyone would aim to shoot through the drywall. She reached over and pulled the door open a crack. No one shot at her.

"Daniel?" she called loudly.

"Alex!" he shouted back—he sounded as relieved as she suddenly felt.

"You're okay?" she checked.

"Yes. Are you?"

"I'm coming out. Don't shoot."

She walked through the front door with her hands raised above her head, just in case. Einstein popped off the floor beside Lola and was at her heels.

She dropped her arms and jogged toward the Humvee. It was lit only by the lamps shining through the front door and windows, but from this vantage it appeared to be totally unharmed by their intentional accident.

Daniel slid out of the front seat.

"The shot?" she asked, her voice quieter as she approached. The dogs around the Humvee seemed relaxed enough, but...

"The last man. He must have climbed the side of the house to get away from the dogs. He was trying to edge around to the roof of the porch."

Daniel gestured with the rifle to a dark mass crumpled on the gravel close to the east corner of the house. She pushed the gas mask back on her forehead, carefully moving the straps on the left side over her ear without touching it. She adjusted her trajectory, edging closer to the broken figure. Einstein shadowed her. A large standard German shepherd was pacing not too far off, seeming uninterested in the body.

Einstein suddenly sped up and passed her. He sniffed the body a few times while she cautiously picked her way forward, and then he turned to her with his tail wagging.

"Is that the all clear?" she muttered.

He kept wagging.

She leaned in for a closer look. It didn't take long to see all there was to see. Impressed, she turned and walked back to the Humvee. Daniel was standing beside the open driver-side door, looking unsure what to do. He still didn't appear to be having any kind of shock reaction.

"Nice shot," she said. One bullet, literally right between the eyes. It couldn't have been more perfect.

"I wasn't very far away."

He stepped toward her, closing the distance, and his gloved hands wrapped tightly around the tops of her arms. Then he gasped and spun to the side, wheeling her around so that the light was no longer behind her.

"How much of this blood is yours?"

"Not much," she said. "I'm good."

"Your ear!"

"Yeah, that's not going to help anything, is it? You handy with a needle and thread?"

His head jerked back in surprise. "What?"

"It's not hard. I can talk you through it."

"Um…"

"One thing first." She shook out of his grasp and ran back up the porch stairs. Lola was still curled in the same spot. She raised her head and thumped her tail limply when she saw Alex.

"Hey, Lola, good girl. Let me take a look at you."

Alex sat cross-legged in front of her. She stroked Lola's side with one hand while searching for the wound with the other.

"Is she okay?" Daniel asked softly. He was on the other side of the porch banister, his elbows resting on the edge of the floorboards. He seemed unwilling to get any closer to the house. She didn't blame him. Lola whimpered as Alex felt along her legs.

"She's lost some blood. It looks like the bullet went

through her back left leg. I can't tell if it hit bone, but the bullet definitely passed through. She was lucky."

He reached through the slats to rub Lola's nose. "Poor girl."

"The stuff in the back of the Humvee must be in total chaos. I'm going to hunt up the first-aid kit. Keep her calm, will you?"

"Sure."

Einstein followed Alex back to the vehicle, just as he'd trailed her to the porch. It surprised her how the silent support buoyed her, made her feel safe despite all the evidence to the contrary.

She opened the back of the Humvee, and an impatient Khan almost knocked her down. She dodged out of his way just in time as he sprang over her. She imagined the cargo hold was tight for him, though she had plenty of space as she crawled inside.

Guns and ammo were strewn haphazardly, loose bullets rolling under her knees. There wasn't time to organize. Her conversation with Hector had been cut short; she hadn't been able to ask one last vital question. *What happens when the job is done?* Who was expecting a call, and when? At least there was the third house still waiting. Unless Hector had made a call between the first and second stops.

Had he called his manager, told him which address had been cleared and which he was heading to next?

Was the manager waiting for another call? Would he have realized that the call was overdue?

She located the duffel that held her first-aid kit. There was nothing she could do now except move fast and make the right decisions. The only problem was she still didn't know exactly what those right decisions were.

"Okay," she huffed as she and Einstein arrived back at Lola's side.

She knelt beside Lola's legs and quickly realized it was too dark for her to see what she was doing.

"I need you to bring the Humvee around and give me some light," she said.

Daniel lurched away from the porch, a massive shadow hulking beside him: Khan still on duty. She wondered how Khan and Einstein had decided to switch assignments. She pulled off her tactical gloves and replaced her bloody latex gloves with a fresh pair. She was just injecting Lola with a mild sedative when the brilliant lights of the Humvee came shooting through the banister slats. She adjusted her position so the glare was out of her face and on the wound. It looked like a clean through-and-through. She waited for Lola's eyes to droop before she started cleaning the wound. Lola's leg twitched a few times, but she didn't cry out. Antiseptic, then ointment, then gauze, then a splint and more gauze. It should heal well, if she could keep Lola off it.

She blew out a sigh. What were they going to do about all these dogs?

"What's next?" Daniel asked when she was done. He was on the ground beside the porch, rifle in hands, scanning the dark plains around them.

"Can you throw a couple of stitches in my ear while I've got the stuff out?"

He balked. "I won't get it right."

"It'll be easy," she assured him. "Haven't you ever sewn on a button?"

"Not through human flesh," he muttered, but he slung his rifle over his shoulder and started up the stairs as he spoke.

She lit a match from the kit and sterilized the needle. It wasn't the highest standard of medical technique, but it was the best she could do under the circumstances. She waved the needle quickly back and forth to cool it, then poked the suture thread through the eye and knotted one end.

She held it out to him along with a fresh pair of gloves. He put the gloves on and then reached slowly for the needle. He didn't seem to want to touch it. She tilted her head back and poured antiseptic across the wound, waiting for the scorching sting to run the course of the cut all the way to her ear. Then she angled her jaw toward him, making sure she was in the brightest beam of light.

"Probably just needs three little ones. Start at the back and pull through."

"What about a local anesthetic?"

"I've got enough painkiller in me already," she lied.

She could feel the slash across her jaw like a brand. But she was out of *Survive*, and anything else she could use would incapacitate her at least partially. This wasn't an emergency, it was only pain.

He knelt down beside her. He put his fingers gently under the edge of her chin.

"This was very close to your jugular!" He gasped, horrified.

"Yeah, he was good."

His face was out of her sight, so she couldn't interpret the little hitching sound in his breath.

"Do it, Daniel. We have to hurry."

He sucked in a deep breath, and then she felt the needle pierce her earlobe. She was braced for it—she kept it off her face and didn't let her hands clutch into fists; she'd learned to localize her reactions. She clenched the muscles in her abdomen, letting the pressure vent there.

"Good," she said as soon as she was sure she could keep her voice even. "You're doing great. Now just fit the pieces together, and stitch them in place."

While she spoke, his fingers moved quickly through the task. She couldn't feel the needle in the severed bottom portion of her earlobe, so she only had to deal with the pain when he perforated the top half. Just three little stabs. It wasn't too bad after the first.

"Do I . . . tie a knot or something?" he asked.

"Yes, in the back, please."

She could feel the pull of the thread tightening as he worked.

"It's done."

She looked up at him and smiled. It tugged at her slashed jaw. "Thank you. I would have had a hard time managing that on my own."

He touched her cheek. "Here, let me bandage this for you."

She held still while he covered the wound with ointment, then taped a strip of gauze to her cheek. He wrapped her ear front and back.

"Probably should have cleaned it first," he muttered.

"It will do for now. Let's put Lola in the Humvee."

"I'll get her."

Daniel gently lifted the sleeping Lola into his arms. Her long front paws and ears dangled out from his arms and wiggled with every step he took. Alex felt a bubble of inappropriate humor rising in her chest, and swallowed against it. There was no time for hysteria. Daniel laid Lola in the space behind the passenger seat. There were only the two front seats in the Humvee. Kevin had removed the rest to leave room for cargo, she guessed.

"What now?" Daniel asked as he walked back to where she was still sitting on the porch. He was probably wondering why she wasn't doing something proactive. He didn't know she was procrastinating.

She took a deep breath and steadied her shoulders. "Give me the phone. It's time to talk to your brother."

"Should we be moving?"

"There's one thing more I need to do, but I want to tell him first."

"What?"

"We really ought to burn the house down."

His eyes widened as he stared at her. Slowly, he pulled the phone from his vest pocket.

"I should make the call," he said.

"He already hates me," she countered.

"But this was my fault."

"You weren't the one who hired a team of hit men."

He shook his head and pressed the button to power up the phone.

"Fine," she muttered.

As she packed up her first-aid supplies, she watched Daniel from the corner of her eye. He pulled up the only number that had ever called, but before he could touch it, the phone rang again.

Daniel sucked in a deep breath, the same way he had before making the first pass on her ear. She imagined this conversation would be the harder of the tasks.

He hit the screen. She could hear Kevin shrieking so loudly that at first she thought the phone was on speaker mode.

"YOU DON'T HANG UP ON ME, YOU—"

"Kev, it's me. Kev! It's Danny!"

"WHAT THE HELL IS HAPPENING?"

"It's my fault, Kev. I was an idiot. I ruined everything. I'm so sorry!"

"WHAT ARE YOU BABBLING ABOUT?"

"Arnie's dead, Kev. I'm so sorry. And some of the dogs, I'm not sure how many. It's all my fault. I wish I could tell you how—"

"PUT THE POISON LADY ON THE PHONE!"

"This is on me, Kev. I messed up—"

Kevin's voice was calmer when he interrupted now. "There's no *time* for this, Danny. Give her the phone. I need someone who can talk sense."

She stood up and reached for the phone. Daniel watched anxiously as she held it a few inches away from her ear.

"Are you secure?" Kevin asked.

Surprised by his businesslike detachment, she answered in the same tone. "For the moment, but we've got to move."

"Have you torched the house?"

"I was just about to."

"There's kerosene in the closet under the stairs."

"Thanks."

"Call me when you're on the road."

He hung up.

Well, *that* had gone better than she'd hoped. She handed the phone back to Daniel. His expression was blank with surprise. The gas in the house would long since have dissipated, so she didn't bother with the mask. Daniel followed her inside, but she made Einstein keep watch at the door.

"Get some clothes out of Kevin's room," she instructed. She could have sent him upstairs for the first set he'd borrowed, but that would take more time, and she didn't know how he would react to the bodies. She could see his eyes cutting away to the sofa that obscured Arnie, and then back to her. They both had to keep it together. They still had a long night ahead of them if they were going to be alive tomorrow. "When you have enough for a few days, get to the kitchen and grab anything that's nonperishable. Water, too, as much as we've got."

He nodded and headed down the hall to Kevin's room. She darted up the stairs.

"Do you want these guns?" he called up after her.

She dodged around the bodies, careful not to slip in the blood slick. "No, those've killed people. If we get caught, I don't want to be linked to anything. Kevin's guns will be clean."

In her room, she stripped off her blood-spattered clothes and pulled on clean jeans and a T-shirt. She gathered up her sleeping bag, wrapping the rest of her clothes in it, then grabbed her lab kit in her open hand and kicked the bloody clothes into the hallway. She hurried back down the stairs and out to the car with her awkward load. While Daniel foraged in the kitchen, she located the kerosene. Kevin had three five-gallon gas cans stashed together. He could only have intended them for lighting up the house. She was glad that he was so prepared and businesslike. It meant his reaction — once Daniel was safe — was likely to be more pragmatic than violent. She hoped.

She started upstairs, making sure her clothes and the bodies were well saturated with the kerosene. The wooden floors wouldn't need as much help. She splashed the baseboards in all three rooms, then trailed the rest down the stairs. She grabbed another can and hurried through the ground floor. It was the first time she'd seen the other bedrooms. They were both large and well appointed with luxurious attached baths. She was glad Arnie had had a comfortable life here. She wished she could have done something to spare him this. But even if she and Daniel had left the first day the missing-person trap had run on the news, Arnie would still have ended up like this. It was a depressing thought.

Daniel's fingerprints were in the dogs' outbuilding, but there was no way to fool Carston's counterpart at the CIA into thinking Daniel — or Kevin — had died here, so it didn't really matter. They would know Daniel was on the run. She didn't want to torch the outbuilding and endanger the animals. It didn't have a wide gravel skirt like the house did, which would hopefully prevent a wildfire. No doubt Kevin had laid the gravel for exactly this reason.

Daniel was waiting for her in front of the Humvee.

"Back this up," she said, waving toward the Humvee. "See if you can get the dogs to move, too."

He got to work. She had the pack of matches from her first-aid kit. She'd left a nice thick trail of kerosene down the middle of the porch steps, so it was easy to set that trail alight and then get out of the way before the blaze really got going. When she turned, the dogs were automatically backing away from the flames. That was good.

Alex opened the driver-side door and called for Einstein. He jumped over the seat in one bound and then positioned himself next to Lola. His ears were up and his tongue out. He still looked eager; Alex envied his energy and positivity.

Daniel was walking through the crowd of surviving animals, giving each one an emphatic "At ease." She hoped that would help when the fire trucks started rolling up. The noise of the shootout wouldn't have carried to any of the distant neighbors, but the orange light of the fire against the black night sky was another matter. They had to run now. She couldn't think of anything else she could do for the dogs. It felt like failure—these animals had saved her and Daniel's lives.

A rumble just behind her head startled Alex. She spun and found herself face to face with Khan. He was staring at her in what seemed like an impatient way, as if he were waiting for her to move. His nose pointed over her shoulder toward Einstein.

"Oh," she said as she realized he was trying to get into the car. "Sorry, Khan, I need you to stay."

She'd never seen an animal look so offended in her life. He didn't move, just stared into her face as if demanding an explanation. She was the more surprised of the two of them when she suddenly threw her arms around his neck and buried her face against his shoulder.

"I'm sorry, big guy," she whispered into his fur. "I wish I could take you with me. I owe you huge. Take care of the others for me. You're in charge, okay?"

She leaned away, stroking the sides of his thick neck. He looked slightly mollified and took an unwilling step back.

"At ease," she said quietly; she patted him once more, then turned to the Humvee. Daniel was already belted into the passenger's seat.

"Are you all right?" Daniel asked quietly as she climbed in. It was obvious he wasn't talking about physical injuries.

"Not really." She laughed once, and there was an edge of the hysteria she was fighting in the sound. Khan was still watching as she pulled away from the house.

Once through the gate, she donned the goggles and turned the headlights off. It was safer to drive the

Humvee across the open plains rather than stay on the only road that led to the ranch. Eventually, they reached another road — it was even paved. She ditched the goggles and put the headlights on as she turned northwest. She didn't have a destination in mind, only distance. She needed to get as far away from Kevin's ranch as possible before the sun rose.

CHAPTER 20

Kevin picked up on the first ring.

"Okay, Oleander, where do we stand?" was his greeting.

"We're headed north in the Humvee. I've got Daniel, Einstein, and Lola with me. We managed to scavenge some of what we need, but not much."

She heard him blow out a relieved breath when she said Einstein's name, but the edge was still there in his voice when he asked, "The Humvee? The truck is blown?"

"Yes."

He thought for a second. "So, only night driving until you can find something new."

"Easier said than done. We've both got major face problems."

"Yeah, I saw Daniel on the news. But yours can't be that bad anymore. Throw some makeup on."

"It's gotten *slightly* worse over the course of the evening."

"Ah." He clicked his tongue a few times. "Danny?" he asked, and she could hear the tension he was trying to hide.

"Not a scratch." The hands didn't count; they'd done that to themselves.

"She made me stay in the car," Daniel yelled loud enough for his brother to hear.

"Good job," Kevin responded. "How many were there?"

"Six."

He sucked a breath in. "Agents?"

"No, actually. Get this—they put a hit out with the *Mob*."

"*What?*"

"It was mostly muscle, but they had at least one authentic professional in the group."

"You took out *all* of them?"

"The dogs did most of the work. They were magnificent, by the way."

He grunted in acknowledgment. "Why'd you bring Lola?"

"Shot in the leg. I was afraid that if someone found her, they would put her down. Speaking of, should I call Animal Control?" she asked. "I worry that when the firemen get there..."

"I'll take care of it. I've got a contingency plan in place for them."

"Good." She would never think of herself as the most prepared again. Kevin was the king of prepared.

"What's your plan now?"

She laughed—and there was the sound of hysteria again. "No idea, actually. I'm thinking we camp out of the Humvee for a few days. After that..." She trailed off.

"You don't have a place?"

"Not one where I can park this beast or hide two large dogs. I've never felt so conspicuous in my life."

"I'll think of something."

"What took you so long to call?" she asked. "I thought you were dead."

Daniel gasped. He stared at her, shocked.

"Getting set up. These things take time. I can't be everywhere at once—I had to plant a lot of cameras."

"A call would have been nice."

"I didn't know you guys were going to blow everything." His voice got suddenly much lower. "What did the idiot do? No, don't answer. I don't want him to hear. Just yes or no. Did he call someone?"

"No," she snapped, irritated.

"Wait—the truck is blown...he didn't leave the house, did he?"

She wanted to say, *No one told him not to,* but Daniel would know they were discussing him. She didn't respond, keeping her eyes straight ahead, though she wanted to sneak a look at Daniel to see if he'd heard any of it.

Kevin sighed. "Not an ounce of common sense."

So many things she wanted to say to that, but she couldn't think of a discreet way to phrase any of them.

He changed the subject. "Arnie... Was it bad?"

"No. He didn't see it coming. He wouldn't have felt anything."

"His real name was Ernesto," Kevin said, but it felt like he was saying it to himself rather than to her. "He was a good partner. We had a good run. A short run, but a good one." He cleared his throat. "Okay, now tell me everything that happened." Then lower: "Except whatever he did to set it off. He's probably traumatized enough."

Alex ran through the events of the evening, keeping it clinical and glossing over the gruesome parts. When she said simply, "I questioned him," Kevin would have a pretty clear picture of what that meant.

"So what happened to your face?"

"He was very flexible. And he had some kind of throwing blade in the lining of his sleeve."

"Hm, that's rough," he said gloomily, and she knew what he was thinking. Facial scars were bad news when you wanted to keep a low profile. They were too easy to remember and recognize. Suddenly the search changed from *Have you seen a short, nondescript female, unknown hair length or color, or a man fitting that same description?* to *Have you seen a person with this scar?*

"Well," she concluded, "it appears the people in

charge pegged you for the win. I won't pretend I'm not insulted. We'll have to tweak the plan. The bait has to come from you, and it needs to go to the right person. Do you have any idea who that would be yet?"

Kevin was quiet for a minute. "When word gets back to my guy about what happened tonight...well, we might not need the e-mail. He's going to have to talk to your guy about this. I'm ready—I'll see them do it. Then we can decide if we need more."

"Sounds good."

"By the way," he said in his covert voice, "I know you sanitized the story for the kid. I want the whole thing when I see you again."

She rolled her eyes. "Right."

"Look, Ollie, don't let this go to your head, but... you did good. Real good. You saved Danny's life. Thank you."

She was so surprised, it took her a minute to respond. "I think we're quits. Without your dogs or your Batcave, we wouldn't have made it out. So... thank you."

"You could have taken off as soon as you saw that first newscast. You knew they thought you were dead, but you stayed to keep a virtual stranger safe, though I'm sure you'd love nothing better than to be rid of both of us. That's honor, right there. I owe you."

"Mmm," she said noncommittally. They didn't need to discuss *everything* tonight.

"Let me talk to him before you hang up," Daniel whispered.

"Daniel wants to talk."

"Put him on."

She handed the phone over.

"Kev—"

"Don't beat yourself up, Danny," she heard Kevin tell him. She wondered if Daniel had been able to hear just as clearly.

"Yeah," Daniel responded, morose, "I'm only responsible for getting Arnie murdered tonight, not to mention the dogs. Why should I suffer?"

"Look, what's done is done—"

"Funny, Alex said that, too."

"Poison girl knows the score. This is a new world, kid. It's got a higher body count. Now, I'm not saying that things like this won't affect you. You just can't let them cloud your vision."

Kevin's voice dropped into a lower register, and Alex was glad to know that Daniel probably hadn't been able to make out the quieter part of their conversation. But she also wanted to know what Kevin didn't want her to hear.

"I think so," Daniel said. A pause. "Maybe not...I will. Yes. Okay. What are you going to do about the dogs? We had to leave Khan."

"Yeah." Kevin's voice was back to normal volume. "I love that monster, but he's not exactly travel-size, is he?

There's a breeder not too far away that Arnie's worked with in the past. He's more a competitor than a friend, but he knows the value of my dogs. Arnie made a deal with him that if we ever wanted out, we'd sell him our stock. Arnie also sort of implied that we might decide to do that suddenly, without any warning and in the middle of the night. I'll call him and he'll meet up with Animal Control before they do anything stupid."

"Won't the cops wonder—"

"I'll coach him. He'll say Arnie called when he heard shots or something. Don't worry, the dogs will be okay."

Daniel sighed, relieved.

"It does piss me off that he's getting his hands on Khan, free of charge. He's been trying to buy him for years."

"I'm sorry—"

"Seriously, kid, don't sweat it. You don't last in this life by getting attached. I know how to start over. Now, be good and do whatever the Oleander says, okay?"

"Wait, Kev, I had an idea. That's why I wanted to talk to you."

"You've got an idea?"

Alex could hear the skepticism from three feet away.

"Yes, actually. I was thinking about the McKinleys' cabin by the lake."

Kevin was silent for a second. "Um, now's not really the time for a trip down memory lane, kid."

"I'm actually two minutes older than you, *kid,* which I'm sure you haven't forgotten. And I don't want to reminisce. I was thinking that the McKinleys only ever used the cabin in the winter. And that your CIA people probably wouldn't know *that* much detail about our childhood. And that I know where Mr. McKinley always kept the key."

"Hey, that's not bad, Danny."

"Thanks."

"That would be about, what? Eighteen hours from the ranch? Just two nights' driving. And that'll bring you closer to my position. Didn't the McKinleys used to keep a Suburban out there?"

"We can't *steal their car,* Kevin."

In the darkness, though more than a thousand miles apart, Alex felt like she was exchanging a loaded glance with Kevin. And maybe an eye roll—on his part, at least.

"We'll talk about finding a car later. Tell the Oleander to take better care of her face next time. We're going to need it."

"Yes, because I'm sure she *so* enjoys having people beat it bloody that it will be hard for her to quit."

"Yeah, yeah. Call me if you have any troubles. I'll make contact when I know more about our friends in Washington."

Kevin disconnected. Daniel stared at the phone for a minute before putting it away. He took a deep breath and let it out slowly.

"How are you holding up?" she asked.

"Nothing feels real."

"Let me see your hand."

He stretched his left arm out to her, and she took his hand with her right. His temperature was warmer than hers. She felt his wrist, and the pulse seemed even. The scratches and punctures on his palm were shallow; they'd already stopped bleeding on their own. She glanced over at him and then looked back to the road. It was too dark to be able to assess his coloring with any degree of certainty.

"What was that?" he asked as she released his hand.

"Looking for signs of shock. Do you feel nauseated?"

"No. But then, I kind of feel as if I *should*, if you know what I mean. Like I will when I can process everything."

"Let me know if you start to feel dizzy, faint, or cold."

"*You* feel cold. Are you sure you're not going into shock?"

"Not entirely, I suppose. If I feel dizzy, I'll pull over and you can drive."

He reached over, took her gloved hand off the wheel, and held it loosely, letting their arms dangle in the space between seats. He took another deep breath.

"I heard all those shots, so close together, and I thought —"

"I know. Thanks for staying in the car like I asked. It's good to know I can trust you."

He didn't say anything.

"What?" she asked.

"Well, when you put it like that," he said, sounding ashamed, "I don't really want to admit this...but I did get out for a few minutes. I was about to go into the house, but Einstein stopped me. And then I realized that one way or another, things were decided inside, and if they *had* got you, my best bet to kill the bastards would be from the Humvee. I wasn't going to let them walk away, Alex. Not a chance."

She squeezed his hand lightly.

"Do you remember what Kevin told me before, about visualization?"

She shook her head. It sounded only vaguely familiar.

"We were at the shooting range for the first time, and I said I didn't think I could shoot another person." He laughed a dark little chuckle. "He told me to visualize someone I cared about in danger."

As he spoke, it came back clearly. "Ah."

"Well, I get it now. And he was right. The second I realized someone had killed Arnie and that he was coming for *you* next..." He shook his head. "I didn't realize I was capable of feeling so...primal."

"I told you that you would get in touch with your

instincts," she said lightly. The joking tone, recalled from that day at the range, felt all kinds of wrong the instant the words were out. Her voice was somber when she added, "I wish it hadn't happened like this."

He squeezed her hand this time. "It's going to be okay."

She made an effort to focus. "So, where exactly are we headed?"

"Tallahassee. We did a couple of Christmases there when we were kids. Some family friends kept a place there so they could get out of the snow. They must have liked their privacy, because the cabin is in the middle of nowhere. It's not actually on the lake, but it's swampy, and the mosquitoes will be murder this time of year."

"You should be in real estate. You're sure no one will be there?"

"I haven't seen the McKinleys since my parents' funeral, but they never went south in the summertime during all the years I knew them. It was always just their winter spot."

"Well, we might as well head that way as any other. If that cabin won't work, maybe we can find something else that's empty."

She saw a sign for State Highway 70, heading north.

"We'll have to turn east, go through Oklahoma City, then down through Dallas. It'll be good, if anyone's looking, to be headed back into Texas. Makes us look innocent."

"We only defended ourselves."

"That won't matter. If we got picked up for what just happened, the police would have to take us in. Even if we explained every detail and they believed every word—which is unlikely, to put it mildly—they'd still have to put us in a cell for a while. It wouldn't take long. The people who hired the hit men would have no trouble getting to us in jail. We'd be sitting ducks."

He felt the tremble in her fingers and rubbed his thumb soothingly across the back of her hand.

"So you're saying a crime spree is a bad idea right now?"

She couldn't believe he was the one trying to cheer her up. "Probably," she agreed, "but it might come to that." She glanced down at the gas gauge, then hissed. "This thing is burning through gas like it *wants* to piss me off."

"What can we do?"

"I'm going to have to go into a gas station, pay with cash."

"But your face."

"There's no help for it. I'll just pretend I was in a car accident...which, actually, is not pretend at all, is it? Anyway, there's nothing else I can do."

The gas-guzzling monster forced Alex to stop much

earlier than she would have liked. She followed the signs in Oklahoma City to the airport, guessing that the gas stations around it would be somewhat busy even late at night. Also, if anyone noticed them there, he might assume they were planning to fly out. Any ensuing search would be concentrated on the airport.

She'd had Daniel find her oversize hoodie while she was driving. She slipped into it now, wishing it were cooler out so that she would look more normal. There were two other vehicles—one taxi and one work truck. Both male drivers eyed the Humvee, of course. She moved in her boy-slouch as she got out and stuck the nozzle into the tank. While it was filling, she slouched her way into the store. She grabbed a box of granola bars and a six-pack of bottled water and took them to the fifty-something woman at the counter. The woman had bleached-blond hair with an inch of dark roots, nicotine-stained teeth, and a name tag that said BEVERLY. At first she didn't pay much attention to Alex, just rang up the goods. But then Alex had to speak.

"Pump six," she said in the lowest register that wouldn't sound put on.

Beverly looked up, and her mascara-smeared eyes opened round.

"Aw, sweet hell, honey! What happened to your face?"

"Car accident," Alex muttered.

"Everyone okay?"

"Yeah." Alex looked pointedly down at the cash in her hand, waiting to count it out. From the corner of her eye, she saw the taxi drive away.

"Well, I hope you feel better soon."

"Um, thanks. What's the total?"

"Oh, is this right? Seems high. One-oh-three fifty-five?"

Alex handed Beverly six twenties and waited for the change. Another truck—a big, black F-250— pulled into the pump behind the Humvee. She watched as three tall thin men got out. As two of them walked into the minimart, she revised her assessment. They were very tall teenage boys; half of a basketball team, maybe. Like her, they wore dark hoodies. At least that made her unseasonable getup look more normal.

"That sure is a big truck you got out there," Beverly commented.

"Yeah."

"Must be a pain to keep that thing full."

"Yeah." Alex held her hand out impatiently.

The boys came in, noisy and boisterous. The smell of beer and marijuana drifted in through the door with them. Outside, the work truck pulled out of the lot.

"Oh, here you go," Beverly said, her voice suddenly impersonal. "Sixteen forty-five."

"Thanks."

Beverly was distracted by the newcomers. She stared over Alex's head, her eyes narrowed. The big boys were headed for the liquor aisle. Hopefully they would be a huge pain as they tried to get fake IDs past Beverly. Anything that would make Alex fade in her memory.

Alex headed for the automatic door with her head down. She didn't need more than one witness.

With a thud, her head knocked into the chest of the third boy. The first thing she registered was the smell; his sweatshirt reeked of whiskey. She looked up automatically when he grabbed her by the shoulders.

"Watch yourself, little playa."

He was a thick white kid, not as tall as the others. She tried to shake him off. He held on tighter with one hand, yanking her hood back with the other.

"Hey, it's a girl." Then louder, toward the boys by the refrigerated cases, "Looky what I found."

Alex's voice was ice. She was not in the mood for this nonsense. "Get your hands off me."

"You leave that gal alone or I'm calling the police," Beverly called shrilly. "I've got the phone in my hand."

Alex wanted to scream. This was all she needed.

"Relax, old bag, we got plenty to go around."

The other two, one black, one Hispanic, were already in place to back their friend up. Alex slid a thin syringe from her belt. This wouldn't help her stay under the radar, but she had to put this kid down and get out of here before Beverly called the cops.

"I've dialed the nine and the first one," Beverly warned them. "You all get out now."

Alex tried to yank herself out of the boy's grip, but the grinning idiot had both hands locked around her upper arms now. She angled the needle.

"Is there a problem, son?"

Nooooo, Alex moaned internally.

"What?" the white kid said aggressively, dropping her and pivoting to face the newcomer. He then took a quick step back, and she had to duck out of his way.

She'd spent so much time around Daniel that she'd forgotten how tall he really was. He had an inch on even the tallest kid, and he stood with wider shoulders and much more assurance. At least he'd put a ball cap on, hiding his hair and shading his face a little. The beginnings of his beard were dark enough to slightly camouflage the contours of his face. That was good. But it was not good that he'd stuck a Glock—in a very obvious way—into the waistband of his jeans.

"No, no problem, man," the black kid said. He grabbed the white kid's shoulder and tugged him back a step.

"Good. Why don't you head on out, then?"

The white kid thrust his chest forward. "When we get what we came for."

Daniel did something different with the way he

held his jaw. Alex couldn't quite put her finger on it, but suddenly his face was the opposite of friendly. He leaned in toward the troublemaker.

"*Now.*"

There was no bluster in how he spoke, just absolute authority.

"C'mon," the black kid insisted. He shoved the white kid past Daniel while tugging on the sleeve of the third boy. They walked quickly to the truck, elbowing each other and scuffling a little. Alex kept her back to Beverly, nudging Daniel so he would turn that way, too. The boys got in the truck and the driver punched the gas, swerving around the Humvee with tires squealing.

"Hey, thanks, buddy," Beverly cooed at him. "I appreciate your help."

"Sure thing," he responded, holding one arm out courteously for Alex to exit first.

Alex hurried back to the Humvee. She could feel Daniel close behind her and just hoped he had the sense to keep his head down and not turn around.

"Well, I don't know how that could have gone worse," Alex said disgustedly when they were back on the road. "That woman will remember us for the rest of her natural life."

"Sorry."

"You just had to go in there like some cowboy, with a gun in your pants."

"We *do* have Texas plates," he pointed out. "And what was I supposed to do? That kid was—"

"Was about to have a violent and prolonged episode of projectile vomiting. It would have incapacitated him totally and perhaps made enough of a mess that Beverly would have forgotten all about me."

"Oh."

"Yeah. *Oh,* indeed. I can take care of myself, Daniel."

His jaw suddenly got hard again, like it had in the gas station store. "I know that, Alex, but there might actually come a time when you need help. When that happens, I'm not going to be waiting in the car again. You should probably wrap your head around that now."

"I'll tell you when I need backup."

"And I'll be there," he snapped.

She let the quarrel drop, and for a moment there was no sound but the roar of the oversize engine burning through the new gas. Then he sighed.

"I should have known you were one step ahead," he said.

She nodded her acceptance of the implied apology, though she had mixed feelings about his declarations.

"Where did you learn how to do that?" she asked after another short lull.

"What?"

"Intimidate people."

"My school isn't exactly an exclusive private prep.

Anyway, most kids just want someone to take control. It makes them feel more secure."

She laughed. "Then those boys will sleep sound tonight."

• • •

THE REST OF the night was less fraught. Daniel dozed against the window, snoring lightly, until the next gas stop, about twenty miles east of Dallas. The sleepy man in the booth showed no interest in Alex's face. When they were away from the gas station's cameras, she pulled off on a dark shoulder and traded seats with Daniel. He claimed to be wide awake and ready. She napped as best she could until the next stop, south of Shreveport, where they switched seats again.

Dawn was coming. Alex searched the fancy GPS for a close-by national park or wildlife reserve and found they were not far from the huge expanse of the Kisatchie National Forest. She headed for the corner of the park that came closest to the I-49, then wandered through back roads until she found an area isolated and overgrown enough that she felt comfortable pulling over into the thick shade of some tightly grouped trees. She backed into a barely wide enough space between the tree trunks and then reversed until there was just room for the rear hatch to open. When she cracked her door, the humid heat outside quickly overpowered the cooler air inside the vehicle.

Einstein was thrilled to get out of the car and

relieve himself. It was harder for Lola. Alex had to redress Lola's wound when she was done. Daniel had food and water out for them before Alex was finished. Then Daniel had the easier job of relieving himself, and Alex got the more complicated version. She'd lived out of a car before, though, and while it wasn't her favorite thing, she was prepared.

She took a look at the front of the Humvee and had to admit she was impressed. To the naked eye, there was no evidence that they'd been in even a minor fender-bender.

The breakfast options were minimal. Alex found herself with the same box of Pop-Tarts that she'd started with her first morning at the ranch. Daniel took a packet, too.

"What are we going to do about food?" he asked.

Alex wiped her arm across her forehead, drying the sweat before it could drip into her eyes. "Tonight I'll stock up a little at each gas station. It will get us through a few days. Let me know if you have any requests." Alex yawned, then hissed when the motion pulled at the cut on her face.

"Do you have aspirin?"

She nodded tiredly. "That might be a good idea. We both need to get some sleep. The dogs will be fine if we just leave them outside, right? I don't want them to have to be cooped up all night and all day, too."

Alex dug up a couple of Motrin while Daniel

shoved the mess in the back of the Humvee to the sides of the bed, leaving a narrow flat space in the middle for them. Satisfied that she'd done everything she could, Alex spread out her sleeping bag and rolled down the top edge for a pillow.

It felt normal in an abnormal way to have Daniel lie down beside her, instinctive and comfortable for him to wrap one arm around her waist and bury his face in the hollow of her neck. The scratch of his short beard tickled her skin, but she didn't mind.

She was starting to drift off when she became conscious of his movement beside her. At first she thought he was beginning to snore, but the shuddering didn't pause. She grabbed his fingers at her waist, and found them trembling. She jerked up and twisted to face him. His eyes flew wide when she moved so suddenly, and he started to sit up. She pushed him down with one hand on his chest.

"What's wrong?" he whispered.

She looked at his face. It was hard to tell in the shade, but he looked paler than before. She should have been watching for this. Now that they had the chance to figuratively lay their weapons down for a moment, of course the severe strain of the night before would catch up to them. Probably not authentic shock; more likely just a traditional panic attack.

"Nothing. Except maybe with you." She touched his forehead; it felt clammy. "Do you feel sick?"

"No, I'm fine."

"You were shaking."

He shook his head and took a deep breath. "Sorry, I was just thinking about...how close it was."

"Don't. It's over. You're safe."

"I know, I know."

"I won't let anything happen to you."

He laughed once, and she could hear the same sound of hysteria that had been in her own laugh last night. "I *know*," he repeated. "*I'll* be fine. But what about you? Are *you* safe?" He pulled her down onto his chest, cradling the damaged side of her face carefully in his long fingers, and whispered into her hair, "I could have lost you, just like that. Everything that means anything to me is gone—I've lost my home, my job, my life...I've lost *myself*. I'm hanging on by my fingernails, Alex, and it's you I'm hanging on to. If something happens to you...I don't know what that means for me. I don't know how I keep going. I'm dealing with the rest, Alex, but I can't lose you, too, I can't."

Another shudder ran through his body.

"It's okay," she murmured uncertainly, reaching up to rest her fingers against his lips. "I'm here."

Was that the right thing to say? She didn't have any experience comforting someone. Even when her mother had been in the last stages of the illness that had killed her, Judy didn't want sympathy and she didn't want lies. If Juliana were to say something like

You look great today, Mom, Judy's response was always along the lines of *Don't bother with that nonsense, I have a mirror.* It never seemed to occur to Judy that Juliana might need comfort; after all, Juliana wasn't the one who was dying.

She'd learned early not to seek sympathy for herself; she'd never really known how to show it to someone else. She would be more comfortable with the clinical, explaining that what he was feeling now was just a natural response to the specter of a violent death, but she'd said things like that to him before and she knew they didn't help. So she found herself mimicking things she'd seen on television, speaking softly, stroking the side of his face.

"We're okay . . . it's over."

She wondered if she should put the sleeping bag over him, just in case, though it was already sweltering and he didn't feel cold. Still, she'd already come to the conclusion that he ran at a warmer temperature than she did. Both physically and metaphorically.

His breathing still sounded rough. She pulled her head free and then propped herself up so she could examine his face.

He was no longer just pale. His soft eyes were haunted, tormented, his jaw tight against the panic he was trying to control. A raised line pulsed in his forehead. He stared at her like he was pleading for a release from pain.

His expression ignited a nightmare of a memory,

the memory of his interrogation, and she impulsively threw her arms around his neck, pulling his head up off the floor of the Humvee and hugging it tight to her chest to hide that face. She felt her own convulsive shiver, and the clinical side of her brain let her know that she was every bit as traumatized as he was. Her nonclinical side didn't care what the reason was. A wave of panic was washing through her and she felt as if she couldn't hold him close enough to reassure herself that he was actually alive and safe and here. As if she might suddenly blink and be back inside her black tent with Daniel screaming in agony. Or, worse, she would open her eyes to the dark upstairs hallway only to find Daniel's bleeding body at her feet instead of the hit man's. Her pulse spiked and she couldn't breathe.

Daniel rolled their bodies so he was at her side, and his hands peeled hers free from his head. For a second she thought he was about to take the comforter's role at which she had failed so spectacularly, but then their eyes met and she was looking into a mirror of all the turmoil and fear in her own head. Fear of loss, fear of *having* because that made the loss possible. Rather than comfort, the depth of his fear multiplied hers. She could lose him, and she didn't know how to live with that.

CHAPTER 21

Their lips crushed together so suddenly she wasn't sure who had moved first.

And then their bodies were tangling together with a kind of desperate fury, lips and fingers, tongues and teeth. Breathing was secondary and she managed it only in broken pants that left her still dizzy. She wanted nothing but to be closer, and then closer, to be *inside* his skin somehow so that he could never be ripped away from her. She felt the scald as the wound along her jaw reopened, and all the bruises, old and new, flared to life, but the pain did nothing to distract from that acute need. They grappled almost like adversaries, turning and twisting together in the limits of the small space, slamming against the duffel bags and then back to the floor. She was amazed at how electrifying his brute strength was—strength in a man had always been something to fear, but now she thrilled to it. Fabric tore, and she couldn't guess who it belonged to. She remembered the texture of his skin, the shape of his muscles under her hands, but she had not imagined they could feel like this against her own.

Closer, her blood pulsed. *Closer.*

And then he suddenly jerked away, his mouth sliding from hers with a choked gasp. An anxious whine sounded at her feet. She leaned over and saw Einstein with his jaws locked on Daniel's ankle. Einstein whimpered again.

"Einstein, *at ease,*" he growled, kicking to free his foot. "Get *off.*"

Einstein let him go, looking to her nervously.

"At ease!" Her voice was husky. "It's okay."

With a hesitant huff, Einstein dropped out of the open hatch.

Daniel rolled up and slammed the door shut. He turned toward her on his knees, his pupils dilated and his eyes wild. He gritted his teeth as if he were fighting for some kind of control.

She reached up for him, her fingers stretching to hook into the waistband of his jeans, and he collapsed into her with a low groan.

"Alex, Alex," he breathed against her neck. "Stay with me. Don't leave."

Even in the frenzy of the moment, she was aware what he was asking. And she meant what she said when she answered, knowing it could be the worst kind of mistake.

"I will," she promised roughly. "I won't."

Their mouths locked together again, and she could feel his heart drumming a syncopated rhythm against her own, aligned beneath their skin because his mirrored hers.

The shrill peal of the phone pierced through the lower register sounds—the double heartbeat, the gasping breaths—and had her pushing away from him in a different kind of panic.

He shook his head quickly once, eyes closed, as if trying to remember where he was.

She sat up, looking for the source of the sound.

"I've got it," Daniel said, gasping. He shoved his hand in his jeans pocket as the phone pealed again.

He looked at the number, then hit Answer with his thumb. With his left hand, he pulled her back against his chest.

"Kev?" Daniel answered between pants.

"Danny—hey, are you guys safe?"

"Yeah."

"What are you doing?"

"Trying to get some sleep."

"Sounds like you're running a marathon."

"The phone scared me. Nerves a little frayed, you know." He lied so smoothly that she almost smiled in spite of the tumult inside her.

"Oh, right, sorry. Let me talk to Oleander."

"You mean Alex?"

"Whatever. Give her the phone."

She tried to slow her breathing, to sound normal. "Yes?"

"What? Don't tell me the phone scared you, too."

"I am not a black ops agent. And it's been a very long night."

"I'll keep it quick. I found my guy. Does the name Deavers mean anything to you?"

She thought for a second, working to pull her mind back to the things that mattered. "Yes, I know the name. It was on some of the files when information was being extracted for the CIA. He never came in to monitor an interrogation, though. Is he a supervisor over there?"

"He's more than a supervisor. He's second in command these days, with an eye to moving up. He was one of several potentials I was monitoring. Early this morning, Deavers gets a call, punches a few walls, then makes his own call. I know this guy—he loves to make the peons scurry. He doesn't leave his office; he sends an aide to bring the person he wants to him. Always the power play. But after that second call, he goes running out to see your man Carston like a gofer. They met up at a random little residential park miles away from both their offices and then went for a leisurely and sweaty walk, looking like they wanted to murder each other the whole time. It's Deavers, for sure."

"What are you thinking?"

"Hmm. I think I still want the e-mail. I need to see who else knows about this. Taking out Deavers won't be too hard, but it just tips the other guys off if he's not alone. Have you got a pen?"

"Gimme a sec."

She crawled to the front seat and located her backpack. She dug for a pen, then scribbled the e-mail address he gave her onto the back of a gas receipt.

"When?" she asked.

"Tonight," he decided. "After you've gotten some sleep and have your nerve back."

"I'll send it from Baton Rouge. Do you have a script or do you want me to wing it?"

"You know the gist. Don't make it sound too cerebral."

"I think I could channel some caveman."

"Perfect. Once you trade cars with the McKinleys, start heading up here." He switched to his library voice, but Daniel was so close it was a wasted effort. "Danny going to give you trouble about staying behind?"

She tilted her face up toward Daniel's. It was easy to read his reaction.

"Yeah. I'm not so sure it's a good idea anyway. Call me paranoid, but I don't believe in safe houses anymore."

Daniel bent down to press his lips hard against her forehead, which made it difficult to pay attention to what Kevin was saying.

"...figure a place for Lola. How bad is your face? Oleander?"

"Huh?"

"Your face. What does it look like?"

"Big bandage across my left jaw and ear." As she spoke, Daniel leaned closer to examine her wounds and then drew in a sharp breath. "Plus all the original fun."

"That could play," Kevin said. "Lola's injured, too. I'll feed them a story that will keep them satisfied."

"Who?"

"The dog-boarding place for Lola. Damn, Ollie, you need some sleep. You're getting dumber by the second."

"Maybe I'll write your e-mail now, while I'm in the right frame of mind."

"Call me when you're on the road again." Kevin hung up.

"You're bleeding through the bandage," Daniel said anxiously.

She handed him the phone. "It's fine. I should have glued it last night."

"Let's take care of it now."

She looked up at his face—the panic and ferocity in his eyes had dimmed to simple concern. His chest was still slick with sweat, but his breathing was regular. She wasn't sure she had reached a similar state of calm.

"*Right* now?" she asked.

He gave her a measured look. "Yes, right now."

"Is it bleeding that much?" She touched the gauze gingerly but felt only a bit of warm wet. From his expression, she'd expected blood to be gushing out in a torrent.

"It's *bleeding;* that's enough. Where is the first-aid kit?"

With a sigh, she turned to the piled duffels. The wrong one was on top, so she had to readjust. While she dug, she felt his fingers cautiously brushing along her left shoulder blade.

"You're all over bruises," he murmured. His fingers followed the line of her arm. "These look fresh."

"I got tackled," she admitted as she pulled out the kit and turned around.

"You never told me what happened in the house," he commented.

"You don't want to know."

"Maybe I do."

"Okay. *I* don't want you to know."

Daniel took the first-aid kit from her hands and then crossed his legs and set it between them. She followed suit with a heavy sigh, angling the left side of her face toward him.

Gently, he started easing the tape from her skin.

"You can do that faster," she told him.

"I'll do it my way."

They sat in silence for a moment while he worked. The stillness allowed her body to remind her how exhausted she was.

"Why don't you want me to know?" he asked as he dabbed a medicated wipe against her skin. "Do you think I can't handle it?"

"No, I just..."

"What?"

"The way you look at me now. I don't want that to change."

From the corner of her eye, she saw him smile. "You don't have to worry about that."

She shrugged in response.

"How do I do this?" he asked, pulling her superglue from the case.

"Push the edges of the cut together, draw a line of glue across the top, then hold it till the glue dries. About a minute."

She suppressed a wince as he pressed his fingertips firmly against her skin. The familiar smell of the adhesive filled the space between them.

"Does this hurt?"

"It's fine."

"Do you ever get tired of being tough?"

She rolled her eyes. "The pain is manageable, thank you."

He leaned away to examine his work. "It looks

messy," he told her. "You should have saved the life of an EMT."

She took the glue from him and screwed the cap back on. She didn't want it to dry out. Who knew how soon she might need it again, the way this trip was going.

"I'm sure it will do the job," she said. "Just hold it for a little longer."

"Alex, I'm sorry about just now." His voice was quiet, apologetic.

She wished she could turn her head and look at him straight on.

"I don't know what that was," he continued. "I can't believe I was so rough with you."

"I wasn't exactly pulling my punches."

"But I'm not injured," he reminded her sourly. "Not a scratch on me, as you put it."

"I don't think that's entirely true anymore," she told him, brushing her fingers against the skin of his chest. She could feel the faint welts her nails had left.

He inhaled sharply, both of them caught for one second in the memory, and her stomach contracted. She tried to turn her head, but he held her face still.

"Wait," he cautioned.

They sat motionless in the charged silence while she counted to sixty in her head twice.

"It's dry," she insisted.

Slowly, he lifted his fingers from her jaw. She turned

to him, but his face was down as he searched the kit. He found the antibacterial spray and applied it liberally to her wound. Then he pulled out the roll of gauze and tape. Gently—and without looking her in the eye—he took her chin between his thumb and forefinger and repositioned her head. He taped the gauze in place.

"We should sleep now," he said as he pressed the last piece tight to her skin. "We're both overwrought and not thinking clearly. We can reopen this...discussion when we're rational."

She wanted to argue, but she knew he was right. They weren't acting like themselves. They were acting like animals—responding to a near-death experience with a subconscious imperative to continue the species. It was primitive biology rather than responsible adult behavior.

She still wanted to argue.

His fingers rested against the side of her neck, and she could feel her pulse begin to jump under his touch. He could, too.

"Sleep," he repeated.

"You're right, you're right," she grumbled, flopping back against the rumpled sleeping bag. She really was bone-weary.

"Here." He handed her his T-shirt.

"Where's mine?"

"In pieces. Sorry."

It was already too warm and stuffy inside the Humvee. She tossed his shirt aside and grinned remorsefully, feeling the glue pull. "For people with quite limited resources, we are not being very careful with our things."

He must have noticed the lack of air circulation as well. He leaned over and opened the back hatch again. "Like I said—we're overwrought."

He lay down next to her, and she curled into his chest, wondering if it would really be possible to sleep with him half naked beside her. She closed her eyes, trying to will herself into unconsciousness. His arms wrapped around her, tentatively at first and then, after a few seconds, more securely, almost like he was testing his resolve.

If she'd been any less tired, she might have made the test harder for him. But despite her heightened awareness of his body and all the little volts of electricity that sparked where her nerve endings met his bare skin, she quickly drifted. As she surrendered to oblivion, one strange word circled through her head.

Mine, her brain insisted as her thoughts faded to black. *Mine.*

• • •

WHEN ALEX WOKE, the sun was still bright in the west, and the sleeping bag underneath her was damp with sweat. The shadows had shifted, and a shaft of light was hitting her full in the face, albeit through the tinted window. She blinked sleepily for a minute, waiting for her brain to wake up.

Then she came to with a jolt as she realized she was alone. She sat up too quickly, making her head ache and spin. The back hatch of the Humvee was still open, and the warm, humid air sat heavily on her skin. Daniel was nowhere in sight. Neither was his T-shirt, so she had to swiftly and silently dig into her things to find something to wear before she could look for him. It was stupid, but if she was about to run into another team of assassins, she didn't want to do it in no more than a worn tan bra. She threw on her thin, oversize gray sweater because it was the first thing her fingers touched, not because it was weather-appropriate. She pulled the PPK out of her bag and tucked it into the small of her back. As she was climbing out the open hatch, she heard the crinkle of paper under her knee.

It was the receipt she'd written the e-mail address on. Underneath that was another neatly printed note.

Taking Einstein for a walk. Back soon.

She shoved the note in her pocket. Still moving quietly, she climbed out of the Humvee. Lola was sprawled out in a patch of shade beside the water and food Daniel had left. Her tail started thumping against the grass when she saw Alex.

Well, at least with Lola there, Alex knew that there was no one else around. Alex gulped down some water, wiped the sweat from her face with the sleeves of the sweater, then shoved them up as high as they could go.

"I don't even know which direction they went," she complained to Lola, scratching her ears. "And you're in no shape to track them down, are you, girl? Though I bet you could pretty fast if you were on your feet."

Lola licked her hand.

Alex was very hungry. She explored the small stash of food Daniel had brought and settled for a bag of pretzels. She would definitely need to replenish their stores tonight, but she so hated leaving a trail. Of course, there were hundreds of possible routes they could have taken to any number of destinations. But if someone were persistent enough and had a little luck on his side, he might be able to put together a pattern. She was out of carefully prepared traps and well-thought-out plans, let alone Batcaves. Her assets were money, guns, ammo, grenades, knives, a variety of venoms and chemical incapacitators, an assault vehicle, and one brilliant attack dog. Her physical liabilities included that same attention-demanding assault vehicle, one lame dog, her own somewhat lame body, one conspicuous face, one face off a wanted poster — more or less — and a lack of food, shelter, and options. Her emotional liabilities were even worse. She couldn't believe how much trouble she'd brought on herself in such a limited time. Part of her wanted nothing more than to rewind, to go back to her cozy little bathtub, her unbroken face, and her safety nets. To choose differently in that distant library and delete the e-mail.

But if she could turn back the clock, would she? Was that life of daily terror and loneliness really such a better option? She'd been safer, yes, but still hunted. In so many ways, wasn't her new, more endangered life a fuller existence?

She was sitting next to Lola, slowly stroking her back, when she heard Daniel's voice approaching. After the first shock of alarm, she didn't panic that he was talking to someone else. There was a special edge in his voice that appeared only when he was speaking with Kevin.

Einstein arrived first. He ran excitedly to Alex and touched his wet nose to her hand. He exchanged a snuffly greeting with Lola, then went to get a drink.

Daniel walked into view, striding quickly down the center of the unkempt dirt road. He had the bulletproof hat on. Beneath it, his brows were furrowed. He held the phone half an inch from his ear.

"I'm back now," he was saying. "I'll see if she's awake... No, I will not wake her if she's still sleeping."

Alex got to her feet, brushing debris from her backside and stretching. The movement caught Daniel's eye, and his expression shifted from annoyance to a slow, wide smile. Though she was a little exasperated, she couldn't help grinning back.

"She's right here. Just one more second of patience, brother dear."

Rather than hand her the phone, Daniel pulled her close for a lingering hug. With her face hidden in his chest, breathing in his smell, she smiled. But when he finally leaned away, she was shaking her head, her eyebrows raised in disbelief.

"Sorry," he said. "Wasn't thinking."

She blew out a frustrated breath, then held her hand out for the phone. He gave it to her with a sheepish grin, his other arm still loosely around her.

"Don't mind me, I'm just trying to keep us alive," she muttered, then spoke into the phone. "Hello."

"Good morning. I see my idiot brother hasn't learned anything from his mistakes."

"What's happened?"

"Not much. A flurry of phone calls, but no one else has implicated himself at this point."

"Then why are you calling?"

"Because it feels like you and Daniel have an infinite capacity to screw things up. It's making me a nervous wreck."

"Well, it's been *lovely* chatting—"

"Don't get mad, Oleander, you know I mean Daniel. I just wish you could somehow put a leash on him."

"He's new. He'll get it."

"Before he kills himself?"

"You know I can hear you, right?" Daniel asked.

"No one likes an eavesdropper," Kevin said loudly. "Give the girl some space."

"Here, just talk to him yourself. I'm going to sort our things out so we'll be ready to go when the sun sets."

She handed the phone back to Daniel and freed herself. He didn't stay on much longer with his brother. They just exchanged a few insults while she walked back to the Humvee and surveyed the damage. The cargo hold was still total chaos. Well, she had plenty of time on her hands now and not much else productive to do. She pulled the PPK from the small of her back and put it away inside a Ziploc bag in her backpack. Next, she rolled up the sleeping bag and stashed it out of the way on the passenger's seat so she could locate all the stray ammo.

She heard Daniel climb in beside her. He went to work combing the space for loose objects.

"I *am* sorry," he said while he worked, not looking in her direction. "It's just, you were sleeping and Einstein was restless, and we seem so alone here. It felt normal. I guess that should have been my first clue that I was committing a crime."

She kept her eyes on her work, too. "Imagine if *you* had woken up here alone."

"I should have thought of that."

"I remember someone recently promising me that he would ask if it was okay before he *breathed*."

He sighed. "Kevin's right, isn't he? I'm terrible at this."

She started organizing the different magazines into Ziploc bags and then sliding each into an outside duffel pocket.

"I see what you're doing there," she told him. "You're making it so I have to either agree with Kevin or forgive you."

"Is it working?"

"Depends. Did anyone see you?"

"No. We saw no signs of life aside from a few birds and squirrels. You know how most dogs chase squirrels? Einstein *catches* them."

"That might come in handy if we have to live out of this Humvee any longer. I'm not much of a hunter."

"One more night, right? We'll survive."

"I truly hope so."

"Er...do you want to save these?" Daniel asked, sounding confused. "Are they...walnuts?"

Alex glanced up to see which Ziploc he was referring to.

"Peach pits," she said.

"Trash?"

She took the bag from his hand and tucked it into the duffel she was reorganizing.

"Not trash," she said. "I use them for the sodium cyanide that occurs naturally in the inner kernel of the pit. There's not much in each—I have to collect hundreds of pits to get a usable amount." She sighed. "You know, I used to like peaches. Now I can't stand them."

She looked over and saw that Daniel was frozen in place, eyes wide. "Cyanide?" He sounded startled.

"One of my security systems. When it reacts with the right liquid acid, it creates hydrocyanic acid. Colorless gas. I make ampoules large enough to saturate a ten-by-ten room. Pretty basic stuff. I don't have access to high-end materials anymore. It's a lot of bathtub chemistry for me these days."

Daniel's expression evened out and he nodded like everything she'd just said was perfectly sane and normal. He turned back to collecting stray ammo. She smiled to herself.

Alex had to admit she felt a little calmer when their gear was all organized and neatly stowed; the best thing about obsessive-compulsive disorder was the cozy high you got from a tidy space. She took stock of all the weapons that remained to her and was comforted by that as well. The earrings could not be replaced, and she was low on several compounds, but the majority of her arms were still in working order.

For dinner they had granola bars, Oreos, and a bottle of water they shared as they sat on the back edge of the open Humvee; her legs dangled a good foot off the ground, but his toes touched. At his insistence, she took more Motrin. At least the over-the-counter pills were easily replaceable. She didn't need to be such a hoarder with those.

"When do we leave?" Daniel asked when they'd cleaned everything up.

She judged the position of the sun. "Soon. Fifteen more minutes, and I think it will be dark by the time we meet the main road."

"I know I'm in terrible trouble and probably deserve, I don't know, to be in solitary confinement or something, but do you think I could kiss you until it's time? I'll be more careful with your face and your clothes, I promise."

"Careful? That's not very tempting."

"Sorry. It's my best offer currently."

She sighed with mock reluctance. "I guess I haven't really got anything else to do."

He took her face in his hands, placing his fingertips delicately again to avoid her injuries, and when his lips touched hers this time, they were so soft there was barely any weight to them at all. She still felt the buzz, the electricity under her skin, but there was an odd kind of comfort to the very gentleness of it. It was like before, like back in the kitchen at the ranch, only a little more cautious. Still, she remembered the morning vividly, and that shifted things. She considered changing the tempo, twisting into his lap and wrapping her legs around him, but she hesitated. It felt so nice just as it was. Her fingers found their way to his curls, as was rapidly becoming her habit.

He kissed her neck, lightly tasting the places where her pulse beat beneath her skin.

He whispered into her good ear, "One thing concerns me."

"Just *one* thing?" she breathed.

"Well, aside from the obvious."

His mouth returned to hers, still careful, but this time more exploratory. It had been a decade, nearly, since anyone had kissed her, but it felt longer. No one had ever kissed her like *this*, with time slowing down and her brain stopping and all the electricity...

"Do you want to know what it is?" he asked a few minutes later.

"Hmm?"

"The thing that concerns me."

"Oh, right. Sure."

"Well," he said, pausing to kiss her eyelids, "I know exactly how I feel about you." Her lips again, her throat. "But I'm not entirely sure how you feel about me."

"It's not obvious?"

He leaned away from her, still holding her face, and stared at her, curious. "We seem to share a level of attraction."

"I'll say."

"But is there anything more for you?"

She stared, not sure what he was looking for.

He sighed. "You see, Alex, I'm in love with you." He searched her face, analyzing her reaction, then frowned and let his hands drop to her shoulders. "And I can tell that you're not buying that, but there it is. Despite what my recent behavior may have implied, sex is not my end goal here. And . . . I guess I'd like to know what your goals are."

"My *goals?*" She looked at him incredulously. "Are you serious?"

He nodded gravely.

Her voice sounded sharper than she'd meant it to when she answered. "I have only one goal, and that's to keep both you and me alive. Maybe, if I can do that long enough, we'll actually have a reasonable expectation of life beyond the next twenty-four to forty-eight hours. Should we ever be in that happy position, I can think about having other goals. Goals imply a future."

His frown spread from his mouth to his eyes. His brows pushed down and together. "Are things really that bad?"

"Yes!" she exploded, her hands clenching into fists. She took a deep breath. "I thought that was obvious, too."

The sun was setting. They should have been on the move five minutes ago. She jumped down from the Humvee and whistled for the dogs. Einstein bounded past her eagerly, ready to be back on the road. She went to pick up Lola, but Daniel was there first.

Alex stretched and tried to focus. She felt decently rested and would probably be fine driving all night. That was all that mattered. Just making it through the night without garnering any more attention than she had to. Sending Kevin's e-mail, and then getting her little traveling circus into a less flamboyant vehicle. That was the limit of her ambition.

They drove in silence for a while. It got dark while they were still on back roads. When they eased onto I-49, Alex relaxed a little. There hadn't been very many cars, and everything they had seen was old and fit the countryside. For now, she was fairly certain that no one knew exactly where they were.

She knew she should be concentrating, but the dark road with the steady flow of anonymous traffic was monotonous, and she couldn't help wondering what Daniel was thinking. It wasn't like him to be so quiet. She thought about turning on the radio, but that felt sort of cowardly. She probably owed him an apology.

"Um, I'm sorry if I was rough back there," she said, the words sounding very loud after the long lull. "I'm not good at this people stuff. There's really no excuse for me. I'm a full-grown adult—I should be able to hold a normal conversation. Sorry."

His sigh didn't sound exasperated; it was more like relief. "No, I'm the one who's sorry. I shouldn't have pushed. My lack of focus landed us in this position. I will get it together."

She shook her head. "You can't think of it that way. You're not responsible for this. Look, someone has decided to kill you. It happened to Kevin six months ago and it happened to me a few years before that. You'll make mistakes, because it's impossible to know what is or isn't a mistake until it's made. But mistakes don't mean you're guilty for what is happening. Never forget that there is a real human being who decided to put his agenda ahead of your existence."

He thought about that for a minute. "I know what you're saying. I believe it. But I need to listen to you more closely—act like you, keep my mind on what matters. It doesn't help us to have me mooning around like a teenager, worrying about whether or not you *like*-like me."

"Honestly, Daniel, I—"

"No, no," he interrupted immediately. "I did not mean to hijack this conversation with that comment."

"I just want to explain. If you're a teenager, I'm a toddler. I'm emotionally backward. Defective, even. I don't know how to do any of this, and while survival is obviously the priority, I'm also using it to deflect questions I should be able to answer. I mean…love? I don't even know what that is, or if it's real. Sorry, it's just…foreign to me. I evaluate things based on needs and wants. I can't deal with anything…*fluffier*."

Daniel laughed his funny *heh-heh-heh* laugh and all the tension bled right out of her. She laughed with him, and then sighed. Everything felt less awful when she could laugh along with Daniel.

He released one final chuckle, then said lightly, "So tell me what you need."

She thought it through. "I need . . . you to be alive. And I would like to be alive, too. That is my baseline. If I get more than that, I would prefer to have you close by. After that, anything else is just frosting."

"Call me an optimist, but I think we may just be dealing with nothing more than some semantic issues here."

"You could be right. If we get a few more weeks together, maybe we'll figure out how to speak the same language."

He took her hand. "I've always been a quick study with linguistics."

CHAPTER 22

A lex chose the gas station outside Baton Rouge based on the age of the cashier. He was eighty if he was a day and she had high hopes that his vision and hearing were past their prime.

Once she ascertained that he was paying her absolutely no attention at all, despite the fact that her thick makeup was far from convincing, she did some thorough shopping. More water, lots of nuts and jerky—any kind of nonperishable protein she could find. She grabbed some cans of V8, though she wasn't a fan, as the convenience store didn't have a fresh produce section. She acknowledged to herself that she would have to go to an actual grocery store at some point, but she hoped they could wait it out a bit longer. Every day her bruises faded a little more.

There was no drama at the twenty-four-hour Internet coffee place, either. It was near the university, so it had no shortage of late-night seat fillers. She kept her hood up and her face down, sat in a secluded corner, and asked for a plain black coffee without looking at the barista who came for her order. She wished she had time to do this from somewhere not on the trail to their destination, but the first priority had to be exchanging the Batmobile. It was currently her biggest disadvantage.

She created a brand-new e-mail account registered to a name that was no more than a random combination of letters and numbers. Then she tried to channel Kevin.

> You should have left it alone, Deavers.
> You shouldn't have involved a civilian.
> I'm not here to do your dirty work, but I
> took care of the little interrogator for
> you. Texas was a nice way to say *you're
> welcome*. Enough is enough.

Not a specific threat, but plenty implied. She hesitated for a second with her finger over the mouse, the little arrow touching the Send button. Was she giving them anything they didn't have? They would know by now that Daniel wasn't among the dead back at the ranch. She couldn't try to fool Deavers on that point. Was there some way she wasn't seeing for this to come back at them? Could this make things worse?

She hit the button. Things couldn't get that much worse, anyway.

As soon as it was sent, she was on her feet. The Humvee was parked in the alley around the back, behind a couple of dumpsters. She walked quickly with her head down, hood up, and a syringe in hand. The side street was mostly empty, just one small knot of people huddled close together in the darkness of a recessed emergency door. She studied the trio for a second before she climbed into the dark vehicle.

Einstein touched his nose to her shoulder. Daniel took her hand.

"Do you know where the night-vision goggles are?" she murmured.

He dropped her hand. "Is something wrong?" he whispered back. He turned to rummage between the seats.

"Nothing new," she promised. "Maybe something helpful."

He handed her the goggles. She switched them on and took a better look at the little conference.

It was just breaking up. This wasn't a particularly rough area of town, and all three participants were expensively dressed, though their clothes were casual. A dark-haired man was holding hands with a blond girl who had so many showy labels on the different pieces of clothing she wore that she looked like a NASCAR driver sponsored by midlevel luxury brands.

These two were walking off now, their path angling away from the Humvee. The blonde bobbled and swayed a little as she walked. The man with her was stuffing something into the pocket of his hoodie.

The third person stayed in the dark door frame, leaning against it casually like he was expecting more guests soon. His clothing was what she would describe as *upmarket frat boy*.

She thought about what she'd just been feeling inside the café before she pushed Send—that things couldn't get much worse. She supposed there were ways this spontaneous idea of hers could go south, but she couldn't think of any that she wouldn't be able to handle quietly. And it would be a big help if the frat boy was what she thought he was.

She pulled the goggles off.

"Where's the cash?" she whispered.

Thirty seconds later, syringe in one hand and roll of fifties in the other, she slid quietly from the Humvee and walked toward the man, who was still relaxed against the wall, like there was no place he'd rather be. She couldn't see very clearly without the goggles, but she thought she caught his minimal reaction when he realized she was approaching him. His body stiffened just slightly, but he didn't move.

"Hello," she said when she was close enough that she could speak quietly and still be sure he could hear.

"Evening," he responded in a lazy southern drawl.

"I was wondering if you could help me. I'm looking for…a specific product." Her inflection went up on the end, like it was a question. She didn't know how to buy drugs off the street. She'd never had to do it before. This was the first time the supply she'd been able to amass during her time in Chicago had run dry. Joey G never minded paying in product.

She expected that the frat boy would accuse her of being a cop, like dealers always did on TV, but he just nodded.

"I might be able to help. What are you looking for?"

It was unlikely *he* was a cop, unless the sale she'd just watched had been faked to draw a real customer in. If he tried to arrest her, she'd knock him out and escape. A manhunt in Baton Rouge would hardly be her biggest problem, and she knew he couldn't see her face well—he hadn't reacted to the damage.

"Opioids—opium or heroin or morphine."

There was a pause as he peered into the darkness under her hood. She didn't think he was successful in seeing much.

"Well—that's an exotic list. Opium? Huh. I have no idea where you could get that around here."

"Heroin will do just as well. I'd prefer the powdered form, if possible. I don't suppose it's likely you'd have anything uncut?" It was all but impossible that he would have pure heroin. Whatever he had would have been modified two or three times before it reached his hands. Not that he would tell her the truth. Purification was a bit of a pain, but she'd make the time.

He laughed once, and she guessed her shopping style was probably not the norm.

"I've got some upscale stuff. It's not cheap, though."

"You get what you pay for," Alex said. "I'm not looking for a deal."

"Two hundred a gram. Pure white powder."

Sure it is, she thought to herself. But corrupted heroin was better than no heroin. "Three grams, please."

He paused. Though it was too dark to really read his expression, she could tell what he wanted from the way he cocked his head to the side. She pulled the cash from her pocket and counted out twelve bills. She wondered for a second if he would try to steal the rest from her. But he seemed to be a businessman. He'd want an apparently affluent customer like her to become a regular client.

He took the money she offered, looked it over quickly, then stowed it in the back pocket of his cargo shorts. She tensed when he crouched down, but he was just pulling a backpack out from behind a pile of garbage bags dumped against the wall. He didn't have to search for what he wanted. He was standing again a second later, holding out three small plastic bags. In the dark she couldn't be positive about the color, but it *looked* close to white. She held out her hand and he laid the bags on her palm.

"Thank you," she said.

"My pleasure, ma'am." He did a funny little nod, almost a bow.

Alex hurried back to the Humvee, glad that it was hard to make out from this angle. The dealer would see a large, dark-colored vehicle, and not much more than that.

Einstein whined quietly as she climbed into the passenger seat.

"Let's go," she said.

Daniel started the engine.

"Turn left down that side street so that guy won't get a good look at the Humvee."

"What just happened?" Daniel whispered as he followed her instructions. Even in a whisper, the tension was easy to hear. No wonder the dog was anxious.

"Just picking up some ingredients I needed."

"Ingredients?"

"I was out of opioids."

As they moved out onto a wider road, Alex could feel his tension easing, probably due to her nonchalance.

"Was that a drug deal, then?"

"Yes. Remember what I said about bathtub chemistry? Getting my raw materials is a little more complicated than it used to be. I didn't want to pass up the opportunity."

It was quiet for a moment.

"I hope that was the right move," she muttered.

"You think he'll tell someone about us?"

She blinked for a second. "What? Oh, no. I'm not worried about the dealer. I was just thinking about sending that e-mail."

"The e-mail was Kevin's call," Daniel responded.

She nodded. "And he has a better batting average than I do."

"No, I just meant that if it goes south, it was *his* call."

She laughed once. It was a heavy sound.

"You don't like it?"

"I don't know. I want to finish this . . . but I'm tired, Daniel. I also want to run away and hide."

"That doesn't sound so bad," he agreed. "Oh, um, if I was invited?"

She glanced at him, surprised. "Of course."

"Good."

There it was again, that automatic *of course*. That crazy assumption that he would be present for whatever future she was allowed.

She didn't know if it was the wearying strain or something more, but an annoying feeling of presentiment haunted her for the rest of the night. Maybe it was just the jitters from finally getting her hands on some coffee for the first time in two days.

She was almost shocked when, seven hours later and with the sun already well above the horizon, they reached the secluded cabin without incident.

Daniel had taken them down only two wrong turns—impressive, considering he hadn't been to the cabin since he was ten years old—and all the roads they'd traveled after sunrise were empty. That meant no one could report seeing an armored vehicle in the vicinity.

She parked the Humvee behind the detached garage for the present. Daniel kicked a few rocks around the base of the stairs until he found the plastic one. He removed the concealed key and then walked up the porch steps with Einstein at his heels.

Alex stood in front of the log cabin—it was a red cedar A-frame, charming despite some evidence that it had been built in the seventies—so tired she couldn't move those last few steps. Though the night had been blessedly uneventful, it had still been a long time on the road. She'd traded seats with Daniel outside Baton Rouge and then been too wired by the sense of apprehension that had troubled her since sending the e-mail to relinquish control again. Daniel had napped off and on, and he seemed almost chipper now. He passed her to go retrieve Lola from the back of the Humvee.

"You look like you might need to be carried, too," he commented as he passed her again, this time with the dog. He set Lola beside the door and then came back for Alex.

"Give me a second," she mumbled. "Brain sleeping."

"Just a few more steps," he encouraged. He put an arm around her waist and pulled her gently forward.

Once she started moving, it was easier. Momentum got her up the stairs and through the front door. She only partially took in a high wall of triangular windows looking out over a swampy forest, aged but comfortable-looking couches, an old-fashioned wood-burning stove, and a short open stairway as he steered her past it all and down a compact hallway.

"The master is over here... I think—Kev and I always got the loft. I'll unload and get the dogs settled, then I'll crash, too."

She nodded as he showed her into a dim room with a large iron bedstead. That was all she noticed before her head hit the pillow.

"Poor darling," she heard Daniel chuckle as she sank into the dark.

.   .   .

SHE CAME BACK to consciousness slowly, drifting up through layers of dreamy nonreality. She was comfortable and calm; nothing had startled her awake, and even before she was fully lucid she was aware of Daniel's body warm beside her. A low, close thrumming caught her attention, but before the sound could frighten her, she felt the breeze of the oscillating fan move gently down the length of her body. She opened her eyes.

It was still dim, but the light was a different color than it had been when she'd collapsed. It leaked in around the lined floral curtains that covered the big window on the opposite wall. Early evening, not as hot as before. She must have been sweating earlier, but it was dried now, a film that felt stiff against the skin of her face.

The room was made of long red logs, just like the outside. More light came from behind her. She rolled over and saw the skylight above the open vanity. Her backpack, her gas mask, and the first-aid kit were by the sink.

Daniel might not be a natural fugitive, but he was more thoughtful than anyone else she'd ever known.

She tiptoed out to the hall and did some quick surveillance. The rest of the cabin was small, just a kitchen with an attached nook for a dining room, the living room with all the windows, the open loft above it, and a small second bedroom with a hall bath. She used that bath to take a quick, much-needed shower. There were shampoo and conditioner in the little blue shower-tub combo, but no soap, so she used the shampoo as body wash. She was glad the soap was missing, just like she was glad the refrigerator was empty and that there was a fine layer of dust on all the counters. No one had been in these rooms for a while.

After she quickly applied new bandages to her face and examined her hands, which looked much better than she'd thought they would, she peeked through the long windows beside the front door to check on the dogs. They were snoozing contentedly on the porch. She was getting used to the comfort of having an early alarm system.

She was a little hungry but felt too lazy to do anything about it right away. She remembered how it felt yesterday to wake up alone, and she didn't want Daniel to experience the same panic. She wasn't really *sleepy* anymore, but she was tired, and the bed still looked pretty good. It was probably avoidance. As long as she kept her eyes closed and her head on the pillow, she didn't have to start planning what needed to happen next.

She returned to her earlier position, curled up against Daniel's chest, and let herself relax. There wasn't anything that she had to do immediately. Twenty minutes of unthinking rest wasn't so much to ask. Or even an hour. She'd gotten them here alive; she'd earned it.

Unfortunately, not thinking was easier said than done. She found herself dwelling on the promise she'd made to Daniel—that she wouldn't leave him behind. On the one hand, she knew she would never be satisfied with any long-distance arrangement for his safety. Even if she could stockpile a year's worth of food, even if she could be positive that the owners wouldn't come back, even if she could arm this place to vaporize any intruder, and even if she could lock Daniel inside like a prisoner so he couldn't wander off and find trouble, she would not be satisfied. Because *what if?* The hunters had found him before, and she'd left a trail, albeit a faint one, to this place. She could take him north to her rental, but the department had contacted her while she was living there. She didn't think they knew her address, but what if? As long as Daniel stayed near her, she could do what was necessary to protect him, things he wouldn't think of himself. She could see the traps he wouldn't see.

On the other hand, was that just her own wants talking? She wanted to be with Daniel. Was her mind coming up with proofs for that necessity? Was her logic flawed—twisting to accommodate her personal wishes? How could she be sure? When she'd told him before that it wasn't a good idea to have her liability close beside her while she went on the attack, she knew that was sound logic. Of course, if they got to him while she was far away, that distance wouldn't remove the hold they'd have on her.

She sighed. How could she see clearly? Her emotions had tangled this whole situation into a knot of Gordian complexity.

Still unconscious, Daniel shifted to wrap his arm around her. She knew what he would say about her dilemma, and she also knew that his perspective would not help her to see more clearly.

He sighed, starting to stir. His fingers traced down the length of her spine, then slowly back up. They played with the wet fringes of hair on the back of her neck.

He stretched with a groan, and then his hands were back in her hair.

"You've been up," he murmured.

His eyes opened slowly, blinking as they worked to focus. In the dusky room, they were dark gray.

"It didn't stick," she answered.

He laughed as his eyes slid shut again. He tucked her more tightly into his chest. "Good. What time is it?"

"Around four, I think."

"Anything to worry about?"

"No. Not for right now, at least."

"That's nice."

"Yeah, it really is."

"*This* is nice," he said.

His hand traced back up her spine again, then trailed over her right shoulder, traced lightly across her collarbone, and finally curved around the good side of her face. He tilted it up until their noses touched.

"Yes, this, too," Alex agreed.

"More than nice," he murmured, and she would have agreed, but he was kissing her. His hand on her face was soft, his lips soft, but the arm around her waist strained her tight against his chest. She wrapped her arms around his neck and held herself closer still.

It wasn't like the car, where the pulse of the hunt had been loud in their ears, when they were still shocked and panicking. There was no horror. Just the rhythm of her heart and his, speeding without fear.

She supposed it was inevitable, the way they'd been carrying on, that given a quiet place far away, for the moment, from any danger, with just the two of them together and no interruptions, there would be nothing to keep them apart any longer.

The strange thing, then, was how it didn't feel at all inevitable. Somehow, it was the biggest surprise of her life. It was all a jumble of opposites tumbling together in a way that left her helpless to analyze any of them. Comfortable, familiar...but also electric and new. Gentle at the same time it was extreme, both soothing and overwhelming. It was like every nerve ending in her body was lit up with dozens of conflicting stimuli simultaneously.

All she was really sure of was the Danielness of him, that core of something pure, something better than anything she'd known before. He belonged to a more excellent world than the one where she resided, and while they were part of each other, she felt like she was allowed to be there with him.

She knew her past experience with relationships was quite limited by most people's standards, so she didn't have much to compare this to. She'd always thought of sex as a single event that had a defined end, an effort at physical gratification that sometimes satisfied and sometimes did not.

This experience didn't fit into the same category on any level. It was less an event and more an ongoing exploration of each other, a satisfaction of curiosity, a fascination over each little detail discovered. It wasn't *about* gratification, but there was no need that wasn't met, whether it was physical or something less definable.

She searched for the right word as they lay kissing quietly, patiently now, with the light turning red around the edges of the curtain. She wasn't sure what to label this emotion that filled her so entirely that she thought it might stretch her skin. It was a little like that bubbly feeling that had left her smiling at the thought of him but multiplied by thousands, millions, and then fired in a crucible until every impurity, every lesser sensation, was burned out, leaving only *this* behind. She didn't have a name for it. The closest she could think of was *joy*.

"I love you," he whispered against her lips. "I love you."

Maybe that was the word. She'd just never thought its definition could be so . . . huge.

"Daniel," she murmured.

"You don't have to say anything back. I just needed to say that out loud. I might have exploded had I tried to keep it in. I will probably have to say it again soon. You are forewarned." He laughed.

She smiled. "I never want to go back to having nothing to lose. I'm glad I have you as my liability. I'm grateful. I'd have you as *anything*."

She laid her head against his chest and listened to his breath moving in and out. For so long now, breathing had been her priority. If she could have spoken to the woman she was even just a month ago, she knew that woman would have been terrified of expanding that priority to include another set of lungs. That woman would have run away from needing anything more than her own life. But what she would have missed! Alex couldn't even remember what she'd been holding on to back then. *This* was the kind of life worth fighting to keep.

"I think I was probably twelve, maybe thirteen, when I sort of gave up on living an extraordinary life," he mused thoughtfully, running his fingers in aimless patterns through her hair. "That's probably about the age that everyone starts to grow up and leave fantasy behind. You realize you're never going to discover that you're actually an alien, adopted by those prosaic human parents, with amazing superpowers that will save the world." He chuckled. "I mean, you *know* that much earlier, but you can't quite let go, not for years. And then the world beats you down a little, and some of the color goes out of life, and you settle for reality...I think I did a decent job of it. I found plenty of happiness in the drab, everyday world. But I want you to know—this time with you has been extraordinary. There has been terror, yes, but along with it, there's been a kind of joy I didn't know existed. And it's because *you* are extraordinary. I'm so glad you found me. My life was destined to change drastically, it seems, in one way or another. I'm just so grateful that it got to be with you."

Her throat was tight, and she marveled as she blinked furiously to keep the moisture in her eyes from pooling. She'd cried in grief, in pain, in loneliness, and even in fear, but this was the first time in her life she'd had tears of joy in her eyes. It seemed a strange response, something she'd never truly taken at face value when she'd read about it. This was the first time she'd understood that joy could be even more severe than pain.

She would happily have never left the bed, but eventually they had to eat. Daniel didn't complain, but she could tell he would be pleased when he had access to real food again. It was strange, as they sat at the little table in the alcove eating jerky, peanuts, and chocolate chip cookies, laughing and scratching the dogs' ears—of course they'd caved quickly and brought Einstein and Lola inside; if you were going to break and enter, you might as well do it in style—to think that they didn't have to get back into the Batmobile and drive tensely through the night again. They had a dozen empty hours ahead of them, open to fill in any way they wanted. She had a fairly good idea of what they would probably choose to do, but the point was the freedom. It felt too good to be true.

So, naturally, Kevin had to call.

"Hey, Danny, you guys good?" she heard him say. His voice was, as always, penetrating.

"I'm excellent," Daniel said. Alex shook her head at him. No need to elaborate.

"Uh, great. You got to the McKinleys', I presume."

"Yeah. The place hasn't changed."

"Good. That means it still belongs to them. Did you get enough rest?"

"Er, yes. Thanks for inquiring."

Alex sighed, knowing Kevin would never ask just to be polite. Too good to be true, indeed. She held out her hand at the same time that she heard Kevin say, "Let me talk to Oleander."

Daniel looked confused, clearly not following, but he handed her the phone.

"Let me guess," Alex said. "You need us to join you as soon as possible."

"Yes."

The corners of Daniel's lips turned down.

"What did Deavers do?" Alex asked.

"Nothing...and I don't like it. Because of course he's doing something, but he's being more cautious now. He's not letting me see anything, because he guesses that I'm watching. He must be making calls from other people's offices so I can't hear. What did the e-mail say?"

She recited it to him word perfect; she'd known he would want the details, so she'd memorized it.

"Not bad, Ollie, not bad. Maybe a little smart for me, but that's okay."

"So what are you thinking?"

"I want to strike within the week, which means you need to get here and get set to move at the same time."

She sighed heavily. "Agreed."

"Is the Suburban still there?"

"Um, I haven't checked yet."

"Why not?" he demanded.

"I slept in."

"You need to toughen up, sweetheart. The beauty sleep can wait for a few weeks."

"I'd like to be in top form for this."

"Yeah, yeah. When can you move?"

"Where are we going exactly?"

"I've got a place for us to crash. Do you have something to write with?"

He gave her an address. It was in a part of DC she wasn't familiar with. She thought the area he was sending them to was in a rather posh part of town, but that didn't fit with her idea of a bolt-hole. She must be picturing the wrong neighborhood. She'd been out of the city for a while.

"Okay, let me get our stuff together. We'll leave as soon as we can... *if* we have another car option available."

"You'll need to stop outside Atlanta sometime after nine a.m. I found a place for Lola."

"What did you tell them? About the bullet hole in her leg, I mean?"

"You were in a carjacking. Both you and the dog were injured. You're heading to Atlanta to stay with your mother for a while, but she's allergic. You're very traumatized, and they shouldn't ask about it. Your name is Andy Wells, and they know you'll pay cash. I'm your concerned brother in this scenario, by the way."

"Nice."

"Of course. Now go check the garage and call me back."

"Wilco, sir," she said sarcastically.

He hung up on her.

"Are we really going to steal the McKinleys' car?" Daniel asked.

"If we're lucky, yes."

He sighed.

"Look, we'll leave the Humvee in the garage. It's got to be worth four or five Suburbans at least. If we aren't able to bring their car back, they won't take a loss, right?"

"I suppose. Kevin won't like his favorite plaything being offered as collateral."

"That part's just the gravy."

The house key fit the garage door. Daniel promised that inside and just to the right of the door, next to the light switch, there would be a little hook with two sets of car keys hanging from it. He flipped the switch.

Alex gasped. "I've died and gone to heaven."

"Huh, they got a new car," Daniel said, less excited. "I guess the old Suburban must have finally quit."

Alex moved around the vehicle, stroking its side with her fingertips. "Look at this, Daniel! Have you ever seen anything more beautiful?"

"Um, yes? It's just a silver SUV, Alex. It looks exactly like every third car on the road."

"I know! Isn't that fantastic? And look at this!" She towed him around the car and pointed to a little chrome plaque by the taillight.

He stared at her, totally confused. "It's a hybrid? So?"

"It's a hybrid!" she half sang, throwing her arms around him. "This is like Christmas!"

"I had no idea you were so green."

"Pssh. You know how many times we're going to have to stop for gas in this thing? Twice! Maybe three times, max, all the way to DC. And look—just *look* at those gorgeous plates!" She pointed with both hands, part of her noting that she must look like a game-show hostess.

"Yes, they're Virginia plates. The McKinleys live in Alexandria most of the year, Alex. That's not a huge surprise."

"This car is going to be invisible in DC! It's like a stealth bomber. If anyone manages to follow the trail we left in the Texan Batmobile, they'll hit a dead end now. This is a beautiful thing, Daniel, and I don't think you're fully appreciating what amazing luck this is."

"I don't like stealing from friends," he grumbled.

"The McKinleys are nice people?"

"Very nice. They were lovely to my family."

"So they probably wouldn't want you to die, right?"

He gave her a dark look. "No, probably not."

"I'm sure, if they knew the whole story, they would *want* you to borrow this car."

"*Borrow* implies we're bringing it back."

"Which of course we will. Unless we're dead. Do you think anything but death could keep Kevin from retrieving his favorite ride?"

Daniel was abruptly much more serious. He folded

his arms across his chest and turned to face the car rather than her. "Don't joke about that."

Alex was a little confused by his mood shift. "I'm not actually joking," she clarified. "I was trying to make you feel better about taking the car. We'll bring it back if we can, I promise."

"Just . . . don't talk about dying. Not like that. So . . . casually."

"Oh. Sorry. It's just, you know, laugh about it or cry about it, that's the only choice. I'd rather laugh while I can."

He looked down at her from the corner of his eye, his posture still rigid for a moment. Then suddenly he softened, freeing one hand to place it on the side of her face.

"Maybe we don't do what Kevin wants. Maybe we just stay here."

She put her hand over his. "We would if we could. They'd find us eventually."

He nodded, almost to himself.

"Okay, then. Shall we start loading?"

"Sure; let me call Kevin first."

Daniel started shifting bags from the Humvee to the Toyota while Alex enthused about the car to Kevin. Kevin wasn't much more excited than Daniel, but he got it immediately.

"That's great, kid. Now hurry up. The clock is ticking."

"We don't want to get to Atlanta before nine, so we don't need to leave here till, what, two a.m.?"

"All right. So I'll expect you here around five p.m."

"Counting down the seconds," she gushed facetiously. The car—or the afternoon with Daniel—had put her in an ebullient mood.

"I'm glad you'll be driving all night," Kevin said. "I think I like you better sleep-deprived." With that, he hung up on her again.

"I should probably walk Einstein," Alex mused. "Redo Lola's bandages. Pack up the food. Then we should try to force ourselves to get a nap. We're flipping our sleeping routine again."

"I suppose I'm not allowed to walk the dog," Daniel said.

"Sorry, America's Most Wanted. My sad little face is better than yours right now, beard or no beard."

"It's dark out—are you sure it's safe for you to go alone?"

"I won't be alone. I'll have a supernaturally intelligent attack dog and a SIG Sauer P220."

He almost smiled. "Tough luck for the hungry gators."

She hid her frown. Alligators. She hadn't been thinking about things like *that*. Well, she'd stay away from the water. And hopefully Kevin had trained Einstein for more than just human attackers.

The walk wasn't long, just enough for Einstein to stretch his legs a little. She couldn't stop thinking about giant reptiles. The road was black, but she didn't want to use a flashlight. She saw no headlights or house lights, heard nothing but swampy noises. It was still hot enough to have the perspiration rolling down her temples, but she was glad she'd brought the hoodie — the mosquitoes were definitely active.

When she returned, the Toyota was in front of the house and the Humvee invisible inside the garage. Daniel had taken care of everything but Lola's dressings. Alex did that, trying to make her work look professional. Hopefully the boarding place would believe a vet had tended her. She stroked Lola's ears sadly. It would be better for Lola to be somewhere people could take care of her, but Alex would miss her. She wondered what would happen to the dog if they weren't able to come back for her. Lola was beautiful. Someone would want her. Alex remembered imagining taking Lola home with her in some safe, unlikely future. If only.

Alex set the alarm clock by the bed for 1:45, but it was obvious that Daniel wasn't interested in stocking up on sleep.

"We're going to regret this around eight a.m.," she promised him as his lips trailed down her sternum.

"I won't ever regret this," he insisted.

He was probably right. Given the abbreviated timeline they were working with, it didn't make sense to waste even a second she got to have with him. Happiness with a deadline, just like she'd thought before. Only the happiness was greater now. And the deadline was crueler.

CHAPTER 23

Alex did manage to get a little bit of sleep, maybe thirty minutes by the time the alarm sounded. Just enough that she was completely dragging as they set off. Daniel was more alert, so he took the first shift and she reclined the passenger seat as far back as it would go. The seats were much more comfortable, the suspension smoother, and it was easier to doze. The dogs seemed happy in the back, as if they appreciated the new ride, too.

She was herself again by the time they got to the dog-boarding facility north of Atlanta. It was after nine thirty; they were running a little behind, thanks to some construction delays on I-65.

Daniel stayed with the car as she carried Lola into the front office. It was a casual place, homey, with lots of fenced acres lining the road in. The dogs that ran alongside the car as they passed looked happy and healthy. Of course, Lola wouldn't be running any-where for a while.

The man behind the desk was all sympathy as Alex came in. He obviously had linked her to the reserva-tion before she introduced herself as Ms. Wells. She followed patiently as he showed her the spacious ken-nel Lola would occupy and explained the visiting vet's schedule. She thanked him and paid him for a month in advance, then gave Lola one last hug. As Kevin had promised, the man never commented on Lola's injury in a specific way, and he didn't mention Alex's face. Twenty minutes later, she and Daniel were back on the road. Alex was glad it was her turn to drive. She needed something to concentrate on so she wouldn't think about leaving Lola behind.

She thought Daniel would crash, but he was still bright-eyed and in a talkative mood. Or maybe he could see how she was trying to fight off the sadness and wanted to help. Knowing him, that was probably it.

"You know almost everything about me from that stupid file," he complained. "But there's so much I don't know about you."

"I've actually told you most of it. When my life wasn't bizarre, it was pretty boring."

"Tell me something embarrassing about you in high school."

"Everything about me was embarrassing in high school. I was a huge nerd."

"Sounds sexy."

"Oh, really? My mother cut my hair at home and I had the most outrageous bangs the nineties had ever seen."

"Please tell me there's a picture."

"You wish. When my mother died, I burned all the incriminating stuff."

"Who was your first boyfriend?"

Alex laughed. "Roger Markowitz. He took me to senior prom. I had the most totally awesome puffy sleeves on my dress. Electric blue, naturally. Roger tried to slip me the tongue in the limo on the way to the ballroom, but he was so nervous that he threw up on me. I spent the whole dance in the ladies' room trying to clean up. I broke up with him that night. One might describe it as an epic romance."

"What a tearjerker!"

"I know. Romeo and Juliet had nothing on us."

Daniel laughed. "Who was your first serious relationship?"

"Serious? Wow. Hmm, I don't know if anyone would qualify besides Bradley. First year of med school at Columbia."

"You went to Columbia med?" he asked.

"I was a very brainy nerd."

"I'm impressed. Back to Bradley."

"Do you want to hear something really and truly embarrassing?"

"Very much."

"The reason I was first attracted to him..." She paused. "Maybe I shouldn't admit this."

"It's too late to turn back. You have to tell me now."

She took a deep breath. "Okay, fine. He looked like Egon. You know, from *Ghostbusters*? Just exactly like that, bouffant hair, round glasses, everything."

Daniel worked to keep a straight face. "Irresistible."

"You have no idea. *So* hot."

"How long were you together?"

"Through that first summer. Then I won a scholarship in my second year. We both applied, and he thought he was a shoo-in. He didn't take it well when I, as he put it, *took it from him*. He went in and demanded to see our scores. Something I noticed multiple times throughout my wild and crazy romantic period: lots of guys don't like girls to be smarter than they are."

"That must have really limited your dating pool."

"Right down to zero."

"Well, rest assured, I've never had a problem with a woman who is smarter than me. I wouldn't want to limit *my* pool by that much. I think that kind of childishness usually goes away when men grow up."

"I'll have to take your word for it. I never dated anyone outside of school. I didn't get to explore the adult stage of the human male. Well, till now."

"Never?" he asked, shocked.

"I was recruited while I was still in school. I told you what it was like after that."

"But...you must have met people outside of work. You got vacation time, didn't you?"

She smiled. "Not very often. And it was hard for me to talk to people outside of the lab. Everything was classified. *I* was classified. I couldn't be myself in any way or talk about any part of my real life with a person on the outside. It was too hard being some imaginary character. I preferred isolation. It embarrassed me to try to play a role. Ironic, isn't it? Now I have a new name every other week."

He put his hand on her knee. "I'm sorry. It sounds horrible."

"Yeah. It frequently was. That's why I'm so backward when it comes to interpersonal relations. But on the plus side, I got to do some really cutting-edge work with monoclonal antibodies—I'm talking about sci-fi stuff here, the kind of thing people don't believe exists. And I had essentially no limits on my practical research. I got everything I wanted in the lab. My budget was amazing. I'm responsible for a larger chunk of the national debt than you know."

He laughed.

"So was your ex-wife smarter than you are?" she asked.

He hesitated for a moment. "It doesn't bother you to talk about her?"

"Why would it? You didn't get jealous over the eternal flame I will always carry for Roger Markowitz."

"Good point. Well, Lainey was very bright in her own way. Not book-smart, but clever, shrewd. When we met, she was so...vivid. She wasn't like other women I'd dated, easygoing girls who were content with easygoing me. Lainey always wanted more— from every aspect of life. She was a little...contrary. In the beginning, I thought she just had very firm opinions and wasn't afraid to disagree. I loved that about her. But then, over time...well, she wasn't really opinionated, she just loved the drama. She would argue if you told her the sun rises in the east. It was always exciting, at least."

"Ah, so you're an adrenaline junkie. This all starts to make sense now."

"What makes sense?"

"Your attraction to me."

He stared at her, blinking owlishly the way he did when he was surprised.

"Admit it," she teased. "You're just in this for the thrill of the near-death experiences."

"Hmm, I hadn't considered that."

"Maybe we should forget this gig in DC after all. If I eliminate my hunters and life gets all safe and boring, you'll be out the door, won't you?" She sighed theatrically.

She couldn't tell if he was serious or playing along

when he answered, "I was never fond of this plan to begin with. Maybe it *is* smarter to run."

"On the other hand, if I do a bad job in DC, it's going to get a lot more dangerous. You'll love that."

He gave her a bleak stare.

"Was that over the line?" she asked.

"A little too close to home."

"Sorry."

He sighed. "Your theory is incorrect, though, I'm afraid. See, I got over my love of drama early on. It was still exciting, but so is drowning in quicksand, I'd imagine. Exciting is not the same thing as enjoyable."

"But you didn't leave."

Daniel stared at his hand—curled tensely around her thigh now—as he answered. "No. I thought… well, this makes me sound like a first-class sucker. I thought I could fix her. She had a lot of issues from her past, and I let those issues be the excuse when she did things to hurt me. I never blamed her; I always blamed her history. Cliff—that's the man she left me for; what a fantastic name to be left for, don't you think?—Cliff wasn't her first fling. I found out about the others later." He glanced up at her suddenly. "Was that all in the file?"

"No."

He stared out the windshield. "I knew I should give up. I knew I wasn't holding on to anything real. The Lainey I loved was just a construct in my head. But I was stubborn. Stupidly so. Sometimes you cling to a mistake simply because it took so long to make."

"It sounds miserable."

He looked over and smiled at her weakly. "Yes, it was. But the hardest part was just admitting none of it had ever been real. It's humiliating, you know, to be duped. So my pride was hurt worse than anything else."

"I'm sorry."

"And I'm sorry, too. My stories are so much less entertaining than yours. Tell me about another boyfriend."

"I have a question first."

He stiffened a little bit. "Go ahead."

"That story you told the hooker, Kate, what was that about?"

"Huh?" His eyebrows pulled together in confusion.

"The one who was supposed to plant your tracker. Kevin said you told her your divorce wasn't final. But he also said this conversation happened two years after you split. You didn't contest the divorce, it went through in months. So why did you say that?"

Daniel laughed. "Thank you, seriously, from the very bottom of my heart, for not voicing that question in front of Kevin."

"You're welcome."

"Yes, the divorce was ancient history by then. But this girl ... girls like *that* did not wander into the dive bar where I used to hang out. And if one happened to, I would not have been the guy she approached."

"What was she like?"

"If memory serves, she was stunning. And predatory. And oddly...frightening. I never believed for an instant that she was really attracted to me. I could sense there was an agenda, and I didn't want to fall for it. I was a little sensitive, at that point, to the idea of being duped again. But of course I didn't want to be rude, so I went with the politest refusal I could think of."

Alex chuckled. "You're right. Never, ever tell Kevin that you were afraid of the stunning hooker."

"Can you imagine?" He laughed with her. "Your turn. Another boyfriend."

"I'm running out...Let's see, I dated a guy named Felix for a couple of weeks in undergrad."

"And what extinguished the flames of your passion?"

"You have to understand, the only place I ever met boys was in a lab."

"Go on."

"Well, Felix worked with animals. Rats, mostly. He kept a lot of them in his apartment. There was a... smell problem."

Daniel threw his head back and howled with laughter. The sound of it was infectious. She couldn't help chortling along with him. It was not as out of control as that first afternoon in Kevin's secret lair, but it was close. All the stress seemed to drain out of her body, and she felt more relaxed than she would have thought possible in light of where she was headed.

Eventually, Daniel fell asleep, midsentence, as he described his fifth-grade crush. He'd been fighting his droopy eyelids for a while, and she suspected again that he'd been trying to keep her mind off the negatives.

It was relaxing to have him sleeping peacefully next to her. Einstein was snoring on the backseat, a nice counterpoint to the even sound of Daniel's breathing. She knew she should be thinking of a variety of plans, ways to get to Carston without exposing herself too greatly, but she just wanted to enjoy the moment. Peace was going to be a limited commodity in her near future. If this was the last moment that she got to be entirely content, then she wanted to experience it fully.

She was in a rare state of calm when she woke Daniel a few hours later, as they were entering the outskirts of DC. The last time she'd pulled into this city, she'd been furious and terrified. She probably had even more reason to feel that way today, but she was still enjoying the time she had left alone with Daniel, and she wasn't going to let that go before she had to.

Daniel read the directions to her as she got closer to their target. As she'd originally thought, this was a nice neighborhood, and it was only getting nicer.

Wasn't that like Kevin, to hide somewhere so incongruous? She circled the building with the matching address twice, doubting whether this could be the place.

"I'd better call him."

Daniel handed her the phone. She hit Redial, and it rang once.

"You're late," Kevin answered. "What's wrong now?"

"Traffic. Nothing. I *think* we're outside, but... this place doesn't look right."

"Why?"

"We're hiding out in a fancy art deco high-rise?"

"Yeah. A friend of mine is letting us crash. There's parking under the building. Go to the fourth level down, I'll meet you." He disconnected.

She handed the phone back to Daniel. "Just once, I want to hang up on him first."

"You did the very first time he called, remember? Fairly spectacularly."

"Oh, right. That does make me feel better."

All the tension came back as they rounded the corner into the parking garage, and the daylight disappeared. She drove in a claustrophobic downward spiral until she reached the right level, and then saw Kevin standing impatiently beside an empty space marked RESIDENTS ONLY. He waved her into it.

She braced herself as she opened the door, expecting a few snide comments about her face or disparaging observations about Daniel's screwups, but Kevin said only, "Don't mind the cameras, I took them offline this morning," and then opened the back of the SUV to let Einstein out.

There was a real reunion with Einstein, who threw Kevin to the ground and attempted to lick the skin off his face. Trying to pretend that she wasn't the slightest bit jealous of Einstein's affection for his man, Alex ignored them both until she and Daniel were loaded up with as much as they could carry.

"Um, which way?" she asked.

Kevin got up with a sigh. "Follow me."

To his credit, he did grab the remaining duffel bags as they went to the elevator.

"Do I need a hat?" Alex asked. "Is there a lobby? I'm not exactly ready for my close-up."

"No worries, Ollie, this goes straight to the apartment. By the way, bro, nice beard. It's a good look on you. In that you don't look like you as much anymore."

"Um, thanks?"

"About this friend…" Alex began.

Kevin sighed again. "They can't all be Arnies. Sorry, shorty, this might get rough."

"You don't trust him?"

The elevator opened into a plush hallway…or was it an anteroom? There was only one door in the space.

"I've paid her through next week, so I trust her about that far."

The hair on the back of Alex's neck stood up. Daniel had gotten her more used to human interaction, but she knew she still had some pretty severe people issues. As they walked the length of the short hall, she struggled with the duffel in her right hand, trying to free some fingers so she could pull a syringe from her belt. Just as she caught hold of the one she wanted, Daniel touched her wrist. She glanced up, and he was giving her a look that seemed to imply she was overreacting. Frowning, she slid the syringe back into place. It wouldn't take long to draw it if the need arose anyway.

Kevin had a key to the single door. He took a deep breath as he pushed it open.

At first Alex wasn't sure they hadn't stumbled into the lobby after all, because she'd never been inside an apartment with a wide marble staircase up to another story. The place was lavish, sleek and modern, and lined with floor-to-ceiling windows that immediately had her feeling exposed. Through the glass, the sun was just beginning to droop toward the DC skyline. There didn't *seem* to be any other apartments close enough to look into this one, but a telescope would make it possible. Or a rifle sight.

"No," a hard—but somehow still velvety—voice announced from behind them.

Alex whirled. The apartment stretched back the other way, too, wrapping around the front door and the hallway beyond. On one side was a huge white kitchen; on the other a dining room with seating for ten, with more window-walls framing each. Leaning against the marble kitchen island was the most exquisite human being Alex had ever seen in real life.

The woman looked exactly like the facetious description Alex had conjured up to describe Kevin's improbable mental image of the Oleander. She had honey-blond hair, thick and long, that stood out from her head in full waves like a Disney cartoon's. Sapphire-blue doe eyes, full red lips turned up at the corners, and a straight, narrow nose, all set with flawless symmetry in an oval face with prominent cheekbones. Swan neck over elegant collarbones. Of course, the generous hourglass figure with a tiny waist and legs that seemed longer than Alex's entire body. The woman was wearing only a short, black kimono and an irritated expression.

"It's temporary," Kevin said in a conciliatory voice. "Obviously, I'll pay you the same for each of them. Three times what we originally agreed on."

The surreally perfect woman raised one eyebrow and looked pointedly at Einstein. His tail was wagging furiously. He stared up at the blonde with the proverbial puppy-dog eyes.

"Four times," Kevin promised. He dropped the bags he was carrying. "You *like* dogs."

"Kate?" Daniel asked suddenly, surprised recognition saturating his tone.

The woman's face dimpled into a toothpaste-commercial-quality smile.

"Hi, Danny," she purred. "I almost didn't know you with all that scruff. Well, that *does* make me feel better. You left a nasty welt on my ego, but at least you didn't forget me."

"It's, er, nice to see you again," Daniel stammered, flummoxed by her greeting.

The blonde's eyes cut to Kevin. "Okay, *he* can stay."

"It's just a few nights," Kevin said. "I need the little one, too."

"You know I don't like women in my space," she said in a flat voice, flicking her eyes to Alex, then back to Kevin.

"Oh, that's okay, Ollie's not a *real* girl," Kevin assured her.

Daniel dropped his bags and took half a step forward before Alex hooked the back of his shirt with her one free finger.

"Not now," she muttered.

Kate — or whatever her real name was — shrugged gracefully away from the island and glided toward them. She looked down her nose at Alex; easy to do, as she was a good six inches taller.

"So what happened to your face? Your boyfriend tune you up?"

Daniel stiffened. Alex wasn't sure what this was — maybe some kind of territorial thing? It was only a guess; Alex didn't have a lot of experience with other women. In the distant past, she'd suffered through a couple of immature roommates, liked a few other lady science geeks, and made small talk with the rare female underling who didn't flee her presence. Mostly she'd worked with men, and she didn't know all the rules for double-X-chromosome interactions. At a loss, she went with the truth, though she probably should have waited to see what Kevin had told the woman.

"Um, no, it was a Mafia assassin." Alex worked her jaw, feeling the bandage pull against her skin. "Oh, and the older stuff was just Kevin trying to kill me."

"If I'd actually been trying to kill you, you'd be dead," Kevin grumbled.

Alex rolled her eyes.

"What, you want to go another round?" Kevin demanded. "Anytime, sweetheart."

"The next time I put you down," Alex promised, "it will be permanently."

Kevin laughed — not derisively, like she expected, but with genuine delight. "See what I mean, Val?"

The woman looked like she was trying not to smile.

"Okay, you've piqued my interest. But I have only the one extra room."

"Ollie's good at roughing it."

"Whatever," the woman said. Apparently it was an agreement. "Get all that mess out of my living room."

She skimmed close by Daniel as she passed them. Without a backward glance, she headed upstairs. The kimono was very short, and both brothers watched her climb with partially open mouths.

"You turned *her* down?" Alex muttered under her breath.

Kevin heard her and laughed again. "Let's move this stuff before she kicks us all out."

• • •

THE EXTRA BEDROOM was bigger than Alex's entire DC apartment had been. And it wasn't as if she'd been living in a dive; her place was what real estate agents described as a luxury apartment. This place, though, was several degrees beyond mere luxury. Kevin had seemed on the level when he said the woman was a hooker, but Alex hadn't had any idea that profession could pay so well.

Kevin stacked the duffels against one wall.

"Ollie, you've still got that cot, right? There's a huge walk-in closet off the bathroom. Check it out and see if it will work for you. You *could* set up on one of those couches out there, but it might be best to keep you out of Val's line of sight as much as possible."

"Of course Alex will sleep in the bed," Daniel said.

Kevin's eyebrows pulled together skeptically. "Really? You're going to get all chivalrous about *Ollie?*"

"It's like you never even met our mother."

"Relax," Alex said as Kevin bridled. "We'll work it out."

"Fine," Kevin said.

"Should I have been more careful with my words out there?" Alex asked Kevin. "You said she's not trustworthy."

Kevin shook his head. "No, you're fine. Val might kick us all onto the street when she's tired of us, but she won't sell us out. I've bought her time and her discretion. What happens with Val stays with Val. She has a reputation to protect."

"Okay," Alex agreed, though she wasn't sure she entirely understood Val's policies.

He moved to the door, then paused with his hand on the knob. "There's plenty of food in the fridge if you're hungry, or we can order something in."

"Thanks," Alex said. "I'll sort my stuff out first."

"Yes," Daniel said. "Let us get situated."

Kevin hesitated one more second, then stepped back into the room. "Uh, Danny, I just wanted to say...it's good to see you. I'm glad you're safe."

Like before, as he was leaving the ranch, Kevin looked

like he wouldn't be opposed to a hug. Daniel stood awkwardly, his body language full of ambivalence.

"Yes, well, thanks to Alex," Daniel said. "And I'm glad you're not dead like she thought you were."

Kevin barked a laugh. "Yeah, me, too. And thanks again, poison woman. I owe you one."

He exited on another laugh, leaving the door cracked behind him.

Daniel gave Alex a long stare, then went to the door and quietly shut it all the way. He turned back to her, and there was clearly an argument about to begin. She shook her head and motioned him to follow her farther into the guest suite.

For a second, the bathroom made her forget why she'd come this way. A swimming pool–size tub was set into the floor, surrounded by marble and a faintly blue tile wall that shimmered like a pale sea. A showerhead the diameter of a truck tire was suspended from the ceiling over it.

"What *is* this place?" Alex gasped.

Daniel shut the door behind them. "Kate—or rather Val—is apparently quite successful."

"Do you think she's really a prostitute, or was that just Kevin trying to make the story better?"

"I didn't come in here to talk about Val."

She turned to face him, her lips twisting sideways into a pucker.

"Alex, I don't like lying to him."

"Who's lied?"

"Acting, then. Pretending that we're nothing to each other."

She huffed a sigh. "I'm just not ready to deal with the inevitable fallout. I have enough stress."

"We're going to have to tell him eventually. Why not get it over with?"

He saw her expression change as she weighed the options.

"You still don't believe we have an *eventually*, do you?" he accused.

"Well...there *is* a good possibility either he or I will be dead within the next week, so why rock the boat?"

Daniel abruptly pulled her into a rough hug that was somehow more reproachful than comforting.

"Don't say that. I can't stand to hear you talk that way."

"Sorry," she said into his shirt.

"We can run away. Tonight. We'll hide. You know how."

"Can we at least wait till we've slept and eaten?" she asked plaintively.

He laughed unwillingly at her tone. "I suppose I could allow that much."

She relaxed into him for a moment, wishing again that running were the right option. It sounded so much easier, restful almost.

"Let's just walk out there hand in hand," Daniel suggested, "and then make out on the sofa for a bit."

"First, eating and sleeping. I am not dealing with the aftermath of some grand reveal until I'm sure I've considered all the possible forms the backlash might take and whether I need to be armed — or, rather, *how* armed I need to be. I can't even think straight right now."

"All right," he said. "I'll give you tonight, because I know how exhausted you are. But we're revisiting this discussion in the morning, and I intend to be quite inflexible."

"Will Kevin be in here too?" she wondered. "The woman said there was only one extra room. That won't make discussing anything very easy."

"I doubt it." She could hear the eye roll in his voice and she pulled away to look at his face. He didn't let her go, but he dropped his arms to rest more casually around her waist.

"Oh, do you think she meant this was the only *empty* extra room?"

"No, I think he's staying with her."

She wrinkled her nose. "Really? She didn't seem to like him very much."

"The women in his life never do."

She was still unconvinced. "But...she could do so much better."

Daniel laughed. "I won't argue with that."

CHAPTER 24

Val's huge double fridge was much better stocked than Arnie's. In fact, it was much better stocked than the average restaurant's. It looked like she was planning to feed a dozen more guests than those she already had in residence—though she apparently had not been apprised of Alex's and Daniel's existence until moments before they arrived.

The incongruity bothered Alex a little, but not enough to deter her from the bowl of grapes. She felt like she hadn't eaten anything fresh in weeks, though it really hadn't been so very long. The ranch seemed months ago. She could barely wrap her head around how short the time actually was.

Alex sat on one of the pure white, ultramodern bar stools. It wasn't terribly comfortable.

Daniel was humming with pleasure as he examined the accoutrements. "Now, this is a kitchen," he murmured. He started sorting through the lower drawers, evaluating the pots and pans available.

"Making ourselves right at home, are we?"

Daniel jerked upright. Alex paused with a grape halfway to her mouth.

Val came into the room laughing, still in the brief kimono. "Relax. All this stuff is here for you. I don't really use this room."

"Um, thank you," Daniel said.

She shrugged. "Kevin paid for it. So, you like to cook?"

"I dabble."

"He's being modest," Alex told her. "He's a five-star chef."

Val smiled warmly at Daniel as she stretched her whole torso across the island toward him so her chin nearly touched the marble. "Well, that's nice. I've never had a live-in chef before. It sounds... fun."

Alex wondered how Val was able to load so many different implications into one common word.

"Er, I suppose so," Daniel said, flushing a little. "Where is Kevin?"

"Walking the dog."

Val turned her face toward Alex, and Alex braced for more aggression.

"I asked Kevin about you. Kevin says you tortured *him*." Val jerked her head toward Daniel.

"Ah, well, technically, that's correct. It was a case of mistaken identity, though."

Val's eyes glowed with interest. "What did you do? Did you burn him?"

"What? No, no... Um, I used injectable chemical treatments. I find them more effective, and they don't leave scars."

"Hmm." Val rolled her body sideways along the marble so she was turned to Daniel again, then pillowed her head against her arm. The kimono was partially dislodged by this maneuver, and Alex imagined his view was quite interesting. He stood awkwardly, one hand on the refrigerator door.

"Was it really painful?" Val demanded.

"Beyond anything I'd ever imagined," Daniel admitted.

Val seemed fascinated. "Did you scream? Did you beg? Did you *writhe?*"

Daniel couldn't help but smile at her enthusiasm. "All of the above, I believe. Oh, and I cried like a baby as well." Still smiling, he seemed suddenly comfortable; he turned back to the fridge and started rummaging.

Val sighed. "I really wish I could have seen that."

"You're into torture?" Alex asked, hiding her concern. Of course Kevin would move them in with a true sadist.

"Not torture per se, but it's so intoxicating, isn't it? That kind of power?"

"I guess I've never looked at it quite that way..."

Val cocked her head, looking at Alex with undisguised interest. "Isn't everything about power?"

Alex thought about it for a moment. "Not in my experience. Back when that was my job, honestly—it sounds naive now, even to me—I was really just trying to save people. There was always a lot hanging in the balance. It was stressful."

Val considered that, pursing her lips. "That does sound naive."

Alex shrugged.

"It never gave you a rush? Being in control?" Val's wide lapis eyes bored into her.

Alex wondered if people felt this way in a psychiatrist's office—this compulsion to speak. Or maybe it was more like being shackled to Alex's own table. "I mean...maybe. I'm not a very dangerous person on the surface. I guess there were times that I appreciated the...respect."

Val nodded. "Of course you did. Tell me, have you ever tortured a woman?"

"Twice...well, once and a half."

"Explain."

Daniel's head was leaning back as he adjusted the flame under the stovetop grill; he was paying close attention. Alex hated talking about this in front of him.

"I didn't actually have to do anything to the first girl. She was confessing before she was even strapped to the table. She didn't belong in my lab anyway—any normal interrogation would have gotten the same results. Poor kid."

"What was she confessing to?"

"A terrorist cell was trying to coerce some suicide bombers in New York. They'd kidnap someone's family back in Iran—in this case, her parents—and kill the hostages if the subject wouldn't do as directed. The NSA had it under control before any of the bombs were detonated, but they lost several of the hostages." She sighed. "It's always messy with terrorists."

"What about the second?"

"*That* was an entirely different situation. Arms dealer."

"Was she tough to break?"

"One of the toughest in my career."

Val smiled as if the answer greatly pleased her. "I've always thought that women can handle a lot more pain than the so-called stronger sex. Men are all just oversize children, really." Then she sighed. "I've made men beg, and I've made them writhe, and maybe there have been some tears here and there, but no one's ever *cried like a baby*." Her full lower lip pushed out into a pout.

"I'm positive they would if you asked them to," Alex encouraged.

Val smiled her glittery smile. "You're probably right."

Daniel was chopping something now. Alex decided she should slow down on the grapes. Dinner was sure to be worth the wait. Val rolled to the side again to watch him, and Alex felt a sudden urge to distract her.

"This is a beautiful place."

"Yes, it's nice, isn't it? A friend gave it to me."

"Oh, does he stay here often?" How many people were going to know about them? She'd already been stupidly and bizarrely honest with this strange woman. It would surely come back to bite her.

"No, no, Zhang and I broke up *ages* ago. He was too stuffy."

"And he let you keep the place?"

Val stared at Alex, disbelieving. "*Let* me? What kind of a gift is it if the deed's not in your name?"

"That's a good point," Alex agreed quickly.

"What was that you were saying earlier, about putting Kevin down?"

"Oh, can I tell the story, please?" Daniel butted in. "It's my favorite."

Daniel stretched the story out, milking it for Val's laughs and coos. He made Alex sound more in control than she had been and fictionalized the parts he wasn't awake for. It was a better story his way, she had to admit. Val's expression as she assessed Alex now was one hundred eighty degrees from what it had been at their first meeting.

Then the food was ready, and Alex stopped caring about much else. It had been a while since she'd had red meat, and her inner carnivore took over. When she came out of the frenzy, she saw that Val was watching her again, engrossed.

Alex glanced down — Daniel had given Val a plate, too, but she'd eaten only a few slivers off the side of her steak.

"Do you always eat so much?" Val asked.

"When it's available, I guess. When Daniel is cooking, definitely."

Val's eyes narrowed. "I'll bet you never gain an ounce, do you?"

"I don't know. I probably must sometimes, right?"

"Do you even own a scale?" she demanded.

"I've got one that weighs milligrams," Alex answered, confused.

Val blew out a puff of breath that ruffled the waves of hair over her forehead. "People with naturally high metabolisms piss me off."

"Seriously?" Alex said, looking her up and down. "You're going to complain to *me* about our relative genetic heritages?"

Val stared at her for a few seconds, then smiled and shook her head. "Well, I suppose a girl can't have everything."

"And you're just the exception that proves the rule?"

"I think I like you, Ollie."

"Thanks, Val. It's actually Alex, though."

"Whatever. You know, you've got a lot of untapped potential. With decent hair, some makeup, and a mid-size boob job, you could do all right."

"Er, I do fine as is, thanks. I have lower expectations out of life. It makes things easier."

"Seriously, you cut your own hair, don't you?"

"I don't have another option."

"Trust me, there's always another option to *this*." She stretched across the counter and tried to touch the hair hanging in Alex's eyes, but Alex flinched out of her way. It was true that it was time for another trim.

Val turned to Daniel, who was trying to be unobtrusive, leaning against the counter directly behind Val as he finished his food, almost like he was hiding from her. Well, Alex could understand that. And she completely understood why Daniel had found Val frightening on their first meeting.

"Back me up, Danny. Don't you think Ollie could be pretty if she tried?"

Daniel did the blinking thing he always did when taken by surprise. "But Alex is pretty now."

"What a gentleman. It's like you're Bizarro Kevin."

"I'll take that as a compliment."

"It *is* a compliment. Maybe the best I've ever given," Val agreed.

"How long have you known him?" Daniel wondered.

"Too long. I don't know why I keep opening the door when he comes begging. I guess it's that power thing." She shrugged, and one shoulder of her silk robe slid down her arm. She didn't fix it. "I like watching someone so strong have to do what I say."

A key jangled in the front door. Alex slipped from the stool to her feet, muscles tensing automatically. Val watched as Daniel looked to Alex, tensing, too, ready to follow her lead.

"You two are funny," she murmured.

Einstein ran panting into the kitchen, and Alex relaxed.

Val eyed the dog, his tongue lolling out and his eyes eager. "Does it want something?"

"He's probably thirsty," Alex told her.

"Oh." She glanced around the kitchen, then grabbed a decorative crystal bowl from the center of the island and filled it in the sink. Einstein licked her hand gratefully and then started lapping up the water.

"Smells good," Kevin commented as he came around the corner.

"You can finish mine," Val said without looking at him. "I'm done." Experimentally, she stroked one of Einstein's ears.

Kevin leaned comfortably against the island, looking very at home as he started cutting into Val's food. "Everyone getting along?"

"You were right," Val answered.

Kevin grinned triumphantly. "I told you she wouldn't bore you."

Val straightened up and smiled back. "Anyone who's chained you to the floor is bound to get along with me."

Kevin's grin disappeared. "It was a draw."

Val threw back her chin and laughed, her long neck looking even more swanlike than before.

Daniel turned the sink on and rummaged for dish soap. Alex joined him automatically, comforted by even just the opening chords of their usual routine. Once again she was in an unfamiliar place, well out of her league, unsure and unsafe, but with Daniel there, she could handle it. He was like a gas mask—a touchstone of refuge. She smiled to herself, thinking how little he would care for that comparison. Well, she wasn't the romantic one.

"Oh, don't bother with that, sweetie," Val told Daniel. "The housekeeper comes every morning."

Alex shot Kevin a loaded glance, which Val caught. "I'll leave a note on the counter, and he'll stay out of the bedrooms," Val assured her. "I know this is all very cloak-and-dagger. Don't worry, you won't be exposed on my account."

"I don't mind," Daniel said. "Dishes relax me."

"What *is* this brother of yours?" Val asked Kevin. "Can I keep him?"

Alex smiled when Daniel's eyes widened in panic, but he kept his face down over the sink so Val didn't see. He handed Alex a clean pair of tongs and she dried them with a dish towel that felt like silk and was probably meant to be ornamental. She had a feeling Val didn't care about things like that.

"He's not your type," Kevin answered.

"I have many types, though, don't I?"

"Fair enough, but I don't think he'll hold your interest long."

She sighed. "They so rarely do."

"So, um, back to this housekeeper—what time will he arrive, leave, et cetera?" Alex asked.

Val laughed. "You take things very seriously."

"People try to kill me a lot."

"That must get irritating," she said casually. "When I'm in residence, Raoul comes early and leaves quickly. He won't even wake you. He's good."

"I'll just lock the door, then."

"If you like."

"We're not sleeping in tomorrow, Ollie," Kevin interjected. "There's a lot to get set before we act, and I don't want to waste more time."

"Give her the one morning off," Daniel insisted. "She's been driving all night for a week, sleeping in the back of cars. She needs rest."

·Kevin made a disgusted face. "She's not a child, Danny. The big kids have work to do."

"It's not a problem," Alex said quickly. She glanced at the clock on the oven; it was only seven. "I'm crashing now anyway, so I'm sure I'll be up long before Raoul arrives."

"I'll walk you through my inventory, then you can tell me what else you need. I've got the video footage of your subject, which I'm sure you'll want to review, and then—"

"Tomorrow, Kevin," Alex interrupted. "Now, sleep."

Kevin inhaled noisily through his nose and rolled his eyes to the ceiling.

Alex almost reached for Daniel's hand as she left the kitchen. She had to curl her fingers into a fist and hope Kevin hadn't noticed. It felt unnatural, and she knew Daniel felt it, too. He followed close behind her, almost as if he were thinking about doing something to instigate the conversation—or possible altercation—that she was trying to avoid. *Not now,* she tried to communicate to him telepathically without turning. She walked faster, but it was a wasted effort. Daniel's legs were too long for her to build any kind of lead.

She felt much better when she heard him close the door behind him and click the lock into place.

"Thanks," she said, turning to wrap her arms around his waist.

"Only because we're exhausted," he reminded her. "I will be much more tenacious tomorrow."

She was really dragging, so she went through only the most important parts of the routine. She didn't want to bother with rebandaging her face, so she decided to let her skin breathe for the night. The wound was still bright red and puckered, and the stitches in her ear — though she'd used a flesh-toned suture thread — were hard to miss. It looked like the two halves of her lobe would rejoin, though. She'd have a nasty scar, but she didn't want to think about that now.

She thought about setting up the cot in the closet for show but decided to wait till morning. It wasn't like Kevin was going to do a room inspection. She also considered stringing a gas-canister line around the door. She didn't think she had the energy, and anyway, an intruder would surely check the master first, if he got past Einstein. She settled for putting her SIG and belt on the bedside table.

Daniel was in the bed before her, but he was still awake.

"Should I leave my rifle out, do you think?" he asked.

"It's a big room, but probably a little tight for the rifle. I can go grab the shotgun."

He gave her an exasperated look. "I was joking."

"Oh. Right."

He held his arms open for her. She switched off the lamp and climbed into her now usual place. The bed was absurd—some kind of soft, supportive cloud that was probably made from spun gold or unicorn mane.

"Good night, Alex," he whispered into her hair, and then she was asleep.

• • •

SHE WOKE WHILE it was still dark outside; the faint light glowing from around the edges of the shades was the unnatural yellow-green of city lights. She couldn't see a clock, but she'd guess it was around four. A solid night's rest and then some. She was glad; today would be long. For years now, all she'd been doing was running and surviving. Now she had to shift into a more proactive mode and she dreaded it. There had been her one uncharacteristic adventure in Texas, but she blamed that on the adrenaline of the moment and the unfamiliar responsibility of having a liability. It wasn't something she would ever have *planned* to do.

So when Daniel, woken by her movements, started to kiss her throat, she didn't mind procrastinating for a bit.

She wondered what it would be like to be a normal person. To be able to expect that mornings like this— waking up with someone you'd chosen—would happen over and over again. To go through the day certain that you'd lie back down at the end of it in the same bed, with that same person next to you. She doubted many people appreciated that certainty when they had it. It would be too much a part of everyday life to them, taken for granted, not something they would think of feeling grateful for.

Well, she couldn't count on another morning like this, but she could be grateful for it now.

She yanked on his T-shirt and he pulled his hands out of her hair long enough to remove it. Alex tugged her own shirt out of the way, greedy for the feeling of his skin next to hers. His kisses, which had begun so tenderly, started to veer more toward the unrestrained, though she could almost hear him reminding himself to be careful with her. She didn't want any of that. She kissed him back in a way designed to make him forget any other consideration.

There was no sound, no warning. She didn't hear the lock turn or the door open. And then, suddenly, the metallic click of a gun safety sliding off, just inches from her head. She froze and felt Daniel do the same. She wasn't sure if he'd recognized the quiet click, as she had, or was just responding to her.

From the sound, she knew the intruder was closer to the gun on the nightstand than she was. She cursed herself for neglecting basic security and worked to think of any move left to her. Maybe if she tried to spin and kick the gun away, it would give Daniel time to get around him.

And then the intruder spoke.

"Step away from the civilian, you poisonous little *snake*."

She blew out the huge gasp of air she'd been holding in. "Hoo! Huh! Okay. Ah! Let's put the gun down now, psychopath."

"Not until you get off my brother."

"This is so far beyond crossing the line, I don't even know what to call it," Daniel said in a harsh tone. "Did you *pick the lock?*"

"Danny, listen to me, she's drugged you again. That's what's happening here."

"As if I would waste my limited supply on recreation," she muttered. She rolled, tugging the sheet up to cover herself, and reached for the lamp. She felt the cool barrel of the gun press into her forehead.

"You're ridiculous," she told him as she switched the light on.

Kevin stepped back, blinking in the light. He still had his long, silenced pistol aimed at her face.

The bed rocked as Daniel vaulted agilely over her body and placed himself between her and Kevin. "What are you *doing?* Don't point that at her!"

"Danny, I don't know what she has you on, but we'll get it out of your system, I promise. Come with me."

"If you know what is good for you, you will turn around and walk away *now*."

"I'm saving you here."

"Thanks, but no thanks. I was quite happy with what I was doing before you so rudely interrupted, and I'd like to return to it. Shut the door behind you."

"What's happened?" Alex asked, yanking her T-shirt on. There was no time for this squabbling. Kevin was wearing only a pair of pajama pants, so whatever the catalyst was, he hadn't had time to prepare himself. It wasn't like Kevin to let something—even something this offensive to him—distract him when there was trouble. She leaned around Daniel to grab her belt and then wrapped it around her waist as she spoke. "Do we need to move?" She reached for the SIG next and shoved it into the back of her belt.

Kevin's gun lowered slowly, and he started to look less confident as he was confronted with her practicality.

"I didn't believe her, so I came to check," he admitted, suddenly sheepish. "I wasn't planning on Danny ever knowing I was here."

"Her?" Daniel asked.

"Val...she said you two were together. She was so sure of herself. I said there was no way in *hell*." His voice was outraged again by the end.

Daniel exhaled, irritated. "Well, I hope you made some kind of bet. With a very humiliating consequence for losing."

"This is punishment enough," Kevin grumbled.

"In all seriousness," Daniel said, "get out, Kevin."

"I can't believe this, Danny. What are you thinking? After what she did to you?"

Daniel was still between Alex and Kevin, so she couldn't see his face, but she could suddenly hear a smile in his voice. "You're supposed to be so tough, so dangerous. And yet you're saying you'd let a little pain come between you and the woman you wanted? Really?"

Kevin rocked a step back and took a few seconds to respond. "But why? Why do you want *her?*" The anger had vanished; when he looked at Alex, there was only bewilderment.

"I'll explain it to you when you've grown up. Now, for the last time, get out, or"—and he reached one long arm around Alex's body and pulled the gun from her back—"I'll shoot you."

He pointed the gun at Kevin's torso.

"Um, the safety is off on that," Alex murmured.

"Counting on it," Daniel replied.

Kevin stared at them—Daniel holding the gun steady, Alex watching from behind his arm—and then his shoulders squared.

He pointed at Alex with his free hand. "You. Just . . .

stop..." He waved his hand in a big, inclusive gesture, taking in the two of them and the bed. "All of this. We leave in fifteen. Be ready."

His hand shifted to Danny. "I..." He blew out a deep breath, shook his head, and then turned and walked out the door. He didn't bother closing it. "Damn it, Val!" he shouted as he headed through the dark hall, as if all of this were somehow her fault. Einstein barked from upstairs.

Alex sighed and stretched. "Well, that went about exactly as I thought it would. No shots fired—this was the best-case scenario, I guess."

"Where are you going?" Daniel asked.

"To shower. You heard the man. Fifteen minutes."

"It's the middle of the night!"

"All the better to hide my face. You're not tired, are you? I think we've been asleep for nine hours, at least."

Daniel scowled. "No, I am not in the least bit tired."

"Well, then..." She started toward the bathroom door.

"Wait."

Daniel jumped up, ruffling his hair as he walked to the bedroom door. He shut it and then locked it again.

"What's the point of that, really?" Alex asked.

Daniel shrugged. "Touché."

He walked to her and wrapped his hands around her upper arms, holding her securely. "I wasn't ready to get out of bed."

"Kevin's not going to knock," she reminded him. "He probably won't even give me the full fifteen."

"I don't like letting him call the shots. Not only was I not ready to get out of bed, I was not ready for you to get out of bed, either."

He bent his head down to kiss her, his hands running slowly up her shoulders till they were cradling her face. She knew that under normal circumstances, it would have taken very little convincing on his part to get her to agree. But these were not normal circumstances, and the idea that Kevin might walk into the room at any moment—probably with gun in hand again—tempered her response.

She pulled back. "What about a compromise?"

The look he gave her was less than thrilled. "I categorically refuse to compromise in any way for Kevin's sake."

"Can I please at least make my case before you dismiss it?"

He kept his expression stern, but she could tell he wanted to smile. "Do what you have to do, but I will not be swayed."

"We have limited time, and we both need to clean up. That shower–slash–lap pool in there will easily fit two—well, actually it could fit twelve—and I was thinking we could multitask."

The hard-line expression disappeared. "I immediately withdraw my opposition and offer my full cooperation."

"I thought you might see it that way."

CHAPTER 25

Because there's no reason for you to go," Kevin objected.

Kevin stood in front of the elevator doors, blocking the call button, arms crossed over his chest.

"Why not?" Daniel demanded.

"You're not going to be a part of the offensive, Danny, so you don't need to be a part of the preparation."

Daniel's lips mashed together into a scowl.

"It doesn't hurt anything for him—" Alex began mildly.

"Except someone could see his face," Kevin growled.

"You mean *your* face?" she countered.

"*I'm* smart enough to keep my head down."

Daniel rolled his eyes. "I'll ride in the trunk if you want."

Kevin evaluated the two of them for a long second. "Are you going to let me focus?"

"What do you mean?" Alex asked.

Kevin closed his eyes; he seemed to be calming himself. He inhaled through his nose, then looked at Daniel.

"Here are my requirements for you to join us on this very boring, standard recon exercise: No one will speak of what happened this morning. I will not be forced to remember the nauseating things I witnessed. There will be no discussion that might allude to said nauseating things. This is business, and you will conduct yourself appropriately. Agreed?"

Daniel's neck started to flush. She was sure he was going to mention the fact that if Kevin hadn't broken in to a locked room in the middle of the night, he wouldn't have seen anything. Before Daniel could object, Alex said, "Agreed. Appropriate businesslike behavior."

Kevin glanced back and forth between them, measuring again. After a second, he turned and hit the call button.

Daniel gave her a *Really?* look. Alex shrugged.

"None of that!" Kevin commanded, though he still had his back to them.

"What?" Daniel complained.

"I can *feel* you two silently communicating. Stop it."

• • •

IT WAS A quiet drive in the average-looking black sedan. She didn't know if it was Val's car or something

Kevin had acquired. It didn't seem like Val's style, but maybe she liked to be incognito sometimes. Alex appreciated the heavily tinted windows. She felt less exposed as she sat with her ball cap pulled low over her face and stared out at the still mostly sleeping city. They were early enough to beat the morning rush.

Kevin drove through a seedier section of town—more the kind of neighborhood she would have expected his hiding place to exist in. He pulled in at a storage facility that seemed to be mostly enormous cargo containers. There was no guard posted, just a keypad and a heavy metal gate with razor-wire coils on top. Kevin drove them to a spot near the back of the fenced lot and parked behind a dingy orange container.

The lot appeared to be empty, but Alex kept her face down and her walk unfeminine as they moved to the wide double doors that made up the front wall of the container. Kevin plugged a complicated sequence of numbers into the heavy-duty rectangular lock, then pulled it out of the way. He opened one door just a few feet and waved them inside.

It was black when Kevin pulled the door shut behind himself. Then there was a low click, and rope lights lining the ceiling and the floor glowed to life.

"Exactly how many Batcaves do you *have?*" Alex demanded.

"Just a few, here and there, where I might need them," Kevin said. "This one's mobile, so that helps."

The inside of Kevin's cargo container was tightly packed but compulsively organized. Like the barn in Texas, there was a place for everything.

Racks of clothing—costumes, really—were wedged against the wall by the double doors. She was sure that was on purpose—if someone got a glimpse inside while the doors were open, all he would see was clothes. A casual observer wouldn't think anything of it. A more careful observer might think it was odd that uniforms for every branch of the military were hanging together, along with mechanic's coveralls and several utility companies' official garb, not to mention the raggedy components of a homeless man's outfit hanging a few feet down from a row of dark suits that ranged from off-the-rack to high-end designer. A person could blend into a lot of situations with these clothes.

The props were in bins over the clothes racks—briefcases and clipboards, toolboxes and suitcases. The shoes were in clear plastic boxes underneath.

Beyond the costumes, deep floor-to-ceiling metal cabinets were installed. Kevin guided her through each; she took note of the things she might need. As in the barn, there was a space for guns, for ammo, for armor, for explosives, for knives. There were other things that hadn't been in Texas, or if they were, they'd been better hidden than the rest. He had a cabinet full of various tech items—tiny cameras and bugs, tracking devices, night-vision goggles, binoculars and scopes, electromagnetic-pulse generators of various sizes, a few laptop computers, and dozens of gadgets she didn't recognize. He identified the code breakers, the frequency readers, the frequency jammers, the system hackers, the mini-drones... She lost track after a while. It was unlikely that she would want to use anything she wasn't familiar with.

The next cabinet was chemical compounds.

"Yes," she hissed, digging past the front row to see what was behind. "*This* I can use."

"Thought you'd appreciate that."

"Do you mind?" she asked, holding up a sealed cylinder of a catalytic she knew she was almost out of.

"Take whatever you want. I don't think I've ever used any of that stuff."

She crouched down to the lower shelf and loaded several more jars and packages into her backpack. *Ah,* this one she needed. "Then why do you have it?"

Kevin shrugged. "I had access. Never look a gift horse—"

"Ha!" She stared up at him triumphantly.

"What?"

"You told me that was a stupid saying."

Kevin raised his eyes to the ceiling. "Sometimes it's really hard not to kick you."

"I know precisely how you feel."

Daniel moved to stand between her and Kevin. She shook her head at him. It was just banter. With the brief lecture on appropriate behavior out of the way, Kevin had shifted back to his normal self—something in between a serial killer and the world's most obnoxious big brother. Alex was getting used to it; she didn't mind him as much anymore.

Grumbling about *silent communication*, Kevin stalked back to the ammo cabinet and started filling a large black bag with reserves.

"First aid?" she asked.

"In the knife locker, top shelf."

There were several zippered black bags over the knives, some of them about the size of a backpack, others smaller, like shaving kits. She couldn't reach any of them, so Daniel pulled them down and she combed through them on the floor.

The first smaller bag she opened had no medical supplies—instead, there were little packets of documents neatly rubber-banded together for easy sorting. She quickly pulled out a Canadian passport and glanced at the ID page. As she'd expected, there was a photo of Kevin with a different name—Terry Williams. She glanced up. Kevin had his back to her. She grabbed two of the packets and stuffed them into the bottom of her backpack, then zipped the bag closed.

These particular items wouldn't be of any help to her, but she had to be prepared for other outcomes.

She peeked at Daniel; he wasn't paying attention to her, either. He was looking at the array of knives with a disbelieving expression. It made her wonder how long he could survive on his own with what he'd learned so far.

Alex pulled open one of the bigger bags but wasn't thrilled with what she found inside. It was a fairly basic kit, with nothing that she didn't already have. She checked the next bag, then the last. Nothing that wasn't in the first.

"What's missing?" Kevin asked.

She jumped slightly; she hadn't heard him approach. He must have read her disappointed expression.

"I'd like access to some decent trauma supplies, just in case..."

"Okay. Grab up whatever else you want here, and then we'll go get some."

"Just that easy?" she asked skeptically.

"Sure."

She raised one eyebrow. "We're going to walk into a medical facility and ask to purchase some surplus?"

"No!" He made a face implying the stupidity of her suggestion. "Haven't you ever heard the phrase *It fell off a truck*? You got some of that knockout stuff on you now?"

"Yes."

"Then hurry, so we can get out there before all the trucks have finished their deliveries."

• • •

ALEX'S BACKPACK WAS now stocked with ammo for her various appropriated guns—the SIG Sauer, the Glock she hadn't abandoned, the shotgun, Daniel's rifle—and her own PPK. She'd taken two extra handguns from the stash, because you never knew, and ammo for those as well. From the tech case she'd grabbed two sets of goggles, some trackers, and two EMP generators of different sizes. She wasn't sure what she would use any of them for, but she might not have time to get back here if there was an emergency. While she shopped through his gear, Kevin reset the lock so that the usual birth-date code would let her back in.

Or Daniel, if things really went south.

"So, what are my options for chemically incapacitating another human being?" Kevin asked when they were back on the road. Alex drove this time.

"Let's see...do you want airborne or contact?"

Kevin gave her a sidelong look. "Which do you recommend?"

"Depends on your approach. Will the target be in an enclosed space?"

"How would I know? I'll be improvising."

She huffed out a breath. "Fine. Take both. Daniel, can you grab the perfume bottle in the outside pocket of my backpack? It's in a Ziploc bag."

"Found it," Daniel said after a minute. "Here." He passed it up to Kevin. Kevin turned it over in his hands.

"Looks empty."

"Mm-hm," Alex agreed. "Pressurized gas. Now," she said, stretching her left arm across her body and holding her hand toward him. "Take the silver one."

He pulled the ring off her third finger, and then his eyebrows mashed down in surprise when the tiny clear tube and attached rubber squeeze pouch came out one after the other, like a couple of handkerchiefs from the sleeve of a mediocre magician. His expression turned skeptical.

"What's this supposed to do?"

"See the little hatch on the inside? Swing it open. Be careful."

Kevin examined the tiny hollow barb, then looked at the little round rubber bag. It was quiet enough to hear the faint sound of liquid sloshing inside.

"Hold the pouch in your palm," she directed, pantomiming as she explained. "Put your hand down hard on your target." She gestured to Daniel, who obligingly held out his arm. She grabbed his wrist—not violently, just forcefully. "The subject will feel the prick and try to pull away automatically. Hold on. If you're doing it right, the liquid in the pouch will be expelled through the barb." She released Daniel when she finished.

"And then what happens?" Kevin asked.

"Your target takes a nap — for an hour, maybe two, depending on his or her size."

"This thing is tiny," he complained, holding the ring between his thumb and forefinger and staring through the hole.

"Sorry. I'll try to have bigger hands for you next time. Put it on your pinkie."

"Who wears a pinkie ring?"

She smiled. "I think it will suit perfectly."

Daniel chuckled.

Kevin shoved the ring onto his littlest finger, but it made it only over his first knuckle. The pouch barely reached his palm. He'd need more tubing if he ever wanted to hide it in his sleeve. He frowned at the apparatus for a moment, then suddenly grinned. "Neat."

Daniel leaned forward and gestured to the rings Alex still wore. "What do those other two do?"

She lifted her right hand, wiggling her ring finger with the gold band. "Kills you easy." She held up the middle finger of her left hand with the rose-gold band. "Kills you hard."

"Oh, hey!" Kevin said in sudden realization. "Is that what that girlie slap back in West Virginia was about?"

"Yes."

"*Damn.* You're one dangerous little spider, Ollie."

She nodded in agreement. "If I were taller or you were shorter, we wouldn't be having this conversation."

"Well, I guess that was your lucky day."

She rolled her eyes.

"Which one did you try to hit me with?"

She held up the middle finger on her left hand again.

"Harsh," Kevin commented. "Why don't those rings have all the extra stuff?" He waved his hand so that the tube and pouch swung beneath his hand.

"Be careful," she warned. "That could detach."

Kevin caught the little bag and cradled it in his palm. "Right."

"My other rings are coated with venom. A little goes a long way. Just one drop of cone snail venom is enough to kill twenty men your size."

"Let me guess, you keep cone snails and black widow spiders as pets back home?"

"No time for pets, and really, black widow venom is on the very weak end of the damage scale. No, I used to have access to a lot of things. I studied cone snail venom briefly because of the way it targets particular classes of receptors. I was never one to waste an opportunity. I kept what I could and I'm careful with my supplies now."

Kevin looked down at the ring he wore again, considering. It kept him quiet, which Alex appreciated.

She chose Howard University Hospital, because it

was a level-one trauma center and she knew her way around the facility—unless a lot had changed in the past ten years.

She did a slow loop around the buildings, scanning for camera placement and police presence. It was not even seven a.m., but there were plenty of people coming and going.

"How about that one?" Kevin asked, pointing.

"No, that will mostly be linens and paper goods," she muttered.

"Take a break before you do another lap; we don't want to be noticed."

"I know how this works," she lied.

She drove a few streets west and stopped at a small green space. A handful of joggers were doing their rounds, but it was otherwise fairly empty. They waited in silence for ten minutes, then she pulled out and drove a wider circle, staying two blocks out from the roads around the hospital. Eventually she spotted something promising—a white truck labeled HALBERT & SOWERBY SUPPLIERS. She was familiar with the company and was pretty sure they would have usable goods on board.

She tailed the truck into a loading area behind the main building of the hospital. Kevin was ready, fingers already wrapped around the door handle.

"Just drop me behind them, then wait a block up," he told her.

Nodding, she slowed to a brief pause just behind the truck, too close for Kevin to be seen in the mirrors. Once he was out, she reversed a couple of feet and then drove away at the exact posted speed. She glanced into the truck from under her hat as she passed; there was only a driver, no passengers. Still, there were plenty of people in scrubs and maintenance uniforms on the sidewalk. She hoped Kevin could be unobtrusive about this.

She braked at the stop sign on the corner, wondering how she was supposed to wait here when there was no parking. Before she could decide, she saw the white truck coming up behind her, one car back. She drove ahead slowly, goading the car between them to pass, then letting Kevin pass, too. She could see the driver—a very young-looking black man—leaning against the passenger-side window with his eyes closed.

"Well, there aren't any cops following him...yet," she muttered as she began following.

"Will it hurt the guy?" Daniel asked. "What Kevin stuck him with?"

"Not really. He'll have an awful hangover when he wakes up, but nothing permanent."

Kevin drove for about twenty minutes, first putting some distance between them and the hospital, then seeking the right place for the transfer of goods. He decided on a quiet industrial park, pulling to the back where there were several empty loading spaces near closed, roll-down access doors. He backed into one and she parked next to him, on the lee side, where she would be invisible to anyone entering the lot.

She yanked on a pair of latex gloves, handed another to Daniel, and shoved a pair into her pocket.

Kevin already had the back door of the truck open. She handed him the extra gloves, then boosted herself up onto the floor of the cargo hold. Everything inside was secured in opaque white plastic bins, stacked high and anchored to the walls with red nylon cords.

"Help me get these open," she instructed. Kevin started pulling the bins down and removing the lids. Daniel climbed in and followed his lead. Alex went behind them, sorting through her options.

Her main worry was being shot. It seemed the most likely fallout from an offensive action. Of course, she couldn't rule out being knifed or beaten with a blunt object. Still, she was very happy when she found a bin with blowout kits; each had tourniquets, gauze impregnated with QuikClot, and a variety of chest seals. She started a pile, adding different kinds of closure strips and gauze packs, dressings and compression bandages, chemical heating and cooling packs, resuscitation kits, a few bag-valve masks, alcohol and iodine wipes, splints and collars, burn dressings, IV catheters and tubing, saline bags, and handfuls of sealed syringes.

"You planning to start your own field hospital?" Kevin asked.

"You never know what you might need," she countered, then added in her mind, *You might be the one who needs this stuff, idiot.*

"Here," Daniel offered, turning one of the half-depleted bins upside down and dumping what was left into another. He took the now-empty bin and started organizing her pile inside.

"Thanks. I think I've got everything I want."

Kevin secured the bins to the wall, then wiped down the door. She followed him again until he found a place to leave the truck and driver, behind a small strip mall. He quickly cleaned his fingerprints from the cab, and they were on their way.

When they got back to the apartment, Raoul the housekeeper had been and gone, and Val was lying across a low sofa watching a big-screen TV that Alex could have sworn was not there yesterday. It was playing a black-and-white movie.

Today Val wore a pale blue jumpsuit with short shorts and a plunging neckline. Einstein lay on the sofa beside her with his muzzle on her arm. She was petting him rhythmically, and he didn't get up to greet them as they came through the door. He only pounded his tail against the sofa when he saw Kevin.

"So, how did all the spying go?" she asked lazily.

"Just boring groundwork," Kevin said.

"Ugh, then don't tell me about it. And don't leave any of that new stuff in here, either. I don't want the clutter."

"Yes, ma'am," Kevin agreed docilely, and he headed back to Alex and Daniel's room to add to the storage pile.

"I'll get you hooked up on my computer, Ollie," he said as he stacked. "You can watch the playback from the cameras I've got on Carston. And you can listen — there's a bug in the car and a directional mike on the office. The car has a tracker, too, so you can follow his movements for the past several days."

Alex exhaled, already exhausted by the mound of intel to assess. "Thanks."

"I'm starved," Daniel said. "Anyone else for breakfast?"

"Yes, please," Alex said at the same time that Kevin answered, "Hell, yeah."

Daniel smiled and turned for the door.

Alex watched him walk away, then realized that Kevin was watching her watch Daniel.

"What?"

Kevin pursed his lips, as if he were looking for the right way to express himself. He automatically glanced at the bed — still rumpled; Raoul had not been allowed in here — and shuddered.

Alex turned her back on him and went to retrieve

her own computer. She'd want to move the important files onto it.

"Ollie..."

She didn't look up from what she was doing. "What?"

"Can I..."

She held her computer to her chest and turned to face him, waiting for him to finish. Unconsciously, she squared her shoulders.

He hesitated again, then asked, "Can I ask you some questions without getting any specific or graphic answers?"

"Like what?"

"This thing with Danny...I don't want him to get hurt."

"That's not a question."

He glared, then took a deep breath, forcing himself to relax. "When we finish up here, where do you go?"

It was her turn to hesitate. "It...well, it kind of feels like a jinx to assume that I'm going to survive. I honestly haven't thought about what's next."

"C'mon, this isn't that hard," he said disparagingly.

"It's not what I do. You handle it your way, I'll handle it mine."

"You want me to take care of Carston, too?"

"No," she growled, though if his tone hadn't been so condescending, she would have been tempted. "I'll take care of my own problems."

He paused, then asked, "So...what? Do you think you're just going to tag along with us after?"

"That wouldn't be my first choice, no. Going with the theory that I'm still alive then, of course."

"You're a real pessimist."

"It's part of the way I plan. Expect the worst."

"Whatever. Back to my point—if you go your own way, what about Danny? Is it just *Good-bye, thanks for the laughs?*"

She looked away, toward the door. "I don't know. That depends on what he wants. I can't speak for him."

Kevin was silent long enough that she finally had to look back. His face was uncharacteristically vulnerable. Like always, when his features were allowed to relax, he looked a lot more like Daniel.

"You think he'd choose to follow you?" Kevin asked very quietly. "I mean, he just met you. He barely knows you. But...I guess he probably feels like he barely knows me, too, at this point."

"I don't know what he'll want," she said. "I would never ask him to make that choice."

Kevin focused on the air a few inches above her head. "I really wanted the chance to make things up to him. To set him up in a life he could live with. I was hoping, after a while, we could be brothers again."

She had an odd urge to walk across the space between them and put her hand on his shoulder. Probably just because he was still looking like Daniel.

"I won't get in the way of that," she promised. She meant it. Whatever was best for Daniel, that was the main thing.

Kevin stared at her for a minute, his face hardening and turning back to normal. He blew out a huge sigh. "Well, damn it, Ollie, I wish I'd just left that Tacoma thing alone. Millions of lives saved — really, what does that add up to in the face of my brother sleeping with Lucrezia Borgia?"

Alex froze. "What did you say?"

He grinned. "Surprised that I know the appropriate historical analogy? I did pretty well in school, actually. I've got just as many brain cells as my brother."

"No, about Tacoma. What do you mean?"

His grin shifted to confusion. "You know all about that — they gave you the file. You interrogated Danny —"

She leaned toward him, unconsciously clutching her computer more tightly against her ribs. "This is about the job you did with de la Fuentes? Does the *T* in TCX-1 stand for *Tacoma?*"

"I've never heard of TCX-1. The de la Fuentes job was about the Tacoma virus."

"The Tacoma Plague?"

"I never heard it called that. What's going on, Ollie?"

Alex yanked open her computer as she climbed onto the foot of the bed. She pulled up the most recent file she'd worked on—her coded case notes. She scrolled through the list of numbers and initials, feeling the bed shift as Kevin put one knee on it, leaning to read over her shoulder.

It felt like a long time since she'd written these notes. So much had happened, and the thoughts she'd attached to these brief lines were faded.

There it was—terrorist event number three, *TP*, the Tacoma Plague. The letters danced in front of her eyes, only some of them resolving into words in her memory. *J, I-P*, that was the town in India, on the Pakistani border. She couldn't remember what the name of the terrorist cell was, only that they originated out of Fateh Jang. She looked at the initials for the connected names: *DH*—that was the scientist, Haugen; *OM* was Mirwani, the terrorist, and then *P*...The other American she couldn't remember. She pressed her fist to her forehead, trying to force her recall.

"Ollie?" Kevin said again.

"I worked this case—years ago, when the formula was first stolen from the U.S. Long before de la Fuentes got hold of it."

"Stolen from the U.S.? De la Fuentes got it out of Egypt."

"No, it was developed in a lab just outside Tacoma. It was supposed to be theoretical, just research. Haugen...Dominic Haugen, that was the scientist." The story came back to her as she concentrated. "He was on our side, but with the theft, the situation became too sensitive for him to continue where he was. The NSA buried him in a lab somewhere under their control. We had the terrorist cell's second in command. He gave up the location of the lab in Jammu that was successfully creating the virus from the stolen blueprints. Black ops razed the lab. They thought they had the biological-weapon aspect locked up, but there were members of the cell who slipped through. As far as I know, the department was still working with the CIA on hunting them down a couple of years later . . . when Barnaby was killed."

She looked up at him, the wheels in her head spinning so fast that she felt physically dizzy.

"When the CIA called you in, when they burned you—you said there were issues you were trying to track down. What were they?"

He blinked fast, reminding her of Daniel again. "The packaging on the vaccinations—the outside was in Arabic, but the inside packaging, the original labels—everything was in English. And the name, too: Tacoma. It didn't make sense. If de la Fuentes had wanted them translated, he would have had it changed from Arabic to Spanish. I wanted to trace the virus back. I was sure it hadn't originated in Egypt. I figured there had to be an American or a Brit working with the developers somewhere. I wanted to find the guy. You're saying this thing started in *Washington State?*"

"It's got to be the same thing. The timing's right. We get some info about this virus, suddenly they start watching me and Barnaby. Two years later—around the time de la Fuentes got his hands on it, right?— they murder Barnaby. That has to be the catalyst. That's why they killed him and tried to kill me. Because the virus was out there again, and if the public found out, we knew something that could connect it back..."

Barnaby had never told her what had triggered his paranoia, why he'd decided they needed to be ready to flee. She looked at the letters on her screen. *DH,* Dominic Haugen. It was unlikely that the bad guys would leave Haugen alive if they'd felt the need to erase her and Barnaby. Had Haugen been the first to die? Probably in some totally normal, expected way. Car accident. Heart attack. There were so many methods to make it look innocent. Had Barnaby seen some notice of Haugen's death? Had that been the tip-off?

She wanted to do a quick search online, but if she was right about this, then Haugen's name was sure to be flagged. Anyone inquiring into his death—no matter how anonymous the method—would be noticed.

Who was the *P?* She couldn't even be positive she had that letter right. It had been a fleeting mention. Something short, she thought, something snappy...

"Ollie, the packaging...it looked...professional? Is that the right word? It wasn't something put together in a makeshift lab somewhere in the Middle East."

They stared at each other for a moment.

"I always thought it was a stretch," she murmured. "That someone could actually fabricate the virus from nothing more than Haugen's theoretical design. It seemed the equivalent of winning the terrorist lottery."

"You think they stole more than notes?"

"Haugen must have done it—actually created the thing. If there was a supply that large, if the vaccine was packaged up so neatly...they must have been producing it. So working on weaponized viruses wasn't just Haugen's weekend hobby. It was a military project. There were hints of that...something about a lieutenant general's involvement. No one wanted to follow up on the American side of things. They kept us focused on the cell. Usually they let us ask the questions that naturally followed...but I remember, this was different. Carston fed me the questions he wanted."

"So we got burned on the same case," Kevin said darkly.

"I don't believe in that big a coincidence."

"Neither do I."

"Who are they protecting?" Alex wondered. "Whoever it is, he's got to be calling the shots. Which means he knows about both of us."

"Which means we've got to get to him, too."

They stared at each other again.

"Alex? Kev? Guys? Is this place soundproofed?"

Alex looked up slowly, her eyes not totally focusing on Daniel walking through the doorway.

"Is something wrong?" Daniel asked in a quieter tone as he took in the tableau. He hurried to the bed and put one hand on Alex's shoulder.

"Just putting a few things together," Kevin said grimly.

Daniel looked to Alex.

"We need to add another name to our list," she told him.

"Who?"

"That's the problem," Kevin said.

"Let me think," Alex said. "If I didn't know the answer to that question, they wouldn't be trying to kill me." She glanced up at Kevin. "I know this is incredibly nonspecific, but did you ever hear a name beginning with a *P* involved with this on your end?"

"A *P?* I'll have to think about it, but not offhand. I'll go through Deavers's calls again, see if I can turn anything up."

"I'll work on it while I go through the Carston stuff."

Kevin nodded, then looked at Daniel. "I hope you came in here because there's some food ready.

Got to feed Ollie's big brain so she can figure this out."

•   •   •

THEY SET THEIR computers up on the big kitchen island and started into it while they ate. Val and Einstein hadn't moved, but they were watching the shopping channel now. Daniel pulled a stool up beside Alex and looked on as she scanned through the video of the front of Carston's very respectable-looking town house. She fast-forwarded through the downtime when no one was in residence, simultaneously listening to Carston's phone calls on her earbuds. Carston was careful—his work conversations were vague, never naming any person or project specifically, and since the office calls were recorded on an exterior microphone, she could only hear his side. He used so many pronouns it was impossible to follow. She could tell only that there were a few *he*s and *him*s that were getting on Carston's nerves in a bad way and that at least one project was not going well. He sounded stressed. That could have been because of what happened in Texas and the e-mail to Deavers. Did Carston feel in danger? Did he think Kevin knew about him? He would have to play it safe, just in case. Carston didn't get to where he was now by not being paranoid enough.

His house had an alarm system, ornamental bars

on the first-floor windows, and exterior cameras. Some of the footage Kevin gave her appeared to be from those cameras—he must have hacked into the system. The street wasn't ideal—lots of close neighbors, lots of activity on the street both morning and night. A plethora of witnesses.

"You have to break into *that?*" Daniel muttered as she pulled up yet another camera angle of the barred windows.

"Hopefully not."

Alex pointed to the small woman who was walking up the front stairs. She had several paper grocery bags weighing her down as she stuck her key in the door and unlocked the dead bolt. From this angle, Alex could see as she paused in the doorway and punched in the code for the alarm. Her hand covered the keypad; there was no way to read the sequence.

"Housekeeper?" Daniel asked.

"Looks like. And she does his shopping."

"Is that good?"

"It might be. If I could get a new face so I would be able to follow her around a bit."

"What about me?" Daniel asked. "I haven't been on the news in a while."

"Daniel, we haven't watched the news in a while," she pointed out.

"Oh. You think they're doing the bad-guy story now?"

"It's possible. We should check it out."

"You want the news?" Val called from the sofa in the adjacent room.

"Um, not if you're using the TV now," Daniel said politely.

"There's another one in the cabinet to the left of the fridge, two over," she told them.

Daniel walked to the indicated cupboard and pulled the door open to reveal a television screen recessed into the space. The door rolled back into a side pocket.

"Sweet," Kevin muttered, glancing up from his own computer for half a second.

Alex went back to her research while Daniel flipped through channels until he found a twenty-four-hour news network. He set the volume low, then came back to sit with her.

Alex didn't hear Val get up, but suddenly the blonde was leaning over her shoulder.

"That looks really dull," she commented.

"Well, adding my mortality into the equation spices it up a bit," Alex told her.

"Did you say you needed a new face?"

"Um, yes. See, the bruises and bandages make me too memorable."

"And being memorable isn't a good thing in your case?"

"No."

"I could do that."

"Huh?" Alex asked.

"Give you a new face."

Alex turned to give Val her full attention. "What do you mean?"

CHAPTER 26

"This would be easier if you'd stop trying to do two things at once," Val complained.

"Sorry. I'm sort of on a deadline."

"Just hold your head still."

Alex did the best she could. She had Kevin's laptop on her knees with her earbuds plugged into it. While Carston was in his car, she could hear both sides of the conversation. Unfortunately, it seemed Carston usually chose to use his driving time to connect with his only daughter, Erin. They spoke almost nonstop about the granddaughter—the one whose picture was in Alex's locket—and after the first forty-minute discussion about which prekindergarten program was most likely to result in an Ivy League happy ending, Alex had started fast-forwarding as soon as she heard the daughter's voice or, if Carston was in the office, the special tone he used only to speak to Erin. They talked a lot more than Alex would have expected. She stretched her fingers down and touched the Play button. Erin was still blathering on, something about taking Livvy to the zoo. Alex hadn't missed anything. She hit fast-forward again.

"I want you to know this is an imperfect job, and it's your fault."

"Any imperfections are on me, agreed," Alex said.

Val had turned Alex away from the wall of mirrors in the bathroom so she couldn't see what was being done. She knew only that it felt like a coat of heavy, oil-based paint had been applied to her skin. Something pulled across the slash on her jaw, tight and constricting.

She'd thought the guest bathroom was opulent, but this palace was insane. Two families of five could live comfortably in just this room.

She focused her attention back on her computer screen. The housekeeper was arriving again at Carston's. It looked like she brought groceries in about every other day. Alex noted the things she could see in the tops of the bags—a quart of organic skim milk, a box of bran cereal, OJ, coffee beans. She had the housekeeper's license plate, and Kevin had gotten an address. After dark, Alex could run out and put a tracker on the woman's car so she could follow her to the store.

She checked the audio again, and Erin was saying

her good-byes. Alex didn't know how Carston was able to devote so much time to listening to his daughter talk. It was a good thing he had only one child. Probably he multitasked, just like Alex was doing.

On his work calls, there had been no names mentioned at all, let alone one that started with a *P*. She felt as though if she could just push this worry to the back of her mind, her subconscious would figure it out for her. Unfortunately, she couldn't stop obsessing about it, so of course she wasn't making any progress.

"Okay, the final touch," Val said, wrestling a wig onto Alex's head.

"Ouch."

"Beauty is pain. You can look now."

Alex stood stiffly—she'd been immobile for too long—and revolved to face the mirrors.

It gave her a start. She didn't recognize herself right away as the short woman standing next to Val.

"How..." Her fingers went automatically to the place where her scabbed wound should be.

Val slapped her hand away. "Don't touch anything, you'll smear it."

"Where did it all go?"

The face of the woman in the mirror was unmarred and perfect. Her skin looked like it belonged to a dewy fourteen-year-old. Her eyes were huge, enhanced without looking overdone. Her lips were fuller, her cheekbones more pronounced. She had shoulder-length, medium brown hair with reddish highlights. It fell in flattering layers around those suddenly high cheekbones.

"Voilà, your new face," Val said. "That was fun. Next time, I'm trying you as a blonde. You have a good skin tone—it will look natural with a lot of shades."

"This is amazing. I can't believe it. Where did you learn how to do this?"

"I play a lot of different roles." Val shrugged. "But it's fun having a model. I always wanted one of those big Barbie styling heads when I was a kid." She reached out and patted the top of Alex's wig. "Or a little sister. But the plastic head was my preference."

"I'm probably ten years older than you," Alex protested.

"What a nice compliment. But whatever my age might actually be, you're still not older when it comes to the things that count."

"If you say so." Alex wasn't about to argue; Val had just handed her an unexpected get-out-of-jail-free card. "My own mother wouldn't know me."

"I can go sexier," Val promised. "But you wanted inconspicuous..."

"This is probably the sexiest I've looked in my whole life. I'd be scared to see what *sexier* looks like."

"I bet Danny would like it," Val purred.

"By the way...where did I screw that up? What tipped you off there?"

Val smiled. "Please. When two people are that into each other, it *radiates* off them. You didn't do anything."

Alex sighed. "Thanks for passing your observations on to Kevin."

"You're being sarcastic, but you *should* thank me. Aren't things easier now, without the secrecy?"

"I guess so...but he nearly shot me in the head, so there's that."

"Little ventured, little gained."

Alex approached the mirror wall and leaned in close to examine the disguise. There was some kind of prosthetic skin covering the wound on her jaw. She moved her mouth carefully, watching for expressions that might pull too far, make the fraud obvious. She could see a slight ripple when she smiled, but the layers of the wig mostly obscured that part of her face anyway. She wouldn't have to worry about someone noticing something wrong with her, even close up. Sure, people would be able to tell she was wearing makeup, but most normal women did. Hardly something that would draw attention.

She could accelerate her plans now. She didn't need to wait for dark. She grinned, then smoothed the expression to ease the tension in her fake skin. The new freedom was a heady thing.

Alex skipped quickly down the stairs, computer tucked under her arm. She already had a pretty workable plan—low risk, minimal exposure—so she was listening to the calls only in the vain hope that Carston would screw up and say something meaningful. It was unlikely, but she'd finish it out. Later. Right now she could get started on the specific preparation.

"Huh," Kevin grunted. Alex saw him look past her to where Val followed. "Hey, Val, how many virgins did you have to sacrifice to make her look like that?"

"I don't need any satanic help to do what I do," Val responded. "And virgins aren't useful for anything."

Daniel got up from the couch where he was watching the news—taking it seriously as his assignment—and came around the stairs to see what Kevin and Val were talking about.

Alex hesitated on the bottom stair, feeling oddly vulnerable. She wasn't used to caring if she looked pretty or not.

Daniel did a small double take, then his face relaxed into a smile.

"I'd gotten so used to seeing you with the bruises, I'd almost forgotten what you looked like without them," he said, and then his grin got wider. "It's nice to see you again."

Alex knew she hadn't looked like *this* on the train, but she let it go.

"I'm headed out to place the tracker," Alex told them. "Shouldn't take me long."

"Do you want me to come?" Daniel asked.

"Better to keep your face hidden in the daytime," she told him. He didn't look happy about it, but his expression was resigned. She imagined how she would feel if he ran out to do some surveillance, and she could understand his reluctance.

"It won't be anything," she promised.

"Take the sedan," Kevin said, gesturing to a set of keys on the counter.

"Wilco," Alex said, imitating his soldier tone. He didn't seem to notice.

Carston's housekeeper would probably be home by now, unless she had errands to run. She only worked mornings there. Of course, she could have other clients, but Alex imagined that Carston would pay well so he wouldn't have to share—he would want her free if he needed something. Alex drove the black sedan across town, not all that far, really, from Daniel's empty apartment. She was glad he was safely tucked away at Val's. She was sure they'd have some kind of surveillance on his place, just hoping he'd be stupid enough to come back for his toothbrush or favorite T-shirt.

The housekeeper's neighborhood had street parking only. She found the decade-old white minivan a block over from the apartments where the woman lived. There was plenty of traffic, both cars and pedestrians. She found a spot near the minimart on the corner and set off for a walk.

The early-summer heat had her sweating almost immediately. Unlike Kevin, she didn't have a myriad of costumes to choose from, so she was in her blazer again today, and it felt twice as thick as usual. Oh, well, she needed the pockets. Hopefully the makeup wouldn't sweat off.

There were enough people around her that she felt invisible, just one of the herd. The numbers dwindled as she crossed over to the next block, but she still didn't stand out.

She pulled her phone out of her pocket and hit Redial.

Kevin answered on the first ring. "What's the problem, Oleander?"

"Just calling to say hi," she told him.

"Ah. Blending?"

"Of course."

"Talk to Danny. I don't have time to blend with you."

"I'd prefer it anyway," she said, but he was already gone.

She heard a thud as the phone hit something, and then Daniel said, "Ouch."

Alex took a deep, calming breath. Kevin always made her want to stab things.

"Alex, are you all right?"

"Absolutely."

Kevin shouted something in the background.

"Kevin says you're trying to look natural," Daniel said.

"That's part of it," she agreed.

She was only two cars from the minivan now. There was a man ahead of her but walking in the same direction so his back was to her. She couldn't hear anyone close behind her, but there could be someone who had her in his sight line. She didn't turn to look.

"So I guess we should talk about something normal people talk about," Daniel was saying.

"Right."

"Um, what would you like for dinner? Do you want to stay in again?"

Alex smiled. "Staying in sounds great. I'll eat anything you feel like cooking."

"You make things too easy for me."

"There are enough difficulties in the world without adding my own." She flipped a few locks of the wig out of her eyes, her fingers knocking into the phone. It skittered across the sidewalk and teetered on the edge of the curb. "Hold on," she called toward it. "I dropped the phone."

She knelt and swiped the phone up, holding on to the edge of the minivan's wheel well for support. She jumped back to her feet, brushing at the knees of her leggings.

"Sorry about that," she said.

"Did you just plant the tracking device?"

She started walking again, heading for the end of the block, where she could begin circling back to the car. "Yes."

"Very smooth."

"I told you it was nothing. I'll see you soon."

"Drive safe. I love you."

Kevin shouted something in the background, and there was another thud close beside the phone.

"Are you *kidding?*" Daniel shouted back. "A knife?"

Alex ended the call and picked up the pace a little. She couldn't leave them alone for twenty minutes.

Things had returned to normal—or her new version of it—by the time she got back to the apartment. Daniel was still studiously watching the news. Val had just brought Einstein back from a walk and was filling the lovely crystal bowl with water for him. Kevin was watching the feed from his cameras and sharpening a machete. Home sweet home.

"Anything?" she asked Daniel.

"Nothing about me. Apparently the vice president is bowing out before the election after all. I guess those recent scandal rumors aren't entirely unfounded. So of course, everyone is speculating about who President Howland will select for his running mate."

"Fascinating," Alex murmured in a tone that implied the opposite. She dumped her bag onto one of the white bar stools, sat on the next one over, and opened her computer. All seemed quiet at Casa Carston, so she started scrubbing backward to see if she'd missed anything while she was out. So far she hadn't discovered any regular visitors besides the housekeeper and the security service that drove by once daily in the afternoon.

Daniel flipped to a different news network, where another version of the same story was running. "You don't care who the president runs with?" he asked. "Howland's pretty popular. Whoever he chooses will probably be the vice president, and possibly the president four years from now."

"Ventriloquist dummies," Kevin grumbled, setting down the machete and starting to work on a long boning knife.

Alex nodded in agreement as she slowed the feed to watch two teenagers amble past Carston's house and up the block.

"What do you mean?" Daniel asked.

"I don't worry about the puppet," Kevin said. "I worry about the guy pulling the strings."

"That's a pretty cynical attitude about the democratic nation you used to work for."

Kevin shrugged. "Yup."

"Alex, Republican or Democrat?" Daniel asked.

"Pessimist."

She reached for the other computer, the one with the bugged calls on it, and plugged in her headphones.

"So nobody cares that the front-runner is some ultra-right senator from Washington State who used to work for the Defense Intelligence Agency?"

The first call Alex had missed was from the daughter again—she could tell from Carston's warm, fatherly voice. She started fast-forwarding.

"Makes sense," Val was saying, pulling a rubber band out of her hair. She was wearing sweaty workout clothes and looked like she should be on a *Maxim* cover anyway. "Howland is soft. Get someone with a conservative edge, pull some voters off the fence. Plus, the new guy is one part grandpa, one part silver fox, with a catchy two-syllable name. Howland could do worse." She shook her golden hair out, and it fell into perfect waves down her back.

"It's sad, but you're probably right. Just a beauty pageant."

"Everything is, honey," Val told him.

Alex stopped to check the recording, but Carston was still just listening and muttering kindly *mm-hmm*s. She sped it up again.

"I suppose I should get used to it, since I imagine I don't get to vote anymore." Daniel frowned. "Vice President Pace. Do you think he was born with that name, or did he alter it to make it voter-friendly? Wade Pace. Is that something you would name a kid?"

"I wouldn't name a kid anything," Val said. "Because I would never be dumb enough to bring one home."

Alex's fingers reached down automatically to stop the recording.

"What was that?" she asked.

"Just explaining that I'm not the mom type," Val said.

"No, Daniel, what was that name?"

"Senator Pace? Wade Pace?"

"That name...it sounds familiar."

"I think everyone knows his name," Daniel said. "He's been positioning himself for this kind of promotion, not exactly low profile."

"I don't follow politics," Alex said. She stared at the TV now, but it just showed some news anchor. "How much do you know about this guy?"

"Just the stuff they're running on the news," Daniel answered. "Sterling service record, all the normal clichés."

"He was military?"

"Yes, some kind of general, I think."

"A lieutenant general?"

"Maybe."

Kevin was paying attention now. "Wade Pace. Pace with a *P*. That our guy?"

Alex stared into space, unconsciously rocking slightly back and forth on her stool. "He's from Washington State...he worked defense intelligence..." She looked up at Kevin. "Let's say the DIA is theoretically exploring some biological-weapons options. This guy's already got some political aspirations, so of course he makes sure the money gets spent in his hometown. They would have had plenty of innocuous goals on the surface—all the outsiders would see was the economic boost. Probably helped get him his seat in the Senate. Great. But then, years later, the fabricated virus is stolen. Obviously, no one can know that he ever had a hand in its creation. No one can know it exists. We track down the bad guys, and they give up too much information. Wade Pace has big dreams. Anyone who heard his name in connection with this virus—"

"Has to be preemptively silenced," Kevin finished. "And who knows exactly what the too-thorough CIA agent might have seen? Better shut him up, too."

"Can't take any chances," Alex whispered. "Not when you're reaching this high."

It was silent for thirty seconds.

"Wow," Val said, so loudly it made Alex jump. "Are you guys going to assassinate the vice president?" She sounded utterly thrilled by the idea.

"He's not the vice president yet," Kevin said. "He's nothing, officially. That means no Secret Service."

Daniel's mouth was hanging open.

Higher stakes again, but not by so very much. In

the end, no matter what else he represented, Wade Pace was just one beating heart.

Kevin locked eyes with Alex. "So he put a hit out on me, my brother, you, your friend...so he could try to be president. Oh, I'm going to *enjoy* this one."

She opened her mouth but then quickly snapped it shut again. It would be a lot easier and safer—for her—to let Kevin do as much of the wet work as possible.

But there was her anonymity—Daniel's, too, so she might as well lump in Kevin's matching face—which had to be protected above all else if this plan was going to work. Kevin might be better at killing people than she was, but she was pretty sure that she was better at doing it with minimal ripples. *If you want something done right...*

"As much as I hate to deprive you of any fun, I think you might want to let me take this one." She shivered slightly. This was probably a big mistake. Was she turning into the adrenaline junkie she'd accused Daniel of being? She didn't *think* so. She felt nothing but dread at the idea of adding another job to her list. "Quiet is the goal, right? It won't get too much attention if our wannabe president dies of a heart attack or a stroke—not the same coverage as if he were found shot in some kind of home invasion."

"I can be quiet," Kevin insisted. His eyebrows were pulling down into a scowl.

"Natural-causes quiet?"

"Close enough."

"*Close enough* puts our other targets on high alert."

"They're already on high alert."

"So how do you see this happening?"

"I'll improvise when I get there."

"Sound plan."

"You know how many people die in household accidents every day in this country?"

"No. But I'm positive that more white men in their early sixties die from health-related problems than from any other reason."

"Okay, great, a heart attack would be the *quietest* way for Pace to die, agreed. How are you going to get in, shorty? Knock on the door and ask to borrow a cup of sugar? Be sure to wear your frilly apron—really sell it."

"I can adapt the Carston plan. I'll just need a few more days of research on Pace—"

Kevin's hand slapped loudly against the counter. "We don't have that kind of time. We've delayed too long as it is. You know Deavers and Carston aren't wasting the prep time we've already given them."

"Rushing just leaves openings they can take advantage of. Proper preparation—"

"You are *so annoying!*"

She hadn't realized how close together she and Kevin had gotten—pretty much spitting in each other's face from about six inches away—until Daniel's hand suddenly shot in between them.

"Can I interrupt to suggest the obvious?" he asked.

Kevin smacked his hand away. "Stay out of it, Danny."

Alex took a deep, calming breath. "What's obvious?" she asked Daniel.

"Alex, you have the best plan for how to . . . um, assassinate the senator." He shook his head quickly. "I can't believe this is real."

"It's real," Kevin said harshly. "And I wouldn't call a plan with no entry point the best plan."

"Let me finish. Alex has the best . . . methodology. Kevin, you have the best chance of getting in undetected."

"Yeah, I do," Kevin said belligerently.

"Oh," Alex said, feeling suddenly disgruntled for some reason. Probably just bruised pride and the irritation of having to cooperate with someone so obnoxious. "You're right," she admitted to Daniel. "Again."

He smiled.

"What?" Kevin demanded. "And stop with the goo-goo eyes, you'll make me vomit."

"Obviously"—Alex drew the word out into almost five syllables—"we have to do this together. You go in with my premixed solution in hand. Actually . . ." Her brain started turning over options. "More than one solution, I think. We'll have to stay in contact so I can guide you to the best application—"

Kevin gave her a withering look. "*You're* in command, and I'm just following orders on the ground?"

Alex stared him down. "Tell me your better plan."

Kevin rolled his eyes, but then refocused. "Fine. It makes sense. Whatever."

Alex felt better already. She could perform her part without any risk. And though she didn't love to admit it, she knew Kevin could do his.

Kevin snorted like he could hear her thoughts, then said, "Can I ask one favor?"

"What do you want?"

"When you're mixing your little beakers of poison, could you make this one hurt? Hurt *bad?*"

Alex smiled in spite of her fear. "*That* I can manage."

He pursed his lips for a minute. "This is weird, Ollie. I...well, I almost like you right now."

"The feeling will pass."

"You're right—it's fading already." He sighed. "How long will you need with your chemistry set?"

Alex calculated quickly. "Give me three hours."

"I'll research my new target, then."

Kevin grabbed his machete and other knives and headed upstairs, whistling.

Alex stood and stretched. Even with the new

pressure and attached dread, it felt good to have the answer. The missing name had been an irritant, like an itch on the inside of her skull. Now she could concentrate on her next move.

· · ·

"ALL RIGHT, I'M in the master bath."

Kevin's voice was muted, for Kevin, but still louder than Alex felt was safe. If she'd mentioned her concern, he would only have reminded her that he was the expert now, but still. He was just so cocky.

Alex wondered if he'd brought Einstein into the house with him. Probably, she thought, but of course the dog made no sound.

"Make sure you've got his side of things. I don't want to kill the wife." Alex couldn't bring herself to speak above a whisper despite his apparent comfort.

"What?"

"Make sure you find *his* stuff," she murmured a little louder. "Nothing unisex, like toothpaste."

"I'm pretty sure the right-hand side medicine cabinet belongs to our guy. Refill safety razor blades, Excedrin, SPF forty-five sunblock, Centrum Silver, some makeup, but it's all flesh tones…"

"Be positive."

"I am. Lots of lipsticks and perfumes on the left side."

"Some things they might share…check the drawers under the medicine cabinet."

Alex pictured the pretty blond woman she'd seen standing beside Wade Pace in the official photos. Carolyn Josephine Merritt-Pace. She was only ten years the senator's junior, but she looked a full quarter of a century younger. Whatever surgeries she had undergone, she'd been circumspect enough to keep things minimal; she'd retained her warm, beaming smile that crinkled the corners of her eyes and had every appearance of being genuine. She'd inherited a fortune from her aristocratic southern family, much of which she used to fund her various causes — literacy, feeding hungry children, saving music programs in inner-city schools, building shelters for the homeless. Never anything controversial. She had been a stay-at-home mother for their two daughters, both of whom had graduated from Magnolia League schools and were now married to respectable men — a pediatrician and a college professor. From everything Alex had learned in her hurried research about the senator's wife, Mrs. Merritt-Pace seemed a pleasant enough woman. Certainly not deserving of the painful death her husband was about to suffer. *Hopefully* about to suffer, Alex amended. There was still so much that was left to luck.

"I've got three boxes of bar soap, a pack of extra toothbrushes, ChapStick in two flavors, cherry and strawberry...pomade, cotton pads, Q-tips...Next drawer down — oh, now here we go. Hemorrhoid cream. That's fitting. Suppositories, too. Whatcha think, Ollie?"

"That might work. I'd love to use something topical rather than going the oral route, just to separate this as much as possible from Carston. But he might not use either the cream or the suppositories regularly."

"A good point. Though it would be so great to literally shove this poison up—oh, hey, is our guy a smoker?"

"Um...hold on one second."

Alex typed the phrase *Does Wade Pace smoke?* into her open browser window. She was immediately flooded with articles and pictures. She clicked on the images—poor-quality photographs taken from behind or at a great distance. Wade Pace—younger than he was now, still some dark in his hair, usually in a military uniform—was never at the center of the photo, but it was easy enough to pick him out, cigarette in hand. And then the more recent photos where he *was* centered; these were after he'd morphed into the "silver fox" Val had called him, and he never held a cigarette. But several photographers had focused in on the nicotine patch just slightly visible through the sleeve of his white button-down. Another on vacation, in a garish Hawaiian shirt, the bottom corner of the tan patch showing just below the sleeve. The vacation picture was from April. Not that long ago.

"Looks like he used to be," Alex said. "Tell me you found the patches."

"NicoDerm CQ. One half-used box, with three unopened packages behind it. I'll check the trash."

Alex waited eagerly through the short silence.

"Affirmative. Used patches in the trash under his sink. I'd say this bin gets emptied regularly. So he's still actively using them."

"This couldn't be more perfect," Alex said through her teeth. "Use the syringe marked with the number three."

"Got it."

She could hear the quiet pull of a zipper.

"Don't let the liquid come in contact with your skin. Come at it from the seam—don't leave an obvious pinhole."

"I'm not an idiot. How much?"

"Depress the syringe halfway."

"It's pretty small, are you sure—you know what, never mind. How soon will it dry?"

"A few hours. Put it—"

"Underneath the top patch, right?" Kevin interrupted. "Second down."

"Yes, that will work."

Alex heard Kevin's low chuckle.

"Mission accomplished. Wade Pace is one very deserving dead man walking. Moving on to target number two."

"Will you check in when you're in position?"

"Negative. Should be less than twenty-four. I'll see you back at the apartment."

"Fine."

"Get on your guy, Ollie."

Her voice was a little higher-pitched when she answered. "Yeah. I'll have that, um, done before you're back."

He tuned in to her nervousness, and his tone became gruff, commanding. "You'd better. If I cause ripples, your plan might not work."

"Right."

He disconnected before she could. Again.

Alex took a deep breath and set the phone and the computer down on the bed next to her.

Daniel was cross-legged on the floor at her feet, one hand curled loosely around her calf. His eyes hadn't left her face throughout the phone call.

"Did you get all that?" she asked.

Daniel nodded. "I can't believe he didn't wake anyone. Tell me my voice isn't so piercing."

She grinned. "It's not."

He leaned forward to put his chin on her knee. She felt his hand tighten around her leg.

"And now it's your turn." He said the words in barely more than a whisper, but the volume didn't disguise his intensity.

"Not quite yet." She glanced automatically at the

digital clock she'd set up as part of her temporary lab. The display read 4:15. "I've got a few hours till showtime."

She felt the shift against her skin as his jaw tightened.

"I'm not doing anything dangerous," she reminded him. "I won't be breaking into anyone's fortress. It's not so different from placing the tracker."

"I know. I keep telling myself that."

Alex stood, stretching, and Daniel leaned back to give her room. She nodded to the corner where her lab equipment was spread out inefficiently across a variety of end tables. She'd taken advantage of the setup to create a healthy supply of *Survive* after she was done with the recipes for Pace.

"I suppose I should clean this up before it upsets Val."

Daniel got to his feet. "Can I help?"

"Sure. Just don't touch anything without gloves."

It didn't take long; she'd had so much practice setting her lab up and taking it down, sometimes with an urgent deadline. Daniel was quick to grasp the order of things, and soon he had the proper case ready before she had the equipment totally dismantled. As she carefully wrapped up the last round-bottomed flask, she glanced at the clock again. She still had hours before Val would need to start on her makeup.

"You look exhausted," Daniel commented.

"We got an early start. Val will fix me up so I'm presentable."

"A nap might not hurt, either."

Alex was fairly sure that she wouldn't be able to fall asleep. She was working to seem composed so that Daniel wouldn't worry, but in truth she could feel the seeds of panic beginning to take root in her stomach lining. Not that she'd lied to him about anything she would be doing, but she wasn't anywhere close to relaxed about the next phase. The actual action part. The truth was, she'd fallen back into her usual mind-set, gotten very comfortable with preparation. Now that it was time for her to implement the plan, her nervous system was in overdrive. Still, even just resting would probably be smart.

"Good idea."

• • •

AS ALEX WATCHED Carston's housekeeper walk through the automatic doors into the huge supermarket, she took a few slow, deep breaths, trying to center herself. She examined her face in the visor mirror and was reassured by the illusion Val had created. Alex was sandy blond today, quite believably so. Her makeup appeared understated, despite all the coverage. Alex was happy to see that her nose was settling into its new shape, probably permanently. Every little bit helped.

A few other shoppers parked and entered, and Alex

knew it was time to move. One more deep breath. This wasn't that hard. Just a normal shopping trip for now.

Inside, the market was busy. It was a diverse group of patrons, and Alex was sure she wouldn't stick out. She was suddenly reminded of Daniel's catastrophic shopping spree in Childress, and she was surprised to find herself smiling. She blamed her reaction on nerves.

Despite the traffic, it wasn't hard to find the woman she was looking for. The housekeeper was wearing a bright yellow cotton wrap dress, and the color stood out. Rather than follow her through the store, Alex worked the opposite pattern and crossed paths with her every other aisle. It put Alex in the woman's sight line more often but seemed more natural, less creepy. The woman—who appeared to be about fifty from close up, in good shape and fairly attractive—paid Alex no attention. Meanwhile Alex filled her cart with random items that seemed innocuous—milk, bread, toothpaste—and then added the few items that mattered.

Carston liked these small bottles of organic orange juice. They must expire quickly, because the housekeeper bought a few every trip but never stocked up. Alex grabbed three—the same number as in the housekeeper's cart—and put them in the front child seat of her own.

She wheeled over to an empty aisle—no one was looking for birthday cards or office supplies this morning—and then uncapped the small syringe in her pocket. It was a very slender needle, and it left almost no mark behind when she pushed it through the plastic of the orange juice bottle, just under the screw-off cap. She kept her body turned toward the cards, as if she were looking for the perfect sentimental phrase. When she was done, she grabbed a glittery congratulations card in hot pink and put it in the cart. Maybe she'd give it to Kevin when he finished his mission. It was the kind of glitter that would stick to someone for days.

She and Barnaby had called this drug simply *Heart Attack*, because that's what it caused. Sometimes after the interrogation was over, the department needed to dispose of a subject in a way that looked natural. After about three hours, *Heart Attack* broke down into a metabolite that was nearly impossible to trace. A man of Carston's age, in his physical condition, and factoring in the high-stress job—well, Alex greatly doubted that anyone would look too carefully at the cause of death, at least in the very beginning. Sure, if he were twenty-five and ran marathons, it might look more suspicious.

Alex moved to the bakery next, because it was near the cashiers and had an unobstructed view of the shoppers waiting to pay. It took about ten minutes as she pretended to dither between a baguette or ciabatta rolls, but then the housekeeper appeared from aisle 19 and got into the checkout line. Alex threw the baguette in her cart and joined the next line over.

This was the tricky part. She'd have to stay pretty close to the woman as they left the store. Alex's inconspicuous black sedan was parked right next to the minivan. As the woman was loading her groceries, Alex was going to trip with her arms full of bags and fall into the minivan's bumper. It shouldn't be too hard to leave her juice in the back of the car. Hopefully snagging the woman's juice bottles would be possible, but if not, she assumed the housekeeper would load them all into the fridge, even if she didn't have the right number.

Alex eyed the conveyor belt next to hers, double-checking that the juice was there. She spotted what she was looking for and glanced quickly away.

As her own purchases slid across the scanner, her brows furrowed. Something was off. Something wasn't matching the mental picture. She glanced back at the other conveyor belt, trying to pin it down.

The bagger was packing a box of Lucky Charms. The housekeeper had never bought that kind of cereal for Carston, as far as Alex had been able to see. Carston was a creature of habit, and he ate the same fiber-heavy cereal every morning. Sugary marshmallows with plastic prizes were not his MO.

Another quick peek, head down. The usual coffee beans, the low-fat creamer, the quart of skim milk, but there was also a half a gallon of whole milk and a box of Nilla Wafers.

"Paper or plastic, miss? Miss?"

Alex quickly refocused, pulled her wallet open, and grabbed three twenties. "Paper, please," she said. The housekeeper always got paper.

Her mind was turning over and over as she waited for her change.

Maybe the housekeeper got groceries for herself while she was shopping for Carston. But if she got her own milk, she'd have to carry it inside and put it in Carston's fridge until she was done for the day, so it wouldn't spoil in the heat. And she'd never done that in the past.

Was Carston expecting guests?

Alex's heart pounded uncomfortably as she followed the woman through the automatic front doors, her two bags both gripped in her left hand.

She needed Carston to be the one who enjoyed that bottle of OJ. But what if a friend grabbed it instead? A friend who *was* twenty-five and a marathoner? It would be obvious what she had attempted. Carston would change his habits, beef up his security. And he would know it was Alex, without a doubt. That she was alive, and nearby.

The hunt would begin again, closer than ever.

Should she go with the odds? The juice was Carston's thing. Probably he wouldn't offer it to someone else. But what if?

As her mind raced through the possibilities, a small piece of meaningless information—or so she'd categorized it—popped into her head and suggested a new prospect.

The zoo. The daughter had kept going on and on about the zoo. And all the calls, every day, some of them hours long. What if Erin Carston-Boyd wasn't always in such close touch with her father? What if Alex, in her hurry to get to the important calls, had fast-forwarded through vital information—like a pending visit from his daughter and granddaughter? The DC zoo was famous. Exactly the kind of place you'd take your out-of-town granddaughter. Just like Lucky Charms was exactly the kind of cereal an indulgent grandpa would have on hand for her breakfast.

Alex sighed, quietly but deeply.

She couldn't risk poisoning the child.

Now what? The coffee beans? But Erin would drink coffee, too. Maybe another kind of toxin, something that looked like salmonella?

She couldn't wait until the family went back where they belonged. Deavers and Pace would be dead by then—if they weren't already—and Carston would be on high alert. This was her one chance to stay ahead of the panicked reaction. There would be six bottles of juice, only one poisoned...odds were Carston would drink it...it was unlikely the child would be hurt...

Ugh, she groaned mentally, and slowed her pace. She knew she wasn't going to do it. And she couldn't go back to his favorite sidewalk café and add an extra ingredient to his chicken parm; he'd surely given up that habit once she'd contacted him there. She'd be stuck with something really obvious and dangerous now, like borrowing Daniel's rifle and shooting Carston through his kitchen window. Her chances of getting caught—and killed—would be much, much higher than she'd planned.

Kevin was going to be disgusted with her. Only one person on her list, and she'd already blown it. She couldn't resent that reaction; she was disgusted with herself, too.

As though he could read her mind, just then Kevin called. She felt the vibration in her pocket, then pulled the phone out and read the number. She hit Answer and put it to her ear, but didn't say anything. She was still too close to the housekeeper, and she didn't want the woman to hear her voice and turn, getting another, closer look at the blond woman shadowing her. Perhaps the housekeeper was still the way in. Alex couldn't afford to be noticed.

Alex waited for Kevin to start in on her, irrationally sure he had somehow sensed that she was failing; *Way to drop the ball, Oleander,* in the half shout that was his normal volume.

Kevin said nothing. She pulled the phone back to look at the screen. Had they been disconnected? Had he dialed her by accident?

The call was live. The seconds counted upward in the bottom corner of the screen.

Alex almost said, *Kevin?*

Four years of paranoia stopped her tongue.

She pressed the phone to her ear and listened intently. There was no ambient sound of a car or movement. No wind. No animal sounds, no human sounds.

Goose bumps erupted on the backs of her arms, raised the hair on her neck. She'd walked past her car, and now she had to keep going. Her eyes darted around while she kept her head still; she focused on a dumpster in the back corner of the lot. Her pace quickened. She was too close to the center of her enemy's power. If they were tracing this call, it would not take them long to get here. She wanted to run, wanted it badly, but she kept herself to a quick, purposeful walk.

Still no sound from the other end of the line. The cold, heavy hollow in the pit of her stomach grew larger.

Kevin wasn't going to suddenly start speaking to her, she knew that. Still, she hesitated for one more second. Once she did what she knew she had to do now, it was over. Her only connection to Kevin was severed.

She hung up. The numbers at the bottom of the screen told her the call had lasted for only seventeen seconds. It felt like much more time had passed.

She walked around the side of the dumpster, where she wasn't visible from the parking lot. She couldn't see anyone, which hopefully meant no one could see her.

She set the groceries on the ground.

In the lining of her purse, she had a small lock-picking kit. She'd never had to use it for its real purpose, but it came in handy now and then when she worked with some of her smaller reflux rings and adapters. She pulled the thinnest probe, then used it to pop the SIM card tray out from her phone. Both card and tray went into her bag.

Using the hem of her T-shirt, she carefully wiped the phone down, handling it only through the fabric. The tether of the shirt's length made it hard to get the phone through the side hatch on the dumpster; it was too high up. She had to toss the phone when she couldn't reach far enough, but she got it through in one try.

Alex grabbed the paper bags, spun back around, and walked quickly to her car. The minivan was just exiting the lot. She couldn't tell if the housekeeper had noticed her side trip. She took the longest strides she was capable of as she hurried back.

The phone was gone, but she could almost see the seconds still ticking away in the corner of the screen. There were two possibilities now, and one of those possibilities gave her a very tight deadline indeed.

CHAPTER 27

"Alex, he just pocket-dialed you," Daniel argued.

"Danny's right," Val agreed. "You're overreacting. It's nothing."

Alex shook her head, feeling the pull in her jaw as her teeth clenched. "We need to move," she said flatly.

"Because the bad guys might be torturing Kevin for information as we speak," Val recapped. She used the patient, humoring voice people used with very young children and the elderly.

Alex's answer was cold and hard. "It won't be a joke if they come for you, Val. I can promise you that."

"Look, Alex, your own plan had just failed," Val reminded her. "You were already upset. Kevin called you and didn't say anything. That is all that happened. I think it's a little bit of a leap to assume it was more than an accident."

"It's what they do," Alex said in a slow, even voice.

Even before Barnaby had gotten her the appropriate classified reading material, she'd seen some of this in action. "The subject has a phone with one number on it. You call that number and see what kind of information you can get from it. You track the signal you've just created. You find the person on the other end."

"Well, there's nothing to find, though, right?" Daniel asked encouragingly. "You tossed the phone. It can't lead them to anything more than a parking lot that's not connected to us."

"The phone is a dead end," she agreed. "But if they have Kevin..."

Doubt rippled across Daniel's face. Val still wore a patronizing expression.

"Do you think they would have killed him?" Daniel asked in a voice that was almost a whisper.

"That's the best-case scenario," she said bluntly. She didn't know how to sugarcoat it or say it in a gentler way. "If he's dead, they can't hurt him anymore. And we're safe. If he's alive..." She took a deep breath and refocused. "Like I said, we need to move."

Val was unconvinced. "You really think he'd sell Danny out?"

"Look, Val, I would never question your understanding on anything remotely feminine. That's your world. This is mine. I am not exaggerating when I say that everyone breaks. It doesn't matter how strong

Kevin is or how much he loves his brother. It may take a while, but he *will* tell them where we are. And for his sake, I hope it doesn't take that long."

It would, though, and she knew it. Rocky as her relationship with Kevin had always been, she had learned to trust him, to *know* him. He would buy her the time she needed to get Daniel and Val somewhere safe. Partly because he did love his brother, and partly because of his pride. He'd never give Deavers what he wanted easily. Kevin would make them work for every word they pried out of him.

She was glad it wasn't her job to break Kevin. She was sure he would be the hardest case she'd ever faced. If anyone could do it—actually take his secrets to the grave with him—that person might be Kevin Beach. Maybe he would have broken her perfect record.

For a second, she could see it vividly—Kevin restrained on the state-of-the-art table in the old lab, herself standing over him. How would she have worked the case? If things had panned out just slightly differently—if her Pakistani subject had never murmured the name Wade Pace—the scenario she pictured could have been her reality.

She shook the image away and looked up at Daniel and Val. Alex could see that her tension—her intensity and dark certainty—were finally getting to Daniel, at least.

"If they did get Kevin...what do you think would

happen to Einstein?" Val asked, still skeptical, but her lapis eyes were abnormally vulnerable.

Alex winced. Why had she learned to care so much about an animal on top of everything else? What a stupid thing to do.

"We don't have time to figure everything out right now," she said. "Do you have a place to go, Val? A place Kevin wouldn't know about?"

"I've got a million places." Val's face hardened. Her perfect features suddenly looked like they belonged to a beautiful doll, cold and empty. "You?"

"Our options are a little more limited, but I'll figure something out. Pack up the things you want to save—it won't be safe to come back here. Can I keep the wig?"

Val nodded.

"Thanks. Do you have another car besides the one we've been using?" Kevin had taken the McKinleys' SUV when he and Einstein had set off just after midnight.

"I've got a couple here. That one isn't mine. Kevin was driving it when he got here."

Val pivoted slowly, gracefully, and then sauntered to the stairs. Alex couldn't tell if she was going to pack or headed up to catch a nap. Val didn't believe her.

Alex's mind was racing in a hundred different directions. They'd have to get a new car quickly and dump the one Kevin knew about. There were so many details she had to think through, and she had to do it fast.

Alex turned and hurried back to the guest room. She had to pack, too.

And think. She hadn't planned for this. She should have.

Daniel followed her down the hallway. "Tell me what I need to do," he said as they walked through the door.

"Can you get everything back into the duffel bags? I . . . I need to think for a few minutes. We can't afford any mistakes today. Just let me concentrate, okay?"

"Of course."

Alex lay down on the bed, then crossed both arms over her face. Daniel worked quietly in the corner; the noise wasn't distracting. She tried to think through all the moves they had available to them, everything Kevin didn't know.

There wasn't much. She couldn't even go back for Lola — Kevin had picked the boarding facility.

She took another centering breath and put that thought away. There was no time for sadness now.

It would be small motels for a while. Cash only. Luckily she had plenty of Kevin's drug money. They'd be able to keep their heads down.

Of course, Carston would expect that. Her face and Daniel's would end up on a police flyer e-mailed to all the potential stops for a thousand miles. Since they'd already rolled the Daniel story, maybe they'd cast her as his captive. It would be hard to sell the other version, given Alex's and Daniel's relative sizes.

They could camp out of whatever car they found, as they'd done before. The scrutiny would be intense. Once Carston's people located Kevin's vehicle, they'd trace every used car sold, every want ad, every stolen car for a hundred miles in any direction. Any description that fit the scenario would go onto a list, and if a cop reported that vehicle, Carston's people wouldn't be far behind.

Maybe it was time to go back to Chicago. Maybe Joey Giancardi wouldn't kill her immediately. Maybe he'd be willing to trade some kind of indentured servitude for two sets of facial reconstruction. Or maybe he'd get one whiff of her desperation and know there was good money to be made in selling her back to the people who wanted her.

She had identities that Kevin knew nothing about, but Daniel didn't. The documents she'd grabbed from Kevin's mobile Batcave wouldn't be safe.

Unless Daniel acted fast enough.

She uncovered her face and sat up.

"Do you think you've grasped the basic principles of hide-and-seek?"

Daniel turned with two clear bags of ammo in his hands. "Maybe the *very* most basic of the basics."

Alex nodded. "You're smart, though. You speak Spanish pretty well, right?"

"I can get by. You want to go to Mexico?"

"I wish I could. Mexico probably isn't totally safe for your face since you've been there so many times, but there are a lot of good hiding places in South America. It's cheap, too, so you won't run out of money for a while. You won't blend in, but there are lots of expats..."

Daniel hesitated for a second, then carefully placed the ammo in one of the duffels. He came to stand next to her.

"Alex, you're using a lot of second-person pronouns there. Are you...talking about us splitting up right now?"

"You'll be safer outside the country, Daniel. If you laid low in a quiet little place somewhere in Uruguay, they might never find—"

"Then why can't we go together? Is it because they'll be looking for a couple...if...if Kevin talks?"

She hunched her shoulders; it was half a shrug, half a defensive motion. "It's because I don't have a passport."

"You don't think they'll be waiting for Daniel Beach to try to board a plane?"

"You won't be Daniel Beach. I've got a couple of Kevin's ID sets. It will be a long while till they get around to asking him about false identities, if they ever do. You'll have plenty of time to catch a flight to Chile tonight."

His expression was suddenly hard, almost angry. He looked like Kevin, and she was surprised at how sad that made her.

"So I just save myself, then? Leave you behind?"

Another almost-shrug. "Like you said, they'll be looking for a couple. I'll slip through the holes in the net."

"They'll be looking for *you*, Alex. I won't—"

"Okay, okay," she interrupted. "Let me think some more. I'll come up with something."

Daniel locked eyes with her for a long second. Slowly, his expression softened until he looked like himself again. Finally, his shoulders slumped and his eyes closed.

"I'm sorry," she whispered. "I'm sorry this didn't work. I'm sorry that Kevin..."

"I keep hoping he'll walk through the door," Daniel admitted, opening his eyes and staring down. "But I can feel it in my gut—that's not going to happen."

"I know. I wish I were wrong."

His eyes flashed up to hers. "If our positions were reversed, he'd do something. He'd find a way. But there's nothing *I* can do. I'm not Kevin."

"Kevin would be in the same position we are. He wouldn't know where they were keeping you. If he did, he'd still be impossibly outgunned. There wouldn't be anything he could do."

Daniel shook his head and sank down onto the bed. "Somehow, none of that would have stopped him."

Alex sighed. Daniel was probably right. Kevin would have some secret informant, or another camera angle, or a way to hack into Deavers's system. He wouldn't give up and run. But Alex wasn't Kevin, either. She couldn't even poison Carston while he was still oblivious. He wasn't anymore, she was sure of that.

"Let me think," she repeated. "I'll try to figure a way out."

Daniel nodded. "But together, Alex. We leave together. We stay together."

"Even if that puts both of us at risk?"

"Even then."

Alex threw herself back onto the bed, hiding her face again with her arms.

If there had been some perfect escape for them, she would have tried it earlier. The whole reason she was here in the first place was that the escape option had failed. Now the attack option had failed. It didn't leave her feeling very optimistic.

It was funny how you didn't realize how much you had to lose until it was gone. Yes, she knew she was in deep with Daniel; she'd embraced that disadvantage.

But who would have thought she would miss Kevin? How had he become her friend? Not even a friend, because you chose your friends. More like family— the brother you tried to avoid at family gatherings. She'd never had anything like that, but this must be what it felt like, the pain of losing something you'd never wanted but had come to count on anyway. Kevin's arrogant self-assurance had made her feel almost safe in a way she hadn't for years. His team was the winning team. His invulnerability was the safety net.

Or used to be.

And the dog. She couldn't even think about the dog or she'd be incapacitated. She wouldn't be able to make her brain work toward any kind of solution.

Again, the image of Kevin on her table flashed across the black insides of her eyelids. If only she could know that he was already dead, that would be something. If she could believe he wasn't in agony right now. Surely he was smart enough to have had a way out. Or was he so certain of himself that failure was never part of the plan?

She thought she knew enough about Deavers from his moves up to this point to be sure he wouldn't waste an opportunity if there were any way to find an edge in it.

She honestly wished the situation were reversed. If she'd been the one caught, she would have been able to take a quick, painless exit, leaving Deavers and

Carston no information about the others. Whatever Kevin had done wrong, however he had failed, he was still the one best qualified to keep Daniel alive. And Val, too, for that matter. Val would have the easiest escape in the short term, but neither Carston nor Deavers seemed like the type to give up on a witness.

If Kevin were the one in Alex's place, trying to come up with a plan, what would he do?

Alex didn't know. He had resources she knew nothing about, resources she couldn't duplicate. But even then, running would have to be his only option. He might come back to try again later, but it wasn't like he could keep going after the potential vice president's kill team today. Now was the time to disappear and regroup.

Or, in her case, disappear and try to stay gone.

That obnoxious image of Kevin on the table wouldn't leave her head. The problem with being a professional interrogator was that she knew, in intimate detail, all the options for what they could be doing to him now. It was impossible not to mark the passing minutes, imagine how the questioning was progressing.

Daniel was quiet. The packing hadn't taken him long; they hadn't spread out here, gotten comfortable. They'd known from the beginning that they might have to leave at any moment, whether because of another disaster or simply wearing out their welcome with Val.

She could guess what he was feeling. He wouldn't want to believe things had gone so wrong. He wouldn't want to believe Kevin could be dead or that death was the best outcome for Kevin now. He would remember how Kevin had come through the roof in the middle of the night to save him and feel guilty that he couldn't do the same. More than guilty—helpless, weak, furious, culpable, cowardly...All the things she was already starting to feel.

But there was nothing she could *do* about Kevin. If she and Kevin switched places, there would be nothing Kevin could do, either. He wouldn't know where they were keeping her. The bad guys wouldn't choose a location that either Alex or Kevin would know about. They had thousands of options open to them. And if there *were* some way to know where their hideout was, they certainly wouldn't be careless about the security there. Kevin would be just as helpless as she was.

She shouldn't waste time thinking about the impossible. She needed to focus.

She had to operate under the assumption that Kevin was still alive, and the bad guys would soon know both she and Daniel were also alive, and nearby. They would know Val's name and address. They would know the make, model, color, and probably plate number of the only two cars they currently had access to. It was time to distance themselves from as many of those facts as possible.

Alex sat up slowly. "We'd better load the car and get moving."

Daniel was leaning against the wall beside the stack of bags with his arms crossed over his chest. Red rimmed his eyes. He nodded.

Val was nowhere to be seen as they ventured out into the great room, both weighed down with bags. The space seemed colder, bigger without the dog in it. Alex walked quickly to the front door.

They didn't speak in the elevator or as they walked to the car. Alex dropped her bags by the trunk and fished the keys out of her pocket.

A hushed scraping sound broke the short silence. It sounded like it was coming from close beside or maybe underneath the car.

I'm an idiot, Alex thought to herself as she dropped into a crouch next to the bag that she desperately hoped contained the guns but most likely held medical supplies. She knew how precarious their situation was, yet she'd walked into the parking garage unarmed.

She'd relied on Kevin to hold out longer. Stupid.

Daniel had the heavier bags. She could tell as soon as her hand rested on the bag in front of her that it contained first-aid gear — first aid she wouldn't have a use for now. At least she had her rings and belt. So she'd have to be close. No resisting at first. That was, if they didn't just shoot her immediately.

Not even a full second passed as she made these calculations. The first noise was quickly followed by another, a low whine that definitely came from under the car. The sound took her back to a different panicked moment, by a dark porch in Texas. It wasn't a human sound.

Alex crouched lower, leaned her head down so it was almost touching the asphalt floor of the garage. The dark shadow beneath the sedan pulled itself closer.

"*Einstein?*" She gasped.

"Einstein?" Daniel echoed behind her.

Alex crawled around to the side of the car to where Einstein was closest. "Einstein, are you okay? Come here, boy."

The dog crept toward her until he was free of the car. She ran her hands along his back and legs.

"Are you hurt?" she crooned. "It's okay. I'll take care of it."

His fur was matted and wet in a few places, but when she pulled her hands away to check, they weren't red—just dirty. His paws were cut up a bit and he panted like he was dehydrated or exhausted or both.

"Is he all right?" Daniel asked, close beside her.

"I think so. It looks like he's had a rough night, though."

"C'mere, boy," Daniel said, reaching for him. Einstein got to his feet, and then Daniel scooped him up. Einstein licked his face over and over again.

"Get him upstairs. I'll load this stuff in the car and follow."

"Okay." Daniel hesitated, then gulped a ragged breath. "It's all true."

"Yes." She popped the trunk without looking up.

She heard him turn and walk away. The sound of Einstein's panting faded.

It didn't take her long to get things squared for their departure. The garage stayed quiet and empty of people, as usual. Maybe this was Val's private floor of the parking garage. Maybe all these cars belonged to her. Alex wouldn't be completely shocked if that was the case.

Shouldn't Alex feel better that the dog was okay? Part of her must have been hoping that she was wrong, that she'd overreacted. That it was just a mistake.

When she walked back into the living room, Val was on the floor with the dog. Einstein was curled in her lap with his head on her shoulder, and Daniel knelt beside them.

Val looked up at her, still wearing the hard-doll face. "Now is when you get to say *I told you so*."

"Do you need help getting out of here?" Alex asked.

"I've had to disappear before. It's been a while, but that's not something you forget."

Alex nodded. "I'm sorry, Val."

"Me, too," Val responded. "Do you think...are you going to take the dog?"

Alex blinked in surprise. "Yes."

"Oh." Val pressed her face into Einstein's fur. "Gimme a minute." Her voice came out muffled.

"Sure," Alex said. They had a few hours. This location was the last thing Kevin would give up. He'd sent the dog back to warn them. He was fighting for them.

Besides, she still had one unlikely avenue of information, and she should probably check that out while she had access to a high-speed Internet connection. She went to the computer on the island.

Carston had been pretty tight-lipped up till now, but maybe he'd finally give something away. At the least, she should be able to construe the approximate time Kevin had been taken. Surely there would be a call to mark that. Maybe some travel. Carston was the expert on this front, not Deavers.

The tracker was an easy check. Carston's vehicle was at his office, as usual for a workday. He might have taken another car, though. She checked the sound feed—Carston was in the office. She scrolled back to listen to his conversations.

Here was something telling. Carston had been in the office for a while—usually he got in at six, but there was activity beginning around three thirty a.m. She wanted to kick herself for not checking backward on the recording before heading out this morning.

His first call was short. Just "I'm here" and "What's the status?" It wasn't hard to draw conclusions from that. Someone had woken Carston up with the news and he'd headed to the office. With zero traffic, it would only have taken him ten minutes to make the drive. Factor in throwing some clothes on, brushing teeth, et cetera, and the call could have come in anywhere from two thirty to three fifteen.

She looked at the clock on her computer, calculating how long they'd had Kevin. They would have had to subdue him in the beginning, then wait for him to be fully cognizant if they'd knocked him out. Then they'd have to decide on a course of action and bring in a specialist...

Was that Carston's second call? At three forty-five, Carston had dialed out.

"What's the play?...I don't like it...Fine, fine, if that's the best option...What?...You know how I feel about it...Like you say, it's *your* problem...I want updates."

He never said much, and the words had probably a thousand possible interpretations, but she couldn't help applying her own.

No, Kevin wasn't dead.

There was a long stretch of silence. Typing, pacing,

breathing; that was all. No calls. It didn't sound like he left the room once. She could almost hear Carston's anxiety and it made her more anxious than she already was. Where were his updates? Was he getting them in e-mails?

Maybe they were lucky. Maybe the specialist had to be brought in from a distance. Maybe Kevin was just being held, anticipating. That was one face of the game, and she'd played the card before—let the subject wait, visualize, panic. Let him lose the fight in his own head before it began.

Not likely, in this case. They knew Daniel was alive. They'd suspect he had other help here in the city. They would not want to give Kevin's confederates time to escape.

The clock was ticking for Carston and Deavers, too. They'd made the call. They'd heard her pick up, then disconnect. She hadn't called back to see if it was an accidental dial. The phone was ditched. They would guess the partner was already running.

Like she *should* be.

Alex came out of her intense reverie, realizing for the first time that Daniel was perched on the stool beside her, watching the reactions play across her face. Val was leaning against the counter by the sink, Einstein at her feet, also watching.

"Just a little longer," she told them, scrubbing through the long silence in Carston's office. She didn't want to miss anything, but she couldn't afford to listen through the empty spaces in real time.

She paused when his voice began, and then carefully backed up. He'd dialed out again. The tone of his voice was one hundred eighty degrees from what it had been. It was such a shift it jarred her. She wondered if she'd somehow messed up the program and pulled up an earlier recording.

It was his kindly-grandpa voice.

"I didn't wake you, did I? How did you sleep? Yes, sorry, I have a small emergency on my plate. I had to come into the office...No, don't cancel the plans. Take Livvy to the zoo. It's going to get hotter tomorrow...You know I don't have a choice in these things, Erin. I am sorry I can't be there today, but there's nothing I can do about it...Livvy will have a great time without me. She can tell me all about it tonight at dinner. Take lots of pictures...I can't make any promises, but I hope to be free by dinnertime...That's not fair...Yes, I remember that I told you this would be a light week, but you know how the job works, honey. No guarantees."

A big sigh.

"I love you. Give Livvy a kiss for me. I'll let you know when I'm free."

She had chills when he hung up. Carston thought it would be over by *dinnertime?* Or was he just placating his daughter?

More silence, more typing. He must be getting the updates electronically. Kevin was in the thick of it, Alex was sure. Was he talking yet? She didn't have a clue.

There was nothing more until she caught up to the present time. She checked the tracker. Carston wasn't going anywhere. Deavers must be handling *his* problem.

Still listening through her earbuds, Alex leaned her forehead against her arms. Carston was typing again.

She pictured him at his desk, poker face in place as he sent out directions or questions. Would he be flushed with anxiety? Would tension sweat drip off his pale, bald head? No, she was sure he would be cool and precise, no more worked up than if he were typing out a request for paper supplies.

He'd know the right things to ask, even if Deavers didn't. He could manage the whole operation from his ergonomically correct desk chair. He'd see Kevin tortured to death, then run out for his dinner reservations without a second thought.

The sudden anger that flared up almost choked her.

What was happening now had nothing to do with national security or saving lives. Carston was running a private vendetta for a man who was quite possibly the kind of person who actually belonged on an interrogation table. Carston had crossed the line from arguably necessary black ops to purely criminal acts a long time ago, and it didn't seem to have affected him at all. Maybe it had always been this way. Maybe everything she'd done for him, every inhuman action she'd performed in the name of public safety, had been a scam.

Did he think he was so untouchable? That these hidden choices would never touch his public life? Did he think he was exempt? Did he not realize that he had liabilities, too?

There were worse things than being poisoned.

Alex's breath caught. Unexpectedly, a new avenue, something she'd never considered before, opened up inside her mind. It was a reach, and she knew it. There were a thousand things that would probably go wrong, a million ways to screw it up. It would be almost impossible, even with a year to plan every detail.

She felt Daniel's hand on her back. Through her earbuds, she heard him ask, "Alex?" in a worried tone.

She looked up slowly. She stared at Daniel, assessing. She examined Val the same way.

"Give me ten more minutes," she said, then she put her head down on her arms and concentrated once more.

CHAPTER 28

Alex spoke quickly as she laid out her plan, emphasizing the details she was sure of a little more than necessary. She tried to make it sound well thought out, like she was confident about it. Daniel seemed to be buying her version, listening intently, nodding at certain intervals, but Alex couldn't read Val at all. Her eyes were focused toward Alex, but almost like she was looking through Alex's face to the back of her head. Her expression was politely distant.

Alex talked through the conclusion, which wasn't nearly as fail-safe as she would have liked it to be, and she could tell she wasn't selling the outcome as well as she had the preliminaries. She looked down at Einstein's face resting on her leg instead of at the human faces, petting him more frequently as her discomfort grew. Trying to wrap it up on a positive note, she went on a little longer than she should have. She was still midsentence when Val interrupted.

"No," Val said.

"No?" Alex repeated. She said the word like a question, but she was already resigned.

"No. I won't do that. You're going to get killed. It's nice that you want to go back for Kevin, but be realistic, Alex. This isn't going to work."

"It might. They won't be expecting this. They won't be ready."

"It doesn't matter if they're ready or not. There will be more than enough of them to make up for it. So you get off a lucky shot and take one down. The guy next to him will get you."

"We don't even know how many people will be there."

"Exactly," Val said in a flat voice.

"Val, they won't pay attention to you. You'd just be an anonymous aide. These people see hundreds of assistants every day. You'll be invisible to them."

"I have never been invisible in my life."

"You know what I mean."

Val looked at her with a perfectly smooth face. "No."

Alex took a deep breath. She knew it wasn't fair to involve Val. She would have to make do.

"Okay," she said, wishing her voice sounded stronger. "I'll do it by myself, then."

"Alex, you can't," Daniel insisted.

She smiled weakly at him. "I can. I don't know how well I'll do, but I have to try, right?"

Daniel looked at her, torn. She could see that he wanted to argue. He wanted to say no, she didn't have to try, but that would mean walking away, leaving Kevin to die in agony. His was an untenable position. Now that there was any hope at all, how could he turn his back on it?

"Together, we'll be able to get the first part done," she told him. "It won't take more than the two of us."

"But the second you're separated from Carston, he'll double-cross you."

Alex shrugged. "I'll just have to sell my threat. If he thinks betraying me means the hostage dies, maybe he'll play it clean."

"You won't know how he's playing it. You won't be prepared."

"Val doesn't want to risk her life. Can you argue with her?"

Val watched Daniel with half-lidded eyes as he hesitated.

"No," he said. "But I can do her part. We'll trade. Val, you could do mine, right?"

Alex squeezed her eyes shut and then slowly opened them again. "Daniel, you know that won't work. Even if you weren't Kevin's twin brother, these are the people who put your face on the news."

"Val can fix me up, can't you, Val? Make me look different enough?"

Val's expression shifted abruptly, became more engaged. She examined his face closely.

"Actually...I think I could." She turned to Alex. "It's not like anyone is going to be looking for him there. Trust me, a lot more people would look at me — even as a nameless assistant. I think I can make him different enough for them not to give him a second glance."

"I'm not doubting your abilities, Val...but they're *twins*."

"Let me try?" she asked, an unfamiliar pleading tone coming into her voice. "I do want to help Kevin." When she said his name, Einstein looked up. "I just won't die to do it. Let me do something."

Einstein put his head on Alex's leg again.

"I guess I could let you try. But it's a waste of time and we don't have enough of that as is."

"It won't take me that long."

"And you'd be willing to do Daniel's part of the plan?"

"Sure, that's easy. No one will be shooting at me."

Alex winced.

What was she contemplating here? People would be shooting at Alex for certain, she'd already come to terms with that. But if Val could disguise Daniel enough, which Alex couldn't even *imagine,* then they might be shooting at Daniel, too. She reminded herself of all the reasons they had to go after Kevin. He had too much vital information. If he told the bad guys everything he knew about Alex and Daniel, the cars they were in, the places they had to go to ground, the way Alex operated, it wouldn't be that hard for the Agency to track them down. Val, too. Most likely, they'd all die anyway.

Die like cowards, running.

But the reasons were moot. If there was a way to save Kevin from what was happening to him, she had to do it. There was a bond there now that she hadn't even realized was forming. He was her friend. Her second liability. They were hurting him, even as she sat here considering. She had to stop it.

"Get to work, Val. This first part will take me two hours, if I'm lucky. When I get done, we'll reevaluate."

• • •

THOUGH SHE'D LIVED in DC for almost a decade, Alex had never visited the National Zoo. She'd always thought of it as something for children, but there seemed to be plenty of adults attending today unencumbered by offspring.

There were still many, many children — it seemed like thousands of them yapping in high-pitched voices and flailing around their parents' feet. All appeared to be under the age of five, so she guessed school wasn't done for the year yet, though it must be close.

She tried to think how long it had been since she'd first met with Carston, but she couldn't tally up the days in a way that made sense. Daniel had had around three weeks left of school then. More time had passed than that...hadn't it? Maybe Daniel's school finished earlier than average.

Alex's first stop was the rental line at Guest Services. It wasn't long. Most of the visitors would have arrived earlier, in the cool of the morning. Lunchtime was approaching, with the sun beating down almost directly overhead. Some people would leave then, avoid the high prices of the food inside the park. Head home for naptime.

She had quite a bit of information about Erin and Olivia, all gleaned from Erin's Facebook page. It was the same place that, months ago, she'd found the picture of Olivia that hung around her neck now.

Alex knew Olivia was three and a half. Still small enough that she would fit in a stroller. Alex knew what Erin looked like from nearly every angle and had a good idea of the kinds of clothes she wore. She knew Erin was a late riser and probably wouldn't have gotten to the zoo right as it opened. She knew Olivia was most excited about seeing the pandas.

Alex paid nine dollars cash for a single stroller, then put her backpack in it and headed into the park. She craned her neck around, searching. It made sense that she would be looking for someone—maybe her sister and nephews, or her husband and their child. There were lots of other patrons looking for their parties. She didn't stand out.

Erin and Livvy would be past the pandas by now, probably thinking about lunch. She analyzed the map she'd gotten with the stroller. She'd try across from the apes first, then near the reptiles.

She walked fast, ignoring the turnoffs and viewing areas.

Erin had the fair skin of a redhead, like her father. She'd posted pictures of herself sunburned and moaned about freckles. Erin would be in a hat and probably light long sleeves. Her hair was bright and hung halfway down her back. It would catch the eye.

Alex scanned the crowds as she moved quickly through them, looking for a woman with a child, ruling out those with friends and spouses and multiple children. For a while, she followed a woman with her hair rolled up under a wide-brimmed straw hat pushing a single stroller, but then the child climbed out to walk with her—it was a boy.

A quick loop around the big cats, and then down toward the petting zoo. All the while, she was conscious of how she looked—map in hand, vigilantly searching for her companions. She wore a straw hat of her own over the dark blond wig and wide-framed sunglasses. She had on a plain T-shirt, boyfriend jeans, and the sport-shoe/ballet-flat hybrids that would let her run if she had to. Nothing about her would be particularly memorable.

Several shades of red hair had grabbed her attention throughout the course of her search, but many of them had been clearly unnatural. Others had been on women too old to be Erin, or too young, or holding extra children. Now she spotted one headed along the trail toward the Amazon exhibit—a long braid of golden-red hair swinging from beneath a white bucket hat. The woman was pushing a single stroller; it looked exactly like Alex's, tan molded plastic with a dark green shade. She wore a sleeveless tank, and her arms were thick with freckles. Alex walked quickly after her.

The woman wasn't moving fast; it didn't take long for Alex to pass her. Alex kept her head down and glanced into the stroller as she walked alongside it.

The little girl looked right. Her face was turned away, but the fluffy blond hair seemed the same. Her size fit the profile.

Alex kept walking and beat the mother and daughter to the exhibit. She parked her stroller in the designated space beside the bathrooms, inconspicuously wiping the handle with the hem of her shirt before she removed her backpack and shrugged into it. Now that she was fairly certain the woman was Erin and that Erin had her own stroller, she didn't need this one.

She located the woman and child dawdling along the trail. A larger group had caught up to them and flowed around them from both sides. Alex could see the woman's face clearly now — it was definitely Carston's daughter. Erin had paused to offer Olivia a sippy cup.

The path was getting more crowded. It was hot, and the wig was making her head itch and sweat. The straw hat wasn't helping.

Alex focused on an empty bench about ten feet ahead of the duo. There was another large crowd behind the first. If she timed it right, she could intercept Erin at the bench while the second crowd was passing.

Alex moved purposefully back the way she'd just come, watching through her dark glasses to see if anyone was paying attention to her. The first group — a loud extended family, it looked like, with several toddlers, multiple parents, and one older woman in a wheelchair — enveloped her for a moment. She dodged through them and then slowed a bit.

The second crowd was all adults — foreign tourists on a day trip, she guessed, many of them wearing fanny packs — and they reached Erin as she was almost to the bench. Alex moved against the flow until she was just ahead of her quarry. As Erin passed a foot away from the bench, Alex turned, twisting around an older man, and pretended to stumble. She reached out and grabbed Erin's hand on the stroller handle. Her palm mashed the pouch of clear fluid and forced it empty with one strong squeeze.

"Hey!" Erin said, turning.

Alex ducked back, twisting partially behind the closest guest. Erin came face to face with the bald septuagenarian.

"Excuse me," he said hesitantly to both of them, not sure how he'd become entangled. He pulled free of Alex and stepped around Erin and the stroller.

Alex watched as Erin blinked once, then again. Her eyelids seemed to get stuck on the second blink. Alex jumped forward and grabbed Erin around the waist as she started to crumple, then jerked her toward the bench so that they fell heavily onto it together. Alex jammed her elbow against the wooden back; it would leave a bruise, but one she could easily cover. Erin was taller and weighed more than Alex, so Alex wasn't able to keep them from slumping awkwardly. Alex loosed a slightly manic laugh—hopefully anyone watching would think they were playing around.

The little girl was singing to herself inside the stroller. She hadn't seemed to notice that she'd stopped moving. Alex extricated herself from the mother and pulled the stroller closer, angling it so that Olivia was facing away from Erin.

Erin lolled on the bench, her head falling onto her right shoulder and her mouth hanging open.

A third conglomeration of visitors moved past them. No one stopped. Alex was operating quickly, so she couldn't keep close tabs on any reaction, but no one had raised an alarm yet.

She pulled the bucket hat lower over Erin's face, shading her lifeless expression. Out of the side pocket of her backpack, Alex drew the little perfume bottle. She reached around the edge of the stroller's shade and pressed the nozzle down for two seconds. The singing ceased, and then Alex felt the light thud through the plastic frame of the stroller as the child fell back against the seat.

Moving as casually as she could, Alex patted Erin's shoulder, then stood up and stretched.

"I'll get her some lunch, you go ahead and rest," Alex said, smoothing the wig under her hat in case her tumble had disarranged it. She glanced around, eyes hidden behind her glasses. No one seemed to be focused on the little tableau she'd created. She grasped the stroller's handle and started moving back toward the parking lot. At first she kept the pace easy. She looked toward the animal cages like the others were doing. As she got farther from the bench, she began moving faster. A mother with an afternoon appointment.

Outside the bathroom at the visitors' center, she parked the stroller and pulled Olivia into her arms. The child had to weigh over thirty pounds and felt heavier because her body was slack. Alex tried to arrange the unconscious child into the same position she'd seen other parents use—straddling one hip, legs on either side, head cradled on the shoulder. It didn't feel like she'd gotten it right, but she had to move anyway. She gritted her teeth and walked as quickly as she could through the gate. She wished she'd been able to park closer, but eventually, with sweat soaking her T-shirt, she reached the car.

Alex hadn't had time to get a car seat. She glanced around surreptitiously to see if anyone was watching, but the area of the parking lot she was in was mostly full, and the people arriving now were far away. The early quitters had already left; she was alone.

She laid the child on the backseat and wrapped a seat belt around her waist. Then she covered Olivia with a blanket to conceal her.

Alex straightened up and checked for witnesses again. No one was nearby; no one was watching her. She pulled a syringe from the inside pocket of her pack and leaned in to administer the drug to the sleeping child. She'd calculated the dose for someone weighting thirty to forty pounds. It should keep Olivia under for about two hours.

Alex turned the car on and cranked up the air-conditioning. She started breathing again for what felt like the first time since she'd entered the zoo.

Phase one was successful. Erin would wake up in forty-five minutes, more or less. Alex was sure that paramedics would be attending to her by then. When she woke, she'd sound the alarm about her missing daughter. The zoo would be searched first, then the police would be brought in. Alex had to be in position when Erin realized her daughter had been taken, that she'd not merely wandered off while her mother was having some sort of seizure. Alex was 85 percent sure which call Erin would make first.

She really hoped that Val would be done working her magic by the time she arrived at the new hiding place so Alex would know exactly which plan was moving forward—not because she'd made up her mind as to which outcome she wanted most. Going in alone...that was suicide. But taking Daniel...was that murder-suicide?

Maybe Val's confidence in herself was misplaced. Maybe Daniel would just look like himself in a wig.

Alex could do it alone. She'd just make it very clear what would happen to Olivia if she, Alex, didn't live through the night. That would keep Carston in line, wouldn't it?

She didn't want to think about the things Carston could set in motion. The traps he could lay so that once he had Olivia back, Alex would be his.

Alex called Val as she approached the new building, and when she pulled into the underground garage, Val was waiting by a set of elevators with a wheeled cart—it looked like something a hotel visitor would receive room service on. The garage was otherwise empty of other people. Alex couldn't spot any cameras, but she kept her body between the open back car door and the best view inside. Neither Val nor Alex spoke. Alex shifted the sleeping child to the bottom shelf of the cart, then rearranged the blanket around her so her shape was obscured.

This elevator was more normal than the one that led to Val's penthouse—just a silver box, as in most of the buildings where Alex had lived. It made her nervous that the box would suddenly slow and the doors would open, exposing them. Val must have felt similarly. She kept her hand on the button for the sixteenth floor, as if holding it down would guarantee them express service.

While the elevator climbed, Alex noticed Val's expression for the first time. It was...a little too stimulated. Alex hoped Val wasn't heading into some kind of power-mad version of a sugar rush.

The elevator doors opened to an empty hallway. It was a nice building, with fancy moldings and marble floors, but it looked pedestrian after Val's other place.

Val pushed the cart down the little hall, motioning for Alex to go ahead.

"Number sixteen-oh-nine, on the end. It's not locked," she said, and the eager tone of her voice made Alex wary again. Though maybe if Val got hyped up enough, she'd change her mind and come with Alex for the main event.

Alex walked into the apartment in a hurry—there was a lot to set up and she needed to be fast. She barely took in the routine living room–kitchen spread, the fabric-shrouded windows, or the beige color scheme. She noted an open door on the far wall, revealing a brightly lit room with a queen bed, and headed for it. She could see some of her duffel bags leaning against the flowered bedspread.

She was halfway to the door before she really absorbed the whole space, and then her eyes focused on the man standing in the dimly lit kitchen.

Even though she'd been expecting *something*, it didn't stop her from spooking. She jumped a step back, her thumbs automatically going to the little hatches of her poisoned rings.

"Well?" he asked.

The tall man in the cheap black suit waited, fighting a smile.

"Told ya," Val said from behind her, and Alex could hear the smug grin on her face without looking.

The man looked Nordic with his fair skin and pale, white-blond hair. His blond beard was neatly trimmed and reminded her of a college professor's. His eyebrows were so pale against his forehead they were nearly invisible, completely changing the look of his eyes and his forehead. The hair around the edges of his head was straight, short, and neatly combed. The top of his head was pale, shiny, and totally bald. It changed the perceived shape of his head and made him look ten years older. He wore thin silver glasses, and his cheeks were unexpectedly round. His most striking features were his bright, icy-blue eyes, framed by nearly white lashes.

"You look like a Bond villain," Alex blurted out.

"Is that good?" Daniel asked, his voice not quite right—it was clipped, somehow, a little slurred.

Alex felt her heart sink as she more closely examined the transformation. If she hadn't been looking specifically for a disguised version of Daniel, she would have walked right past this man on the street. Even if she had been looking for Daniel, only his height would have made this man a suspect. As the despair settled sickeningly into her stomach, Alex knew she'd really been counting on Val's failing.

"Val did a good job," Alex said, and then she started moving again. "Let's get Olivia set up."

Einstein was sniffing around the blanket-covered child. He whimpered quietly, ill at ease.

"Is it good *enough?*" Daniel persisted while pulling the child out from under the cart and cradling her against his chest.

"Let me think about it while I do this," Alex hedged.

Daniel laid Olivia on the flowered coverlet, smoothing the sweaty fluffs of hair back from her forehead. It took Alex only a few seconds to get the IV bags hanging. One clear, one white and opaque, and then a very small bag with a dark green fluid inside. She quickly placed the IV catheter using the smallest needle she had and then started the fluids.

"Back out of the way," she told Daniel.

Alex pulled up the camera on a phone Val had given her—left behind by a *friend,* Val said—and snapped a few pictures of Olivia sleeping. She flipped through them and found one that she decided would do.

"This is my least favorite part of the plan," Daniel muttered.

She glanced up and saw his pained expression. It looked strange on his new face.

"Let's hope Carston feels similarly."

His frown deepened. Alex took his hand and pulled him from the room. The way he was holding his mouth made the round shape of his cheeks more prominent.

"What did she do to your face?" Alex asked.

Daniel stuck two fingers in his mouth and pulled out a little piece of plastic. "These make it a little hard to talk." With a sigh, he replaced the plastic, and his cheek rounded out again.

Val waited for them in the big living room, eyes still lit up with her success.

"That baby's not going to wake up, right?" she asked.

"Right."

"Good. I wouldn't know what to do with a kid. Now, what do you think? Totally altered, yes?"

Alex looked at Daniel again, and her shoulders slumped. He was thicker around the middle, too; she hadn't noticed that before. It all looked so real.

"You don't think it's good enough, do you?" Daniel asked.

"It's good enough," Val answered for her. "And she knows it. That's why she looks so glum. She'd much rather risk my life than yours."

Daniel looked at Alex, waiting for her answer.

"Val's right. Except for the part about risking her life. I don't want to risk anyone's."

Val snorted.

Daniel grabbed Alex's hand and pulled her against his chest. "It's going to be fine," he murmured. "We can do this together. Your plans always work. I will follow your instructions to the letter, and we'll make it through. I promise."

Alex squeezed her eyes tight, trying to force the tears back into their ducts.

"I don't know, Daniel. What am I doing?"

He kissed the top of her head.

"Cut it out," Val interrupted. "You two are making me jealous, and that's never a safe thing to do."

Alex opened her eyes and pulled away, brushing at Daniel's suit to make sure she hadn't left any makeup on it.

"I see you had time to get the things I needed from the Batcave. This toolbox is perfect."

"More than perfect—check the fifth drawer down. I packed the rest how you asked," Daniel told her. "Do you want to go through it before I put it in the car?"

"That's a good idea."

The silver toolbox—one of the props from Kevin's stash, she assumed—had wheels and a pull-up handle, like a suitcase, but unlike a suitcase, many locking drawers that pulled forward out of its face. She went swiftly through the top drawers, identifying the location of the different drugs by the color rings on the syringes. The syringes were stacked in the rubber trays she usually stored them in. The next drawer down had a variety of scalpels and razor blades. She wouldn't need so many; the point was to make the drawer look full. Saline bags and tubing were next, along with needles and catheters in different sizes. The next compartment was deeper. It held her pressurized canisters and several random chemicals from Kevin's stores.

The second-to-last drawer was key. It held another tray of syringes—these empty—and seemed shallower than the last. She traced the edges of the bottom of the drawer—of course Kevin would have something like this. She could fit her fingernails around and lift up the false bottom. She peeked at what was underneath.

"Let's hope Carston's up for some Oscar-level acting," she murmured to herself.

She went through the final, deepest drawer, where Daniel had stowed her more ostentatious props — the blowtorch, the wire snips, the pliers, along with several arbitrary tools Daniel had added from the items available in Kevin's hoard.

There was one more useful thing she needed — just a tiny configuration of wires that she'd picked up the first time they'd visited the local Batcave. She pulled it from her backpack now and hid it in the third tray of the first drawer, under a syringe. She would want easy access to that one.

Alex straightened. "Perfect. Thank you."

"You," Val said, pointing to Daniel. "Get to the rendezvous point. You," she continued, moving her index finger toward Alex's face. "Let's fix you up and get going. The clock is ticking." She motioned to a set of double doors across the room.

"I'll be there in thirty seconds," Alex promised.

Val rolled her eyes. "Fine, have your little good-bye scene." She turned and walked through the doors.

"Alex —" Daniel began.

"Wait."

She took his hand again and led him out the front door, pulling the toolbox with her free hand. He had the big first-aid bag slung over his shoulder. Einstein tried to follow and then whined when she shut the door on him.

They walked down the quiet hall to the elevator. Alex pressed the button. When the doors slid apart, Daniel walked in and she followed, putting one foot across the breach to hold it open. She dropped the toolbox's handle and reached up to hold Daniel's face between her hands.

"Listen to me," she said quietly. "In the glove compartment of the sedan there's a manila envelope. There are two sets of IDs—passports, driver's licenses, and a bunch of cash."

"I don't look that much like Kevin now."

"I know, but people age, lose hair. You can toss the glasses, shave, dye your hair back to brown. And if things go badly, you'll need to do all of that. Then get to the nearest airport. Get on any plane that's leaving North America, okay?"

"I won't leave you behind."

"When I say *go badly*, I mean that I won't be around for you to wait for."

He stared at her with that odd new version of his troubled face.

"Okay?" she repeated insistently.

He hesitated, then nodded.

"Good," she said, trying to sound like that discussion was closed. She wasn't feeling the conviction behind his nod, but there wasn't time to argue about it.

"You stay quiet tonight," she instructed. "Don't speak to anyone unless you have to. Think like an underling. You're just there to drive the car and carry the bags, okay? This is just a paycheck. None of what's happening means anything to you. No matter *what* you see, it doesn't affect you. You have no emotional response. You got that?"

He nodded seriously. "Yes."

"If things get dicey, it will make sense for you to run. This isn't your problem."

"Right," he agreed, but his answer was less decided this time.

"Here." She yanked the gold ring from her finger. It was the bigger of the two. She removed his arms from around her and tried it on all his fingers. As with Kevin, it fit only on his pinkie. At least she was able to get it all the way down over his knuckles. Hopefully it wouldn't look too out of character.

"Be *extremely* careful with this," she told him. "Slide this little hatch out of the way if you need to use it. Whatever you do, don't touch the barb. If you're not in the act of using it, keep it closed. But if you're trying to get out, and someone's in your way, all you have to do is put that barb in contact with his skin."

"I got it."

Alex looked into the startling blue eyes, searching

for Daniel behind the strangeness of his oddly simple disguise. She was out of instructions, and the feelings she wanted to share with him didn't seem to have corresponding words.

"I . . . I don't know how to go back to my old life," she said, trying to explain. "I don't know how to do that anymore, without you. Having you as my liability is the best thing that ever happened to me."

He smiled just a little bit, though it didn't reach his eyes. "I love you, too," he whispered.

She tried to smile back.

Daniel put his hands on her shoulders and kissed her for one lingering second. Then he smiled at her again, unfamiliar and familiar at the same time. She took a step away from him.

"I told you I'd be there when you needed backup," he said.

The elevator doors closed.

CHAPTER 29

There was no wig involved this time, just a quick trim that left her real hair looking like it had an actual style. A pixie cut; that's what people called it, she thought. The color was medium blond now, and it lightened up her complexion. It was also flattering to her face shape the way her real hair hadn't been since...she couldn't remember the last time her hair had been attractive.

"Seriously," Alex said. "Did you go to cosmetology school?"

Val applied mascara with a hand as steady as a surgeon's. "No. I never liked school that much. It always seemed a little bit like prison to me—I wasn't going to sign up for extra. I just liked playing with my appearance, having a face for every mood. I practice a lot."

"I think you've got a real aptitude. If being the most

beautiful woman on the planet ever gets dull, you could open a salon."

Val flashed her brilliant teeth. "I never thought I would want an actual woman friend. It's more fun than I imagined."

"Ditto. Just curious, and you don't have to answer, but is Val for Valerie?"

"Valentine. Or Valentina. It changes, depending on mood and circumstance."

"Ah," Alex said. "That fits better."

"It's very *me*," Val told her. "It's not the name I was born with, of course."

"Whose is?" Alex murmured.

Val nodded. "It's only logical. My parents didn't even *know* me when they picked a name out. Of course it didn't fit."

"I never really thought of it that way, but it does make sense. My mother picked a name for a much more... feminine kind of girl."

"My parents evidently assumed I would be very boring. I cleared that misconception up pretty quickly."

Alex chuckled once. As was so often true lately, the laugh carried with it the barely disguised sound of panic. It was nice to talk like she imagined normal people did, to try to forget that this might be the last friendly, mundane conversation she would ever have, but she couldn't keep her thoughts focused on pleasantries.

Val patted her head. "It's going to be okay."

"You don't have to pretend to have faith in the plan. That's only for us suckers who are putting ourselves into the line of fire."

"It's not a bad plan," Val assured her. "I'm just not a risk taker. I never have been." She shrugged. "If I were brave, I would do it."

"It wasn't fair for me to ask you."

"No, it was. I do...care about Kevin. Part of me just can't believe that what you say is happening to him is actually happening. He's always seemed so invulnerable. That's what pulls me to him. Like I said, I'm not brave, so I'm fascinated with people who are. The other part of me..."

Val leaned back for a moment, the little brush with lip gloss on it trembling suddenly. Her face was still perfect, but suddenly it was the doll's face again. Exquisite, but empty.

"Val, are you okay?"

Val blinked and her face came back to life. "Yes."

"You'll leave here, after your part, right?"

"Absolutely. I have lots of friends who can protect me. Maybe I'll go visit Zhang. I'm sure he's still stuffy, but he has an amazing place in Beijing."

"Beijing sounds lovely," Alex half sighed. If she lived through tonight, she'd do whatever she had to in order to get her hands on a passport. She'd blow the rest of her savings—all of Kevin's drug money. To be out of the easy reach of the American government sounded like a practical version of heaven.

"If..." *Though* when *was probably more appropriate,* Alex thought to herself. "If you don't hear from any of us by sunrise, go see Zhang. If I can, I'll call you from a pay phone."

Val smiled a little. "You have my number." Her lips pursed. "You know, there's a guy... I might be able to get my hands on a service-dog vest."

Alex stared at her for a moment, then felt her face start to crumple. With the new plan, the suicidal plan, there was really no way for Alex to keep Einstein safe.

"That's a brilliant idea. That makes me feel better." Her positive words didn't match her expression.

Val reached out with one bare foot and stroked it along Einstein's back. His tail thumped once against the marble floor, but without much enthusiasm.

"Okay," Val said in a brighter voice. "You're done. I'll throw on my things, and we're off."

While Val disappeared into the closet, Alex checked out her face. Val had done another excellent job. Alex looked pretty, but not flashy. The hair was obviously hers, which was important; she would definitely be scrutinized tonight, and a wig would be the most obvious tell. She looked more or less credible for the role she'd chosen. Of course, she'd feel more comfortable with no makeup at all — in her experience, that was the way people in this specific role presented themselves, without fuss or vanity. But that was just baggage from her past.

She knelt down on the floor beside Einstein. He looked up at her with eyes that were unmistakably pleading. She stroked his muzzle, then rubbed his ears.

"I'll do everything I can," she promised. "I won't come back without him. If I screw this up, Val will take care of you. It will be okay."

Einstein's eyes didn't change. They accepted no excuses or consolation prizes. They just begged.

"I'll *try*," she vowed. She laid her forehead against his ear for just a moment. Then, with a sigh, she got to her feet. Einstein put his head on his paws and huffed out his own sigh.

"Val?" Alex called.

"Two seconds," Val called back. Her voice sounded far away, like she was at the other end of a football field. This bathroom was nice—like the bathroom in a fancy hotel suite—but not insane like Val's other place. Maybe the excess here was saved for the closet.

She heard Val shut the closet door and glanced up; she felt a brief jolt of shock at the change, then nodded.

"That looks about right," she approved.

"Thanks," Val replied. "Some parts of being a spy I could handle."

The outfit Val was wearing was not inconspicuous.

She had on a long flowy dress kind of thing that covered her from chin to wrist to floor, similar to a sari, but with more coverage; it had scarf-like pieces that cascaded around her, obscuring the shape of her body. It looked like something straight off an avant-garde runway, and probably was. It was memorable. But from behind, all you could see about her body was that she was tall. She wore a thick, dark wig with corkscrew curls that jutted out wildly in every direction. It, too, called attention at the same time that it obscured the shape of her head and covered parts of her face. With the wide-framed black sunglasses she held in her hand, she would be well hidden.

"Shall we?" Val asked.

Alex took a deep breath and nodded.

· · ·

ALEX PARKED VAL'S tacky green Jaguar at a meter on the hill overlooking a large, dingy-gray concrete office block. Val had insisted on the green car—a gift from another admirer, naturally. It was the one, she said, that she wouldn't miss if she had to submerge it in a lake.

From this angle, Alex could see the entrance to the underground parking garage. It was kind of sad, actually, that Carston had never moved to a better office. Maybe he liked the depressing surroundings. Maybe it seemed appropriate to the job and he liked things to conform. Making things easier for Alex had probably not been on his agenda, but it was nice it had worked out this way.

She and Val sat in the Jag for more than an hour, Val getting out to feed the meter once. They didn't talk; Alex's mind was miles away, working overtime to think through the flaws in her plan and try to fix them insofar as that was possible. There was so much that had to be left up to chance; she hated chance.

Alex imagined Val's mind was in Beijing. It was a good place to run to. Val might even be safe there. Alex wished she and Daniel were getting on a plane to Beijing right now.

Daniel probably wasn't enjoying the wait any more than she was. He'd be at the park now, nothing to fill his time until Alex arrived, no way to know what was happening. At least she had Val to sit with, even if neither of them was very good company at the moment.

Finally there was movement below, and she sat up straighter. The white-and-red-striped arm at the mouth of the garage was rising to let someone out. The last two alarms had both been delivery trucks, but this time a dark sedan was pulling out of the garage. Alex started the engine and rolled out onto the street. Someone honked behind her, but she didn't spare him a glance. She didn't take her eyes off the car. From this distance, it appeared to match Carston's black BMW. It was only just after four o'clock now, not quite time for government employees to be heading out.

Here was the first big chance. Once Erin Carston-Boyd was sure her daughter was missing, she would have called her father in a panic. Right? She knew he had some kind of important government job. She would consider him powerful and capable. She wouldn't rely on just the police with her daughter kidnapped. Should it have taken this long? When Alex had last been able to check, no call had come and Carston was still in his office. Managing Kevin's interrogation, no doubt.

She thought he would head to his daughter's side. It seemed the only response. But what if Carston had other options? What if he sent a special ops team instead? Was he that cold? If he had to be . . . probably yes.

But surely Deavers could manage the interrogation by himself for a few hours. Right?

Alex's driving was much more offensive than defensive as she weaved her way forward, refusing to stop for even the pinkest of yellow lights. She knew the two best routes from Carston's office to the zoo, where she assumed Erin's call had come from. Would the terrified mother leave the last place she'd seen her daughter before she was positive the child wasn't hiding somewhere in the foliage? If the call came from a police station, of which there were several possible options, Carston could take a number of different routes.

So many things left to chance.

The BMW was heading down the correct street, the one she would have chosen as the quickest route to the zoo. He was driving a little erratically as well. She carefully moved up from behind two other cars. She didn't want to spook him.

It was the right car. The plates matched. It looked like the back of Carston's mostly bald head.

Alex watched for eyes in the rearview mirror, but he seemed to be focused on the road. She maneuvered into the parallel lane.

She supposed she should feel better that this part was going according to plan. But it felt like someone was drilling a wide hole into the bottom of her stomach; she thought she might gag as she pulled alongside his car. Because if this part worked, that meant she had to go forward with the rest of the plan.

The light turned yellow ahead. Cars streamed through, but Carston was slowing. He knew he was too far back to make it. The car in front of him braked, too. Alex could have pulled up to the line in her lane — the car in front of her had turned right. Instead, she stopped directly beside Carston.

She waved, her face pointed straight toward his profile. The motion was deliberately large, meant to catch his peripheral vision.

Carston glanced over automatically at the movement, his mind clearly far away, worry making a crinkled mess of his forehead. It took him a second to realize what he was seeing. In that instant of shock, before he could smash down the accelerator, pull a gun, or dial a number, she held up the phone in her hand. She had the image zoomed in on the girl's sleeping face.

He locked down his expression as the facts began falling into place.

Quickly, she hopped out of her car and reached for the passenger door of his. She didn't look back to watch Val slide over into the driver's seat, but she heard the door close behind her. Alex waited with her fingers on the BMW's passenger-door handle until she heard the locks click open. She climbed in next to him. The whole wordless exchange had taken less than two seconds. The cars behind them might be curious, but they would probably forget the transfer by the next light.

"Turn left," she told Carston as Val went right and headed east. The Jag disappeared around the corner.

Carston was quick to recover. He put on his blinker and pulled across the left lane, nearly hitting the van headed through the light. Alex took his phone out of the cup holder, powered it down, and shoved it in her pocket.

"What do you want?" he asked. His voice sounded

calm, but she could hear the strain in his lack of inflection.

"I need your help."

He took a moment to digest that.

"Turn right at the next corner."

He complied carefully. "Who is your partner?"

"Someone for hire. Not your concern."

"I really believed you were dead this time."

Alex didn't respond.

"What have you done to Livvy?"

"Nothing permanent. Yet."

"She's only three." His voice quavered uncharacteristically.

She turned to give him an incredulous look, which was wasted, as he never glanced away from the road in front of them. "Really? You expect me to care about civilians at this point?"

"She's done nothing to you."

"What did three innocent people in Texas do to you, Carston? Never mind," she said when he opened his mouth to answer. "That was obviously rhetorical."

"What do you want from me?"

"Kevin Beach."

There was another long pause as he rearranged things in his mind.

"You're going to turn left at the next block," she instructed.

"*How* did you..." He shook his head. "I don't have him. The CIA does."

"I know who has him. And I know Deavers is following your direction in his interrogation," she bluffed. "Your specialist is the one leading the case. I'm sure you know where they're working on him."

He stared stone-faced through the windshield.

"I don't understand what is happening," he muttered.

"Let's talk about what you do understand, then," Alex said in a bleak voice. "Of course you remember a little concoction Barnaby and I created for you called *Deadline*."

His pasty skin started to mottle, blotches of puce blooming on his cheeks and neck. She held her phone out and his eyes flickered to it automatically. The photo was back to its original size now, and the IV hooked into his granddaughter's arm was conspicuously in the foreground. There was a saline bag, the nutrition bag, and a smaller, dark green bag attached underneath it.

He stared at the photo for one long second, then his eyes were back on the road.

"How long?" he asked through his teeth.

"I was generous. Twelve hours. One hour has passed. This operation shouldn't take more than four, at most. Then Livvy is delivered safely back to her mother, no worse for wear."

"And I'm dead?"

"I'll be honest, the odds aren't good that either of us makes it through unscathed. A lot is riding on your acting abilities, Carston. Lucky for you, we both know how convincing you can be."

"What happens if, through no fault of mine, you die?"

"Bad luck for Livvy. And her mother, for that matter. Things have been set in motion. If you care about your family, you'll do your very, very best to get me out alive."

"You could be bluffing. You were never this cold-blooded."

"Policies change. People change. Shall I share a secret?"

She gave him a moment to respond, but he just stared straight ahead with his jaw locked.

"Kevin Beach wasn't in Texas when Deavers sent the kill squad. *I* was." She let those two words hang in the air for a moment before she went on. Carston wasn't the only one with acting abilities. "I'm not the person you used to know, Carston. You'd be surprised at the things I'm capable of now. Take the next right."

"I don't know what you hope to accomplish here."

"Let's get down to it," Alex said. "Where is Kevin?"

Carston didn't hesitate. "He's in a facility west of the city. It used to be a CIA interrogation suite, but they haven't used it in years. Officially, it's abandoned."

"The address?"

He listed it from memory without a pause.

"What kind of security?"

He glanced over, his eyes studying her for a second before he responded. "I don't have that information. But knowing Deavers, it's more than is necessary. He'll go overboard. He's terrified of Kevin Beach. That's why he came up with the whole charade with the brother. *No risk,* that's what he called it." Carston chuckled once. It was a bitter sound, in no way amused.

"Does he know my face?"

Carston's eyes jerked to her in surprise. "You're going in?"

"Will he recognize me?" she demanded. "How much of my file did he see? Did you show him the footage from the Metro?"

Carston pursed his lips. "We agreed from the beginning to keep our…situations separate. It was need-to-know. Years ago, he would have had access to your old recruitment file, your write-ups from a few interrogations. He might still have those, but nothing more current. The only picture in that old file was from your mother's funeral. You were very young, your hair was longer and darker…" He paused, seeming lost in thought. "Deavers isn't a detail guy. I doubt he'd be able to link you to the picture. You don't look that much like nineteen-year-old Juliana Fortis anymore."

She hoped he was right. "It's more than my life on the line," she reminded him.

"I'm aware. And . . . that much is a bet I'd take. But I don't know what you think you're going to do when you get inside."

"*We,* Carston, we. And, probably, we go down in a hail of bullets."

"And Livvy pays? That's not acceptable," he growled.

"Then give me more to work with."

He took a deep breath, and she glanced over at him. He looked exhausted.

"How about this," she suggested. She was going on intuition. She'd listened to Carston's aggravation with that one particular *him* in the phone calls, and she thought she could guess who it was. After all, it was Deavers's plan that had failed so spectacularly, over and over. "Would it be accurate to characterize you as unhappy with Deavers's management of this joint operation?"

He grunted.

"Have you and Deavers disagreed on how to proceed?"

"You could say that."

"Does he think that you trust him to handle the interrogation of Kevin Beach?"

"No, at this point, I would say he does not believe that I trust him to zip up his own fly correctly."

"Tell me about your interrogation specialist."

Carston made a sour face. "Not mine. He's Deavers's lackey, and he's an imbecile. I told Deavers that someone like Beach was going to die before he talked to an ordinary interrogator. You can rest easy, if that's your concern. They won't break him. Beach hasn't said anything about you, except that he killed you. I don't think they even followed up on that. To be fair, I believed it, too."

She was surprised. "So you never replaced me?"

Carston shook his head. "I've tried. I wasn't lying about that in the beginning—you remember? 'True talent is a limited commodity.'" He quoted himself and sighed. "Deavers has had a stranglehold on the department for a long time now, ever since I 'lost a dangerous asset.' The CIA has blocked my recruitment process and shut down all but the lab. The things we're producing now could be created by any halfway decent pharmacist." He shook his head. "They act as if they aren't the reason why you're dangerous in the first place."

"You still pretend you weren't part of that decision?"

"If I had been, I'm being punished for it now." Carston stared morosely through the windshield.

"Would Deavers be shocked to learn that you were developing talent on the side?"

Carston was always quick. He pursed his lips and nodded as he talked it through. "For about half a second, then he'll just be angry. He's one hundred percent on board with the current program, but he knows my doubts have been increasing. No, he won't be that surprised."

"You don't like how Pace gets things done? He seems like a pragmatic person, I thought you'd get along."

"So you did put it together. I thought you might. But I'll bet you never would have if Pace hadn't over-reacted in the first place. Machiavellianism doesn't bother me—stupidity does. Mistakes happen, but Pace has a penchant for compounding one error with a second that's worse. And then a third. He's put us all in this mess."

"What are you saying, Carston? That we're on the same side? Everybody makes mistakes, like you said, but you shouldn't rely on my gullibility again."

"I don't expect you to believe me, but it is what it is. I have nothing to gain from the current agenda. If Pace succeeds, Deavers's star will rise. He'll end up director of the CIA. My life's work is already being dismantled. We're more on the same side than you know."

"If it makes you happy to say so. It doesn't change the plan."

"We go in together," he mused. "You're my secret protégée. I insist that you take over for Deavers's butcher. It can work, up to that point. I don't know what you think happens then."

She tried to hide her flinch when Carston said the word *butcher*. So much depended on how much was left of Kevin.

"We'll see," she said, working to keep her voice smooth.

"No, don't tell me. That's smart. Just as long as you have a plan."

She didn't answer. Her plan wasn't strong enough.

"Just out of curiosity," she asked, trying to distract Carston from her reaction. "When did Dominic Haugen die?"

"Two weeks after the lab in Jammu was destroyed."

She nodded. Then it was as she'd suspected. Barnaby had seen something and begun his preparations.

"I have an idea," Carston volunteered.

"This should be good."

"How do you feel about faking some injuries? A sling, maybe? We had a situation in Turkey nine days ago, got some good information from a quick-thinking corporal. Exactly the kind of person I would have been interested in recruiting, but the situation went dark. The corporal didn't survive the hostile force's rescue attempt. But maybe the information was actually acquired by my secret side project, who *did* make it out alive."

She stared at him.

He held a hand up, as if in surrender. "Okay, we

don't have to do it my way. It was just an idea. Deavers knows the story; it would make my bringing you in feel anchored, less spur of the moment."

"I think I can manage some injuries," Alex said dryly.

• • •

THEY'D GONE OVER the story a few times before they reached the rendezvous point, and he'd described the interrogation room in detail. It wasn't a pretty picture, and she felt their chances for survival getting more bleak.

Carston pulled into the lot attached to the small municipal park and stopped the Bimmer next to the only other car in the lot, as directed. It gave Alex a start, even though she was expecting it, to see the big blond man waiting on the park bench.

This was the first test, and if Daniel didn't pass, she was pulling the plug. Carston had surely seen the photos of Daniel on the news, no matter how separate he and Deavers had kept their operations. She watched Carston from the corner of her eye, assessing his reaction. His face was a blank.

"Who's this?" he asked.

"Your new aide."

"Is that necessary?"

"Cut the engine."

Daniel got up and walked quickly toward them.

Alex watched Carston for any change in expression as Daniel approached.

"I can't watch you every second, Carston," she said sweetly. "Pop the trunk."

She and Carston waited in silence as Daniel moved the gear from the back of the sedan into the BMW's cargo space. When he was done, he stood beside Carston's door, waiting.

"Get out," Alex said.

Slowly, always keeping his hands in view, Carston opened the door and stepped out. As Alex got out, she saw the way he was eyeing Daniel. She tried to appraise Daniel impartially. He was a large man and looked able to handle himself, even with the glasses and the extra paunch. It made sense under these circumstances that Carston would be cautious and probably frightened, though he hid it well.

As instructed, Daniel said nothing. He met Alex's eyes only briefly and kept his expression neutral. His jaw jutted out just a bit, the way it had when he'd intimidated the drunk boys in Oklahoma City. It made him look dangerous, but also slightly more like Kevin. Had Carston seen photos of Kevin?

Daniel stopped beside the driver's door, his arms loose at his sides, ready.

"Hands on the roof," Alex ordered Carston. "Don't move until I get back."

Carston assumed the position of a suspect braced

against a police car. He kept his head down, but Alex could tell he was examining what he could see of Daniel in the window's reflection. There was no sign of recognition, but Alex couldn't be sure if Carston was hiding his response. Alex was distracted by the way the parking-lot lights glinted off their bald heads in the same spots.

"This is Mr. Thomas," she told Carston. "If you try to give me away, or escape, or hurt me, you'll be dead in approximately two and a half seconds."

A bead of sweat was forming at Carston's temple. If he was faking that, she was truly impressed.

"I'm not going to do anything to endanger Livvy," he snapped.

"Good. I'll be right back. I'm going to go give myself some injuries."

Daniel's bright blue eyes flickered to her when she said the word *injuries;* he forced them back to Carston.

All her things were neatly stowed in the cargo hold of the BMW. She unzipped the first-aid duffel bag and rummaged around quickly till she found what she needed, then cut off a short section of gauze and tape. She grabbed her handbag and turned away, leaving the trunk open. The public restroom was just on the other side of the little playground. She walked quickly to the ladies' room and turned on the lights.

There was no counter, and nothing had been cleaned in days, maybe weeks, so she kept the bag on her shoulder. She used the gritty powdered soap to scrub off Val's lovely makeup job. It was better this way. The makeup was out of character, and the patch of fake skin would have been a red flag to anyone who looked closely. Her bruises and bandages would draw attention, obviously, but they would also make her less recognizable. People would be less likely to examine the face underneath.

She was happy to see the remnants of her black eyes, the yellow shape of the lingering bruise on her cheek. The glue job on her jaw was too amateur, but a normal person would keep it bandaged regardless.

There were no towels, just a broken air dryer. She used her T-shirt to dry her face, then taped the gauze to her jaw and ear, taking the extra seconds to do the job right, so it looked like a doctor had done it. Her black T-shirt and thick leggings worked—comfortable clothes were part of the job, and the lab coat in the trunk would give her the professional appearance she wanted.

As she walked back to the car in the encroaching darkness, she could hear Carston trying to engage Daniel, but Daniel was staring down at the man with his lips tightly closed.

Alex retrieved the lab coat from the trunk and put it on, then ran her palms down the front of it to smooth out the folds. When she was satisfied, she shut the trunk and opened the back door.

"At ease, Lowell," she told Carston. He straightened up warily. "You'll ride with me in the back. Mr. Thomas will drive."

"Taciturn fellow," Carston commented as he ducked in through the open door.

"He's not here to entertain you; he's here to keep you in line."

Alex shut the door behind him, then walked around the car to climb in the other side. Carston stared at her.

"Your face...that's very realistic work, Jules. Subtle. It doesn't look like you're wearing any makeup at all now."

"I've developed many new skills, and the name is Dr. Jordan Reid. Please direct Mr. Thomas to our destination. When we're five minutes out, you get your phone back."

Her eyes met Daniel's in the mirror. He gave one tiny shake of his head. Carston hadn't said anything to make Daniel think he'd been recognized during the time they were alone.

Daniel started the engine. Carston gave him the address and a short set of directions. Daniel nodded once.

Carston turned to Alex and asked, "I assume someone is with Livvy now?"

"Assumptions are never a safe bet, you know that."

"If I do my best, Jules, if I do everything I can..." Carston began. His voice was suddenly raw. "Please. Please let Livvy go. Make the call, whatever you have to do. Even if...even if you're not getting out. I know you have every reason to hurt me, but, please, not the baby." He was only whispering by the end. She rather thought he was speaking from the heart, as much as he had one.

"I can't do anything for her if I don't make it out. I'm sorry, Carston, I wish I could have done things differently, but I didn't have the time or the resources."

He clenched his hands in his lap and stared at them. "You better know what you're doing."

She didn't answer. He probably could guess what that meant.

"If we go down," he said, his voice stronger, "at least take that bastard Deavers with us. Can you do that?"

"I'll make a point of it."

. . .

"WE'RE FIVE MINUTES out, approximately."

"Okay, here."

Alex handed Carston his phone. He turned it on, then, after a second, selected a number from his address book. The phone rang twice over the car's speaker.

"Why are you interrupting me?" a man answered.

His voice was pitched to be quiet, almost a whisper, but Alex could hear that it was a deep baritone. He sounded annoyed.

Carston was annoyed, too. "I'm assuming there's been no progress."

"I don't have time for this."

"None of us have time for this," Carston snapped. "Enough is enough. I'll be at the gate in two minutes. Make sure they're expecting me and my assistants."

"What—" Deavers started, but Carston hung up.

"Combative," Alex commented.

"It's our normal form of interaction."

"I hope so."

"I'll do my part, Jules. If Livvy weren't involved, I think I would actually enjoy this. I am so *tired* of that pompous fool."

The building they pulled up to would have looked abandoned if there weren't two cars parked beside the entrance. The small lot was protected by steep, man-made hills that surrounded it on three sides, the unassuming, one-story concrete building taking up the fourth. The front of the building wasn't visible until you were already in the lot. The location was hidden in the middle of miles of warehouses and Soviet bloc–style office buildings, all certainly owned by some arm of the government and all seemingly empty. As was the maze of roads weaving through them. She doubted anyone would wander back here by accident, and she was glad she'd had Carston to guide them through the maze. She hoped Daniel had paid attention. She'd tried to memorize the route, but it was unlikely she'd be there to guide him back out.

There were no lights in the small, shaded windows, but that was expected. The ground floor was nothing but camouflage.

Carston got out and came around to hold the car door for her, already acting his role. She almost smiled, remembering what it had been like when she had been *the talent*. Well, that was her part to play tonight. She would have to get into character.

Daniel pulled the steel toolbox on rollers out of the trunk and brought it around to her. Someone was probably already watching, though she couldn't see where the cameras were hidden.

"Careful with that," she admonished in a stern tone, taking the handle from him. She straightened her left cuff, and brushed an imaginary speck of dust off her sleeve. Daniel went to stand just behind Carston's right shoulder. She noticed the gold pinkie ring. It didn't quite fit the picture, but the rest of him did—even in the dark lot, his black suit looked just right, conservative, not expensive; every FBI agent in the country had something exactly like it in his or her closet. No badge, but then, anyone working as an aide to *this* department wouldn't be expected to carry identification. It wasn't a badge kind of organization.

She squared her shoulders and faced the dark building, trying to come to terms with the fact that she'd probably never see this ugly parking lot again.

CHAPTER 30

This way, Dr. Reid," Carston said, and he led them to a blank gray door. Daniel stayed close on his heels, his back to Alex. She walked briskly behind them, struggling to keep up with her shorter legs.

Carston didn't knock on the door; he merely stood directly in front of it. Expectant, like he'd already rung the bell.

The door opened a second after Carston planted himself. The man who answered it wore a suit not unlike Daniel's, though this man's was so new it still had a sheen on it. He was shorter than Daniel and wider through the shoulders. There was an obvious bulge under his left arm.

"Sir," the man said, and saluted Carston. His hair was high and tight, and she guessed he'd feel more at home in a uniform. But his appearance was still part of the camouflage. The uniforms would be downstairs.

"I need to see Deavers immediately."

"Yes, sir, he informed us you'd be arriving. This way."

The soldier turned abruptly and paced inside.

She followed Daniel into a drab office space: gray carpet, a few tight cubicles, some uncomfortable-looking chairs. The door closed behind her with a solid-sounding thud and an ominous click. No doubt someone was still watching; she couldn't afford a glance back to look at the lock. She would have to hope it was meant to keep people out and not in. It hadn't taken the soldier long to open the door to them.

The soldier turned sharply down a dim hallway, took them past several darkened rooms with open doors, then stopped at the very end. There was a door there labeled JANITORIAL SUPPLIES. He reached into his left sleeve and pulled out a spiral cord with a key. He unlocked the door and led the way inside.

The room was dimly lit by an emergency exit sign over another door opposite the first. Mops and buckets lined the wall, presumably for show. The soldier opened the emergency door, revealing a featureless, metal-lined box. An elevator. She'd known to expect this; she hoped Daniel was controlling his expressions.

They joined the soldier in the elevator. When she turned to face the doors, she saw that there were only two buttons. He pressed the bottom one, and she felt the descent begin immediately. She couldn't be sure, but it felt like at least three floors. Not entirely necessary, but definitely disconcerting. Though this building had not been used for the same kind of interrogations she had conducted, it would still be part of the routine to make the subject feel alarmed and isolated.

It worked; she felt an increase in both.

The elevator came to an abrupt halt, and the doors opened on a brightly lit anteroom. It looked like an airport security post, only much less crowded and more colorless. There were two more men, these in dark blue army uniforms, and a standard metal detector with a short counter and even the little plastic trays for belt buckles and car keys. The uniforms made Alex think these must be Pace's men.

The surveillance cameras were very obvious in this room.

Carston moved forward, impatient and sure of himself. He put his phone in the tray, and a handful of change. Then he stalked through the square frame. Daniel moved quickly behind him, putting the car keys in another tray, then retrieving Carston's belongings and handing them back to him before reclaiming the keys for himself.

Alex wheeled the steel toolbox to the side of the detector.

"I'm afraid you'll have to search that by hand," she said as she walked through the frame. "I have a lot of metal tools. Please be careful, some of my things are breakable, and some are pressurized."

The two soldiers looked at each other, obviously uncertain. They looked at her damaged face, then at her toolbox. The taller one knelt down to open the top compartment while the shorter one stared at her face again.

"Please be careful," she repeated. "Those syringes are delicate."

The short soldier watched now as the tall soldier lifted the top tray of syringes, only to find an identical tray below it. He carefully replaced it, not checking the two trays beneath. He opened the second compartment, then looked up quickly at his companion. Then at Carston.

"Sir, we aren't supposed to let weapons past this point."

"Of course I'll need my scalpels," Alex said, letting some irritation bleed into her tone. "I'm not here to play Scrabble."

The soldiers looked at her again, understanding beginning to dawn in their eyes.

Yes, she wanted to say, *I'm* that *kind of guest.*

They might have read the words in her expression. The tall one straightened up.

"We're going to have to get authorization for this." He turned on his heel and strode through the metal double doors behind them.

Carston huffed out a big, exasperated breath and folded his arms across his chest. Alex schooled her expression into one of impatience. Daniel stood very still by Carston's right shoulder, his face blank. He was doing well. No one had paid him any attention at all. To the soldiers, he was just one of those anonymous briefcase holders, which was exactly what she'd hoped for. Val was right thus far—they would have paid much more attention to her.

It was only a few minutes before the doors opened again. The tall soldier was back with two other men.

It was easy to tell which was Deavers. He was smaller and more gaunt than the voice had suggested, but he moved with an obvious authority. He didn't watch to see where the other men walked; he expected them to move around him. He wore a well-cut black suit, several pay grades in price and style above what Daniel and the door guard were wearing. His hair was steel gray, but still thick.

From his lack of formality, Alex guessed the man behind Deavers was the interrogator. He was dressed in a rumpled T-shirt and black pants that looked like scrubs. His lank brown hair was greasy and disheveled; there were substantial bags under his bloodshot eyes. Though he'd obviously had a long day, there was fire in those eyes as he focused on her lab coat, then her toolbox, the scalpel tray still exposed.

"What is this, Carston?" he blustered.

Neither Carston nor Deavers looked at him. Their eyes were focused on each other.

"What do you think you're doing?" Deavers asked in an even voice.

"I'm not going to let that hack kill the subject when I have a better option."

Deavers looked at her for the first time. She tried to project calm, but she felt her heart racing as he examined her, his eyes lingering on the damage to her face.

He turned back to Carston. "And where did you suddenly get this better option?"

At least he hadn't recognized her immediately. And he hadn't so much as looked at Daniel. The two men were focused on each other again, antagonism running between them like an electric current.

"I've been developing alternatives to save the program. This alternative has already proven herself more than capable."

"Proven how?"

Carston's chin moved up an inch. "Uludere."

The current seemed to break on that word. Deavers took an unconscious step back and blew out an annoyed breath. He looked at Alex's bandaged face again, then at his adversary.

"I should have known there was more going on in Turkey. Carston, this is beyond your authority."

"I'm currently being underutilized. Just trying to make myself more valuable."

Deavers pursed his lips and glanced back at her again. "She's good?"

"You'll see," Carston promised.

"But I'm at a critical point," the interrogator protested. "You can't pull me off the case now."

Carston gave him a withering glance. "Shut up, Lindauer. You're out of your league."

"All right," Deavers said sourly. "Let's see if your better option can get us what we need."

.   .   .

THE ROOM WAS as Carston had described. Plain concrete walls, plain concrete floor. One door, a large one-way mirror between this and the observation room, a round overhead light flush with the ceiling.

At one time, there would have been a desk in this room, two chairs, and a very bright desk lamp. Subjects would have been questioned, harangued, threatened, and pressured, but that would have been the extent of it.

Now a surgical table took the place of the desk. It was like something from a World War I movie, one solid piece of unpadded stainless steel with the kind of wheels a gurney had. There was a folding chair in the corner. This facility was nowhere near as functional as the state-of-the-art suites back at the department, but clearly, this interrogation was off even the most covert section's records.

She kept her inspection clinical and prayed that Daniel would have the restraint necessary for this.

Daniel had accompanied Carston and the others into the observation room, and he was invisible to her behind the glass. Before the group divided, neither Deavers nor any of the others had looked at his face. She desperately hoped he would do nothing now to change their indifference to suspicion.

Kevin lay on the table under the one light, hand-cuffed and shackled in place. He was naked, his body gleaming wet with sweat and blood. Long burns blistered a multitude of uneven parallel lines down his chest. Thin slices ran up his ribs, ragged skin blanched at the edges — probably with acid. The soles of his feet were covered in blisters and bleached white as well. Lindauer had poured acid into those burns. Kevin was missing another toe on his left foot, the one next to the first stump.

Lindauer's tools littered the floor, messy with blood and his dirty handprints. She knew there was a toe down there, too, but she couldn't find it at first glance.

She'd expected a clean, clinical setup; that was what she was used to. This was savagery. Her nose wrinkled in disgust.

Kevin was alert. He watched her as she walked in behind the interrogator, his face tightly controlled.

With a precision meant to mock Lindauer's unprofessional work habits, she bent to her toolbox and carefully laid out a few of her syringe trays.

"What's this?" Kevin asked hoarsely. She glanced up automatically to see that he was addressing the mirror, not her. "You think a little girl can break me? I thought this flunky was the low. Honestly, you guys never cease to disappoint."

Lindauer, who had insisted on being in the room, leaned furiously over the table. He jammed one finger into a slash wound that cut across a burn on Kevin's chest. Kevin grunted and clenched his jaw.

"Don't worry, Mr. Beach. The *little girl* is just a nice rest period for you. Get your strength back. I'll return later, and then we'll have some productive conversations."

"Enough, *Doctor*," Alex snapped in a ringing tone. "I agreed to let you observe, but you will kindly step away from my subject now."

Lindauer glanced at the mirror as if expecting backup. When he got only silence in response, he frowned sullenly and went to sit in the lone chair. Once he was down, he seemed to collapse a little, whether from exhaustion or disgrace, she couldn't tell.

Alex turned her back on Lindauer and pulled on a pair of blue latex gloves. The small piece of metal she'd palmed in the process was invisible beneath the right glove.

She stepped to the edge of the table, gingerly clearing a swath in Lindauer's mess with one foot.

"Hello, Mr. Beach. How are you feeling?"

"Good to go a few more rounds, sweetheart. Looks like somebody already had a nice time with you, eh? Hope it was fun for him."

While he spit the words through his teeth, she began examining him, shining a small flashlight in his eyes and then assessing the veins in his arms and hands.

"A little dehydrated, I think," she said. She looked directly at the mirror while she put his right hand back on the table, leaving the thin key under his palm. "I assumed there would be an IV in place. Could I get a pole, please? I have my own saline and needles."

"I'll *bet* you know your way around a pole," Kevin said.

"No need to be crass, Mr. Beach. Now that I'm here, things will be much more civilized. I do apologize for the current conditions. This is all very unprofessional." She sniffed scornfully, giving Lindauer her most cutting side-eye. He looked away.

"Honey, if this is the good-cop routine, sorry, but you're not really my type."

"I assure you, Mr. Beach, I am not the good cop. I am a specialist, and I should warn you now, I won't play the same silly games this . . . *interrogator*" — the desire to use a less flattering word was clear in her inflection — "has wasted your time with. We'll get down to business immediately."

"Yeah, sugar, let's get down to business, that's what I'm talking about." Kevin tried to keep his voice loud and his tone derisive, but she could see the effort it was costing him.

The door opened behind her. She watched in the mirror as the tall soldier brought in an IV pole. So far she'd seen only four others besides Deavers and Lindauer, but there were probably more hidden from view.

"Just put that at the head of the table, thank you," she said without turning to look at him, voice dismissive. She bent to retrieve the syringe she wanted.

"You gonna dance for me now?" Kevin muttered.

She looked at Kevin coldly as she straightened. "This will be just a sample of what we'll be doing tonight," she told him as she circled the table. She placed the syringe by his head while she hung the saline bag and the tubing. The door closed, but she didn't look away from Kevin. She examined his veins again, then chose his left arm. He didn't resist. While she carefully inserted the needle, she tried to spy the key she'd given him, but it was nowhere in sight. She picked up the largest blade she could see on the floor and laid it next to his right arm. "You see, I don't need such crude weapons; I have something better. I always think it's fairer to let the subject understand what he's up against before I go full strength. Let me know what you think."

"I'll tell you what I think, you—" Kevin launched into an avalanche of profanity that put all his previous creative descriptions to shame. The man had a talent.

"I appreciate your bravery, really, I do," Alex said when he was done. She held the point of the syringe against the IV port. "But please know, it's a wasted effort. Playtime is over."

She stabbed the needle through the plastic and depressed the plunger.

The response was nearly immediate. She heard his breathing accelerate, and then he started shrieking.

Lindauer's head snapped up. She could tell he'd never gotten a reaction like this from Kevin, despite his best efforts. She heard movement behind the glass as the audience edged closer, and the faint murmur of voices. She thought she could pick out a surprised tone, and it was gratifying. Though, honestly, it was all due to Kevin's acting.

She knew how he would be feeling now as the strength raced through his veins and all the pain vanished. She'd used more than double the highest dose of *Survive* she'd ever used on herself, taking into account his greater mass and need. His screams were primal, almost triumphant. She hoped she was the only one to notice that nuance and that he'd remember that the damage done to his body was still very real, whether he felt it any longer or not.

She waited only five minutes—tapping her foot and watching him dispassionately—while he did his part, keeping his screams loud and constant. She wanted him to have as much time with the drugs in his system as possible. When they wore off, he would be incapacitated.

"There, Mr. Beach," she said as she shot ordinary saline into the IV line. She gave him the cue he would need. "I think we understand each other now, so I can let this end. Shall we talk?"

Kevin took longer to recover than he should have, but then, he didn't know her drugs. He pretended to come out of it slowly, and she was glad Daniel was standing close to Carston with the venom-coated ring ready. Only Carston would recognize the fraud.

Kevin was still breathing heavily after a minute, and he actually had tears streaming down the sides of his face. It was easy for her to forget he was an under-cover professional, because she'd never seen him in the field, but she should have known he would nail this performance.

"Well, Mr. Beach, what now? Shall we continue to full strength, or would you like to talk first?"

He turned to stare at her, his eyes wide with convincing fear.

"Who are you?" he whispered.

"A specialist, as I told you. I believe the *gentleman*"— sarcastically, with a nod toward Lindauer—"had some questions for you?"

"If I talk," he said, still in a whisper, "do you go away?"

"Of course, Mr. Beach. I am merely a means to an end. Once you have satisfied my employers, you will never have to see me again."

Lindauer was openly gaping now, but Alex was worried. They had to keep moving forward, but at the same time, would anyone believe Kevin could fold so easily?

Kevin moaned and closed his eyes. "They won't believe me," he said.

She wasn't sure how, but she thought his right handcuff was no longer locked to his wrist. There was just the tiniest misalignment of the two halves of the bracelet. She didn't think anyone could see it but her.

"I'll believe you, if you tell me the truth. Just tell me what you want to say."

"I did have help . . . but . . . I can't . . ."

She took his hand in hers, as if she were soothing him. She felt the key drop into her palm.

"You *can* tell me. But please don't try to buy time. I have little patience."

She patted his hand, then walked around his head to examine the IV line.

"No," he mumbled weakly. "I won't."

"All right, then," she said, "what do you want to tell me?" She dropped her hand onto his left, inserting the key between his fingers.

"I had help . . . from a traitor on the inside."

"What?" Lindauer gasped out loud.

She shot him a dirty look, then turned to the mirror.

"Your man is unable to control himself. I want him removed from this room," she said severely.

An electronic crackle sounded through the room. She glanced up for the speaker but couldn't find it.

"Continue," Deavers's disembodied voice commanded. "He will be escorted out if there is any more misconduct."

She frowned at her own reflection, then turned to lean over Kevin.

"I need a name," she insisted.

"Carston," he breathed.

No!

Nerves already frayed and strained, she had to fight back the urge to slap him. But of course Kevin had no way of knowing how she'd gotten here.

She heard a commotion in the observation room and hurried on in a louder voice. "I find that very hard to believe, Mr. Beach, as Mr. Carston is the reason I am here with you. He wouldn't send me in if he wanted to avoid the truth. He knows what I'm capable of."

Kevin shot her one disgusted look under half-lowered lids, then groaned again. "That's the name my contact gave me. I can only tell you what he told me."

Nice save, she thought sarcastically.

The commotion hadn't ended with either her pronouncement or Kevin's. She could hear raised voices and some movement. Lindauer was distracted, too, staring at the glass.

She tried again, pulling a new syringe and slipping a small device from beneath it into her pocket. "Forgive me for thinking that was all a bit too easy—"

"No, wait," Kevin huffed, pitching his voice a little louder. "Deavers sent the guy; he knows who I'm talking about."

Well, maybe that would muddy the water a bit. Get both names on the table.

It wasn't stopping whatever was happening in the observation room, though. She had to make a move. The one good thing about the unanticipated situation on the other side of the glass was that they obviously weren't watching her very carefully. Time was up.

"Mr. Lindauer," she called sharply without looking in his direction. In the mirror, she could see that he was preoccupied with the other room as well. His head whipped around to her.

"I'm worried these ankle restraints are a little too tight. I need his circulation performing optimally. Do you have the key?"

Kevin could guess what this was about. His muscles tensed in readiness. Lindauer hurried to the foot of the table. One voice was raised above the others in the observation room, shouting.

"I don't know what you're talking about," Lindauer complained, his eyes on Kevin's ankles and mangled feet. "These aren't cutting off his circulation. It wouldn't be safe to have them any looser. You don't know what kind of man you're dealing with."

She stepped close to him, speaking softly so that he would have to lean in toward her. Inside her pocket, she pressed her thumb against the tiny flash capacitor of the electromagnetic-pulse emitter.

"I know exactly what kind of man I'm dealing with," she murmured.

She switched on the capacitor with her left hand and stabbed the syringe into Lindauer's arm with her right.

The light overhead flickered and popped; the shattered bulbs tinkled against the Plexiglas face of the fixture. Luckily the pulse didn't blow out the Plexiglas or it would have been bad for Kevin's exposed skin. The room went black.

The pulse wasn't strong enough to reach the other room. Muted light shone through the mirror, and she could see dark figures moving on the other side of the glass, but she couldn't tell who was who or what was happening.

Lindauer managed only half a scream before he was convulsing on the floor. She could hear Kevin moving, too, though those sounds were much quieter and more purposeful than Lindauer's thrashing.

She knew precisely where her toolbox was in the dark. She whirled and fell to her knees next to it, yanked the second-to-last drawer open, emptied the tray of syringes to the floor, and felt for the hidden compartment beneath.

"Ollie?" Kevin breathed. She could hear he was off the table now, near the IV pole.

She grabbed the first two guns she touched and lurched toward the sound of his voice. She collided with his chest, and his arms came up to keep her from falling backward. She shoved the guns against his stomach just as two shots rang out in the other room. There was no shatter of glass—they weren't shooting into the interrogation room. A third, and then a fourth shot.

"Danny's in there," she hissed as he yanked the guns out of her hands.

She fell back to her knees as he spun away and slid into the toolbox. She grabbed the other two guns, the familiar shape of her own PPK and another she didn't recognize by touch. She'd given Kevin her SIG Sauer by accident.

It didn't matter. She'd accomplished the main objectives of her strategy: free Kevin and get a loaded gun into his hands. Now she was primarily backup. She just had to hope that the star performer was in good enough shape to do what she needed him to do. If that sadist Lindauer had injured him too greatly... well, then they were all dead.

Lindauer had gotten his. He was probably still alive, but not for much longer. He wouldn't enjoy what was left of his life at all.

A full second hadn't passed when another shot echoed deafeningly through the small concrete room, and this time there was the muffled crunch of buckling safety glass.

Cracks of yellow light spider-webbed through the window as four shots responded back in quick succession. The answering shots didn't change the splintered pattern of light; again, they weren't aimed into the interrogation room. They were still shooting at each other inside the observation room.

She stayed low as she moved forward, guns pointed at the fractured square in case someone burst through it. But the movement came from her side; a dark shadow hurtled into the mosaic of glass fragments and crashed through it into the next room.

The men in the observation room were only ten feet away from her, so much closer than the hay bales she'd practiced on that it seemed too easy. She braced her hands against the steel table and fired toward the uniforms that filled the room. She didn't allow herself to react to the fact that she couldn't see Daniel or Carston. She'd told Daniel to get down when the shooting started. He was just following directions.

A storm of shots rang out now, but none of them were aimed at her. The soldiers were firing at the bloody, naked man who had exploded into their midst with a volley of bullets. There were six uniformed men still on their feet now, and she quickly dropped three before they could realize the attack was coming from two fronts. As they crumpled, they revealed the man in the suit they'd been protecting. His eyes were focusing toward her as she aimed, his body already in motion when the bullet left her gun; she wasn't sure she'd done more than just wing him as he ducked down out of her range.

She couldn't see Kevin's position, but the other three soldiers were now on the ground. She had nothing left to aim at from this vantage.

Alex darted to the edge of the open window, glass crunching beneath her shoes, and put her back against the wall beside it.

"Ollie?" Kevin called, his voice strong and controlled.

Relief flooded through her body in a hot rush at the sound of his voice. "Yes."

"We're clear. Get in here. Danny's down."

Ice washed down the same path the heat had just blazed.

She dropped the guns into her pockets, wrapped her hands in the folds of her lab coat, and boosted herself over the jagged ledge of the window. The floor was a mass of bodies in dark uniforms, with deep red splatters marking everything light enough to show it—the faces, the floor, the walls. Kevin was shaking off a body he'd evidently used as a shield. There was still movement, and more than one gasping murmur. So, not entirely clear, but he must feel it was under control, and, obviously, the need was urgent.

Daniel was in the back right corner—she could see the white-blond hair ringing his pale scalp, but most of him was obscured by two bodies in uniform that looked to have crumpled on top of him. Carston was down a few feet away, blood blossoming across his white shirt from multiple wounds. His chest was still moving.

It took less than a second for her to absorb all this, already in motion as she assessed, heading straight for Daniel.

"Deavers is alive," she muttered as she passed Kevin, and in her peripheral vision, she saw him nod and start moving in a crouch toward the far left corner of the room.

There was very little blood on the soldier lying across Daniel's chest, but his face was an unhealthy shade of purple and there were pink bubbles on his lips. A quick glance at the man draped over Daniel's legs revealed the same manifestations. Both of these men were dying from the venom on Daniel's ring. A new froth of bloody bubbles foamed on the first man's lips as she tried to pull his paralyzed body off Daniel.

Part of her was very far away from what was happening—the part that needed to scream and panic and hyperventilate. She let the ice of her fear keep her focused and clinical. Later there would be time for hysterics. Now she had to be a doctor on the battlefield, quick and certain.

She finally rolled the man off Daniel's chest, and suddenly there was blood everywhere. She ripped Daniel's crimson-drenched shirt out of the way and found the source only too easily. All of her training, all of her time as a trauma doctor for hire, told her she was far too late.

It was a perfect kill shot, right through the upper left side of his chest. Whoever had placed that bullet knew exactly what he was doing. It was one of the few shots that would fell a person instantly, straight through the heart, dead before he hit the ground.

Dead probably before he could even register the pain.

There was nothing she could have done, even if she'd never left his side. She'd let him come here to protect her, and that choice had killed him just as surely as the bullet in his heart.

CHAPTER 31

It wasn't supposed to have happened like this. The guns should have been pointed at Alex and Kevin. In the confusion, no one had shot at her—not even once; she was totally unscathed. Daniel was supposed to be in the background, invisible. There was no reason to waste such a perfect shot on an anonymous aide. That skilled shooter was supposed to be aiming for Alex.

She'd known the plan was deeply flawed, but she had never dreamed she'd walk through the firefight untouched. Daniel was supposed to be the survivor.

A line of nameless faces—gangsters she hadn't been able to save—flashed through her mind. One had a name—Carlo. He'd died exactly the same way. She hadn't been able to do anything. What had Joey G said? *You win some, you lose some.* But how did she live through this loss?

The shrieking part of her was very near the surface. Only shock kept the paroxysm of grief at bay. The frozen pause was endless, crystal clear, with every detail defined. She was aware of the sound of a struggle somewhere very far away from her, and Kevin shouting in his harshest voice, *"Where's your deep perimeter now, Deavers?"* She could smell the fetid musk of her ring's victims and the warm, *alive* scent of fresh blood. She could hear labored breathing at her back where Carston lay dying.

Then, suddenly, the sound of another shallow, sucking wheeze close beside her bowed head.

Her eyes, which she hadn't even realized were closed, snapped open. She knew that sound.

Frantically, she ripped the glove from her hand and stretched it tight over the hole in Daniel's chest. She watched incredulously as the pull of his struggling lung tried to suck air through the latex. She lifted the edge of the glove for the exhale, letting the air vent, and then strained the glove against his skin again for the inhale.

He was *breathing*.

How? The shot must have somehow missed his heart, though it seemed perfectly placed. She took stock quickly and realized that there wasn't actually as much blood as she'd first thought. Not enough to suggest a hole in his heart. And he was breathing, which he wouldn't have been if the bullet had gone true.

She thrust her other hand under his shoulder, searching frantically for an exit wound. Her fingertips found the tear in his jacket, and she shoved them through the hole, then into the hole in his back, trying to seal the airflow. It didn't feel any bigger than the hole in his chest. The bullet had passed straight through him.

"Kevin!" Her raw shriek held all the panic she was too numb to feel. "I need my toolbox. Now!"

Movement again, but she didn't look up to see if it was Kevin helping her or a victorious Deavers moving in for the kill. She found she didn't even care if it was Deavers; she wasn't afraid of anything he could do to her. Because if Kevin was down and unable to get her the things she needed immediately, Daniel could die in minutes.

She had more of what she needed in the car, but she had no idea how to get Daniel back to the surface.

A metallic crash sounded at her right elbow.

"Ziploc bags," she instructed frantically. "The bottom compartment, on the left, and tape—should be near the top."

Kevin laid the things she needed on Daniel's chest, next to her hand. Quickly, on the exhale, she traded her glove for the plastic bag and instructed Kevin to tape it down tightly on three sides. She didn't have anything that would work as a valve to vent the excess air, so she had to leave the fourth side open. It should suck against the hole as he inhaled, and then let the air release as he breathed out.

"Roll him toward me, I need to seal the exit wound."

Kevin carefully moved his unconscious brother onto his side. She hoped the position would take some of the pressure off Daniel's undamaged lung. She had to break contact with the wound briefly as Kevin moved him, and then another precious second as she used a scalpel to cut his shirt and jacket out of the way. She taped a second plastic bag against his skin while she analyzed the pool of blood beneath him. Not so much, really. The bullet had miraculously missed his heart entirely, and the major vessels as well. The exit wound looked clean and she didn't see any bone fragments. If she could just keep him breathing, she could get him through the next hour.

Kevin's voice interrupted her frantic planning. "Carston's still alive. What do you want me to do with him?"

"Can he be saved?" she asked while she checked Daniel's airway and pressure. He'd lost too much blood. He was in shock. She could still make out a pulse at his wrist, but it was weak and fading. She grabbed a syringe from the top tray and injected him with ketamine and a separate painkiller.

"Doubt it. Too much damage. He probably only has a few minutes. Oh, um, hey. Sorry, man."

His voice had changed at the end. He wasn't speaking to her anymore.

"Is he lucid?" she asked. She ran her hands down Daniel's arms and legs, searching for any other wounds.

"Jules?" Carston rasped weakly.

"Kevin, bring the operating table over here. We've got to get Daniel up to the car." She took a deep breath. "Lowell, it's okay. I never poisoned Livvy. Of course not. She's only sedated. She'll be with her mother by morning, whether I come home or not."

While she reassured Carston — her eyes never leaving Daniel — she heard Kevin leave and then return. There was a heavy metal groan as he shoved the table through the window and a moist thud when it hit the bodies on the floor. She bit her lip as she continued to work on Daniel, pulling the rubber pieces of his disguise out of his mouth so he couldn't choke on them, carefully wiping the contacts from his eyes. How long till Kevin collapsed? He still had a good fifty minutes to enjoy the drugs in his system, but that wouldn't affect how much his body could actually endure. She needed to try to remember that he wasn't the same Kevin, the one who could do anything. She had to go easier on him. But how? Daniel needed speed. If she could just get him to the car...

"Proud of you, Jules," Lowell Carston wheezed quietly. "You managed to hold on to your soul. Impressive..." The last word trailed off with a low, rattling exhalation. She listened for more, but it was silent behind her now.

She'd outlived Carston, a feat she never would have put money on. Instead of feeling the triumph she'd always expected, she was ambivalent. Perhaps the triumph would come later, when the panic gripping her was gone.

"Is it safe to lift him?" Kevin asked.

"Carefully. Try to keep his chest as immobile as possible. I'll get his legs."

Together they hefted Daniel carefully onto the silver tabletop. She took his wrist again, willing his pulse to stay discernible.

"Give me two seconds, Ollie," Kevin said as he began stripping the soldier who'd fallen over Daniel's legs, the one with the least blood on him. "How many more are upstairs?"

She glanced at the faces on the floor. She thought she recognized the shorter guard from the metal detector.

"At least one isn't here, for sure. He was at the door. It seemed empty up there, but I didn't see most of these guys beforehand."

He was already in the pants, pulling socks over his mangled feet and then trying the shoes. They were too small. He yanked another pair off the other poisoned soldier. Those looked a little big, but Kevin tied the laces tight.

"You're going to have to cut those off," she said.

He buttoned the white shirt, then threw the dark navy coat over the top, not bothering with the tie. "I'll do what I have to do when we live through this. Lose the lab coat, it's covered in blood."

"Right," she agreed, awkwardly shoving the guns into the elastic band at the back of her leggings. It was barely strong enough to hold them both in place. She shrugged out of the coat and let it drop to the floor.

"Okay, let's get this table past all the bodies, then you should be able to handle it in the hall. I'll sweep ahead and take out anybody who's left."

In seconds she was rolling Daniel down the hall, half running while Kevin disappeared into the darkness, somehow at a full sprint. Then she was in the metal-detector room, and Kevin was waiting, holding the elevator for her. The room was empty; everyone must have rushed to the observation room when the shooting started. She darted into the elevator.

Kevin reached out to hit the button as the doors shut silently behind her. She stared at his right hand on the button, his dominant hand, and a sudden burst of understanding had her coughing out one half-delirious laugh.

Kevin eyed her sharply. "Keep it together, Ollie."

"No, no, see, it's his *heart*, Kev. It's on the wrong

side—the *right* side. That's why the shooter missed." She choked out another laugh. "He's alive because he's your opposite."

"Lock it up," he ordered.

She nodded once, taking a deep breath to steady herself.

The elevator stopped and the door opened to the supply closet. The outer door was closed. Kevin lifted the edge of the table over the lip of the elevator, then went to the door.

She expected him to ease it open, but instead he threw it wide with a loud bang.

"Help!" he yelled. "We need help down here!"

Then he was racing forward silently. She could hear louder footsteps coming for them from the other room—just one set, she was sure. She pushed Daniel forward as quietly as she could.

Kevin was in place before the guard came around the corner. The guard ran right past him, gun in hand but held low by his side, pointed at the ground. Kevin's gun was high. He shot the guard in the back of the head. The man crumpled to the floor. Kevin stepped forward and put one more bullet into his head to be thorough.

The hallway was too narrow to maneuver the gurney around the body. Kevin grabbed it with both hands and lifted it over. Alex did what she could to help, but she knew Kevin was taking most of the weight. She didn't know how he was still performing at this level, and she was afraid he was going to kill himself trying.

There was no other guard.

"Get him to the car," Kevin commanded. "Let me finish up here."

No one tried to stop her; no one shot at her from a darkened window while she ran into the parking lot. The sky was completely black now. The single streetlight near the front door cast only a dim yellow circle toward the parked cars. She fumbled in Daniel's pockets till she found Carston's keys. She popped the trunk and ran for her souped-up first-aid kit.

She knew exactly where the blowout gear was. She'd expected either she or Kevin — or both — would be shot, and she'd prepared accordingly. She didn't need the tourniquet or the QuikClot gauze, but she had several HALO seals, and they would work better than her plastic sandwich bags. She also had a Mylar survival blanket, more saline, and some strong intravenous antibiotics. Bullets were dirty things, and infection would be a concern... if she could keep Daniel alive that long.

She knew she couldn't. Maybe for twenty-four hours at most with what she had here. Despair made her hands shake as she ripped open the packages.

Then Kevin was right beside her. He threw a heavy black-and-silver square into the trunk.

"Hard drive the cameras recorded to," Kevin explained. "I'll get him into the back."

She nodded, filling her arms with stopgap measures.

When she crawled into the foot space of the backseat, she could see that Kevin had done everything right. Daniel was on his left side. His head was propped up on the driver's headrest, which Kevin had ripped out of place—violently, it appeared. She checked Daniel's airway again, his pulse. She could still just make it out in his carotid. The ketamine would keep him under for a while. He couldn't feel any pain. His system would remain as unstressed as possible under the circumstances.

The car started to move. She could feel Kevin was trying to keep the motion smooth for her, but it wouldn't be smooth enough.

"Stop," she said. "Give me a minute to get things in place."

He hit the brakes. "Hurry, Ollie."

It took only seconds to switch her makeshift seals for the real thing. She got the IV in quickly and then pinned the bag to the top of the seat back.

"Okay." As she spoke this time, she could barely recognize her own voice—she knew there wasn't anything more she could do, and the despair was starting to suck her down. "You can drive."

"Don't quit on me now, Oleander," Kevin growled.

"You're stronger than that. I know you can do this."

"But there's nothing more I can do," she choked out. "I've done everything. It's not enough."

"He's going to make it."

"He needs a level-one trauma center, Kevin. He needs a thoracic surgeon and an operating suite. I can't clean his wounds or put in a chest tube in the backseat of a damn *Bimmer!*"

Kevin was silent.

Tears streamed down Alex's cheeks, but she didn't feel grief yet. Just rage — at the injustice, at the limitations of their situation, at herself for this ultimate failure.

"If we dropped him off at an ER —" She sobbed.

"We'd be handing him over to the bad guys. They'll be looking at the hospitals."

"He's going to die," she whispered.

"Better that than he end up in a room like the one you just busted me out of."

"Didn't we just kill the bad guys?"

"Pace is still in charge, Ollie, till he slaps the right patch on, and given the current stress level, he might just start smoking again. If he doesn't die…even without his partners, he has no shortage of muscle at his command. The hospital is out."

She bowed her head, defeated.

The seconds ticked by. She marked them by the

faint, steady pulse in Daniel's neck. She should probably be driving. She didn't know how Kevin was still going, but he didn't even seem fazed by his ordeal, not slowed in the slightest by his myriad of wounds. He was a machine. At least Daniel shared the same iron constitution...But finding any excuse for hope right now was kind of stupid.

"If..." Kevin began thoughtfully.

"Yes?"

"If I could get you to an operating space...if I could get you the things you needed...Could you fill in for the thoracic surgeon?"

"It's not my specialty, but...I could probably handle the basics." She shook her head. "Kev, how could we get a suite up and running? If we were in Chicago, sure, I might know a guy, but—"

Kevin laughed once—more of a bark, really.

"Ollie, I've got an idea."

•   •   •

ALEX HAD NO sense of what time it was. Maybe three a.m., maybe four. She was ragged with exhaustion, but also wired and jittery. The hand that held her seventh Styrofoam cup of coffee was trembling so badly that the surface of the liquid looked like a miniature storm at sea. Well, that was okay. She didn't need steady hands anymore.

Joey Giancardi. She never would have thought she

could feel so much warmth toward her old Mafia handler, but tonight she blessed his name. If she hadn't done what amounted to an intensive trauma course with the Mob, she never would have been able to pull Daniel through. Each thug and gangster she'd repaired had given her just that much more experience, all of it adding up until she could play both EMT and surgeon tonight. Maybe she should send Joey a thank-you card.

She ran her quivering free hand through her hair and suddenly found herself wishing she were a smoker, like Pace. Smokers always seemed so serene with a cigarette in hand. She needed something to bring her down, to slow her agitated heart, but the only physical comfort she could find was the cup of strong black sludge she held, and that wasn't exactly helping her relax.

Dr. Volkstaff was snoring on a battered couch squeezed between two large storage cabinets against the back wall of his workspace. He'd been surprisingly capable—despite his age and specialty. They'd had to cobble together much of what they'd needed in his operating theater, but he was inventive and familiar with his tools, and she was inspired by desperation. Together, they'd made a potent team. They'd even done a decent job of patching together a makeshift Heimlich valve that appeared to be working perfectly. The gentle beeping of Daniel's heart monitor was the most soothing sound she'd ever heard. Not that it could do anything about the caffeinated overstimulation of her nervous system. Unthinkingly, she took another gulp of coffee.

Daniel's color was good, his breathing even. He did share all of Kevin's physical characteristics, it seemed; he was engineered to survive. Dr. Volkstaff said he'd never seen a smoother procedure, and he'd dealt with plenty of lung injuries in his time, though usually puncture wounds. It was possible that Daniel would be walking out of here tomorrow.

She carefully set her cup on the counter and then gripped her shaking hands into fists as she walked slowly back to the stool by Daniel's bed and sat. It was actually two operating beds bungeed together. Nothing here had been near long enough for Daniel.

After a second, she leaned her head against the thin, plastic-covered cushion and closed her eyes.

She thought about what they had accomplished tonight, what she had almost traded Daniel's life for.

Deavers and Carston were dead. There might not be another person alive—besides Wade Pace—who knew she existed. And his hours were numbered. Hopefully.

Kevin was snoring on the floor, an old dog bed under his head for a pillow. She'd given him the largest dose of painkillers that was safe, and Volkstaff had cleaned his wounds once Daniel was in the clear. Sleep was the best thing for Kevin now.

By this time, Val should have dropped Livvy at the urgent-care center—chosen for its lack of exterior cameras—with Alex's grammatically unsound, tearstained apology note. She wondered how seriously the police would continue their search for the kidnapper. Livvy was unharmed, with no memory of her time away from Erin. The DC police would surely have little time to track down a frenzied mother who'd thought the little girl looked exactly like an older version of her own child, stolen two years ago by an estranged father. There had to be several missing-children cases that would match the loose information she'd given them. It would keep the authorities focused in the wrong direction. Maybe they'd tie Livvy's kidnapping to the death of her grandfather on the same day, but probably they wouldn't. There was an entirely separate cornucopia of motives to sift through for Carston's violent death. It would look like nothing more than a horrible coincidence.

The shadowy powers that be, the people who pulled the puppet strings, would *have* to cover everything up. One fact was going to stand out to them— the CIA's second in command and the director of a black ops program that wasn't supposed to exist had shot each other and a handful of American soldiers. The puppet masters would probably demolish the entire complex before they'd even had time to make sense of the evidence there. They'd call it a horrible accident, a building collapse due to a structural flaw, what a shame.

She thought of the last things Kevin had said to her before he crashed.

"You can do this, Ollie. I know you'll save his life. Because you have to. And then we'll all be safe. This isn't going to happen to Danny again, so you *pull him through it.*"

She wondered if he really did have that much faith in her or if he was just trying to keep her from panicking. But would he have allowed himself to pass into unconsciousness if he hadn't believed his own words?

"Alex?"

Her head whipped up so fast the wheeled stool beneath her rolled back a few inches. She jumped off it and leaned over Daniel, taking the hand that was weakly groping for hers.

"I'm right here." She glanced at his IV. The ketamine must be out of his system now, but he had an intravenous painkiller that would keep him from feeling too much discomfort.

"Where are we?"

"Safe, for the moment."

His eyes slowly opened. It took them a moment to find her, and then another to focus.

She'd known with decent certainty for at least two or three hours now that he was going to open his eyes again, but the familiar gray-green nearly knocked the wind out of her anyway. She felt tears overflow her own eyes.

"Are you hurt?" he asked.

She sniffed. "Not a scratch on me."

He smiled slightly. "Kevin?" he asked.

"He's fine. That's him snoring you hear—not a buzz saw."

The corners of his mouth turned down as his eyes slipped closed again.

"Don't worry about him. He'll be fine."

"He looked...really bad."

"He's tougher than any person should be—kind of like you."

"Sorry." He sighed. "I got shot."

"Yeah, I noticed that."

"Carston took the gun from the guy next to me when Deavers pulled a gun on him," Daniel explained, his lids pulling back just a few millimeters. "He moved fast for an older guy. They were shouting at each other, but all the soldiers lined up with Deavers."

Alex nodded. "Those were their orders."

"Deavers gave the order, and one of them shot Carston and then me. Carston fell to his knees but started shooting. I didn't have a gun, so I grabbed the ankles of the people near me with your ring."

"You did good."

"I wanted to get to a gun, but the two guys I hit fell

on me. I couldn't lift them. My arms weren't working right."

"The one on your chest probably saved your life, actually. He kept the wound covered till I could get there."

Daniel blinked his eyes open again. "I thought I was dead."

Alex had to swallow. "Honestly, so did I for a while."

"I wanted to stay until you got there. I wanted to tell you some things. It felt horrible when I knew I couldn't."

She stroked the side of his face. "It's okay. You did it. You stayed."

The comfort thing was coming to her more easily these days. She'd changed a lot since meeting Daniel.

"I just wanted you to know that I don't regret any of it. I'm grateful for every second I've had with you— even the bad ones. I wouldn't have missed it, Alex, not for anything."

She leaned her forehead against his. "Neither would I."

They didn't move for a long moment. She listened to the sound of his breathing, the sound of his evenly beeping monitors, and Kevin's robust snores in the background.

"I love you," he murmured.

She laughed once—a quick, jittery sound that

matched the tremors in her hands. "Yeah, I've sort of figured that one out, I think. Took me long enough, didn't it? Anyway, though, I love you, too."

"Finally speaking the same language."

She laughed again.

"You're shaking," he said.

"I've had so much caffeine, I need a detox."

It was still middle-of-the-night quiet outside, so the sound of a car pulling up to the back of the building was hard to miss. Alex was surprised by how little her nerves reacted—there wasn't much left in her, she could tell. She just felt weary as she straightened up and freed her hands. She pulled her PPK from the small of her back.

"I really hope that's Val," she muttered.

"Alex—" Daniel whispered.

"Don't move even a fraction of an inch, Daniel Beach," she whispered back. "I spent too long patching you up for you to go and tear something now. I'm just being cautious. I'll be back in a sec."

She hurried to the rear door and peeked past the side of the little curtain. It was the car she was expecting—the ugly green Jag—Val in the driver's seat. She could see Einstein standing up on the passenger side.

Alex knew she should feel more, knowing that all of it was over, that almost every loose end was wrapped up. She should be elated, relieved, grateful, possibly shedding tears of joy. But her body was completely done. Once the coffee wore off, she'd be comatose.

"It's Val, like I thought," she told Daniel quietly as she set the gun on the end of his improvised bed.

"You look like you're going to pass out."

"Soon," she agreed. "Not quite yet."

"Alex?" Val called quietly as she came through the door.

"Yes."

Einstein bounded into the room, head whipping back and forth as he searched for Kevin. He paused and made a little whimper when he found him on the floor. Einstein's head cocked to the side, and then he licked Kevin's face twice. Kevin's snore stuttered.

Alex expected Einstein would curl up with his best friend, but, his tail wagging vigorously, he turned and ran to her. He jumped both paws onto her hips so he could lick her face. She had to hold on to Daniel's bed to keep from being knocked over.

"Careful, Einstein."

He coughed a quiet bark, almost like an answer. Then he dropped back to all fours and trotted over to Kevin, nestled into his side, and licked his neck again and again.

Alex was shocked when Kevin spoke. The drugs she'd given him should have kept him out for . . . well, she wasn't actually sure how long it had been. Her brain was too exhausted even for simple addition.

"Hey, buddy, hey there," he said, sounding just like he usually did—too loud. His voice seemed impossibly vigorous for the way his body must be feeling. "Did you miss me? Good boy. You told them what happened. I knew you would do it."

"Kev?" Daniel asked. Alex put her hand firmly on his forehead when he twitched like he wanted to sit up.

"Danny?" Kevin nearly shouted. Volkstaff snorted and rolled onto his side.

Kevin pulled himself up, wincing.

"You probably shouldn't move..." Alex began, and then, when he completely ignored her, "Hey, at least keep off your feet!"

"I'm fine." Kevin grunted.

"You're an idiot," Val said harshly. "Just stay put for two seconds."

Val was out of the strange, avant-garde-runway sari-thing and in sweats and a T-shirt now. She strode out through a door marked LOBBY. Kevin waited, puzzled, kneeling on the linoleum with one hand braced against the wall. She was back almost immediately, pushing a wheeled office chair, her expression set in angry lines. If Alex had any energy left, she would have sighed with envy. Val looked absolutely ridiculous for someone in a ponytail and no makeup who'd gotten no more sleep than the rest of them.

"I'm fairly sure they don't keep wheelchairs here, but this ought to work for now," Val said. "Sit."

Though her voice sounded deeply annoyed, she offered both hands to pull him up. He hissed and staggered when the soles of his feet touched the ground, but as soon as he was seated, he was trying to use them to roll himself closer to Daniel.

"Ugh, stop it," Val complained. She guided the chair across the room while Kevin held his feet gingerly a few inches off the floor. Val stopped when Kevin was right beside Alex. Alex shuffled over a step to make room.

Kevin stared at Daniel's open eyes and good color with shock. Carefully, he patted Daniel's hair, obviously afraid to touch any other part of him.

"Looks like your poison woman got it done," Kevin said in a gruff voice. "I'm not sure about the balding Swede thing you've got going on, though."

"Val's idea."

Kevin nodded absently for a moment. "You shouldn't have come in after me. I didn't want you to do that."

"You would have done it for me."

"That's different." He shook his head when Daniel started to protest. "But you're going to be okay?" Kevin looked up at Alex for the answer.

She exhaled through her nose and nodded. "He looks like he's going to be totally fine. I don't know what it is with you two. Are you sure your mom didn't have a one-night stand with a genetically engineered superhuman?"

When Kevin's hand darted toward her, Alex's first instinct was that she'd crossed the line with the mother comment. But before she could brace for a blow, he'd grabbed her roughly and yanked her into an awkward bear hug. She found herself half on his lap, her arms pinned under his, and there was nothing she could do when he decided to kiss her full on the lips with a wet, resounding *smack*.

"Hey!" Daniel protested. "Get your face off my poison woman!"

Alex wrenched her head to the side, finally feeling something again — nausea. "Ugh, get *off* me, you psychopath." She heard Val laughing.

Kevin managed to spin the chair in a complete revolution. "You're a genius, Ollie. I can't believe you did it."

"Go make out with Volkstaff, he did half the work."

He wouldn't free her. It was like he didn't even notice that she was trying — violently — to wriggle away. "What a performance! I can't *believe* you just walked in there and busted me out! Never tell me you aren't black ops — honey, you're what black ops *dreams* about being!"

Einstein whined and Alex felt his jaws close lightly around her wrist. He yanked, trying to help her escape. Kevin didn't seem to notice.

She knew where Kevin's worst injuries were. She'd use that knowledge soon if she had to. "Let me go!"

"Kevin," Daniel said, his voice measured but icy. "If you don't set Alex down right now I'm going to shoot you with her gun."

Finally Kevin dropped his arms. She ducked free and they both spun anxiously to Daniel.

"Don't move," they said in unison.

Alex breathed again when she could see that Daniel hadn't actually tried to reach for the gun.

"Volkstaff?" Daniel asked. "I know that name... where are we?"

"You remember Dr. Volkstaff," Kevin said. "He saved my best friend's life in fifth grade—after he got caught in the bear trap. You can't have forgotten that."

Daniel blinked. "Tommy Velasquez got caught in a bear trap?" he asked, bewildered.

Kevin smiled. "Tommy wasn't my best friend." He stroked Einstein's head, and the dog rubbed his face against Kevin's leg, still delirious with joy.

"Wait... *Volkstaff?*" Daniel repeated, finally putting it together. "You took me to the *vet?*"

Alex laid a hand on his forehead. "Shh. It was the right place to go. Volkstaff is a rock star. He saved your life."

"Now, now," Volkstaff's gravelly voice broke in. "I was merely the assistant, Dr. Alex. Don't be trying to give me the credit for saving Danny."

Volkstaff was sitting up on the couch, patting the unruly tufts of white hair that were arrayed in a jagged halo around his head. It made her think of Barnaby, and she realized why she'd felt so comfortable working with the friendly old man who was apparently still quite devoted to the Beach family.

"It was an honor to work beside you, Doctor," Volkstaff continued as he tottered over to them. He appeared frail with age now, but he'd shown no feebleness during the long night. He smiled down at Daniel. "Good to see you awake, son." He dropped his voice into a stage whisper. "You've found a winner, kid. Don't mess things up with this one."

"Oh, I know it, sir."

Alex frowned. She hadn't said anything about her feelings for Daniel, and Daniel had been unconscious. How were they always so obvious?

Volkstaff turned. "What a gorgeous shepherd. This can't be Einstein, can it? It's been years."

"His grandson, actually," Kevin told him.

"Isn't that something!" He reached down to caress Einstein's ear. "Such a beauty."

Einstein licked his hand. The dog was full of goodwill for all mankind tonight.

"Now, Kevin," Volkstaff said, straightening, "would you like to walk again? Because if so, you'll need to get those feet elevated, and all of you needs to rest. Don't you dare give me that look, young man. You can use my couch over there. Er, Miss..." Volkstaff's eyes bugged a little as he took in Val for the first time. Alex had warned Volkstaff that the fourth member of their party would show up later, but he clearly hadn't expected a Victoria's Secret model.

"You can call me Valentine," Val purred.

"Yes, thank you, well. Miss Valentine, could you push Kevin over to the sofa and help him onto it? Exactly—thank you."

Alex watched, feeling numb again, her head disconnected from every part of her body, while Val half shoved Kevin from the chair to the couch. Her expression was irritated, her hands rough, but Alex saw her duck in suddenly to kiss his forehead.

"And you, Doctor..."

Alex turned slowly to look at Volkstaff.

"There are more couches in the waiting room. Go use one of them. That's an order."

She hesitated, swaying in place, staring at Daniel.

"Yeesh, you two," Val said as she stalked back across the room. "Sleep before you collapse, Alex. I've had a few hours. I'll keep an eye on him."

"If anything *at all* changes on his monitors, the slightest variation—"

"I'll drag you back in here by your much-improved hair," Val promised.

Alex bent down and kissed Daniel softly. "Volkstaff and I went through a lot of trouble to put you back together again," she murmured against his lips. "Don't screw up our work."

His lips brushed hers as he spoke. "Wouldn't dream of it. Be a good girl and get some sleep like my old family vet ordered you to."

"I'll have you know I'm in the prime of my life," Volkstaff objected.

"C'mon," Val said, suddenly right in Alex's ear. "Let's go while you can still walk. I'm sure I could carry you, but I don't *want* to."

Alex let Val guide her through the door and down the unlit hallway. She concentrated on moving her feet and nothing else. Her surroundings were just a dark blur. Val had to lower her to the couch, but Alex was sure she would have been just as happy on the floor. Unconsciousness took her while she was still falling.

CHAPTER 32

It was a strange morning.

For Alex, it was also a very late morning. It was peaceful in the empty veterinary hospital, and no one disturbed her. She learned later that Volkstaff had called his office team, canceled all the appointments, and put a sign in the window that read CLOSED FOR FAMILY EMERGENCY.

It was an odd place to feel so safe—an unfamiliar place, a place where she'd prepared no traps or defenses.

But things had changed. She'd only really thought of rescuing Kevin, but their actions last night had also shifted their position significantly.

Kevin was as energetic as ever, despite the fact that he was stuck in the rolling office chair again, his gauze-wrapped feet elevated on the wheeled stool. Val disappeared as soon as she saw Alex to take her turn on the couch. Daniel had had his eyes closed to ignore his brother but quickly "woke up" when he heard Alex's voice. Volkstaff was apparently out getting lunch. The others had left her a bagel and cream cheese.

As soon as Alex had finished her examination of Daniel — who was recovering more quickly than anyone who hadn't worked with Kevin Beach would believe — Alex grabbed her breakfast and the newspaper Volkstaff had brought in with the bagels. She read furiously while she chewed. They'd made the front page — though only the people in the room knew that.

"This all feels anticlimactic, Ollie," Kevin complained, using a broom to push his chair in circles around the room. "It would have been more fun to shoot him."

The big headline for the day was Wade Pace's fatal aneurysm. The journalists had barely paused for a moment of silence before they were on to guessing what President Howland's strategy would be for finding his new running mate.

"Well, you did get to shoot Deavers."

"I was too stressed about Danny to really enjoy it, though," he mused.

Kevin had been terse in his explanation about how Deavers had gotten the upper hand. Alex could tell he was embarrassed, but she didn't think less of him. How could anyone have prepared for the extremes that Deavers's paranoia had pushed him to? More than forty men, deployed into three perimeters, one more than a mile out from Deavers's position. Once Deavers hit the panic button, the perimeters had collapsed in. Kevin maintained that if he hadn't ignored his gut and brought a rocket launcher along, he would have made it out.

There was nothing else in the news, nothing about a violent shootout in an underground bunker on the outskirts of town. No word about a missing CIA deputy director. No mention of Carston, not even the relatively public kidnapping of his granddaughter. Maybe in tomorrow's news.

Kevin didn't think so.

"It'll be a gas-line explosion or something like that. That real story is all going to get buried so deep, they'll name Jackie Kennedy as the Dallas shooter before any of it gets out."

He was probably right.

They couldn't be 100 percent sure, of course, and they would continue to behave with caution, but the pressure was significantly decreased. Alex knew she would feel the lightness like a layer of helium under her skin, if she could ever convince herself to believe in their good luck.

After lunch, Volkstaff removed the stitches from Alex's ear and complimented Daniel's even hand when she gave him the credit. Alex was bemused by how much the white-haired old man took in stride. None of them had tried to explain their unusual injuries or even make up a cover story, but Volkstaff asked no questions and showed no obvious curiosity. He didn't comment on the fact that Kevin was supposed to have died in prison, though apparently—Daniel informed her in a whisper—Volkstaff had been at the funeral. He asked only about old acquaintances from their childhood and, more particularly, the animals they'd known together. Though Alex had just barely learned to recognize love at all, she thought she might be falling for Volkstaff just a little, too.

Still, they couldn't live in the animal hospital forever. Volkstaff had other patients. After a few minutes of discussing options, Val surprised Alex by volunteering to house them again, back in her palatial penthouse, now that it was safe. For a fee, naturally. Kevin seemed the most shocked at her offer.

"Don't let it go to your head," she told him. "I want the dog. And I actually *like* Alex and Danny. Almost as much as I can't stand you." Then she'd kissed him— long enough that it got uncomfortable for everyone. Volkstaff politely turned his back, but Alex just stared. She would never understand what Val saw in Kevin.

•   •   •

"SOOO . . ." KEVIN BEGAN.

Alex turned from her organizing; it wasn't quite

packing yet. Kevin was lounging in the doorway of the room Alex and Daniel had always shared in Val's home, his left arm braced against the top of the frame. For one second, Alex was irrelevantly jealous of tall people in general. It wasn't an uncommon feeling these days, always surrounded by giants as she was. She put it away.

"So what?"

"So how did the appointment go today? What did you and Volkstaff conclude?"

He didn't have to ask where Daniel was now — Daniel's normal shower-serenade volume would have gotten him in trouble if the other tenants were any closer. The Bon Jovi phase hadn't passed yet; he was particularly fond of "Shot Through the Heart" at the moment. Alex didn't find it so funny, but she tried not to let it irritate her.

"The vet thinks Daniel's good to go. I concur. You Beaches are a charmed breed." She shook her head, still a little incredulous at how quickly and thoroughly Daniel had healed. "Also, he wants to look at your feet."

Kevin scowled. "My feet are fine."

"Don't shoot the messenger. I mean that literally."

His frown faded into his normal expression, but he continued to stand there in the doorway, staring at her.

"Sooo...?" she echoed.

"So…do you have any ideas about where you're heading now?"

Alex twitched her shoulders noncommittally. "Nothing too specific yet." Like a coward, she turned back to her worn duffel and looked over her stowed chemicals again, checking that they were all appropriately protected from jostling. She might have been going overboard with the organization, she admitted to herself. They probably didn't need to be alphabetized. But she'd had a lot of time on her hands, and other than surfing the web for possible new digs, she was at loose ends. Daniel had objected to being examined more than four times a day.

"Have you talked to Danny about it?"

She nodded with her back still turned to him. "He says wherever I want to go is fine by him."

"He's planning to tag along with you, I guess."

Kevin's voice was casual, but Alex knew it must be a strain to keep it that way.

"I haven't discussed that part specifically with him, but, yes, it does seem to be the assumption."

He didn't say anything for a moment, and she really had nothing left to do with the bag. She turned slowly to face him.

"Yeah," he said, "I could tell it was going to go that way." His expression was indifferent. Only his eyes revealed the depths of his hurt.

She didn't want to tell the full story, but she felt

guilty holding it back. "If it makes you feel any better, he seems to be assuming you'll be there, too."

Kevin's eyebrows eased back from their normal compressed position.

"Really?"

"Yes. I don't think he's envisioned any more splitting up at this point."

Kevin inclined his chin. "I can understand that. Kid's been through a lot."

"He's bouncing back pretty well."

"True, but we wouldn't want to traumatize him again. Don't want him to have a setback."

Alex knew where Kevin was going with this. She suppressed both a sigh and a smile, keeping her face neutral.

"True," she said in her serious-doctor tone. "It might be best to keep his environment as stable as possible, aside from all the unavoidable changes."

Kevin didn't suppress *his* sigh. He blew out a huge breath and crossed his arms over his chest. "It'll probably be an enormous pain, but I guess I can stick close until he's adapted."

Alex couldn't resist pushing back just a tiny bit. "I'm sure he wouldn't want you to put yourself out. He'll survive."

"No, no, I owe the kid. I'll do what I have to."

"He'll appreciate that."

Kevin met her gaze for one long second, his expression candid, and then suddenly sheepish. The moment passed, and he grinned.

"What's the general area you're looking at?" he asked.

"I was thinking maybe the Southwest or the Rocky Mountains. Medium-size city, settle in the suburbs. The usual."

No one was looking for them, as far as they knew, but Alex was always a fan of playing it safe, just in case. She'd have to use a fake name regardless— Juliana Fortis was legally dead.

Daniel's singing cut off, then picked up again, muffled by a towel.

"I know a town that might work."

Alex shook her head slowly. He'd probably already rented a house and set up the new identities. She'd choose her own name no matter what he'd done. "Of course you do."

"How do you feel about Colorado?"

EPILOGUE

A dam Kopecky sat today's files on his desk and reached for the phone with a smile already in place. He had the best job in the world.

Working as an assistant producer for a famous chef's reality road show could have meant many things, but for Adam, it meant flexible hours, a quiet little office, and a near-constant stream of positivity.

He was in charge of managing the visits to the various mom-and-pop eateries his chef would be featuring on the show, and while he was sometimes jealous of Bess and Neil, who were always on the road trying out every hole-in-the-wall they could find, he believed what he was doing suited his temperament better. Plus, Bess and Neil had to eat a lot of garbage to find the diamonds in the rough, and Neil had gained at least twenty-five pounds in this past year with the show; Adam had cobbled together a standing desk so that his more stationary job would not start to affect him the same way. And then, out of necessity, no one knew who Bess and Neil were, so no one was particularly excited to hear from them.

Thursday afternoon was Adam's favorite. Today he would call the chosen ones.

The show was heading to the Denver region in a month, and the lucky winners were a barbecue place in Lakewood, a bakery right in downtown, and then the outlier, a bar and grill that was closer to Boulder than Denver. Adam had been skeptical, but Bess insisted that the Hideaway would be the highlight of the episode. If possible, they should be there on a Friday night. The place was a local karaoke hot spot. Adam hated karaoke, but Bess was insistent.

"It's not what you're thinking, Adam," she'd promised. "This place is so cool, Chef'll need a parka. Doesn't look like much from the outside, but the style is there. *Je ne sais quoi* and all that. Plus the owners are seriously camera-ready. The cook's name is Nathaniel Weeks—so *fine,* let me tell you. I hate to admit to being unprofessional, but I did make a play. I got zero response. The waitress tipped me off that he was married. The good ones are always taken, right? But he's got a hot brother, apparently. Plays bouncer for the bar at night. I may tag along with Chef for this one."

She'd taken a bunch of pictures on her iPhone. As she'd mentioned, the outside was forgettable. It could have been anyplace in the West. Saloon-ish, dark wood, rustic. Most of the other photos were of plates of food that seemed to have too much style for such an unremarkable location. A few of the pictures must have been of the cook she liked so much—tall, full beard, thick curly hair. Adam didn't think he was especially attractive, but what did he know? Lumberjacks could be Bess's thing. A small woman with short dark hair was in a lot of the backgrounds, never facing the camera... maybe this was the chef's wife. He had the names of all the owners off the alcohol license. Nathaniel Weeks was the chef, so Kenneth must be the bouncer brother, and Ellis the wife.

Adam had remained hesitant, but the Hideaway had gotten Neil's enthusiastic thumbs-up as well. Best food he'd had in the past three seasons.

There were always a couple of backups—a coffee shop in Parker and a breakfast-only diner in Littleton were on this list—but Adam very rarely had to contact the backups. The show had a track record of boosting business by a healthy percentage for the first two months after an episode aired, with an ongoing lift for the rest of the year. There were even a bunch of groupie types who tried to follow Chef's journey and eat at every place he featured. Chef was always complimentary, and the show regularly pulled in almost a million viewers every Sunday night. It was the world's best advertisement, and it was free.

So Adam was prepared for the reaction at the Lakewood barbecue place, Whistle Pig. As soon as he said the name of the show, the owner was screaming. Adam thought he could even hear her feet pounding against the floor as she jumped up and down. It was like showing up at someone's door with one of those huge Publishers Clearing House checks.

Once the owner had calmed down, Adam went through the usual spiel, getting the date on her calendar, giving her the contact info she would need, prepping her for the kinds of access the show would require, et cetera. All the while, she kept thanking Adam and occasionally shouting the good news to someone who'd just walked into the room.

Adam had made this same call over eight hundred times now, but it always left him grinning and feeling like Good Saint Nick.

The call with the bakery was similar, but instead of screaming, the head pastry chef had an infectious belly laugh that Adam couldn't help but laugh along with. This call took longer than the first, but eventually Adam was able to compose himself, even if the local chef never did.

Adam had saved the Hideaway for last, knowing that a Friday-night karaoke event would be a little more complicated to arrange. Adam thought it might be too much of a departure for the show, but he supposed they could get some footage from both the dinner hour and the performances, then cut it together to see what would work.

"This is the Hideaway," an alto female voice answered his call. "How can I help you?"

In the background, Adam could hear the expected sounds—the clinking of clean dishes being put away, the *chop, chop, chop* of the prep work, the murmur of a few conversations lowered for the sake of the phone call. Soon they'd be plenty loud.

"Hello," Adam greeted her heartily. "Could I please speak to Mrs. Weeks—Mrs. Ellis Weeks—or either of the Mr. Weekses?"

"This is Mrs. Weeks."

"Great. Hi. My name is Adam Kopecky, and I'm calling you on behalf of the show *The Great American Food Trip*."

He waited. Sometimes it took a minute to sink in. He wondered if Mrs. Weeks was a screamer or a gasper. Maybe a crier.

"Yes," Mrs. Weeks responded in a cool tone. "What can I do for you?"

Adam coughed out an awkward laugh. It happened sometimes. Not everyone was familiar with the show, though it really was a household name these days.

"Well, we're a cuisine-focused reality show that follows the food journeys of Chef—"

"Yes, I know the program." There was a hint of impatience in the voice now. "And what can I help you with?"

Adam was a bit thrown. There was the strangest sort of suspicion in her reaction, like she thought this was a scam. Or maybe something worse. Adam couldn't quite put his finger on it.

He hurried to set her straight. "I'm calling because the Hideaway has been chosen for our show. Our spies"—he laughed lightly—"came home raving about your menu and your entertainment. We hear you've become quite a local hot spot. We'd love to profile your establishment—get the word out to anyone who hasn't heard of you yet."

Surely now it would click for her. As one-third owner of the restaurant, she had to be adding up the financial possibilities in her head. He waited for the first squeal.

Nothing.

He could still hear the clinking, the chopping, the murmuring, and in the distance, a couple of dogs barking. Otherwise he would have thought the call had dropped. Or that she'd hung up on him.

"Hello, Mrs. Weeks?"

"Yes, I'm here."

"Well, then, um, congratulations. We plan to be in your area the first part of next month, and we can be somewhat flexible within that time frame to work with your schedule. I've heard that Friday nights are a highlight, so we might want to plan for that—"

"I'm sorry—Mr. Kopecky, did you say it was?"

"Yes, but call me Adam, please."

"I'm sorry, Adam, but while we're...flattered, I don't think it will be possible for us to participate."

"Oh," Adam said. It was half gasp, half grunt.

He'd had a few instances where schedules could not be made to fit, where exigent circumstances of the most weighty kind—weddings, funerals, organ transplants—had gotten in the way, but the dream had never died without a major effort on the part of the owners and major disappointment to follow. One poor woman in Omaha had sobbed into the receiver for a solid five minutes.

"Thank you so much for thinking of us..."

As if this were no more than an invitation to a distant relative's backyard birthday party.

"Mrs. Weeks, I'm not sure you realize what this could do for your business. I could send you some statistics—you'd be amazed at what a difference in your bottom line a spot on the show would mean."

"I'm sure you're right, Mr. Kopecky—"

"What is it, Ollie?" a voice interrupted. This one was deep, and very loud.

"Excuse me a moment," Mrs. Weeks said to Adam, and then her voice was slightly muffled. "I've got it," she said to the loud voice. "It's that show—the *American Food Trip* thing."

"What do they want?"

"To feature the Hideaway, apparently."

Adam took a slow breath. Maybe one of the other owners would respond appropriately.

"Oh," the deep voice said, and his tone reminded Adam of the woman's first response. Flat.

How was this bad news? Adam felt like he was being pranked. Was this Bess and Neil's idea of a joke?

"Really?" someone called out from a distance— another deep voice, but this one more enthusiastic. "They want to put us on their show?"

"Yes," Mrs. Weeks responded. "But don't—"

A few cheers interrupted whatever she was going to say. Adam didn't relax. He couldn't feel any change directly on the other end of the line.

"You want me to talk to him, Ollie?" the loud voice asked.

"No, go deal with *them*," Mrs. Weeks said. "Nathaniel might need a stiff drink. Maybe the wait-staff, too. I'll take care of this."

"Wilco."

"I apologize for the interruption, Mr. Kopecky," Mrs. Weeks said, her voice clear again. "And truly, thank you so much for the offer. I'm very sorry it won't work out."

"I don't understand." Adam could hear the defla-tion in his own tone and was sure she could, too. "We can be flexible, like I said. I've...I've never had any-one who didn't want this."

Now her voice was more animated—soothing,

kind. "And we would want this, absolutely, if it was possible. You see . . ." A short pause. "There's an issue, a legal issue, that we're dealing with. A lien situation with my brother-in-law's former girlfriend. Was it a business loan, was it a personal gift? Yada yada; you get the picture. It's all very delicate—sticky, you know, and no press is good press for now. We have to keep a low profile. I hope you can understand. We *are* very flattered."

He could hear the loud brother arguing with someone in the background, more barking, and some quieter mumbles that sounded like complaints.

This was more like it. A concrete reason, even if he didn't totally understand how a legal case would be negatively impacted by the restaurant's involvement with the show . . . unless they thought they were going to have to pay out some percentage of what the place was worth?

"I'm sorry to hear that, Mrs. Weeks. Maybe sometime in the future? I could give you my—"

"Absolutely. Thank you so much. I'll be in contact if we are ever in a position to accept."

The line went dead. She hadn't even let him give her his phone number.

Adam stared at the papers in front of him for a few seconds, trying to shake off what felt very much like being shut down after asking a charity date to the prom.

A few minutes passed while he stared at the phone. Finally, he shook his head and reached for the file with the backups. The coffee shop in Parker would be only too grateful to be chosen. Adam needed a few good screams.

ACKNOWLEDGMENTS

This story wasn't one I could have written by myself, and I'm immensely grateful to all the people who gave me so much of their time, patience, and expertise.

My MVP was Dr. Kirstin Hendrickson of Arizona State University's school of Molecular Sciences and her colleague Dr. Scott Lefler. Dr. Hendrickson spent an incredible amount of time working out realistic ways for me to kill, torture, and chemically manipulate fictional people, and I am so appreciative for her help.

My favorite RN, Judd Mendenhall, was also a huge help in keeping Daniel Beach alive by talking me through a sucking chest wound and coming up with the veterinarian solution.

Without Dr. Gregory Prince's brilliant help with molecular biology and monoclonal antibodies, I would not have been able to give Alex the backstory she deserved.

An enormous thank-you to each of the following awesome people: Tommy Wittman, retired special agent, ATF, who gave me an excellent crash course in gas masks; Paul Morgan and Jerry Hine, who were frighteningly helpful with the mechanics of building a functional death trap; Sergeant Warren Brewer of the Phoenix Police Department, who vetted my drug deals; S. Daniel Colton, former captain, USAF JAG Corps, for his expertise in the creation of Kevin's backstory; Petty Officer First Class John E. Rowe, who is always happy to talk guns with me or any other random thing I might be curious about.

And a huge thank-you also to my sources who preferred to remain anonymous. Your help is so appreciated.

All my love to the usual suspects: My very understanding family, who are so patient with my sleepless, manic writing spells; my brilliant and kind editor, Asya, who never tells me I'm crazy even when I am; my ninja agent, Jodi, who inspires fear in all who oppose her (and sometimes those who don't); my super-classy film agent, Kassie, whom I aspire to be when I grow up; my production partner, Meghan, who carries all the weight of Fickle Fish so it doesn't burn to the ground in my absence. And, of course, my heart is full of love for all the people who pick my books up and give them a chance — thank you for letting me tell you stories.

And finally, thank you to Pocket, my gorgeous and IQ-challenged German shepherd, who, at the very slightest hint of danger, immediately cowers behind my legs. Who will never love me the way he loves my husband. Who still doesn't understand the basic principles of the game of fetch. I love you, too, you big, dumb, beautiful chicken.

ABOUT THE AUTHOR

Stephenie Meyer graduated from Brigham Young University with a degree in English literature. She lives with her husband and three sons in Arizona. Read more about Stephenie and her other books at stepheniemeyer.com.